BOLLINGEN SERIES XCV: 1

overleaf: C. G. Jung: New York, 1912

C.G.JUNG LETTERS

selected and edited by	GERHARD ADLER
in collaboration with	ANIELA JAFFÉ
translations from the German by	R. F. C. HULL
in two volumes	1: 1906–1950

BOLLINGEN SERIES XCV : 1   PRINCETON UNIVERSITY PRESS

THIS TWO-VOLUME WORK IS THE
NINETY-FIFTH IN A SERIES OF BOOKS
SPONSORED BY BOLLINGEN FOUNDATION

*Library of Congress Catalogue Card
Number: 74-166378*
ISBN 0-691-09895-6

MANUFACTURED IN
THE U.S.A.

TABLE OF CONTENTS

LIST OF ILLUSTRATIONS

Frontispiece

C. G. Jung: New York, 1912. *Campbell Studios, New York*

Plates

FOLLOWING PAGE 282

Illustrations in the Text

INTRODUCTION

In May 1956—Jung was then nearly 82—I broached to him the question of the publication of his letters. Jung's ready response made it clear that this project had been on his mind for some time. Thus my inquiry came at a favourable moment, and Jung asked his secretary, Mrs. Aniela Jaffé, to select two file folders of letters, all of them to clergymen, labelled "Pfarrerbriefe" in Jung's own handwriting, for my opinion concerning the advisability of their publication.

Over many years Jung had frequently used the medium of letters to communicate his ideas to the outside world and to rectify misinterpretations about which he felt sufficiently strongly, quite apart from answering people who approached him with genuine problems of their own and corresponding with friends and professional colleagues. In this way many of his letters contained new creative ideas and a running commentary on his work.

In his later years it became his practice to send copies of letters which he regarded as important to people whose judgment he trusted. This he did partly to communicate ideas to them which, on account of his age, he no longer felt willing or able to put into book form, and partly because the question of the publication of his letters had been on his mind for some time.

Originally the idea of such publication had come not from himself but from friends who were aware of the unique literary and psychological value of Jung's correspondence. At first Jung had reacted against the whole notion, since he felt that the spontaneity and immediacy of his letters were not for the general public; but in his later years he changed his attitude, and he even mentioned occasionally in a particular letter that it was not only directed to the addressee but was also meant for later publication.

Thus it was just the right moment when I put my own thoughts to Jung, and he responded by asking me if I were willing to undertake the editorial task. The final result of my talk and of the ensuing correspondence with him was formulated in Jung's decision, stated in a letter to me of 15 November 1957, to appoint an Editorial Committee consisting of his daughter Mrs. Marianne Niehus-Jung as representative of the family, Mrs. Aniela Jaffé, who had been Jung's secretary since the autumn of 1955 and was familiar with the archives kept at his house in Küsnacht, and finally myself as chairman of the Committee and chief editor who was to direct the whole project. The matter was formalized in a letter of 29 January 1959 from Jung to Mr. John D. Barrett, president of the Bollingen Foundation, which sponsored the publication of Jung's Collected Works. The original plan had been to bring out the letters as part of the Collected Works, a plan which was later modified so as to publish the letters independently.

There the matter rested until after Jung's death in 1961. Active work on the project started in January 1962, and early in 1963 appeals for Jung's letters were published in various newspapers and journals in the United States, Great Britain and Switzerland. This appeal was all the more important since the archives in Küsnacht were, to put it conservatively, incomplete. For years, Jung had no regular secretary, except for occasional help from his unmarried sister Gertrud. He wrote most letters in longhand and apparently kept no file copies. It was not until April 1931, when his daughter Marianne (later Mrs. Walther Niehus-Jung) began helping her father with secretarial work, that carbon copies of typewritten letters sent out were kept and filed together with letters received. But it was only in 1932, with the advent of Marie-Jeanne Schmid (later Mrs. Marie-Jeanne Boller-Schmid, daughter of Jung's friend Dr. Hans Schmid-Guisan), that files were established in a systematic way. Marie-Jeanne Schmid remained Jung's secretary until her marriage in 1952.* Without her accuracy and devoted care, the publication of these letters would have been virtually impossible, and to her is due the gratitude of all interested in Jung's work.

Marie-Jeanne once told me that one of the reasons why Jung did not bother to keep his addressees' letters or copies of his own was that he realized only later in life that he was a "famous man" in whose correspondence people might some day be interested. He was particularly neglectful of letters of a more personal and intimate nature—in short, of letters not immediately connected with his scientific work. The situation was complicated by Jung's habit of writing many letters by hand, particularly from his country retreat,

* Between her departure in 1952 and Aniela Jaffé's arrival in 1955 Jung had three other secretaries who, however, stayed only for short periods.

his Tower at Bollingen, without having them copied, although later on Mrs. Jaffé succeeded in saving many such letters from oblivion by typing copies before they were sent off.

This explains the relative dearth of letters before 1931–32. For earlier letters we were almost completely dependent on the result of published appeals. Thanks to the generosity of individuals and several libraries or archives, about sixty letters of the early period, up to the end of 1930, were received, not counting the letters to Freud (about which more later on). So small a number must be very disappointing, considering that it covers a period of several decades, and it is to be hoped that the publication of these volumes will lead to the discovery of more letters of the early period. This period could have been much more adequately covered with regard to both quantity and valuable material had the Jung heirs, to my deepest regret, not proscribed the publication of any of Jung's letters to his family (the earliest, to his mother, dating from 1896), the great majority of them to his wife. I can only hope that this embargo will be lifted at a later time, since these letters, on account of their personal character, warm feeling, and gay tone, are a very necessary complement to the letters published here with their predominantly scientific content. (It seemed superfluous to republish the seven letters to his wife printed in Jung's *Memories, Dreams, Reflections.*) The only letters to his closer family are two to his daughter Marianne, which were given to me by her personally. There exist also many intimate and very personal letters to other recipients, mostly analysands or pupils, who, however, felt it too early to allow their publication. Jung's letters to his close friend and collaborator Miss Toni Wolff were returned to him after her death in 1953 and were destroyed by Jung, together with her letters to him.

The correspondence between Freud and Jung is of particular importance. It consists of 167 letters from Freud to Jung and of 196 letters from Jung to Freud. It starts with Freud's letter of 11 April 1906, thanking Jung for the present of a volume of his *Diagnostische Assoziationsstudien*, and ending with Jung's letter of 27 October 1913, announcing his resignation as editor of the *Jahrbuch für psychoanalytische und psychopathologische Forschungen*. When Jung agreed to the plan for the publication of his letters he explicitly excluded these to Freud, which he did not want to be published until at least thirty years after his death (a period which he later reduced to twenty years). In a letter to me of 24 May 1956 he wrote: "Separate treatment of this correspondence is justified, because it touches in parts upon very personal problems, whereas the planned publication refers to scientific subjects. I consider it inopportune to expose the personal material as long as the waves of animosity are still running so high (*so lange die Wogen der Gehässigkeit noch so hoch schlagen*). At the date suggested by me Freud and I will be 'historical personalities,' and the necessary detachment from events will prevail by then." For these reasons I felt justified in publishing only a very few and quite uncontroversial letters of Jung's to Freud, eight in all.* However, Jung's heirs, in conjunction with the heirs of Freud, decided for an earlier publication of the Freud/Jung correspondence. In consequence the two sons met in London in 1970, and Ernst Freud and Franz Jung exchanged the letters of their respective fathers. As a result of these changed conditions the complete Freud/Jung correspondence is now to be published in translation in the United States by Princeton University Press, and in the United Kingdom in a joint edition by Hogarth Press and Routledge and Kegan Paul; and in the German original by Fischer Verlag, Frankfurt.

After eliminating all purely "business" letters, such as routine correspondence with publishers, notes of appointments with patients, etc., I had in the end to choose from about 1600 letters. Since these letters were frequently written in Jung's capacity as a psychiatrist in answer to people's personal questions, the first principle of selection had to be that of medical discretion, and many such letters had perforce to be omitted. Furthermore, there are numerous references to people who themselves, or whose relatives, are still alive, which necessitated either omissions or the substitution of initials for names. Besides this principle of discretion the chief criterion of selection was that of intrinsic interest, whether scientific, personal, or historical. Some letters which were too long or too technical have been omitted but will be published in volume 18 of the Collected Works. The long correspondence between Jung and H. L. Philp and David Cox, published in Philp's book, *Jung and the Problem of Evil* (1958), has also been omitted—with the exception of three short letters—on account of both its bulk and its availability in the said book. So has the correspondence between Jung and Dr. Löy, published in volume 4 of the Collected Works.

The reader may notice a certain repetitiveness. Although I have

* Seven letters of Freud's to Jung were included in a selection edited by E. L. Freud (1960). See Freud, 5 Oct. 06, n. □.

tried to eliminate this to some extent, I felt that such repetitions—
apart from Jung's frequent complaint about too much work or correspondence—tended to emphasize his great concern with certain
problems. They also show his feeling of being constantly misunderstood (as on the distinction between God and God-image, or on his
empirical approach to psychological problems) and his equally constant attempt—sometimes expressed with great patience and tolerance, sometimes with some affect—to clear up such misunderstandings.

As far as humanly possible, I, with the help of Mrs. Jaffé, tried
to obtain permission for publication from every single addressee
after the year 1930. The same applies to dream material or other
data mentioned in the notes. Since the earlier letters date back many
decades, some degree of liberty had to be taken with letters to people
who we knew had died. In some cases, arrangements were made
through friendly relations with families or estates of addressees (such
as Countess Keyserling and the Hermann Hesse and Richard Wilhelm archives); in others, where the contents seemed to justify
and allow it, we had to take personal responsibility for publication.
As far as living addressees are concerned, we tried to consult every
one who could be identified. In this task we were only partially
successful, since many of the inquiring letters we sent out were returned marked "addressee unknown" or "addressee moved." This is
not surprising. But it was gratifying to receive almost exclusively
positive answers from those who responded, very often with kind
personal remarks and helpful information, and I want to express my
thanks to all these people for their cooperation. Only a handful of
outright refusals were received. Some of the addressees requested
anonymity, or the omission of certain passages, or the anonymity of
some person mentioned in a letter; some letters were sent in with
deletions made by the addressees. Others asked specifically for inclusion of their name or of certain passages which it had been my
intention to treat differently. A few omissions have been made where
the meaning was too obscure. This was the case with untraceable
allusions, as when a letter referred to previous correspondence which
could not be recovered, or to a conversation with the addressee.

The annotations are intended to provide the reader with facts it
might prove difficult for him to find out for himself. I had started off
with considerably more detailed and extensive notes than those I
decided to include in the end. Such elaborate annotation would have

burdened the volumes with facts that were not absolutely necessary or about which the reader could be expected to inform himself without too much trouble. Some notes which may appear unduly elaborate or unnecessary are included for personal or historical interest: the more time passes, the more difficult it will become to elicit the information given in them. On the other hand, many a time I had to admit defeat: there will be quite a few places in Jung's letters where the reader might look in vain for a numeral signalling a note. In such places, lengthy editorial research has failed to elucidate the reference. This regrettable fact is often due to Jung's habit of not keeping the addressees' letters; and he usually returned the numerous manuscripts and related material to the sender, so that very often identification was impossible. A special problem is that of giving details concerning addressees. This has been done wherever possible in a preliminary note designated with a □ ; in some cases, discretion precluded such annotation, and in many more cases the addressee could not be located. It should be borne in mind that many of the letters Jung received were from people completely unknown to him.

As a matter of principle and in order to prevent the notes from becoming too bulky, publications by addressees are included chiefly in the □ notes referring to analytical psychologists (and even here occasionally only in selection; generally only published books are cited). However, a few exceptions are made where it seems desirable for the understanding of the correspondence. Where the requisite information is available, biographical notes on addressees are regularly attached to the first letter, but the index contains every reference to them in other letters. The aim has been, when nothing else is known of an addressee, to give in the □ note at least the city or town to which the letter was addressed or, when the addressee is anonymous, the country. Such a place may not, obviously, have been a permanent residence. In so far as possible, the professional status of recipients is indicated, as well as the birth and death dates of those who are deceased; correspondents whose photographs appear as illustrations are limited to close friends who are no longer living. Names, book-titles, events, and subjects of importance are, with a few exceptions, annotated at their first occurrence; here again the index can be consulted for information on subsequent occurrences. While the notes are as concise as possible, abbreviations are kept to a minimum, the chief being CW for the Collected Works (19 vols., all published except the Miscellany and the Bibliography/ Index vols.) and *Memories* for the autobiographical *Memories*,

Dreams, Reflections, by Jung in collaboration with Aniela Jaffé. As the London and New York editions of the latter differ in pagination, double page references are given.

In spite of the great care taken and much time-consuming research, a fair number of gaps remain. I would be most grateful for any important information or corrections to letters and notes which readers might be able to provide.

The sources of the letters are varied. The largest group, from the files at Küsnacht, consists of carbon copies of dictated and typed letters and secretarial typed copies of handwritten letters. A second category includes letters sent to us by the recipients or their heirs, some in the original, some in xerox copies, some in the recipient's own typed copy. Handwritten letters are so indicated in the □ notes, and likewise previously published letters, but it has not been possible to give full details of the various documentary states of typed letters —originals with signature, xerox copies of the same, file carbon copies, typed copies of holograph letters, etc.

Although the greatest care has been taken to establish the authentic text, this was not always possible owing to Jung's habit of writing in corrections and adding handwritten postscripts. These changes were as a rule transferred by the secretaries to the carbon now in the files. However, some omissions of this procedure cannot be ruled out, e.g., where Jung's letters were posted at the village of Bollingen. Another problem was Jung's habit of filling in by hand Greek words or phrases for which a blank space had been left by the secretary. In most cases inquiries have enabled us to fill in these gaps; sometimes, however, clarification has not been possible. All such omissions, as well as doubtful restitutions, are mentioned in the notes. There are also instances of letters published by an addressee, who changed Jung's English, sometimes rightly and sometimes wrongly.

Occasionally we received copies of letters through third hands without knowing the name of the addressee. In such cases we had no means of checking the text. I have nevertheless assumed the accuracy of the copies.

Omissions are of two kinds: of repetitive or quite unimportant passages, and of passages of a too intimate or confidential nature. All omissions are indicated by ". . .". Changes in the letters written in English are limited mainly to punctuation (Jung's followed the German style and would be confusing to the English reader), obvious spelling mistakes, and corrections of secretarial errors (for instance, the incorrect "septem reges lapis" in the letter to Miss Nanavutty of 11 Nov. 1948, or a hearing mistake in a letter to Schoening of 24 Mar. 1955: the incorrect "what are they giving an aim to" for "what are they giving a name to"). We may suppose that such secretarial errors were corrected by Jung on the top copies. More important changes concern Jung's English style, which because of Germanisms and other idiosyncrasies makes Jung's difficult to understand for the English reader, particularly if he is unfamiliar with German. Un-English locutions like "in a hundred miles distance," "I wish you would elucidate me," "according to my humble idea," "on the one side/on the other side" have been changed to "a hundred miles away," "I wish you would enlighten me," "in my humble opinion," "on the one hand/on the other hand." Typically German is Jung's use of prepositions: "I object against," "independent from," "with other words," and similar phrases have been regularly altered to the customary English usage. Germanisms like "I succeeded to find" and "incapable to do" have also been changed. Jung's use of tenses is often highly erratic, and he frequently uses the classical subjunctive after "if"; these have been normalized. Jung's use of capitals in English (Anima, Unconscious, Psychology, Man, etc.) was so irregular that I felt justified in standardizing it and bringing it into line with the Collected Works. The same applies to the uniform use of forms like "psychic" instead of Jung's "psychical." In revising, I have followed the advice of Mr. R.F.C. Hull, the translator of the Collected Works. I am sure that Jung would not only not have objected but would have approved such changes, seeing that he submitted all of his English lectures and writings to the criticism of English-speaking people for revision. On the other hand, where Jung's English is highly personal and idiosyncratic but clearly understandable, no changes have been made, so that the English reader may come across passages that sound slightly strange to his ears.

In both the original English and the translated letters, certain conventions have been adopted. Titles of books have uniformly been put in italics, those of articles and essays have been put in quotation marks. For quotations in Latin, French, etc., italics are regularly used. As a rule, titles of Jung's works (and non-English works in general) are given in their translated forms. Paragraphs—often very long, as is usual in German—have occasionally been subdivided in order to make the text easier to read. Jung's address is not given except in the case of letters not written from his home at Seestrasse

228, Küsnacht. In a few cases, the address is uncertain, e.g., where Jung wrote letters from Bollingen, Locarno, etc., without the place being mentioned in the letter. Dates are conventionalized to the form "1 January 1909" (in notes, abbreviated "1 Jan. 09"). Jung's letters were dated almost without exception. To save space, the complimentary closings have usually been run in with the body of the letter and the signature.

A special problem is raised by the German salutations and complimentary closings. It is quite impossible to find precise equivalents in English. "Sehr geehrter Herr Doktor" and "Lieber Herr Doktor" are both bound to become "Dear Dr. —," "Verehrter Herr Graf" (Honoured Count) must be reduced to "Dear Count," and "Liebe gnädige Frau" (Dear gracious lady) to the prosaic "Dear Frau —." Recipients without honorifics are addressed "Dear Herr/Frau/Fräulein" or "Dear Mr./Mrs./Miss" according to language. Letters to Swiss, German, or French Protestant clergymen begin "Dear Pastor —," as the formal English "Dear Mr. —" would be inappropriate. The names of anonymous recipients are replaced by "N."; in the few cases where he or she received several letters, another capital has been substituted. As for the comparatively elaborate nuances of the German and French endings, often untranslatable, we have had in the main to use the conventional English forms that come closest while having a natural, idiomatic ring. No English translation can, most unfortunately, do complete justice to the nuances of the Continental formalities and distinctions.*

In some cases the reader may find it regrettable that the letter of the addressee is not published as well. However, I have tried to give in the notes the gist of the essential points—sometimes at considerable length—and to fill in the background wherever it seemed necessary for an understanding of Jung's answer. Here again, unfortunately, explanations are lacking only too frequently, because it was impossible to recover the addressee's letter.

*

As mentioned at the outset, the original Editorial Committee consisted of three members: Mrs. Marianne Niehus-Jung, Mrs. Aniela Jaffé, and myself. It was a very sad loss when Marianne Niehus died

---

* The availability of the Swiss edition of these Selected Letters will facilitate the comparison of the texts for those interested in the precise nuances. Cf. p. xvi.

in March 1965 after a prolonged illness. By that time the task of collecting the letters had virtually come to an end, but the work of
selection and annotation was just beginning, and her co-operation
was sorely missed. I would like to express my profound appreciation
of her warmth and generosity, her tact and understanding, and her
constant willingness to further my work. I am deeply grateful to her
for all she had done right up to the end of her life.

After her death I had to carry the full responsibility with the
support of Aniela Jaffé. Here again I would like to express my deep
gratitude for the help she has given me all through the many years
of the work. Her intimate knowledge of Jung's later years, her close
contact with him both as his secretary and as his collaborator, her
complete grasp of his ideas, were of the greatest assistance to me. I
regularly sent her my notes for possible additions or corrections;
and equally the selection and omission of letters were the subject
of continuous correspondence. Thus a most friendly co-operation
developed over more than ten years of work on these letters. It was
the natural consequence of this co-operation that Aniela Jaffé from
1968 onwards assumed responsibility for the Swiss edition of the
Briefe, published by the Walter-Verlag, Olten and Freiburg (which,
in 1971, took over the interests of Rascher Verlag, Zurich, in the
publication of Jung's works). With a very few exceptions, owing to
the relative interest of some letters to the British/American or the
German/Swiss reader, the selection of letters in the two editions is
identical.

I am also much indebted to all those scholars in various fields
who helped me in the formulation of notes. Jung's immense range
of interests as shown in his letters makes it practically impossible
for *one* person to provide the necessary annotations, and here I have
been greatly helped in my researches by many experts, too numerous
to be mentioned individually. However, I want to single out the
Rev. W. Baddeley, of Cambridge, England, who gave me invalu-
able help with the Greek and Latin quotations. Particular thanks
are due to Mr. R.F.C. Hull, the translator of the Collected Works.
His remarkable knowledge of Jung's texts, terminology, and style
and his wide interest in other fields were a constant stimulus to me
and occasioned many improvements. Mrs. Jane A. Pratt very kindly
contributed the English translation of the letters written in French.
Equally helpful was Mr. William McGuire, of Bollingen Series and
Princeton University Press, whose editorial and research experience

was of the greatest value and who succeeded in locating a considerable number of letters, in particular of correspondents in the U.S.A. Mr. Kurt Niehus, Jung's son-in-law, accepted responsibility on behalf of the family for reading and approving the final selection of letters. I wish also to thank my faithful secretary Mrs. Hertha Manheimer, who over many years of complicated work never lost patience in spite of the continuous changes, deletions, and additions and my all but illegible handwriting.

Last but certainly not least, my particular thanks are due to the Bollingen Foundation, without whose moral and financial support these letters could not have been collected, edited, and published in their present form.

London, 1971   GERHARD ADLER

An important letter of 1919 to Hermann Hesse, which was discovered too late for chronological placement, and two significant letters by Hesse are given as addenda.

G. A.

London, September 1972

CHRONOLOGY

1875	26 July: born to Johann Paul Achilles Jung (1842–1896), then parson at Kesswil (Canton Thurgau), and Emilie, née Preiswerk (1848–1923).
1879	The family moves to Klein-Hüningen, near Basel.
1884	Birth of sister Gertrud (d. 1935).
1885–1900	Medical training (and qualification) at Basel U.
1900	Assistant Staff Physician to Eugen Bleuler at the Burghölzli, the insane asylum of Canton Zurich and psychiatric clinic of Zurich U.
1902	Senior Assistant Staff Physician at the Burghölzli. — M.D. dissertation (Zurich U.): *Zur Psychologie und Pathologie sogenannter occulter Phänomene* (= "On the Psychology and Pathology of So-called Occult Phenomena," CW 1).
1902–1903	Winter semester with Pierre Janet at the Salpêtrière in Paris for the study of theoretical psychopathology.
1903	Marriage to Emma Rauschenbach, of Schaffhausen (1882–1955); one son and four daughters.
1903–1905	Experimental researches on word associations, published in *Diagnostische Assoziationsstudien* (1906, 1909) (= *Studies in Word-Association*, 1918; CW 2).
1905–1909	Senior Staff Physician at the Burghölzli; after that in private practice at his home, 1003 (later 228) Seestrasse, Küsnacht (Zurich).
1905–1913	Lecturer (Privatdozent) on the Medical Faculty of Zurich U.; lectures on psychoneuroses and psychology.
1907	*Über die Psychologie der Dementia Praecox* (= *The Psychology of Dementia Praecox*, 1909; CW 3). — First meeting with Freud in Vienna.
1908	First International Psychoanalytical Congress, Salzburg.
1909	First visit to U.S.A. with Freud and Ferenczi on the occasion of the 20th anniversary of Clark University, Worcester, Mass., where Jung lectures on the association experiment and receives hon. degree of LL.D.

1909–1913   Editor of *Jahrbuch für psychoanalytische und psychopathologische Forschungen.*

1910   Second International Psychoanalytical Congress, Nuremberg.

1910–1914   First President of the International Psychoanalytical Association.

1911   Third International Psychoanalytical Congress, Weimar.

1912   Another visit to U.S.A. for series of lectures at Fordham U.,
New York, on "The Theory of Psychoanalysis" (CW 4).
— "Neue Bahnen der Psychologie" (= "New Paths in
Psychology," later revised and expanded as "On the Psychology of the Unconscious"; both CW 7). — *Wandlungen
und Symbole der Libido* (= *Psychology of the Unconscious,*
1916; for revision, see 1952) leading to

1913   break with Freud. — Fourth International Psychoanalytical
Congress, Munich. — Jung designates his psychology as
"Analytical Psychology" (later also "Complex Psychology").
— Resigns his lecturership at Zurich U.

1913–1919   Period of intense introversion: confrontation with the unconscious.

1916   "VII Sermones ad Mortuos"; first mandala painting. —
Collected Papers on Analytical Psychology. — First description of process of "active imagination" in "Die transzen-
dente Funktion" (not publ. until 1957; in CW 8). —
First use of terms "personal unconscious," "collective/su-
prapersonal unconscious," "individuation," "animus/an-
ima," "persona" in "La Structure de l'inconscient" (CW
7, App.). — Beginning of study of Gnostic writings.

1918   "Über das Unbewusste" (= "The Role of the Uncon-
conscious," CW 10).

1918–1919   Commandant of camp for interned British soldiers at
Château d'Oex (Canton Vaud). — First use of term
"archetype" in "Instinct and the Unconscious" (CW 8).

1920   Journey to Algeria and Tunisia.

1921   *Psychologische Typen*; first use of term "self" (= *Psychological Types,* 1923; CW 6).

1922   Purchase of property in village of Bollingen.

1923   First Tower in Bollingen. — Death of mother. — Richard
Wilhelm's lecture on the *I Ching* at the Psychological Club,
Zurich.

1924–1925   Visit with Pueblo Indians in New Mexico.

1925   First English seminar at the Psychological Club, Zurich.

1925–1926   Expedition to Kenya, Uganda, and the Nile; visit with the Elgonyi on Mt. Elgon.

1928   Beginning of encounter with alchemy. — *Two Essays on Analytical Psychology* (= CW 7). — *Über die Energetik der Seele* (various essays, now in CW 8).

1928–1930   English seminars on "Dream Analysis" at the Psychological Club, Zurich.

1929   Publication, with Richard Wilhelm, of *Das Geheimnis der goldenen Blüte* (= *The Secret of the Golden Flower*; Jung's contribution in CW 13). — *Contributions to Analytical Psychology.*

1930   Vice-President of General Medical Society for Psychotherapy, with Ernst Kretschmer as president.

1930–1934   English seminars on "Interpretation of Visions" at the Psychological Club, Zurich.

1931   *Seelenprobleme der Gegenwart* (essays in CW 4, 6, 8, 10, 15, 16, 17).

1932   Awarded Literature Prize of the City of Zurich.

1933   First lectures at the Eidgenössische Technische Hochschule (E.T.H.), Zurich (Swiss Federal Polytechnic), on "Modern Psychology." — *Modern Man in Search of a Soul.* — Eranos lecture on "A Study in the Process of Individuation" (CW 9, i).

1934   Founds International General Medical Society for Psychotherapy and becomes its first president. — Eranos lecture on "Archetypes of the Collective Unconscious" (CW 9, i). — *Wirklichkeit der Seele* (essays in CW 8, 10, 15, 16, 17).

1934–1939   English seminars on "Psychological Aspects of Nietzsche's *Zarathustra*" at the Psychological Club, Zurich.

1934–1939   Editor of *Zentralblatt für Psychotherapie und ihre Grenzgebiete* (Leipzig).

1935   Appointed Professor at the E.T.H., Zurich. — Founds Schweizerische Gesellschaft für Praktische Psychologie. — Eranos lecture on "Dream Symbols of the Individuation Process" (expanded to Part II of *Psychology and Alchemy*, CW 12). — Tavistock Lectures at the Institute of Medical Psychology, London (not published until 1968: *Analytical Psychology; Its Theory and Practice*; CW 18).

1936   Receives hon. doctoral degree from Harvard U. — Eranos lecture on "Ideas of Redemption in Alchemy" (expanded as part III of *Psychology and Alchemy*); "Wotan" (CW 10).

1937   Terry Lectures on "Psychology and Religion" (CW 11) at Yale U., New Haven, Conn. — Eranos lecture on "The Visions of Zosimos" (CW 13).

1938   Invitation to India by the British Government on the occasion of the 25th anniversary of Calcutta U.; hon. doctorates from the universities of Calcutta, Benares, and Allahabad. — International Congress for Psychotherapy at Oxford with Jung as President; he receives hon. doctorate of Oxford U. — Appointed Hon. Fellow of the Royal Society of Medicine, London. — Eranos lecture on "Psychological Aspects of the Mother Archetype" (CW 9, i).

1939   Eranos lecture on "Concerning Rebirth" (CW 9, i).

1940   Eranos lecture on "A Psychological Approach to the Dogma of the Trinity" (CW 11).

1941   Publication, together with Karl Kerényi, of *Einführung in das Wesen der Mythologie* (= *Essays on a Science of Mythology*; Jung's contribution in CW 9, i). — Eranos lecture on "Transformation Symbolism in the Mass" (CW 11).

1942   Resigns appointment as Professor at E.T.H. — *Paracelsica* (essays in CW 13, 15). — Eranos lecture on "The Spirit Mercurius" (CW 13).

1943   Hon. Member of the Swiss Academy of Sciences.

1944   Appointed to the chair of Medical Psychology at Basel U.; resigns the same year on account of critical illness. —*Psychologie und Alchemie* (CW 12).

1945   Hon. doctorate of Geneva U. on the occasion of his 70th birthday. — Eranos lecture on "The Psychology of the Spirit," expanded as "The Phenomenology of the Spirit in Fairy Tales" (CW 9, i).

1946   Eranos lecture on "The Spirit of Psychology" (expanded as "On the Nature of the Psyche," CW 8). — *Die Psychologie der Übertragung* (= "The Psychology of the Transference," CW 16); *Aufsätze zur Zeitgeschichte* (= *Essays on Contemporary Events*; in CW 10); *Psychologie und Erziehung* (CW 17).

1948   *Symbolik des Geistes* (essays in CW 9, i, 11, 13). — Eranos lecture "On the Self" (expanded to ch. IV of *Aion*, CW 9, ii). — Inauguration of the C. G. Jung Institute, Zurich.

1950   *Gestaltungen des Unbewussten* (essays in CW 9, i and 15).

1951   *Aion* (CW 9, ii). — Eranos lecture "On Synchronicity" (CW 8, App.).

1952   Publication, with W. Pauli, of *Naturerklärung und Psyche* (= *The Interpretation of Nature and Psyche*; Jung's contribution "Synchronicity: An Acausal Connecting Principle," CW 8). — *Symbole der Wandlung* (= *Symbols of Transformation*, CW 5: 4th, greatly revised edition of *Psychology of the Unconscious*). — *Antwort auf Hiob* (= "Answer to Job," CW 11).

1953   Publication of the 1st vol. of the American/British edition of the *Collected Works* (tr. by R.F.C. Hull): *Psychology and Alchemy* (CW 12).

1954   *Von den Wurzeln des Bewusstseins* (essays in CW 8, 9, i, 11, 13).

1955   Hon. doctorate of the E.T.H., Zurich, on the occasion of his 80th birthday. — Death of his wife (27 November).

1955–1956   *Mysterium Coniunctionis* (CW 14); the final work on the psychological significance of alchemy.

1957   *Gegenwart und Zukunft* (= "The Undiscovered Self (Present and Future)," CW 10). — Starts work on *Memories, Dreams, Reflections* with the help of Aniela Jaffé (pub. 1962). — BBC television interview with John Freeman.

1958   *Ein moderner Mythus* (= "Flying Saucers: A Modern Myth," CW 10). — Publication of initial vol. in Swiss edition of Gesammelte Werke: *Praxis der Psychotherapie* (Bd. 16).

1960   Hon. Citizen of Küsnacht on the occasion of his 85th birthday.

1961   Finishes his last work 10 days before his death: "Approaching the Unconscious," in *Man and His Symbols* (1964). — Dies after short illness on 6 June in his house at Küsnacht.

Letters 1906–1950

To Sigmund Freud

Dear Professor Freud,   Burghölzli-Zurich, 5 October 1906

Please accept my sincerest thanks for the present[1] you kindly sent me. This collection of your various short papers should be most welcome to anyone who wishes to familiarize himself quickly and thoroughly with your mode of thought. It is to be hoped that your scientific following will continue to increase in the future in spite of the attacks which Aschaffenburg,[2] amid the plaudits of the pundits, has made on your theory—one might almost say on you personally. The distressing thing about these attacks, in my opinion, is that Aschaffenburg fastens on externals, whereas the merits of your theory

☐ (Handwritten letter.) This and the following letters of Jung to Freud (1856–1939) form part of an extensive correspondence, which is commented on fully in the Introduction, pp. xi f. Jung at one time stipulated that the correspondence not be published until thirty years after his death (cf. letter to Eissler, 20 July 58). However, by mutual agreement between the Freud and Jung families, the entire correspondence is now to be published. Previously, seven letters of Freud's to Jung were published in *Letters of Sigmund Freud, 1873–1939,* ed. E. L. Freud (1960), several brief excerpts in Ernest Jones, *Sigmund Freud: Life and Work,* II (1955), and excerpts of three more letters of Freud's in Jung, *Memories, Dreams, Reflections,* recorded and edited by Aniela Jaffé (1963), pp. 361–64/333–35 (hereinafter called *Memories;* the second page numbers refer to the London edn.). The letters in the present selection are published by friendly permission of Ernst L. Freud. — Jung had become interested in Freud's teachings as early as 1900 when he had read the latter's *The Interpretation of Dreams,* now Standard Edn., IV/V (cf. Jung, *Memories,* pp. 146f./144f.), and he refers to this book in his doctoral dissertation of 1902, "On the Psychology and Pathology of So-Called Occult Phenomena" (CW 1). In 1906, when he sent the first vol. of his *Diagnostische Assoziationsstudien* (*Studies in Word-Association;* now in CW 2) to Freud, the latter, impatient to see the work, had already bought it himself (cf. Jones, II, p. 34; London edn. cited in the present work). The two men actually met for the first time in Feb. 1907 in Vienna.

[1] The first volume (1906) of Freud's *Sammlung kleiner Schriften zur Neurosenlehre* (Collected Short Papers on the Theory of the Neuroses, in various vols. of Standard Edn.).

[2] Gustav Aschaffenburg, M.D., (1866–1944), German professor of psychiatry and neurology, later in U.S.A. Concerning his attacks, cf. Jones, II, p. 124. Jung's rejoinder, "Freud's Theory of Hysteria: A Reply to Aschaffenburg," is in CW 4.

are to be found in the psychological realm of which modern psychiatrists and psychologists have somewhat too scanty a grasp. Recently I conducted a lively correspondence[3] with Aschaffenburg about your theory and espoused this standpoint, with which you, Professor, may not be entirely in agreement. What I can appreciate, and what has helped us here in our psychopathological work, are your psychological views, while I am still pretty far from understanding the therapy and the genesis of hysteria because our material on hysteria is rather meagre. That is to say your therapy seems to me to depend not merely on the affects released by abreaction but also on certain personal rapports, and it seems to me that though the genesis of hysteria is predominantly, it is not exclusively, sexual. I take the same view of your sexual theory. Harping exclusively on these delicate theoretical questions, Aschaffenburg forgets the essential thing, your psychology, from which psychiatry will one day be sure to reap inexhaustible rewards. I hope to send you soon a little book[4] of mine, in which I approach Dementia praecox and its psychology from your standpoint. In it I have also published the case[5] that first drew Bleuler's[6] attention to the existence of your principles, though at that time still with vigorous resistance on his part. But as you know, Bleuler is now completely converted.

Respectfully and gratefully yours, C. G. JUNG

[3] This correspondence now seems to be lost.
[4] *The Psychology of Dementia Praecox* (orig. 1907, CW 3), "a book that made history in psychiatry" (Jones, II, p. 34). This book led to Freud's invitation to Jung to visit him in Vienna. Cf. Jung, *Memories*, p. 149/146.
[5] This is most likely the case of "B. St.," CW 3, pars. 198ff.
[6] Eugen Bleuler, M.D., (1857–1939), professor of psychiatry at the U. of Zurich, director of the Burghölzli Hospital (i.e., the Clinic of the U.). Jung began his psychiatric career at the Burghölzli in 1900. In 1905 he became lecturer in psychiatry at the U. and senior physician at the Hospital, a position he held until 1909, when he resigned in order to have more time for his scientific and private work. Cf. *Memories*, Ch. IV: "Psychiatric Activities." Bleuler was one of the most prominent psychiatrists of his time and his "conversion" was most valuable to Freud. (See pl. II.)

To Karl Abraham

Dear Colleague,   Burghölzli-Zurich, 3 January 1908

First of all, my best wishes for the New Year! Then please forgive me for not having reacted until now to your earlier news. I am still

4

DR. C. G. JUNG
Privatdocent der Psychiatrie

Burghölzli-Zürich, 3.I.08.

Lieber Herr College!

Zuvor meine besten Wünsche zum neuen Jahr! Dann entschuldigen Sie bitte, dass ich auf Ihre bisherigen liebenswürdigen bisjetzt noch nicht reagiert habe. Ich leide eben immer noch unter den Nachwehen der assistentenlosen schrecklichen Zeit. Wie ich höre, hat Ihre Praxis einen ermuthigenden Anfang genommen. Ich wünsche ebensoerfreulichen Fortschritt. Es wird Sie nicht nur vom theoretischen, sondern auch vom praktischen Standpunkt aus interessieren zu erfahren, dass der junge Binswanger bald ein kleines Buch über Hysterieanalyse publicieren wird, wozu der alte Binswanger in Jena eine Einleitung verfassen wird. Das wird ein Bombenloch in die deutsche Opposition reissen, und die Vorurtheile ein bischen erschüttern. Binswanger jun. war gestern hier und hat mir über die Fortschritte der Freud'schen Sache in Jena allerhand berichtet. Ich habe auch wieder eine Hysterianalyse einer Pat. mit schweren Dämmerzuständen von 8–10 tägiger Dauer. Bisjetzt macht die Analyse glänzende Fortschritte. Noch selten ist mir bei einer Analyse die Klarheit der Neurose so aufgefallen wie bei dieser Patientin. Die Construction und der Ablauf der Träume ist von seltener aesthetischer Schönheit. Die Analyse ist zwar sehr anstrengend,

Abraham, 3 Jan. 08

täglich 2–3 Stunden harte Arbeit, aber ungemein befriedigend, sodass ich immer nur mit Schadenfreude constatiere, dass alle diejenigen, die gegen Freud opponieren, auch des Anblickes dieser Dinge sich nicht erfreuen dürfen.

Die Idee von wegen einer Freud'schen Zusammenkunft in Salzburg stammt von den Backpettern. Ich werde Ihnen nächstens ein Circular schicken mit den Vorschlägen der Zeit und der Dauer. Der Ort dürfte mit Salzburg endgültig festgelegt sein.

Meine Frau hat mir zu Weihnachten eine wirklich ausgezeichnete Photographie von Freud geschenkt, ca 12 × 20 cm. Reflectieren Sie auf einen Abzug?

Ob Bleuler auch nach Salzburg kommt, weiss ich nicht. Es hängt davon ab, ob es sein Gewissen zulässt, die Anstalt für 3 Tage Dr. Maier anzuvertrauen. Ich möchte ihn furchtbar gern in Berlin hören. Sein Vortrag wird jedenfalls ein Muster von Gediegenheit. Er hat jetzt schon eine Reihe von feinen Gesichtspunkten.

Mit besten Grüssen an Sie und höflichen Empfehlungen an Frau Gemahlin

Ihr sehr ergebener

Jung.

Abraham, 3 Jan. 08 (verso)

suffering from the after-pains of the frightful time without assistants. I hear your practice has made an encouraging start, and I hope its progress will be equally gratifying. You will be interested to know not only from the theoretical but from the practical side as well that the young Binswanger[1] will soon be publishing a little book on the analysis of hysteria,[2] with an introduction by the old Binswanger[3] in Jena. It will come as a bombshell to the German opposition and shake their prejudices a little. Binswanger junior was here yesterday and told us all sorts of things about the progress of Freud's cause in Jena. Again I am doing an analysis of hysteria—a woman patient with severe twilight states lasting 8–10 days. So far the analysis is going ahead splendidly. Seldom in my analytical work have I been so struck by the "beauty" of neurosis as with this patient. The construction and course of the dreams are of a rare aesthetic beauty. The analysis is very exacting, 2–3 hours of hard work every day, but extraordinarily satisfying, so I can only take malicious glee [*Schadenfreude*] in asserting that all those who oppose Freud should not enjoy the spectacle of these things either.

The idea of a Freudian meeting in Salzburg[4] originates with the

☐ (Handwritten.) Karl Abraham, M.D., (1877–1925), German psychiatrist, one of the most outstanding followers of Freud, founder and president of the Berlin Society of the International Psycho-Analytical Association. He was on the staff of the Burghölzli Hospital 1904–7, and then moved to Berlin. Cf. Freud, "On the History of the Psycho-Analytic Movement," Standard Edn. 14, pp. 34, 44; Jones II, pp. 39, 79, 81; A *Psycho-Analytic Dialogue: The Letters of Sigmund Freud and Karl Abraham, 1907–1926*, ed. H. C. Abraham and E. L. Freud (1965).

[1] Ludwig Binswanger, M.D., (1881–1966); director of the Kreuzlingen Mental Hospital. He was one of Jung's pupils (cf. his contribution in Jung's *Studies in Word-Association*: "On the Psychogalvanic Phenomenon in Association Experiments," orig. 1907/8) and in 1910 became the first president of the Swiss Society of the International Psycho-Analytical Association. Co-founder of "Daseinsanalyse" (existential analysis), largely based on Martin Heidegger's philosophical ideas.

[2] "Versuch einer Hysterieanalyse," offprint from the *Jahrbuch für psychoanalytische und psychopathologische Forschungen* (Leipzig/Vienna), I (1909). (Hereinafter called *Jahrbuch*.)

[3] Otto Binswanger, M.D., (1852–1929; uncle of Ludwig B.). Professor of psychiatry and director of the Psychiatric Clinic, Jena. He had written what was then considered the standard work on hysteria: *Die Hysterie* (1904).

[4] On 27 Apr. 1908 forty-two of Freud's followers met in Salzburg (Jones, II, pp. 45ff.). Jung read a paper "On Dementia Praecox," which has not been preserved (most likely a summary of "The Psychology of Dementia Praecox"). The "Budapestians" were Sandor Ferenczi and Philip Stein.

Budapestians. Shortly I will send you a circular with suggestions as to the date and duration. The place should definitely be Salzburg.

For Christmas my wife gave me a really superb photograph of Freud, ca. 12 x 20 cm. Are you thinking of buying a copy?

I don't know whether Bleuler will come to Salzburg.[5] It depends on whether his conscience allows him to entrust the Clinic for 3 days to Dr. Maier.[6] I terribly much want to hear him in Berlin. In any event his lecture will be a model of thoroughness. Just now he has a lot of subtle ideas.

With best greetings to yourself and please remember me to your wife,

Yours sincerely, JUNG

[5] Bleuler did attend the meeting.
[6] Hans Wolfgang Maier, M.D., (1882–1945), Bleuler's first assistant at Burghölzli. Later, professor of psychiatry at the U. of Zurich; 1928–1941 director of Burghölzli.

To Karl Abraham

Dear Colleague,   Burghölzli-Zurich, 30 January 1908

I am pleased to see from your letter that you are not only coming to Salzburg but will also give us the pleasure of lecturing.[1] I would ask you to keep it short, limiting it to about 20 minutes, as we must make room for a lecture by Freud. I shall announce in the programme that the speaking time is restricted to 20 minutes. So far we are sure of four lectures, one of them by Dr. Jones,[2] London: "Rationalism in Everyday Life."

The Freud discussion in Berlin makes dismal reading—they have even filched the method from Breuer-Freud.[3] It is nothing but a ri-

□ (Handwritten.)
[1] He read a paper, "The Psychosexual Differences between Hysteria and Dementia Praecox" (tr., *Selected Papers*, 1927).
[2] Ernest Jones, M.D., (1879–1958), a prominent follower of Freud and his biographer (*Sigmund Freud: Life and Work*, 3 vols., 1953–57). In 1911 he founded the American Psycho-Analytical Association and in 1913 the British Psycho-Analytical Society. In 1920 he founded the *International Journal of Psycho-Analysis*, which he edited until 1933. (See pl. II.)
[3] Josef Breuer, M.D., (1842–1925), Austrian neurologist. In 1880–82 he discovered that hysteria could be cured by the recall of painful memories. Later he collaborated with Freud and together they published *Studies on Hysteria* (orig. 1895), introducing the "cathartic method." The sexual content of neuroses caused him to abandon further treatment and research.

diculous farce and a piece of impudent knavery besides for Bezzola[4] to assert that he has a new method. Freud has done all that already, only with less masquerading and other suggestive humbug, but more intelligence. It is depressing that Juliusburger,[5] who is obviously an honest man, didn't spot the trick. Can't you instil a little insight into him? Liepmann's[6] attitude is—well, what can one call it? Maybe you have a good Berlin expression for this, for there must be other people of that ilk there. Freud was naturally moved by this discussion—he did get mentioned and a crumb even fell to him from the Lord's table. A man of Freud's modest achievements can wax fat on that.

You know, of course, that Bezzola called Freud a "psychological swine." In order to spare the moral susceptibilities of this gentleman I have not sent him an invitation to Salzburg. On the other hand Juliusburger, who evidently still doesn't quite know how matters stand, perhaps would be interested in our meeting. Unfortunately I don't know how far he has been immunized against further understanding by Bezzola's injections of antifreudin. Perhaps you would sound him out sometime if you are better acquainted with him. I'd rather not send him a direct invitation.

The photograph can be obtained on request from our Zurich photographer for fr. 10. It is an enlargement of my excellent little snapshot and is wonderfully handsome. The best picture of Freud I have ever seen.

If you can round up in Berlin a few more participants for the meeting, that would be very nice provided that they are people with pro-Freudian interests. Please would you stress in each case the private nature of the project.

With best wishes for the continued successful development of your practice and remembrances to your wife,

Ever sincerely yours, JUNG

---

[4] Jones (II, p. 267) mentions D. Bezzola as the most important of some writers who "had drawn the conclusion that an analysis should logically be followed by a synthesis, a demand still occasionally made by the misinformed, but Freud animadverted strongly against this."

[5] Otto Juliusburger, M.D., a Berlin psychiatrist, had in 1907 published a paper friendly to psychoanalysis, and in 1908 joined the newly founded Berlin Society. Later he withdrew from psychoanalysis.

[6] Hugo Karl Liepmann, M.D., (1863–1925), neurologist and brain anatomist at the U. of Berlin.

To Sandor Ferenczi

Dear Colleague,   Burghölzli-Zurich, 6 January 1909

Following your wish I will write at once to Dr. Brodmann[1] to ask whether he will take your paper,[2] although I would have liked to see you represented in our 1909 *Jahrbuch*.[3] I hope you won't fail to collaborate with us. Freud has already written to me about your work with many expressions of praise, so that I must here give vent to an ignoble feeling of envy, as Freud has not always taken Olympian delight in certain of my works. Still, someone is always destined to come afterwards who does it better. As you see, I am sublimating our rivalry into the philosophy of the fate of all things earthly. So if you don't get accepted by Brodmann, you will find a resting-place with us in the *Jahrbuch*. Moreover, perhaps Bresler[4] would not be unwilling, or the *Allgemeine Zeitschrift für Psychiatrie*.

Do you know Strohmayer's paper?[5] It is an arrow that hits the mark. Cordial greetings,

Yours, JUNG

☐ (Handwritten.) Sandor Ferenczi, M.D., (1873–1933); Freud's closest friend and collaborator, founder of the Hungarian Psycho-Analytical Society. (See pl. II).
[1] Editor of the *Journal für Psychologie und Neurologie* (Leipzig).
[2] "Introjection and Transference" (tr., *Contributions to Psychoanalysis*, 1916; cf. Ferenczi, 6 Dec. 09, n. 3); orig. published in the *Jahrbuch*, I:2 (1909).
[3] At the meeting of psychoanalysts in Salzburg, Apr. 1908 (cf. Abraham, 3 Jan. 08, n. 4), it had been decided to issue a periodical, *Jahrbuch für psychoanalytische und psychopathologische Forschungen*. It was to be directed by Bleuler and Freud and edited by Jung. The first volume appeared in 1909. Jung remained editor until 1914, when he resigned in consequence of his break with Freud. Cf. Freud, "On the History of the Psycho-Analytic Movement," Standard Edn. 14, pp. 27, 46; Jones, II, p. 49.
[4] Johannes Bresler, M.D., editor of the *Psychiatrisch-neurologische Wochenschrift* (Halle); founder and co-editor (with Freud) of the *Zeitschrift für Religionspsychologie* (Halle).
[5] "Ueber die ursächlichen Beziehungen der Sexualität zu Angst und Zwangszuständen," *Journal für Psychologie und Neurologie* (Leipzig), XII (1908).

To Sigmund Freud

Dear Professor Freud,   Burghölzli-Zurich, 2 April 1909

Worry and patients and all the other chores of daily life have beset me again and quite got me down for the first 2 days. Now I am slowly coming to the surface and beginning to bask in the memory of the days in Vienna.[1] I hope you will have received my offprints in good time for Wednesday evening.[2]

12.IV.

After a 10-day interruption I have at last succeeded in continuing my letter. From this interlude it appears that the above complaint was premature, because, as usual, worse was to follow. Today I have put the last bad day behind me. All during the Easter holidays, when other people were out walking, I was able to snatch only one day's breath of air. On 15.IV I shall wrench myself free without fail and start my bicycle tour. Since Vienna all scientific work has been out of the question. But in my practice I have accomplished much. At the moment a madly interesting case is stretching me on the rack. Some of the symptoms come suspiciously close to the organic borderline (brain tumour?), yet they all hover over a dimly divined psychogenic depth, so that in analysing them all one's misgivings are forgotten. First-rate spiritualistic phenomena occur in this case, though so far only once in my presence. Altogether it makes a very peculiar impression. The patient is a man-slaying Sara, Raguel's daughter.[3]

The case I told you about—evil eye, paranoiac impression—was cleared up as follows. She was abandoned by her last lover, who is altogether pathological (Dem. praec.?);[4] abandoned also by an earlier lover—this one even spent a year in an asylum. Now the infantile pattern: hardly knew her father and mother, loving instead her brother, 8 years older than she and at 22 a catatonic. Thus the psychological stereotype holds good. You said the patient was merely *imitating* Dem. praec.; now the model has been found.

When I left Vienna I was afflicted with some *sentiments d'incomplétude* on account of the last evening I spent with you. It seemed to me that my spookery[5] struck you as altogether too stupid and

☐ (Handwritten.)

1 Jung and his wife had stayed in Vienna 25–30 Mar. 1909 (cf. Jones, II, p. 57).
2 The Viennese group used to meet every Wednesday evening for discussion in Freud's waiting room (Jones, II, p. 9). The offprints were probably "The Significance of the Father in the Destiny of the Individual" (CW 4) and some of the studies in word-association (CW 2).
3 Tobit (Apoc.) 3:7ff. and 8:1ff. Cf. also Jung, "Significance of the Father," pars. 742f.
4 Dem. praec., D. pr.: abbreviations for dementia praecox, the older term coined by the German psychiatrist Emil Kraepelin for the mental disorder now known as schizophrenia, the term coined by Bleuler.
5 Cf. the episode related by Jung in *Memories*, pp. 155f./152f. While visiting

perhaps unpleasant because of the Fliess analogy.[6] (Insanity!) Just recently, however, the impression I had of the last-named patient smote me with renewed force. What I told my wife about it made the deepest impression on her too. I had the feeling that under it all there must be some quite special complex, a universal one having to do with the prospective tendencies[7] in man. If there is a "psych-analysis"[8] there must also be a "psychosynthesis" which creates future events according to the same laws. (I see I am writing rather as if I had a flight of ideas.) The leap towards psychosynthesis proceeds via the person of my patient, whose unconscious is right now preparing, apparently with nothing to stop it, a new stereotype into which everything from outside, as it were, fits in conformity with the complex. (Hence the idea of the objective effect of the prospective tendency!)

That last evening with you has, most happily, freed me inwardly from the oppressive sense of your paternal authority.[9] My unconscious celebrated this impression with a great dream which preoccupied me for some days and which I have just finished analyzing. I hope I am now rid of all unnecessary encumbrances. Your cause must and will prosper, so my pregnancy fantasies tell me, which luckily you caught in the end. As soon as I get back from Italy I shall begin some positive work, first of all for the *Jahrbuch*.

I hope you had a good Easter holiday and feel the better for it.

Freud he brought up the subject of parapsychology. Freud "rejected this entire complex of questions as nonsensical," and there then occurred a "catalytic ex-teriorization phenomenon" which Jung predicted would be repeated the next moment—and it was. Freud reacted in a long letter of 16 Apr. 09 (ibid., pp. 361ff/333ff). Jones does not mention this incident.

[6] Wilhelm Fliess, M.D., (1858–1928), German ear, nose, and throat specialist, founder of the theory of periodicity. He was Freud's closest friend for about ten years until they clashed in 1900 (Jones, I, ch. XIII, and Freud, *The Origins of Psychoanalysis: Letters to Wilhelm Fliess, Drafts and Notes, 1887–1902*, ed. M. Bonaparte, A. Freud, E. Kris, 1954). Subsequently Freud became increasingly critical of Fliess's scientific work because of its highly speculative character. Jones (I, p. 320) speaks of the "mystical features" in his writings and quotes (II, p. 117) Freud's letter of 6 Apr. 14 to Abraham on Fliess's "incapacity in the psychological field." Apparently Jung refers to this mistrust which Freud may well have expressed to him at their meeting.

[7] Defined in 1902 as "attempts of the future personality to break through." Jung, "On the Psychology and Pathology of So-called Occult Phenomena," CW 1, par. 136.

[8] The first form of the word "psychoanalysis."

[9] For Freud's reaction see the letter mentioned in n. 5 supra

N. Ossipow,[10] head physician of the Psychiatric University Clinic in Moscow, has published a fine report on our affairs. They seem to be working along our lines.

I have heard that Abraham with some others has issued a "psychanalytical questionnaire."[11] Let's hope it's a canard! Cordial greetings,

Gratefully, J U N G

[10] N. Ossipow had started translating Freud's works into Russian, and in 1911, together with others, founded a Russian psychoanalytical society (Jones, II, pp. 84, 97).

[11] Issued by Magnus Hirschfeld (1868–1935), a Berlin sexologist and one of the first members of the Berlin Society (resigned 1911), in collaboration with Abraham and the Hungarian psychoanalyst Philip Stein.

To Auguste Forel

Dear Professor Forel,   Küsnacht/Zürich, 12 October 1909

Unfortunately your letter of 26.VIII.09 came into my hands only shortly after my return from America.[1] Hence my delay in answering. Naturally I sympathize with your project for the coalition of all psychotherapists, but, given the present irreconcilability of opposites, I doubt very much whether we of the Freudian school would be welcome guests.

Yours very sincerely, c. g. J U N G

☐ (Handwritten.) Auguste Forel, M.D., (1848–1931), Swiss psychiatrist and entomologist; Bleuler's predecessor at the Burghölzli. — In 1909, when Jung left the staff of the Burghölzli, he moved from Zurich into his new home at Seestrasse 1003 (from 1915, numbered 228), in Küsnacht, suburb of Zurich, and thereafter he conducted his practice at his residence. For the rest of his life, unless otherwise noted, his letters were written from Küsnacht (earlier spelling: Küsnach) or, after the late 1920's, from his retreat at Bollingen, at the southeastern end of the Lake of Zurich. — This letter is published in Forel, *Briefe, Correspondance* 1864–1927, ed. H. W. Walser (1968).

[1] Jung had been invited by Clark University, Worcester, Mass., to lecture on his association experiments. Freud was invited too, and they travelled together from Bremen, joined by Ferenczi. (Cf. *Memories*, p. 156/152 and Appendix II: "Letters to Emma Jung from America"; Jones, II, pp. 6off.) Jung's three lectures on "The Association Method" were first published in the *American Journal of Psychology*, XXI:2 (Apr. 1910). The first two, "The Association Method" and "The Family Constellation," are in CW 2; the third, "Psychic Conflicts in a Child," is in CW 17.

To Sandor Ferenczi

Dear Colleague,   6 December 1909

Your letter has certainly hit the mark. These things were in the air. You can well imagine that I often felt a proper fool when, because of your position, I found myself thrust into the role of a usurper. But I don't feel like a usurper at all, rather one of the workers who is doing a special bit of work. Whether I am recognized or not recognized as the "crown prince"[1] can at times annoy me or please me. Since I gave up my academic career[2] my interest in science and knowledge has become purer and amply compensates for the pleasures of outward esteem, so that it is really of greater importance to me to see clearly in scientific matters and work ahead for the future than to measure myself against Freud. No doubt my roving fantasy caters to this and particularly the unconscious, but that must be so and is the necessary undercurrent of all creativity. I believe that if we succeed in putting the work above ourselves (so far as this is possible at all) we free ourselves from a lot of unnecessary encumbrances and unwanted responsibilities brought by ambition, envy, and other two-edged swords. What does one want actually? In the end it is always the one who really is or was the strongest that remains king, even if only posthumously. As always, we have to submit trustingly to this natural law, since nothing avails against it anyway. Ambition is for the most part the same as jealousy, and therefore crippling and nonsensical. Haven't we seen that with the American mania for setting up records? All beauty gets lost in the process—a grave loss which our science can hardly afford.

Won't you translate your lectures into German? They would surely be accepted by Bresler, for instance. Have you anything in mind for the 2nd half of *Jahrbuch* II?

Congratulations on Freud's recognition!!![3]

Best greetings, JUNG

□ (Handwritten.)

1 Freud had frequently suggested to Jung that he should become his successor (cf. *Memories*, p. 157/154, and Freud's letter of 16 Apr. 09, ibid., p. 361/333: "my successor and crown prince"; also in the Freud-Jung Letters).

2 Cf. Freud, 5 Oct. 06, n. 5.

3 In the autumn of 1909 Ferenczi published a paper on "Introjection und Uebertragung" (cf. Ferenczi, 6 Jan. 09, n. 2) which met with Freud's warm approval. Ferenczi put together a volume of collected papers for which Freud wrote a preface. It was published in Hungarian in 1910 in Budapest under the title *Lélekelemzés* ("Psychoanalysis"). Later translated into German and English (*Contributions to Psychoanalysis*, 1916).

To Sandor Ferenczi

Dear Colleague,   25 December 1909

I consider it impossible to keep up our analytical relationship by correspondence. One simply hasn't the time for so many and such long letters. Now and then, as you say, a sign of life and no diplomatics when we meet—that is possible.

I am very pleased to welcome you among the collaborators, this time for the second volume.[1] Sadger[2] tells me that for the 1st half of vol. II he is contributing a case in which he too will expatiate on homosexuality. I am looking forward to comparing your findings. Incidentally, your paper on "Introjection"[3] made a great impression here, as also did your previous paper on "Actual" (etc.)[4] The latter particularly on Pfister.[5]

At present I am once again in terminological difficulties. The reason why this always seems to happen only to me lies in my teaching activity. Recently I took issue with Binswanger about Freud's concept of regression,[6] as to whether it included the infantile element or not. Now it turns out that the concept crops up in two variants. When Adler[7] demonstrates repressed homosexuality in the dreams of a prostitute, there is a distinct collision with the clinical concept of homosexuality as it actually exists. In this sense homosexuality is

☐ (Handwritten.)

[1] Ferenczi did not publish a paper in vol. II of the *Jahrbuch* but in vol. III (1911), "Ueber die Rolle der Homosexualität in der Pathogenese der Paranoia."
[2] Isidor Sadger, M.D., Austrian neurologist and psychoanalyst. His article was "Ein Fall von multipler Perversion mit hysterischen Absenzen," *Jahrbuch*, II:1 (1910).
[3] Cf. previous letter, n. 3.
[4] "Actual- and Psycho-neuroses in the Light of Freud's Investigations and Psychoanalysis," *Further Contributions to the Theory and Technique of Psychoanalysis* (1926). Originally published in *Gyógyászat*, nos. 15 and 16 (1908), one of the leading Hungarian medical weeklies, and the same year in the *Wiener Klinische Rundschau*, nos. 48–51.
[5] Oskar Pfister (1873–1956), Swiss Protestant clergyman. He became interested in psychoanalysis in 1908 and was a prominent Freudian. His correspondence with Freud has been edited by H. Meng and E. L. Freud, *Psycho-Analysis and Faith* (1963).
[6] Cf. "Notes upon a Case of Obsessional Neurosis," Standard Edn. 10 (1955). The case was originally published in the *Jahrbuch*, I:2 (1909). Reference in letter is to Ludwig Binswanger.
[7] Alfred Adler (1870–1937), Austrian psychiatrist. Originally a follower of Freud's, he seceded in 1911 and founded his own school, called "Individual Psychology."

the dominance of this same component in overt acts because of a permanent cathexis, and for that reason it differs from the temporary cathexis of the homosexual component due to displacement of the heterosexual component. These and similar difficulties make teaching unspeakably tiring and lead to everlasting misunderstandings.[8]

Freud's paper on obsessional neurosis[9] is marvellous but *very hard to understand*. I must soon read it for the third time. Am I particularly stupid? Or is it the style? I plump cautiously for the latter. Between Freud's speaking and writing there is "a gulf fixed" which is very wide. Most of all I have disputed with Freud the "symptom of *omnipotence*"[10] (!) because the term is too clinical. Naturally he is right, and the term is artistic too. But if you have to *teach* that kind of thing in a systematic context, you get goose pimples and take to swearing.

With best greetings, J U N G

[8] Jung apparently felt that the two different uses of the term "homosexuality" presented great difficulties to his students: the one, clinical, concept which denotes actual and expressed homosexuality "on the basis of a permanent cathexis"—the other of a "fleeting cathexis on account of (a temporary) displacement of the heterosexual component," not expressed in actual homosexual acts.

[9] Cf. n. 6 supra.

[10] See next letter, n. 1.

To Sigmund Freud

Dear Professor Freud,   25 December 1909

My attempt at criticism, though it looked like an attack, was actually a defence, which is why I apparently had to tilt at the "*omnipotence* of thoughts."[1] Of course the term is dead right as well as elegantly concise and trenchant, for that's how it is, especially in D. pr. where new fundamentals are constantly being uncovered by it. All this has shaken me very much, in particular my faith in my own capacities. But most of all I was struck by your remark that you longed for archaeologists, philologists, etc. By this, I told myself, you probably meant that I was unfit for such work. However, it is in pre-

□ (Handwritten.)

[1] In a letter of 14 Dec. 09 Jung expressed his doubts about the term "omnipotence of thoughts" (Jones, II, 495) which Freud used in his "Notes upon a Case of Obsessional Neurosis," as generalizing from an individual case.

cisely these fields that I now have a passionate interest,[2] as before only in Dem. pr. And I have the most marvellous visions, glimpses of far-ranging interconnections which I am at present incapable of grasping, for the subject really is too big and I hate impotent bungling. Who then is to do this work? Surely it must be someone who knows the psyche and has the passion for it. D. pr. will not be the loser. Honegger,[3] who has already introduced himself to you, is now working with me with *great* understanding, and I shall entrust to him everything I know so that something good may come of it. It has become quite clear to me that we shall not solve the ultimate secrets of neurosis and psychosis without mythology and the history of civilization, for *embryology* goes hand in hand with *comparative anatomy*, and without the latter the former is but a freak of nature whose depths remain uncomprehended. It is a hard lot to have to work alongside the father creator. Hence my attacks on "clinical terminology."

31.XII. The Christmas holidays have eaten up all my time, so I am only now in a position to continue my letter. I am turning over and over in my mind the problem of antiquity. It's a hard nut! Without doubt there's a lot of infantile sexuality in it, but that is not all. Rather it seems to me that antiquity was ravaged by the struggle with *incest*, with which sexual *repression* begins (or is it the other way round?). We must look up the history of family law. The history of civilization, taken by itself, is too skimpy, at least what there is of it today. For instance, Burckhardt's[4] *History of Greek Civilization* remains wholly on the surface. A particularly significant topic is Greek demonology, which I hope to penetrate into a little via Rohde[5] (*Psyche*). I'd like to tell you many things about Dionysos were it not too much for a letter. Nietzsche seems to have intuited a great deal of it. I have an idea that the Dionysian frenzy was a backwash of sexuality, a backwash whose historical significance has been insuffi-

[2] At this time Jung had embarked on a serious study of mythology, which he regarded as necessary for the understanding of latent psychoses. Cf. *Memories*, p. 131 and Freud, 12 June 11, n. 2.

[3] J. Honegger, M.D., a prominent pupil and an analysand of Jung's; he committed suicide in Mar. 1911. Cf. Jung, *Symbols of Transformation*, CW 5, par. 200 & n. 23; Jones, II, p. 75.

[4] Jacob Burckhardt (1818–97), Swiss historian. His *History of Greek Civilization* was published posthumously, ed. Jakob Oeri (1898–1902).

[5] Prof. Erwin Rohde (1845–98), classical scholar, friend of Nietzsche. His *Psyche, Seelenkult und Unsterblichkeitsglaube der Griechen* was published 1890–94 (tr., *Psyche*, 1925).

ciently appreciated, essential elements of which overflowed into Christianity but in another compromise formation. I don't know whether I am writing you banalities or hieroglyphics. An unpleasant feeling. How much I'd prefer to talk it over with you personally!

Will it suit you to hold the Nuremberg meeting[6] on Easter *Tuesday*? As soon as I know, I will work up the idea in a circular and send it to you.

I note that my difficulties regarding the question of libido and also of sadism are obviously due to the fact that I have not yet adjusted my attitude sufficiently to yours. I still haven't understood properly what you wrote me. The best thing is to postpone it until we can *talk* in peace. I would really have to question you on every sentence in your letter.

.   .   .

As regards Nuremberg I must add that I am naturally counting very much on your taking first place as lecturer. That, as in Salzburg,[7] is what we all hope.

.   .   .

Tomorrow I must prepare a lecture for the students here on "symbolism,"[8] which fills me with horror. God knows what I shall scribble together. I have read Ferrero,[9] but what he writes about is not our kind of symbolism. Let's hope a good spirit will stand by me. With many cordial greetings and wishes,

Most sincerely yours, JUNG

[6] The Second International Psycho-Analytical Congress, held in Nuremberg, 30–31 Mar. 1910 (cf. Jones, II, p. 75).

[7] Cf. Abraham, 3 Jan. 08, n. 4.

[8] No MS exists of this lecture. But in a letter of 30 Jan. 10 to Freud, Jung says of this lecture: "I have tried to put the 'symbolic' on a psychogenetic foundation, i.e., to show that in the individual fantasy the primum movens, the individual conflict, material or form (whichever you prefer), is mythic, or mythologically typical."

[9] Guglielmo Ferrero (1871–1942), author of *I simboli in rapporto alla storia e filosofia del diritto* (1893). A quotation from the French translation, *Les Lois psychologiques du symbolisme* (1895), forms the motto to Jung's *Symbols of Transformation* (and its 1911 original version).

To Sigmund Freud

Dear Professor Freud,   11 February 1910

I am a lazy correspondent. But this time I have (as always) excellent excuses. Preparing the *Jahrbuch* has taken me an incredible amount of time, as I had to work mightily with the blue pencil. The bulk of the manuscripts goes off today. It will be an impressive affair.

Enclosed is a list of addresses.[1] Please let me know if I have forgotten anyone from abroad. You will see that I am setting about it on a rather large scale—I hope with your subsequent approval. Our cause is forging ahead. Only today I heard from a doctor in Munich that the medical students there are taking a massive interest in the new psychology, some of them poking fun at the gentlemen at the Clinic because they understand nothing about it.

Meanwhile I too have now received an invitation from the apothecary Knapp in Bern to join the I.O.[2] I have asked for time to think about it and have promised to submit the invitation to the Nuremberg Congress. Knapp wanted to have me also for lectures. The prospect appals me. I am so thoroughly convinced that I would have to read myself the longest ethical lectures that I cannot muster a grain of courage to promote ethics in public, let alone from the psychoanalytical standpoint! At present I am sitting so precariously on the fence between the Dionysian and the Apollinian that I wonder whether it might not be worthwhile to reintroduce a few of the older cultural stupidities such as the monasteries. That is, I really don't know which is the lesser evil. Do you think this Fraternity could have any practical use? Isn't it one of Forel's coalitions[3] against stupidity and evil, and must we not love evil if we are to break away from the obsession with virtue which makes us sick and forbids us the joys of life? If a coalition is to have any ethical significance it should never be an artificial one but must be nourished by the deep

---

□ (Handwritten.)

[1] Of people to be invited to the Nuremberg Congress.

[2] Knapp had tried to enlist Freud's support for the "International Fraternity for Ethics and Culture" ("I.O." is Jung's abbreviation for "Internationaler Orden"). One of its aims was to "fight against the authority of the State and the Church in cases where they are committing manifest injustice" (letter from Freud to Jung, 13 Feb. 10, quoted in Jones, II, pp. 74f.). Freud asked Knapp to get in touch with Jung.

[3] Forel was president of Knapp's "Fraternity." Like Bleuler, he was a fanatic teetotaller. For a time Jung, under Bleuler's influence, joined their ranks (Jones, II, pp. 61, 165).

instincts of the race. Somewhat like Christian Science, Islam, Buddhism. Religion can be replaced only by religion. Is there perchance a new saviour in the I.O.? What sort of new myth does he hand out for us to live by? Only the wise are ethical from sheer intellectual presumption, the rest of us need the eternal truth of myth.

You will see from this string of associations that the problem does not leave me simply apathetic and cold. The ethical problem of sexual freedom really is enormous and worth the sweat of all noble souls. But 2000 years of Christianity have to be replaced by something equivalent. An ethical fraternity, with its mythical Nothing, not infused by any archaic-infantile driving force, is a pure vacuum and can never evoke in man the slightest trace of that age-old animal power which drives the migrating bird across the sea and without which no irresistible mass movement can come into being. I imagine a far finer and more comprehensive task for ψa[4] than alliance with an ethical fraternity. I think we must give it time to infiltrate into people from many centres, to revivify among intellectuals a feeling for symbol and myth, ever so gently to transform Christ back into the soothsaying god of the vine, which he was, and in this way absorb those ecstatic instinctual forces of Christianity for the *one* purpose of making the cult and the sacred myth what they once were—a drunken feast of joy where man regained the ethos and holiness of an animal. That indeed was the beauty and purpose of classical religion, which from God knows what temporary biological needs has turned into a Misery Institute. Yet how infinitely much rapture and wantonness lie dormant in our religion, waiting to be led back to their true destination! A genuine and proper ethical development cannot abandon Christianity but must grow up within it, must bring to fruition its hymn of love, the agony and ecstasy over the dying and resurgent god,[5] the mystic power of the wine, the awesome anthropophagy[6] of the Last Supper—only *this* ethical development can serve the vital forces of religion. But a syndicate of interests dies out after 10 years.

ψa makes me "proud and discontent," I don't want to attach it to Forel, this hair-shirted John of the Locusts,[7] but would like to affiliate

---

[4] Abbreviation for "psychoanalysis."
[5] Dionysus–Zagreus was one of the Near Eastern dying and resurgent gods (cf. Jung, *Symbols of Transformation*, par. 527). Regarding the significance of this figure see ibid., par. 175: ". . . the young dying god, who has ever been our hope of renewal and of the world to come." (Also in 1911 original edn.)
[6] Cf. Jung, "Transformation Symbolism in the Mass," CW 11, pars. 340ff.
[7] An allusion to Forel's teetotalism. Cf. Matthew 3:4.

18

it with everything that was ever dynamic and alive. One can only let this kind of thing grow. To be practical: I shall submit this crucial question for ψa to the Nuremberg Congress. I have abreacted enough for today—my heart was bursting with it. Please don't mind all this storming.[8] With many cordial greetings,

Very sincerely yours, J U N G

[8] Fifty years later one of Jung's pupils wrote him a letter quoting the above remarks about Christianity. In a letter of 9 Apr. 59 (not in this selection) Jung replied: "Best thanks for the quotation from that accursed correspondence. For me it is an unfortunately inexpungable reminder of the incredible folly that filled the days of my youth. The journey from cloud-cuckoo-land back to reality lasted a long time. In my case Pilgrim's Progress consisted in my having to climb down a thousand ladders until I could reach out my hand to the little clod of earth that I am."

To Sigmund Freud

Dear Professor Freud,   17 June 1910

I answered Adler today. His first letter went to Riklin,[1] who filed it. Unfortunately his letter of 1.VI. remained unanswered because I first had to wait for the founding of the Zurich group[2] in order to give Adler positive news. As I hold the view that the International Association[3] has been founded since Nuremberg, I cannot imagine why the Viennese group[4] could not consolidate itself. Perhaps I have misunderstood something? We were of the opinion here that a group already existed in Vienna just as in Berlin and now also in Zurich. Please forgive me for the delay in answering. The break with Bleuler[5]

☐ (Handwritten.)

[1] Franz Riklin, M.D., (1878–1938), Swiss psychiatrist, from 1910 secretary to Jung as president of the International Psycho-Analytical Association, editor of the *Correspondenzblatt* or *Bulletin* (Jones, II, p. 77). He collaborated with Jung on "The Associations of Normal Subjects," *Studies in Word-Association*, now in CW 2.

[2] In June 1910 a psychoanalytical group was founded in Zurich.

[3] The International Psycho-Analytical Association, founded at the Nuremberg Congress in Mar. 1910.

[4] Adler became president of the Viennese group of the Association in Oct. 1910 (Freud, "On the History of the Psycho-Analytical Movement," p. 44; Jones, II, p. 8).

[5] Bleuler's attitude to psychoanalysis had been constantly vacillating, and in 1910 a break occurred between him and the Zurich group (Freud, ibid.; Jones, ibid., pp. 8of.).

has not left me unscathed. Once again I underestimated my father complex. Besides that I am working like mad. I just keep alive in a breathless rush. It's high time I got some help. Unfortunately Honegger is coming only at the end of next week. Till then I'll have to let the correspondence pile up unanswered. I have at last succeeded in getting the Juristic-Psychiatric Society, of which I was president, off my neck.

The founding of our group was a painful affair. We have about 15 members, several of them foreigners. As yet we haven't got down to debating the statutes because of the difficulties at the Burghölzli. But we have elected Binswanger[6] president and my cousin Dr. Ewald Jung[7] secretary—he is coming along very nicely. Now the hair in the soup: I proposed holding *occasional* public meetings and then inviting Burghölzli, etc. Binswanger declared he would accept the vote for president only if all meetings were held in common with non-members. I put it to the vote and my proposal fell through. So now we have a Society with a few regular members and a public that doesn't belong, that has all the privileges and itself does nothing. I don't like it a bit. But what can I do? I suggested asking your fatherly advice beforehand but this was turned down. So we in Zurich limp along making a poor show. You won't be happy about it. Neither shall I.

Leonardo[8] is wonderful. Pfister tells me he has seen the vulture[9] in the picture. I saw one too, but in a different place: the beak precisely in the pubic region. One would like to say with Kant: play of chance, which equals the subtlest lucubrations of reason. I have read Leonardo straight through and shall soon come back to it again. The transition to mythology grows out of this essay from inner necessity,

---

[6] Ludwig.

[7] Swiss psychiatrist. See Jung's letter to him of 31 July 35.

[8] "Leonardo da Vinci and a Memory of his Childhood" (1910; now in Standard Edn. 11).

[9] Freud discusses at great length a childhood memory of Leonardo's in which, as Freud assumed, a vulture played an important part (in fact, he mistranslated the Italian *nibio,* mod. *nibbio,* "kite"). Pfister believed he had discovered a hidden vulture in certain outlines of Leonardo's "Madonna and Child with St. Anne" (in the Louvre), a painting which Freud expatiates on in his essay (cf. Pfister, "Kryptolalie, Kryptographie und unbewusstes Vexierbild bei Normalen," *Jahrbuch,* V, p. 115; Freud, "Leonardo," pp. 115ff. & n.; Erich Neumann, "Leonardo da Vinci and the Mother Archetype," *Art and the Creative Unconscious,* 1959). For Jung's comments on Freud's interpretation of the painting see "Concerning the Archetypes, with Special Reference to the Anima Concept," CW 9, i, par. 140 & n. 27.

actually it is the first essay of yours with whose inner development I felt perfectly in tune from the start. I would like to dwell longer on these impressions and brood quietly on the thoughts which want to unroll in long succession. But the present rush that has already gone on for several weeks leaves me no peace any more.

Again many thanks for your friendly advice about Honegger.[10] Your advice has been anticipated by events. I had already told Honegger that things simply couldn't go on as they were. You can hardly imagine the uproar in my office and the German-French-English caterwaulings my bloodsuckers have set up. So I beg your forgiveness once more for the delay. Be patient with me—when Honegger is here I shall be able to breathe more freely and cope with my outer obligations a bit more decently.

I think I have already told you that I received the manuscripts safely, with best thanks.

Cordial greetings and again a plea for forgiveness,

Most sincerely, JUNG

[10] In a letter of 9 June 10 Freud had advised Jung to be more tolerant with Honegger and to "take him as he is."

To Sigmund Freud

Dear Professor Freud,   13 December 1910

I have postponed my answer so as to give you time to come to terms with Bleuler.[1] I take it that you have now reached agreement. Any day between Christmas and New Year will suit me. Only not New Year's Day. I would like if possible a few days' rest in the mountains at Sylvester.[2]

I am greatly looking forward to Munich,[3] where the Schreber case[4] will play a not unimportant role. I hope my hands won't be empty

☐ (Handwritten.)
[1] Freud had tried to come to terms with Bleuler (cf. Freud, 17 June 10, n. 5) because of his influence in the psychiatric world.
[2] On the Continent, New Year's Eve = Sylvester.
[3] Freud arranged to meet Bleuler in Munich, 25–26 Dec., and he and Jung used this occasion to meet after Bleuler's departure.
[4] Freud's analysis of the Schreber case is in "Psycho-Analytic Notes on an Auto-biographical Account of a Case of Paranoia (Dementia Paranoides)," 1911, Standard Edn. 12. Cf. Schreber, *Memoirs of My Nervous Illness* (tr., 1955).

either, though unfortunately I cannot bring my manuscript[5] along with me. For one thing it has still to be copied out, and for another it is only the first half. The earlier lecture I sent you has been vastly expanded. Moreover the second half, the so-called drama of Chiwantopel,[6] has proved to be so rich in archaeological[7] material that I haven't yet been able to put everything in order. I have still a lot more reading to do, so that I can publish the second half only in the summer issue [of the *Jahrbuch*]. It seems to me, however, that this time I have hit the mark, or nearly so, as the material is falling into a surprising pattern. Too much shouldn't be revealed yet. But be prepared for some strange things the like of which you have never yet heard from me. I have thoroughly revised and documented the introductory section on the two kinds of thinking.[8] I think it is now presentable and expresses what I want to say though not in a masterly fashion. For me it has become something of a chore. Besides, the problem really is a difficult one. I shall take shelter behind a motto from Guglielmo Ferrero,[9] which defends the scholar who exposes himself to criticism. My conscience is clear, for I have done honest work and drawn nothing out of a hat. There is little to report about our work in Zurich although all sorts of things are being produced. I would only like to ask you if you have any objection in principle to *experimental studies* occasionally appearing in the *Jahrbuch* which have to do with the psychophysiology of complexes. Dr. Beauchant[10] is, I believe, an acquaintance of Dr. Assagioli.[11] I cannot complain about my martyrdom.[12] Not only do people abuse me, but this winter

[5] Draft of Part I of *Wandlungen und Symbole der Libido* (tr., *Psychology of the Unconscious*, 1916), rev. 1952 as *Symbole der Wandlung* (tr., *Symbols of Transformation*, CW 5, 1956). Part I was first published in the *Jahrbuch*, III (1911); Part II, ibid., IV (1912). The book led to the break with Freud and finally to Jung's resignation (1914) as editor of the *Jahrbuch*.
[6] The book is an analysis of the fantasy material of Miss Frank Miller, which was published by the Swiss psychiatrist Théodore Flournoy as "Quelques faits d'imagination créatrice subconsciente," *Archives de psychologie* (Geneva), V (1906). In these fantasies the figure of "Chiwantopel," an Aztec, plays an important role (cf. *Symbols of Transformation*, Appendix, pp. 457ff.).
[7] The more correct term would be "mythological."
[8] Cf. ibid., Part I, ch. 2.
[9] Cf. Freud, 25 Dec. 09, n. 9.
[10] R. Moricheau-Beauchant, M.D., professor of medicine in Poitiers (cf. Jones, II, pp. 85, 97).
[11] R. Assagioli, M.D., of Florence had joined the Swiss "Freud Society" in Zurich in 1910 (ibid., pp. 82, 85).
[12] In a letter of 3 Dec. 10 Freud mentioned "the negative aspect of my fame" and added "sometimes it makes me angry that nobody abuses you."

22

I haven't even brought off my course of lectures—for want of an audience. With cordial greetings,

Sincerely, JUNG

To Sigmund Freud

Dear Professor Freud, 12 June 1911

Since last writing to you (long enough, alas!) I have made good use of my time. I was at the Congress of Swiss Psychiatrists in Lausanne and spoke on "forms of unconscious fantasy."[1] These things are contributions to, and elaborations of, the work in the current *Jahrbuch*, which, incidentally, is taking shape terribly slowly (because of the wealth of material). Everything I am doing now revolves round the contents and forms of unconscious fantasies. I think I've already got some really fine results. You will see that this investigation is the necessary preliminary work for the psychology of Dem. praec.[2] Spielrein's case[3] is proof of that (it's in the *Jahrbuch*). Often I longed for you to be here so that I could discuss an extremely difficult case: Dem. praec. with, one can well say, a tremendous unconscious fantasy system which I have to drag into the light of day with unspeakable effort and patience. On top of that, constant danger of suicide. A really devilish case, but extraordinarily interesting and instructive. The case is particularly painful because I am now beginning to see what I did not see with Honegger. It seems that in Dem. praec. you have at all costs to bring to light the inner world produced by the introversion of libido, which in paranoiacs suddenly appears in distorted form as a delusional system (Schreber), as I have apparently

☐ (Handwritten.)
[1] This lecture undoubtedly contained material from *Wandlungen und Symbole* but no MS seems to exist.
[2] At the psychoanalytical Congress in Weimar, Sept. 1911, Jung read a paper on symbolism in the psychoses and mythology (Jones, II, p. 96). Cf. Freud, "On the History of the Psycho-Analytical Movement," p. 36: "A deep impression was made on all hearers at one of the psycho–analytical Congresses when a follower of Jung's demonstrated the correspondence between schizophrenic phantasies and the cosmogonies of primitive times and races." Jung's "follower" was Jan Nelken; cf. his "Analytische Beobachtungen über Phantasien eines Schizophrenen," *Jahrbuch*, IV (1912); also Jung, *Mysterium Coniunctionis*, CW 14, index *s.v.* Nelken.
[3] Sabina Spielrein, "Ueber den psychologischen Inhalt eines Falls von Schizophrenie," *Jahrbuch*, III (1912). There are numerous references to her case study in *Symbols of Transformation*.

succeeded in doing in the present case but failed to do with Honegger because I had no inkling of it. I tell myself that this lack of knowledge of mine led to his death. What if this view should be confirmed? I have the feeling I am practising vivisection on human beings with intense inner resistance. It seems that introversion leads not only, as in hysteria, to a recrudescence of infantile memories but also to a loosening up of the historical layers of the unconscious, thus giving rise to perilous formations which come to light only in exceptional cases.

My evenings are taken up very largely with astrology. I make horoscopic calculations in order to find a clue to the core of psychological truth. Some remarkable things have turned up which will certainly appear incredible to you. In the case of one lady, the calculation of the position of the stars at her nativity produced a quite definite character picture, with several biographical details which did not belong to her but to her mother—and the characteristics fitted the mother to a T. The lady suffers from an extraordinary mother complex. I dare say that we shall one day discover in astrology a good deal of knowledge that has been intuitively projected into the heavens. For instance, it appears that the signs of the zodiac are character pictures, in other words libido symbols which depict the typical qualities of the libido at a given moment.

I still haven't finished my popular exposition for the Zurich Jahrbuch.[4] This week I must start work on my Brussels lecture.[5]

.   .   .

With cordial greetings,

Very sincerely, JUNG

[4] "Neue Bahnen der Psychologie," *Raschers Jahrbuch für Schweizer Art und Kunst* (1912); now "New Paths in Psychology," *Two Essays on Analytical Psychology*, CW 7, Appendix I.

[5] "Ueber Psychoanalyse beim Kinde," held at the Ier Congrès International de Pédagogie, Brussels, Aug. 1911. Later incorporated in "Versuch einer Darstellung der psychoanalytischen Theorie," *Jahrbuch*, V (1913); now Lecture 9 ("A Case of Neurosis in a Child") of "The Theory of Psychoanalysis," *Freud and Psychoanalysis*, CW 4, pars. 458ff. The nine lectures comprising "The Theory of Psychoanalysis" were delivered at Fordham U., New York, Sept. 1912.

To Alphonse Maeder

Dear Colleague,   Kaserne St. Gallen, 28 October 1911

Please forgive me for answering your letter only now. It was impossible to do so earlier because I was detailed for a very strenuous mountain exercise. I find it very boring that people are so lazy. The next meeting[1] would be a good opportunity to cover some elementary ground, for instance the cathartic and psychoanalytical method, or trauma and sexual constitution. In case of necessity I could bring my Brussels lecture with me (child analysis).[2] Then we must set aside some time for discussing matters bearing on the Association. The Burghölzli racket must be stopped. . . . The whole analytical tradition is going to the devil there. In accordance with our psychoanalytical principles I would only like to speed up this process of reverting to anatomy and classification by dissociating ourselves from the Clinic. We can expect nothing good from those people. With best greetings,

Sincerely, JUNG

☐ (Handwritten, from an army camp where Jung was a medical officer.) Alphonse Maeder, M.D., (1882–1971), Swiss psychotherapist, member of the Swiss Freudian group. After Jung's break with Freud he was one of the very few who supported Jung. Later he became associated with the Oxford Movement of the American evangelist Frank Buchman, founder of "Moral Rearmament."
[1] Of the Swiss Branch Society of the International Psycho-Analytical Association (cf. Jones, II, p. 79).
[2] Cf. Freud, 12 June 11, n. 5.

To Sigmund Freud

Dear Professor Freud,   17 May 1912

. . .

As regards the question of incest,[1] I am afraid of making a very paradoxical impression on you. I only venture to throw a bold con-

☐ (Handwritten.)
[1] Jung's different interpretation of incest and his modification of the libido theory as put forward in *Wandlungen und Symbole* were the crucial points of disagreement with Freud leading to the final break. While working on the last chapter of the book he realized what the consequences of his theories would be, and "for two months I was unable to touch my pen, so tormented was I by the conflict" (*Memories*, p. 167/162, cf. also pp. 208f.; Jones, II, pp. 162f.; Freud, "History of the Psycho-Analytical Movement," pp. 59ff.).

jecture into the discussion: the large amount of free-floating anxiety in primitive man, which led to the creation of taboo ceremonies in the widest sense (totem, etc.), produced among other things the *incest taboo* as well (or rather: the mother and father taboo). The incest taboo does not correspond with the specific value of incest *sensu strictiori* any more than the sacredness of the totem corresponds with its biological value. From this standpoint we must say that incest is forbidden *not because it is desired* but because the free-floating anxiety regressively reactivates infantile material and turns it into a ceremony of atonement (as though incest had been, or might have been, desired). Psychologically, the incest prohibition doesn't have the significance which one must ascribe to it if one assumes the existence of a particularly strong incest wish. The aetiological significance of the incest prohibition must be compared directly with the so-called sexual trauma, which usually owes its aetiological role only to regressive reactivation. The trauma is *seemingly important* or real, and so is the incest prohibition or incest barrier, which from the psychoanalytical point of view has taken the place of the sexual trauma. Just as *cum grano salis* it doesn't matter whether a sexual trauma really occurred or not, or was a mere fantasy, it is psychologically quite immaterial whether an incest barrier really existed or not, since it is essentially a question of later development whether or not the so-called problem of incest will become of apparent importance. Another comparison: the occasional cases of real incest are of as little importance for the ethnic incest prohibitions as the occasional outbursts of bestiality among primitives are for the ancient animal cults. In my opinion the incest barrier can no more be explained by reduction to the possibility of real incest than the animal cult can be explained by reduction to real bestiality. The animal cult is explained by an infinitely long psychological development which is of paramount importance and not by primitive bestial tendencies—these are nothing but the quarry that provides the material for building a temple. But the temple and its meaning have nothing whatever to do with the quality of the building stones. This applies also to the incest taboo, which as a special psychological institution has a much greater—and different—significance than the prevention of incest, even though it may look the same from outside. (The temple is white, yellow, or red according to the material used.) Like the stones of a temple, the incest taboo is the symbol or vehicle of a far wider and special meaning which has as little to do with real incest as hysteria with the sexual trauma, the animal cult with the bestial tendency and the temple with the stone (or better, with the primitive dwelling from whose form it is derived).

I hope I have expressed myself a bit more clearly this time. With many cordial greetings,

Very sincerely, JUNG

To Trigant Burrow

[ORIGINAL IN ENGLISH]

My dear Burrow,   26 December 1912

I am very glad to have your letter and the manuscript. I suppose you heard of the great change in Vienna, where Freud and Stekel[1] are in full disagreement. Stekel behaved in a most impertinent and foolish way, so that Freud had to give up the editorship of the *Zentralblatt*.[2] Unfortunately the publisher remained on the side of Stekel, hence Stekel kept the *Zentralblatt* and Freud was dismissed. Freud founded a new journal[3] of international character and we all have gone over to this new journal, leaving Stekel with his mutilated *Zentralblatt*. I think you agree with me, sending your article to Freud with the request that your name is mentioned among the regular contributors of the journal. This place will be more commendable than the *Zentralblatt*.

I am pretty sure to have left my fountain-pen in your house probably as a present symbolizing literary fertility; it is the pen I wrote my *Libido-Arbeit*[4] with. I very much regretted this loss, but if it is in your hands it may stay there.

Yours very truly, JUNG

☐ (Handwritten.) Trigant Burrow, M.D., (1875–1950), American psychiatrist and psychoanalyst, pupil of Jung's (Jones, II, p. 75). Jung had visited him in Baltimore in September.
[1] Wilhelm Stekel, M.D., (1868–1940), Austrian nerve specialist and psychoanalyst.
[2] *Zentralblatt für Psychoanalyse und Psychotherapie*, published by J. F. Bergmann (Wiesbaden). The first number appeared in Oct. 1910 under the editorship of Adler and Stekel (Jones, II, pp. 77, 79; Freud, "History," pp. 44f.). Freud gives Sept. 1910 as the date of the first issue.
[3] *Internationale Zeitschrift für ärztliche Psychoanalyse* (Leipzig) (Freud, ibid., p. 47).
[4] *Wandlungen und Symbole der Libido*.

To Alphonse Maeder

Dear Colleague,   29 October 1913

The *Jahrbuch* affair is a private matter to be settled between myself and Freud. If the Zurich people are also affected by it, then it is very painful for me. As you can well imagine, I am not giving up the *Jahrbuch* for fun but because it is impossible to collaborate with Freud's attitude. I still have no news from Vienna. But I shall take care to create for the Zurich people a new organ in the style of the *Jahrbuch*, perhaps called "*Psychologische Untersuchungen*. Works of the Zurich School of Psychoanalysis."[1] In the event, Deuticke is ready to accept it. If our works are dropped from the *Jahrbuch*, maybe the *Jahrbuch* will pack up too.

I have by no means walked into Freud's trap, for I consider it of no advantage to Freud to have sickened me off.

A committee of inquiry is out of the question, because the *Jahrbuch* is not after all run by a club and I *won't* collaborate with Freud any longer. It will make a very bad impression all round. But inner successes count more with me than the howling of the mob.

I shall soon be able to give you news of Deuticke and Freud, if the latter does not deem it beneath his papal dignity to answer me.

Yours sincerely, J U N G

☐ (Handwritten.)
[1] The first volume in a series actually called *Psychologische Abhandlungen*, edited by Jung, was published by Rascher in 1914. It contained 5 essays by his followers but none by Jung himself. He retained this designation for most of his major works; thus *Ueber die Energetik der Seele* (included in CW 8) appeared as Vol. II in 1928. X/XII, the last to appear, were the 3 vols., of *Mysterium Coniunctionis*, 1955/57.

To the Psychoanalytical Review   [O R I G I N A L   I N   E N G L I S H ?]

Fall 1913

It is most welcome news to learn of Doctors Jelliffe and White's foundation of a broadly planned journal, which aims at the compila-

☐ As published in the *Psychoanalytic Review* (New York), I:1 (fall 1913), 117–18, headed "Letter from Doctor Jung." The original has not been discovered. This was the inaugural issue of the *Review*, which was founded and edited by Smith Ely Jelliffe (see 24 Feb. 36) and William Alanson White. The same issue and the four issues following contained Jung's "The Theory of Psy-

tion of general psychological literature, and which therefore may be expected to fill a gap that the existing forms of psychology have rendered painfully evident. Each of these forms deals with a special domain, such as philosophical psychology, which is largely transcendental, experimental or physiological psychology, which has been accused, not without cause, of being physiology rather than psychology, and medical psychology, which through the psychoanalytical method of Freud has now come to encroach freely upon the domain of normal psychology. The complex psychic phenomena are left practically unexplained by the first two forms of psychology, whereas the psychoanalytical method of medical psychology has started a line of inquiry which would seem to have a general range of application.

Two problems in particular are adapted to exert an activating effect upon normal psychology. One of these is the recently elaborated dynamic interpretation of the psychological experience, which endeavours to explain the psychic manifestations as equivalent energy transformations. The other problem is represented by symbolism, which comprises the structural analogy of the intellectual functions, in their onto- and phylogenetic evolution. Medical psychology naturally came closest to these problems, as being most likely to observe, examine and analyze the mode or origin of powerful affects or extraordinary psychic structures. The delusional structures of the insane, the illusions of the neurotic, and the dreams of normal as well as abnormal individuals have also afforded abundant opportunities for studying the remarkable analogies with certain ethnological structures.

In my paper on the "Changes and Symbols of the Libido,"[1] a faint attempt has been made at sketching these relations, not in order to propound a finished theory, which would be beyond me, but simply to stimulate further research in a direction which appears extremely promising. It is beyond the powers of the individual, more particularly of physicians, to master the manifold domains of the mental sciences which should throw some light upon the comparative anatomy of the mind. Hence I welcome as a most opportune plan the idea of the editors to unite in their journal the contributions of competent specialists in the various fields. We need not only the work of medical psychologists, but also that of philologists, historians, archaeologists,

---

choanalysis" (see CW 4, pp. 83ff.), which he had given as lectures at the medical school of Fordham U., New York, in 1912. For Jung's relations with White, see *Psychological Types*, CW 6, par. 747, n. 62.

[1] *Wandlungen und Symbole der Libido*.

mythologists, folklore students, ethnologists, philosophers, theologians, pedagogues and biologists.

I am free to admit that this enterprise is ambitious and highly creditable to the liberal and progressive spirit of America. The collection of comparative material, to place on a firmer footing the available results of medical psychology, is an inviting task for the near future. Especially in the realm of symbolism, a wide territory is here opened up for students of the several mythologies and religions. Another task is set in the transference of the dynamic interpretation to the problems of the history of culture. The collaboration of all these forces points towards the distant goal of a genetic psychology, which will clear our eyes for medical psychology, just as comparative anatomy has already done in regard to the structure and function of the human body.

I wish the best of success to this new venture and trust that it will not fail to arouse an active interest also on the part of the non-medical faculties.

C. G. JUNG

To Hans Schmid

Dear friend,   6 November 1915

. . .

In the meantime, and after long reflection, the problem *of resistance to understanding* has clarified itself for me. And it was Brigitta

☐ (Handwritten.) Hans Schmid or Schmid-Guisan, M.D., (1881–1932), Swiss psychotherapist, friend and pupil of Jung's with whom he exchanged a lengthy correspondence 1915/16 on the question of types, more specifically the (later abandoned) equation of thinking with introversion and feeling with extraversion. At the end of his foreword to *Psychological Types* (CW 6, p. xii) Jung pays the following tribute to Schmid: "I owe a great deal of clarification to this interchange of ideas, and much of it, though of course in altered and greatly revised form, has gone into my book. The correspondence belongs essentially to the preparatory stage of the work, and its inclusion would create more confusion than clarity. Nevertheless, I owe it to the labours of my friend to express my thanks to him here." The correspondence was brought to light again by Schmid's daughter, Marie-Jeanne Boller-Schmid, Jung's secretary from 1932 to 1952, in 1966. The Editors of CW concurred with Jung's view that its inclusion, as an Appendix, in CW 6, "would create more confusion than clarity," and held it to be too technical and prolix for inclusion in CW 18, a volume of miscellaneous and posthumous writings, some hitherto unpublished. The passage reproduced here forms a wholly unexpected personal codicil to Jung's long letter of 6 Nov. 15, too valuable and moving to pass into oblivion. Jung's

of Sweden[1] (1303–1373) who helped me to gain insight. In a vision she saw the devil, who spoke with God and had the following to say about the psychology of devils:

"Their belly is so swollen because their greed was boundless, for they filled themselves and were not sated, and so great was their greed that, had they but been able to gain the whole world, they would gladly have exerted themselves, and would moreover have desired to reign in heaven. A like greed is mine. Could I but win all the souls in heaven and on earth and in purgatory, I would gladly snatch them."

So the devil is the devourer. Understanding = *comprehendere* = κατασυλλαμβάνειν,[2] and is likewise a devouring. Understanding swallows you up. But one should not let oneself be swallowed if one is not minded to play the hero's role, unless it be that one really is a hero who can overpower the monster from within. And the understander in turn must be willing to play the role of Fafner and devour indigestible heroes. It is therefore better not to "understand" people who might be heroes, because the same fate might befall oneself. One can be destroyed by them. In wanting to understand, ethical and human as it sounds, there lurks the devil's will, which though not at first perceptible to me, is perceptible to the other. Understanding is a fearfully binding power, at times a veritable murder of the soul as soon as it flattens out vitally important differences. The core of the individual is a mystery of life, which is snuffed out when it is "grasped." That is why symbols want to be mysterious; they are not so merely because what is at the bottom of them cannot be clearly apprehended. The symbol wants to guard against Freudian interpretations, which are indeed such pseudo-truths that they never lack for effect. With our patients "analytical" understanding has a wholesomely destructive effect, like a corrosive or thermocautery, but is banefully destructive on sound tissue. It is a technique we have learnt from the devil, always destructive, but useful where destruction is necessary. But one can commit no greater mistake than to apply the principles of this technique to an analysed psychology. More than that, all understanding in general, which is a conformity with general points

---

obituary for Schmid in the *Basler Nachrichten* (23 Apr. 32) and his foreword to Schmid-Guisan's *Tag und Nacht* (1931) are in CW 18.
[1] St. Bridget, the most famous saint of the Northern Kingdoms. She had eight children, one of whom became St. Catherine of Sweden. *Ca.* 1346 St. Bridget founded the Order of Brigittines (Ordo Sanctissimi Salvatoris).
[2] Cf. *Symbols of Transformation*, par. 682.

of view, has the diabolical element in it and kills. It is a wrenching of another life out of its own course, forcing it into a strange one in which it cannot live. Therefore, in the later stages of analysis, we must help people towards those hidden and unlockable symbols, where the germ lies hidden like the tender seed in the hard shell. There should truly be no understanding in this regard, even if one were possible. But if understanding is general and manifestly possible, then the symbol is ripe for destruction, as it no longer conceals the seed which is about to break from the shell. I now understand a dream I once had, which made a great impression on me: *I was standing in my garden and had dug open a rich spring of water that gushed forth. Then I had to dig another deep hole, where I collected all the water and conducted it back into the depths of the earth again.* So is healing given to us in the unlockable and ineffable symbol, for it prevents the devil from swallowing up the seed of life. The menacing and dangerous thing about analysis is that the individual is apparently understood: the devil eats his soul away, which naked and exposed, robbed of its protecting shell, was born like a child into the light. That is the dragon, the murderer, that always threatens the newborn divine child. He must be hidden once more from the "understanding" of humanity.

True understanding seems to be one which does not understand, yet lives and works. Once when Ludwig the Saint[3] visited the holy Aegidius[4] incognito, and as the two, who did not know each other, came face to face, they both fell to their knees before each other, embraced and kissed—and *spoke no word together.* Their gods recognized each other, and their human parts followed. We must understand the divinity within us, but not the other, so far as he is able to go by himself and understand himself. The patient we must understand, for he needs the corrosive medicine. We should bless our blindness for the mysteries of the other; it shields us from devilish deeds of violence. We should be connivers at our own mysteries, but veil our eyes chastely before the mystery of the other, so far as, being unable to understand himself, he does not need the "understanding" of others.

[UNSIGNED]

[3] Louis I, the Pious (778–840), Holy Roman Emperor, King of France, third son of Charlemagne (d. 814).

[4] St. Giles (? 8th cent.), reputedly an Athenian of royal descent who fled to France, where he lived as a hermit. One of the most popular saints in the Middle Ages, he was invoked as the patron of cripples, beggars, and lepers.

To Fanny Bowditch

Dear Miss Bowditch,   22 October 1916

It is understandable that, as long as you look at other people and project your psychology into them, you can never reach harmony with yourself. I am afraid that the mere fact of my presence takes you away from yourself so that it will be necessary for you to devalue me to such an extent that you can concentrate your libido on your own individuality. I have no objection as long as this procedure serves your best interest. I know that this is the way of not a few people. However, I must ask you for patience. I have to enter military service at the end of the week and shall return only at the beginning of December. But then I am willing to start work with you.

I realize that under the circumstances you have described you feel the need to see clearly. But your vision will become clear only when you can look into your own heart. Without, everything seems discordant; only within does it coalesce into unity. Who looks outside dreams; who looks inside awakes. With best regards,

Yours sincerely, DR. JUNG

□ (Handwritten.) Fanny Bowditch (1874–1967), daughter of Henry Pickering Bowditch (1840–1911), Harvard physiologist, 1871–1906. 1912, James Jackson Putnam, M.D., referred her to Jung for treatment (see N. G. Hale, Jr., ed., *Putnam and Psychoanalysis*, 1971, p. 40, and Payne, 23 July 49, n. 6). 1916, she married Dr. Rudolf Katz, of Amsterdam. Letters to her published by courtesy of the Harvard Medical Library in the Francis A. Countway Library of Medicine, Boston.

To Alphonse Maeder

Dear friend,   19 January 1917

Please permit this more intimate form of address! I have the need to tell you once again of the special joy I felt yesterday evening when I saw how close we are in spirit to one another in our different ways. This impression was a great satisfaction to me after the tiresome experiences of last week.

Allow me to give you personally the enclosed little present—a fragment[1] with far-reaching associations. I deserve no credit for it, nor

□ (Handwritten; likewise the next letter.)
[1] *Septem Sermones ad Mortuos*, printed privately and pseudonymously ("Basilides

does it want or pretend to be anything, it just *is*—simply that. Hence I could not presume to put my name to it, but chose instead the name of one of those great minds of the early Christian era which Christianity obliterated. It fell quite unexpectedly into my lap like a ripe fruit at a time of great stress and has kindled a light of hope and comfort for me in my bad hours. Of course it won't mean anything more to you than what I mean by it: a token of my joy over our wordless understanding yesterday evening.

I would ask you to find the little book a discreet resting place in your writing desk. I don't want a profane hand to touch my memory of those limpid nights. With cordial greetings,

Very sincerely, JUNG

---

in Alexandria") in 1916. Published in *Erinnerungen, Träume, Gedanken* (Zurich, 1962), pp. 388ff. The 1963 edn. of *Memories* does not contain the *Sermones*. The translation of the latter by H. G. Baynes (privately printed 1925) appears, however, in the 2nd paperback edn. of *Memories* published by Vintage Books (1966) and in the 4th hardbound edn. by Pantheon Books (1967), and has been published independently by Stuart and Watkins (London, 1967). For the history of the *Sermones* see *Memories*, pp. 189ff./182f.

To Alphonse Maeder

Dear friend,   26 February 1918

Please accept my heartfelt sympathy over the passing of your mother. Death is a faithful companion of life and follows it like its shadow. We have still to understand how very much wanting to live = wanting to die.

Very cordially, JUNG

To Fanny Bowditch Katz

[ORIGINAL IN ENGLISH]

Dear Madam,   30 July 1918

I think such an important and delicate question cannot be solved by medical advice only. The main question is your psychological attitude towards this problem. From a purely medical standpoint you have the opinion of the competent gynaecologists, according to which the physical possibility seems to exist. But this statement

☐ (Handwritten.) See Bowditch, 22 Oct. 16.

doesn't solve the question. There is a most important psychological side to this problem. If the unconscious is with your conscious decision, or if there is a very positive hint from the unconscious concerning a real child, then you can be sure that the powers of nature also are with you and will help you in a successful overcoming of the strain of gravidity and childbirth. But if your dreams should show a considerable amount of resistance against a real child, then I would say that pregnancy is not advisable, for the time being at least. Because, if you act against the tendency of the unconscious, you will be counteracted by the unconscious, which is always a most important obstacle. You should be absolutely at one with yourself, if you want a real child. It must be a *fate*, and not a personal wish, if you want to have all guarantees that the child should be as sound as possible. The factor of inheritance has to be considered as a serious point in the discussion of the problem, *but not as an absolute counter-argument*. The quality and disposition of the whole family and of the ancestors play a much greater rôle in the creation of the child's disposition than the individual disposition of father or mother.

I was astonished not to find an allusion to the unconscious material in your letter. In such a serious problem you should be aware of the standpoint of the unconscious. If you feel a resistance against the unconscious, you resist yourself. If the unconscious agrees with your conscious standpoint, then the child seems to be required, *no matter whether the enterprise will be hard or not*. Under such circumstances you have the guarantee that, in so far you and your husband are concerned, the child will be all right—all right as far as ancestral inheritance and physical conditions allow it.

I am not astonished that Dr. Katz as well as yourself come to such a conclusion, and I wouldn't wonder if you really would give birth to a child. This problem is absolutely on the way, as I had the honour to foretell it once to Dr. Katz. Only be careful in examining your own attitude, so that you know that you fully agree or disagree.

Yours sincerely, JUNG

Anonymous

Dear Dr. N.,   3 August 1918

Naturally I am overjoyed to hear of your success. Don't let it upset you that you needed not only a good deal of time but also a bad attack of exam fright to reach this goal. The neurotic constitution

35

demands a bit more sacrifice and a bit more effort and a bit more patience than does the normal. In return this moral seriousness is rewarded, whether by outward successes or by the blessing of deepened insight into the world and the soul. The rebellions of the evil spirit are also valuable experiences which strengthen one's patience and perseverance if, as you have done, one has taken the trouble to prove to oneself that the expenditure of effort is its own reward.

From the bottom of my heart I wish you every success in the future. With best regards to yourself and your wife,

Yours sincerely, DR. JUNG

☐ (Handwritten.) To a resident of Zurich.

To Marianne Jung

Dear Marianne,   London,[1] 1 July 1919

It was sweet of you to write me a letter. It has made me so happy that I am writing you a letter too. If you can't read it, Mama will read it to you. I have bought a doll here. It is carved from brown wood and comes from India. But it is for Mama. I shall bring it with me in my trunk. I am staying here in a big house. About fifty thousand cars go by every day. Every morning at half past ten the Guardsmen ride past in golden breastplates with red plumes in their helmets and black cloaks. They are going to the King's castle and guard the King and the Princes and Princesses. The King has his golden throne and his golden sceptre in another castle, in a high tower. It has windows with thick bars and iron doors. By day the crown is in the tower on top and you can see it, in the evening it sinks down with the sceptre into a deep cellar which is shut with iron plates. So no one can steal it. In the crown are precious stones as big as pigeon's eggs. Round the castle are three walls and moats and soldiers stand at the gates. London lies on a big river where the seaships go. Every day the river flows downwards for 6 hours and then upwards for 6 hours. When it flows downwards, the ships that are going away float out into the sea, and

☐ (Handwritten.) Jung's third daughter Marianne (Frau Niehus-Jung; 1910–65). Co-editor of Jung's Gesammelte Werke until her death; also member of the Editorial Committee for the Selected Letters.
[1] Jung spent the first part of July 1919 in London, where he read several papers to various learned societies. Cf. "Instinct and the Unconscious" and "The Psychological Foundation of Belief in Spirits" (CW 8), and "The Problem of Psychogenesis in Mental Disease" (CW 3).

when it flows upwards the ships that have waited outside come into
the city.

Just think, more than twice as many people live in London as in
the whole of Switzerland. Chinamen live here too.

Many loving greetings to you and Lilli,[2]

from your Papa

[2] Jung's youngest daughter Hélène (Frau Hoerni-Jung).

[*To Hermann Hesse*, 3 Dec. 1919; see Addendum, p. 573.]

To Albert Oeri

Dear friend,   11 December 1920

I have still to express my heartfelt condolences on the death of
your mother. I heard this sad news only when I got back to Switzerland after a long absence in England. The mass of work that had
piled up in the meantime has prevented me from attending to my
correspondence.

I hope all goes well with you, your family and my godchild,[1] to
whom I send special greetings. Unfortunately I never go to Basel, but
I hope she will come to visit me sometime next summer. We will then
take the big sailing boat to the enchanted island in the Upper Lake,
where the wild ducks, plovers, and crested grebes nest in the reeds.
This will be sure to please her.

Cordial greetings, JUNG

□ (Handwritten.) Albert Oeri, Ph.D., (1875–1950), editor-in-chief of the *Basler
Nachrichten*, member of the Swiss National Council; friend of Jung's since their
student days. Cf. *Erinnerungen, Träume, Gedanken*, pp. 102ff. (these pages are
omitted in the English edn.); also Oeri, "Some Youthful Memories of C. G.
Jung," *Spring* 1970, 182ff. In 1945 Jung contributed "The Enigma of Bologna"
(now in *Mysterium Coniunctionis*, pars. 51ff.) to the *Festschrift Albert Oeri*.
[1] Oeri's eldest daughter, Marianne Flügge-Oeri.

To Hermann Hesse

Dear Herr Hesse,   28 January 1922

Heartiest thanks for your beautiful poems,[1] and at the same time
congratulations on their publication. I see from the papers that you

have given the Hottingen Literature Fraternity[2] a touch of the horrors with your far-ranging autobiography.[3] Who is the literary reporter on the N.Z.Z.[4] anyway? He is the possessor of a truly lamentable style. In my thoughts I had to pity you for this, but I hope the sun of Montagnola will rapidly bleach away these cisalpine vulgarities.

For a person like me, who never reads poetry, your poems are simply beautiful. With best greetings,

Sincerely, JUNG

☐ (Handwritten.) By courtesy of the Landesbibliothek, Bern. — Hermann Hesse (1877–1962), German/Swiss novelist and poet. He then resided at Montagnola, in Canton Ticino. Received Nobel prize for Literature, 1946. (See pl. III.)
[1] *Gedichte des Malers* (1920).
[2] Lesezirkel Hottingen, a literary society in Zurich.
[3] "Aus einem Tagebuch des Jahres 1920." Hesse read parts of this MS at a meeting of the Lesezirkel on 23 Jan. 22. The enlarged fragment appeared later in *Corona*, and in 1960 in "Die Kleinen Bücher der Arche" (Arche-Verlag, Zurich).
[4] *Neue Zürcher Zeitung*, no. 120, 27 Jan. 22.

To Theodor Bovet

Dear Herr Bovet,   25 November 1922

Much as I admire your courage, I cannot conceal from you that this is a problem "with horns" which you are setting out to discuss.[1] Have you appreciated the fact that only very few people have the courage to talk about it honestly, and that the thousand-headed hydra twines round the neck of anyone who dares to tell the truth? Most people lie, whether they will or no, when they come to speak of this question. And yet you are quite right when you say that the problem of love is the most important in human life. Also, the most important is the most difficult to talk about. People have a natural shyness about it, a sort of reverence, such as all great and powerful things inspire. Therefore I find your plan very risky, to say the least. That you have picked on me, of all people, as a speaker arouses very mixed feelings, because the problem of love seems to me a monster of a mountain

☐ (Handwritten.) Theodor Bovet, M.D., Th.D., Swiss psychiatrist. Founder of the Zentralinstitut für Ehe- und Familienwissenschaft.
[1] B. asked Jung to lecture to students in Zurich on the love-life of students. The lecture, "The Love Problem of a Student," is in *Civilization in Transition*, CW 10.

which, for all my experience, has always soared to still greater heights whenever I thought I had almost reached the top. But no doubt such a discussion belongs to our age of reorientation and I am willing to do what I can to make it a success. Please would you schedule the discussion rather late in December, so that I have time to write a decent paper? And would you also let me know *where* the evening is to be held. A Friday or Tuesday evening would suit me best.

Yours truly, DR. C. G. JUNG

To Oskar A. H. Schmitz

Dear Herr Schmitz,   26 May 1923

I have read your book[1] with attention, and must again thank you for your kindness in sending it to me.

Permit me a few remarks: to the extent that I regard the psycho-analytic and the psychosynthetic method as an instrument for self-improvement, your comparison with the method of yoga seems to me extremely plausible. But I feel it necessary to emphasize that this is merely an analogy, because nowadays far too many Europeans are inclined to accept Oriental ideas and methods uncritically and to translate them into the mental language of the Occident. In my view this is detrimental both to ourselves and to those ideas. The products of the Oriental mind are based on its own peculiar history, which is radically different from ours. Those peoples have gone through an uninterrupted development from the primitive state of natural poly-demonism to polytheism at its most splendid, and beyond that to a religion of ideas within which the originally magical practices could evolve into a method of self-improvement. These antecedents do not apply to us. The Germanic tribes, when they collided only the day before yesterday with Roman Christianity, were still in the initial state of a polydemonism with polytheistic buds. There was as yet no proper priesthood and no proper ritual. Like Wotan's oaks, the gods were felled and a wholly incongruous Christianity, born of monothe-

□ (Handwritten.) Oskar A. H. Schmitz (1873–1931), German author, pupil of Jung's. He introduced Jung's psychology to Count Hermann Keyserling (cf. Keyserling, 21 May 27, n. □); at his instigation Jung was invited to K.'s "School of Wisdom" in Darmstadt. Schmidt's work includes *Psychoanalyse und Yoga* (1923); cf. also *Sinnsuche oder Psychoanalyse: Briefwechsel Graf Hermann Keyserling/Oskar A. H. Schmitz* (1970).
[1] *Psychoanalyse und Yoga.*

ism on a much higher cultural level, was grafted upon the stumps. The Germanic man is still suffering from this mutilation. I have good reasons for thinking that every step beyond the existing situation has to begin down there among the truncated nature-demons. In other words, there is a whole lot of primitivity in us to be made good.

It therefore seems to me a grave error if we graft yet another foreign growth onto our already mutilated condition. It would only make the original injury worse. This craving for things foreign and faraway is a morbid sign. Also, we cannot possibly get beyond our present level of culture unless we receive a powerful impetus from our primitive roots. But we shall receive it only if we go back behind our cultural level, thus giving the suppressed primitive man in ourselves a chance to develop. How this is to be done is a problem I have been trying to solve for years. As you know, I am a doctor, and am therefore condemned to lay my speculations under the juggernaut of reality, though this has the advantage of ensuring that everything lacking in solidity will be crushed. Hence I find myself obliged to take the opposite road from the one you appear to be following in Darmstadt. It seems to me that you are building high up aloft, erecting an edifice on top of the existing one. But the existing one is rotten. We need some new foundations. We must dig down to the primitive in us, for only out of the conflict between civilized man and the Germanic barbarian will there come what we need: a new experience of God. I do not think this goal can be reached by means of artificial exercises.

On this point I must part company with Darmstadt, much as I admire your efforts. Your brilliantly written book, with its many profound and true thoughts, will assuredly have a most beneficial influence. But so far as practical life is concerned I cannot suppress my misgivings. I have hinted at some of them in my chapter on Schiller.[2]

Though it would be wrong to draw a parallel between Darmstadt and theosophy, it does seem to me that the same danger exists in both cases: of a new house being built on the old shaky foundations, and of new wine being poured into old bottles. Though the old damage is covered up, the new building does not stand firm. Man must after all be changed from within, otherwise he merely assimilates the new material to the old pattern.

Do you not find it also rather suspect to nourish the metaphysical needs of our time with the stuff of old legends? What would have

[2] *Psychological Types* (CW 6), ch. II, e.g., pars. 189ff.

happened in the 1st century of our era if people had taken the Dionysus legend as the material and occasion for meditation?

Shouldn't we rather let God himself speak in spite of our only too comprehensible fear of the primordial experience? I consider it my task and duty to educate my patients and pupils to the point where they can accept the direct demand that is made upon them from within. This path is so difficult that I cannot see how the indispensable sufferings along the way could be supplanted by any kind of technical procedure. Through my study of the early Christian writings I have gained a deep and indelible impression of how dreadfully serious an experience of God is. It will be no different today. Yet nowhere in the views put forward by Rousselle[3] can I discover that shattering conflict with the world which is the unfailing concomitant of the primordial religious experience. In Rousselle personally, as you know, the darkness lies buried deep. We need it, however, and also the fear of it, otherwise we do not know what light is.

I fully understand that you can scarcely dwell upon such abysses in a book, so I do not conclude from the character of your book that you are not aware of these abysses.

Do you know Keyserling's dreams? And do you think he could safely stand the shock of glimpsing the face of his own shadow?[4] I have yet to meet a man who has done so without shuddering, and who did not talk a little deliriously afterwards. You can hear echoes of it in Meyrink's gruesome fantasies.[5] And it is characteristic that (at least in his books) he has still not got over it. Of course I have no idea of his personal attitude to what he writes.

Please excuse my outspokenness. I have never written such a long letter about a book, from which you can judge how vital your book is to me.

With best thanks and kind regards,

Yours very sincerely, JUNG

[3] Erwin Rousselle (1890–1949), Sinologist and Buddhist scholar. 1923, lecturer at Darmstadt; later, professor at the U. of Peking; after 1930, director of the China Institute at U. of Frankfurt a. M.; lectured at Eranos.

[4] Jung's term for the inferior side of the personality. Cf. Martin, 20 Aug. 37.

[5] Gustav Meyrink (1868–1923), Austrian author. Best-known works: *Der Golem* (1915) and *Das grüne Gesicht* (1916).

To Henry A. Murray

[ORIGINAL IN ENGLISH]

My dear Murray,   2 May 1925

Thank you for your nice letter! Don't say too many good things, as I have to be careful not to be swayed away by megalomania. It is so important to keep close to the earth, as the spirit is always soaring up to heaven like a flame as much destructive as enlightening. I appreciate your genuine reactions and I sympathize with your enthusiasm, because I am deeply convinced that those ideas that came to me are really quite wonderful things. I can easily say that (without blushing) because I know how resistant and how foolishly obstinate I was when they first visited me, and what a trouble it was until I could read this symbolic language, so much superior to my dull conscious mind.

Your visit has been a joy and a refreshment to me as there are so few people capable of understanding the clarity of the *profunda coeli.*

I just spent about 3 weeks in the tower,[1] where I finished the 3rd edition of a little book of mine,[2] much inspired by the peculiar atmosphere of the place. . . .

Yours sincerely, C. G. JUNG

☐ (Handwritten.) Henry A. Murray, M.D., now professor (emeritus) of clinical psychology, Harvard U.; formerly director of the Harvard Psychological Clinic.
[1] Jung's house at Bollingen. Cf. n. ☐ to the next letter.
[2] *Das Unbewusste im normalen und kranken Seelenleben* (1926), later revised, and in CW 7 as "On the Psychology of the Unconscious."

To Hans Kuhn

Dear Hansli,   Bunambale Bugisu, Uganda, 1 January 1926

I promised to write you a letter from Africa.[1] We left England on 15 Oct. for Lisbon, Malaga, Marseille, Genoa. On 7 November we were in Egypt, in Port Said. Then we went through the Red Sea,

☐ (Handwritten.) Hans Kuhn was a boy of 16, living in Bollingen, on the Upper Lake of Zurich. Jung met him by chance in 1922 when he landed there with his sailboat. Later he assisted Jung in the construction of the "Tower" (cf. *Memories*, ch. VIII), and helped him with gardening, cooking, and sailing.
[1] Cf. ibid., ch. IX:iii, "Kenya and Uganda."— For snapshots from the African trip, see pl. IV in the present vol.

desert on both sides, high cliffs and not a blade of grass. At night the temperature was 30° [86° F.] and by day 32° [nearly 90° F.]. On 12 Nov. we reached Mombasa, East Africa. Before sunrise it was already 28° [82° F.]. The whole town consists of huts which are thatched with grass, Negroes and Indians everywhere. Tall coconut palms. Two days later we took the train (narrow gauge) up into the interior, where the great plains are. We travelled for 24 hours. The earth there is quite red, and red dust swirled about the train so that our white clothes turned all red. We saw wild Masai with long spears and shields, they were quite naked and had only an ox skin draped on. They had bored through the lobes of their ears and hung such heavy brass rings in them that the lobes were 10 cm. long. The women wear iron rings round their ankles, sometimes up to the knee. We travelled through jungle where monkeys were sitting in the trees, then we came on unending plains where we saw whole herds of antelope and zebra —two ostriches raced the train. Finally we were in Nairobi, capital of Kenya. There we bought two guns and 400 cartridges. We also hired four black servants and a cook. Then we went on by train for a whole day until the line ended. We hired a truck for all the baggage, tents, utensils, etc. and drove 100 km. We came into the jungle and then into the land of the Kavirondo. Then we marched 5 days with 48 bearers until we reached the foot of an extinct volcano. This mountain is called Elgon or Masaba, it's 4300 metres high and about 60 km. wide from base to top. We trekked our way up for about 12 km. until we came to huge and impenetrable forests. There we camped. Almost every night we heard lions, often leopards and hyenas prowled round the camp. We stayed there for 3 weeks and climbed the mountains and took a look at the wild natives. I learned their language. We slaughtered an ox. Immediately great eagles came to steal the meat. We shot at them. Then the natives came and begged us for the guts and feet of the ox. They at once put them on sticks, made a fire, waggled the guts through the flames and ate them half raw. We dried the meat in the sun. The camp was pitched at 2100 metres. I climbed up to 2900 metres. Up there the bamboo forests are full of black buffalo and rhino. These animals are very dangerous. We always had to keep our guns at the ready. We killed three big poisonous snakes. One of them suddenly came down a hill and wanted to attack Mr. Beckwith,[2] but he was able to shoot it in the head in time.

---

[2] George Beckwith, a young American friend of Jung's and an excellent shot. The party also included H. G. Baynes (cf. Baynes, 6 Mar. 37) and Ruth Bailey.

It was all green and about 8 feet long. I am bringing 2 snakeskins home. A week ago we travelled westwards round the southern foot of the mountain and are now 2000 metres high. Lots of buffalo and leopard here, also giant snakes. Tomorrow we set out for Lake Victoria. It is so big that it takes a steamer 13 days to go round it. On 15 Jan. we journey up the river for 6 weeks as far as Egypt. I am coming home at the beginning of April and shall soon be in Bollingen again.

Many greetings to you, your parents and brothers and sisters,

DR. C. G. JUNG

To Frances G. Wickes

[ORIGINAL IN ENGLISH]

My dear Mrs. Wickes, Sils-Maria, Engadin, 9 August 1926

I feel profoundly moved by the bad news about your health, especially the matter with your eyesight. You want me to tell you something about Africa. You know, that is not easy at all. There is too much to tell and that would not be much worthwhile, and then there are a few things and I don't know exactly what to say about them. The one is the fact that we discovered a new form of a very primitive psychological religion with the tribes on the slopes of Mt. Elgon, where nobody advised us to go. They apparently worship the sun. But it isn't the sun, it is the moment of dawn: that is God. I think it's rather amazing. It is the origin of the Egyptian Horus idea.[1] The other thing is how Africa affects oneself.[2] That latter point is not yet fully worked out. I had no time to think. But I am going to. For the time being I have finished some old papers. Patients eat me. But my resistances against them are gathering like thunderclouds. I should write much. I have not said yet all I ought to.

I remain with my warmest wishes for your health,

Yours sincerely, C. G. JUNG

☐ (Handwritten.) Frances Gillespy Wickes (1875–1967), American analytical psychologist. Cf. her *The Inner World of Childhood* (1927, rev. 1965); *The Inner World of Man* (1938/1950); *The Inner World of Choice* (1963). Jung's foreword to the first book is in CW 17; to the second, in CW 18. (See pl. VI.)
[1] Cf. *Memories*, pp. 268f./251.
[2] Ibid., pp. 244ff./230f.

To Frances G. Wickes

[ORIGINAL IN ENGLISH]

My dear Mrs. Wickes,   Bollingen, 27 August 1926

It is too terrible.[1] Was there anything wrong with the thymus gland? There might be a reason for such a sudden death in youth. Anyhow he did not know that he died. He vanished at the moment of joy. But what a loss to you! I wish I could hold your hand and tell you how deeply I feel with you.

Yours affectionately, C. G. JUNG

□ (Handwritten.)
[1] Her only son Eliphalet, 21, had died while sailing on the coast of Maine. It was supposed that he had either had a heart attack or been struck by the boom of the sailboat.

To Louis S. London

[ORIGINAL IN ENGLISH]

My dear Dr. London,   24 September 1926

I suppose the news you heard of my successes in the treatment of Dementia praecox is greatly exaggerated. As a matter of fact I only treated a limited number of cases, and these were all what one might call in a liquid condition, that is to say, not yet congealed. I avoid the treatment of such cases as much as possible. It is true they can be treated, and even with the most obvious success, but such a success costs almost your own life. You have to make the most stupendous effort to reintegrate the dissociated psychic entities, and it is by no means a neat and simple technique which you can apply, but a creative effort together with a vast knowledge of the unconscious mind. These are not merely big words but simple statements of the actual truth. It is not too easy to cure a neurosis, but to cure a case on the borderline of D.p. is worse. Moreover the treatment of D.p. is entirely based upon the empirical knowledge gained from the neuroses. Therefore if you want to know anything about the treatment of D.p. you ought to begin with the study of the analytical treatment in general. . . .

Yours sincerely, C. G. JUNG

□ (Handwritten.) M.D., psychiatrist in New York City. Most of this letter was published in London, *Mental Therapy: Studies in Fifty Cases* (1937), vol. 2, p. 637.

To Frances G. Wickes

[ORIGINAL IN ENGLISH]

My dear Mrs. Wickes,   6 November 1926

Nobody, as long as he moves about among the chaotic currents of life, is without trouble. So I say again: Don't worry about myself. I am on my road and I carry my burden just as well as I can do. You got worries enough—more than enough. Thus, inasmuch as it is not for your own sake, don't worry about the things I have to deal with. There is no difficulty in my life that is not entirely myself. Nobody shall carry me as long as I can walk on my own feet.

If you are troubled about me, ask yourself what the thing is in you that troubles you, but don't assume that *I* trouble you. I am doing my best to be up to myself. Nobody can do it for me.

Yours cordially, C. G. JUNG

To Count Hermann Keyserling

Dear Count,   21 May 1927

I am sorry I am behindhand in answering your letter.

As regards X. I have simply noticed that he has a predominantly intellectual attitude like Scheler[1] and is therefore taken in by intellectual conjuring tricks. But that has nothing to do with his beautiful dreams. Dreams like that can occur no matter what the conscious attitude may be. Dreams are always beautiful when the development of the personality has to proceed via the unconscious. "Beauty" is synonymous with "being allured or attracted."

Your case seems to be different. Your own execution[2] accompanied by feelings of pleasure means that you should execute yourself consciously, i.e., choose another attitude and want it. Your development

☐ Hermann Alexander Graf Keyserling (1880–1946), German philosopher and author, founder of the "Schule der Weisheit," Darmstadt, Germany, where Jung lectured in 1927 (see "The Structure of the Psyche," CW 8, and "Mind and Earth," CW 10) and 1930 ("Archaic Man," CW 10). His best known work is *The Travel Diary of a Philosopher* (1925; orig. 1919). — Jung's letters to him are published by courtesy of the Keyserling Archive, Darmstadt. The Archive have asked us to mention the forthcoming publication of a volume of K.'s letters under the editorship of Hans G. Wiebe, Toronto. It will contain his answers to Jung's letters.—Cf. Schmitz, 26 May 23, n. ☐. (See pl. v.)
[1] Max Scheler (1874–1928), German philosopher.
[2] K. had frequent dreams of execution.

is evidently proceeding at present via the conscious will and not via the unconscious. In other words, the scope of your experience of external life and the world is not yet exhausted for you. With best regards,

Yours sincerely, C. G. JUNG

To J. Allen Gilbert

[ORIGINAL IN ENGLISH]

My dear Dr. Gilbert,   19 June 1927

. . .

Analysis is not only a "diagnosis" but rather an understanding and a moral support in the honest experimental attempt one calls "life." For the *individual* you never can know better or ahead. You only can help people to understand themselves and to gather up courage enough to try and risk. The invisible part of the work goes much further than whatever you can publish in a scientific journal. You have got to leave room for the irrational factor, although you hate it.

Cordially yours, C. G. JUNG

☐ (Handwritten.) J. Allen Gilbert, M.D., (1867–1948), American physician and psychotherapist, of Portland, Oregon.

To Count Hermann Keyserling

Dear Count,   19 June 1927

About your dream[1] I would only remark that "hanging" signifies "suspense"—a provisional or expectant state with swings of the pendulum which are represented by your excursions into the most diverse spiritual spheres. If you talk too much, then by the law of contrasts "stillness" accumulates within you and will one day come to expression (perhaps merely symptomatically and indirectly). With best regards,

Yours sincerely, C. G. JUNG

☐ (Handwritten.) In a letter of 23 May, K. reported an odd dream in which he had been repeatedly executed by hanging. After each "death" an inner voice called out: "The stillness increases." In his answer of 28 June K. expressed his full agreement with Jung's interpretation, particularly with the idea of hanging as "suspense."

47

To Christiana Morgan

[ORIGINAL IN ENGLISH]

My dear Christiana Morgan,   28 December 1927

Don't think you are forgotten. You would be far from the truth. First of all you ought to realize that I lived in the happy illusion that I had written to you—presumably because I so often thought of you and I had the intention to write to you so often that eventually I felt as if I had written. Well you know, it's all overwork. There is just too much to do! Let me thank you most sincerely for your pictures and the text. I went through the pictures, but not yet through the text. I think your technique has most marvellously improved. One of your pictures is almost exactly like one of St. Hildegard's[1] from the early 13th century—I just discovered it. (The one with a naked figure in the centre of the circle.[2]) This seems to be specifically feminine. With a man it is nearly always some abstraction; a geometrical figure f.i. that expresses the ultimate form of his essence. It is probably Logos and Eros,[3] impersonal and personal, which are the most fundamental differences between man and woman. Your material is *most valuable* to me. I often think of working through it, because it seems to me as if it were a most beautiful example of the original initiation process.

In early December your face haunted me for a while. I should have written then but there was the question of time.

Thank you for everything. "Don't blame me!" You are always a living reality to me whereas other former patients fade away into oblivion, becoming unreal shadows in Hades. You are keeping on living. There seems to be some sort of living connection (but I should

☐ (Handwritten.) Christiana Drummond Morgan (1897–1967), an American, had been a patient of Jung's, and Jung later used part of her analytical material extensively in his Seminars held in English at the Psychological Club, Zurich. The Seminar Notes, *The Interpretation of Visions*, were edited by Mary Foote and privately published for the use of members only, in 11 vols. (1930–34; new edn., 1939–41). Long excerpts, edited by Jane A. Pratt, appeared in the annual *Spring* (pub. by the Analytical Psychology Club of New York), 1960–69. Cf. Körner, 22 March 35, n. 1.

[1] St. Hildegard of Bingen (1098–1179), the first German woman mystic. She is particularly well known for her visions.

[2] The picture appears as Fig. 27 in Jung, "Concerning Mandala Symbolism," CW 9, i.

[3] Logos and Eros are the terms used to describe the basic principles of masculine and feminine psychology. Cf. Jung, "Woman in Europe," CW 10, pars. 235ff.

have said that long ago I suppose). You probably need a confirmation from my side of the ocean just as well.

Please do tell Jonah[4] as well as your husband that they are real to me. If I don't write, it is just that hell of letters and papers and patients.

But my dear ~~dear~~ (!!)[5] Christiana Morgan, you are just a bit of a marvel to me. Now don't laugh, there is nothing to laugh about. You were quite right in scolding me.

Yours affectionately, c. g.

[4] Cf. Jones, 6 Jan. 31.
[5] Jung inadvertently repeated "dear," then crossed it out.

To Count Hermann Keyserling

Dear Count,   2 January 1928

. . . Your return to yourself, enforced by illness, is on the right track and is something I have wished and expected for you.

You identify with the eternally creative, restless and ruthless god in yourself, therefore you see through everything personal—a tremendous fate which it would be ridiculous either to praise or to censure! I was compelled to respect Nietzsche's *amor fati*[1] until I had my fill of it, then I built a little house way out in the country[2] near the mountains and carved an inscription on the wall: *Philemonis sacrum—Fausti poenitentia*,[3] and "dis-identified" myself with the god. I have never regretted this doubtless very unholy act. By temperament I despise the "personal," any kind of "togetherness," but it is so strong a force, this whole crushing unspiritual weight of the earth, that I fear it. It can rouse my body to revolt against the spirit, so that before reaching the zenith of my flight I fall lamed to earth. That is the danger you too must reckon with. It is also the fear that prevents our friend X. from flying. He can be nothing else but intellectual.

☐ (Handwritten.)
[1] Nietzsche had a great influence on Jung during his student years; in his *Memories* (p. 102/106) Jung reports that *Thus Spake Zarathustra* was "a tremendous experience" comparable to *Faust*. Regarding Nietzsche's *amor fati*, cf. *Zarathustra* (tr. R. J. Hollingdale, Penguin Classics), Part III, "The Wanderer": "Ah, this sorrowful, black sea beneath me! Ah, this brooding reluctance! Ah, destiny and sea! Now I have to go down to you!"
[2] The "Tower" in Bollingen; cf. Kuhn, 1 Jan. 26, n. ☐.
[3] "Shrine of Philemon—Repentance of Faust." Cf. *Memories*, p. 235/222, n. 5.

You have paid a salutary tribute to the earth with your illness. Let's hope your gods will be equally gracious to you next time! With best wishes for the New Year,

Yours sincerely, C. G. JUNG

To Count Hermann Keyserling

Dear Count,   12 May 1928

Now that my assistant has succeeded in deciphering your crypto-gram[1] to the point where I can think of an answer, I hasten to give you the information you want.

My lecture tour in London was arranged by the New Educational Movement.[2] Mrs. Beatrix Ensor in particular. So far as I remember, we shared the profits. I think it was Mortimer Halls where I lectured.

My expression "resentment"[3] was perhaps unhappily chosen—the slovenly idiom of medical psychology—one could also say: the *feeling of alienation* caused by your collision with the world. This is aptly characterized by your dream arrival in the cosmic stillness and your role as the last man.[4] One doesn't leave what one loves, so you prob-ably have little love for earth and man. This is called, or can be called, an indirect expression of resentment. This is the resentment I mean.

By the way, the *Neue Schweizer Rundschau* has urged me to write an article on your *Spektrum*, which I have done, with the title "The Swiss Line in the European Spectrum."[5] I shall not fail to send you an offprint as soon as it is out. In it I have said much more than in my letter.

I don't believe the "last man" laughs "heartily," nor "like a homeric

---

[1] K.'s handwriting was very difficult to read.

[2] In English. Correct name is the New Education Fellowship, of which Mrs. Ensor was director; she was also one of its founders.

[3] From a letter of K.'s dated 4 Apr., it appears that Jung, in a letter which has not been preserved, had criticized K. for the resentment he expressed in his book *Das Spektrum Europas* (tr. *Europe*, 1928).

[4] In the same letter of 4 April, K. reported a recurrent dream: he was the last man on earth and "laughed like a homeric hero," full of happiness about the "cosmic stillness" surrounding him.

[5] In *Civilization in Transition*, CW 10. First published as "Die Bedeutung der schweizerischen Linie im Spektrum Europas," *Neue Schweizer Rundschau* (Zurich), XXIV:6 (1928).

50

hero," but, if I may say so, rather like Nietzsche. No doubt tremendously comic—no longer even a tailor to sew the last button on the last pair of trousers, sliding down the slope of the Beyond on the last Saturday evening, breakfastless and dinnerless—a gorgeous sight never to be beheld, marvellously absurd as a fantasy. The "humour" of your book sounds like the laughter in your dream, which explains to me what you understand by humour. I was never forced to laugh when I read your book, or only once over the "ha-ha-hairy" clergy— otherwise never. Nor can one laugh when reading Nietzsche. The laughter of alienation is not infectious.

Always sincerely yours, C. G. JUNG

To Meinrad Inglin

Dear Herr Inglin,   Bollingen, 2 August 1928

Please excuse my irresponsible silence. I had to wait for the holidays before I could write any letters at all. But I didn't want to fail to thank you personally for your beautiful book,[1] which I <u>could</u> read with passionate understanding. I underline *could* because contemporary literature, particularly German, is to me the epitome of boredom coupled with psychic torture. But with your book I knew what you were talking about—you talk about the great mystery of the Swiss lakes and mountains in which from time to time I blissfully immerse myself. You are *the only* Swiss who had reacted personally to my article[2] and on your own initiative! I have to write to this unique personage. If your name were not Meinrad Inglin, and if this genuine-sounding name were a pseudonym, I would almost doubt you were Swiss. But since I cannot doubt your authenticity, I say thank God there is at least one person whose head has grown out of the earth and who can consequently see it. I would have liked to dedicate a copy of my criticism to you, but just now I am rapt in daily contemplation of the Buchberg in Schwyz facing me on the Upper Lake. And shall be for several weeks. If you look across from Nuolen[3]

□ (Handwritten.) Meinrad Inglin (1893–1971), Swiss author; resident of Canton Schwyz.

[1] *Lob der Heimat* (privately printed, 1929).

[2] "The Swiss Line in the European Spectrum."

[3] Village on the southern side of the Upper Lake of Zurich, opposite Bollingen on the northern side.

51

you can see my little tower where I am now living. With best greetings and thanks,

Yours sincerely, c. g. j u n g

To Count Hermann Keyserling

Dear Count, 25 August 1928

The negative relationship to the mother[1] is always an affront to nature, unnatural. Hence distance from the earth, identification with the father, heaven, light, wind, spirit, Logos. Rejection of the earth, of what is below, dark, feminine. Negative relationship to material things, also to children. Flight from personal feelings.

On the subjective level[2] the "father" is an imago:[3] the image of your relationship to the father and to everything he stands for. In your dream this imago is dark, on the point of disappearing; that is to say a different attitude to the father imago is brewing (and to everything it stands for). Your *one-sided spiritual* tendency is probably meant, for anyone whose stature requires the size of a continent is not so very far away from Father Heaven (Zeus). This is too much for our human stature. It is an *inflation*[4] by the universal, suprapersonal spirit. (Originally this was forced on you by the negative attitude of your mother.) This spiritual inflation is compensated by a distinct inferiority of feeling, a real *undernourishment* of your other side, the feminine earth (*Yin*)[5] side, that of personal feeling. Hence your

□ (Handwritten.)

[1] This letter is in answer to one from K. of 20 Aug. in which he mentioned his negative attitude to his mother and his great affection for his father, also an obsessive fear of starvation. He reported a recurrent dream in which his father, long dead, had not really died but lived in sad and reduced circumstances. A meeting with the father was always frustrated by his father's hopelessness about himself and his wish to disappear.

[2] Interpretation on the subjective level takes the dream figures as "reflections of inner psychic factors and of the inner situation of the dreamer" (Toni Wolff, *Studien zu C. G. Jungs Psychologie*, 1959, p. 116). Cf. also Jung, *Two Essays on Analytical Psychology*, par. 130.

[3] The parental imago is composed of two factors: the personally acquired image of the personal father or mother plus the parental archetype. In later years Jung equated the imago with the archetype, but the equation is not applicable in this case.

[4] Inflation is identification with an archetype. It is generally compensated by feelings of inferiority in some other area of the personality.

[5] *Yang* and *Yin* are the two cosmic principles of Chinese philosophy, *Yang*

feeling appears in negative form, as an obsessive symptom = *fear of starvation*. Symptoms are always justified and serve a purpose. Because of your negative relation to the earth side there is a danger of actual starvation; you arouse enmity because you give out no warm feeling but merely autoerotic emotions which leave other people cold, also you are ruthless and tactless in manner. But your inferior feeling[6] is *genuine*, hence anyone who sees behind your heavenly cloak with its ten thousand meteors has confidence in you. (There aren't many of them.)

By having too much libido in the father imago you give the spirit of your father too much blood, therefore he cannot get out of the chthonic shadow world into non-spatiality (eternal rest) as he would like to. He is still in a sorry condition, for Hades is a gloomy place. One shouldn't attach the dead to the living, otherwise they both get estranged from their proper spheres and are thrown into a state of suffering.

. . .

Yours very sincerely, JUNG

---

representing the masculine principle (heaven, light, spirit, creativity), Y*in* the feminine principle (earth, darkness, matter, receptivity).
[6] The Keyserling Archive have asked for an explanatory addition to this letter. They write: "Keyserling's answer shows that he regarded Jung's correlation of the dominant spirit with inferior feeling as erroneous. He associated the truly valuable content of feeling, such as Christian or Platonic love, with the spirit, and because of his affinity with the spirit he judged enmity quite differently and took it as one has to take the weather."

To Oskar A. H. Schmitz

Dear Herr Schmitz,   Bollingen, 20 September 1928

. . .

I greatly appreciate your not having burst in on me unannounced in Bollingen with Frl. X. I do in fact dislike being disturbed, especially when working. One of the most important and difficult tasks in the individuation process is to bridge the distance between people. There is always a danger that the distance will be broken down by one party only, and this invariably gives rise to a feeling of violation followed by resentment. Every relationship has its optimal distance,

☐ (Handwritten.)

which of course has to be found by trial and error. The problem is a particularly delicate one with women, where sexuality is apt to rear its ugly head. Scrupulous attention must be paid to *resistances*. They can hardly be taken seriously enough, since one is only too prone to self-deception. With kind regards,

Yours very sincerely, c. g. j u n g

P.S. I completely forgot to answer your earlier question. The advantage of an hourly arrangement is that the patient is less likely to be drawn into the atmosphere of a personal relationship, and the financial aspect is easier to calculate. In the present case I think you might charge 50–70 fr. a day. If you want to work during the day, you should make a fixed charge for the half day, e.g., ½-day = 4 hours = 60 (or 50) marks. The more hours you work, the higher the fee.

In cases of inferior feeling, a trauma very often has pathological consequences in the realm of sensation, e.g., *physical pain* unaccompanied by feeling. In cases of inferior sensation, therefore, the trauma can precipitate intense feeling-symptoms. Very often the shock obliterates the function in question, just as excruciating pain blots out consciousness ("witch's sleep" under torture), and leaves "marginal symptoms" behind.

To Count Hermann Keyserling

Dear Count,   20 October 1928

. . .

You must pay especially careful attention to your body because your intuitive extraversion, stretching over continents, pulls energies into its vortex which are drawn from the body. This causes a lack of resistance in the body, with the result that stomach ulcers, digestive troubles, and infections (especially skin diseases) are not uncommon among intuitives.

I am looking forward to your America book.[1] Europe is an overcrowded peninsula and not a continent. Everyone is jealous of his little place in the sun and the European is then essentially petty. The outcry against Eckener[2] is another proof of this. At bottom the public only wants you to write every now and then such letters as that to

☐ (Handwritten.)
[1] *America: Der Aufgang einer neuen Welt* (1930; tr. *America Set Free*, 1930). For Jung's review of this book, see "The Rise of a New World," CW 10.

Herr V. They clamour for attention too—the everlasting "woe is me" of little people! With best wishes for a speedy recovery,

Very sincerely yours, C. G. JUNG

[2] Hugo Eckener (1868–1954), successor to Count Zeppelin (1838–1917), inventor of the rigid airship. He commanded the *Graf Zeppelin* (LZ-127) on a 21,700-mile world flight around the world in 1929.

To Jolande Jacobi

Dear Frau Jacobi,   20 November 1928

This letter will not give you the same pleasure as I received when I read yours with the clipping. I congratulate you on the fluency of your pen!

The purpose of my reappearance today is a letter—I have it before me—from a pitiable female, obviously physically *and psychically* in black misery, a derelict from the deluge of 1914, unknown to me, filling me with pity yet not with hope—forgive me, I have written to tell her that perhaps you can give her advice! Foreigners aren't allowed jobs in Switzerland, so I can do nothing. She is odd and has a knot in the unconscious that sets up a vibration. I am mildly curious. One should never be curious with women. But please do take a look at her. Perhaps she will write to you. (She knows nothing of this letter.) Please forgive me this imposition. It's not what I usually do.

Cordial greetings to Herr v. Trentini,[1] whom I congratulate on his 50th birthday. On *my* 50th birthday there was a beautiful sunset, the waterfowl called to one another, a chill night wind came down from the mountains, and I drank an extra bottle of wine and smoked a birthday cigar. I also got a letter from one of my friends, who said: they really ought to bring out a *Festschrift* on this occasion. I found that touching. With very best regards,

Yours sincerely, C. G. JUNG

☐ (Handwritten.) Jolan (later Jolande) Jacobi, Ph.D., analytical psychologist, originally of Budapest and Vienna, later Zurich. Cf. her *The Psychology of C. G. Jung* (6th edn., 1962), *Complex/Archetype/Symbol* (1959); *The Way of Individuation* (tr., 1967); *Frauenprobleme/Eheprobleme* (1968); *Vom Bilderreich der Seele* (1969); *Psychological Reflections, An Anthology of Jung's Writings* (2nd edn., 1970). Around 1928, as leader of the Kulturbund, she brought Jung to Vienna to lecture.
[1] Albert von Trentini (1878–1933), Austrian author and government official.

To L. Oswald

Dear Colleague,   8 December 1928

Please do not consider it a presumption on your part to interrogate me. On the contrary, I am glad you found my lecture[1] interesting. I have experienced nothing of the kind in Switzerland yet.

You are quite right in supposing that I reckon astrology among those movements which, like theosophy, etc., seek to assuage an irrational thirst for knowledge but actually lead it into a sidetrack. Astrology is knocking at the gates of our universities: a Tübingen professor has switched over to astrology and a course on astrology was given at Cardiff University last year.[2] Astrology is not mere superstition but contains some psychological facts (like theosophy) which are of considerable importance. Astrology has actually nothing to do with the stars but is the 5000-year-old psychology of antiquity and the Middle Ages. Unfortunately I cannot explain or prove this to you in a letter.

You are also quite right in your view that people who subscribe all out to any of these movements exclude *authentic* experience for the sake of *believed* hypotheses, not knowing that they are mere hypotheses but believing them to be *knowledge*.

But in all these dubious fields there is at least something that is worth knowing and that our present-day rationalism has cast aside rather too hastily. This something is projected psychology.

Always gladly at your service,

Yours sincerely, C. G. JUNG

☐ (Handwritten.) Zurich.
[1] "The Spiritual Problem of Modern Man," CW 10. In this lecture (at the Lesezirkel Hottingen, Zurich, Nov. 1928) there are several references to astrology (pars. 169, 172, 176, 188), and Oswald, surprised by what appeared to him a positive evaluation of it, asked for further elucidation.
[2] Evening lectures by J. M. Thorburn, B.Sc., M.A., then lecturer in philosophy. The course continued for several years. Cf. Thorburn, 6 Feb. 52.

To J. Allen Gilbert

[ORIGINAL IN ENGLISH]

My dear Dr. Gilbert,   2 January 1929

Please be kind to your fellow beings! Don't think that they are all damned fools, even if they say excitingly foolish things, even if they are the most inconsistent idiots. Allow for one grain of wisdom in all their foolishness. Can't you conceive of a physicist that thinks and speaks of atoms, yet is convinced that those are merely his own abstractions? That would be my case. I have not the faintest idea what "psyche" is in itself, yet, when I come to think and speak of it, I must speak of my abstractions, concepts, views, figures, knowing that they are our specific illusions. That is what I call "non-concretization." And know that I am by no means the first and only man who speaks of anima, etc. Science is the art of creating suitable illusions which the fool believes or argues against, but the wise man enjoys their beauty or their ingenuity, without being blind to the fact that they are human veils and curtains concealing the abysmal darkness of the Unknowable. Don't you see that it is life too to paint the world with divine colours? You never will know more than you can know, and if you proudly refuse to go by the available "knowledge" (or whatever you like to call it) you are bound to produce a better "theory" or "truth," and if you should not succeed in doing so, you are left on the bank high and dry and life runs away from you. You deny the living and creative God in man and you will be like the Wandering Jew. All things are *as if* they were. *Real* things are *effects* of something unknown. The same is true of anima, ego, etc. and moreover, there are no real things that are not *relatively real*. We have no idea of absolute reality, because "reality" is always something "observed." And so on. I am sure all this stuff gets your goat, but that's not the point. The point is that if you create a better theory, then I shall cock my ears.

Cordially yours, C. G. JUNG

☐ (Handwritten.)

To Albert Oeri

Dear It,[1]   4 January 1929

Heartiest thanks for your letter! It was a great joy. I applaud your idea that occasionally there are individuals who, like "accumulators" or condensers, precipitate upon themselves and embody the expectations of the people and thus fulfil them. I am entirely of this opin-

[1] "Es" (It) was the student name given to O. in his and Jung's Zofingia fraternity.

ion. Joffre[2] and Hindenburg[3] are probably such figures, without significance under normal conditions, heroes under exceptional ones. Generally they are almost peasantlike by nature, attached to the soil, profoundly unconscious, somehow deeply rooted in their collectivity. Their strength is ten thousandfold, as it flows to them invisibly from the masses. I don't know if one can speak of telepathy. So far as I can grasp the nature of the collective unconscious, it seems to me like an omnipresent continuum, an unextended Everywhere. That is to say, when something happens here at point A which touches upon or affects the collective unconscious, it has happened everywhere—hence the strange parallelism of the Chinese and European periods of style, which Wilhelm recently demonstrated to me at the China Institute,[4] or the unfathomable simultaneity of the Christ and Krishna myth.[5]

As we know from the Yezidis,[6] it is characteristic of most primitive religions that they have an extremely nebulous, remote kind of Trinity or some other highly spiritual principle that plays no role at all in actual religious practice, which is pre-eminently magical. I wonder which devil Karl Barth[7] (with his absolute God) worships in practice. It's very likely one of them has him by the collar.

Cordially, Your Barrel[8]

[2] (1852–1941), Commander-in-Chief of the French Army during World War I; Marshal of France, 1917.
[3] (1847–1934), Field Marshal of Germany during World War I; President, 1925–34.
[4] Cf. "Richard Wilhelm: In Memoriam," CW 15, par. 81.
[5] It was originally supposed by Indologists that the Krishna myth took definitive shape at the beginning of our era, but today this is uncertain. Nevertheless there are striking similarities between certain motifs in the Christ and Krishna myths, for instance the child motif, the Christophorus motif, and the identity of the two figures with a supreme God.
[6] The Yezidis are a small religious sect, scattered from northern Iraq to the Caucasus, speaking a Kurdish dialect. They distinguish between a supreme god and the devil as a creative agent, producing evil.
[7] Karl Barth (1886–1968), Swiss Protestant theologian. He taught that man can have no direct communication with God since God is wholly "cut off" (= absolute) from man and completely incomprehensible. God's sole revelation is in Christ and the Word of God is his one and only means of communication with man. One of Barth's most influential books is Commentary on Romans (orig. 1919; tr. H. C. Hoskyns, 1933).
[8] "Walze" (Barrel), the Zofingia fraternity name given to Jung.

Anonymous

[ORIGINAL IN ENGLISH]

Dear Mrs. N.,   4 January 1929

There is some likeness in the upper storey[1] but the ensemble is not satisfactory. Have you got some of the many snapshots Mrs. X. got of me through her niece? They might be helpful. My exterior is in strange contrast to my spirit. When I am dead, nobody will think that this is the corpse of one with spiritual aspirations. I am the clash of opposites. That makes it so frightfully difficult to get me right. Should my portrait be the reconciling symbol of your own contradictions?

The very best wishes for a happy New Year,

Yours sincerely, C. G. JUNG

☐ Eastern U.S.A.
[1] N. had made a portrait of Jung in 1928.

To Kurt Plachte

. . .   10 January 1929

I can agree with your statements in all details and merely regret I am not in a position to give you practical examples of my views. Everything in me has arisen from direct experience of the mentally ill or "seekers after truth."

For me a symbol is the sensuously perceptible *expression of an inner experience*. A religious experience strives for expression and can be expressed only "symbolically" because it transcends understanding. It *must* be expressed one way or another, for therein is revealed its immanent vital force. It wants to step over, as it were, into visible life, to take concrete shape. (The spirit shows its effective power only in the reshaping of matter.)

An idol is a petrified symbol used stereotypically for "magical" effects. It can have this fascinating effect so long as it touches those layers of the unconscious from which the symbol arose (somewhere else, i.e., with other people). Its effect is just the opposite of the symbol's.

The symbol is an expression of the enrichment of consciousness

☐ Beginning and end of letter incomplete; reproduced from identical file typescript copy. Plachte resided in Kiel.

through experience. The idol betokens a regression to the unconscious, i.e., an impoverishment of consciousness.

The Master speaks a "power word" born of the richness of his vision, the disciple merely conjures with it. For the Master the Communion means: I give you myself, my flesh, my blood. For the disciple this means: I eat the god, his flesh and blood. The ritual anthropophagy of primitive man (the cave dweller) echoes fascinatingly deep down in us: we can do it again, mysteriously sanctified, and yet we are not primitive brutes but are sanctified by the god's flesh. In a few cases I have found a quite unquestionable *blood lust* in connection with the Communion! Here we have religious license for what is primitive and no longer permissible. The magical word is one that lets "a primordial word resound behind it"[1]; magical action releases primordial action.

I am indeed convinced that creative imagination is the only primordial phenomenon accessible to us, the real Ground of the psyche, the only immediate reality. Therefore I speak of *esse in anima*,[2] the only form of being we can experience directly. We can distinguish no form of being that is not psychic in the first place. All other realities are derived from and indirectly revealed by it, actually with the artificial aid named science.

We should think of the collective unconscious neither as order nor as disorder. Experience corroborates both. With a disordered consciousness order can come out of the unconscious, just as conversely unconscious chaos can break into the too narrow cosmos of consciousness. At the founding of the great religions there was to begin with a collective disorientation which everywhere constellated in the unconscious an overwhelming principle of order (the collective longing for redemption). Through his inner vision the prophet discerns from the needs of his time the helpful image in the collective unconscious and expresses it in the symbol: because it speaks out of the collective unconscious it speaks for everyone—*le vrai mot de la situation*! Hence it has a fascinating effect on everyone, it is "true"— temporarily valid because it is meant *only for a particular situation*. If the situation changes, a new "truth" is needed, therefore *truth is always relative to a particular situation*. So long as the symbol is the true and redeeming answer to the corresponding situation, it is true

[1] Cf. Gerhart Hauptmann: "Poetry is the art of letting the primordial word resound through the common word." *Symbols of Transformation*, par. 460.
[2] "Being in the soul." Cf. *Psychological Types*, pars. 66f., 77.

and valid, indeed "absolute." But if the situation changes and the symbol is simply perpetuated, it is nothing but an idol, having an impoverishing and stultifying effect, because it merely makes us unconscious and provides no explanation and enlightenment. Justin Martyr,[3] for instance, spoke of Christianity as "our philosophy." The symbol is doctrine, the idol delusion.

I regard Hegel's "perceptual" thinking as a thinking analogous with the archetypes. "Perceptual" or "apperceptive" thinking[4] has greater meaning and value because it unites at least two functions. The highest form of the intellectual process would be symbolic experience and its symbolic expression.

You are right—the symbol belongs to a different sphere from the sphere of instinct. The latter sphere is the mother, the former the son (or God). For my private use I call the sphere of paradoxical existence, i.e., the instinctive unconscious, the Pleroma,[5] a term borrowed from Gnosticism. The reflection and formation of the Pleroma in the individual consciousness produce an image of it (of like nature in a certain sense), and that is the symbol. In it all paradoxes are abolished. In the Pleroma, Above and Below lie together in a strange way and produce nothing; but when it is disturbed by the mistakes and needs of the individual a waterfall arises between Above and Below, a dynamic something that is the symbol. Like the Pleroma, the symbol is greater than man. It overpowers him, shapes him, as though he had opened a sluice that pours a mighty stream over him and sweeps him away.

Our difficulty is that we understand the psyche as what we make and regulate ourselves, and we can't get it into our heads that we are the helpless victims of psychic forces. Take the professor who suffers from a "compulsion neurosis." Compulsion neurosis is a magic word used by the modern medicine man, which means (apotropaically!)[6] nothing but neurosis (imaginary illness). Yet real compulsion neurosis is one of the most hellish, devilish tortures, far worse than

---

[3] Christian apologist, born A.D. *ca.* 100, martyred between 163 and 167.

[4] Lit. "vernehmendes/wahrnehmendes Denken." It is not clear whether this is Hegel's characterization of a particular type of thinking or Jung's characterization of Hegel's thinking.

[5] Fullness, plenitude. In Gnostic theology, "the spiritual universe as the abode of God and of the totality of the Divine powers and emanations" (SOED).

[6] Apotropaism: attempt to banish the effect of an evil or frightening thing by giving it a good name; e.g., the Erinyes (Furies) were called the Eumenides (Kindly Ones).

any organic disease. It would be better if the professor thought he were possessed by the devil! That would be considerably nearer the truth.

The term "symbol" in Freud's psychoanalysis has nothing to do with the *symbol*. He should have said "symptom" or "metaphor" instead.

The symbol never arises in the unconscious (the Pleroma) but, as you rightly say, "in self-formation." It comes from the unconscious raw material and is formed and expressed consciously. (Cf. my definition of the symbol in *Psychological Types*.[7]) The symbol needs man for its development. But it grows beyond him, therefore it is called "God," since it expresses a psychic situation or factor stronger than the ego. (I call it the self.[8]) This factor is pre-existent in the collective unconscious, yet powerless until I experience it consciously; then it takes the lead. ("Yet not I, but Christ liveth in me."[9]) It supplants the ego in essential respects. Hence the deliverance from the feeling of ineptitude, etc. ("Thy Will be done.")

. . .

[7] Def. 51, esp. pars. 825ff.
[8] The concept of the self, the archetype of order and psychic totality, became central to Jung's theories. Preliminary formulations occur in *Psychological Types* (orig. 1921), par. 623 and under Def. 16, "Ego" (Def. 46, "Self," in CW 6, was specially written for the 1960 Swiss edn.), but it was formulated in detail for the first time in "The Relations between the Ego and the Unconscious" (orig. 1928), CW 7. Cf. also *Aion*, CW 9, ii, ch. IV.
[9] Galatians 2:20.

To Richard Wilhelm

My dear Professor Wilhelm,   6 April 1929

Warm thanks for everything you have sent me. I am giving up the Rosicrucian symbols.[1] Without the text I can make nothing of them.

□ (Handwritten.) This and the following letters to W. are published by courtesy of the Richard Wilhelm Archive, Bad Boll, Germany. — Richard Wilhelm (1873–1930), German author, theologian, and missionary in China, director of the China Institute, Frankfurt am Main. He is best known for his translations of Chinese classical writings, particularly the *I Ching, or Book of Changes*. In 1929 in conjunction with Jung he published *Das Geheimnis der goldenen Blüte* (tr., *The Secret of the Golden Flower*, 1931; rev. edn., 1962). Jung's contribution, "Commentary on *The Secret of the Golden Flower*," is also contained in

I hope your health is better. It was surely the cold mayonnaise at X.'s which ruined our care.

I arrive in Frankfurt on 11 April at 2.24 p.m. and shall stay till 5.15 p.m. The next day I have to lecture in Nauheim.[2] Could I visit you then? And where? Please drop me a line. I shall soon be able to make a start on our MS.[3]

Are you overworked? We should impose a retreat on you somewhere on a wild rocky mountain with the pleasantest company for at least 3 months. Why are there no secular monasteries for people who ought to be living outside time? The world eats them up from inside if it doesn't from outside.

Excuse this pious ejaculation. It is for your sake!

Cordially, JUNG

Alchemical Studies, CW 13. Cf. also "Richard Wilhelm: In Memoriam," CW 15, and *Memories*, Appendix IV. (See pl. III.)

[1] Cf. Boner, 8 Dec. 38, n. 2.

[2] Cf. next letter, n. 1.

[3] *Das Geheimnis der goldenen Blüte*, of which a part was published under the title "Tschang Schen Schu. Die Kunst das menschliche Leben zu verlängern," in the *Europäische Revue*, V:2/8 (Nov. 1929).

To Richard Wilhelm

My dear Professor Wilhelm,   26 April 1929

Please don't be horrified at my writing to you again. I rushed in vain to your house in Frankfurt—not to bother you but because I was somehow worried about you. Please don't be offended. You are *too important* to our Western world. I must keep on telling you this. You mustn't melt away or otherwise disappear, or get ill, but wicked desires should pin you to the earth so your work can go on.

The result of my lecture[1] at the Nauheim Psychotherapeutic Congress[2] is that, without my previous knowledge, the board of the Psychotherapeutic Society has decided to ask *you* to give a lecture next year[3] (presumably in Baden-Baden). This will make history! Think what it means if medical practitioners, who get at the ordinary person

□ (Handwritten.)

[1] "The Aims of Psychotherapy," CW 16.

[2] 11–14 Apr. 29.

[3] The lecture was never held. W. died 1 Mar. 30.

so brashly and in the most vulnerable spot, were to be inoculated with Chinese philosophy! It is simply inconceivable. I am delighted and only hope that no devils will keep you away from this historic occasion. This really goes to the heart of the matter. Medicine is switching over to psychology with a vengeance, and that's where the East comes in. There's nothing to be done with the theologians and philosophers because of their arrogance.

Excuse this new intrusion! I hope you are restored in health. Don't overwork yourself. The Lamaic mandala[4] has been copied. I will send back the original soon.

Your ever devoted, C. G. JUNG

[4] The frontispiece to *The Secret of the Golden Flower*, also Fig. 1 in "Concerning Mandala Symbolism," CW 9, i, and Fig. 43 in *Psychology and Alchemy*, CW 12. — Mandala (Skt.) means "circle," more specifically the "magic circle" used in Yoga meditation. Jung introduced the term to describe the infinite variety of circular images or patterns drawn by patients which symbolize the self, "a psychic centre of the personality not to be identified with the ego" (*Psychology and Alchemy*, par. 126). Mandalas belong to the oldest archetypal patterns of mankind, and they arise spontaneously in the dreams and visions of modern people. The commentary on *The Golden Flower* was Jung's first public account of mandalas; they are constantly mentioned in his later writings. Cf. in particular "Concerning Mandala Symbolism" and "A Study in the Process of Individuation," CW 9, i.

To Walter Robert Corti

Dear Herr Corti,   30 April 1929

It doesn't surprise me that you were rather offended by my letter. I had to write to your father and tell him honestly what my "diagnosis" is. "Diagnosis" does not mean saying someone is pathological; it means "thorough knowledge," that is to say of your psychological state. "Hypertrophy of intellectual intuition" is a diagnosis I would apply also to Nietzsche and Schopenhauer and many others. I myself am one-sided in this respect. One compensates for it with a feeling

☐ (Handwritten.) Walter Robert Corti, Ph.D., Swiss writer, philosopher, and teacher, founder of the Pestalozzi Village for Children (1946); 1942–57, editor of the Swiss monthly *Du*; editor of the *Archiv für genetische Philosophie*; 1954, founder of the Bauhütte der Akademie, an educational institution. He met Jung in Mar. 1929 through the mediation of his father, who had been warned by a doctor of the young man's emotional state.

of inferiority. Diagnoses like this merely hurt our vanity. But we must see where we stand, otherwise we are immoral illusionists. This isn't to say that a person is pathological, let alone mad. Your medical man is a stupid shitbag who ought to become a psychiatrist so that he can get better acquainted with X., whose sister I saved from the madhouse. There is too much of this sorry medical rabble running around Switzerland judging me without knowing me.

I expected my letter would dismay you, because you don't yet have the distressing capacity of seeing yourself from outside. You must hasten to acquire it without letting it upset you. Jesus said to the man who was working on the Sabbath: "Man, if indeed thou knowest what thou doest, thou art blessed; but if thou knowest not, thou art cursed, and a transgressor of the law."[1] We live not only inwardly, but also outwardly.

O you carriers of ideas, why do you have to make buffoons of them by the idiotic life you lead? Nietzsche preached: "You should make friends with the nearest things."[2] I would hold his world-negating life responsible for this did I not know that syphilis lurked in him and that paralysis hung over him like the sword of Damocles.

Look, the Catholic priest is the most faithful, the closest to the earth. He is living history, and no Holzapfel.[3]

That you "live for God" is perhaps the healthiest thing about you —"He that is near me is near the fire,"[4] so runs a Gnostic saying of the Lord. But where God is nearest the danger is greatest.[5] God wants to be born in the flame of man's consciousness, leaping ever higher. And what if this has no roots in the earth? If it is not a house of stone where the fire of God can dwell, but a wretched straw hut that flares up and vanishes? Could God then be born? One must be able to suffer God. That is the supreme task for the carrier of ideas. He must be the advocate of the earth. God will take care of himself. My inner principle is: Deus et homo. God needs man in order to become conscious, just as he needs limitation in time and

[1] Non-canonical saying of Jesus in Codex Bezae Cantabrigiensis (5th cent. text of the Gospels and Acts) to Luke 6:4. Cf. M. R. James, *The Apocryphal New Testament* (1924), p. 33.
[2] *Human All Too Human*, II: "The Wanderer and his Shadow," sec. 16.
[3] Rudolf Maria Holzapfel (1874–1930), philosopher and poet; his main work is *Panideal* (1901; rev. 1923). (The name contains a pun: *Holzapfel* = crab-apple.)
[4] Quoted from Origen, *Homiliae in Jeremiam*, XX, 3, referring to Isaiah 33:14. Cf. James, p. 35.
[5] Cf. opening lines of Hölderlin's "Patmos": "Near is God, and hard to apprehend. But where danger is, there arises salvation also."

space. Let us therefore be for him limitation in time and space, an earthly tabernacle.

Jesus—Mani—Buddha—Lao-tse are for me the four pillars of the temple of the spirit. I could give none preference over the other.

Sometime I will show you some Manichean Turfan frescoes.[6]

Next Saturday I shall be at my country seat, a tower by the Upper Lake, halfway between Bollingen and Schmerikon. You can come to see me there.

With best regards, DR. C. G. JUNG

[6] The Turfan oasis, where important frescoes, some dating back to the 7th cent., were discovered, is situated in Sinkiang (W. China).

To Richard Wilhelm

Dear friend,   25 May 1929

It is lovely to hear the word "friend" from you. Fate seems to have apportioned to us the role of two piers which support the bridge between East and West. I thank you with all my heart that you are willing to give the lecture.

For the time being, however, you must get thoroughly well again. Please let me know how things are with you (indirectly through your secretary or wife). All of us here are concerned about your health and would be glad to have news of you now and then. I hope Baden-Baden is doing you good.

At present I am overworked, so my MS[1] must wait a bit. I am taking a holiday at the end of June and then I shall have leisure to finish the work. No harm has been done by my putting it off, because I have had a number of experiences that have given me some very valuable insights. With heartfelt wishes for your speedy and thorough recovery,

Your devoted JUNG

☐ (Handwritten.)
[1] Jung's commentary on the *Golden Flower*.

To Richard Wilhelm

Dear friend,   27 August 1929

Best thanks for your letter and the good news about your health, which until now has caused me great worry. Please abstain from doing too much. Don't let the devil of action lure you to Barcelona. There they make mayonnaises that poison the soul and the bowels.

If I understand your proposals correctly, the questions at issue are 1. the MS on meditation,[1] which I am hatching out now, will be published by Grete Ullmann in book form after first appearing in the *Europäische Revue*, 2. your interpretation of the *chakras*[2] (in which I play no part) is to be published by the same firm.

As regards 1, I agree with this provided I get a decent fee or 15% of the proceeds.

As regards 2, this is entirely up to you. Naturally I shall be glad to make a contribution of my own on "primordial images."[3] No list or anything of the sort exists. The mythological motifs have never yet been classified, as their name is legion. You will find a large number of them if you look up the index of my book *Wandlungen und Symbole der Libido*. Perhaps I can contribute something if you send me your description of the original characters.[4] But it may be a ticklish job. Or do you want us to undertake this work in common as we did the first? With the very best wishes,

Your sincere and devoted JUNG

☐ (Handwritten.)

[1] *Das Geheimnis der goldenen Blüte* was published by Dorn Verlag Grete Ullmann (Munich, 1929).

[2] *Chakra* or *cakra* (Skt.), "wheel": the seven ascending centres or "lotuses" of the human body as described in Hatha Yoga and Kundalini Yoga. Cf. A. Avalon, *The Serpent Power* (1924), ch. V; H. Zimmer, *Philosophies of India* (1951), pp. 584ff. W.'s work on *chakras* was never published.

[3] The early term for archetypes.

[4] Cf. next letter, n. 4.

To Richard Wilhelm

temporarily (till end of Sept.) Tower, Bollingen,

Dear friend,   Ct. St. Gallen, 10 September 1929

My commentary is now more or less finished. It has turned out to be rather more extensive [than I expected], because it represents a European reaction to the wisdom of China. Please would you read it first so that you can correct any Chinese blunders. I have tried my hand at interpreting Tao.[1]

☐ (Handwritten.)

[1] The exact translation of Tao, one of the fundamental concepts of Chinese

I haven't inserted any mandala pictures but can easily do so afterwards if you think it expedient.

Naturally the whole thing is too long for the *Revue*. I would therefore suggest that the *Revue* picks out a few plums and publishes them.

Further, I would like to tell you that a philological introduction or commentary from your side would be in the highest degree desirable. For this purpose I enclose the notes you gave me in Küsnacht. The reader ought to know something of the philosophical and religious background of the ideas in the text. Its approximate date should be indicated. The extremely interesting amalgamation of Taoism with Mahayana[2] was quite new to me. A reference to similar texts (such as the *Hui Ming Ching*[3]), if any are accessible, would also be most desirable. Please excuse these importunate suggestions, but I am inspired by these texts that are so close to our unconscious.

My MS will go off to you as soon as it is copied out. You won't need it for the philological part. It would be useful to have a short explanation of the concepts *tao, sin, ming, shen, gui, hun,* and *po*[4] from the characters, which should be reproduced along with them.

. . .

In my commentary I have explained the symbols and psychic states in some detail, exclusively of course from the psychological standpoint, and at the same time drawn parallels with our psychology. It runs to some 53 written folio sheets of about 39 lines each. The Table of Contents is included.

I hope your health continues to make good progress.

---

philosophy, is extremely difficult. W. translated it as "meaning" (*Sinn*), Arthur Waley as "way" (*The Way and the Power*, 1934); other translations like "Logos" or even "God" (by Jesuit missionaries) have been used. Originally it meant the revolution (or way) of the heavens about the earth; action in accordance with Tao is "heaven's way." Jung interprets it as "the method or conscious way by which to unite what is separated . . . the attainment of conscious life" ("Commentary on *The Secret of the Golden Flower*," par. 30).

[2] The "Great Vehicle," one of the later schools of Buddhism, prevalent in China, Tibet, and Japan.

[3] By Lin Hua Yang, "The Book of Consciousness and Life," trans. Lo, *Chinesische Blätter für Wissenschaft und Kunst*, I:3 (1926). The text appears in the 1962 edn. of *The Golden Flower*, pp. 69ff.

[4] *Sin (hsin)* = heart, *ming* = life, *shen* = spirit, soul, *gui (kuei)* = demon, departed one, *hun* = light, *yang*-soul (animus), *po (p'o)* = dark, *yin*-soul (anima). Cf. W.'s "Discussion of the Text" in ibid., pp. 13ff.

To save time it would probably be better if you sent the whole MS, your discussion (or introduction), the text, and my commentary direct to the *Revue*. The main thing is the book edition. With very best greetings,

Your devoted J U N G

P.S. It has just struck me that in my commentary I have suggested using "logos" for *hun* instead of "animus," because "animus" is a suitable term for the "mind" of a woman, corresponding to the "anima" of a man.[5] European philosophy must take into account the existence of feminine psychology. The "anima" of a woman might suitably be designated "Eros."

[5] Animus/anima, terms coined by Jung to denote the masculine, Logos aspect of a woman's psychology and the feminine, Eros aspect of a man's. Cf. *Aion*, ch. III.

To Walter Robert Corti

My dear Corti,   Bollingen, 12 September 1929

I have read no letters for 4 weeks as I had to cope with a thousand-year-old Chinese text which the China Institute sent me for a commentary. We live in the age of the decline of Christianity, when the metaphysical premises of morality are collapsing. (Recently I saw Wells[1] at my house, who said the same thing and rubbed his nose with his finger, which meant: Then we ought to know—or smell— what we can do now.) That's why the young are experimenting like young dogs. They want to live experimentally, with no historical premises. That causes reactions in the unconscious, restlessness and longing for the fulfilment of the times. (This is called "chiliasm."[2]) When the confusion is at its height a new revelation comes, i.e., at the beginning of the fourth month of world history.[3] This follows

☐ (Handwritten.)
[1] H. G. Wells (1866–1946), British writer.
[2] Doctrine of the millennium, the return and thousand-year reign of Christ.
[3] In astrological tradition the transition of the vernal equinox into the zodiacal sign of Aquarius (taking place towards the end of the 20th cent.) will coincide with a new advance in human development. Jung argues in *Aion* that whereas the aeon of Pisces was ruled by Christ and Antichrist (par. 141) and the archetypal motif of the hostile brothers, Aquarius will constellate the union of opposites (par. 142). The "4th month" puts the beginning of world history into the aeon

psychological rules. Wyneken[4] is also homosexual. (Trial!) The young today can be forbidden no stupidities since they thereby increase the salutary confusion. People like you must *look at* everything and *think* about it and communicate with the heaven that dwells deep within them and listen inwardly for a word to come. At the same time organize your outward life properly so that your voice carries weight.

You must first ask the publisher whether Wells's book[5] has been translated already. Then ask Wells if he'll let you translate it. Then, if the publisher accepts it, everything will be all right.

With best regards, JUNG

The fear is not of myself, but of the myth in you.

---

of Taurus, i.e., 6–7,000 years ago, when man first became conscious of historical time (each "Platonic month" lasts about 2,000 years). Cf. Baur, 29 Jan. 34, n. 1.
[4] Gustav Wyneken (1875–1964), German pedagogue, founder of the progressive school community Wickersdorf. Tried and condemned for homosexuality.
[5] On Jung's recommendation C. read Wells's *God the Invisible King* and planned to translate it. The plan did not materialize.

To Christiana Morgan

[ORIGINAL IN ENGLISH]

My dear Christiana Morgan,   13 September 1929

You are unforgotten but hard to be reached, i.e., it takes a hell of a long time until I can find the right moment for writing. Now I do write. I think your countryhouse has been an interesting experience. I found that it takes three or four months or more until the upheaval of the local elfs and other ghosties is laid, when one has built a house in their hitherto undisputed realm. When I built my Tower my oldest daughter,[1] then about 14, said, This place contains spirits of the deceased, not only elfs. There must be a corpse somewhere. In 1927 (4 years later) when we dug up the foundations for an annexe to the Tower, we found a male skeleton with a bullet in the right forearm. Careful investigations proved that it was the body of a French soldier that was drowned nearby, in 1799! I made him a nice "tombeau du soldat inconnu."[2]

☐ (Handwritten.)
[1] Now Frau Agathe Niehus-Jung.
[2] Concerning this episode cf. *Memories*, pp. 231f./219.

I have just finished a paper that goes into a book I am publishing together with Prof. Wilhelm, the Director of the China Institute in Frankfort. In that paper (which is a commentary to an old, but recently discovered Chinese text) I say more. That old text contains f.i. my anima theory and something more about the self—you will enjoy it.

I had a letter from Jonah.[3] When shall we all meet again?

My very best greetings and wishes to yourself and to your husband.

Cordially yours, C. G.

[3] Cf. Jones, 6 Jan. 31.

To Richard Wilhelm

Dear friend,   28 October 1929

I entirely agree with your alterations to the contract. I am very glad you have chosen the old title[1] as it accords much better with the real meaning of the book than the other. I am pleased that my comments meet with your approval and, even more, that your own train of thought proceeds along parallel lines. As for the mandalas I would like the publisher to see, none of the numerous mandalas in my possession gets anywhere near the perfection of the Tibetan mandala, because the one lays more stress on this idea and another on another. Consequently I have picked out a series of mandalas that represent the various modulations of the central ideas. Shortly I will send the photographs to the publisher and hope he will reproduce them all. I also hope you will agree with this proposal. The mandalas complement one another and by their very variety give an excellent picture of the efforts of the European unconscious to grasp the eschatology of the East. I will send you copies of these mandalas soon. You say nothing at all about your health, so I hope the improvement you reported earlier has kept up. In any event you should never forget to spare your body, as the spirit has the unpleasant quality of wanting to eat the body up.

With warm greetings and best wishes, C. G. JUNG

□ (Typewritten.)
[1] The old title is "The Secret of the Golden Flower," which had been changed by a Chinese editor to "The Art of Prolonging Human Life." Cf. Wilhelm, 6 Apr. 29, n. 3.

To J. Allen Gilbert

[ORIGINAL IN ENGLISH]

My dear Dr. Gilbert,   20 December 1929

Thank you for the article! It is no small enterprise to embark on such a treatment. I found sometimes that it is a great help, in handling such a case, to encourage them to express their peculiar contents either in the form of writing or of drawing and painting. There are so many incomprehensible intuitions in such cases, fantasy fragments that rise from the unconscious, for which there is almost no suitable language—I let my patients find their own symbolic expressions, their "mythology." I don't analyse these products in a reductive way (if it is not absolutely indicated), but I rather try to understand or get at the meaning the patient tries to express. It would be a more synthetic kind of understanding. There are many borderline cases that are merely crazy, because they themselves as little as anybody else understand their peculiar contents. I must say I learned a lot about the unconscious in trying to understand what the patients were driving at.

I wish you every good luck and a happy New Year.

Sincerely yours, C. G. JUNG

☐ (Handwritten.)

To Count Hermann Keyserling

Dear Count,   20 December 1929

I still haven't heard anything from X.[1] It goes without saying that I shall treat your letter as non-existent. Your excellent description of the fateful intermezzo with her clearly shows that it is an encounter with an "earth woman," fraught with meaning. Concealed and revealed in it is one of the most beautiful animus-anima stories I have ever heard. Unfortunately poetic stories usually end in disappointment because, when one meets one's own soul, one never recognizes it but confuses it with the poor human creature who has functioned unconsciously as a symbol-carrier. X.'s longing for identification

---

[1] In a long and confidential letter of 25 Nov., K. described a strangely intense and at the same time unreal relationship that had developed between a well-known South American writer and himself, in which she clearly played the role of the "femme inspiratrice." Her ambivalence led to considerable complications during his stay in S. America.

72

actually refers to the animus which she should like to possess in you, but she mixes it up with you personally and then of course is deeply disappointed. This disappointment will be repeated, always and everywhere, until man has learnt to distinguish his soul from the other person. Then his soul can return to him. This lesson is a hellish torture for both, but extremely useful, *the* experience one would have wished for you, and assuredly the most fitting torture of all for X., who is still possessed by her earth demons. Perhaps she prefers to be torn to pieces by the titans, as happens to many such anima figures. Hence you should always remember, with reverence and devotion, what has been revealed to you in the human shell of X., so that your soul may remain inalienably with you, and your access to the earth may never be blocked. Let us hope the same for her, that besides tigers and serpents and eternal spirit there is still a human being in her who can remember with gratitude the revelation of her own spirit in you. But it is only too easy to make a personal tragedy out of what was ultimately a "Divina Commedia," and then a spark of the eternal fire hisses out in a puddle. With best regards,

Ever sincerely yours, C. G. JUNG

P.S. Please excuse the spot of paraffin on the paper. My lamp suddenly seems to have got symptoms of incontinence.

To J. Allen Gilbert

[ORIGINAL IN ENGLISH]

My dear Dr. Gilbert,   4 March 1930

Oppenheim's[1] statement isn't literally true. Freud had accepted my copy,[2] but he told me that my whole idea meant nothing but resistances against the father. Particularly he incriminated my idea that the libido has a contradictory character, wanting life as much as death. Twenty years later he brought the whole thing out as his own discovery.[3] He didn't take my book seriously at all and that's the reason why I had to leave him.

Yours sincerely, C. G. JUNG

[1] Cf. Oppenheim, 12 Aug. 33.

[2] Of *Wandlungen und Symbole der Libido* (1912).

[3] Jung's memory for dates was at fault if this refers to Freud's hypothesis of life and death instincts, first formulated in "Beyond the Pleasure Principle" (orig. 1920), Standard Edn., 18. Cf. Jung, *Two Essays*, CW 7, par. 33 & n. 4.

Anonymous

My dear Frau N.,   26 April 1930

It is obvious that you have inwardly coalesced with your husband. Formerly he assimilated so much of you that you yourself are now in him too. Nothing is so binding as affects and unconscious states let loose on the other person. Now you must suffer your husband as he has suffered you. You must take it for granted that you'll have to endure everything that affects him. Naturally he is now confused and disoriented because his unconscious side is coming up. The whole situation is turning around.

He wrote me recently and accused me of teaching psychology instead of living. I know this accusation. All those people make it who misuse psychology to shirk their own life. He has lived too long *through you* instead of through himself. But now it has caught him by the scruff of the neck. He has, as a matter of fact, killed the old man (in me) since he has thrown out the baby with the bathwater and no longer gets any benefit from psychological insight. That comes from misuse. I have answered him but have mislaid his address. Perhaps I had an unconscious resistance to answering him because his letter didn't tell me the truth. I enclose my answer. You can send it to him if you wish. Your dream:[1]

The elephant is the largest *animal*. It represents the crushing weight of the unconscious life in you. It has to decompose, that is to say you mustn't let yourself be driven to extremes any longer by the unconscious but must act according to your conscious insight. This transformation process expresses itself in your body. It is the same process your husband is going through, only in reverse. It is a dangerous crisis and you must cling with might and main to consciousness. You need insight and understanding in the highest degree, for only this can ensure that the animal will decompose in you in such a way that you are not too much affected by it. It's a question of becoming human. Man is distinguished by the supremacy of consciousness, but the animal is the victim of instincts, impulsive moods, affects and illusions.

Your husband has still to experience all this in his own body. Until now he has been much too reasonable because for him you have

---

[1] An elephant is being eaten up by worms so that all its bones show. An unknown person tells her to observe this process closely as it symbolized her illness (pulmonary tuberculosis).

74

represented too much of his own unreason. Now the boot is on the other leg.

You can be absolutely sure of my discretion. With heartfelt sympathy,

Very sincerely, C. G. JUNG

To Hugh Walpole

[ORIGINAL IN ENGLISH]

My dear Mr. Walpole,   15 August 1930

When I talked to you in Zurich[1] I was under the painful impression that I never read a book you have written. Since then I have found out that I have read a very decent number of them. I usually can't stand the typical literary writing. It bores me too much. But some of your novels, particularly the story of the student who committed a murder, have left absolute traces in my mind. I think the *Prelude*[2] is a psychological masterpiece. If only such people had more often the chance to commit a decent murder—but I have seen "pale criminals"[3] only. Minor crimes done by the right people have ordinarily a wonderfully humanizing effect, a decided moral improvement. This seems to be the true reason why God is good and even better than any mortal.

I hope the day when you come to Zurich again will not be too far off. There are too few intelligent people in the world.

Yours cordially, C. G. JUNG

☐ (Handwritten.) Hugh Walpole (1884–1941), English novelist.
[1] "Walpole gave a lecture on some literary subject at Zurich in July 1930, and was delighted to find Jung was in the audience. In his diary Walpole wrote of Jung: 'He's like a large genial English cricketer! We sat together at supper after and he delighted me with his hatred of hysterics.'" (From a letter by Rupert Hart-Davis, Walpole's literary executor, to the editor, quoted with his permission. I am indebted to him for Jung's letters to Walpole.)
[2] *The Prelude to Adventure* (1912).
[3] Cf. Nietzsche, *Thus Spake Zarathustra*, Part I, ch. 6.

To Count Hermann Keyserling

Dear Count,   9 September 1930

I still owe you many thanks for your new book on America.[1] However, I have not got down to reading it yet as I myself have some writing to do. But I shall set about it soon.

75

When you write about South America,[2] the continent of your inferior function,[3] and at the same time your body forces itself unpleasantly upon your attention, this may well be because body and earth somehow feel irritated by your writing. Your nausea bears this out. Why don't you let your bowels say something too in your new book?

With best greetings and again heartiest thanks, JUNG

□ (Handwritten.)
[1] *America Set Free* (tr., 1930).
[2] *South-American Meditations* (tr., 1932).
[3] In Jung's theory of psychological types, the differentiated function is opposed by an inferior, undifferentiated function. K.'s intuition was his best function, and accordingly sensation his worst, expressing itself in physical symptoms.

To Alice Raphael Eckstein

[ORIGINAL IN ENGLISH]

Dear Mrs. Eckstein,   16 September 1930

Thank you very much for your long and interesting letter. It is surely a very interesting problem, the question of the relation between brain and consciousness. Everyday experience tells us that consciousness and brain are in an indispensable connection. Destruction of the latter results in an equal destruction of the former. Bergson is quite right when he thinks of the possibility of a relatively loose connection between the brain and consciousness,[1] because despite our ordinary experience the connection might be less tight than we suppose. There is no reason why one shouldn't suppose that consciousness could exist detached from a brain. Thus far there is no difficulty for our assumption. But the real difficulty begins when it comes to the actual showdown, namely when you should prove that there is consciousness without a brain. It would amount to the hitherto unproven fact of an evidence that there are ghosts. I think it is the most difficult thing in the world to produce evidence in that respect entirely satisfactory from a scientific point of view. As a matter of fact, it is the hardest thing I could imagine. I frankly confess I don't know at all how such a

□ Alice P. Raphael, American writer and analyst. She published translations of *Faust I* (1930) and of Goethe's *Parable* (1963), and wrote *Goethe and the Philosophers' Stone* (1965).
[1] Cf. Bergson, *Creative Evolution* (orig. 1907; tr., 1911), p. 190: ". . . the more complicated the brain becomes . . . the more does consciousness outrun its physical concomitant."

proof would look. How can one establish indisputable evidence for the existence of a consciousness without a brain? I might be satisfied if such a consciousness would be able to write an intelligent book, invent new apparatuses, provide us with new information that couldn't be possibly found in human brains, and if it were evident that there was no high-power medium among the spectators. But such a thing is quite unthinkable. I therefore consider the possibility of proving an incorporeal consciousness an extremely unlikely one.

Trance conditions are certainly very interesting and I know a good deal about them[2]—though never enough. But they wouldn't yield any strict evidence, because they are the conditions of a living brain.

Yes, I know of the Tarot.[3] It is, as far as I know, the pack of cards originally used by the Spanish gypsies, the oldest cards historically known. They are still used for divination purposes.

If ever you should have new experiences I shall be most interested to hear of them.

Very sincerely yours, C. G. JUNG

[2] Cf. "On the Psychology and Pathology of So-called Occult Phenomena," CW 1; also *Memories*, pp. 118f./119.
[3] Card game, probably of Italian origin, with symbolic figures of esoteric significance. Widely used for fortune-telling.

To Dr. S.

Dear Dr. S.,   16 October 1930

You are quite right: such views do indeed prevail among the German public, unfortunately not without justification. An essentially reductive analysis like Freud's and the collectivizing psychology of Adler, which erases all differences, are the most virulent poison imaginable for the attitude of the artist and the creative person in general. As you know, my own views differ from both. I work directly with the creative principle within us. A few years ago I wrote an article[1] on the relation between analysis and poetry in the Swiss literary magazine *Wissen und Leben* and have also made a contribution[2] to *Philosophie der Literaturwissenschaft,* published by Ermat-

☐ A physician in Germany.
[1] "Ueber die Beziehungen der analytischen Psychologie zum dichterischen Kunstwerk," *Wissen und Leben*, XV:19/20 (1922); tr. "On the Relation of Analytical Psychology to Poetry," CW 15.

inger, on psychology and literature. My standpoint can easily be ascertained from these two works if people would read them. But these days the voice of the single individual is almost completely drowned in the chaos of newspapers and the flood of books. It reaches only a few. Therefore one must always wait until a false view has belaboured itself to death.

Anyway I am grateful to you for your stimulation. With best regards,

Yours sincerely, C. G. JUNG

[2] "Psychologie und Dichtung," *Philosophie der Literaturwissenschaft* (Berlin), 1930; tr. "Psychology and Literature," CW 15.

Anonymous

Dear Herr N., 27 October 1930

The wonderful Chinese statuette not only came as an extraordinary surprise but has also given me much pleasure. As I am a great admirer of Chinese art I can appreciate your gift all the more highly.

May I take this opportunity to express the hope that the latest developments have not shaken anything essential in you. In the last resort the value of a person is never expressed in his relation to others but consists in itself. Therefore we should never let our self-confidence or self-esteem depend on the behaviour of another person however much we may be humanly affected by him. Everything that happens to us, properly understood, leads us back to ourselves; it is as though there were some unconscious guidance whose aim it is to deliver us from all ties and all dependence and make us dependent on ourselves. This is because dependence on the behaviour of others is a last vestige of childhood which we think we can't do without.

. . .

Yours sincerely, C. G. JUNG

□ Germany.

To Hugh Walpole

[ORIGINAL IN ENGLISH]

My dear Mr. Walpole, 14 November 1930

I was delighted with your letter, which I should have answered right away if time had permitted. Unfortunately I can't write letters when *I* want. Being a doctor I am *à la merci* of circumstances. And, in a way, it is still necessary for me to be a doctor, because as such I am in the position to gather experiences which I could not have otherwise.

I wish I had the time to write a book. It is always the best time one possibly can have. The gods live only in creativeness. Your place must be lovely indeed. I saw a picture of it in a paper. You were in it too with a German writer, quite recognizable. I am enclosing a photo of mine.

I am most indebted to you for the books your publisher keeps on sending me. I shall dive into them as soon as I have a moment of respite. To give you some idea of my work I have ordered my publisher to send you a copy of my *Two Essays*.[1] I wanted to send you the English translation of *The Secret of the Golden Flower*, an old Chinese text which I have published together with the late Professor Wilhelm. But I don't know when the thing is going into print.

I hope the day will soon come when you return to Switzerland. I should like to continue our conversation.

Cordially yours, C. G. JUNG

☐ (Handwritten.)
[1] *Two Essays on Analytical Psychology*, tr. C. F. and H. G. Baynes (1929).

To H. Langenegger

Dear Herr Langenegger,   20 November 1930

The psychology of the 16th century is not entirely unfamiliar to me. I have studied Colonna's *Polifilo*[1] with great care and have come to the conclusion that one can never decide whether certain materials are derived from reading or spring from autochthonous roots. Something that has been read can appear genuine and the genuine can appear like something read. Moreover in that age the capacity for thinking in symbols was considerably greater than it is today. We must also remember that what now seems to us rigid orthodoxy was once the most vital expression and essential formulation of the needs of the unconscious psyche. In such cases there is one thing you have to

☐ Zurich.
[1] *Hypnerotomachia Poliphili*, a work of the early Italian Renaissance, ascribed to a Venetian monk, Francesco Colonna. Cf. Linda Fierz-David, *The Dream of Poliphilo* (tr., 1950), with a foreword by Jung also published in CW 18.

guard against very carefully, and that is reduction to the personal. The whole sphere of the mind is influenced in an infinitely higher degree by collective factors than by personal ones. Besides which the personal aspect of this Magdalena is probably the same banality you can expect of all Magdalenas.

Yours sincerely, C. G. JUNG

To Charles Roberts Aldrich

[ORIGINAL IN ENGLISH]

My dear Aldrich, 5 January 1931

I am glad you could appreciate my foreword to your book.[1] I surely shall recommend it to my patients because it is an excellent introduction to primitive psychology, one of the few books about this subject that is blessed with common sense, and common sense means a sound dose of philosophy. You are quite right, as soon as psychology becomes anything like useful and practical, for instance in psychotherapy, it needs must be philosophical. What else is behaviourism and mechanism and all that than a sort of unsound philosophical prejudice?

I'm enclosing a review about Keyserling's book on America[2] which might interest you. I am about to publish a book of lectures and essays in German.[3] I can send you a copy of it because it might be helpful in your actual work. It will contain my most recent formulations.

Joggi[4] is in excellent health and keeps on being the most delightful companion. For New Year's Eve I performed the rule [rite?] you obviously often have taught him, namely I made a parcel of a rich meal of mutton chops and brought it home to him in your memory. I talked English with him in order to bring back happy childhood souvenirs to his actual consciousness.

My best wishes for a happy New Year.

Yours, C. G. JUNG

☐ American psychologist and writer (d. 1933), who had worked with Jung in Zurich.
[1] *The Primitive Mind and Modern Civilization* (1931), with a foreword by Jung also published in CW 18.
[2] Cf. Keyserling, 20 Oct. 28, n. 1.
[3] *Seelenprobleme der Gegenwart* (1931). The essays are distributed in CW 4 (Appendix 3), 8, 10, 16, 17.
[4] A.'s dog, given to Jung on A.'s return to England.

To Robert Edmond Jones

[ORIGINAL IN ENGLISH]

My dear Jonah,   6 January 1931

Thank you very much for sending me a copy of the wonderful book. Having read *Ol' Man Adam and his Chillun*[1] I was quite able to appreciate the particular beauty of the play and of your share in it. I wish we could see such a thing over here. But, alas, it is not even to be seen in England. The censors[2] there must be completely possessed by the devil. No wonder, it is a piece of true religion. I once said in the seminar it would be by no means impossible that the next saviour might be a coloured man for the better humiliation of the white man's spiritual inflation.

Thank you again! My best wishes for a happy New Year.

Yours sincerely, C. G. JUNG

☐ (1887–1954), American theatrical designer.
[1] J. designed the set for Marc Connelly's play *The Green Pastures*. The play was based on Roark Bradford's stories of Negro life in the Deep South, *Ol' Man Adam an' his Chillun* (1928). Connelly's play opened in New York in Feb. 1930 and won the Pulitzer Prize for Drama, 1929/30.
[2] The Lord Chamberlain, the Earl of Cromer, refused a license for a London production. Although no reason was given, the general impression was that exception was taken to the impersonation of God by a Negro.

To Jolande Jacobi

Dear Frau Jacobi,   7 February 1931

Heartiest thanks for your friendly telephone call! I was happy to know that you are well and also that the flowers reached you safely. You have conjured up again everything I experienced in those days in Vienna. Scarcely back home, I am swamped with work again. In spite of all the work I have often remembered the last evening with you.

.   .   .

I cannot begin to tell you how much your royal hospitality meant to me. I felt absolutely grand in Vienna and for that I am indebted to you. But what I most value and admire was your humanity.

Please accept, dear lady, once more the expression of my deepest gratitude,

Ever sincerely, C. G. JUNG

81

To Oskar A. H. Schmitz

Dear Herr Schmitz,   23 February 1931

I consider the *puer aeternus*[1] attitude an unavoidable evil. Identity with the *puer* signifies a psychological puerility that could do nothing better than outgrow itself. It always leads to external blows of fate which show the need for another attitude. But reason accomplishes nothing, because the *puer aeternus* is always an agent of destiny.

With best regards, C. G. JUNG

[1] The eternal youth, divine child. Cf. "The Psychology of the Child Archetype," CW 9, i, pars. 268f., and *Symbols of Transformation*, pars. 392f.

To Count Hermann Keyserling

Dear Count,   23 April 1931

From your description I have the impression that your South American experience, especially the encounter with X., has constellated contents in your unconscious that are the source of continued disturbances.[1] For better or worse we must (in collaboration with the South American earth) take X. as the *anima*, who (like South America) stands for the whole unconscious. The unconscious has a different rhythm from consciousness and different goals. Until now you have been accustomed, by means of intuition and literary work, to subordinate everything the psyche offered you to the aims of your conscious mind, or to create out of it a conscious view of the world. You have made South America out of X. Now it is a question of expressing those contents which can be located neither in X. nor in S.A. (and which seem to you still completely unknown), not by moulding them into a picture of the external world or incorporating them in such a picture, but, on the contrary, by subordinating your philosophical skill and descriptive powers to those unknown contents. Then those contents will be able to mould an inner picture of the world without your guidance or intention. The initial question to be

☐ (Handwritten.)

[1] K. described in letter of 31 Mar. how obsessed he was by the thought of death. He had been suffering from heart and lung trouble and felt quite devitalized and unable to write. He wondered to what extent his encounter with X. could have been the cause of his state.

directed to the Invisible would be: "Who or what has come alive in S.A.? Who or what has entered my psychic life and created disturbances and wants to be heard?" To this you should add: "Let it speak!" Then switch off your noisy consciousness and listen quietly inwards and look at the images that appear before your inner eye, or hearken to the words which the muscles of your speech apparatus are trying to form. Write down what then comes without criticism. Images should be drawn or painted[2] assiduously no matter whether you can do it or not.

Once you have got at least fragments of these contents, then you may meditate on them *afterwards*. Don't criticize anything away! If any questions arise, put them to the unconscious again the next day. Don't be content with your own explanations no matter how intelligent they are. Remember that your health is seriously at stake, and that the unconscious has an unknown and far-reaching control over it.

Treat any drawings the same way. Meditate on them afterwards and every day go on developing what is unsatisfactory about them. The important thing is to let the unconscious take the lead. You must always be convinced that you have mere after-knowledge and nothing else. In this case the unconscious really does know better.

Forgive me for delaying my answer so long! With best wishes,

Yours sincerely, C. G. JUNG

[2] The advice given here is a summary of Jung's method of "active imagination" by which a content of the unconscious, e.g., a dream or fantasy image, is activated and amplified. It is a technique of introspection in which the stream of inner images can be observed and made to come alive by active participation in the interior drama. It was described for the first time under the concept of "The Transcendent Function," an essay written in 1916 but not published until 1957. Cf. CW 8, esp. pars. 166ff. Also *Two Essays*, pars. 323ff., 342ff.; *Mysterium Coniunctionis*, pars. 706, 753ff.; and *Analytical Psychology: Its Theory and Practice* (1968), pp. 190ff.

To Katharine C. Briggs

[ORIGINAL IN ENGLISH]

Dear Mrs. Briggs,   4 July 1931

Thank you for your news of the X. family. It is indeed an unfortunate end to your attempts; yet an almost unavoidable one in such a

□ (1875–1968), Washington, D.C.; student of Jung's typology and co-author of *The Myers-Briggs Type Indicator* (Educational Testing Service, Princeton, N.J., 1962).

case. You overdid it. Your attitude was altogether too Christian. You *wanted* to help, which is an encroachment upon the will of others. Your attitude ought to be that of one who offers an opportunity that can be taken or rejected. Otherwise you are most likely to get into trouble. It is so because man is not fundamentally good, almost half of him is a devil.

. . .

Sincerely yours, c. g. j u n g

To Count Hermann Keyserling

Dear Count, 13 August 1931

First I must ask you to forgive me for not reacting earlier to your interesting MS.[1] It is rich and significant in content. You are inaugurating a new and contemporary style of "sentimental journey," though it is considerably bloodier than its predecessors. South America has also brought you face to face, plainly and honestly, with the dark underworld, the chthonic unconscious. It is a classic case of the collective unconscious being constellated by the activation of the inferior function, which because of its contamination with the contents of the collective unconscious always drags this up with it. Simultaneously the anima emerges in exemplary fashion from the primeval slime, laden with all the pulpy and monstrous appendages of the deep. And outside, conjured up by her appearance inside, X. is forced into your magic circle—a meaningful adventure whose continuation arouses my curiosity! That was an encounter with the daemonism of the earth and it has never yet been described better.

I wish you all luck with the continuation, but would advise you to cut down on "cultural speculation" as much as possible, otherwise you will blur what is most impressive about your work—the personal experience with its exemplary subjectivity.

I hope you are all right in health. With best regards,

Yours sincerely, c. g. j u n g

☐ (Handwritten.)
[1] Part of *South-American Meditations.*

84

To Count Hermann Keyserling

Dear Count,   30 August 1931

Best thanks for your MS. I have read it with great interest and find your description of earthbound dying perfectly correct, as well as of primitivity. Will you write a chapter on South American "spirituality?" I am sure you will find striking proofs of the primitiveness of the South American mentality.

At all events you have stressed the importance of personal experience in your chapter on death. This seems to me rather to contradict what you said in your letter about wanting to leave out the personal aspect. The totality of life and experience can be attained only by including the personal, otherwise we succumb to the modern European disease of the merely imaginary life, the "provisional life"[1] as I usually call it.

Unfortunately I shall be away from Zurich until the end of September, as I still have some work to do which allows of no disturbances.

I am glad to hear that your health is better. No doubt giving concrete shape to the turmoil in your unconscious has done much to calm your nervous system and will do so still more in the future if not counteracted too much by adverse circumstances. With best wishes and greetings,

Yours sincerely, C. G. JUNG

□ (Handwritten.)
[1] Cf. "The Practical Use of Dream Analysis," CW 16, par. 336.

To Count Hermann Keyserling

Dear Count,   24 December 1931

Your dream[1] eludes my understanding as I don't know what conscious situation it is compensating. Academically speaking, "bath" always signifies "change," "rebirth," "renewal." "Sea" = the collective unconscious. X. is undoubtedly the anima, representing the coll. unc.

□ (Handwritten.)
[1] In the dream K. finds himself at a seaside resort and meets X., the "femme inspiratrice" (cf. Keyserling, 20 Dec. 29, n. 1). She is detached but tender and anxious to help him with the translation of his latest book, *South-American Meditations*. There are several swimming pools which are alternately filled with sea water in flood, but he is trying despite obstacles to reach the open sea.

In the psychological sense your South America book corresponds to a "night sea journey,"[2] i.e., another rebirth ritual. Could this dream be connected with the fact that you have as good as finished the book? As a rule a book or work of art amounts to an external ritual action, which does not by itself produce a change in the subject since it merely deputizes for him. Often the (ritual) work can grip the author retroactively and afterwards bring about a psychic change in him if he has not gone through the initial experience or has not done so sufficiently. This is a fateful question I cannot decide. But if it should be your destiny to go through further changes in order to arrive at an illumination and detachment of consciousness you have not yet attained, then this dream would be a message and a warning that you are again confronted with the collective unconscious and the anima just as you were in South America.

I have regretted very much not having seen you in the summer. Unfortunately you were within reachable distance just at the time when I had shut myself away from the world for a month. These retreats are so important to me that nothing can interrupt them. Please forgive me. I am at home in January, from the 15th on. If you came on the 20th I would be most happy to see you again.

I need hardly say how much I am looking forward to your "Divina Commedia." I hope you have been sent my new book.[3] It is only a collection of essays. With best wishes for the New Year,

Yours sincerely, C. G. JUNG

[2] The "night sea journey," a term coined by the German ethnologist Leo Frobenius (1873–1938) in his book *Das Zeitalter des Sonnengottes* (1904), describes a type of myth in which the hero, after being swallowed by a sea monster, travels in its belly from West to East (the "night sea journey" of the sun), cuts his way out of its belly on landing, and slips out, together with all the other people the monster has devoured. Jung takes this worldwide myth as an illustration of psychological rebirth. Cf. *Symbols of Transformation*, pars. 307ff. and 538, n. 85.
[3] *Seelenprobleme der Gegenwart.*

Anonymous

. . .   8 January 1932

I have attacks of feeling horribly inferior. I have to digest a whole span of life full of mistakes and stupidity. Anyway feelings of in-

□ This letter was sent in as printed, without beginning or end.

feriority are the counterpart of power. Wanting to be better or more intelligent than one is, is power too. It is difficult enough to be what one is and yet endure oneself and for once forgive one's own sins with Christian charity. That is damnably difficult.

. . .

To A. Vetter

Dear Dr. Vetter,   25 January 1932

You rightly say that it is as if my work "reached out beyond philosophy and theology." You could also say it begins "behind" both of them. But it is not due to any intention or activity of mine that the spiritual and historical analogy with the East gets into my way of looking at things. The intrusion of the East is rather a psychological fact with a long history behind it. The first signs may be found in Meister Eckhart, Leibniz, Kant, Hegel, Schopenhauer, and E. von Hartmann. It is not, however, the actual East we are dealing with but the collective unconscious, which is omnipresent. You have seen very rightly that I have landed in the Eastern sphere, so to speak, through the water of this unconscious; for the truths of the unconscious can never be thought up, they can be reached only by following a path which all previous cultures right down to the most primitive level have called the way of initiation.

It is much to be regretted that talk is not possible. That's what would really be needed. With best regards,

Yours sincerely, c. g. j u n g

☐ Berlin.

To M. Fuss

Dear Professor Fuss,   20 February 1932

So far as we know, psychological events, whether conscious or unconscious, are bound up with the organic nervous system. It is simply impossible to imagine any experimental set-up which could prove that the psyche exists independently of living matter. This is not to say that it *could* not exist without matter, since we also take it for

☐ Sibiu (Hermannstadt), Romania.

granted that matter exists without psyche, doubtful as this appears in the light of the latest findings of quantum physics.[1] The only answer to this question is *non liquet*, if asked in absolute terms. But within our human experience the psyche cannot be found at all except in connection with living matter.

Yours truly, C. G. JUNG

[1] Cf. "On the Nature of the Psyche," CW 8, pars. 438f. & n. 130.

To Max Rychner

Dear Dr. Rychner,   28 February 1932

Here are my answers to your questions about Goethe:

1. My mother drew my attention to *Faust* when I was about 15 years old.

2. Goethe was important to me because of *Faust*.

3. As a "poet," perhaps Hölderlin.

4. In my circle *Faust* is an object of lively interest. I once knew a wholesaler who always carried a pocket edition of *Faust* around with him.

5. Young people today try to be unhistorical. Goethe does not seem to mean much to them because, for them, he is too close to the fishy ideals of the 19th century.

6. Everything to do with the masses is hateful to me. Anything popularized becomes common. Above all I would not disseminate Goethe, rather cook books.

7. Apart from a few poems, the only thing of Goethe's that is alive for me is *Faust*. For me this was always a study—for relaxation I prefer English novels. Everything else of Goethe's pales beside *Faust*, although something immortal glitters in the poems too.

What one could "enjoy" of Goethe is, for me, too patriarchal, too

☐ (1897–1965), Swiss author; cf. his article on Jung in *Arachne, Aufsätze zur Literatur* (1957). As editor of the *Kölnische Zeitung*, he sent Jung and other notabilities a questionnaire on their attitude to Goethe (1932 was the centenary of Goethe's death). The questions were: 1. Who first drew your attention to Goethe? 2. By which of his works were you influenced? 3. Has any other poet meant more to you? 4. Are people in your professional and social circle interested in Goethe? 5. Have you drawn the attention of young people to Goethe and with what result? 6. Which work of Goethe's would you disseminate among the masses? 7. Which work would you take with you on a long holiday? Jung's replies were published in the *Kölnische Zeitung*, 22 Mar. 1932.

much *de l'époque*. What I value in Goethe I cannot "enjoy"; it is too big, too exciting, too profound. *Faust* is the most recent pillar in that bridge of the spirit which spans the morass of world history, beginning with the Gilgamesh epic,[1] the *I Ching*,[2] the Upanishads, the *Tao-te-Ching*, the fragments of Heraclitus, and continuing in the Gospel of St. John, the letters of St. Paul, in Meister Eckhart and in Dante. It seems to me that one cannot meditate enough about *Faust*, for many of the mysteries of the second part are still unfathomed. *Faust* is out of this world and therefore it transports you; it is as much the future as the past and therefore the most living present. Hence everything that to me is essential in Goethe is contained in *Faust*.

Yours sincerely, C. G. JUNG

[1] Gilgamesh is the hero of the ancient Akkadian epic of Gilgamesh, dating from the turn of the 2nd millennium B.C. It relates Gilgamesh's quest for the secret of immortality, which ends in failure but leads to quiet resignation. For a résumé see *Analytical Psychology: Its Theory and Practice*, pp. 117ff.

[2] *The I Ching or Book of Changes*, rendered into English by Cary F. Baynes from Richard Wilhelm's German translation of the Chinese text (Bollingen Series, 3rd edn., 1968). Originally considered a book of oracles (as which it is still used today in China and Japan), it was reputedly edited by Confucius and regarded as a book of wisdom, exerting great influence on Confucianism and Taoism. Cf. Jung's foreword to the English translation, which he fostered; the foreword is also published in CW 11.

To M. Vetter

Dear Frau Vetter,   12 March 1932

So far as I can gather from your letter, an essentially intellectual thinking that takes pride in having no relation with the heart appears inconceivable to you. I can understand that very well. This kind of thinking never comes from the whole personality and is therefore bloodless and lifeless. Nor can it ever produce anything that could be described as truth, whereas the thinking that comes from the whole man cannot be anything but a truth. But this thinking is a great rarity nowadays, because our time suffers like none other before it from a deplorably one-sided differentiation about which I have written a thick and—let me tell you in confidence—difficult book, beware![1] I

□ Ammersee, Bavaria.
[1] *Psychological Types*.

think, though, that you would understand one or two chapters. With best regards,

Yours sincerely, c. g. j u n g

To H. Dänzer-Vanotti

Dear Frau Dr. Dänzer-Vanotti,   6 April 1932

My work is not connected in any way with university institutes. Consequently we have no polyclinical material at our disposal. Also, you cannot possibly learn analytical psychology by studying its object, since it consists exclusively of what you don't know about yourself. You can see in another person only what you yourself know. But what you yourself already know you don't need to learn. Also it is quite impossible for two of you to conduct a real analysis of a third person. In that way you would never get at the other person at all. When I suggested that you work on your own material, I did so not because I was of the opinion that this is a treatment but because it is the *sine qua non* for learning analysis. You yourself must be able to fulfil everything you expect of your patient. If you expect him to hand out his intimate experiences, you must first of all be in a position to do it at least three times better. No analysis of another person will ever provide this unique experience which the analysis of your own material can give you. Only in this way do you learn to recognize the living psychic process which is not identical with consciousness. No one who has not experienced analysis in his own person has a right to practice it. This is my firm conviction and I shan't budge from it under any circumstances. If you agree with this, then we can consider further possibilities.

Yours sincerely, c. g. j u n g

□ Karlsruhe.

To A. Vetter

Dear Dr. Vetter,   8 April 1932

The chief difficulty seems to be the concept of transcendence. For me this concept is only epistemological, but for you, if I understand you correctly, it is something almost theological. Cf. the Christian concept of the Trinity, resulting from the efforts of the old theologians to push God out of the sphere of psychic experience into the Absolute. We all know that this was done for the (necessary) purpose of bolstering up the authority of the Church against continual erosion by Gnosis and heresy. Thus man was most effectively separated from God and the intercession of *Ecclesia Mater* became unavoidable. It is in fact the great achievement of Protestantism that this transcendence, in practice at least, came a cropper. Actually it is not correct to say that there is no mother goddess in the Christian Trinity. The mother is simply veiled by the Holy Ghost (Sophia), which is the connecting link between Father and Son. It is the breath that moves to and fro between them, according to the Catholic view. This veiling of the mother (for the reasons mentioned above) had the result that the mother then appeared in an all the more concrete and authoritarian form as *Ecclesia.*

You are perfectly right when you say that an orthodox theologian could never equate God and the unconscious. In my opinion he cannot do so because he imagines he can make assertions about God. I don't imagine I can, so that it doesn't matter to me in the slightest whether God and the unconscious are ultimately identical or not. The mother is, I maintain, only one aspect of the unconscious. There is also a father aspect, though I wouldn't attribute to these aspects more than a necessary illusionary character, due to the mental difficulty of conceiving anything that is not concrete and the incapacity of our language to express anything that is not a verbal image. In a certain sense I could say of the collective unconscious exactly what Kant said of the *Ding an sich*—that it is merely a negative borderline concept, which however cannot prevent us from framing . . .[1] or hypotheses about its possible nature as though it were an object of human experience. But we do not know whether the unconscious *an sich* is unlimited, whether it is experienceable in part or not at all. It could be absolute, i.e., inexperienceable. At all events it is absolutely necessary for us to give up the anthropomorphism of the Christian concept of transcendence if we do not want to commit flagrant transgressions. I grant you that I am on the best way to delivering up the Christian concept of the spirit to the chaos of Gnosis again, from which it was so carefully insulated. But in my view the spirit is alive only when it is an adventure eternally renewed. As soon as it is held fast it is nothing but a man-made expression of a particular cultural form. Of

---

[1] Lacuna in file carbon copy. Most likely a Greek word handwritten by Jung, a frequent procedure in his letters.

course the cultural form owes its very existence to the intervention of a true and living spirit, but once it is fixed it has long ceased to be. In my view the woolliness of our present-day thinking comes from our illegitimately granting it prerogatives which appear to endow thinking with faculties it doesn't really possess. Hence my function theory.

I hope we can meet again sometime and that we can then [continue] our discussion by word of mouth.[2]

. . .

[2] The end of the letter is missing.

To Gustav Schmaltz

My dear Schmaltz, 9 April 1932

. . .

Your dream[1] is extremely remarkable. Taken in conjunction with other, similar dreams it always seems to me quite extraordinary with what precision the unconscious anticipates events and you really have to ask yourself what degree of consciousness should be attributed to anticipations of this nature. Sometimes one cannot avoid the impression that a superior agency is at work. Our immanent causality then seems to me like a tissue of deception, a reckoning we make without our host. With best regards to your wife and yourself,

Yours sincerely, c. g. jung

□ M.D. (hon.), Dr. Ing., (1884–1959), German analytical psychologist. Cf. his *Oestliche Weisheit und westliche Psychotherapie* (2nd edn., 1953); *Komplexe Psychologie und körperliches Symptom* (1955). Jung's foreword to the latter is in CW 18.
[1] The dream has not been preserved.

To Count Hermann Keyserling

Dear Count, 10 May 1932

Just now I am wading through the South American "steam of creation," and not a little of its *grouiller et pulluler* comes to light in your *Meditations*. But I am not yet through by a long way, because I am unpleasantly pedantic when I read. Your *Meditations* face me with yet another task.

Now as for your dream,[1] I must begin by saying that a recurrent dream is of special importance for the integration of the psyche, and secondly that it must refer to something that has been in existence for a long time and is particularly characteristic of the mental attitude of the individual. Quite apart from the possible personal significance of the father, which I naturally don't know about, the father imago also has a quite general significance as Logos or spirit with specifically parental characteristics. As you know, the Logos as such is not necessarily paternal; it can also be filial. In the latter case the paternal quality is missing. The filial Logos is the begotten Logos, while the paternal Logos is the Begetter, protective and solicitous. The filial Logos generally has the character of an heroically uncompromising confession of faith, challenging anyone who receives it to make equally independent decisions. The Father Begetter, on the contrary, introduces, guides, accompanies, teaches. He does not explode like a bomb or a firework, but takes the ignorant or unwilling by the hand and leads them by a safe path through the inhospitable darkness. It is an outstanding characteristic of your spirit that it totally lacks the paternal quality and unexpectedly bursts on the public like a sudden, lowering storm or a dazzling mirage. The paternal quality feels responsible for understanding, smoothes the way towards it, and seeks to avert the ill consequences of misunderstanding. Hence it always makes use of a differentiated feeling function, whose greatest virtue is human empathy. This side of your Logos is unquestionably atrophied, that is, too callow, too thin, and too irresponsible. At your age, however, recognition of the paternal quality is imperative. Hence your dream. With best regards,

Yours sincerely, C. G. JUNG

[1] The dream repeats with slight variations the dream about the father reported in Keyserling, 25 Aug. 28, n. 1.

To Gerhard Adler

Dear Dr. Adler,   7 June 1932

Best thanks for kindly sending me the interesting drawing.[1] The symbolism is clear enough, only it has a quite different value for the

☐ Ph.D., analytical psychologist, in Berlin until 1936, now practising in London; co-editor of the Collected Works of Jung. Cf. his *Entdeckung der Seele* (1934);

young boy from what it would have for an adult. For an adult it would mean the individuation he is seeking, for the boy it means what he should leave behind him—a burdensome prenatal memory, a still existing link with the collective psyche. It is these vestiges that prevent the inferior function from being born, that impede its separation from the contamination of the unconscious. Because it is tied to the timeless, the inferior function never wants to affirm the world of the moment, the world of time, since it would rather cling on to timelessness. The separation is a real and conscious sacrifice of that very dangerous tie to the past. That is your problem. With best regards,

Yours sincerely, C. G. JUNG

Studies in Analytical Psychology (2nd edn., 1966); *The Living Symbol* (1962). Jung's forewords to the first two books are in CW 18.
[1] Reproduced in Adler, *Studies in Analytical Psychology*, Pl. 12: "The Fight with the Dragons," and in Jung, "The Philosophical Tree," CW 13, Fig. 9.

Anonymous

Dear Frau N.,   20 June 1932

Sincerest thanks for kindly sending me the mandala.

Please forgive me if I don't go into your questions, lack of time unfortunately makes it quite impossible for me to write long letters. I would only remark that our proper life-task must necessarily appear impossible to us, for only then can we be certain that all our latent powers will be brought into play. Perhaps this is an optical illusion born of inner compulsion, but at any rate that is how it feels. With best regards,

Yours sincerely, C. G. JUNG

☐ Germany.

Anonymous

Dear Frau N.,   23 June 1932

Unfortunately I am so very busy at the moment that I can see you only today week, Thursday, June 30th, at 11 in the morning.

☐ Switzerland.

94

The rumour that I do not recommend analytical treatment for elderly people is quite erroneous. My eldest patient—a lady—has reached the stately age of 75. The psyche can be treated so long as a person has a psyche. The only people you can't treat are those who are born without one. And of these there are not a few.

Hoping the appointed time will suit you also, I remain, dear lady,

Yours sincerely, c. g. jung

To O. Curtius

Dear Colleague,   27 June 1932

Best thanks for kindly sending me the beautiful drawings.

I see from your address that you are taking a holiday on your island. Unfortunately I haven't got to that point yet. A mass of work has still to be coped with before then.

I wouldn't like to miss this opportunity of telling you how much pleasure our work together has given me, though it was only a beginning to be continued in real life. What is glimpsed in analysis actually has to be rediscovered there, for on entering into life it apparently gets lost. And indeed it must get lost, otherwise the symbol is taken as a model for living. With best wishes,

Yours sincerely, c. g. jung

□ (1886–1956), M.D., German psychotherapist, Schliersee (Bavaria), Germany.

Anonymous

[ORIGINAL IN ENGLISH]

Dear Mr. N.,   5 July 1932

You will realize the extraordinary difficulty of telling anything about dreams of people one doesn't know. Your dream[1] has interested me indeed. The second part of it, the secretary-bird and the snake, has been correctly interpreted, in spite of the fact that the snake is not exactly Kundalini[2] because the Kundalini serpent actually dissolves into

□ Eastern U.S.A.
[1] A secretary-bird (*Serpentarius secretarius*) swallows a snake.
[2] Concerning the Kundalini serpent cf. Avalon, *The Serpent Power*; also Jung, "The Realities of Practical Psychotherapy," CW 16 (1966 edn.), pars. 558ff., and "The Psychology of the Transference," ibid., par. 380.

light. But sure enough the two animals represent a pair of opposites, which represent spirit and matter, or the spiritual and chthonic principle. Yet the fact that they are represented by two animals means, according to the rules of dream interpretation, that this peculiar conflict does not take place in a human consciousness, but outside it in the collective unconscious. Since olden times the bird and the snake are the symbols which typify this conflict. It is a peculiarity of our Western mind that we can think such a conflict consciously without having it. This is rather a peculiar fact which, I find, is most difficult to explain to the said Westerner. It's rather a curse to be able to think a thing and to imagine one possesses it while one is miles away from it in reality.

So this dream has a peculiar introduction which you omitted completely in attempting an interpretation. You behave exactly as if you were possessing the two opposites, like any good Westerner. What happened in reality was the following thing: you did try some Yoga stunt,[3] and then the dream said, "Look out, that lovely young lady is threatened by the presence of the gila monster,[4] pregnant with sensuality!" You see, in spite of being a man in advanced age,[5] you still have a young soul, a lovely anima, and she is confronted with the dangerous lizard. In other words, your soul is threatened by chthonic poison. Now this is exactly the situation of our Western mind. We think we can deal with such problems in an almost rationalistic way, by conscious attempts and efforts, imitating Yoga methods and such dangerous stuff, but we forget entirely that first of all we should establish a connection between the higher and the lower regions of our psyche. Such a connection exists in Eastern man, while we are cut off from our earth through more than a thousand years of Christian training. Thus the Western man has to develop that connection with his unconscious first, and then only he will understand really what the Eastern methods aim at. If he can't establish the connection, then the conflict between bird and snake remains a sort of vicious circle that turns round and round in his mind and never even touches our reality, it remains a mere fantastical pastime which as a rule creates an unwholesome inflation.

---

[3] The (unanalysed) dreamer wrote of some Yoga exercises "for the unfoldment of the Golden Flower" which he had tried a few hours before the dream.

[4] *Heloderma suspectum.* "With its relative *H. horridum* of Mexico, the only lizards known to be poisonous . . . inhabits deserts in the southwestern United States" (*Enc. Brit.*). In the dream it endangered "a lovely young lady."

[5] The dreamer reported he was 64, "virile and in good health."

Now watch what the bird is doing: he plunges his head backward, out of your sight, which is a very unusual thing for the secretary-bird to do. Now that is a hint of what one really ought to do: if you look down in front of you, you are in the sphere of your consciousness, but if you look backward, you look into the region of your unconscious which is always there where we haven't got the eyes of our consciousness. So the bird tells you, you ought to look behind your back and then you would discover the means by which you can attain your end. Your aim is to kill the lizard that threatens the anima. You are the secretary-bird that should protect the anima. You can't protect your anima by Yoga exercises which only procure a conscious thrill, but you can protect her by catching the unconscious contents that well up from the depths of yourself. Try to see what your fantasies are, no matter how disreputable they seem to be; that is your blackness, your shadow that ought to be swallowed. The serpent is the bird, and the bird is the serpent.

You know, Eastern Yoga is based upon man as he really is, but we have a conscious imagination about ourselves and think this is our Self, which is an appalling mistake. We are also our unconscious side, and that is why the bird swallows the black snake, namely to show what you ought to do in order to be complete. Not perfection, but completeness is what is expected of you.

Yours sincerely, C. G. JUNG

To Pastor Damour

Dear Pastor Damour,   15 August 1932

Best thanks for kindly sending me your article.[1] It is a pity that it was turned down by the editor of the N.Z.Z. The tutelage of the public by the intellectual censorship of prejudiced editors always gets my goat.

Your article is really very sensible and much better than X.'s feckless balancing act. You can't tear people into two parts and assign one of them to the doctors and the other to the theologians.

Today theologians are up against the same thing doctors are faced

□ Resident of Canton Thurgau.
[1] The *Neue Zürcher Zeitung* published two articles (20 July and 4 Aug. 32) on "Medizinalgesetz und Seelsorge." D. wrote an article in reply which was not accepted.

with. Just as the doctor has to go on relearning endlessly in order to understand the psychic problem of a neurotic, the theologian will have to make sacrifices if he is to wrestle with this most difficult of all problems with any prospect of success.

Incidentally, the *Neue Zürcher Zeitung* has never asked me to write a concluding article. I don't use the press if I can help it.

Barth's[2] objection to the psychologizing of religious experiences, which I see you also have defended, is a totally unjustified prejudice. Does Barth or anyone else know what the unconscious is, or does Barth want to prove to us perhaps that religious experience, as we know it, comes from some other source than the psyche? The theological authorities I appeal to in this connection are Tertullian and Meister Eckhart, not to mention my own experience, which has given me more insight into the nature of the human psyche than the editorial pulpit of Herr Barth. This is precisely why the theologians, on their own admission, don't know how to cope with the psyche of the sick. The human psyche and the psychic background are boundlessly underestimated, as though God spoke to man exclusively through the radio, the newspapers, or through sermons. God has never spoken to man except in and through the psyche, and the psyche understands it and we experience it as something psychic. Anyone who calls that psychologism is denying the eye that beholds the sun.

I have taken the liberty of keeping your article in case I should have to write something on this subject. In that event I would quote you, with your permission. Again with best thanks,

Yours sincerely, C. G. JUNG

[2] Prof. Hans Barth, literary editor of the N.Z.Z. (later professor of philosophy at the U. of Zurich), published a review of Jung's *Die Beziehungen der Psychotherapie zur Seelsorge* (orig. 1932; "Psychotherapists or the Clergy," CW 11), on 3 Aug. in which he criticized Jung for "psychologizing religion."

To James Joyce

[ORIGINAL IN ENGLISH]

Dear Sir,   27 September 1932

Your *Ulysses* has presented the world with such an upsetting psychological problem that repeatedly I have been called in as a supposed authority on psychological matters.

☐ Joyce (1882–1941) was then living in Zurich. — This letter is published in Richard Ellmann, *James Joyce* (1959), p. 642, and also in his *Letters of James*

Ulysses proved to be an exceedingly hard nut and it has forced my mind not only to most unusual efforts, but also to rather extravagant peregrinations (speaking from the standpoint of a scientist!). Your book as a whole has given me no end of trouble and I was brooding over it for about three years until I succeeded in putting myself into it. But I must tell you that I'm profoundly grateful to yourself as well as to your gigantic opus because I learned a great deal from it. I shall probably never be quite sure whether I did enjoy it, because it meant too much grinding of nerves and of grey matter. I also don't know whether you will enjoy what I have written about *Ulysses*[1] because I couldn't help telling the world how much I was bored, how I grumbled, how I cursed and how I admired. The 40 pages of non-stop run in the end is a string of veritable psychological peaches. I suppose the devil's grandmother knows so much about the real psychology of a woman, I didn't.

Well, I just try to recommend my little essay to you, as an amusing attempt of a perfect stranger who went astray in the labyrinth of your *Ulysses* and happened to get out of it again by sheer good luck. At all events you may gather from my article what *Ulysses* has done to a supposedly balanced psychologist.

With the expression of my deepest appreciation, I remain, dear Sir,

Yours faithfully, C. G. JUNG

Joyce, III (1966), pp. 253, 262. — For Joyce's encounter with Jung cf. Patricia Hutchins, *James Joyce's World* (1957), pp. 181ff. Cf. letter to Greacen (P. Hutchins), 29 June 55, part of which is published in her book.
[1] Jung's essay on *Ulysses* was originally published in *Europäische Revue*, VIII:2/9 (Sept. 1932); now in CW 15, where this letter is also published.

To L. M. Boyers

[ORIGINAL IN ENGLISH]

Dear Dr. Boyers,   30 September 1932

I have written nothing about Geley's[1] point of view, which by the way is a very interesting and important one, provided that the material it is based on is absolutely reliable. If the parapsychological [data] are what they now seem to be, then science will have to

□ Berkeley, California.
[1] G. Geley, *From the Unconscious to the Conscious* (1920; tr. from the French).

discuss Geley's point of view very seriously. I am however not in a position to judge the physiological side of this theory because I am merely concerned with the psychological aspect of the things below the threshold of consciousness. Concerning the psychological aspect I must say that Geley is not a psychologist and has no experience whatever of the psychology of the unconscious. He knows a good deal about the physiological aspect, which we are unable yet to link up with our psychological observations. Geley's book has taught me nothing with reference to my particular sphere of interest, since it is not concerned with it at all.

I'm personally convinced of the existence of connections between our psychological observations and the parapsychological phenomena, but the connection is just as evasive as for instance the management of a Bank and the dreams of a philosopher, or better still: childbirth and mythological images. I know however that certain archetypal figures of the unconscious literally appear as ghostly controls with materialization mediums. I can't deny the possibility that certain figures that might appear in our dreams could materialize just as well as ghosts, though I'm in no way capable of proving such a possibility. From my experience with unconscious phenomena I must even admit that what we call thoughts or emotions could be in a way independent psychic agencies of which we perceive only the psychological aspect, but not their potentially physical nature. Analytical psychology is full of unsolved riddles and is teeming with mysteries. I'm therefore following up very closely the facts of parapsychology, because it is quite conceivable that these phenomena will throw a new light on the psychology of the unconscious, perhaps in the near future already.

Sincerely yours, C. G. JUNG

To Dr. Brupbacher

Dear Colleague,   30 September 1932

Although I am absolutely opposed to war and make no bones about it in my words and writings, I am simply not in a position to burden myself with actual propaganda work. As I have said I do what I can here and there in publications, but it is quite impossible for me to spare any time for meetings and suchlike. Unfortunately

☐ Zurich.

100

I have only one life instead of a dozen and am therefore far from being able to fulfil all the expectations I am asked to meet. With lively regrets,

Yours sincerely, C. G. JUNG

To Antonio Mirabal

[ORIGINAL IN ENGLISH]

My dear friend Mountain Lake,   21 October 1932

It was very nice of you indeed that you wrote a letter to me. I thought you had quite forgotten me. It is very good that this woman Schevill[1] from California has come to see you and to remember you of myself. It is good that she could give you my address. I often thought of you in the meantime and I even talked of you often to my pupils. And whenever I had the opportunity to talk to Americans, I tried to give them the right idea about your people and how important it would be for them to give you all the rights of the American Citizen. I believe that things are getting better in the future.

I'm glad to hear that your crops were good. I wish you would write to me once, what your religious customs are in order to secure a good harvest. Have you got corn-dances, or other ways by which you make the wheat and the corn grow? Are your young men still worshipping the Father Sun? Are you also making occasionally sand-paintings[2] like the Navajos? Any information you can give me about your religious life is always welcome to me. I shall keep all that information to myself, but it is most helpful to me, as I am busy exploring the truth in which Indians believe. It always impressed me as a great truth, but one hears so little about it, and particularly over here, where there are no Indians. Times are very hard indeed and un-

---

□ Antonio Mirabal = Ochwiay Biano (Mountain Lake), chief of the Taos Pueblo, whose acquaintance Jung made during his travels in Arizona and New Mexico, 1924–25. Cf. *Memories*, pp. 247ff./232ff.

[1] Cf. Schevill, 1 Sept. 42.

[2] Sand-paintings are traditional symbolic designs made on the ground with coloured sands and used for various ceremonial purposes, mainly by North American Indian tribes of the Southwest. Several examples are reproduced in Schevill, *Beautiful on the Earth* (1945). Cf. J. King, M. Oakes, J. Campbell, *Where the Two Came to Their Father* (with a portfolio of Navaho pollen-paintings; 2nd edn., 1969) and G. A. Reichard, *Navaho Religion* (1950). Cf. also "Concerning Mandala Symbolism," figs. 45 and 46, and *Psychology and Alchemy*, fig. 110.

fortunately I can't travel as far as I used to do. All you tell me about religion is good news to me. There are no interesting religious things over here, only remnants of old things. I will send you something which is still alive in this country of the old beliefs.

I was glad to hear that you are in better health than when I saw you. I'm sure your tribe needs you very much, and I wish that you will live still many happy years.

If you ever see Mrs. Schevill again, please give her my best greetings.

As ever your friend, C. G. JUNG

To Werner Kaegi

Dear Herr Kaegi, 7 November 1932

Thank you very much for kindly sending me your offprint.[1] I am glad you have drawn my attention to Walser.[2]

As you are obviously well acquainted with Walser's writings, I would like to ask you whether Walser has also taken an interest in the *Ipnerotomachia* of Francesco Colonna. I find that it gives us a key to the backdoors of the Renaissance. It is strange that the broad, shining surface of things always interests me much less than those dark, labyrinthine, subterranean passages they come out of. Civilizations seem to me like those plants whose real and continuous life is found in the rhizome and not in the quickly fading flowers and withering leaves which appear on the surface and which we regard as the essential manifestation of life. Burckhardt mentions Colonna's work[3] but for understandable reasons he sees nothing in it.

Of the more recent writers, it seems to be chiefly Luigi Valli[4] who has ventured into the background. I almost believe that the real history of the human mind is a rhizome phenomenon. With best thanks,

Yours sincerely, C. G. JUNG

☐ Ph.D., later professor of history at Basel U.

[1] "Prof. Dr. Ernst Walser," *Basler Jahrbuch* 1930.

[2] Professor of Italian language and literature at Basel, 1878–1929.

[3] Jacob Burckhardt, *The Civilization of the Renaissance in Italy* (tr., 1944), p. 113.

[4] Valli, *Il Linguaggio segreto de Dante e dei 'Fedeli d'amore'* (1928/30). (German translation in *Europäische Revue*, VI, 1930.)

To J. Wilhelm Hauer

Dear Professor Hauer, 14 November 1932

. . .

I want to tell you of certain negotiations I am at present engaged in. That is, I would like to extend our collaboration in a special way. For this purpose a publisher[1] has made me an interesting proposal. He wants to bring out a magazine aiming at a synthesis of the various branches of science. He considers my psychological viewpoint particularly suited to achieve this. His plan is to invite a number of specialists from the various branches of science to participate. I think of this collaboration somewhat as follows: certain questions would be put to specialists by an editorial committee. Each of them would answer the question in an essay based on the factual material available to him. The relevant psychological material would be supplied by me and my school, thus effecting a synthesis which would make it possible to understand the living meaning of facts and ideas gathered from all times and places. I hope very much that if the invitation is extended to you, you will not refuse us your cooperation. I would like to ask you not to make use of this information for the time being, though I would be very much obliged if you could let me know whether you are willing to support our undertaking.

With regard to the "associative displacement of symbols"[2] I must say that this belongs to the very essence of symbol formation. Usually the fact to be expressed by the symbol is something that cannot be expressed directly anyway and can therefore be formulated only approximately. As a result, its surmised content attracts everything, however unsuitable, into its orbit and gives it a definite colouring. Thus it comes about that the Holy Ghost can endow even the static mast with a propulsive function. With cordial greetings, also to your wife,

Yours sincerely, C. G. JUNG

☐ (1881–1962), German Indologist (U. of Tübingen) and theologian. Founder of the "German Faith Movement." Cf. Jung, "Wotan," CW 10, pars. 397f. & n. 16.
[1] Daniel Brody, proprietor of Rhein Verlag, Zurich, publisher of the *Eranos Jahrbücher*. Cf. Brody, 18 Mar. 58.
[2] Cf. *Symbols of Transformation*, par. 659.

To Alfred Kubin

Dear Herr Kubin,   19 November 1932

Thank you very much for your kind letter, which I appreciate all the more as it occurred to me afterwards that you might have misunderstood my remark about your book *Die andere Seite*.¹ With reference to *Ulysses*, the epithet "peasant-like"² is really a compliment. In a way I value your book much more because it gives an exact and faithful description of the things you have seen. I have mentioned your book several times in my writings³ as a classic example of the direct perception of unconscious processes. Our late mutual friend Schmitz had also learnt to descend into those depths and in his Hannickel fairytale⁴ he struck chords that are reminiscent of Kubin.

I am also glad that you wrote to me because our paths have already crossed in Schmitz's book of fairytales.⁵

In spite of all the confusions that may beset you, you can take comfort in the fact that in your book as well as in your art you have anticipated truths which are now affecting the whole world. You were born out of your time and it was therefore more difficult for you than for others to orient yourself in an age which is still too unconscious to understand what lies behind the wall of the future. With friendliest greetings,

Yours sincerely, C. G. JUNG

□ (1877–1959), Austrian artist and author. Dreams and the unconscious play an important role in his artistic and literary work.

¹ *The Other Side* (orig. 1908; tr. 1967), an autobiographical novel illustrated by the author.

² Cf. Jung, "Ulysses," CW 15, par. 194, where he calls K.'s novel "a country-cousin of the metropolitan Ulysses." (Actually the German word is "ländlich" = rural, not "bäuerlich" = peasant-like.)

³ *Psychological Types*, par. 630, n. 9, and *Two Essays*, CW 7, par. 342.

⁴ Schmitz, "Wege nach Atlantis," *Märchen aus dem Unbewussten*, 1932.

⁵ Jung wrote a foreword to the book and K. illustrated it. The foreword is in CW 18.

Anonymous

Dear Herr N.,   19 November 1932

I am sorry that other business has prevented me from thanking you for your letter. You wish to hear my views. I have the following remarks to make:

Every person who possesses even a modicum of intelligence and the necessary educational urge will, after thorough reflection on his experiences during the analytical treatment of his neurosis, hit upon trains of thought which agree in a remarkable way with the religious ideas of all times and peoples. The neurosis brings the unconscious nearer to the surface, and since the unconscious consists partly of instinct and partly of these primordial ideas of humanity, it is not at all surprising that after year-long reflection you too should have stumbled on these universal ideas. The danger of having this kind of consciousness is that you are drawn away from your own individual tasks in the real world and wafted into an inferior irreality where you only make demands and no longer want to achieve anything. It is all very fine when you discover what sort of parallels the unconscious-made-conscious has in the history of the human mind. But this discovery remains a useless fact as long as it has no effect on reality. It is even harmful because, as I have said, it alienates you from your own reality. This alienation from reality gives rise to what you call a sexual blockage. Actually it is a blockage of vital energy in general, not merely of sexuality, for a person who does not fulfil his life-task in any way is necessarily blocked. And then he will build a theory that everything morbid comes from this blockage, and this theory is correct. But it is not a theory that applies to the world as a whole, since this is mainly populated by people who love, suffer hunger, work, etc. It applies only to a person who, like a neurotic, goes on uselessly vegetating and spinning fantasies. His fantasy activity would have a meaning only if he were capable of transforming into action the insights gained from contact with the unconscious, this is, into something that seizes hold of people and changes them, and for this purpose ceaseless creative activity on human beings is needed. Pertinax[1] doesn't fulfil a single one of these tasks. He simply plays about with his neurosis and has no idea of how he ought to work on people because he has no idea of how he ought to work on

---

[1] Pseudonym of the addressee (residing in Switzerland), who wrote pamphlets on sex.

himself. He preaches his sexual tension theory and hasn't even brought himself to the point of at least getting married or taking up a profession or earning a cent. Any theory proclaimed by someone who belies himself like that is foredoomed from the start; it is just an illusion that only serves to extricate people from their tasks and duties in life.

I would ask you to stick this document at the back of your mirror and to contemplate it daily, and if anyone asks you what Dr. Jung thinks of your theory please show it to him.

Yours truly, C. G. JUNG

To Heinrich Zimmer

Dear Professor Zimmer,   21 November 1932

First of all, best thanks for your beautiful essay in *Corona*.[1] Also please give your wife my best thanks for her kindness in sending me *Andreas*.[2]

I must now tell you about a special project which got under way during my last visit in Vienna. A wealthy publisher has invited me to edit, or to be the nominal editor of, a magazine which might appear under the title of "Weltanschauung" or something like that. He has been discussing this subject with me for a long time and our discussions have led to the conclusion that we must first see who would be willing to collaborate on such a magazine.

Since I also mentioned your name, I am taking the liberty of writing to you about this matter. I have been thinking that in view of the tremendous fragmentation of the sciences today we might well have an organ that could fish out from the ocean of specialist science all the facts and knowledge that are of general interest and make them available to the educated public. Everyone who wants to find his way about nowadays has to rummage through dozens of periodicals he can't subscribe to, and thousands of books, wasting a vast amount of time until he comes to what he thinks might be

□ (1890–1943), German Indologist (U. of Heidelberg), later at Columbia U., New York. Cf. Jung, "Heinrich Zimmer," in *Erinnerungen, Träume, Gedanken*, pp. 385f. (The American/English edn. does not contain this tribute.) (See pl. v.)
[1] "Der indische Mythos," *Corona* (Zurich), III:1 (Oct. 1932).
[2] Hugo von Hofmannsthal's novel *Andreas* (orig., 1912–13; tr. in *Selected Prose*, Bollingen Series, 1952). Zimmer's wife was Hofmannsthal's daughter. See Zimmer, 14 Dec. 36.

helpful to him. We have therefore concluded that for every specialist field under consideration we should seek out one or two suitable spokesmen who would be willing to act as a centre for information and advice, or even become members of a many-headed editorial committee. In practice the duty of the person concerned would be to use this magazine as a forum for all data of general interest from his specialist field, or at least to indicate what authors might be approached by the editors for a suitable contribution. What I myself would like best would be a series of short papers dealing with eschatological ideas, doctrines of redemption, fundamental concepts of God, cosmogonic theories, initiation rites, and so on. Special weight would have to be laid on the communication of facts, considerably less weight on the originality of the contributions, since the magazine would be aimed not at any particular group of specialists but at the educated public in general. The fact that I am supposed to head such a project will show you in what sort of spirit it ought to be conducted. It should be an instrument of synopsis and synthesis—an antidote against the atomizing tendency of specialism which is one of the greatest obstacles to spiritual development.

I now want to ask you whether you would be willing to assist us and to take on the duty of serving as a centre for information and advice. It wouldn't be any particular burden on your time. I should be grateful for an affirmative answer.

Yours sincerely, c. g. j u n g

To Walter Mertens

Dear Walter, 24 November 1932

I am entirely in agreement with the spirit of your essay on Picasso. I am only against artists getting away with it like the theologians, about whom one may not say anything critical. I don't see why artists should not have exactly the same human psychology as everybody else. The claim to be the infallible mouthpiece of God is as odious to me in art as in theology. From the artistic standpoint I can well appreciate the achievements of modern art, but from the standpoint of the psychologist I have to say what the nature of these achievements is. In my article in the N.Z.Z.[1] I expressly pointed out that I

☐ Zurich.
[1] "Picasso," *Neue Zürcher Zeitung*, 13 Nov. 32; now in CW 15.

wasn't talking of art but of psychology. Yet psychology seems to be as hateful to artists as it is to theologians, and as I say I find this extremely repugnant.

Moreover, art fails entirely in its educative purpose if people don't see that it depicts the sickness of our time. That is why this art is neither enjoyable nor elevating, but as you rightly say a "scream." But a scream is always just that—a noise and not music. Hence I shall hold unswervingly to the view that modern art is much more correctly judged from the psychological rather than from the artistic standpoint. "Kunst" [art] comes from "Können" [ability, skill]; "stammering" is not skill but only a miserable attempt to speak. Naturally I don't want to discourage modern art; it must continue its attempts and I wish it luck. The creative spirit cannot be discouraged anyway, otherwise it would not be creative. So nothing untoward has happened.

With best greetings,

Yours, CARL

Anonymous

[ORIGINAL IN ENGLISH]

My dear Mrs. N.,   25 November 1932

I am glad you put your questions so plainly, it is much easier then to answer them.

It is under all conditions a most advisable thing to keep to the conscious and rational side, i.e., to maintain that side. One never should lose sight of it. It is the safeguard without which you would lose yourself on unknown seas. You would invite illness, indeed, if you should give up your conscious and rational orientation. On the other hand, it is equally true that life is not only rational. You are not fully adapted to life by a merely rational attitude. To a certain extent you have to keep your senses open to the nonrational aspects of existence. Among the latter is the unconscious. Such a nonrational factor has to be carefully observed.

If you observe the unconscious at all you are instantly drawn to it, and if you haven't sufficient foothold in your real conscious life the dragon of the unconscious will swallow you. You know what that means! Only if you maintain your consciousness with all its power of criticism can you begin to observe the unconscious.

The unconscious itself is neither tricky nor evil—it is Nature, both

☐ Berlin (though English-speaking).

beautiful and terrible. If the unconscious shows itself in a hostile and malignant form, it is due to your own attitude that indulges carelessly in its seductive imagery. If you have to deal with the unconscious at all, it must be done in an active way only. First of all nothing the unconscious produces ought to be taken for granted or literally. It must be subjected to a just criticism, because it is as a rule highly symbolic. You can dismiss a thing entirely, but you have to search for its symbolic meaning, and the symbolic meaning is the thing that has to be accepted. The best way of dealing with the unconscious is the creative way. Create for instance a fantasy. Work it out with all the means at your disposal. Work it out as if you were it or in it, as you would work out a real situation in life which you cannot escape. All the difficulties you overcome in such a fantasy are symbolic expressions of psychological difficulties in yourself, and inasmuch as you overcome them in your imagination you also overcome them in your psyche.

Now think of what I've written to you, and in case you should not understand something or other, ask Dr. X. Then try to understand what I say by all means, and if you don't, write again. Because you must learn to deal with such a dangerous attitude to the unconscious as you have.

You should not throw up your situation with your husband unless he insists upon it. It is always better to have the sparrow in your hand than to gaze at the pigeon on the roof. Life doesn't offer many opportunities. Therefore don't gamble away with them.

Sincerely yours, C. G. JUNG

Anonymous

[ORIGINAL IN ENGLISH]

Dear Mrs. N., 28 November 1932

. . .

There are great news happening here. Last week I got the "Literaturpreis der Stadt Zürich," which means that I'm no longer a prophet in my own country. A sad end to a hopeful young prophet's career. It is always sad when one loses a perfectly good reason for grumbling. I'm afraid I shall have to look elsewhere for good causes. I guess from your letter that you haven't lost yours yet.

I deeply wonder how you look at New York, or how New York looks at you.

□ U.S.A.

Please give my best regards to Mr. N. With warmest wishes I remain,

Yours devotedly, C. G. JUNG

To the Town Council of Küsnacht

Mr. President, Gentlemen! 3 December 1932

Allow me to express my most cordial thanks for your congratulations[1] and also for the beautiful flowers. I am quite particularly touched by your participation in the unexpected and unhoped-for honour that has been done to me, because, living as I do in quiet seclusion and constantly working, I have had little opportunity to play any kind of public role and to share in the social life of the community. But I am all the more thankful that a benevolent fate has made it possible for me to spend my life here in Küsnacht, where I can devote myself to my work undisturbed, surrounded by the beauties of nature.

Please accept once again, Mr. President and Gentlemen, the expression of my best thanks,

Yours sincerely, C. G. JUNG

[1] On the award of the Literature Prize of the City of Zurich.

To H. Knoll

Dear Colleague, 9 December 1932

Best thanks for kindly sending me your brochure. I can appreciate your work in Bellelay very highly because I myself have had sufficient experience of asylums. It is salutary and gratifying to see how an institution flourishes under expert and devoted management.

You shouldn't believe that the view prevails in my immediate circle that the schizophrenics looked after in institutions merit psychological attention. Whenever the talk turns on schizophrenia, it concerns those cases which the psychiatrist never sees because they crop up, if at all, among neurologists. There are plenty of them. When I started practising I was amazed to see how many cases there are of this kind, who never come near an asylum and whose psychotherapeutic treatment is not by any means always hopeless.

☐ Bellelay, in the Bernese Jura.

I would like to take this opportunity to ask you a question: do you have among your patients any who draw or paint? I would be most grateful if you could perhaps send me a few such drawings. Or do you have patients who would like to draw? In that case I would ask you to let them draw just as their fantasy dictates. I would be very pleased to have more comparative material of this kind.

Thank you for congratulating me on my award. To me it came as the greatest surprise. Interestingly enough, the choice fell on me not from above but from below—directly from the public. With best regards,

Yours sincerely, C. G. JUNG

Anonymous

Dear Frau N.,   10 December 1932

Best thanks for kindly sending me your book of visions.[1] I shall read it as soon as my time allows and then tell you something of my impressions.

Wanting to know the truth is also a striving for power and pleasure. Actually you shouldn't want to have visions, they should just come to you—*quod bonum felix faustum fortunatunque sit!*[2] My patients, for instance, have to seek visions as a punishment, and not in order to discover some kind of truth but rather to see their own errors. The secrets of the world's depths reveal themselves when *they* want and not when *we* want. I hope to find in your book something of the eternal images if it is the genuine article. Hang it, that affair of the madwoman—why did it have to happen to you? Excuse the interjectory character of my thought! Meanwhile with best regards and sincere thanks,

Yours sincerely, C. G. JUNG

☐ Vienna.
[1] Unidentifiable, but probably a private record of N.'s own visions.
[2] "May it be good, happy, favourable, and propitious."

To R. Pfähler

Dear Colleague,   12 December 1932

I was indeed very beleaguered when I lectured in Vienna.[1] Even so, we managed a handshake.

111

I have every sympathy with your impressions of Vienna. Of course as an outsider you get to see only the outside of things, but this outside is very important. The whole of psychiatry is also an outside and the views one hears on such an occasion have an hallucinatory air. But in reality, that is, in practice, there are neuroses one has to do something about and one can only do what one can. Faced with the patient, you see at once, if you are not totally blinded, that all theorizing is absurd. Everything depends on how you strike the patient as a human being. In the end the personality is the most powerful therapeutic agent. The effort to form views of one's own moulds the personality, and the personality expresses itself through the kind of insight that has been won, because one's views, insights, and convictions are ultimately only an expression of the personality still lying in the darkness of the unconscious. So it is very important to go through a whole lot of negative experiences, as you always learn more from them than from the positive. With friendly greetings,

Yours sincerely, C. G. JUNG

☐ Vienna.
1 "Die Stimme des Innern," lecture at the Kulturbund, Nov. 1932. Now "The Development of Personality," CW 17.

To E. Haesele

Dear Frau Dr. Haesele,   23 December 1932

. . .

With reference to your question I must tell you that once definite outbreaks of insanity have occurred there is always a permanent lowering of the threshold of consciousness which facilitates the repetition of these outbreaks. Consequently, the results of psychic treatment are always a bit hazy. But if the conscious personality is still in good shape and in addition a decent amount of intelligence and goodwill are present, then an attempt should be made to carry the treatment through. It is always better that something happens rather than nothing at all. Occasionally there are even cases that can be cured. However, I am not very optimistic because, as you rightly say, psychoses often reach deep into the organic realm where psychic influence becomes ineffectual.

Yours sincerely, C. G. JUNG

☐ Salzburg.

To Jolande Jacobi

Dear Frau Jacobi,   23 December 1932

. . .

This business of the magazine lies heavy on my stomach. I must fully concur with your views. Nothing would be more sterile than to squeeze the whole world into a psychological straitjacket. As you rightly say, the psychological viewpoint should only be a centre. I would therefore suggest "Weltanschauung" as the name of the magazine, under which title everything could be collected that is of general interest, including psychology.

The editorship is definitely the burning question. Heyer's[1] intuition and aggressive temperament would be welcomed by me. To give him an assistant editor would be technically impossible. It would have to be an editorial committee, though in my opinion the financing of it belongs to the realm of impossibilities. I can imagine, however, that the editor could submit doubtful contributions to a wider editorial staff for an opinion, and in case of necessity consult me. This editorial staff would be made up of a large number of specialists with sufficient general interests to recognize the value or otherwise of a contribution. Equally, this staff would be prepared to supply the relevant information.

I have already received affirmative answers from Prof. Hauer, Prof. Zimmer, Prof. Pauli[2] (for modern physics). For philosophy and the history of the medieval mind I have two younger people in view (I would always give preference to younger people). Kranefeldt[3] might be considered for psychotherapy. For Buddhist studies I would suggest Prof. Rousselle,[4] to whom I have not yet written. Ziegler[5] and Keyserling would be best for original contributions. Would Broch[6] be suitable for modern literature? I still lack suitable contributors for biology, astrophysics, geology, physiology, Egyptian, Assyrian-Babylonian and American archaeology, and for antiquity (mysteries!). A clever and perspicacious editor could probably come up with something.

[1] Cf. Heyer, 20 Apr. 34, n. □.
[2] Cf. Pauli, 29 Oct. 34, n. □.
[3] W. M. Kranefeldt, M.D., German psychotherapist. Cf. his *Secret Ways of the Mind* (orig. 1930; tr., 1932/34). Jung's introduction is in CW 4.
[4] Cf. Schmitz, 26 May 23, n. 3.
[5] Leopold Ziegler (1881–1959), German philosopher.
[6] Hermann Broch (1886–1951), Austrian novelist, later in U.S.A. Cf. Jaffé, 22 Oct. 54.

The monthly publication of the magazine, though it would pay off commercially, seems to me very difficult. A very forceful and self-sacrificing editor would be needed for that.

I cannot conceal from you that I still have a profound doubt about the whole thing: *it might be premature.* It is only now that I am becoming known in the German-speaking world. The public at large still knows far too little of me for my name to be used as a particularly alluring advertisement. At all events this project needs your energetic support, from which you can judge how much confidence I have in you. For the imponderables and the window-dressing in this world the Church Fathers, as we know, always need an especially shrewd St. Cathérine d'Alexandrie.[7] As such you would have to figure in the list of the editorial staff.

. . .

Meanwhile, my heartiest greetings for the New Year. I also hope that things will go better with X.

Yours sincerely, c. g. jung

[7] Martyred 307 by command of the Emperor Maxentius, whose wife and many of whose courtiers she had, according to legend, converted to Christianity. — Jung's flattering comparison refers to the role Saint Catherine played in Anatole France's *Penguin Island.* She was always called in for advice when the heavenly council reached a deadlock on theological points. Cf. *Mysterium Coniunctionis*, par. 227, and White, 30 June 52, n. 6.

To Hans Welti

Dear Dr. Welti,   23 December 1932

Best thanks for kindly sending me the photograph of your hieroglyphic object. As an utter dilettante I am of course completely nonplussed by it. It would be a lie if I said I liked it, because it does not move me aesthetically in the least. On the other hand it has something that intrigues me, although this, as I have sometimes found, often appear absurd to the artist—I look for the meaning. Things that are neither useful nor beautiful usually have at least a *meaning.* Why, for instance, does this thing not have three, five, or more prongs but precisely four? Why, when you photograph it, does it cast such a deep shadow? Why is its base corrugated like that? If I find such an object in the hut of a primitive, I know at once that it is *ju-ju*,[1] i.e.,

□ Zurich.
[1] West African term for a magic fetish or charm.

medicine, and thus has a meaning. A fetish is as a rule neither useful nor beautiful, but it has meaning, magical meaning. This analogy helps me to gain some understanding of these things.

From the artistic standpoint, I have thoroughly understood your article in the N.Z.Z.,[2] but for all that I cannot approve of modern art, i.e., find it beautiful. I find it perfectly frightful. The reason for this, it seems to me, is that art, without being aware of it, has invaded the realm of the mind and is trying to work out the unconscious meaning pictorially. I can understand modern works of art only as idols from the underworld, and they become accessible to me only through a knowledge of the psychology of the unconscious. They do not affect me aesthetically. It may very well be that my attitude is that of a Philistine, but God knows I can't find them beautiful. Perhaps other centuries will, in which case I am thankful to the Creator that man doesn't live for 200 years, otherwise he would suddenly find himself in an age in which he would choke to death.

As to your concluding question, phenomena of decay naturally occur in all epochs, but in some they pile up. High points are the decline of antiquity, and the 12th and 16th centuries. With best regards,

Yours sincerely, C. G. JUNG

[2] "Picasso auf dem Zürichsee," *Neue Zürcher Zeitung*, no. 1693 (14 Sept. 32).

Anonymous

Dear Dr. N.,   28 January 1933

I understand your difficulties, but I have to tell you that it fares with every civilized man as it formerly did with Doctor Faustus, who also was unable to follow the Mephistophelean advice that he live the simple life of a peasant. This for the simple reason that civilized life is no longer the simple life. The civilized man must be able to change his whole attitude accordingly. You know that Faust finally had to approach the unsavoury witches' cauldron. Today this is called analysis.

You rightly surmise that I am an expensive customer. I have to be, otherwise I would be eaten up skin, bones, and all. Therefore I wanted to give you good advice and save you a lot of money. From earlier days you naturally still have the amiable habit of expecting

□ Switzerland.

effects from others. You have yet to learn how one can produce effects on oneself, and you can learn that from simpler people than me. Nor, in the last resort, could I conjure them up for you as if by magic, but you would have to do the ultimate and best yourself. You must only learn how to make the effort, and that was what I meant when I once advised you to talk over your problems with my wife. I thought you would continue these discussions.

I am sorry it is not possible for me to see you for the next four weeks as I am soon going to Germany on a lecture tour. Therefore I would advise you to try once again and this time more thoroughly. You know very well that what you put into something with a serious effort will always come out again.

Yours sincerely, c. g. j u n g

To E. Sabott

Dear Herr Sabott, 3 February 1933

Your letter pleased and interested me very much. Time and again I have had the unfortunate experience—which also befell my illustrious predecessor Heraclitus—of being named "the Dark." Heraclitus probably understood this darkness as little as I do, but I have so often come up against this judgment that I have finally accustomed myself to thinking that either my views or my style must be so involved that they confront ordinary so-called sound commonsense with insoluble riddles. I admit I have always wished for readers like you. And in later years I have gradually come to the conclusion that the muddle is not located in my head but in the heads of others, and that besides me there are a whole lot of people who still possess an uncontorted intelligence and can therefore think straight. The reading of my books has never caused them any digestive troubles.

I also realize that his master's voice is far less enlightening than immediate experience. In fact, this is what so easily happens to students—they give up working on their own intellectual development when it is so easy to repeat the words of the master. Being a student also has its advantages. But I hope that X. will win through in time. The intellectually greedy atmosphere of Berlin has put too great a strain upon him—temporarily, let's hope.

Moreover it is a law of fate that where there are teachers there must also be students. All learning was originally imitation and it is

□ Berlin.

not always indolence on the part of the student if he renounces his individuality and effaces himself in favour of the *verbum magistri*. Were it not for these followers the voice of the teacher would be too weak to be heard above the hubbub of the crowd. Therefore many must repeat the bare word even though this repetition is not a new birth sprung from the heart. The picture of Goethe, for instance, would be incomplete without Eckermann[1]—to cite a famous example (no presumption intended). To be a student in this sense is not a stigma, and no one has ever become a teacher without having been a student first.

Yours sincerely, C. G. JUNG

[1] Johann Peter Eckermann (1792–1854), German author of *Conversations with Goethe*, in which he acted as a Boswell to Goethe in old age.

To Pastor W. Arz

Dear Pastor Arz,   17 February 1933

. . .

It is of little use having any convictions about the question you ask. I therefore determine the probability of certain views whenever possible by the empirical method. It is naturally quite out of the question that we shall ever be able to furnish a proof of the immortality of the soul. On the other hand, it does seem to me possible to establish certain peculiar facts regarding the nature of the soul[1] which at least do not rule out the immortality affirmed by religious belief. What is commonly understood by "psyche" is certainly an ephemeral phenomenon if it is taken to mean the ordinary facts of consciousness. But in the deeper layers of the psyche which we call the unconscious there are things that cast doubt on the indispensable categories of our conscious world, namely time and space. The existence of telepathy in time and space is still denied only by positive ignoramuses. It is clear that timeless and spaceless perceptions are possible only because the perceiving psyche is similarly constituted. Timelessness and spacelessness must therefore be somehow inherent in its nature, and this in itself permits us to doubt the exclusive temporality of the soul, or if you prefer, makes time and space appear doubtful. Every ephemeral phenomenon requires limitation in time and space,

□ Kleinwittenberg, Germany.
[1] Cf. "The Soul and Death," CW 8, pars. 813ff., and *Memories*, ch. XI: "On Life after Death."

but if time and space are doubtful, then the peculiar limitation of such phenomena becomes doubtful too. It is sufficiently clear that timelessness and spacelessness can never be grasped through the medium of our intelligence, so we must rest content with this borderline concept. Nevertheless we know that a door exists to a quite different order of things from the one we encounter in our empirical world of consciousness. This is about all that science can contribute to this question. Beyond that there is still the subjective psychological experience which can be in the highest degree convincing for the individual even though it cannot be shared by the wider public.

Yours sincerely, C. G. JUNG

To Pastor Josef Schattauer

Dear Pastor Schattauer,   20 February 1933

. . .

I can only agree with you when you equate St. Francis with the essence of primitive religiosity, but even so a special illumination is needed for a person living in more highly developed centuries to become as simple again as a primitive. Equally I share your conviction that genuine religiosity is the best cure for all psyche suffering. The pity of it is that it is exceedingly difficult nowadays to inculcate into people any conception of genuine religiosity. I have found that religious terminology only scares them off still more, for which reason I always have to tread the path of science and experience, quite irrespective of any tradition, in order to get my patients to acknowledge spiritual truths. When you say that the Reformation undermined very many of them, I must add that modern science has undermined them still more thoroughly, so thoroughly that in the psyche of educated people today there is only a big black hole. This has forced me to build up a psychology which will open the door again to psychic experience. The Catholic Church must hold fast to what still remains from earlier times of living religiosity; I on the contrary must do pioneer work in a world where everything pristine has vanished. With kind regards,

Yours sincerely, C. G. JUNG

☐ Salzburg.

To Pastor W. Arz

Dear Pastor Arz,   10 April 1933

Of course I have no objection to your discussing my private communications to you among your circle of friends.

Scientifically speaking, nothing whatever can be made out about the phenomenon of the spirit. These things are so delicate that they completely elude our scientific grasp. The idea that man alone possesses the primacy of reason is antiquated twaddle. I have even found that men are far more irrational than animals. Since we know from experience that the psyche can be grasped to only a very limited degree, it would be best to regard it as a tiny conscious world influenced by all sorts of unknown factors lurking in the great darkness that surrounds us. Among these factors we can perhaps include what we call spirit; thus far science may go, but no further.

I have discussed what spirit means to me in my essay "Geist und Leben"[1] (*Seelenprobleme der Gegenwart*, Rascher, Zurich, 1931). There you will find a formulation of my views on the place of our psyche in the cosmos.

It seems to me therefore quite right if man, conscious of his limitations, feels himself only in modest degree a creator, but in far higher degree a creature or object of a (scientifically unknown) factor that evidently has the tendency to realize itself in human life. One should never confuse oneself with this determinant, otherwise there is always an inflation. In this connection I would like to draw your attention to my book *Die Beziehungen zwischen dem Ich und dem Unbewussten*,[2] published by Reichl (Darmstadt [1928]). Perhaps you also know the book I brought out together with the late Richard Wilhelm, *Das Geheimnis der goldenen Blüte*. With best regards,

Yours sincerely, C. G. JUNG

[1] "Spirit and Life," CW 8.
[2] "The Relations between the Ego and the Unconscious," CW 7.

To Jolande Jacobi

Dear Frau Jacobi,   10 April 1933

I assume you will already have heard from Brody what has happened to the falcon that flew out of your hand into the blue.[1] It came

[1] The project to found a magazine "Weltanschauung" was a failure.

119

home again bedraggled and crept into its own egg, just as Noah's dove found no rest for the sole of her foot. The highly implausible story that the dove returned with an olive leaf has not yet come to pass; the ark still tosses on the waters, which are higher than ever.

I personally do not regret this deflation in the least, as I am not at all set on making more work for myself. I am convinced that people who could do it by themselves do not exist.

The fate of X. seems to me far sadder. I have heard indirectly how badly it goes with him, and from the talk I had with him in Vienna this catastrophic decline could be foreseen, as nobody can defy life's laws with impunity.

I know how very hard your lot is these days. With best wishes,

Ever sincerely yours, C. G. JUNG

To Jolande Jacobi

Dear Frau Jacobi,   21 April 1933

Many thanks for your detailed letter. From what you say of him, Dr. N. seems to be the right man. If he can win over Frau S., in whose sound judgment I have the fullest confidence, he must be quite something. An ordinary idiot of a neurologist couldn't do that. X. is an extraordinarily difficult case, unfortunately far advanced in neurotic degeneration. The danger is that the treatment will get lost in trivialities. With X. one must always keep the whole in mind. He should be cured from "above," for ultimately it is a question of the great conflict for a *Weltanschauung*, which in his case has collided with an antiquated infantile attitude embodied by his wife. Hence on the one hand this great question must be considered, and on the other his infantilism and the junk shop of trivialities. No small task! I would be glad to know of an intelligent neurologist in Vienna. I have often been asked.

My wife has told me of all the garbage that has piled up round the magazine project. Oh this anima! I hope I won't need to do any more explanatory work. For instance the essence of the "famous" meeting in Munich was my *private* talk with Heyer, where only the two of us were together. I had to see what sort of programme he would commit himself to. Even then I had my private doubts, but had still to wait for the official document, the prospectus, where it was bound

☐ (Handwritten.)

120

to come out how those gentlemen were planning the project. I then saw that *everything* would devolve upon me and that I would be boundlessly overburdened. An absolutely unworkable proposition! The stuff men talk on such occasions, sniffing around each other like dogs, is what the English call "eyewash." Everything null and void, valueless, until there's a signed contract. *That alone counts.* Everything else a capricious, deceptive anima intrigue that simply drives women crazy, because they always want to know why and how. The main thing is to know how things are *not* done.

Please give X. my best greetings and tell him—because his love is all too easily injured—he should meditate on Paul's words in the Epistle to the Corinthians: "Love endureth all things." With cordial greetings,

Yours ever, JUNG

To G. Meyer

Dear Colleague,   20 May 1933

I am sorry to say that continuing pressure of work makes it quite impossible for me to see you, especially at the time you mention, when I urgently need my rest.

It is, moreover, a very useful thing to experience a conflict of opposites. Nobody can solve this conflict for you, as it is a conflict in your own nature. A man must be able to stand this struggle. This act of courage is essential for a doctor. Anyone who solved the conflict for you would have got the better of you, for he would rob you of a reward on which all self-respect and manliness are ultimately grounded. You can find in my books all the necessary indications that might make the solution possible on a human and intellectual level. If you need human help, there are enough simple folk who from the simplicity of their hearts could give you the support you need.

With best regards, C. G. JUNG

☐ Guebwiller, Alsace, France.

To Christian Jenssen

Dear Herr Jenssen,   29 May 1933

I have rapidly skimmed through the article you so kindly sent me. I can only thank you for its general tenor, for there are indeed only

121

a few people who have noticed that I am saying something different from Freud. Unfortunately, it is only in Germany that I am not known. In the Anglo-Saxon world I have been known for a long time (whether I have been understood is another matter).

You will find my debate with Freud in *Seelenprobleme der Gegenwart,* in the essay "Der Gegensatz Freud-Jung."[1]

I would like to take this opportunity to rectify the error that I come from the Freudian school. I am a pupil of Bleuler's and my experimental researches had already won me a name in science when I took up the cudgels for Freud and opened the discussion in real earnest in 1905.[2] My scientific conscience did not allow me, on the one hand, to let what is good in Freud go by the board and, on the other, to countenance the absurd position which the human psyche occupies in his theory. I suspected at once that this partly diabolical sexual theory would turn people's heads and I have sacrificed my scientific career in doing all I can to combat this absolute devaluation of the psyche.

Incidentally, I should be much obliged if you would let me know on a postcard whereabouts in my work you have found "intellectual shadow boxing" and other such yarns. I am essentially an empiricist and have discovered to my cost that when people do not understand me they think I have seen visions.

Yours very truly, C. G. JUNG

☐ Cologne.

[1] "Freud and Jung: Contrasts," CW 4.

[2] In 1905 Jung published an article on "Cryptomnesia," CW 1, in which Freud is briefly mentioned (pars. 170, 172). But it is more likely that the reference is to "Freud's Theory of Hysteria: A Reply to Aschaffenburg" (orig. 1906), CW 4. He had mentioned Freud appreciatively as far back as 1902, in "On the Psychology and Pathology of So-called Occult Phenomena," pars. 97, 117, 119 and n. 90, and 133.

To Paul Maag

Dear Colleague, 1 June 1933

Many thanks for kindly confirming my expectations. You are, of course, quite right: I have not yet given up struggling for a philosophy of life and I very definitely hope that this struggle will not come

☐ Dr. Maag was superintendent of a sanatorium in Thurgau, Switzerland.

to an end too soon, for I cannot see that possessing the absolute truth is a state in any way to be envied. I would therefore rather not make any specific prognoses about the future, since the modest share of the light of knowledge that has been vouchsafed me does not enable me to see whither and to what goals the tortuous paths of fate are wending.

Theology and the Church do not embarrass me in the least. On the contrary, I am indebted to both for extraordinarily valuable insights. It was kind of you to recommend Martensen's *Jacob Böhme's Leben und Autorenschaft*. Böhme's writings have long been familiar to me. As you have observed, I am also well aware of the difference between myth and revelation, having concerned myself solely with myths and never with revealed truths. Hence I found it exceedingly odd that you should amiably take me for an atheist. You must surely have noticed that my principal concern is psychology and not theology. So when I treat of the concept of God I am referring exclusively to its psychology and not to its hypostasis. I have voiced this scientifically necessary epistemological proviso many times in my writings. I must also confess that I have never yet been taken for an atheist by my readers, because for educated people today the principles of the theory of knowledge have already become pretty much part of their flesh and blood. Certainly in Kant's time[1] there were still a few theologians who cherished the regrettable error that Kant was an atheist, but even then there was a bigger educated public who were capable of distinguishing between criticism of the concept of God and belief in God. I think you do me an injustice when you hold the view that I have not mastered even the elements of gnoseology.[2] If you would submit the epistemological statements in my *Psychological Types*[3] to a well-disposed examination, you could clearly discern my philosophical position. You would also see that nothing is further from my mind than to deny the contents of religious experience. With collegial regards,

Yours sincerely, C. G. JUNG

---

[1] By denying the sweeping claims of dogmatic theology in his *Critique of Pure Reason*, Kant laid himself open to the charge of atheism.
[2] The more general term would be "epistemology."
[3] Cf pars. 59–67.

To J. H. Schultz

Dear Professor Schultz,   9 June 1933

Dr. Cimbal[1] has now given me a full report and explained the situation. The Society is not being dissolved, so the resignation of the Committee *en masse* is superfluous. As Prof. Kretschmer[2] has resigned from the presidency it is now my turn. Earlier I had drawn Dr. Cimbal's attention to the possible inconveniences of a foreign president. But he thought that wouldn't be a drawback. Hence I have declared my willingness to take over the presidency until further notice, that is, until the knotty problems that have arisen have been definitely straightened out. I have named Dr. Heyer as deputy.

I am in entire agreement with the formation of the proposed commission.[3]

Yours sincerely, C. G. JUNG

☐ M.D., (1884–1970), German neurologist, author of *Das autogene Training* (1932).
[1] Walter Cimbal, honorary secretary of the General Medical Society for Psychotherapy. Cf. Cimbal, 2 Mar. 34, n. ☐.
[2] Ernst Kretschmer, M.D., (1888–1964), at that time professor of psychiatry at Marburg, had been president of the Society for Psychotherapy since 1930 but resigned 6 Apr. 1933. As Jung had been elected vice-president, it became his turn to step in after K.'s resignation. Cf. CW 10, Appendix, pars. 1014 and 1016 and n. 2. He remained acting president until 1940.
[3] S. suggested forming a committee of psychiatrists, one of whose members would be Jung, to deal with all questions arising during an interregnum.

To Paul Maag

Dear Colleague,   12 June 1933

Best thanks for your kind letter. You assume, unjustly, that your specifically orthodox position arouses in me a feeling of mockery. Nothing could be further from my mind. I can only emphasize yet again that I must fulfil my scientific duty as a psychologist and therefore may not go beyond the bounds proper to science without making myself guilty of intellectual presumption. I cannot under any circumstances square it with my scientific conscience to presume to make any arrogant assertions about God that spring from a belief or a subjective opinion. Even what I may personally believe about the ultimate things is, regarded as an object of science, open to scientific criticism. But that in no way prevents me from having views of my

124

own. These views cannot possibly be known to you since I have never expressed them. When therefore you state in your estimable letter that you know exactly what kind of God I believe in, I can only marvel at your powers of imagination. In my humble opinion you would perhaps have done better to ask me first what I actually think about God outside the bounds of my science. It might then have turned out that I am a Mohammedan, or a Buddhist, or possibly even an orthodox Christian like you. Whatever my subjective opinions may be, I would consider it absolutely immoral to use them to antici-pate what is scientifically knowable. My subjective attitude is that I hold every religious position in high esteem but draw an inexorable dividing line between the content of belief and the requirements of science. I consider it unclean to confuse these incommensurables. Even more, I consider it presumptuous to credit human knowledge with a faculty that demonstrably exceeds its limitations. We must admit in all modesty the limitations of all human knowledge and take it as a gift of grace if ever an experience of the Unfathomable should come our way. What men have always named God is the Unfathom-able itself. Were that not so, it would be as possible for an ant to know man and his nature as it is for us to know the nature of the ant.

As you see, I am wholly incorrigible and utterly incapable of com-ing up with a mixture of theology and science. This was, as you well know, the prerogative of the early Middle Ages and is still the pre-rogative of the Catholic Church today, which has set the *Summa* of Thomas Aquinas above the whole of science. It has been one of the greatest achievements of Protestantism to have separated the things of God from the things of the world. With our human knowledge we always move in the human sphere, but in the things of God we should keep quiet and not make any arrogant assertions about what is greater than ourselves. Belief as a religious phenomenon cannot be discussed. It seems to me, however, that when belief enters into practical life we are entitled to the opinion that it should be coupled with the Christian virtue of modesty, which does not brag about absoluteness but brings itself to admit the unfathomable ways of God which have nothing to do with the Christian revelation. Even though the apostles and Paul and John of the Apocalypse himself emphasize its unique-ness and exclusiveness, we nevertheless know that they were all mortal men who for that reason were also subject to the limitations of hu-man knowledge.

Hoping I have made my standpoint sufficiently plain,

With collegial regards, C. G. JUNG

To S. Malkinson

[ORIGINAL IN ENGLISH]

Dear Sir,   12 June 1933

I'm afraid there will be little hope in the future as I have to reduce my time spent on the treatment of patients next October. The
reason is that I have to give lectures here and in Germany and this
occupation will take a great deal of my time. It is true, I don't deny
my sympathy to suffering humanity, but I'm only one man against a
host of patients and it is just impossible that one man can do the
whole job.

It is a mistake when you think that only the authority in this field
could help you. You have a mind just as well as any other human
being and you can use it if you only know how to apply it. Any of my
pupils could give you so much insight and understanding that you
could treat yourself if you don't succumb to the prejudice that you
receive healing through others. In the last resort every individual alone
has to win his battle, nobody else can do it for him.

Sincerely yours, C. G. JUNG

□ Bern.

To Paul Maag

Dear Colleague,   20 June 1933

I gather from your letter that when I said it was "presumptuous to
credit human knowledge with a faculty that demonstrably exceeds its
limitations," this seemed to you to contradict my remark about the
possibility of a subjective "experience of the Unfathomable." You
seem to forget that I have never contested the possibility of subjective
experience. Subjective experience can be an object of scientific investigation only if it is taken as a psychologem. You write: "Lack of
prejudice belongs to the very nature of science." This sentence plainly
excludes the admixture of belief, for belief is a prejudice precisely
because it is not scientific knowledge. All scientific knowledge is open
to discussion, belief isn't. What do you do with a Buddhist who regards the Buddha as a world redeemer, believes in no God, and yet
believes his particular view just as steadfastly as any Christian? How
do you prove that the one is right and the other is not? If you do not
separate belief and science, you subordinate all science to theology
as in the Middle Ages. And to what does theology appeal in order

to support its highest scientific theory? To belief, which is beyond all possibility of discussion and hence is absolutely untenable as a scientific principle, since otherwise science would be prejudiced, which on your own admission it should not be, because it belongs to its nature to be unprejudiced.

How subjective belief is you can see from the fact that I positively do not believe that Christianity is the only and the highest manifestation of the truth. There is at least as much truth in Buddhism, and in other religions too. If for instance I had to choose between the Greek Orthodox Church and Islam, I would opt for Islam. If you brag about your belief, others brag about theirs. Thus all discussion is only a religious war, but any real discussion remains impossible. With collegial regards,

Yours sincerely, c. g. jung

To Linda Gray Oppenheim

[ORIGINAL IN ENGLISH]

Dear Mrs. Oppenheim,   12 August 1933

A year ago I heard through a friend of Mr. Oppenheim's most unexpected death. Yes, it is true, such a death and such suffering seem to be pointless if one assumes that this life is the acme of all existence. I have seen quite a number of people who died when they had reached the most they could. Obviously then the measure of their life was fulfilled, everything said and everything done and nothing remained. The answer to human life is not to be found within the limits of human life.

Sincerely yours, c. g. jung

☐ Widow of James Oppenheim (1882–1932), American poet and writer on psychology. His *American Types* (1929) was based on Jung's typology.

To Daisetz T. Suzuki

[ORIGINAL IN ENGLISH]

Dear Professor Suzuki,   22 September 1933

Being an admirer of your former work on Zen Buddhism, it has been a very great pleasure indeed to receive such a precious gift as your *Essays in Zen Buddhism, Second Series.*[1]

☐ Daisetz Teitaro Suzuki (1870–1966), Japanese philosopher and authority on Zen.

Zen is a true goldmine for the needs of the Western "psychologist." Formerly one would have called such a man a philosopher, but as you know, philosophy with us has been usurped by the philosophical departments of universities and thus removed from life. But as souls could not be removed to the shelves of an academic science, people who by profession have to be busy with human souls, as for instance a nerve doctor like myself, have to concoct a philosophy of their own and they have to call it psychology for the reasons above mentioned. My acquaintance with the classical works of the Far East has given me no end of support in my psychological endeavours. Thus I feel deeply obliged to you for your kind and generous gift.

Most sincerely yours, c. g. j u n g

¹ London, 1933. In 1939, Jung wrote a foreword to the German edition of Suzuki's *Introduction to Zen Buddhism*, now in CW 11.

To Albert Oppenheimer

Dear Herr Oppenheimer,   10 October 1933

Not being a prophet, it is impossible for me to predict where the world is going to. But I know from my own experience of very many individuals of our time that a very definite instinctive tendency is at work to bring them back to consciousness of themselves. The catastrophe of the World War is no doubt responsible for this. What happens to the individual also happens to nations after a time, by a process of natural summation. The economic crisis operates as a contributory causative factor. Nations will become more and more entrenched in their idiosyncrasies and we may expect an increase in nationalism everywhere. Contrary to the rational expectation of worldwide understanding, the individuality of each nation is going to be built up for a long time to come. Economic hardship makes people egoistic as well as increasing mistrust between them.

It is clear that civilization, if not exactly threatened, is being held up in its advance. This is to be welcomed in that our advance has been much too rapid for the real man, which is why we have become lopsidedly intellectualistic and rationalistic and have quite forgotten that there are other factors which cannot be influenced by a one-track rational intellect. Hence we see on all sides a mystic emotion-

□ The Hague.

128

ality flaring up, which had been declared extinguished ever since the Middle Ages. It fares with nations as with the individual: if he grows too high in the air his roots go down too deep, which means that however fast he progresses he will after a time be overtaken by his own shadow, where he will find plenty of work to do on himself at home. In the individual one calls it a conflict, in the nation it's a civil war or revolution.

I think the continuing divisions and upheavals will gradually lead to a state of balance which will form the basis for a reconstruction. But I think the phase of disintegration will last at least several decades more. I see no special social or political gain for our generation but an all the greater spiritual one. This, of course, is not identical with what used to be called the march of civilization.

Yours sincerely, c. g. jung

To Hans Schäffer

Dear Dr. Schäffer,   27 October 1933

Sincerest thanks for your friendly and interesting letter. Your individual attempt at a typization[1] shows that the typological problem can be approached from any number of angles, and usually with considerable advantage for the inventor of the scheme in question.

Your attempt is essentially characterological, which I cannot assert of my own typology. Nor was it ever my intention to characterize personalities, for which reason I did not put my description of the types at the beginning of the book; rather I tried to produce a clear conceptual scheme based on empirically demonstrable factors. Hence my typology aims, not at characterizing personalities, but at classifying the empirical material in relatively simple and clear categories, just as it is presented to a practising psychologist and therapist. I have never thought of my typology as a characterological method and have never applied it in this sense. For any such application it would be much too general and therefore much too scanty. As you very rightly observe, one needs 27 categories and probably a few more besides in order to give an adequate characterization of mentally differentiated persons. For the psychologist, who has to deal with people in prac-

□ Stockholm.
[1] S. wrote about his special system of typology based on a complicated combination of 9 basic characteristics, later expanded to 27.

129

tical terms, a characterological diagnosis of the patient is of secondary importance; for him it is far more important to have a terminology in which at least the crassest differences between individuals can be formulated.

Your characterological aim is to sketch an adequate picture of a person's character. My typology aims at elucidating conceptually the empirical psychological material presented by any one individual and thus subordinating it to general points of view. This intention of mine has often been misunderstood, for the simple reason that the layman can form absolutely no conception of the peculiar material the psychotherapist is confronted with. In practical dealings with people it is certainly of the greatest importance to know with whom one is dealing. For the therapist this is a matter of indifference, since he has to deal with him anyway and the patient's psychology is such that the only thing to do is change it. Consequently, categories like "sensitivity," "good-naturedness," "intellect," etc. can be considered only as more or less pleasant concomitants.

I should like to add, however, that your findings may well be of great importance biographically and are obviously an extremely valuable contribution to our knowledge of contemporary personalities. With collegial regards,

Yours sincerely, C. G. JUNG

To Elisabeth von Sury

Dear Fräulein von Sury,   14 November 1933

I have been pondering over your suggestion for a lecture in Paris[1] and have come to the conclusion that in view of the present intellectual situation in France it would be premature if I lectured at the Sorbonne. It would look too much like making propaganda for my own cause. I would regard such a procedure as not only unintelligent but misleading as well. I have always acted on the principle that if people have the need to hear me they could also invite me to speak. I would therefore prefer to wait and see whether something will stir spontaneously in Paris or not.

I have found over and over again that it is not worthwhile speaking

☐ Swiss analytical psychologist.
[1] Jung had lectured in Paris in 1916 on "La Structure de l'inconscient," now "The Structure of the Unconscious," CW 7, Appendix II.

to an unprepared public. My whole psychology is such that it can be accepted only by someone who is ready for it. It is too little in accord with the conscious expectations of the time to be grafted on to something known. So let us wait and leave it to the intellectual development of France whether or not to adopt a positive attitude to this kind of psychology.

I am sorry to disappoint you now after I had already expressed my willingness to oblige. With best regards,

Yours sincerely, C. G. JUNG

To Rudolf Allers

Dear Colleague,   23 November 1933

The reason why no communication has reached you concerning the state of affairs in Germany is that nobody was clear about what was happening and what is going to happen. I will give you a brief description of how things stand at present.

The Zentralblatt[1] is to continue. As president of an international medical Society for Psychotherapy[2] I am the more or less involuntary editor of this organ. As such I would like to secure your valuable cooperation for the Zentralblatt in your former capacity as editor of the reviews section. At present the Zentralblatt will have to consist mostly of reviews until conditions in Germany have become somewhat clearer.

The German section of the Society for Psychotherapy has been "gleichgeschaltet" [conformed] and placed under the direction of Prof. Göring[3] in Elberfeld. (G. is a cousin of the Prime Minister!) As I was recently informed in Germany, all societies, advisory centres, and other medical organizations concerned with psychotherapy are to be under him. Göring will also undertake the publication of a special German issue of the Zentralblatt,[4] which is to express what psycho-

---

☐ M.D., Austrian "non-Aryan" psychotherapist, follower of Alfred Adler; later emigrated to U.S.A. where he taught at Georgetown U., Washington, D.C.

[1] Zentralblatt für Psychotherapie und ihre Grenzgebiete (Leipzig), organ of the International General Medical Society for Psychotherapy.

[2] Cf. Schultz, 9 June 33, n. 2.

[3] M. H. Göring, of Wuppertal, cousin of Reichsminister Hermann Göring (cf. CW 10, Appendix, par. 1016, n. 2). The common surname gave rise to numerous misunderstandings.

[4] This was number VI:3 of the Zentralblatt, which appeared in Dec. 1933 and caused considerable controversy. Cf. Brüel, 2 Mar. 34, n. 1.

therapy signifies under the present political conditions in Germany. I must confess that I am still in the dark on this score.

In Switzerland as well as in Holland and Sweden I have secured reviewers in order to ensure a tolerable continuance of the *Zentralblatt*. It is not yet certain who will take over the editorship. As the German section is by far the strongest, I thought of Cimbal[5] or possibly Heyer in Munich. A foreign editor, I fear, would in the present circumstances meet with not a few difficulties, because the German government, as you know, seems to like having the editors of all periodicals appearing in Germany in safe and uncomfortable proximity. Otherwise I would have proposed you as editor. I have written to Cimbal on this matter but so far have received no answer. It must unquestionably be a "conformed" editor, as he would be in a far better position than I to have the right nose for what one can say and what not. In any event it will be an egg-balancing dance.

Thank you very much for sending me the announcement of this new journal.[6] I have declined with thanks to cooperate because I propose to turn my interest more to the *Zentralblatt*. Psychotherapy must see to it that it maintains its position inside the German Reich and does not settle outside it, regardless of how difficult its living conditions there may be. Göring is a very amiable and reasonable man, so I have the best hopes for our cooperation.

As soon as I know more I will let you know. Meanwhile with collegial regards,

Yours sincerely, C. G. JUNG

[5] Cimbal subsequently became editor.
[6] Probably *Psychotherapeutische Praxis*, ed. W. Stekel, Vienna, and A. Kronfeld, Berlin. The first number appeared in March 1934.

To Frau V.

Dear Frau V.,   15 December 1933

Your questions are unanswerable because you want to know how one *ought* to live. One lives as one *can*. There is no single, definite way for the individual which is prescribed for him or would be the proper one. If that's what you want you had best join the Catholic Church, where they tell you what's what. Moreover this way fits in with the average way of mankind in general. But if you want to go

☐ Switzerland.

your individual way, it is the way you make for yourself, which is never prescribed, which you do not know in advance, and which simply comes into being of itself when you put one foot in front of the other. If you always do the next thing that needs to be done, you will go most safely and sure-footedly along the path prescribed by your unconscious. Then it is naturally no help at all to speculate about how you ought to live. And then you know, too, that you cannot know it, but quietly do the next and most necessary thing. So long as you think you don't yet know what this is, you still have too much money to spend in useless speculation. But if you do with conviction the next and most necessary thing, you are always doing something meaningful and intended by fate. With kind regards and wishes,

Yours sincerely, c. g. j u n g

To H. Oberhänsli

Dear Herr Oberhänsli,   16 December 1933

Best thanks for your friendly letter of Nov. 8th, which I am sorry I can answer only now. I must also thank you for sending me the brochure on Christ and the Pope.

You are quite right when you say that the real task of religion would be to cure psychic suffering. I have always advocated this idea even in medical circles.

As for the different denominations, it is no longer a question today of the rights of each but of the existence of religion as such, so that I do not lay too much weight on the differences between them. To my mind Catholicism, in its ecclesiastical organization, is an absolute secularization of Christianity, and has nothing whatever to do with the intentions of the founder of the Christian religion. It is a religion in itself, just like Buddhism, Confucianism, Taoism, etc. We must modestly leave it to the wit of the Creator to resolve these irregularities, obviously foreseen in the divine plan of creation, and be satisfied with the fact that from the worldly point of view we are Protestants who do not lag behind the Creator in tolerance. With kind regards,

Yours sincerely, c. g. j u n g

☐ Schaffhausen.

To J. Allen Gilbert

[ORIGINAL IN ENGLISH]

My dear Gilbert,   8 January 1934

I have just finished reading your MS[1] from the first to the last letter. I must say I enjoyed it unreservedly. It is a most savage onslaught of intellect on itself. Building up and pulling down again—what has happened after all? Oh, I quite agree with you, intellect is a great sorcerer: it can make even itself disappear. The chapters about psychology, religion, and philosophy are splendid. The bit of personal biography you produce in the sociological chapter is enormously to the point. I guess they liked you all right for your candidness.

But I say you would be a perfect model of a Nazi if you were in Germany, where they are going to castrate about 400,000 individuals. That's what you call a *thrust*? But why the devil are you still so intellectual? Your critique is exceedingly logical and intellectual, not less your fair recognition of what belongs and what does not belong to the jurisdiction of the intellect. Nowhere do I find you kicking your intellect about a bit, juggling, shifting, moulding, tricking and that sort of thing, which life seems to do so often. You were most faithfully intellectual. Surely you would not let that lazy beggar starve to death, would you? No, you would feed him and tomorrow you would kick him in the bottom. That's life, isn't it? And he was made for it, otherwise he never could have grown a bottom. Life is marvellously inconsistent. It even wants some sympathy with the poor old Harlequin Intellect. Isn't that delight-maker[2] life's useful instrument in its attempts at tricking the human mind into the belief in so-called reality? Isn't it remarkable that it's just you who make such a bad case for the intellect? You sit at the microscope and see it as a very black thing indeed. Would you say, black for yourself? I would.

Sorry that I have kept you waiting so long, but I wanted to read your book. And I have enjoyed it profoundly.

Cordially yours, C. G. JUNG

[1] The MS was never published. The proposed title was "The Curse of the Intellect," for which Jung wrote a foreword, now in CW 18.
[2] Cf. Michaelis, 20 Jan. 39.

To Poul Bjerre

Dear Colleague, 22 January 1934

I would like to express my best thanks for your willingness to take part in the reorganization of the General Medical Society for Psychotherapy. I am very glad of your help.

The main concern at present is the organization of the International Society. As you know, the German Society has been compelled by the political change in Germany to form a national group under a leader. This group has to comply with the strictest political guidelines, as you can well imagine. Its existence would have been impossible without absolute submission to the National Socialist State. I have therefore advised the Germans to submit without hesitation, for what matters above all is that psychotherapy in Germany, now gravely threatened, should survive the adversities of the time. Therefore I have also got into touch with the leading circles in order to do everything possible to ensure the continued existence and recognition of psychotherapy. All the German organizations are now under the uniform direction of Prof. Göring in Elberfeld. He is the responsible leader.

Through this founding of a national group influenced by the special political conditions, the international section of the Society has been compelled to form national groups in turn, constituting an organization within the framework of which the German group is absorbed. By means of this organization I am trying to prevent the special political currents in the German group, which is numerically the strongest, from spilling over into the Society as a whole. This is what many foreigners fear, particularly the Jews, who as you know are very numerous. If we succeed in organizing some national groups in neutral countries, this will act as a counterweight and at the same time afford the Germans a much needed opportunity to maintain a connection with the outside world in their present spiritual isolation. This connection is essential for the continued development of psychotherapy in Germany, since at present she is even more cut off than during the war.

I should be very grateful to you if you would take the initiative in Sweden for the founding of a national group which would be a member of the International Society. It would be sufficient for individual

☐ M.D., (1876–1964), Swedish psychotherapist. His attempt to form a Swedish group failed at the time. He succeeded, however, in 1936 (cf. Bjerre, 8 May 36).

members to declare their enrolment in this Society. Naturally you are free to organize your group in such a way that it also holds local meetings in Sweden itself, though this is not necessary. Dr. W. Cimbal is secretary-general of the whole Society and I would ask you to get in touch with him as regards both the membership fees and the subscription to the *Zentralblatt*. Perhaps there would also be an opportunity to discuss preferential terms for subscribers.

Further, I want to tell you that I would be very pleased if you could assure us of your cooperation with the *Zentralblatt*. For the present it would be a matter of your now and then bringing to our notice, either personally or through one of your co-workers, new publications of a psychotherapeutic nature by means of reviews. We should also be grateful for original contributions. Submissions to the *Zentralblatt* should be sent to the secretary-general, Dr. Cimbal. With collegial regards,

Yours sincerely, C. G. JUNG

P.S. I have just received word from Copenhagen that a Danish national group, under the presidency of Dr. Paul Reiter, St. Hans Hosp. near Roskilde, has been formed under the name "Selskab for Psykoterapi" [Society for Psychotherapy].

To Alphonse Maeder

Dear friend, 22 January 1934

I am writing to you about the organization of a Swiss national group[1] in the General Medical Society for Psychotherapy. In consequence of the revolutionary changes in Germany the Germans have been compelled to form a national group under a "leader." This group has to pledge loyalty to the National Socialist State and is obliged to adhere most strictly to political guidelines within its organization. The leader is Professor Dr. M. H. Göring (Platzhoffstr. 26, Wuppertal-Elberfeld). Through the resignation of Professor Kretschmer, for whom things evidently got too "complicated," I have been pushed forward from the position of vice-president to that of president. I would never have accepted this doubtful pleasure had not the Ger-

---

[1] The group was founded in Jan. 1935 by a committee consisting of, among others, Jung, K. von Sury, C. A. Meier, K. Binswanger, and G. A. Farner. Maeder did not take part in the organization. The name of the group was "Schweizerische Gesellschaft für praktische Psychologie."

mans particularly insisted on having a foreign president for the International Society. The secretary-general is Dr. W. Cimbal (Allee 87, Altona).

Essentially it is simply a question of someone taking the initiative and bringing together all those doctors in Switzerland who are interested in psychotherapy with a view to getting them to join the General Medical Society for Psychotherapy. What is needed at present is only the loose organization of a national group. Of course it would be desirable if this group could decide to hold one or two meetings annually, though this is not necessary since the International Society will also meet only once a year. I would be very gratified if you organized this national group and took over its presidency.

I am in the midst of similar negotiations with Bjerre in Stockholm. The Dutch want to wait until they see what happens in other countries. I am convinced that if such groups were formed in Sweden and Switzerland, Holland would agree to do something along these lines. Under the present political conditions probably nothing can be arranged with Austria, moreover the psychotherapists there are practically all Jews. It seems that many people are afraid to go along with Germany because of the existing regime. But with the Germans, as I know from experience, it is just the other way round. Prof. Göring himself wrote me that foreigners should take a psychotherapeutic view of the present German situation. The position of German science is really not to be envied. Hence I think it necessary for outside neutrals, by founding a broad organization as a framework, to give it an opportunity to make international connections. Germany is spiritually more cut off at present from the outside world than during the war and is therefore in particular need of spiritual contacts.

I don't want to interfere with the practical arrangements. I will only tell you how I think of them. The founding of the group could be done by a circular letter[2] which would simply need signing. Membership fees could be kept low since we are not bound by the German statutes. Nevertheless it would be a good thing if you got in touch with Dr. Cimbal for further information. Particularly in regard to subscriptions to the *Zentralbatt*, more favourable terms might be reached for subscriptions in large numbers.

In case anything is still unclear to you, I am ready to give you more information. A personal meeting is probably not necessary at present.

---

[2] In all probability this is the letter which was inserted as a separate sheet in *Zentralblatt*, VII:6 (Dec. 1934). Cf. CW 10, Appendix, "Circular Letter," pars. 1035f.

Best thanks for kindly sending me the two offprints, one of which I knew already.

With friendly greetings, JUNG

To B. Baur

Dear Dr. Baur, 29 January 1934

Best thanks for your kind information. So far as the argument of the precession[1] is concerned, this is no objection to the validity of astrology but rather to the primitive theory that the stars themselves radiate certain effects. The precession argument says that a person born today in Aries 1, when ostensibly Aries has risen one degree over the Eastern horizon, is not born at this point of time at all but in Pisces 1. The secret powers of the sun are in Aries 1. Moon for instance in Cancer 7, Venus, Jupiter in similar positions, are therefore not right astronomically and so cannot be derived from these merely apparent and arbitrarily fixed positions. Choisnard quite correctly says: "Le bélier reste toujours à la 12ᵉ partie du zodiaque,"[2] etc., obviously meaning that "sun in Aries" is not an astronomical statement but an indication of time. It is "springtime" that contains the active forces no matter in which real astronomical zodion the sun is standing. In a few thousand years, when we say it is Aries time, the sun will be in reality in Capricorn, a deep winter sign, though the spring will not have lost its powers.

The fact that astrology nevertheless yields valid results proves that it is not the apparent positions of the stars which work, but rather

□ Zurich.

[1] The precession of the equinoxes (reputedly discovered by the Greek astronomer Hipparchus, born *ca.* 190 B.C.) is the slow western motion of the equinoctial points along the ecliptic, caused by the conical motion of the earth's axis; a complete revolution takes about 26,000 years, called the "Platonic Year." As a consequence, the vernal equinox moves clockwise through the twelve zodiacal signs, the precession through each taking about 2,000 years, a "Platonic Month." Thus at the beginning of our era the vernal equinox entered the sign of Pisces and is now moving into Aquarius. Astrology, in its horoscopic calculations, does not take account of the precession but bases them on the vernal equinox fixed by Hipparchus at 0° Aries. This discrepancy is a main objection to astrology. (Cf. Corti, 12. Sept. 29, n. 3.)

[2] Paul Flambart (= Paul Choisnard), *Preuves et bases de l'astrologie scientifique* (2nd edn., 1921), p. 162: ". . . aujourd'hui comme dans l'antiquité on peut appeler Bélier la douzième partie du zodiaque que traverse le soleil aussitôt après l'equinoxe de printemps."

the times which are measured or determined by arbitrarily named stellar positions. Time thus proves to be a stream of energy filled with qualities and not, as our philosophy would have it, an abstract concept or precondition of knowledge.

The validity of the results of the *I Ching* oracle points to the same peculiar fact. Careful investigation of the unconscious shows that there is a peculiar coincidence with time, which is also the reason why the ancients were able to project the succession of unconsciously perceived inner contents into the outer astronomical determinants of time. This is the basis for the connection of psychic events with temporal determinants. So it is not a matter of an indirect connection, as you suppose, but of a direct one. Conjunctions, oppositions, etc. are not in the least affected by the fact that we arbitrarily designate Pisces 1 as Aries 1.

. . .

With best regards,

Yours sincerely, c. g. j u n g

To Olga Fröbe-Kapteyn

Dear Frau Fröbe,   29 January 1934

I see that the programme is already a feast of riches and will certainly more than satisfy your public. I therefore feel it is almost superfluous to pile on still more lectures. I would like to leave the floor to the Sinologists and Indologists and keep psychology in the background as a difficult and unsavoury subject for the Asiatic enthusiast, which nobody bothers about unless he must. But psychology in the stricter sense is bound up with the practical use of the *I Ching*. One must have a far-reaching psychological understanding in order to enjoy the *I Ching* with advantage. Too much Oriental knowledge, however, takes the place of immediate experience and thus blocks the way to

□ (1881–1962), originally Dutch; founder of the annual Eranos meetings in Ascona, Switzerland, at which an international group of scholars lectured and exchanged views. The first meeting took place in Aug. 1933, when Jung delivered a lecture "Zur Empirie des Individuationsprozesses" (revised and expanded as "A Study in the Process of Individuation," CW 9, i). Up to 1951 he was a frequent lecturer and the spiritual centre of the meetings. The lectures are published annually in the *Eranos Jahrbücher* (cf. Hauer, 14 Nov. 32, n. 1). A selection in English has been published under the auspices of Bollingen Foundation (6 vols., 1954–68). (See pl. v.)

psychology. Still, it is understandable that people should first try all passable ways before they can decide to set foot on the path into the untrodden.

These are the reasons that have decided me to keep psychological questions in the background. I would therefore like to comport myself at your meeting essentially as a sympathetic listener.[1]

Yours sincerely, C. G. JUNG

[1] In actual fact, Jung did lecture at this meeting, on "The Archetypes of the Collective Unconscious," CW 9, i.

To Erich Neumann

Dear Colleague,   29 January 1934

It is possible that a Dr. X. will turn to you. He pants for therapy, needs it too, because he consists essentially of only an intellectual halo wandering forlorn and footless through the world. He could be not uninteresting, but there's no money in it. With best greetings,

Yours sincerely, C. G. JUNG

☐ M.D., Ph.D., (1905–1965), originally German, later Israeli. His works include *Origins and History of Consciousness* (orig. 1949), *Amor and Psyche* (orig. 1952), *The Archetypal World of Henry Moore* (1959), *The Great Mother* (1955), *Art and the Creative Unconscious* (orig. 1954), *Depth Psychology and a New Ethic* (1969), *The Child* (orig. 1963), and contributions in the *Eranos Jahrbücher* XVI/XXIX. (See pl. in vol. 2.)

To Bernhard Baur-Celio

30 January 1934

. . .

I cannot leave your "question of conscience" unanswered. Obviously I speak only of what I know and what can be verified. I don't want to addle anybody's brains with my subjective conjectures. Beyond that I have had experiences which are, so to speak, "ineffable," "secret" because they can never be told properly and because nobody

☐ According to a communication from Prof. Baur-Celio, this letter reached him in the form reproduced here, without beginning or end. It is in answer to the question whether Jung possessed any "secret knowledge" surpassing his written formulations.

can understand them (I don't know whether I have even approximately understood them myself), "dangerous" because 99% of humanity would declare I was mad if they heard such things from me, "catastrophic" because the prejudices aroused by their telling might block other people's way to a living and wondrous mystery, "taboo" because they are an ἄδυτον[1] protected by δεισιδαιμονία[2] as faithfully described by Goethe:

> Shelter gives deep cave.
> Lions around us stray,
> Silent and tame they rove,
> And sacred honours pay
> To the holy shrine of love.[3]

And already too much has been said—my public might be fatally infected by the suspicion of "poetic licence"—that most painful aberration!

Can anyone say "credo" when he stands *amidst* his experience, πιστεύων ὁράματι δεινῷ,[4] when he knows how superfluous "belief" is, when he more than just "knows," when the experience has even pressed him to the wall?

I don't want to seduce anyone into believing and thus take his experience from him. I need my mental and physical health in fullest measure to hold out against what people call "peace," so I don't like boosting my experiences. But one thing I will tell you: the exploration of the unconscious has in fact and in truth discovered the age-old, timeless *way of initiation.* Freud's theory is an apotropaic attempt to block off and protect oneself from the perils of the "long road"; only a "knight" dares "la queste" and the "aventiure." Nothing is submerged for ever—that is the terrifying discovery everyone makes who has opened that portal. But the primeval fear is so great that the world is grateful to Freud for having proved "scientifically" (what a bastard of a science!) that one has seen nothing behind it. Now it is not merely my "credo" but the greatest and most incisive experience of my life that this door, a highly inconspicuous side-door on an unsuspicious-looking and easily overlooked footpath—narrow and indistinct because only a few have set foot on it—leads to the secret of transformation and renewal.

[1] Holy (numinous) precinct, sanctuary.
[2] Fear of the gods (or demons).
[3] *Faust II*, Act 5, last scene (tr. P. Wayne, p. 279).
[4] "In faith trusting the terrifying apparition."

141

> Intrate per angustam portam.
> Quia lata porta et spatiosa via est,
> quae ducit ad perditionem,
> Et multi sunt qui intrant per eam.
> Quam angusta porta et arcta via est,
> quae ducit *ad vitam*,
> *Et pauci sunt qui inveniunt eam!*
> Attendite a falsis prophetis qui veniunt
> ad vos in vestimentis ovium—
> *intrinsecus autem sunt lupi rapaces.*[5]

Now you will understand why I prefer to say "scio" and not "credo" —because I don't want to act mysterious. But it would infallibly look as though I were acting mysterious if I spoke of a real, living mystery. One *is* mysterious when one speaks of a *real* mystery. Therefore better not speak of it in order to avoid that evil and confusing look. Like all real life it is a voyage between Scylla and Charybdis.

. . .

[5] Matthew 7:13–15 (Vulgate).

Anonymous

Dear Dr. N.,   5 February 1934

You will surely appreciate that it is quite impossible to clear up your whole psychic situation by letter. Very much could be said in answer to what you have written me. Above all things you must be clear that the uncovering of the unconscious, as it happens in analysis, is only the beginning of a journey that cannot be halted but must be continued to the end. Behind all the rationalizations of Freud's theory there are still facts that need to be understood. It is futile to devalue them with the famous "nothing but"[1] formula. If in exceptional cases the inner demand can be reduced to silence, people have lost something and they pay for their apparent calm with inner desiccation. The irrational factors that manifest themselves indirectly as "incest complexes" and "infantile fantasies," etc. are susceptible of a quite

☐ Netherlands.

[1] A term frequently used by Jung to denote the common habit of explaining something unknown by reducing it to something apparently known and thereby devaluing it. It is borrowed from William James, *Pragmatism* (1907), p. 16: "What is higher is explained by what is lower and treated for ever as a case of 'nothing but'—nothing but something else of a quite inferior sort."

different interpretation. They are psychic forces which other ages and other cultures have viewed in a different light. To experience this other side one should have the courage, for once, not to rationalize the statements of the unconscious but to take them seriously. That, to be sure, is saying much in a few words—perhaps too much. I don't know whether you are acquainted with my essay "The Relations between the Ego and the Unconscious." There you will find a clarification of what I have said here.

The psychosis phobia is always a sign that the irrational psychic factors are piling up and want to be assimilated. As you have correctly seen, there is a danger here of the apparent unity of your consciousness falling apart into pairs of opposites. This problem is discussed in *Psychological Types,* in the chapters on Schiller and Spitteler. The unconscious wants to force you into a serious confrontation, with the obvious intent of defending its position against your conscious attitude. The unconscious is on no account an empty sack in which the refuse of consciousness is collected, as it appears to be in Freud's view; it is the whole other half of the living psyche. More than that, it is a psychic reflection of the whole world. If you go into these problems you will soon see that our ego is situated between two antithetical worlds—the so-called outer world open to the senses, and the unconscious psychic substrate which alone enables us to grasp the world at all. This psychic substrate must necessarily be different from the so-called outer world, otherwise there would be no possibility of grasping it, for like cannot cognize like.

Psychically you are, so to speak, directly confronted with the realization of the collective unconscious. During this process borrowed knowledge will help you only indirectly, i.e., only when you have made the encounter with your own individual unconscious a part of your deepest experience. I doubt whether you can go this way entirely alone. At all events you should have someone to give you at least moral support, if not competent advice. You can get a few practical hints from the above-mentioned essay. In any case you can be certain that it is a natural process of development. If only one has the patience to let the existing opposites do their work they will produce a third thing. Dreams can be very helpful in this respect. Only, you shouldn't interpret the symbols produced by dreams reductively, but must understand them as true symbols, that is, as the best possible formulation for unknown facts that cannot be reduced to anything else.

• • •

Yours sincerely, c. g. jung

143

Anonymous

Dear Herr N.,   20 February 1934

Nobody can set right a mismanaged life with a few words. But there is no pit you cannot climb out of provided you make the right effort at the right place.

When one is in a mess like you are, one has no right any more to worry about the idiocy of one's own psychology, but must do the next thing with diligence and devotion and earn the goodwill of others. In every littlest thing you do in this way you will find yourself. It was no different with X. He too had to do it the hard way, and always with the next, the littlest, and the hardest things.

Yours truly, c. g. j u n g

☐ Germany.

To Oluf Brüel

Dear Dr. Brüel,   2 March 1934

I am very much obliged to you for your efforts to organize national groups in Sweden and Norway. The inquiry I sent to Dr. Bjerre has remained unanswered.

The organization of the German group is not yet in a satisfactory condition. Also, the running of the *Zentralblatt* is still very much disturbed by political interference. Thus Göring's Manifesto,[1] which

☐ M.D., Danish psychotherapist. He met Jung at the Nauheim Congress of 1934 (see Heyer, 20 Apr. 34) and together with Jung and others was one of the founders of the International General Medical Society for Psychotherapy. He founded a Danish group of this Society in 1934, under his presidency. His attempt to organize similar groups in Sweden and Norway failed. Cf. CW 10, Appendix, pars. 1048, 1055.

[1] A statement which appeared in the Dec. 1933 issue of the *Zentralblatt*. It had been planned that Prof. Göring, as president of the German section of the International Society, would bring out a special supplement for exclusive circulation in Germany (cf. Allers, 23 Nov. 33, n. 4). It was to contain a signed declaration by Göring—the so-called "Manifesto"—committing the members of the German section to Hitler's political and ideological principles. Whether by accident or design the Manifesto appeared not only in the supplement (*Deutsche Seelenheilkunde*, Leipzig, 1934) but, in slightly altered form, also in the *Zentralblatt* without Jung's having been apprised of this fact (cf. CW 10, Appendix, par. 1021). For a comprehensive account of the situation cf. Jaffé "C. G. Jung and National Socialism," *From the Life and Work of C. G. Jung* (1971).

144

it was agreed would come out in a special German issue, has been put in the *Zentralblatt* under my name. This against my express demand that the special German issue should be signed by Göring and not by me. I can hardly make our very deserving managing editor, Dr. Cimbal, responsible for this irregularity. The fault lies with the peculiar internal political conditions that still aggravate the organization of the *Zentralblatt* in a high degree. I consider it a tactical blunder if exclusively German manifestos intended only for Germany are put in a journal intended for foreign consumption.

Chiefly for political reasons I am meeting with great difficulties in founding a national group in Switzerland. I find the shortsightedness of my countrymen deplorable.

I shall try everything possible in the future to eliminate political influences from the *Zentralblatt*. According to the latest news I have received, the ministerial decree that was to sanction the German group has still not come out. As soon as I know more I will report to you again. Meanwhile with collegial regards,

Yours sincerely, C. G. JUNG

To Walter Cimbal

Dear Colleague,   2 March 1934

I am sorry that an indisposition has prevented me from writing to you earlier. I now take this opportunity of informing you that the fact that Göring's Manifesto, which should have appeared only in the special German issue, has nevertheless come out in the *Zentralblatt* has displeased me. As you will remember, I told you of my express wish that the German issue should be signed by Prof. Göring. I as a foreigner do not fit into German internal politics. Also, with regard to foreign subscribers, it is a regrettable tactical blunder when purely domestic political manifestos, which can at a pinch be taken as German necessities, are rammed down the throats of foreign readers who are critical enough as it is. I don't want to reproach you personally for this, because I know what unspeakable trouble you are having with the reorganization of the Society and its organ. I assume that you were driven to this step by the exigencies of domestic politics. I would, however, urgently request you to make the *Zentralblatt* intended for

☐ M.D., German psychotherapist; honorary secretary of the General Medical Society for Psychotherapy, of which Jung became vice-president in 1930.

145

foreign circulation unpolitical in every respect, otherwise it is quite impossible for foreign subscribers to join the Society. Understandably, they don't want to commit themselves to a definitely political declaration of faith.

The *Zentralblatt* blunder has already set off a campaign against me in Zurich.[1] You will appreciate that as its editor I must have some influence on its make-up at least in certain respects. You may rest assured that I will not under any circumstances use this influence for the publication of anything that is politically inadmissible. But as president of the International Society I must make absolutely sure that the periodical under my direction maintains a scientific form outside all politics. With best regards,

Yours sincerely, c. g. jung

[1] The campaign was sparked off by the Swiss psychiatrist G. Bally, in an article "Deutschstämmige Psychotherapie?" published in the *Neue Zürcher Zeitung*, 27 Feb. 34. He attacked Jung for drawing attention, at this critical juncture, to the differences between Germanic and Jewish psychology in his Editorial to the Dec. 1933 issue of the *Zentralblatt*, VI:3 (cf. CW 10, Appendix, pars. 1014 f.). Jung's reply in the N.Z.Z. (13/14 March), "A Rejoinder to Dr. Bally," is in ibid., pars. 1016ff.

To J. H. van der Hoop

Dear Colleague, 2 March 1934

As you will have seen, the last issue of *Zentralblatt* contains a political edict by Göring, president of the German Society. This edict was intended for a special German issue which on my instructions was to have been signed by him alone. To my utter amazement this edict has got into the *Zentralblatt*, against my express wish that the *Zentralblatt* should be reserved for exclusively scientific contents. It was not within my power to forestall this regrettable event. Internal politics are to blame. In the present circumstances it is incredibly difficult to get a scientific project going without its being immediately scorched by the political fire. I certainly don't want to make either Cimbal or Göring personally responsible for this unpardonable tactical blunder, as I know that both of them are under overwhelming political pressure.

□ M.D., Dutch psychotherapist, President of the Dutch group of the International Medical Society for Psychotherapy. Cf. CW 10, Appendix, pars. 1048, 1055.

If the foreign groups do not support my efforts to maintain scientific contact with Germany, my strength alone is not sufficient to build up a counterweight to the political tidal wave that threatens to engulf everything. Maeder has written to me that he intends to do nothing in this matter, as he is now devoting himself entirely to the Christian work of conversion in the Oxford Movement. With best regards,

Yours sincerely, c. g. j u n g

To A. *Pupato*

Dear Colleague, 2 March 1934

The question I broached regarding the peculiarities of Jewish psychology[1] does not presuppose any intention on my part to depreciate Jews, but is merely an attempt to single out and formulate the mental idiosyncrasies that distinguish Jews from other people. No sensible person will deny that such differences exist, any more than he will deny that there are essential differences in the mental attitude of Germans and Frenchmen despite the fact that the French liver functions exactly like the German. The mental attitude is only very tenuously connected with the liver, however. When, on the other hand, it is a question of psychological theories, we must, for the sake of scientific justice, always criticize very carefully all conscious and unconscious assumptions, since the whole mass of an individual's assumptions inevitably gets into any psychological theory. Psychology differs from other sciences in that the object of investigation is at the same time the instrument of investigation. That is why there is an infinity of psychological theories, each of which is patently connected with the historical assumptions of the individual in question. Even in the phenomenology of the neuroses there are very distinct differences between German and French clinics, a fact that struck the old nerve doctors. For instance, the typical "grande hystérie" we find in the Salpêtrière[2] is almost completely absent in the German clinical domain. Again, nobody with any experience of the world will deny that the psychology of an American differs in a character-

□ Zurich.
[1] Cf. "The State of Psychotherapy Today," CW 10, pars. 352ff., and "A Rejoinder to Dr. Bally," ibid., pars. 1024ff.
[2] Famous mental hospital in Paris, where Jung studied for some months under Pierre Janet in 1902 (cf. Jeliffe, 24 Feb. 36, n. 2).

istic and unmistakable way from that of an Englishman. It seems to me the height of absurdity. . .[3] To point out this difference cannot possibly, in my humble opinion, be in itself an insult to the Jews so long as one refrains from value judgments. If anyone seeking to pin down my peculiarities should remark that this or that is specifically Swiss, or peasant-like, or Christian, I just wouldn't know what I should get peeved about, and I would be able to admit such differences without turning a hair. I have never understood why, for instance, a Chinese should be insulted when a European asserts that the Chinese mentality differs from the European mentality. Or is the well-known fact that the average Chinese gets along better with the French than with the English an insult to the French or to the English or to the Chinese?

It is my opinion that the peculiarity of the Jews might explain why they are an absolutely essential symbiotic element in our population. If there actually were no differences between them and other people, there would be nothing to distinguish them at all and then there would also be nothing in the characteristic influence, amply attested by history, which they have exerted on their environment. It must after all be supposed that a people which has kept itself more or less unadulterated for several thousand years and clung onto its belief in being "chosen" is psychologically different in some way from the relatively young Germanic peoples whose culture is scarcely more than a thousand years old.

It is true that I fight Freud's psychology because of its dogmatic claim to sole validity. The monotony of Freudian explanations obliterates the wealth of differences that do indeed exist. I am persuaded that I am not doing another person a favour by tarring him with the brush of my subjective assumptions. If I want a proper knowledge of his nature I must ascertain where and to what extent he is different from me. Then only is it possible for me to know him really objectively. I would consider it most fortunate if, for example, Germany and France took the trouble to understand each other better and could appreciate and acknowledge each other's characteristic values. But the way things are, each explains the other in terms of the assumptions of its own psychology, as you can convince yourself daily by reading the French and German newspapers.

[3] The rest of the sentence is missing in a photocopy that was supplied of the original letter, and it could not be restored. From the context it may have read somewhat as follows: "to deny that the Jew possesses a psychology characteristically different from that of the non-Jew."

That people in some respects are also all alike is by this time a familiar fact, but it leads to no misunderstandings. These come from the differences, which should therefore be a worthy object of investigation.

Yours very truly, C. G. JUNG

To J. H. van der Hoop

Dear Colleague,   12 March 1934

It goes without saying that the International ("überstaatliche") Society is totally independent of the German group, which as you know cannot exist without being conformed. This necessity which has been imposed on the German group applies only inside Germany. The International Society would consist essentially of separate national groups. Since it is not possible, for political and other reasons, to form national groups everywhere, the necessity will arise of having to accept individual members who do not belong to any national group. There are no regulations about this at present, as I have purposely not yet worked out the statutes for the International Society. I want to carry through this work at the next Congress.[1]

As you will have seen from the *Zentralblatt*, the German Society considers itself an independent Society which, however, is affiliated as a unit to the International Society. This state of affairs, which is occasioned by the peculiar political conditions, does not apply to the organization of the International Society. The latter can accept any kind of member. Race, religion, and suchlike things are not taken into account, nor of course political sentiments. As a medical Society we are rather like the Geneva Convention,[2] which internationalizes doctors as politically neutral. I do not, however, disguise the fact that in individual cases all sorts of difficulties might arise for the Germans, for instance at Congresses if they take place in Germany. It may

[1] The statutes of the International Medical Society for Psychotherapy, drawn up by Jung, were ratified in May 1934 at the 7th Congress for Psychotherapy in Bad Nauheim. The constitution was approved by delegates from Switzerland, Holland, Sweden, Denmark, and Germany. It contained a clause enabling German Jewish doctors to become members of the International Society. Cf. "Circular Letter," CW 10, Appendix, pars. 1035ff., and ibid., par. 1060.

[2] The Geneva Convention of 1906 (preceded by one in 1864) gave international protection to the Red Cross and secured humane treatment for wounded or ill prisoners of war.

149

prove necessary under the circumstances to hold the Congresses abroad.

Certain necessities will also arise in connection with the general statutes. That is to say, in order to prevent the large number of German members from having the decisive voice in the conduct of the International Society, it is necessary that national groups be organized, or rather separate Societies which nominate some kind of representatives or delegates. In this way it will be possible to paralyze in a constitutive assembly what might be an overwhelming German influence. The Germans have a great interest in getting affiliated abroad and for this reason I do not fear that they will make special difficulties. (Errors excepted!) At any rate the experiment is worth trying.

Whether German psychotherapists can join the International Society without belonging to their own national group is a very delicate question. From our side we would naturally make no difficulties. But it is not impossible that the German political authorities would take steps against it. In that case the matter would not be in our hands. At any rate I shall suggest that individual psychotherapists be allowed membership alongside the national groups regardless of where they come from. But in the interests of the counterweight against Germany one would have to insist that these individual members are entitled to a vote for the election of the Committee only when they join a national group. For the reasons indicated above, as you can well understand, I would like the Committee to be elected by the delegates of the national groups.

The question of membership fees is a technicality to be cleared up at the ratification of the statutes at the next Congress.

With regard to the next Congress one of the major difficulties is that no general statutes yet exist and we are therefore not in a position to appear with delegates from national groups. So I would like to ask you to select a few colleagues privately, who are to take part in the constitutive assembly in Nauheim. We shall then discuss the statutes with these delegates and ratify them. We must do this with a limited number of people because experience has shown that it is quite impossible to discuss statutes properly when a Congress is in plenum. This can only be done in committee. For the rest, I think you can be assured that the Nazi outpourings of the German members are due to political necessity rather than to the religious convictions of the gentlemen in question.

I am very grateful to you for your positive cooperation. Without this it would be altogether impossible to cope with this insanely complicated situation in a fruitful way. If there is anything unclear in my letter I am ready to give you further information. With best regards,

Yours sincerely, c. g. jung

P.S. I have just heard that the Congress is fixed for May 10th in Nauheim.

To Claire Kaufmann

Dear Fräulein Kaufmann,   12 March 1934

I have nothing against your wish to write me letters "that reach him," on the contrary I must say that I am interested in what you think. Though I don't know who you are and your name conveys nothing to me, your philosophical discussion is none the less interesting for that. So if you don't expect me to give detailed answers, everything is in order.

It is serenely feminine of you to define a man as a philosopher "if his life is realized in the concept." We know very well that a man's ambition is for his concepts to be realized in life, whereas it is the most secret longing of all women for their lives to be realized in concepts. This is not a fundamental criticism, only a friendly hint at the very natural fact that a man wants to understand, whereas a woman wants to be understood. For this purpose she tries to make her life understandable to herself. With best regards,

Yours sincerely, c. g. jung

□ Berlin.

To Oluf Brüel

Dear Colleague,   19 March 1934

The disagreement between your views and Dr. Bjerre's is known to me.[1] I would not like to advocate an independent lay analysis. In this respect I hold a position in the middle. My experience over the years has convinced me that lay assistants of doctors can often do very useful work, but I abide by the principle that lay analysis should always

---

[1] Their disagreement concerned the role of lay analysts and their admission to the Society for Psychotherapy. Cf. Bjerre, 11 Jan. 35.

remain under the control of the doctor. If you cannot come to agreement with Dr. Bjerre, it is quite conceivable that the founding of two Societies should be kept in mind. Because of the political conditions the German Society is a separate Society anyway and our future international organization must be prepared to take these facts into account.

For the Nauheim Congress of the German Society, which takes place on May 10th, I shall work out a draft of new statutes which will then be submitted for ratification to a committee of delegates from all the national groups.

I too have regretted that Göring's Nazi manifesto appeared in the *Zentralblatt*. I erroneously assumed that this edict was intended for the German issue. Owing to the distance and the delay this causes I am not always *au courant* with everything that is going on. But I have given the managing editor strict instructions to keep the *Zentralblatt* neutral. For this reason I have also refused to let my introductory article,[2] coming out shortly in the *Zentralblatt*, appear in the special German issue, against the wishes of my German colleagues.

I shall also endeavour to keep the international organization on absolutely neutral ground and to regulate the relations between the groups by special statutes in such a way that it is impossible for any one group, no matter how numerous its members may be, to influence the policy of the Society as a whole.[3] At present I plan to have two delegates selected from each national group who will sit on a special committee that has to ratify the statutes. Germany like any other group will also be represented by only two members. I shall get the complicated legal conditions clarified so far as possible beforehand by a competent jurist. I have also charged Dr. Cimbal with the task of getting information from a competent quarter as to whether ratification of international statutes is possible at all in present-day Germany. If it is not, I would send my draft of the statutes as a circular to the various representatives of the national groups.

I have told my publisher of your wish to review my book.[4]

In conclusion, I would ask you to inform all those who have misgivings because of the political conditions in Germany that I stand

[2] "The State of Psychotherapy Today," CW 10, published in the *Zentralblatt*, VII:1 (1934).

[3] In order to avoid domination by any national group—in this case the German—it was stipulated that no group could muster more than 40% of the votes.

[4] *Wirklichkeit der Seele* (1934). The essays are distributed in CW 8, 10, 15, 16, 17.

on strictly neutral ground and that the German doctors are compelled only by the special circumstances of the time to make a political declaration of faith. Medical work, however, is an international affair, as already laid down by the Geneva Convention.

Thank you very much for kindly sending me your interesting offprints, also for the Danish communication,[5] which I shall pass on to the managing editor. With collegial greetings,

Yours sincerely, C. G. JUNG

[5] Cf. Bjerre, 22 Jan. 34, P.S.

To Wilhelm Laiblin

Dear Herr Laiblin,   19 March 1934

Best thanks for your letter, which interested me very much. Also for your two open letters to the bishop.[1]

As to your dream,[2] I entirely agree with you that the falling stars and moons refer to the collapse of a whole world of ideas that has become obsolescent. I think we may also hazard the conjecture that the three moons refer to the Trinity concept. The second part of the dream unquestionably refers to the anima, who offers you food and drink at an exorbitant price. There is nothing in the dream to indicate that there is any necessity, or a personal reason, to take up an attitude in public. The stars are falling anyway, one cannot and need not accelerate their fall. I think I can understand why the bishop has not replied to your letters. Anyone who has to run a church under these circumstances cannot concern himself with problems that cast doubt on the validity of this same church. The meaning of the dream is only that when the churches keep silent the psyche gives you food and drink. I certainly understand that in the present atmosphere, which strives for collective solutions, it was obvious that you should speak out for yourself. We are in fact not absolutely dependent on the unconscious but can and should on occasion act on our environment at our own discretion. For my part I would have looked at the dream in another light. It would

☐ Then schoolmaster in Stuttgart, later (from 1937) analytical psychologist.
[1] L. had addressed two letters to the bishop of the Evangelical Church, Württemberg, and, receiving no answer, published them as "Open Letters" in *Kommende Gemeinde* (Stuttgart), 5. Jahrg., vol. 4/5 (Dec. 1933). Prompted by a conflict of conscience he criticized certain problems of dogma.
[2] The sky changed, stars fell as in a cloudburst, and two, or even three, moons disintegrated into small fragments which finally disappeared.

have occurred to me that the unconscious, in a very unchristian manner, was urging me to go home and nourish myself in silence and bear the costs of such an undertaking.

So long as the Church does not practice restraint of conscience, it can safely be kept alive for all those, the weak ones, to whom no offence should be given. I am therefore extremely conservative and reserved in these matters, for I am convinced that the Catholic as well as the Protestant form of faith have not by any means lost their *raison d'être*. A renewal of religious beliefs has no form at present, so that the weak and those who are dependent on forms should not be prematurely precipitated into formlessness.

I am naturally in complete agreement with the content of your letters. If one says it at all, then one has to say it like that. I only ask myself whether it is the right time to say such things now. With best regards,

Yours sincerely, C. G. JUNG

To B. Cohen

Dear Dr. Cohen,   26 March 1934

I would like to thank you for your understanding and decent article[1] in the *Israelitisches Wochenblatt*. Such an event at a time like this, when stupidity is celebrating veritable orgies, is a rarity.

Your criticism of my lack of knowledge in things Jewish is quite justified. I don't understand Hebrew. But you seem to impute a political attitude to me which in reality I do not possess. I am absolutely not an opponent of the Jews even though I am an opponent of Freud's. I criticize him because of his materialistic and intellectualistic and—last but not least—irreligious attitude and not because he is a Jew. In so far as his theory is based in certain respects on Jewish premises, it is not valid for non-Jews. Nor do I deny my Protestant prejudice. Had Freud been more tolerant of the ideas of others I would still be standing at his side today. I consider his intolerance—and it is this that repels me—a personal idiosyncrasy.

The editorial comment, for which you are not responsible, treats itself to the joke of taking my reference to the Chinese[2] as an anti-

☐ Friedrichstadt, Germany.
[1] "Ist C. G. Jung 'gleichgeschaltet'?" (Has Jung Conformed [to Nazi ideology]?), *Israelitisches Wochenblatt für die Schweiz*, 35. Jahrg., No. 11 (16 Mar. 1934).
[2] Cf. "Editorial (1933)," CW 10, Appendix, par. 1014. In 1928 Jung had written

Semitic allusion. What do these people know of the Chinese? They have no inkling that I have been cudgelling my brains over the *I Ching* ever since 1919.

At present I am a . . .³ who cannot be interpreted politically. If one nevertheless does so, one falls from one astonishment into the next. My relation with Germany is very recent and is due to idiotic altruism and not at all to political sentiment. The problem of "anti-Semitism" has been thrown up for the psychotherapists but not for the political daily press. Or must it always go on as it used to in France, when they wouldn't accept the concept of Dementia praecox because it was "made in Germany"? Thirty years ago a French scholar told me: "Savez-vous, il y a des frontières politiques même en science." In psychotherapy the last thing one should do is to tar everything with the same brush. Infinite nuances are needed if justice is to be done to human beings.

Very sincerely, C. G. JUNG

---

in *Two Essays,* par. 240, n. 8: ". . . it is a quite unpardonable mistake to accept the conclusions of a Jewish psychology as generally valid. Nobody would dream of taking Chinese or Indian psychology as binding upon ourselves. The cheap accusation of anti-Semitism that has been levelled at me on the ground of this criticism is about as intelligent as accusing me of an anti-Chinese prejudice."
³ Lacuna in file carbon copy: possibly the word was ζῷον (animal).

To Max Guggenheim

Dear Colleague,   28 March 1934

I realize that it is very disquieting when one sees somebody in my position having anything to do with the conformed ["gleichge-schaltet"] Germany. But you should not forget that "Gleichschalt-ung" in Germany is a political fact which, however, does not get rid of the other fact that there are human beings in Germany. You may be sure that if I had done for Russia what I have done for the Germans I would undoubtedly have been condemned as a Bolshevist, for everything there is just as politicized and thoroughly conformed. But the work of Nansen and the Quakers continues nevertheless and no one would assert that the Quakers are Bolshevists.

If you disregard the persecution of the Jews in Germany, you must

☐ Lausanne.

admit that there is a medical Society there which is very important for us in Switzerland. It is therefore not a matter of indifference what happens to psychotherapy in that country. At critical moments I had to look behind the scenes and what I saw has prompted me to intervene, not least because I was thinking of what will happen in Switzerland in the future. You will perhaps have noticed that we Swiss are not very inventive, but in many of our innovations are influenced in the highest degree from abroad. So if I have attempted to forestall certain developments in Germany, I have done so at the source from which sooner or later it is quite sure that effects will flow into Switzerland. As a psychotherapist I cannot be indifferent to the future of psychotherapy. Its development in Germany will also be crucial for us. Freud once told me, very rightly: "The fate of psychotherapy will be decided in Germany." To begin with it was doomed to absolute perdition because it was considered wholly Jewish. I have broken this prejudice by my intervention and have made life possible not only for the so-called Aryan psychotherapists but for the Jewish ones as well. What with the hue and cry against me it has been completely forgotten that by far the greatest number of psychotherapists in Germany are Jews. People do not know, nor is it said in public, that I have intervened personally with the regime on behalf of certain Jewish psychotherapists. If the Jews start railing at me this is shortsighted in the extreme and I hope you will do what you can to combat this idiotic attitude. The existence of the Society for Psychotherapy, which has very many Jewish members, is now assured, also the membership of Jewish doctors.[1] Actually the Jews should be thankful to me for that, but it seems that the—as you say—paranoid attitude prevents them from seeing clearly. Also the *Zentralblatt* has now been placed on a secure footing and I have successfully ensured that the Jewish editor of the review section, Allers in Vienna, can do his work as before. During the war people moaned that the Allies used the hunger blockade against Germany. The understandable opposition of the Jews to the Hitler regime now makes it quits: everything German is outlawed, regardless of whether people are involved who are entirely innocent politically. I find that shortsighted too. With collegial regards,

Yours sincerely, c. g. j u n g

[1] Cf. Hoop, 12 Mar. 34, no. 1.

To E. Beit von Speyer

Dear Frau von Speyer,   13 April 1934

As you have probably noticed, your letter has not been answered. The reason is that I was away from home and found it only on my return. I am very sorry this has happened, but it was holiday time.

Thank you very much for your interesting picture. It is a correct representation of your basic psychic attitude. It is characteristic that the four functions are represented by four animals. This means that the principles of these functions still have an instinctive form. There are possibilities of further development.

I have fallen foul of contemporary history. From abroad one can hardly have anything to do with Germany without becoming politically suspect on one side or the other. People now think I am a blood-boltered anti-Semite because I have helped the German doctors to consolidate their Psychotherapeutic Society and because I have said there are certain differences between Jewish and so-called Aryan psychology which are mainly due to the fact that the Jews have a cultural history that is 2,000 years older than the so-called Aryan.[1] There has been a terrific shindy over this. It is no pleasure to be well known. You are then like a city on a mountain and cannot remain hidden. With cordial greetings,

Yours sincerely, C. G. JUNG

☐ Frankfurt a. M.
[1] Cf. Pupato, 2 Mar. 34, n. 1.

To Gustav Richard Heyer

My dear Heyer,   20 April 1934

Although the prospect is not at all rosy, I must nevertheless go to Nauheim[1] to keep the promise I made the Germans that I would do everything possible to promote the cohesion of the Society. Whether I shall succeed is another matter. Personally I doubt it. If Prof. Göring

☐ M.D., (1890–1967), German analytical psychologist. Cf. his *Seelenführung* (1929); *The Organism of the Mind* (orig. 1933/ tr. 1935); *Praktische Seelenheilkunde* (1935); *Vom Kraftfeld der Seele* (1949); *Seelenkunde im Umbruch der Zeit* (1964). Jung's reviews of the 1935 publications are in CW 18.
[1] The 7th Congress for Psychotherapy in Bad Nauheim, 10–13 May 1934. Cf. Hoop, 12 Mar. 34, n. 1.

turns a purely medical affair into a political one there is nothing we foreigners can do about it. But we must first wait and see.

I must tell you that I should be very pleased, not least also for personal reasons, if you came to Nauheim too. I have the feeling I am treading on ground the nature of which I know far too little, and I must have somebody near to give me the necessary information. I cannot possibly rely on Cimbal and the others as their interests and motives are so obscure that an outsider like me cannot see through them.

I regard this Congress as a unique and perhaps final attempt to promote a general cohesion though it may not be at all timely. But one must have done so in reality before one can withdraw with a good conscience. I am thinking anyway of not retaining this presidency for too long, which was forced on me only because of the precarious situation, and of passing it on as quickly as possible, since for me it involves a load of work which I would never have accepted under normal conditions.

I would like to ask you to let me know by return postcard whether you consider it opportune if I lecture in Nauheim.² I personally have the feeling I had better not, as I want to adopt a waiting and watchful attitude. I gave Prof. Göring my consent to lecture only very hesitantly and with reservation, so that I could withdraw without further ado. Meanwhile with best regards,

Yours ever, JUNG

² Jung did in fact deliver a lecture: "A Review of the Complex Theory," CW 8. His favourable references to Freud enraged the Nazis.

To Leslie Hollingsworth

[ORIGINAL IN ENGLISH]

Dear Mr. Hollingsworth, 21 April 1934

Of course one can guess what the religion of the future might be, but it's hardly worthwhile guessing. Surely the Christians of 80 A.D. guessed too, but they never would have guessed the splendours of the Vatican and Alexander VI on St. Peter's throne and the popes of Avignon and 10,000 Christian heretics burnt in Spain, etc. So one never can tell how the future religion will look or what it will be based on. Also one can't say whether the religion will be based upon

□ New York City.

love or upon fear, because Christianity has shown that even a religion of love can be based on fear, and moreover it can cause fear just as well as love. We also don't know whether it will be a brotherhood of man or anything as lovely as that.

Religions are not necessarily lovely or good. They are powerful manifestations of the spirit and we have no power to check the spirit. Surely great catastrophes such as earthquakes or fires are no longer convincing to the modern mind, but we don't need them. There are things much more gruesome, namely man's insanity, the great mental contagions from which we actually suffer most indubitably. Everybody wants peace and understanding and with an infernal fatality the nations are working for war and misunderstanding. Not even the most modest disarmament has been possible. That shows where our real catastrophes come from. Curiously enough people are still too unconscious to become aware of the real dangers they are threatened with.

By the way, my so-called article in the *Cosmopolitan Magazine*[1] was an interview with a reporter and not an article written by myself. I have not even seen a copy of it.

Sincerely yours, C. G. JUNG

[1] "Does the World Stand on the Verge of Spiritual Rebirth?" *Hearst's International Cosmopolitan* (New York), Apr. 1934, pp. 179–82, 245. Included with other interviews in the forthcoming collection *C. G. Jung Speaking.*

To B. Cohen

Dear Dr. Cohen, 28 April 1934

Best thanks for your friendly letter. My reference to China seems to have given rise to all sorts of misunderstandings. If I understand your letter aright, you appear to assume that I think there are parallels between Jewish and Oriental teachings. I wouldn't dream of making such an assertion and it was not intended under any circumstances. I mentioned China only because I wanted to show drastically how nonsensical it is to accuse me of anti-Semitism when I declare there are differences between Jews and so-called Aryans. I therefore said one could just as well accuse me of an anti-Chinese bias because I stressed in my book *The Secret of the Golden Flower*, which I brought out with Richard Wilhelm, that there is an essential difference between the Western and the Eastern mentality, in consequence of which we cannot directly take over Oriental teachings and methods without impairing our own psyche. I am convinced from my own experience of Orientals that they have never misunderstood this critical attitude of mine as European snobbery. The unfortunate prejudices and mis-understandings that exist between Jews and Christians have given rise to so much touchiness that one has only to allude to certain differences and one is instantly accused of hostility. I must emphasize again and again that it makes an enormous difference whether some-one has a 1,000- or a 3,000-year-old culture behind him. In the same way, one can see at once whether he has an ancestral line of educated people or of primitives. Especially among Indians and in Indian mys-ticism I have seen how enormous this difference is. There are doc-trines which suit the Indians themselves very well but which one cannot even mention to a European because they provoke the most violent misunderstandings. The same is true of Freud's views. They can be discussed in a cool and abstract atmosphere but they have a destructive effect on the general public, as I have unfortunately seen only too often. This is perhaps the deeper meaning in that story of the Rabbi, which you surely know: He knew that a dog that barks doesn't bite but was not certain if the dog also knew it, so he pre-ferred to take to his heels before the barking dog. Again with best thanks and kind regards,

. . .

Yours sincerely, c. g. j u n g

To James Kirsch

My dear Kirsch,   26 May 1934

I am very glad you have written to me once again. It appears that amusing rumours are being spread about me. The only unquestion-able fact behind all this stupid gossip is that as honorary president of the International Society for Psychotherapy I could not leave the Society in the lurch at the moment when Kretschmer resigned. I have been urgently requested by the German doctors to retain this po-

□ M.D., analytical psychologist, then in Palestine, formerly in Germany, now in Los Angeles. Cf. his *The Royal Self* (1966). — Lengthy extracts from this letter have been published in Ernest Harms, "Carl Gustav Jung—Defender of Freud and the Jews," *The Psychiatric Quarterly* (Utica, N.Y.), April 1946; also in *Psychological Perspectives* (Los Angeles), III:1 (1972).

sition and have subsequently done what anyone would have done in my place, namely, my duty towards the International Society. This consisted essentially in preserving the framework of the international organization and in affiliating to it the German Society. This has now been accomplished at the last Nauheim Congress. We can also record the satisfying fact that at my suggestion a special provision was adopted whereby German Jewish doctors can individually join the International Society. They have thus become members with equal rights.

I need hardly go into the other rumours. It is a downright lie to quote me as saying that Jews are dishonest in analysis. Anyone who believes I could say anything so idiotic must think me extraordinarily stupid. Neither have I addressed Hitler over the radio or in any other manner, nor have I made any political statements.

With regard to my opinion that the Jews so far as we can see do not create a cultural form of their own,[1] this opinion is based on 1. historical data, 2. the fact that the specific cultural achievement of the Jew is most clearly developed within a host culture, where he very frequently becomes its actual carrier or its promoter. This task is so specific and demanding that it is hardly conceivable how any individual Jewish culture could arise alongside it. Since very specific conditions do in fact exist in Palestine, I have inserted a cautious "so far as we can see" in my sentence. I would in no wise deny the possibility that something specific is being created there, but so far I do not know it. I simply cannot discover anything anti-Semitic in this opinion.

Coming to your suggestion that I should write a special work on this question, this has already been anticipated, as I have proposed a correspondence with Dr. Neumann,[2] who has worked with me and is now also in Palestine, that will deal with all controversial questions. So far I have heard nothing from him.

The Jewish Christ-complex is a very remarkable affair. As you know, I completely agree with you in this matter. The existence of this complex makes for a somewhat hysterical attitude of mind which has become especially noticeable to me during the present anti-Christian attacks upon myself. The mere fact that I speak of a difference between Jewish and Christian psychology suffices to allow anyone to voice the prejudice that I am an anti-Semite. Or, in the opinion of the *Schweizer Israelitisches Wochenblatt*, my assertion that I am as

[1] Cf. "The State of Psychotherapy Today," par. 353.
[2] This plan did not materialize.

little an anti-Semite as an anti-Chinese proves my intention to compare the Jews with a Mongolian horde.[3] This hypersensitivity is simply pathological and makes every discussion practically impossible. As you know, Freud previously accused me of anti-Semitism because I could not abide his soulless materialism. The Jew directly solicits anti-Semitism with his readiness to scent out anti-Semitism everywhere. I cannot see why the Jew, unlike any so-called Christian, is incapable of assuming that he is being criticized personally when one has an opinion about him. Why must it always be assumed that one wants to damn the Jewish people? Surely the individual is not the people? I regard this as an inadmissible method of silencing one's adversary. In the great majority of cases I have got along very well with my Jewish patients and colleagues. It happens with other people, too, that I have had to criticize the individual, but they do not ascribe it to the fact that they are English, American or French. However, there is one exception worth mentioning, and that is the German. It has happened more than once that when I criticized a German he immediately concluded that I hate the Germans. It is really too cheap to try to hide one's inferiority behind a political prejudice. . . .

. . . You ought to know me sufficiently well to realize that an unindividual stupidity like anti-Semitism cannot be laid at my door. You know well enough how very much I take the human being as a personality and how I continually endeavour to lift him out of his collective condition and make him an individual. This, as you know, is possible only if he acknowledges his peculiarity which has been forced on him by fate. No one who is a Jew can become a human being without *knowing* that he is a Jew, since this is the basis from which he can reach out towards a higher humanity. This holds good for all nations and races. Nationalism—disagreeable as it is—is therefore a *sine qua non*, but the individual must not remain stuck in it. On the other hand, in so far as he is a particle in the mass he must not raise himself above it either. As a human being I am a European, as an atom in the mass I am a Swiss bourgeois, domiciled at Seestrasse 228, Küsnacht near Zurich.

. . .

If you see Dr. Neumann, please give him my greetings and remind him that I am waiting to hear from him.

In conclusion, I want to tell you that my new book *Wirklichkeit*

---

[3] Cf. Cohen, 26 Mar. 34, n. 1. In an Editorial Comment to C.'s article the editor took exception to Jung's argument that he was as little anti-Semitic as anti-Chinese. (The expression "Mongolian horde" was not used by the editor.)

der Seele has appeared. I have included in it an essay by a Jewish author[4] on the psychology of the Old Testament, just to annoy the Nazis and all those who have decried me as an anti-Semite. The next thing that will be invented about me is that I suffer from a complete absence of convictions and am neither an anti-Semite nor a Nazi. We happen to live in a time which overflows with lunacy. *Quem Deus vult perdere prius dementat.*[5] With kindest regards,

Yours, C. G. JUNG
et semper idem.

[4] Hugo Rosenthal, "Der Typengegensatz in der jüdischen Religionsgeschichte."
[5] "Those whom the gods would destroy they first drive mad."

To M. H. Göring

Dear Professor Göring,   7 June 1934

Dr. Cimbal informs me that difficulties have arisen with Professor Kretschmer. Naturally I do not want to meddle with these domestic German matters, but would only like to clarify my position so that you are oriented about my intentions.

Should it ever happen that psychotherapy in Germany is subordinated to psychiatry it would simply be a catastrophe. The psychiatrists have always made it their business to suppress psychotherapy in any form. We have never had any encouragement from psychiatry, and psychiatry has never taken any interest in our endeavours. The psychiatrist understands nothing of psychotherapy in principle because he is never in the position of having to practise it. One could just as well subordinate internal medicine to surgery. So if it came to the point where German psychotherapy was annexed by psychiatry and thus lost its independence, I would not hesitate to resign, for I would then lose faith in the future of psychotherapy in Germany. I would have to do this as a token of protest vis-à-vis my own country, where I have always staked my life on keeping psychotherapy separate from both psychiatry and neurology.

Yours sincerely, C. G. JUNG

☐ See Allers, 23 Nov. 33, n. 3.

To Gerhard Adler

Dear Dr. Adler,   9 June 1934

Best thanks for your detailed letter,[1] the tenor of which I find completely acceptable. I have pointed out in several places in my article that Freud does not appear to me as the typical exponent of the Jewish attitude to the unconscious. In fact I expressly state that his view of it is not binding for all Jews. Nevertheless there is something typically Jewish about his attitude, which I can document with your own words: "When a Jew forgets his roots, he is doubly and triply in danger of mechanization and intellectualization." With these words you have laid your finger on exactly what is typically Jewish. It is typically Jewish that Freud can forget his roots to such an extent.[2] It is typically Jewish that the Jews can utterly forget that they are Jews despite the fact that they know they are Jews. That is what is suspicious about Freud's attitude and not his materialistic, rationalistic view of the world alone. Freud cannot be held responsible for the latter. In this respect he is simply a typical exponent of the expiring 19th century, just like Haeckel,[3] Dubois-Reymond,[4] or that *Kraft und Stoff* ass Büchner.[5] These people, however, are not as completely rootless as the Jewish rationalist, for which reason they are also much more naïve and therefore less dangerous. So when I criticize Freud's Jewishness I am not criticizing the *Jews* but rather that damnable capacity of the Jew, as exemplified by Freud, to deny his own nature. Actually you should be glad that I think so rigorously, for then I speak in the interests of all Jews who want to find their

[1] A. wrote a long letter expressing concern about certain passages in "The State of Psychotherapy Today."
[2] Freud always felt himself to be a Jew by race but at the same time quite estranged from Judaism as a religion, the commandments of which he hated. He was "very conversant with the Bible," thinking highly of its ethical teachings (Jones, II, pp. 375f.), but felt "a radical opposition to the practices of traditional Judaism." Cf. Ernst Simon, "Freud, the Jew," *Yearbook II of the Leo Baeck Institute of Jews from Germany* (1957), pp. 277, 279. Cf. also Neumann, "Freud und das Vaterbild," *Merkur* (Stuttgart), Aug. 1956.
[3] Ernst Heinrich Haeckel (1834–1919), German biologist, professor of zoology at Jena, enthusiastic supporter of Darwin. He developed a materialistic, monist philosophy based on the theory of evolution.
[4] Emil Dubois-Reymond (1818–1896), German physiologist, professor of physiology at Berlin; adhered to a materialistic philosophy.
[5] Ludwig Büchner (1824–1899), German physician and philosopher. Apostle of extreme materialism in his main work *Kraft und Stoff* (1855).

way back to their own nature. I think the religious Jews of our time should summon up the courage to distinguish themselves clearly from Freud, because they need to prove that spirit is stronger than blood. But the prejudice that whoever criticizes Freud is criticizing the Jews always demonstrates to us that blood is thicker than spirit, and in this respect anti-Semitism has in all conscience learnt much from the Jewish prejudice.

As to my assertion that the Jews have not created a "cultural form" of their own, please note that I did not say "culture." I expressly stated that the Jews have a culture nearly 3,000 years old, but one can have a culture without possessing a cultural form of one's own. For instance, Switzerland has a culture but no cultural form. It has still to be proved conclusively that the Jews have ever created a cultural form of their own. At any rate they haven't in the last 2,000 years. It is also difficult to see how a relatively small folk ranging from India through Europe to America would be in a position to create such a form. I came across the same objection in a letter from a Jew a few days ago. Considering the proverbial intelligence of the Jews it has always seemed to me incomprehensible that they can no longer see the simplest truths because they are blinded by hypersensitivity. Blood is undoubtedly thicker than spirit, but, as you very rightly say, it is a tremendous danger for the Jew to get lost in the viscosity of sheer materialism.

As to your third point, the negative value of the unconscious,[6] I ought to have said the personal unconscious. But I thought it would be sufficiently clear from the context that the personal unconscious was meant, since when Freud speaks of the unconscious he always means just that.

Hoping that I have cleared up at least these misunderstandings, and with cordial greetings, I remain,

Yours sincerely, C. G. JUNG

[6] Cf. "The State of Psychotherapy Today," CW 10 par. 353: "As a member of a race with a three-thousand-year-old civilization, the Jew, like the cultured Chinese, has a wider area of psychological consciousness than we. Consequently it is *in general* less dangerous for the Jew to put a negative value on his unconscious."

To Mark Wyman Richardson

[ORIGINAL IN ENGLISH]

Dear Dr. Richardson,   14 June 1934

Thank you very much for kindly sending me the offprints of the Margery case.[1] I know the case from the Proceedings of the American Society for Psychical Research, but I'm indeed very glad to have the whole collection of offprints, as the Margery case has interested me to an extraordinary extent. The phenomena you have observed are really most illuminating, particularly from the philosophical point of view. For many years I'm closely following the progress of mediumistic research, but I must say that I hardly ever came across a more wonderful case of mediumism than the Margery case. Though I appreciate the enormous contribution to science which is due to the exact observation of mediumistic phenomena, I always miss the ideological, i.e., psychological side of the reports of such a case. I would be very much interested to know something about the personal biography of the medium and at the same time whatever the medium knows about the spiritual agencies involved in her mediumistic performances. I'm not afraid of unaccountable spirit messages because I'm interested in their psychology which provides material to me for comparison with what I already know of the contents of the unconscious. Would it be possible, for instance, for the medium to write a careful biography of herself, f.i. in the way Mrs. Espérance has written a story of her life? Her little book[2] is a most valuable psychological document and I wish we could possess more of such honest and straightforward statements. It would help our psychological research considerably. At all events I'm most indebted to you for your kindness in letting me know of the results of your observations. They truly throw a light upon the darkest and yet most important side of the human soul, namely upon the spot where it touches transcendent reality. I quite agree with you that such observations enlarge the horizon of man and give him a deeper insight into the [. . .][3]

☐ M.D., (1867–1947), of Boston.
[1] Margery, pseudonym of Mrs. L.R.G. Crandon, a highly controversial American medium (d. 1941). Investigators discredited the physical phenomena she produced as trickery, but the question of her direct-voice mediumship remains unresolved. Cf. reports of séances with Margery in *Proceedings of the Society for Psychical Research* (Glasgow), XXXVI (1928) (by E. J. Dingwall); XXXVIII (1928–29), (book review by T. Besterman); XXXIX (1930–31), (by V. J. Woolley and E. Brackenburg).
[2] Elizabeth d'Espérance, *Shadow Land, or, Light from the Other Side* (1897). She was a medium famous for her alleged materialization phenomena.
[3] The rest is missing in the file carbon copy and cannot be restored.

To C. E. Benda

Dear Colleague, 19 June 1934

Best thanks for kindly sending me your offprints.

I wonder what can have caused you to misconstrue my article[1] to the point where you consider it necessary to defend Jewish culture against me. No one is more deeply convinced than I that the Jews are a people with a culture. Between culture and cultural form there is, as we know, an essential difference. The Swiss, for instance, are a people with a culture but no cultural form of their own. For this, as you rightly remark, certain conditions are needed, such as the size of a people, its ties to the soil, etc. In my opinion the Bible is not a cultural form but a document.

A people with no ties to the soil, having neither land nor homeland, is commonly called nomadic. If you will submit these two points to which you took exception to unprejudiced scrutiny, you will probably come to the conclusion that there is no unjustified criticism in them. Had I said of the Jews what I said of the Germans in the same article, there might have been some cause for excitement, since "barbarism"[2] comes close to a value judgment.

That psychoanalysis is, so to speak, a Jewish national affair is not my invention but Freud's.[3] When I wrote my book *Wandlungen und Symbole der Libido* and deviated at one point from orthodox theory, Freud suddenly accused me of anti-Semitism.[4] From this I must conclude that I had somehow trespassed against the Jews. This prejudice has stuck to me ever since and has been repeated by all Freudians, thereby confirming every time that psychoanalysis is in

□ Berlin.
[1] "The State of Psychotherapy Today."
[2] Cf. ibid., par. 354.
[3] Cf. Freud's letter (1908) to Abraham in Jones, II, p. 53: "Be tolerant and don't forget that really it is easier for you to follow my thoughts than for Jung, since to begin with you are completely independent, and then racial relationship brings you closer to my intellectual constitution, whereas he, being a Christian [here Jones adds in a note: "The customary Jewish expression for 'non-Jews.'"] and the son of a pastor, can only find his way to me against great inner resistances. His adherence is therefore all the more valuable. I was almost going to say that it is only his emergence on the scene that has removed from psycho-analysis the danger of becoming a Jewish national affair."
[4] "On the History of the Psycho-Analytical Movement" (orig. 1914), Standard Edn. 14, p. 43: "[Jung] seemed ready to enter into a friendly relationship with me and for my sake to give up certain racial prejudices which he had previously permitted himself."

fact a Jewish psychology which nobody else can criticize without making himself guilty of anti-Semitism.

Incidentally, if I were a Jew-eater I would hardly bring out books together with Jews[5] as I have just done, or introduce books by Jewish authors.[6] In the present overheated political atmosphere it is of course understandable that clear vision is somewhat obfuscated. Hence I cannot blame my critics if they themselves succumb to the childish idea that I wrote my books out of sheer resentment. The impassioned delusions of our time impair our judgment and cause spectres to appear where none exist. With collegial regards,

Yours sincerely, C. G. JUNG

[5] Cf. Kirsch, 26 May 34, n. 4.
[6] Cf. his foreword to Gerhard Adler, *Entdeckung der Seele* (1934), now in CW 18.

To G. A. Farner

Dear Dr. Farner,   29 June 1934

Best thanks for kindly sending me your travel book.[1] I am no despiser of such fare, and it tastes all the better to me when it is brought into the house with friendly feelings.

You could easily have spoken to me on Sunday. When I am in evidence I am accessible. Only invisibility means: Leave me in peace!

As a matter of fact I did build the round tower myself with two workmen.[2] I learnt to split stones in the Bollingen quarries and the masons also taught me a lot and I learnt their art relatively quickly with a certain native intelligence. You correctly surmise that one of the motives was the workableness of matter to compensate the airiness of psychology. The historical form had to be there in order to give the ancestral souls an abode pleasing to them. I can tell you that the doyen of that corps chuckled when he found himself again in the accustomed frugal rooms, smelling of smoke and grits, and occasionally of wine and smoked bacon. As you know, in olden times the ancestral souls lived in pots in the kitchen. *Lares* and *penates* are important psychological personages who should not be frightened away by too much modernity.

Yours sincerely, C. G. JUNG

☐ Ph.D., Swiss psychologist. Cf. Maeder, 22 Jan. 34, n. 1.
[1] *Sturmfahrten im Faltkajak* (1930).
[2] Cf. *Memories*, ch. VIII.

Anonymous

Dear Frau N., 13 July 1934

If X. feels particularly well when he studies religion and philosophical literature it is a sure sign that this activity is vital to him. So there is nothing for it, aside from physical treatment, but to support this tendency in his nature. It is, however, striking that a young man of 30 should have such a vital relation to ideas of this kind, a relation which even affects the body. Whatever the reason for this may be, it seems to be a matter of the greatest importance. But one question remains to be answered: is it absolutely certain that X. is not somewhere circumventing a vitally important collective demand, and that as a result an unnatural intensification of his spiritual activity has set in? If so, the impairment of his working capacity would signify a resistance from the side of instinct. Unfortunately I know far too little of X.'s personal life to presume to an opinion, but with young people one must always be careful in this respect, because the demands of instinct are only too easily covered up by deceptive spiritual interests. But if that is not the case, there is probably no alternative for him than to come to terms with the unconscious, for better or worse. I would conjecture that this is so because middle life has set in too early in consequence of a relatively short life expectancy.[1]

. . .

With best regards,

Yours sincerely, C. G. JUNG

☐ Berlin.
[1] In fact, X. died at 55.

To Elined Kotschnig

[ORIGINAL IN ENGLISH]

Dear Mrs. Kotschnig, 23 July 1934

The symbol of the bee,[1] though belonging to the general class of the insects, is a very particular one. Insects in general always point

☐ Analytical psychologist, Washington, D.C.
[1] K. described a picture done by a patient of hers consisting "of a score or more of bees . . . distributed pretty evenly over the sheet of drawing-paper, and grouped in a general way about a pink rose . . . which occupied the centre of the page." The patient was completely "unaware of the whole erotic field."

169

to the sympathetic system, usually demonstrating a certain activity therein, owing to the fact that insects possess only a sympathetic system which is highly automatic and mechanical. The bee in the case of your patient shows an intense activity, a continuous vibration that produces a sort of humming sound like a swarm of bees. It is a peculiar restlessness in the lower centres closely associated with sex. The bee is the symbol of the dormant Kundalini that is ready to strike. Therefore in the Tantra Yoga[2] it is said that she produces a humming sound like a swarm of erotically excited bees. It shows a peculiar restlessness which draws all the attention to itself, so that the conscious becomes almost inaccessible to outward impressions and arguments.

The purpose of such an activity is never what the conscious would assume, namely an immediate erotic experience. On the contrary, it is an intense enhancing of the Self. This is the reason why such people always fall in love with those who don't love them in return. It is in order to prevent the erotic experience, because such an experience would alienate the person from her secret purpose, which, at least for the time being, is individuation. In this case it would mean a greater awareness of herself. As a matter of fact the bee symbolizes that instinct which makes her thoroughly autoerotic. This is not wrong for the moment, as she is not grown up enough. In certain respects she is still like a child who needs all her libido for her own development. The bee as it is now presumably symbolizes erotic fantasies and thoughts that sting her. The picture she has drawn proves that the bee-instinct is seeking the Rose, i.e., the mandala, the symbol for the Self.

Sincerely yours, C. G. JUNG

[2] In Tantra Yoga the Kundalini serpent lies coiled up in *muladhara*, the nethermost *chakra* (cf. Wilhelm, 27 Aug. 29, n. 2) and in meditation is experienced as moving upwards through the other *chakras*. Cf. also Anon., 5 July 32, n. 2.

To Hermann Hesse

Dear Herr Hesse,   18 September 1934

Thank you for your letter and enclosures. I am much amused that you think I have "become professorial."[1] Evidently I have success-

□ (Handwritten.)

[1] In an essay "Ueber einige Bücher," *Die Neue Rundschau*, vol. 45, II (1934), Hesse used this phrase in his review of Jung's *Wirklichkeit der Seele*.

fully deceived even your eagle eye. One must have a good exterior "dans ce meilleur des mondes possibles";[2] for there is no point in having none. Pearls should not be cast before swine.

You do me an injustice with your remarks on sublimation.[3] It is not from resentment that I fight this idea, but from copious experience of patients (and doctors too) who shirk the difficulty every time and "sublimate," i.e., simply repress. *Sublimatio* is part of the royal art where the true gold[4] is made. Of this Freud knows nothing, worse still, he barricades all the paths that could lead to the true *sublimatio*. This is just about the opposite of what Freud understands by sublimation.[5] It is not a *voluntary and forcible* channeling of instinct into a spurious field of application, but an *alchymical transformation* for which *fire* and the black *prima materia*[6] are needed. *Sublimatio* is a great mystery. Freud has appropriated this concept and usurped it for the sphere of the will and the bourgeois, rationalistic ethos. *Anathema sit!* But who understands any of these things today? Therefore they remain in darkness. With best regards,

Yours sincerely, C. G. JUNG

[2] Leibniz, *Essais de Theodicée sur la bonté de Dieu, la liberté de l'homme et l'origine du mal* (1710), declared this world to be the best of all possible worlds since God, in his power, wisdom, and goodness, could choose only the best.

[3] In his review H. defended Freud's use of the term "sublimation" against Jung's criticism of it in "Sigmund Freud in His Historical Setting," CW 15, par. 53.

[4] The meditative, symbolic aspect of alchemy was concerned with producing the "true gold," which is both chthonic and spiritual, male and female, body and spirit, light and darkness. It represents the union of opposites, for which reason it was also called the *res simplex*, simple substance, which "refers, ultimately, to God." Jung, "The Visions of Zosimos," CW 13, par. 117, n. 117.

[5] Freud, "Five Lectures on Psycho-Analysis," Standard Edn., 11, pp. 53f., defines sublimation as a "process of development . . . in which the energy of the infantile wishful impulses is not cut off [as in repression] but remains ready for use—the unserviceable aim of the various impulses being replaced by one that is higher, and perhaps no longer sexual."

[6] The origin and end (*lapis*) of the alchemical opus. Cf. *Psychology and Alchemy*, pars. 425ff.

To James Kirsch

My dear Kirsch,   29 September 1934

Unfortunately I had so many urgent tasks to cope with that I never got down to writing to you in peace. Though I thoroughly approve of the tone and tendency of your article,[1] there is one thing I object to, and this is that I identify the Jew with Freud. First of all I don't, and secondly it is always being pointed out just from the Jewish side (as recently by Kronfeld)[2] that psychoanalysis (= Freud and Adler) is Jewish in spirit.[3] If that is said by the Jews themselves, I am forced to assume that at least a large number of authoritative Jews flatly identify themselves with Freudian psychology. From this one must conclude that they feel the reductive standpoint is largely in accord with their own psychology, especially as no other standpoint has been espoused from that quarter. Silence may be taken as consensus. I think entirely as you do, that it would be extremely important and salutary for the Jews to see the positive side of the unconscious.

What is of the greatest concern to me is that a way should be found to combat the touchiness and affectivity that poison everything. As it is one can never reach an objective understanding. Formerly I was counted a hater of Germans because I criticized their barbarism, now the Jews are accusing me of trying to curry favour with them. . . .

With regard to your patient, it is quite correct that her dreams are occasioned by *you*. The feminine mind is the earth waiting for the seed. That is the meaning of the transference. Always the more unconscious person gets spiritually fecundated by the more conscious one. Hence the guru in India. This is an age-old truth. As soon as certain patients come to me for treatment, the type of dream changes. In the deepest sense we all dream not *out of ourselves* but out of what lies *between us and the other*.

Cordial greetings,

Ever sincerely, C. G. JUNG

☐ (Handwritten.) Last par. in *Psychological Perspectives*, III:1 (1972).
[1] "Einige Bemerkungen zu einem Aufsatz von C. G. Jung," *Jüdische Rundschau* (Berlin), No. 43 (29 May 34), a discussion of "The State of Psychotherapy Today" from the Jewish angle. Other contributions were made by Erich Neumann (No. 48, 15 June 34) and Gerhard Adler (No. 62, 3 Aug. 34).
[2] Arthur Kronfeld, Berlin, psychiatrist and psychotherapist.
[3] Cf. Benda, 19 June 34, n. 3.

Anonymous

[ORIGINAL IN ENGLISH]

My dear N.,   29 September 1934

Thank you for your letter! Marriage is indeed a brutal reality, yet the *experimentum crucis* of life. I hope you learn to *endure* and not to struggle against the suppressing necessities of fate. Only thus you remain in the centre.

I should like to come over to England once more. But I find it exceedingly difficult to prepare new lectures. I have almost no time.

Please give my best regards to Mrs. N.

Cordially yours, C. G. JUNG

☐ (Handwritten.) London.

To Hermann Hesse

Dear Herr Hesse,   1 October 1934

Best thanks for your detailed answer.[1]

Naturally we shouldn't quarrel about words. Nevertheless I would note in all humility that the expression "sublimation" is not appropriate in the case of the artist because with him it is not a question of transforming a primary instinct but rather of a primary instinct (the artistic instinct) gripping the whole personality to such an extent that all other instincts are in abeyance, thus giving rise to the work of divine perfection.

Excuse this terminological hair-splitting, but we have to deal with

---

[1] H. sent a long and detailed answer to Jung's letter of 18 Sept. 34 in which he defined his attitude to sublimation. The following passages are quoted for their intrinsic interest: "I share and agree with your view of Freud's sublimation . . . but the concept as such is important to me for the whole question of culture. . . . To me, it's true, sublimation is in the last resort also 'repression,' but I use the exalted word only when it seems to me permissible to speak of 'successful repression,' that is, when an instinct is effectively channelled into a lofty field of culture though not properly belonging to it, for instance into art. I regard the history of classical music, for instance, as the history of a technique of expression and frame of mind in which whole generations of composers, mostly without even being aware of it, channelled instincts into a field which, because of this genuine 'sacrifice,' came to perfection, to classicism. . . . What seems to me impermissible in psychoanalysis, namely the escape into pseudo-sublimation, seems to me permissible, indeed most valuable and desirable, when it is successful, when the sacrifice bears fruit. . . . Within our category of art, we artists perform a true *sublimatio*, not by will or from ambition, but by grace. This does not mean the 'artist' as he is commonly and by dilettantes thought to be, but the servant and Don Quixote, who even in his craziness is still a knight, a sacrifice [to art]." (Quoted with kind permission of Suhrkamp Verlag.) The letter is published in Hesse, *Briefe* ("Bücher der Neunzehn," vol. 117, 1965), pp. 126ff.

173

a wicked world in which innumerable flies get caught in the cobwebs of concepts. With best regards,

Yours sincerely, C. G. JUNG

To Samuel D. Schmalhausen

Dear Sir,

[ORIGINAL IN ENGLISH]

19 October 1934

Thank you very much for kindly sending me your interesting book.

From the psychological point of view it is important to look at the problem of further development of man from the standpoint of collective influences as well as from his individual standpoint. Being a doctor I'm naturally concerned with the suffering individual and not with the Marx movement. What the Marx movement can do to man you can only study where this movement really influences the individual, as f.i. in Russia or in Germany or in Italy. There always are and there always will be the two standpoints, the standpoint of the social leader who, if he is an idealist at all, seeks salvation in a more or less complete suppression of the individual, and the leader of minds who seeks improvement in the individual only. I don't see the way to a reconciliation between the two since they are necessary pairs of opposites which keep the world in balance.

Sincerely yours, C. G. JUNG

□ New York City.

To Wolfgang Pauli

Dear Professor Pauli,

29 October 1934

Best thanks for kindly sending me Jordan's paper.[1] I think this paper should be published, as it is concerned with the actual change-

□ (1900–1958), Austrian theoretical physicist, later in Zurich. He received the Nobel prize for physics in 1945 for his formulation of the "exclusion principle" (also called the "Pauli principle"). Lectured in Zurich (where he died) and frequently met Jung for a fruitful exchange of ideas on the relations between nuclear physics and psychology. Cf. Jung and Pauli, *The Interpretation of Nature and the Psyche* (orig. 1952). P.'s contribution was "The Influence of Archetypal Ideas on the Scientific Theories of Kepler"; Jung's was "Synchronicity: An Acausal Connecting Principle," CW 8. This letter is published with the kind permission of Frau Franka Pauli.

over of the physicist's mode of observation to the psychological field. This paper was inevitable. Having come to the conclusion that the observed is also a disturbance by the observer, the consistent investigator of the unknown interior of the atom could not help seeing that the nature of the observing process becomes perceptible in the disturbance caused by the observation. To put it more simply, if you look long enough into a dark hole you perceive what is looking in. This is also the principle of cognition in yoga, which derives all cognition from the absolute emptiness of consciousness. This method of cognition is thus a special instance of the introspective investigation of the psyche in general.

With regard to Jordan's reference to parapsychological phenomena, clairvoyance in space is of course one of the most obvious phenomena that demonstrate the relative non-existence of our empirical space picture. In order to supplement this argument, he would also have to adduce clairvoyance in time, which would demonstrate the relativity of our time picture. Jordan naturally sees these phenomena from the standpoint of the physicist, whereas I start from that of the psychologist, namely, from the fact of the collective unconscious, as you have so rightly noted, which represents a layer of the psyche in which individual differences of consciousness are more or less obliterated. But if individual consciousnesses are blotted out in the unconscious, then all perception in the unconscious takes place as though in a single person. Jordan says that senders and receivers in the same conscious space simultaneously observe the same object. One could invert this proposition and say that in unconscious "space" senders and receivers are the same perceiving subject. As you see, I as a psychologist would speak from the standpoint of the perceiving subject, whereas the physicist speaks from the standpoint of the common space in which two or more observers are present. Jordan's view, carried to its logical conclusion, would lead to the assumption of an absolutely unconscious space in which an infinity of observers observe the same object. The psychological version would be: in the unconscious there is only one observer who observes an infinity of objects.

If you should draw Jordan's attention to my writings, perhaps I may recommend you to mention—besides the essay already cited by you[2]—"Basic Postulates of Analytical Psychology" in the same vol-

---

[1] "Positivistische Bemerkungen über die paraphysischen Erscheinungen," later published in *Zentralblatt für Psychotherapie*, IX (1936).
[2] "The Soul and Death," CW 8.

ume.[3] As regards the collective unconscious, there is in an earlier volume, *Seelenprobleme der Gegenwart*, an essay where I treat this theme in greater detail, namely "The Structure of the Psyche."[4] I would be grateful if I could keep Jordan's paper a while longer.

It has just occurred to me that with regard to the relativity of time there is a book by one of Eddington's pupils, Dunne, *An Experiment with Time*,[5] in which he treats clairvoyance in time in the same way as Jordan treats clairvoyance in space. He postulates an infinite number of time dimensions roughly corresponding to Jordan's "intermediate stages." It would interest me very much to hear what your attitude is to Dunne's arguments.

I also thank you for your personal news and wish you further progress. With kindest regards,

Yours sincerely, C. G. JUNG

[3] Ibid.; orig. in *Wirklichkeit der Seele*.
[4] In CW 8.
[5] John William Dunne, *An Experiment with Time* (1927). Cf. Jung, "Synchronicity," pars. 852f.

To Pascual Jordan

Dear Professor Jordan,   10 November 1934

Thank you very much for kindly sending me your offprints,[1] some of which I already knew.

Although I am no mathematician, I am interested in the advances of modern physics, which is coming ever closer to the nature of the psyche, as I have seen for a long time. I have often talked about it with Pauli. One is, to be sure, concerned here with aspects of the psyche which can be mentioned only with the greatest caution, as one is exposed to too many misunderstandings. Probably you will get a taste of them in time. So long as you keep to the physical side of the world, you can say pretty well anything that is more or less provable without incurring the prejudice of being unscientific, but if

☐ German physicist, professor in Rostock, Berlin, and Hamburg; made important contributions to quantum physics. Cf. Jung, "On the Nature of the Psyche," CW 8, par. 440, n. 131, and "Synchronicity," CW 8, par. 862, no. 55.
[1] The exact titles are not identifiable, but from a letter of Jordan's to the editor, 18 Apr. 66, they dealt with general principles of quantum mechanics and their relation to causality.

you touch on the psychological problem the little man, who also goes in for science, gets mad.

With respect to your paper[2] I can only tell you that I have read it with the greatest interest. It marks an extremely memorable moment in the history of the mind, the moment when the circle closes,[3] or when the cutting of the tunnel from opposite sides of the mountain is complete. I don't know whether Pauli has told you of the letter I wrote him after reading your MS. If not, I am taking the liberty of sending you a carbon copy. At the same time I would like to tell you that I have asked my bookseller to send you the book containing my essay "The Structure of the Psyche."

As to the hypothesis of the collective unconscious, not nearly all the material bearing on this matter has yet been published. For the reasons mentioned above, I must restrict myself at present wholly to the parallelism of psychic phenomena. With this in mind, I have also brought out a little book with the late Richard Wilhelm, which deals with a Taoist text called *The Secret of the Golden Flower*. There you will find those parallels of which I speak. The strange cases of parallelism in time, which are commonly called coincidences but which I call synchronistic phenomena,[4] are very frequent in the

---

[2] In a letter of 2 Nov. 34 accompanying the above-mentioned offprints J. wrote of his "Positivistische Bemerkungen über die paraphysischen Erscheinungen": "I am very pleased to hear from Pauli that he sent you a copy of an MS in which I try to integrate telepathic etc. phenomena into our scientific picture of the world—or rather to integrate them into a fundamental extension of this picture. This extension seems to me necessary on the basis of the epistemological considerations resulting from the most recent discoveries in physics and of the modern psychology of the unconscious. Pauli also drew my attention to the relationship between the concepts presented in my MS and your concept of the 'collective unconscious.' I am trying to get two of your works which Pauli mentioned to me. I have read with great interest your essay 'The Soul and Death' which Pauli sent me." (For the telepathic phenomena see ibid., pars. 813ff.)

[3] Cf. "On the Nature of the Psyche," par. 439, n. 130, quoting Pauli: "As a matter of fact the physicist would expect a psychological correspondence at this point, because the epistemological situation with regard to the concepts 'conscious' and 'unconscious' seems to offer a pretty close analogy to the . . . 'complementarity' situation in physics. . . . It is undeniable that the development of 'microphysics' has brought the way in which nature is described in this science very much closer to that of the newer psychology."

[4] Jung coined the term "synchronicity" to characterize "the simultaneous occurrence of a certain psychic state with one or more external events which appear as meaningful parallels to the momentary subjective state" ("Synchronicity," par. 850). One of the earliest formulations of synchronicity is to be found in the Seminar Notes on *Dream Analysis*, I, autumn 1929, p. 103: "I have invented

observation of the unconscious. In this connection there is a rather crazy book by Kammerer, *Das Gesetz der Serie*,[5] which may be known to you. It may be said in passing that Chinese science is based on the principle of synchronicity,[6] or parallelism in time, which is naturally regarded by us as superstition. The standard work on this subject is the *I Ching*, of which Richard Wilhelm brought out a translation with an excellent commentary.

.   .   .

Again with best thanks and kindest regards,

Yours sincerely, C. G. JUNG

---

the word *synchronicity* as a term to cover these phenomena, that is, things happening at the same moment as an expression of the same time content."

[5] Paul Kammerer, *Das Gesetz der Serie* (1919). (Cf. "Synchronicity," pars. 824f.) No further letter of Jung's to Jordan before that of 1 Apr. 48 has been preserved. That there must have been some intermediate correspondence is evident from a letter of Jordan's, 17 Feb. 36, in which he thanks Jung for sending him an offprint of "Traumsymbole des Individuationsprozesses" (*Eranos Jahrbuch* 1935), now revised as Part II, "Individual Dream Symbolism in Relation to Alchemy," in *Psychology and Alchemy*. He writes: "I am deeply impressed to see how a posthumous understanding of alchemy is opening up. I myself have felt for a long time that the utterly superficial assessment of alchemy, existent until now, ought to be liquidated. Up till now, however, I have sought in vain for a deeper understanding of this phenomenon, so significant in the history of civilization."

[6] Cf. "Richard Wilhelm: In Memoriam," CW 15, par. 81.

To Hans Conrad Bänziger

Dear Colleague,   26 November 1934

You will have discovered as I have done that the viewpoints of modern psychotherapy[1] go far beyond the boundaries of medicine and have aroused an interest in the general public which is becoming a menace. No doubt you are also aware that Freud, despite his intense resistance to "wild" psychoanalysis, could not help trusting

□ M.D., (1895–1956), Swiss psychiatrist and psychoanalyst. Cf. his *Persönliches und Archetypisches im Individuationsprozess* (1947).
[1] The gist of this letter appears in "Contribution to a Discussion on Psychotherapy," CW 10, Appendix, pars. 1062f., which is much the same in substance as Jung's presidential address to the Nauheim Congress (ibid., par. 1035, n. 2).

the competence of his medically unqualified daughter[2] and even expressed very heretical views[3] in public about the medical future of psychoanalysis. I am therefore of the opinion that doctors would do well to keep an eye on this trend. For this reason I emphasized at the last Psychotherapeutic Congress in Nauheim how important it is that the non-medical movement should remain under the control of the doctor and that a fixed course of studies and a fixed relation to the doctor should be prescribed for non-medical psychologists. There are unquestionably a lot of cases who need psychological education although they cannot be assigned to any clinical group of neuroses. There are also people who for that reason never visit the doctor but, if they belong to the Catholic Church, turn to the father confessor. Perhaps such people make up the clientele of psychological counsellors. As you very rightly surmise, among these people there are also definitely neurotic cases who for these and other reasons belong much more to the doctor. If, then, doctors close their eyes from the start to the large psychological lay movement that already exists, the lay movement will not be suppressed, as experience has amply shown, but will on the contrary be made independent of them. In that way the doctor loses all control over the activity of lay therapists. In my humble opinion a far-sighted policy would strive without reserve to establish a carefully normalized cooperation between lay psychologists and doctors in order to prevent quackery from running riot.

Medical psychology, however, like any other branch of the healing art, needs technical assistants who require a careful training. Hence there is already a paedagogic therapy which with us, at least, does not lie in the hands of doctors but which they should know something about. If doctors adopt the position of not wanting to know anything about these developments, they will one day be confronted with the fact that this development has passed over their heads. On the basis of long experience I have come to the conclusion that one would do better to consolidate these dissident groups and if possible work out a normalization which would clearly delimit the various fields of work and facilitate the much needed medical control over the activities of non-medical psychologists.

I must now confess that I do not understand your reasons for holding aloof from these endeavours. I think that under no circum-

[2] Anna Freud, Freud's youngest daughter (b. 1895), a leading exponent of psychoanalysis.
[3] Freud, "The Question of Lay Analysis," Standard Edn. 20, pp. 179ff.

stances is it appropriate to practise an ostrich policy with developments that are actually going on. In Germany they are now trying to bring non-medical psychological work into a definite relationship with medicine, and this alone will make proper control possible. In this respect it is just like the fight against venereal diseases: pushing prostitution out of sight in no wise prevents infection.

I do not find it so bad that mechanistic and hormonistic points of view are repudiated, for in the last resort we treat neuroses neither with mechanisms nor hormones but psychically, and at present the idea that the psyche is a hormonal system still belongs to the realm of mythology. Hence I am all for the psychotherapist calmly acknowledging that he treats and cures neither with diet nor pills nor with the surgeon's knife. With collegial regards,

Yours sincerely, c. g. jung

To J. B. Rhine

[ORIGINAL IN ENGLISH]

Dear Sir,   27 November 1934

I have received a copy of your most interesting book *Extra-Sensory Perception*,[1] but I didn't know that I owed the book to your personal kindness.

I am highly interested in all questions concerning the peculiar character of the psyche with reference to time and space, i.e., the apparent annihilation of these categories in certain mental activities.

I am quite ready to give you any information concerning my own experiences in such matters, but I should like you to tell me exactly what you expect of me.

☐ Then professor of psychology at Duke U., Durham, North Carolina; well known for his experimental researches into extra-sensory perception (ESP). Cf. Jung's numerous references to Rhine's work in "Synchronicity: An Acausal Connecting Principle," CW 8. In 1965 he established the Institute for Parapsychology, sponsored by the Foundation for Research on the Nature of Man, at Durham.

[1] *Extra-Sensory Perception* (1934). R. sent it to Jung after having read his *Modern Man in Search of a Soul* (1933). In a letter of 14 Nov. 34 he mentioned "some experiments which are designed to test the capacity of the human mind to exteriorize or externalize itself." He also asked Jung to contribute his personal observations on the subject, in particular the case of the "exploded knife." In a private communication (1972), Professor Rhine stated that he had learned the story of the knife (previously unpublished) from Professor William McDougall (1871–1938), formerly head of the Department of Psychology, Duke U., and earlier an associate of Jung's. Cf. CW 16, pars. 255ff.

Concerning the case of the exploded knife[2] I only can tell you that it happened in 1898 under apparently simple circumstances. The knife was in a basket beside a loaf of bread and the basket was in a locked drawer of a sideboard. My aged mother was sitting at a distance of about 3 meters near the window. I myself was outside the house in the garden and the servant was in the kitchen which is on the same floor. Nobody else was present in the house at that time. Suddenly the knife exploded inside the sideboard with the sound of an exploding pistol. First the phenomenon seemed to be quite inexplicable until we found that the knife had exploded into four parts and was still lying scattered inside the basket. No traces of tearing or cutting were found on the sides of the basket nor in the loaf of bread, so that the explosive force apparently did not exceed that amount of energy which was just needed to break the knife and was completely exhausted with the breaking itself.

Within a few days of this fact under very similar circumstances a round table with the diameter of about 130 cm. suddenly tore about 3/4 through.[3] The table then was 90 years old, its shape hadn't been altered and there was no central heating in the house. I happened to be in the adjoining room with the door open in between and it was the same sound as of an exploding pistol.

According to my idea these two facts are connected with an acquaintance I had made just in these days. I met a young woman with marked mediumistic faculties and I had made up my mind to experiment with her.[4] She lived at that time at a distance of about 4 km. She hadn't come anywhere near to my house then, but soon after the

[2] Cf. *Memories*, p. 105/108.
[3] Ibid., pp. 105ff./108ff.: "The table top had split from the rim to beyond the centre."
[4] Ibid., pp. 105f./109f. The results of these experiments formed the basis of Jung's doctoral dissertation (1902): "On the Psychology and Pathology of So-called Occult Phenomena."

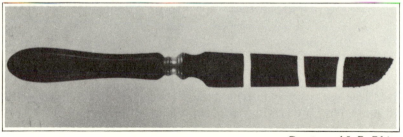

Courtesy of J. B. Rhine

series of séances with her began. She told me that she had vividly thought of these séances just in those days when the explosions occurred. She could produce quite noticeable raps in pieces of furniture and in the walls. Some of those raps also happened during her absence at a distance of about 4 km.

I am going to send you a photograph of this knife. Thanking you again for your most valuable book,

Sincerely yours, C. G. JUNG

To P. Schmid

Dear Herr Schmid,   21 December 1934

In itself the fact of having frequent dreams is not abnormal. There are very many people who have a very active dream life, but this could not be said to be in any way extraordinary or pathological. If, on the other hand, people who ordinarily dream very little suddenly get into a phase of dreaming very much, this is a sure sign that an overloading of the unconscious has set in, usually because there is a problematical situation which the dreamer has tended to overlook or has not mastered. In such cases one can say that the unconscious would have all sorts of things to contribute to his conscious life provided he understood what the unconscious meant. But even such an activation of the unconscious is not in itself a pathological phenomenon. Only when the dreamer is basically disturbed by the dreams, for instance in sleeping, or feels nervous the next day, can one speak of a real disturbance of the psychic equilibrium. But that is not in itself a disquieting fact either, for the equilibrium can often be temporarily upset without there being any fear of a more deep-seated injury.

Yours truly, C. G. JUNG

☐ Zurich.

To Poul Bjerre

Dear Colleague,   11 January 1935

As I have a virtually international practice and the views regarding psychotherapy[1] are very different from ours especially in Anglo-Saxon

[1] Concerning the subject of this letter, cf. Brüel, 19 Mar. 34, n. 1.

countries, I very early—that is, more than 20 years ago—found myself in the position of training people for psychotherapy who were able to work in their own countries as consulting psychologists or practical psychologists at paedagogic institutes or as free practitioners. Then after the war a whole lot of Germans, especially teachers, came to me for training in practical psychology. A large number of such lay psychologists work together with doctors and I must emphasize that this collaboration has generally had very favourable results. The very fact that four eyes see more than two, and that teachers or even educated laymen often possess an understanding of practical psychology that should not be underestimated, is often of the greatest assistance to the work of the doctor.

I have therefore, as you know, several times publicly advocated that a special standing should be created for practical psychologists who supplement the doctor's work in paedagogics and the social sciences. From the medical side it would be an unwarrantable presumption to think that the human psyche is an object for exclusively medical influence. Nervous patients just as often need a bit of quite ordinary education and training to learn how to cope better with their psychic complications. Every surgeon has one or more efficient theatre nurses who work under his direction and who usually perform much better than his assistants. Given time, we shall reach a similar situation in psychotherapy. I find it positively irresponsible of doctors simply to ignore the tremendous spread of psychological knowledge in our day and to try to keep psychotherapy an exclusively medical preserve. In that way they merely create a psychological movement split off from medicine in the field of general paedagogics, which is then of necessity completely outside the doctor's control. I therefore take every available opportunity of advocating that all paedagogically minded psychotherapists, clergymen, and educationists in the stricter sense should work together instead of against each other, but every time I meet with the highly inopportune and shortsighted resistance of the doctors.

I hope I have now fulfilled your wish to know what my position is. With collegial regards,

Yours sincerely, C. G. JUNG

To J. H. van der Hoop

Dear Colleague,   19 January 1935

With regard to the negotiations for the next Congress I have asked the Swiss representative of the secretariat, Dr. Meier,[1] to send you the programme as it looks at present. The preparations are bedevilled by all sorts of difficulties. Not only have very different wishes to be considered, but one must also reckon with the withdrawal of delegates and much else besides.

Naturally I would be very pleased if someone from Switzerland could be found for lectures. . . . The few younger people who are on my side are not yet representative enough to be considered. I myself have my good reasons for keeping in the background because of the preconceived opinion that I am a mere antipode of Freud and Adler. Consequently one is exposed to all sorts of misunderstandings which are no encouragement to general collaboration.

I have done my utmost to prevent nationalistic outbursts at the International Congress and to create a basis of a purely scientific nature, but if you have seen Gauger's book[2] you will understand that my efforts are meeting with very great difficulties. The snag is that an international movement can only come into being if everyone goes along with it. But if everyone holds back and waits to see whether it will come into being or not, naturally nothing happens. Recognizing this fact, I have not hesitated to place myself at the disposal of such a movement in the hope that other sensible people will do the same. For it is solely up to us to put an international movement on its feet. If we attempt such an undertaking at all under the existing circumstances, we cannot do it without Germany. The "neutrals" are too weak and moreover the repercussions of the present political situation and of the psychic epidemic that has broken out in Germany would reach us in some form in the end. It therefore seems to me better to take the bull by the horns and to confer directly with the Germans.

Here in Switzerland I have succeeded after much effort in bringing together a number of doctors and psychologists so that a meeting can

---

[1] C. A. Meier, M.D., Swiss psychiatrist and analytical psychologist; since 1961 professor of psychology at the Swiss Federal Polytechnic (ETH), Zurich. Cf. his *Ancient Incubation and Modern Psychotherapy* (orig. 1949; tr., 1967); *Die Empirie des Unbewussten* (1968).

[2] Kurt Gauger, *Politische Medizin, Grundriss einer deutschen Psychotherapie* (1934). It propagated a psychotherapy based on Hitler's concepts.

take place on Jan. 22nd to celebrate the founding of the Swiss national group. Not one of the older psychotherapists is attending since practically all of them prefer to live in sectarian seclusion.

In my humble opinion a "sufficiently international beginning" has been made, so that, if every national group is really willing to join in, an International Society is altogether possible. That this Society is not at present all-embracing is certainly not the fault of our intentions but of political conditions beyond our control, and also of the undoubted sectarian tendency of psychotherapists to go it alone. Again it is up to us to do our utmost to combat these pathological symptoms.

So far as my lectures in Amersfoort are concerned, I am quite willing to give a lecture at the Dutch Society of Psychotherapy on "Principles of Practical Psychotherapy."[3] As to the other lectures in Amersfoort, I have arranged with Dr. van der Water[4] that there should be a kind of seminar where fundamental concepts will be debated. From what he says I have the impression that it will not be an exclusively medical public, and I therefore had a general exposition of the complex theory and of practical dream analysis in mind, since I was of the opinion that specifically medical questions about indicia etc. should be reserved for the discussion. I should be grateful if you would let me know whether this plan meets with your approval. You must remember that the nature of these Amersfoort proceedings is completely new and unknown to me. With kind regards,

Yours sincerely, C. G. JUNG

[3] CW 16. The lecture was first delivered to the Zurich Medical Society in early Jan. 1935.
[4] Then director of the International School for Wijsbegeerte, in Amersfoort.

To Dr. S.

Dear Colleague, 28 January 1935

. . .

Your question about dreams relates to the little explored problem of the attitude of the dreamer to what is dreamt. There are various levels of realization, different degrees of intensity and enfeeblement of the dream experience. So far as I can judge, it seems that a certain degree of waking consciousness is correlated with an inner distance from the dream event; in other words, when I am on the point of awaking from a dream, this expresses itself in a kind of pushing away of the dream experience, so that it looks as if someone else were experiencing the dream and I were getting only a report of it. Conversely, it very often happens that at the beginning of a dream one merely experiences something like a cinema show, or that one knows something has been said earlier, or that one has maintained an opinion, and that only with deeper sleep does one enter into the real action as an active protagonist. Then, suddenly, one is in the dream. I would be very chary of the assumption of "make-believe." I have good reasons for doubting whether there is such a thing in dreams at all. With best regards,

Yours sincerely, C. G. JUNG

To G. A. Farner

Dear Dr. Farner,   18 February 1935

. . .

With regard to *Psychological Types,* I must say that I always use typology in the stricter sense as a critical apparatus, just as the idea of a psychological typology is really an attempt at a critical psychology. But I regard this as only one side of my book. The other side deals with the problem of opposites arising out of such criticism. I have discussed this chiefly in Chs. 2 and 5 on Schiller and Spitteler. There lies the gravamen of the book, though most readers have not noticed this because they are first of all led into the temptation of classifying everything typologically, which in itself is a pretty sterile undertaking. I have therefore stressed in the preface to the Spanish edition[1] that my typology is essentially a critical apparatus for sifting the empirical material collected by analysis. So it is not the case at all that I begin by classifying my patients into types and then give them the corresponding advice, as a colleague of mine whom God has endowed with a peculiar wit once asserted. In general I use these technical terms in my practical work only when I have to explain to certain patients the one-sidedness of their behaviour, their remarkable relations with other people, and such things.

I hope these hints will suffice. Please do not upset yourself on account of possible criticism.[2] In our Club we are in the habit of

[1] Actually the Argentine edition, *Tipos Psicológicos* (Buenos Aires, 1936). Jung's foreword is included in *Psychological Types,* CW 6, pp. xiv–xv.
[2] F. was going to read a paper "Begegnung mit Jung" at the Psychological Club, Zurich.

treating our speakers very civilly. With best regards and wishes for a thorough recovery,

Yours sincerely, c. g. j u n g

Anonymous

[ORIGINAL IN ENGLISH]

Dear Mrs. N.,   12 March 1935

I have read with interest that you are busy on your book and I'm particularly glad to know that you see some life in that job. I'm sure it will do you a lot of good to revise and clarify an important part of your past.

I'm busy as usual and I am going to give a seminar at the ETH[1] in spring for the most elementary beginners, i.e., very young students who know nothing whatever. If things are going on like this, I shall in a few years' time be giving a seminar in a nursery which I think would be still more profitable because this kind of teaching forces me to the utmost simplicity of expression. To my horror I have discovered that I can be pretty complicated over complicated matters. This is only good when you want to seem profound but as a matter of fact it is nothing but a damnable participation with the subject-matter. It needs some self-abnegation which is after all the most healthy sort of exercise.

. . .

With my best wishes for patience, endurance, and concentration upon the baby-book, I remain,

Yours cordially, c. g. j u n g

□ U.S.A.
[1] Eidgenössische Technische Hochschule (Swiss Federal Polytechnic), where Jung lectured 1933–1940. At the time of writing his subject was "Modern Psychology," Oct. 1933–July 1935; 2 vols., multigraphed for private circulation in English and the original German.

To Otto Körner

Dear Colleague,   22 March 1935

Thank you for your letter. I am in some doubt as to whether the faithful account you have given of the meaning of my psychology will be properly understood by anyone who, coming to it from out-

□ M.D., psychotherapist in Dresden.

side, has not the necessary knowledge to understand what it is really all about. To such people I usually say nothing about its deeper intentions and its background, but apprise them of the fact that for many years there has been an English Seminar[1] in Zurich. Moreover I hold public lectures and from the next semester on I have a seminar for students. In addition, I have undertaken numerous training analyses myself or have had them undertaken by my pupils. If nothing of this sort has been organized in Germany, it is chiefly because the Germans have noticed much later than the Anglo-Saxons that there are other psychic things besides the intellect. Also, as you know, there are still very few people in Germany nowadays who are capable of looking beyond this. To me, it is just this academic restriction to the intellect that makes anti-Semitism explicable.

To my mind it would be an advantage if you told Prof. X. what my views are about the training course. In this connection I have sent a memorandum to Prof. Göring. Above all, I demand knowledge of clinical psychiatry and of organic nervous diseases. Secondly a training analysis, 3. a certain amount of philosophical education, 4. study of primitive psychology, 5. of comparative religion, 6. of mythology, 7. of analytical psychology, beginning with knowledge of the diagnostic association technique, the technique of interpreting dreams and fantasies, 8. training of one's own personality, i.e., development and differentiation of functions which are in need of education. These are the demands I put to a pupil. Naturally there are only a few people who can fulfil them, but I have long ago given up producing manufactured articles. Above all, I don't want to evoke the impression that I think psychotherapy is intellectual child's play, and I always take pains to make it clear to people that real knowledge of the human psyche requires not only a vast amount of learning but a differentiated personality. In the last resort the psyche cannot be handled with any one technique, and in psychotherapy it is just the psyche we are dealing with and not with any old mechanism that can be got at with equally mechanistic methods. One should therefore avoid giving the impression that psychotherapy is an easy technique. Such a view un-

[1] Jung held regular weekly seminars in English for his pupils and selected patients at the Psychological Club. The subjects included *Dream Analysis* (1928–30, 5 vols.), *The Interpretation of Visions* (1930–34, 11 vols.), and *Psychological Aspects of Nietzsche's Zarathustra* (1934–39, 10 vols.). The reports of these seminars, edited by Mary Foote, were multigraphed for private circulation, but a selection in several volumes, ed. R.F.C. Hull, is to be published under the auspices of Bollingen Foundation. Cf. Morgan, 28 Dec. 27, n. ☐.

dermines the dignity and prestige of our science, which I regard as the highest of them all.

With best regards,

Yours sincerely, c. g. jung

To Dr. S.

Dear Colleague,   22 March 1935

The working out of the dreams[1] you sent me contains all the viewpoints needed for their interpretation. In other words, you have found an adequate interpretation through your discussion of them. I would only add that there is obvious alteration of the anima figure. That may also be the reason why she seems to vanish away. She disappears in her earlier form and grows clearer in another, which very often happens in the course of this process. She can change from a child into an old woman and from an animal into a goddess. If she is old, this is an indication that one's consciousness has become considerably more childish. If she is young, then one is too old in one's conscious attitude. The puerilization of the conscious attitude should not be understood as a regression; it is often necessary in order to produce an unprejudiced, naïve, receptive consciousness. This is needed to understand the spiritual side of the anima figure. I won't say anything more about this so as not to anticipate your further work along these lines.

The psoriasis of the anima figure is due to certain contents which the anima has within her, as though in the blood, and which sweat out on the surface. This is also indicated by the snakelike patterns of the psoriasis. It is a kind of painting that appears on the skin. Very often this points to the need to portray certain contents or states graphically, and in colour. This is sometimes necessary because they cannot be grasped conceptually but only concretely. This "art" activity is also indicated by the fact that the anima discovers all sorts of feminine handicrafts in her trunk. That is to say, all these works of the anima are products of the feminine mind in a man. The feminine mind is pictorial and symbolic and comes close to what the ancients called Sophia.

No fee required. With best regards,

Yours sincerely, c. g. jung

[1] The dreams have not been preserved.

To J. B. Rhine

[ORIGINAL IN ENGLISH]

Dear Dr. Rhine,   20 May 1935

I was glad to be able to contribute to your researches, but being of a less optimistic outlook than you Americans I never put my experiences on show. I have learned too much from the past in that respect. There are things which are simply incomprehensible to the tough brains of our race and time. One simply risks being taken for crazy or insincere, and I have received so much of either that I learned to be careful in keeping quiet. I would ask it as a favour from every psychologist in Europe not to put that photograph[1] on the wall, but since North Carolina is very far away from Europe, so far away, indeed, that probably very few are even aware of the existence of a Duke University, I shall not object. I have found that there are very few people who are interested in such things from healthy motives and fewer still who are able to think about such and similar matters, and so in the course of the years I arrived at the conviction that the main difficulty doesn't consist in the question how to tell, but rather in how not to tell it. Man's *horror novi* is so great that in order not to lose his modest brain capacity he always prefers to treat the fellow who disturbed him as crazy. If you are really serious in teaching people something good, you must do your best to avoid such prejudices. Those are the reasons why I prefer not to communicate too many of my experiences. They would confront the scientific world with too upsetting problems.

Sincerely yours, C. G. JUNG

---

[1] Of the exploded knife mentioned in Rhine, 27 Nov. 34.

Anonymous

Dear Fräulein N.,   23 May 1935

. . .

As it is at the moment essentially a question of consolidating your personality, I would strongly advise you to do this bit of analysis with a woman, since experience has shown that analysis with a man always has an effect on the animus, which for its part loosens up

□ Eastern France.

the personality again, whereas analysis with a woman tends on the contrary to have a "precipitating" effect. With best regards,

Yours sincerely, c. g. JUNG

To Jolande Jacobi

24 June 1935

. . . When I treat Catholics who are suffering from neurosis I consider it my duty to lead them back to the bosom of the Church where they belong. The ultimate decisions rest with the authority of the Church for anyone who is of the Catholic faith. Psychology in this context therefore means only the removal of all those factors which hinder final submission to the authority of the Church. Anyone who puts another "factor" above the authority of the Church is no longer a Catholic. . . .

To Pastor Fritz Pfäfflin

Dear Pastor Pfäfflin,   5 July 1935

Understandable though your question[1] is, I find it difficult to answer by letter and in a few words. Whatever future developments may bring, I think that despite everything it is not necessary at present for you to hang your cassock on the nail. So long as there is a parish for you to look after, you have work enough to do. Christianity as bequeathed to us by our fathers will be a necessity for a long time to come. What is worrying you does not conflict with Christianity but has to do with experiences which a Christian-minded person, who takes his religion seriously, must go through provided he has the necessary vocation. The great majority of people can and should be content with Christianity as it is today. But it would not surprise me if among those who are entrusted with the care of a parish there were some who have also to experience the inner meaning of what they are doing.

Behind all religions, as you know just as well as I, there are certain experiences which in the course of hundreds or thousands of years have formed a precipitate of rites and cult ideas. "The way to the

☐ Würzbach, Germany.

[1] P. had read Jung's 1934 Eranos lecture, "Archetypes of the Collective Unconscious," CW 9, i, and wrote about his doubts concerning his vocation.

191

water"[2] is, in Christian terms, "the way to baptism." Through historical development "the way to baptism" has departed so far from its original meaning that the idea of baptism is left hanging in mid-air because the actual experience of baptism has somehow disappeared. If your unconscious now comes up with the water symbol, this means that it is trying to give you back the experience of baptism in its original form. Originally it was an immersion to the point of death and thus had the significance of rebirth. So it is hedged about with fear. The treasure lying in the water can be compared with the treasure hid in a field or the pearl of great price which signifies the kingdom of Heaven. If these symbols are translated into the language of dogma, the peculiar sense of gratuitous experience is stripped from them. It is therefore necessary that the symbols be experienced in their original form. Hence one must let oneself go and carefully observe and write down what one is experiencing. This objectivity of observation is absolutely necessary, because otherwise one is overcome by panic and there's no point in that. Naturally the dreams must be considered too, because they often contain important hints. If vivid vision-like images occur, they should if possible be drawn or painted, no matter whether one has any artistic talents or not. The path you tread in this way leads to those inner experiences which underlie Christianity. The experiences you go through permit an interpretation of Christian dogma whereby the latter appears as a symbol, as an expression for certain fundamental psychic happenings.

You will surely understand that, as I have said, it is impossible to go into more detail by letter. I must therefore content myself with a rather general orientation. But I would like to emphasize again that what the unconscious is trying to bring you is not something absolutely different from Christianity, but rather a deepening of Christian symbolism and a revivification of the foundations upon which Christianity as well as other great religions are built.

Yours sincerely, C. G. JUNG

[2] Cf. ibid., pars. 39ff.

To Ewald Jung

Dear Ewald,   31 July 1935

Hearty thanks for your birthday congratulations!

What I call transformation is at bottom a question of fate. Although we may wish to keep within our own limits, or to overstep them, it is never done by wishing but only by happening. Only when it happens to us that we overstep our limits can we be sure that we have overstepped them and that it had to be so. In the end there is no legitimate having-to-go-beyond-ourselves. Hence I would not recommend anybody to wish to go beyond himself. Moreover this expression is false; we cannot go beyond ourselves but only deeper into ourselves, and this self is not identical with the ego because in this self we appear wondrously strange to ourselves.

As for your question about the anima, it can be answered with yes and no. It is really the same problem as that of the constitution. You are not responsible for your constitution but you are stuck with it, and so it is with the anima, which is likewise a constitutional factor one is stuck with. For what we are stuck with we have a certain responsibility, namely for the way we act towards it, but not for the fact that it exists. At any rate we can never treat the anima with moral reprimands; instead of this we have, or there is, wisdom, which in our days seems to have passed into oblivion.

Please thank your wife and your sister for their kind wishes,

With best greetings, CARL

☐ M.D., psychiatrist in Bern, cousin of Jung (d. 1943). He was secretary of the psychoanalytical group founded on Jung's initiative in Zurich, 1910 (cf. Freud, 17 June 10, n. 6; also Jones, II, p. 79).

To Erika Schlegel

Dear Erika,   31 July 1935

Your letter and the little picture of Tobias's father's miraculous cure[1] gave me great pleasure, for which I thank you with all my heart. This picture must obviously come from a very old edition of the Bible. The woodcut and type suggest a very early incunabulum. Your

☐ Wife of Jung's friend, Eugen Schlegel, Dr.jur. She was convalescing in Bavaria.
[1] In the Apocryphal Book of Tobit, chs. 6 and 11, it is related how Tobias heals his father's blindness with the liver and gall of a fish which he caught on a journey accompanied by the angel Raphael. — Jung discusses his own father's religious doubts in *Memories*, pp. 91ff./96ff. In connection with the "very old edition of the Bible" it is of interest to note Jung's dreams concerning his father and the fish motif in ibid., pp. 213–19/203–8, esp. p. 217/207, where his father holds a Bible "bound in shiny fishskin."

brother will probably know what early printing it comes from. I shall have the little picture framed *tel quel*, for it is of an unusual quality and has an inner connection with my own fate. Indeed I have often thought: if only I could have opened my own father's eyes! But he died before I had caught the fish whose liver contains the wonder-working medicine.

I am particularly touched that your son Werner also sent me his congratulations. Please give him my best thanks.

I hope you can recuperate in Elmau in a congenial atmosphere. With best wishes,

Your devoted CARL

To Friedrich Seifert

Dear Colleague,   31 July 1935

Heartiest thanks for your kind birthday congratulations. I owe you particular thanks for your contribution to my Festschrift.[1] I have read it already and have learnt a whole lot from it. It was always my view that Hegel was a psychologist *manqué*, in much the same way as I am a philosopher *manqué*. As to what is "authentic," that seems to be decided by the spirit of the age. Or perhaps the decisive factor is the historical development of the functions, as I have always suspected, but whose history would have to be written by a professional philosopher. This development is a very complicated affair, since it would have to be treated not in terms of the contents that have remained more or less the same in the history of civilization but in terms of form.

Hegel seems to me a romantic thinker in contrast to Kant and hence a typical child of his time; and as a romantic he is already on the way to psychology. The thinking form is not authentic any more but is a vehicle. Your essay is a highly significant *novum* in the interpretation of Hegel's philosophy. I am extremely pleased that you have gone to all this trouble to contribute to my Festschrift.

□ (1891–1963), professor of philosophy at the Technische Hochschule, Munich, later analytical psychologist. Cf. his *Tiefenpsychologie: Die Entwicklung der Lehre vom Unbewussten* (1955); *Bilder und Urbilder: Erscheinungsformen des Archetypus* (together with R. Seifert-Helwig; 1965). Cf. Nelson, 17 June 56.
1 "Ideendialektik und Lebensdialektik: Das Gegensatzproblem bei Hegel und bei Jung," *Die kulturelle Bedeutung der komplexen Psychologie* (Berlin, 1935), edited by the Psychology Club, Zurich, on the occasion of Jung's 60th birthday.

I would also like to thank you for sending me your fantasies, which I find extraordinarily interesting and valuable. So far I haven't had a chance to study them thoroughly and have only skimmed through them, but I have seen already that they are worth thorough study. In case I should come across something that seems to me particularly worth mentioning, I will write to you again. Meanwhile with best thanks,

Yours sincerely, C. G. JUNG

To Pastor Ernst Jahn

Dear Pastor Jahn,   7 September 1935

I am sorry that pressure of work has prevented me from answering your kind letter. Please forgive me. It is very kind of you to have gone into my work so thoroughly. With your permission, I would like to draw your attention to a few points that have struck me.

It seems to me that you approach my views too much from the angle of the theologian. You seem to forget that I am first and foremost an empiricist, who was led to the question of Western and Eastern mysticism only for empirical reasons. For instance, I do not by any means take my stand on Tao or any Yoga techniques, but I have found that Taoist philosophy as well as Yoga have very many parallels with the psychic processes we can observe in Western man. Nor do I get anybody to draw or contemplate mandala pictures as in Yoga, but it has turned out that unprejudiced people take quite naturally to these aids in order to find their bearings in the chaos of unconscious processes that come to light.

A point which theologians very often overlook is the question of the reality of God. When I speak of God, I always speak as a psychologist, as I have expressly emphasized in many places in my books. For the psychologist the God-image is a psychological fact. He cannot say anything about the metaphysical reality of God because that would far exceed the limits of the theory of knowledge. As an empiricist I know only the images originating in the unconscious which man makes of God, or which, to be more accurate, are made of God in the unconscious; and these images are undoubtedly very relative.

Another point is the relation between the psychological I and Thou.

□ Berlin.

The unconscious for me is a definite *vis-à-vis* with which one has to come to terms. I have written a little book[1] about this. I have never asserted, nor do I think I know, what the unconscious is in itself. It is the unconscious region of the psyche. When I speak of psyche, I do not pretend to know what it is either, and how far this concept extends. For this concept is simply beyond all possibility of cognition. It is a mere convention for giving some kind of name to the unknown which appears to us psychic. This psychic factor, as experience shows, is something very different from our consciousness. If you have ever observed a psychosis in a person you know intimately, you will know what a dreadful confrontation that can be. It seems to me that it is difficult for a theologian to put himself in an empiricist's shoes. What the theologian takes to be spiritual realities are for the empiricist expressions of psychic life, which at bottom is essentially unknown. The empiricist does not think from above downwards from metaphysical premises, but comes from below upwards from the phenomenal world and, conscious of the limitations of his mind, must be content with understanding the psychic processes reconstructively. And so it is with my therapy. I have chiefly to do with people in whom I cannot implant any values or convictions from above downwards. Usually they are people whom I can only urge to go through their experiences and to organize them in a way that makes a tolerable existence possible. The pastor of souls is naturally not in this position as a rule; he has to do with people who expressly demand to be spiritually arranged from above downwards. This task should be left to the pastor of souls. But those rarer people who cannot accept traditional values and convictions, who in other words do not possess the charisma of faith, must perforce seek advice from the empiricist, who for his part, in order to do justice to his task, can appeal to nothing except the given realities. Thus he will on no account say to his patient, "Your psyche is God," or "Your unconscious is God," because that would be just what the patient has fled from in disgust. Rather he will start off the psychic process of experiencing unconscious contents, whereby the patient is put in a position to experience his psychic realities and draw his own conclusions. What I described in the *Golden Flower* are simply the results of individual developments which closely resemble those arrived at through Eastern practices. Centuries ago Yoga congealed into a fixed system, but originally the mandala symbolism grew out of the unconscious just as

---

[1] "The Relations between the Ego and the Unconscious," CW 7.

individually and directly as it does with Western man today. I had known about the spontaneous emergence of these symbols for 17 years but deliberately published nothing on this subject so as to prevent the regrettable but undeniable imitative instinct from getting hold of these pictures. In these 17 years I had ample opportunity to see again and again how patients quite spontaneously reached for the pencil in order to sketch pictures that were meant to express typical inner experiences. Yoga, however, as we know it today, has become a method of spiritual training which is drilled into the initiands from above. It holds up the traditional pictures for contemplation and has precise rules as to how they should be executed. In this respect Yoga is directly comparable to the *Exercitia* of Loyola. But that is the exact opposite of what I do. I am therefore an avowed opponent of taking over Yoga methods or Eastern ideas uncritically, as I have stated publicly many times before.

So what I have said on these matters is the result of empirical work and does not constitute the technical principles of my therapy. Perhaps I may draw your attention to a book that has just been published (*Die kulturelle Bedeutung der komplexen Psychologie*, Jul. Springer, Berlin 1935), in which the first contribution[2] deals with my method. There you will find a philosophical basis for my whole work, which will doubtless elucidate for you any points that may still be obscure.

Yours sincerely, C. G. JUNG

[2] Toni Wolff, "Einführung in die Grundlagen der komplexen Psychologie," now in Wolff, *Studien zu C. G. Jungs Psychologie* (1959). Jung's introduction to this book is in *Civilization in Transition*, pars. 887ff.

Anonymous

Dear N.,   7 September 1935

Best thanks for your kind letter. I was very interested to hear of your experiences with the Oxford people. What you tell me accords by and large with my expectations. I can very well imagine that such a milieu is a great relief for you. One of the great advantages of this movement is that it gives people all those collective alleviations which they do not possess or cannot create for themselves, together with a shared religious confession. That was always the meaning of

□ Switzerland.

the Christian community. I hope very many more people will recognize this meaning. The world is in dire need of it. I have heard the same reports from many people I know well, so that I am sufficiently convinced that the movement has positive results to show. It would therefore be quite superfluous for me to convince myself personally of it again. I have as little need to convince myself of how good the Catholic Church is for very many people. I have seen this only too well with people whom I also know well. I could cite other religions that rescue man from his isolation in the ego. This typically individualistic isolation is in fact the sickness of our time, the essential cause of which is that a real communal religion no longer exists and most people have forgotten that Christianity is one. I have always known this as I had the advantage of a Christian education and have consequently never felt isolated or dried up.

I am sincerely happy to know that you have found the atmosphere that agrees with you and that the meaning of the nearly two-thousand-year-old Christian religion has dawned upon you.

With best regards, CARL

To Henry A. Murray

[ORIGINAL IN ENGLISH]

My dear Dr. Murray, 10 September 1935

Thank you for your interesting letter. I think going to Samoa is a very wonderful plan, but nothing for myself as I'm fettered to all sorts of obligations in Zurich. Next summer I'm going to Harvard University,[1] as you probably will have heard, which is adventurous enough. I'm sorry that I will not be able to see you, as you just then sail for the happy isles. Look out that the paradise doesn't eat the bottom out of your soul. It is dangerous ground, all the more so as one is not aware of it.

While writing this letter I received your second one. I'm sorry for the delay of my answer, but I'm so overburdened with work that I'm really often quite unable to answer or even to read long letters.

. . .

My plans for summer 1936 are not yet fixed at all except that, as I say, I'm going to Harvard to endure a tercentenary. I don't know

---

[1] Jung had been invited to lecture at Harvard on the occasion of its tercentenary in 1936. The lecture was "Psychological Factors Determining Human Behaviour," CW 8.

exactly what that means, but I imagine all sorts of tiresome things. I'm also certain that many of my friends and acquaintances want to see me. A bit of nature, I admit, would be rather heaven-sent, but it shouldn't be too far away and not too adventurous, as my wife is probably accompanying me. Airplanes and such devilish inventions ought to be avoided. To write the book you suggest[2] would be a very difficult and expensive enterprise.

Concerning your trouble with the question of the causality of fantasy images, I want to say that it is certainly true that external conditions are the cause of inner reactions, but the external cause is only one condition of the reaction, the other condition is always the quality of the thing that reacts. One cannot assume that at any time the thing that reacts has been a thing without quality. In other words, the psyche as an inherent quality of the living body always had its peculiar and specific quality which is not equal to the nature of the external things. A psychic image is, as you know, by no means identical with the external object itself. It would be an unjustified assertion to assume that the psyche wholly derives from the influences of external facts, as it would be to assume that all external objects are nothing but projected images of the mind. When you carefully study the primitive mind, you will see that primitives are in no way concerned with their personalities, but their personalities are very much concerned with themselves. So the unconscious in them produces actions and images without their consciousness, as is the case in our dreams. These images are surely answers to external facts and conditions, but they are *the answers of the psyche* and therefore produce accurate pictures of the psychic facts. If you compare the sun-myth to the actual experience of the senses, then you see the whole difference. The conscious mind perceives the sun as a round celestial body, the unconscious produces a myth which in its imagery has nothing but a very faint relation with the actual perception of the senses. If the Freudians say that this is nothing but infantile, then they are right in so far as these images begin to become actual already in childhood. But they are all based upon the inherent qualities of the inherited psyche. That's the reason why with children you not too rarely find dreams that are anything but childish. If one holds that the images the child produces always were childish impressions in the history of mankind, one only repeats what has been said before,

[2] M. suggested that Jung should "make a book of the Seminars on the Trances," referring to the Seminars on *The Interpretation of Visions*.

199

namely that the peculiar reactions of the psyche already begin to manifest themselves in early childhood. It is certainly a very great error to assume that the psyche is without qualities except those that are insinuated or suggested by external objects. If that were the case, then our unconscious would only produce exact replicas of external facts, which is by no means the case.

I'm chiefly concerned with the psyche itself, therefore I'm leaving out body and spirit. Philosophy and theology know all about spirit. Physiology and medicine know all about the body, but I'm a humble psychologist whose particular métier is to investigate the peculiar nature of the psyche. Body and spirit are to me mere aspects of the reality of the psyche. Psychic experience is the only immediate experience. Body is as metaphysical as spirit. Ask the modern physicist what body is, they are coming fast across to the recognition of the reality of the psyche.

Sincerely yours, C. G. JUNG

Anonymous

[ORIGINAL IN ENGLISH]

Dear Mr. N., 25 October 1935

I absolutely share your appreciation of the I Ching and whatever good things you have to say about it, but most certainly I'm not going to sympathize with your very Western idea of making an institute of it. You may know a great deal of the soul of the spiritual nobleman of the East, but you seem to be fundamentally ignorant of the soul of Western man. You don't know what a hell of trouble I have to instill the smallest drop of wisdom into the veins of the "Technicalized Savage" called European. The technique and wisdom of the I Ching is something so subtle that it needs the refined culture of an age-old Eastern education to understand it truly. Most of the educated Chinamen of today haven't an inkling of an idea of the I Ching any more. Nor have Chinese scholars with us any adequate understanding. What we need is a psychological education so that we slowly become able to understand the I Ching. But an institute that hands out the wisdom is the quintessence of horror to me. I know enough of them in Europe and in America.

Wisdom is not and never has been something for the many, because foolishness for ever will be the main thing the world craves for.

☐ New York City.

If that were not so, the world would have been cured of its own existence already in the times of old Pythagoras. Wisdom may be good for you but to hand it out to other people means just as much as corruption of the truth. Wisdom is the thing that one individual enjoys all by himself, and if you keep silent about it, then they will believe you, but when you talk it, you have no effect. I sincerely hope that the *I Ching* has not put that idea into your head, otherwise I would lose my belief in the *I Ching*. Even those people who use the *I Ching* as the Taoist priests in China do have degenerated into ordinary soothsayers and they enjoy the bad reputation which they thoroughly deserve. If I understand anything of the *I Ching*, then I should say it is *the* book that teaches you your own way and the all-importance of it. Not in vain has the book been the secret treasure of the sages. Compare it to what Confucius said to the masses and you will see the difference. He was a sage that made use of the *I Ching*, but he didn't teach it. He spoke the language of the masses, because he enjoyed teaching. Lao-tse didn't enjoy teaching: see what he said and how many there are that understand what he said. Neither Kung Fu-tse[1] nor Lao-tse nor Chuang-tse[2] had institutes as far as I'm informed.

I have no objection against an honest attempt to introduce the wisdom of the *I Ching* to the Western mind, but such a thing has to be done with the utmost care in order not to arouse a flood of most pernicious misunderstandings. I don't know in what way you have acquitted yourself of this task. If you want to avoid the disastrous prejudice of the Western mind you have to introduce the matter under the cloak of science. Thus I should advise you to apply for an introductory word rather to Prof. Rousselle who is a competent Chinese scholar, while I'm nothing but a psychologist and the world doesn't see what psychology has to do with the *I Ching*.

I hope you don't mind my very frank statements, but I'm a jealous lover of the *I Ching* and I know that such things thrive the best and unfold in a natural way as long as they are not technicalized.

Faithfully yours, C. G. JUNG

[1] Confucius is the Latinized form of Kung Fu-tse, meaning "the philosopher, or master, Kung."
[2] Chinese Taoist philosopher, *fl.* 4th–3rd cent. B.C.

To Claire Kaufmann

Dear Fräulein Kaufmann,   29 October 1935

You are quite right that on the philosophical level the concept is always a symbol even though it is an expression for something known. I absolutely agree with you when you understand knowing at the same time as not-knowing, but one must go pretty far before one finds people who admit that this is so. Your view fully accords with the standpoint of St. Paul that thinking opens the way to God. "For the spirit," as Paul says, "searcheth . . . the deep things of God."[1]

What you say about the theoretical development of my empirical views is also very true. I found long ago that further building needed to be done. But I am still working on the foundations. With kind regards,

Yours sincerely, C. G. JUNG

[1] I Cor. 2:10.

To J. A. Hadfield

[ORIGINAL IN ENGLISH]

Dear Dr. Hadfield,   4 November 1935

You know perhaps that I am president of the Internationale Aerztliche Gesellschaft für Psychotherapie. This is an organization of medical psychotherapists which originally included German, Austrian, Dutch, Danish, Swedish, Norwegian, and Swiss members. Through the revolution in Germany this original organization has been blown up. Since then I have done my best to stitch that organization together again. But it is an almost hopeless attempt to organize an international society in an atmosphere poisoned by all sorts of political and racial prejudices. The actual persecution of the Jews in Germany is causing so much hatred that it is almost impossible for the smaller countries to keep their organization together because we are far outnumbered by the Germans.

We are therefore considering the possibility of a closer contact with an Anglo-Saxon organization. A proposition has been made to try the Society for Mental Hygiene.[1] Now I must confess that I know

□ (1882–1967), English psychiatrist and psychotherapist, then Director of Studies at the Institute of Medical Psychology (the Tavistock Clinic), London.
[1] Probably a misnomer for The National Council for Mental Hygiene, one of the parent bodies of the later National Association for Mental Health.

very little of this Society and I should therefore be much obliged if you could frankly tell me what you think of it, or whether you could make any other suggestion. I assume that it would also be of a certain advantage to an Anglo-Saxon Society to have the collaboration of continental physicians. I would be very much obliged if you would tell me whether any other medical society existing in England would be accessible to the proposition of a closer connection with the continental groups. Our purpose would be to create a really international organization of psychotherapists in which Germany wouldn't play a predominating role any more.

I should be very grateful to you for any suggestion and advice you can give me in that matter.

Sincerely yours, C. G. JUNG

To M. Patzelt

Dear Frau Patzelt, 29 November 1935

I have read a few books by Rudolf Steiner[1] and must confess that I have found nothing in them that is of the slightest use to me. You must understand that I am a researcher and not a prophet. What matters to me is what can be verified by experience. But I am not interested at all in what can be speculated about experience without any proof. All the ideas that Steiner advances in his books you can also read in the Indian sources. Anything I cannot demonstrate in the realm of human experience I let alone and if someone should assert that he knows more about it I ask him to furnish me with the necessary proofs.

I have read a few books on anthroposophy and a fair number on theosophy. I have also got to know very many anthroposophists and theosophists and have always discovered to my regret that these people imagine all sorts of things and assert all sorts of things for which they are quite incapable of offering any proof. I have no prejudices against the greatest marvels if someone gives me the necessary proofs. Nor shall I hesitate to stand up for the truth if I know it can be proved. But I shall guard against adding to the number of those who use unproven assertions to erect a world system no stone of which rests on the surface of this earth. So long as Steiner is or was not able

☐ Munich.
[1] Rudolf Steiner (1861–1925), German philosopher, founder of anthroposophy ("wisdom of humanity").

to understand the Hittite inscriptions yet understood the language of Atlantis which nobody knows existed, there is no reason to get excited about anything that Herr Steiner has said.

Yours very truly, C. G. JUNG

To Hélène Kiener

Dear Fräulein Kiener,   6 December 1935

Suffering in sympathy with the psychic difficulties of the sick is a peculiarity which none escapes who has to do with such people. It is a well-known childhood ailment. In the beginning it is very exhausting and burdensome. When I started analysing I could usually endure only two cases a day because it was too much of a strain for me. This apparent weakness disappears with time and practice. Only, at the beginning one must not overexert oneself, otherwise one becomes discouraged and disappointed. It is advisable to use all the available time to recover by doing something quite different. In this way you accustom yourself to change round quickly and to concentrate only on the hours you spend with the sick person. May you have patience and sufficient instinct to learn to overcome as soon as possible the infection that emanates from every sick psyche.

Best thanks for your *a posteriori* birthday wishes. With kindest regards,

Yours sincerely, C. G. JUNG

☐ Analytical psychologist of Strasbourg.

To the Praesidium of the Dutch Group of the International Society for Psychotherapy

Gentlemen,   21 December 1935

I note with regret from your letter of 15 December 1935 that the Dutch group has withdrawn the invitation[1] it voluntarily extended in spring 1935. The reasons given for this decision, namely the political views prevailing in Germany, the persecution of the Jews, and the suppression of free speech, are to be sure emotional motives but objectively considered can hardly be validated as reasons against a

[1] The Dutch group had offered to organize the next Congress of the International Medical Society for Psychotherapy in Holland.

Congress held outside Germany. At a neutral Congress there would be no restriction on free speech, moreover the Jews would not have been excluded, and finally the attitude customary in scientific circles towards political questions has for the last 150 years stood by the principle of establishing the scientific truth irrespective of the political views and needs of individual scientists. I must resolutely emphasize that our German colleagues were not the makers of the Nazi revolution, but live in a State that demands a definite political attitude. If the association with Germany is now to be jeopardized on political grounds, we are falling into the same error we accuse the others of: politics is simply pitted against politics. This religious war in miniature is in truth not the business of science, and I must protest against political resentments cloaking themselves under its name.

The fact that the Dutch group will not hold the Congress which it itself proposed and that there is also a decided tendency within the group to sever all connections with the International Society is of fundamental importance in that Holland has the strongest group after Germany. In these circumstances the convening of a Congress outside Germany is of course completely hopeless, and that free expression of opinion which was so ardently postulated before is thereby rendered impossible. I am convinced that if Russian doctors who believe in the religion of Communism sought to join the International Society the present opposition would raise no objections. I would also regard it as a mistake to exclude such doctors on account of the religion prevailing in their country. Neither would we exclude Mohammedans despite the fact that we couldn't agree on the Koran. Why, then, should German doctors be excluded when it is now possible for German Jewish doctors to become direct members of the International Society? Really one might expect psychotherapists and psychologists not to insist on political resentments as an argument against international cultural endeavours.

Naturally it is quite impossible to run an International Society under these conditions. If the smaller national groups get infected with political resentment there will be no possibility, either, of establishing contact with England, for instance. I have in fact done this already and have received word that two delegates from the Institute of Medical Psychology[2] will attend the next Congress.

I am now compelled to inform the German group of Holland's attitude. This attitude cannot be described as anything other than

[2] Cf. Hadfield, 4 Nov. 35, n. □.

a disavowal of the true purpose of our International Society. We Swiss cannot form an International Society with Germany alone. Denmark has too few members to be considered, and in Sweden Dr. Bjerre has met with no success so far. The logical outcome of this situation is that I tender my resignation as president[3] of the International Society and I shall address myself in this sense to the head of the German group.

Copies of this letter will go to the heads of the other national groups as well as a copy of your letter of 15 December 1935.

Yours truly, C. G. JUNG

[3] This resignation did not become effective.

To Erich Neumann

My dear Neumann,   22 December 1935

Don't grow any grey hairs for having overlooked my 60th birthday! To me the abstract number means nothing. I much prefer to know, or to hear from you, what you are doing. What the European Jews are doing I know already, but I am extraordinarily interested in what the Jews are doing on their own archetypal soil. Analytical psychology (or as it is now called, complex psychology) has its roots deep in Europe, in the Christian Middle Ages, and ultimately in Greek philosophy. The connecting-link I was missing for so long has now been found, and it is alchemy as Silberer[1] correctly surmised. Unfortunately, rationalistic psychologism broke his neck for him.

. . .

The "cultivated Jew" is always on the way to becoming a "non-Jew." You are quite right: the way does not go from good to better, but dips down first to the historical data. I usually point out to most of my Jewish patients that it stands to reason they are Jews. I wouldn't do this had I not so often seen Jews who imagined they were something else. For them "Jewishness" is a species of personal insult.

[1] Herbert Silberer, M.D., (1881–1923), Austrian psychoanalyst. In his *Problems of Mysticism and Its Symbolism* (orig. 1914; tr., 1917), he attempted the first psychological interpretation of alchemy. His concept of a dual aspect of dreams, the one psychoanalytical/retrograde, the other spiritual/anagogic, was rejected by Freud (cf. Jones, II, p. 248). He ended by suicide.

. . . I find your very positive conviction that the soil of Palestine is essential for Jewish individuation most valuable. How does this square with the fact that Jews in general have lived *much longer* in other countries than in Palestine? Even Moses Maimonides[2] preferred Cairo Fostat although he had the opportunity of living in Jerusalem.

Is it the case that the Jew is so accustomed to being a non-Jew that he needs the Palestinian soil *in concreto* to be reminded of his Jewishness? I can scarcely feel my way into a psyche that has not grown up on any soil. With heartiest wishes for your continued well-being,

Your ever devoted, C. G. JUNG

[2] Moses Maimonides (Rabbi Moses ben Maimon; 1135–1204), the greatest Jewish philosopher of the Middle Ages. After many migrations he settled in Cairo Fostat, where he practised as a physician and became personal physician to the Sultan Saladin.

To J. H. van der Hoop
President of the Dutch Group of the
International Society for Psychotherapy

Dear Mr. President,   3 January 1936

I consider it my self-evident duty to keep the heads of the national groups informed about all essential events. Accordingly I shall send a copy of your letter of 30.XII[1] to the national groups.

In explanation of my "indignation" I would like to inform you that I was urged from various quarters to arrange a Congress abroad. Holland had declared itself ready to take this on. The justification for this foreign Congress was that no free expression of opinion was possible in Germany and that one therefore could not go to German Congresses either. Now, after this Congress was agreed upon, the impossibility of a foreign Congress is again justified by a negative mood towards Germany. All this looks as if the existence of an international association is going to be torpedoed. Under these circumstances there is little sense in organizing an International Society.

[1] H.'s reply to Jung's letter of 21 Dec. 35, explaining that the mood of the Dutch group caused by developments in Germany was unfavourable to the organization of the Congress.

Just now it would have been desirable for many reasons if at least the will for international cooperation had been publicly demonstrated by neutral countries. The Congress could indeed, as I had already suggested to you in my letter of 21.XII, have taken place in a small setting, for instance in Amersfoort.[2] As to the possibility of a meeting in Switzerland, the same reasons which I set forth at the Congress in Nauheim still militate against it.

The reasons for tendering my resignation are not to be laid exclusively to the decisions of the Dutch group. Another reason was that I had the feeling, reinforced by information I had received, that I personally was a stumbling block on account of my different attitude. However, under no circumstances do I want to encumber the existence of an international association, difficult enough already under present conditions, with an additional impediment if there is any prospect of a more neutral personality than I causing less general offence. My fears relate chiefly to the faint possibility of founding an Austrian group, with regard to which I know for certain that the predominantly Freudian influence insists that my personality is the chief obstacle. I can easily imagine that a similar situation exists in Holland. I have no ambition whatever to be an international president and I accepted election only because I was minded to do everything I could to set the Society on its feet again. If it should turn out that I am just as much an obstacle I shall not hesitate for a moment to resign.

Yours truly, C. G. JUNG

[2] Jung's slip. Amersfoort is not mentioned in the letter of 21 Dec., but in his letter to Hoop of 19 Jan., and apparently not in connection with the Congress.

To Baroness Tinti

Dear Baroness,   10 January 1936

Many thanks for your interesting letter. Indeed, many of the peculiarities of the figures in the unconscious could be explained by a long-lasting primeval matriarchy if only we knew for certain that it ever existed, just as the flood myths could be explained by the myth of Atlantis if only we knew that there ever was an Atlantis.

□ Maribor, Yugoslavia.

208

Equally, the contents of the unconscious could be explained by reincarnation if we knew that there is reincarnation. These hypotheses are at present articles of faith, and science is always in the modest role of a beggar since it has to be content with what it has. If it didn't it would be a fraud. This is the reason why I restrict myself essentially to facts and observations and fight shy of mythological explanations.

The book you very kindly promised me is unfortunately not yet in my hands. All the same I thank you for it.

Yours sincerely, c. g. j u n g

To J. Wilhelm Hauer

Dear Professor Hauer,   14 February 1936

By the same post I am sending you an offprint of my last year's Eranos lecture.[1] This is not intended as a *captatio* but rather an *anticipatio benevolentiae*, since a little later I shall send you an essay in which I have included you as a symptom,[2] this time without mentioning your humanity which I know very well.

We in Switzerland are near enough to Germany and also far away enough to have to come to terms with the spiritual events there and perhaps we can. But if we embark on this venture we must look beyond the personal and regard the German Faith Movement, including yourself, as a symptomatic occurrence connected with the hidden history of the German mind. I don't know whether you will be irritated by this attempt. At any rate I have refrained from value-judgments and have been content with pure observation of the facts. I am deeply convinced that historical events cannot be evaluated but at best interpreted. I know from experience that being interpreted is not the pleasantest of things even when it is done to the best of our knowledge and conscience. It is precisely then that it very often is not! Meanwhile, with best regards and wishes,

Yours ever, c. g. j u n g

[1] Now "Individual Dream Symbolism in Relation to Alchemy," Part II of *Psychology and Alchemy*.

[2] Cf. "Wotan," CW 10, pars. 397f., where Jung discusses the "German Faith Movement," founded by Hauer, as a symptom of German identification with Wotan.

To Smith Ely Jelliffe

[ORIGINAL IN ENGLISH]

Dear Dr. Jelliffe,   24 February 1936

The reports of my seminars[1] are mere protocols which are exclusively destined for members of the said seminars. They wouldn't be fit for scientific use. I don't think that my volume *Wirklichkeit der Seele* has any interest for you because it is merely psychological and has nothing to do with your medical point of view.

I'm quite willing to answer your questions. I owe a great deal of mental stimulation and of knowledge to Janet,[2] whose lectures I followed in 1902 in Paris. I also got a great deal from his books. I certainly owe a very important psychological point of view to his psychology. I never denied the fact that my psychiatry comes from Bleuler's clinic. I was there already in 1900.

The concept of the "Gefühlsbetonter Komplex"[3] as it is used in the association test is really my own invention, if one doesn't insist that the word "complex" has been used in many other ways before my time. But I'm not aware that it has been used in the particular way I have been using it. When you study Kraepelin's[4] experimental work about associations (Aschaffenburg, etc.) you don't find any systematic consideration of this fact, nor in the experiments of Wundt's[5] school.

I quite agree with you that normality is a most relative conception. Yet it is an idea which you can't do without in practical life. It is quite certain that from century to century or even from month to month our point of view changes, yet there is always a stock of

---

□ M.D., (1866–1945), American neurologist. He had been instrumental in arranging Jung's lectures on "The Theory of Psychoanalysis" (CW 4) at Fordham U., New York, 1912 (cf. supra, letter to *Psychoanalytical Review*, 1913).

[1] Cf. Körner, 22 Mar. 35, n. 1.

[2] Pierre Janet (1859–1947), French psychiatrist and neurologist, known for his researches on hysteria and neurosis. Jung studied theoretical psychopathology under him at the Salpêtrière for one term in 1902.

[3] "Feeling-toned complex." Cf. "Occult Phenomena," CW 1, par. 168, n. 2a, and *Experimental Researches*, CW 2, index, s.v.

[4] Emil Kraepelin (1856–1926), German psychiatrist. He was a pioneer of modern psychiatry and introduced the distinction between dementia praecox (schizophrenia) and manic-depressive psychosis. Concerning his and Aschaffenburg's work on associations cf. "Occult Phenomena," p. 167, n. *; "The Associations of Normal Subjects," CW 2, par. 22 and passim; "The Psychology of Dementia Praecox," CW 3, par. 22, n. 43; "The Significance of the Father in the Destiny of the Individual," CW 4, par. 695.

[5] Wilhelm Wundt (1832–1920), German psychologist and physiologist, founder of experimental psychology.

human beings or of facts which represents the average functioning, and which is called "normal." If this conception didn't exist, we couldn't speak of something abnormal, by which term we express the fact that certain functions or events are not conforming to the average course of events.

It is quite true that the reason why I couldn't continue to collaborate with Freud was that everything in his psychology was reductive, personal, and envisaged from the angle of repression. A thing which seemed to me particularly impossible was Freud's handling of dreams, which looks to me like a distortion of facts. The immediate reason for my dissension was that Freud in a publication identified the method with his theory,[6] a fact that seemed inadmissible to me, because I am convinced that one can apply a scientific method without believing in a certain theory. The results obtained by this method can be interpreted in several ways. Adler for instance interprets neurosis in a very different way, and the same Freud's pupil Silberer has quite clearly shown, independently of myself, that one can interpret in what he called an anagogic way.[7] I think a psychologist has to consider these different possibilities and it is my sincerest conviction that it is much too early for psychology to restrict itself to a one-sided reductive point of view. If you carefully study Freud's paper *Die Zukunft einer Illusion*[8] you see what the results are. Freudian psychology reaches into a field that simply cannot be reduced to Freudian premises, if one studies the actual facts without bias.

. . .

Yours truly, C. G. JUNG

[6] This could refer to Freud's "On Psycho-analysis," Standard Edn. 12, p. 207: "Psycho-analysis is a remarkable combination, for it comprises not only a method of research into the neuroses but also a method of treatment based on the aetiology thus discovered."
[7] Cf. Neumann, 22 Dec. 35, n. 1.
[8] *The Future of an Illusion*, Standard Edn. 21.

To J. Wilhelm Hauer

Dear Professor Hauer,   10 March 1936

By the same post I am sending you my little essay "Wotan." Fear not, I have not stripped you bare! I have only used your public figure to illustrate the nature of *Ergriffenheit*.[1] I have no desire to

[1] = possession (lit. "being seized or gripped"). Cf. "Wotan," pars. 386f., 397f.

211

stab anyone in the back. But as a German you must put up with serving as a model of the German.

I have sincerely regretted that it was not possible for you to come here for your lecture. We would have been able to talk about many things that cannot be dealt with by correspondence or by writing articles. But I think I have honestly taken pains to understand the German phenomenon from outside, at least so far as this is possible for anyone who has experienced the same thing though in quite a different way. With cordial regards,

Yours ever, C. G. JUNG

To Elined Kotschnig

[ORIGINAL IN ENGLISH]

Dear Mrs. Kotschnig, 16 April 1936

The symbol of losing teeth has the primitive meaning of losing one's grip because under primitive circumstances and in the animal kingdom, the teeth and mouth are the gripping organ. If one loses teeth, one loses the grip on something. Now this can mean a loss of reality, a loss of relationship, a loss of self-control, etc. The English word grip is contained in the German word *Begriff* (conception or notion). The Latin word *conceptio* means the same, i.e., catching hold of something, having a grip on something.[1] Thus the lost tooth also can mean that one loses a certain conception of things, a hitherto valid opinion or attitude. For instance pregnancy can have such an effect that one loses one's grip on the psychic continuity as the physiological condition takes the lead over the mind. The dream of the bone in the skull seems to point to the hole in the skull through which the soul escapes according to primitive belief. This can mean a fear of death or a somewhat dangerous communication with the unconscious. That the bone comes out of the mouth in the form of a tooth would convey the idea that a certain old opinion has been lost or is to be lost. Occasionally it can also mean getting old or older, particularly so with women that have children, because there is a saying that each child cost a tooth.

. . .

Sincerely yours, C. G. JUNG

[1] Cf. Jung, "Foreword to the *I Ching*," CW 11, par. 981.

212

To Wilhelm Laiblin

Dear Herr Laiblin,   16 April 1936

. . .

The toad that appears in your book generally signifies an anticipation of the human being on the level of the coldblooded creatures, and actually stands for the psyche associated with the lower spinal cord. Like the snake, it is a symbol of the creative unconscious.

What interested me most in your letter[1] was that you as the *Ergriffener* look at the situation more from the feminine side. This fits exactly, because the *Ergreifer* is the man and the *Ergriffener* is the woman. But the *Ergriffener* whose *Ergreifer* one does not see is taken for the *Ergreifender*[2] and also functions as such (i.e., dangerously). The counterpart of sentimentality is as we know brutality. Wotan's inner meaning, represented by his lost eye, is Erda, the *Magna Mater*.

I understand perfectly why you feel the German phenomenon differently. It would be the same with me, but I am caught in my outsiderness and dare not let myself see it too exclusively from the inside. That would also rob me of the capacity to make the German character comprehensible to the non-German world. The West knows too much about sentimentalities to believe in them. With best regards,

Yours sincerely, C. G. JUNG

[1] L., to whom Jung had sent "Wotan," asked why the outsider was more impressed by the masculine aspect of events in Germany whereas to one judging from inside the feminine aspect was more impressive.
[2] *Ergriffener* = he who is gripped; *Ergreifer/Ergreifender* = he who grips.

To Claire Kaufmann

Dear Fräulein Kaufmann,   30 April 1936

I cannot possibly answer your question in a letter. I think you would do best to take the whole problem of love as a *miraculum per gratiam Dei* which nobody really understands. It is always fate, whose ultimate roots we shall never dig out. One shouldn't let oneself be upset by God's doings. The sublime nonsense or nonsensical sublimity of love may invite us to philosophic wonder. The symbolic form of love (animus-anima) shrinks from nothing, least of all from

213

sexual union. There is a "real" partner only if you make him real. Reality is an anthropomorphism.

You really ought to have asked this question when you were here. Volumes could be written about it, which I shall on no account do, however. With best regards,

Yours sincerely, C. G. JUNG

To Poul Bjerre

Dear Colleague,   8 May 1936

Best thanks for the gratifying news that the Swedish group exists. I was not yet fully in the picture, as you told me in your letter of 3 Feb. 1935 that you had not succeeded in forming the national group in face of the resistance from the psychiatric-neurological section. Since then you have sent me no further communication about the constitution of the Society. I shall immediately get our editor to announce the founding of a Swedish group in the *Zentralblatt*.

I shall ask our colleague Brüel whether he intends as before to take in hand the organization of an International Congress in spring 1937.[1] As soon as I have his official consent, I shall, supported by this and by your initiative, turn to the other groups and inform them that there is an invitation from the Scandinavian groups to hold a Congress in Copenhagen.

For your information I would like to tell you that the German group is in a very difficult situation at present. The psychiatrists in Germany are trying to cripple psychotherapy and efforts are now being made to thwart this tendency. I am sorry I cannot give you more details and I would ask you to treat this information with discretion.

I would like to take this opportunity to tell you also that on the 19th of July a psychotherapeutic meeting of an international character will take place in Basel, on the occasion of the "Congrès des Aliénistes et Neurologistes de France et des Pays de Langue Française." This meeting was arranged by the Swiss Commission for Psychotherapy,[2] which was nominated by the Swiss Society for Psychi-

[1] The 9th International Medical Congress for Psychotherapy in Copenhagen, 2–4 Oct. 1937, organized by Bjerre and Brüel. For Jung's presidential address cf. CW 10, pars. 1064ff.
[2] The members of this Commission were Jung, G. Bally (Zurich), O. L. Forel (Prangins), W. Morgenthaler (Bern), de Saussure (Geneva). In 1936 Forel was

atry. I am myself a member of this Commission and at my suggestion four speakers[3] have been appointed, representing the four different psychotherapeutic movements: Freud, Adler, Jung, and the phenomenological school. This is the first attempt to get the various schools to cooperate. Invitations will be sent to you. I wanted, however, to apprise you of this important meeting. Meanwhile with best regards,

Yours sincerely, C. G. JUNG

---

president of the Commission. It was enlarged in 1937 by the election of H. Flournoy (Geneva).
[3] Jung, de Jonge (Prangins), Morgenthaler, Trüb (Zurich).

To Pastor Walther Uhsadel

Dear Pastor Uhsadel,   4 August 1936

Best thanks for kindly sending me the "Johannesbrief 1936,"[1] also for your words on prayer,[2] about which I would have all sorts of things to say though I cannot do so in writing.

By a twist of fate, an acquaintance of mine drew my attention a little while ago to the Berneuchener Circle and especially to its liturgical endeavours. I received a very sympathetic impression. "In the wide ocean you must make a start. There you begin with small things of the seas,"[3] says Proteus to Homunculus. Everything that happens in reality must obey the laws of growth. If a renewal, or I would be inclined to say a justification, of the Protestant Church is to ensue, this can only be done step by step by individuals who do not merely talk about it but to whom it is also a fact. Mass success is a bad sign. If the Church is not something self-evidently eternal it is nothing at all, and for this reason I think the continuity of the rite is extraordinarily important.

☐ Professor of theology, U. of Hamburg.
[1] One of the Jahresbriefe ("yearly letters"—there were actually five letters each year) of the Berneuchener Circle, a German Protestant movement aiming at a deepening of religious life and a liturgical renewal. The name derives from the place of their first meetings, the estate Berneuchen, Neumark, Germany. The letters appeared later as "Evangelische Jahresbriefe," renamed still later "Quatember, Evangelische Jahresbriefe."
[2] An offprint of his "Dein Wille geschehe. Vom Sinn und Wesen des Gebetes" (Thy Will be done. On the Meaning and Essence of Prayer).
[3] Faust II, Act 2 (tr. Wayne, p. 148).

215

As soon as I have more time I will read your words on prayer more closely. Perhaps I shall be able to say something about it. Meanwhile with best thanks,

Yours sincerely, C. G. JUNG

To Pastor Walther Uhsadel

Dear Pastor Uhsadel,   18 August 1936

I have now read your little book on prayer with great interest and I have to agree with all of it on the assumption that you are speaking to believers or at least to people who are capable of believing. You simply take belief for granted. But this presupposition is to a large extent no longer valid and therein lies the whole difficulty. If we believe, then any discussion about prayer is superfluous because it is self-evident. But if we don't believe, it seems to me pointless to talk about prayer. The question then is: Why don't we believe any more? How does one get to believe? Whence does modern man derive any certainty that the circle of the world is open towards the Divine? The unbeliever knows as well as anybody else that this world is in a frightful mess and always was. This knowledge alone has probably never yet prompted any modern man to believe. On the contrary! God's perfection would lead one to expect a perfect work of creation and not this sorry semi-hell of laziness, stupidity, and wickedness. Misery does not always teach prayer by any means but far more often cursing, violence, and criminality.

Among the educated today I have as a rule to deal with people who are incapable of believing and whom I cannot condemn on that account. They are profoundly alienated from the Church as well as from religion because all they hear is "Thou shalt" when they don't know anyway how they could fulfil this commandment. What modern man needs and what would afford the only possibility of a religious attitude is precisely *not* an effort of the will and *not* moral compulsion, but rather the experience that his view of the world, which reflects his hybris of consciousness, is really and truly inadequate. This experience is possible only when something happens to him personally which is not of his conscious doing. It is only the experience of the spontaneous activity of the psyche, independent of his will and consciousness, that has this power of conviction. It seems to me that the most important task of the educator of the soul would be to show people the way to the primordial experience which most clearly befell St. Paul, for example, on the road to Damascus. In my experience this way opens up only during the psychic development of the individual. Naturally I'm speaking of educated people. That collective effects also occur is shown by the amazing success of the Oxford Movement. My own personal view is that this is merely a *psychologie des foules*[1] with a prognosis to match.

The turning away of educated people from the churches is a momentous loss, for it means a slipping of the Church down to a lower, popular level and hence an impoverishment of spiritual life. A Church that has only the support of the masses can hardly be distinguished from the State. It seems to me that Protestantism has lost contact with the individual personality in the most disastrous way. The absence of personal confession and of the exceedingly important function of the *directeur de conscience* is, in a sense, the cause of a dangerous alienation of minds.

I hope you will not be offended by the candour of my remarks. Nobody is more poignantly aware of the necessity of religious convictions than I, but just for that reason I am concerned most of all about the technical question of the way in which religious experience may, so to speak, be induced. With kind regards,

Yours sincerely, C. G. JUNG

[1] Cf. Gustave Le Bon, *The Crowd, A Study of the Popular Mind* (orig. 1895).

Anonymous

Dear Fräulein N., 18 August 1936

With regrettable tardiness I am answering your letter of May 18th. My correspondence is more like a flood than anything that can be kept within reasonable bounds.

As for your question,[1] I am reluctant to answer people I don't know personally, so I can only go into it in a general way. In principle I am always in favour of children leaving their parents as soon as possible once they have reached maturity. Parents must realize that they are trees from which the fruit falls in the autumn. Children don't belong to their parents, and they are only apparently produced by them. In

□ Germany.
[1] N. asked about the problem of her relationship to her apparently tyrannical and possessive parents.

reality they come from a thousand-year-old stem, or rather from many stems, and often they are about as characteristic of their parents as an apple on a fir-tree. Beyond the human obligation to look after ageing parents and to maintain a friendly relation with them, there should be no other dependences, for the young generation has to start life anew and can encumber itself with the past only in case of the greatest necessity. With kindest regards,

Yours sincerely, C. G. JUNG

To Kurt Breysig

Dear Professor Breysig,   20 August 1936

I must apologize many times over for my negligence and forgetfulness. I have just found your article[1] together with your letter of Dec. 1929 and must thank you for your kindness in sending it to me.

It has interested me to see what view a sociologist takes of our psychology. As you have rightly seen, I have no sociological intentions whatever and have therefore left the world of action completely out of account. From the psychological standpoint action is an extremely complicated thing. Only half of it can be understood in terms of the psychology of the individual. For the rest it is an irrational occurrence which is so complicated by a thousand chance conditions that a scientific investigation is practically impossible. As a rule the psychologist can only determine the nature of an attitude, but the action that proceeds from it belongs to the realm of history because of its irrational character. If my psychology had any sociological intentions I would naturally have had to include the world of action. But it purports to be no more than a system for classifying empirically observable attitudes and also symbolic products. The latter aspect in particular may be completely alien to the sociologist, and it does in fact concern only the psychologist who has to do with psycho-phenomenology in the stricter sense.

Again with best thanks, C. G. JUNG

□ (1866–1940), German historian and sociologist, then professor of history in Berlin.
[1] "Seelenbau, Geschichts- und Gesellschaftslehre," *Kölner Vierteljahreshefte für Soziologie und Kölner Sozialpolitische Vierteljahresschrift*, VIII (1929), 1–26.

To Abraham Aaron Roback

[ORIGINAL IN ENGLISH]

Dear Sir,   [Bailey Island, Maine?], 29 September 1936

I am sorry I cannot accept President Moore's kind invitation as I am leaving this country already Oct. 3rd.

Since we are bilingual in Switzerland my name is "Carl" as well as "Charles" (French), so there was not much of a mistake.

Concerning my so-called "Nazi affiliation" there has been quite an unnecessary noise about it. I am no Nazi, as a matter of fact I am quite unpolitical. German psychotherapists asked me to help them to maintain their professional organization, as there was an immediate danger that psychotherapy in Germany would be wiped out of existence. It was considered as "Jewish science" and therefore highly suspect. Those German doctors were my friends and only a coward would leave his friends when they are in dire need of help. Not only did I set up their organization again but I made it clear that psychotherapy is an honest-to-God attempt and moreover I made it possible for Jewish German doctors, being excluded from professional organizations, to become immediate members of the International Society at least. But nobody mentions the fact that so many perfectly innocent existences could have been completely crushed if I had not stepped in.

It is true that I have insisted upon the *difference* between Jewish and Christian psychology[1] since 1917, but Jewish authors have done the same long ago as well as recently.[2] I am no anti-Semite.

From all this I gained neither honours nor money, but I am glad that I could be of service to those in need.

Faithfully yours, C. G. JUNG

☐ Ph.D., American psychologist (1890–1965). — This letter was written in the U.S.A., after Jung had lectured at the Harvard Tercentenary Conference of Arts and Sciences. Cf. Murray, 10 Sept. 35, n. 1.

[1] Cf. "The Role of the Unconscious" (orig. 1918), *Civilization in Transition,* CW 10, pars. 17ff., and "A Rejoinder to Dr. Bally," ibid., pars. 1025ff. & n. 5.

[2] Cf. Freud's letter to Ferenczi, 8 June 13, quoted in Jones, II, p. 168: "Certainly there are great differences between the Jewish and the Aryan spirit [*Geist*]. We can observe that every day. Hence there would assuredly be here and there differences in outlook on life and art." Cf. also Erich Neumann, "In Honour of the Centenary of Freud's Birth," *Journal of Analytical Psychology* (London), I:2 (May 1956).

To Hermann Hesse

Dear Herr Hesse,   27 October 1936

Best thanks for kindly sending me "Josef Knecht's Dream."[1] Is it a dream? And who is the dreamer? Excuse this question of a psychologist who, deeply impressed by the beauty of the form and content, cannot suppress his curiosity. But you need not answer the question.[2] With best greetings,

Yours sincerely, C. G. JUNG

[1] A poem later incorporated in Hesse's novel *Das Glasperlenspiel* (1943) as "Ein Traum" (tr. R. and C. Winston, *The Glass Bead Game* (1969); the poem on pp. 437ff.). The poem was originally published in a private edition, Erasmusdruck, Berlin, Sept. 1936.
[2] Hesse's answer, if there was one, seems to be lost.

To Jolande Jacobi

Dear Frau Jacobi,   27 October 1936

Best thanks for your kind letter. I have just got back from America, where I had a pretty gruelling time. I am thinking of severely restricting my work this winter because I am working on a book that has long been due. I have also suspended most of my lectures and therefore cannot, unfortunately, accept your kind invitation to lecture in Vienna. I regret very much that I cannot duplicate or triplicate myself, which would make things decidedly easier.

With regard to your dream,[1] I entirely agree that it is a "big" one. It is obviously dreamt in a state of introversion. In such a state the deeper layers of the unconscious become activated, and since the collective unconscious does not keep strictly within the limits of time and space as we conceive them, shifts in time and space may easily occur. If in a dream there is an intense regression in time, for instance back to earlier centuries, this also indicates a progression covering the same span of time. Such a dream has always to be understood under two aspects. On the one hand the historical root, on the other the freshness of the tree. The tree is what grows in time.

· · ·

[1] A dream about numbers in relation to time and the aeons of Pisces and Aquarius. Jung's commentary has been omitted except for the concluding paragraph.

The youth always signifies enterprise, hastening ahead, anticipation. The tree expresses spiritual growth in time. The planting of the tree means the beginning of a development whose fruits will appear in the new Platonic month. The two historical vagabonds are the opposite of the youth, namely the historical, primitive element, the deposit of the past in the body. The blood potion seals the union of opposites, the *coniunctio oppositorum* from which new growth will come. The dream is in my opinion a look behind the scenes into the age-old processes of the human mind, which might explain your special feeling of happiness. With best regards,

Yours sincerely, C. G. JUNG

To Oluf Brüel

[ORIGINAL IN ENGLISH]

Dear Dr. Brüel,   12 December 1936

Your news is somewhat disappointing. Fortunately the notice about the Congress has not appeared in the *Zentralblatt* yet. Your proposition to postpone the Congress[1] until September, on the other hand, is an inevitable issue. Concerning the date: 4–6 September, I should plead rather for a later date, end of September or beginning of October. In September I'm usually having my vacations abroad or I'm busy with scientific work which then I should hate to interrupt. I should be much obliged if you could kindly look into this matter and tell me whether it couldn't be the later date.

Concerning your proposition to deal with the theme of "Nationale Bedingtheit der Psychotherapie"[2] I must say that this is an exceedingly ticklish topic. First of all it would demand a very thorough formulation of the differences of national psychologies and then it would challenge all the different political convictions that are actually raging in Europe. It would most certainly provoke a National Socialist outburst of devastating sterility. The general political atmosphere is such that one couldn't dare to introduce any topic that would come anywhere near to politics or nationalistic prejudices. Yes, if psychotherapists were philosophically minded and *au dessus de la mêlée*, nothing would be better and more fruitful than such a discussion, but as things and human beings are what they actually are, I'm afraid that any such discussion is absolutely out of question.

---

[1] Cf. Bjerre, 8 May 36, n. 1.
[2] "Nationalism as a Conditioning Factor in Psychotherapy."

Please let me know as soon as possible what you think about a postponement of our Congress to the end of September or beginning of October.

Sincerely yours, C. G. JUNG

To Heinrich Zimmer

Dear Professor Zimmer,   14 December 1936

First of all I want to thank you most heartily for your very friendly review of *The Tibetan Book of the Dead*.[1]

Secondly, I enclose letters of recommendation to various Americans.[2] I give you these letters sealed, because they also contain personal matters.

1. Prof. W. E. Clark[3] of Harvard University, whom I know personally. I had some delightful talks with him on the occasion of my visit there. He is a very introverted man who must be approached with the politeness due to animals in the bush, that is to say one must act as if one had not seen him and must talk softly and slowly so as not to scare him off. It is also advisable to whistle before going into the forest so that the rhinos won't be startled out of their slumbers but are gently and melodiously prepared for your coming and have time to make themselves scarce. He has a very nice wife who is the exact opposite.

2. I also recommend you to Prof. W. E. Hocking[4] of Harvard University. This one is "correct." He wears a stiff collar day and night. But once you have deeply acknowledged his correctness and conventionality and given him a chance to explain that he is not what he looks like, the way is paved for a useful conversation. His rebellion against American Christianity, or rather against the *Genius Agri Harvardensis*, has brought about a strong link with Taoist philosophy. A few sublimities dropped *sotto voce* from Chuang-tsu and Chu-hsi[5] should strike the right note. His wife overflows with feeling and it is very advantageous to display a certain helplessness.

---

[1] Review of Jung's "Psychological Commentary on *The Tibetan Book of the Dead*," CW 11. The review cannot be traced.
[2] Zimmer, whose wife was partially of Jewish ancestry, had decided to leave Germany. Cf. Zimmer, 21 Nov. 32.
[3] Walter Eugene Clark (1881–1960), professor of Sanskrit.
[4] Cf. Hocking, 5 May 39.
[5] Chinese philosopher (1130–1200).

3. The third recommendation is to Prof. Harry Caplan[6] at Cornell University.

4. The fourth is to Prof. Blake,[7] director of the Widener Library at Harvard. He is Gargantuan in every respect and helpful like all fat people. He is a linguist (Slavic languages).

5. Don't omit to visit my friend Leonard Bacon, the American poet, whose most important work appears to be his "Animula Vagula."[8] He lives in his private theatre where it is all tremendously noisy and diverting.

6. In New York I can recommend you to our Psychological Club, whose president is Dr. E. Henley. . . .

I should be greatly obliged if you could tell me whereabouts in Indian literature Surya[9] or the sun is described as one-footed. I think I have read it somewhere but cannot find the note. With best wishes,

Yours sincerely, c. g. jung

[6] 1930–67 professor of classics.

[7] Robert Pierpont Blake, 1928–36 director of Harvard U. Library; linguist and Byzantinist.

[8] "Little wandering soul," the opening words of a poem by the Roman emperor Hadrian. Bacon (1887–1954), poet and formerly professor of English at Berkeley, wrote his *Animula Vagula* (1926) in Zurich while working with Jung. Pulitzer Prize for Poetry, 1941.

[9] In the *Atharva Veda*, XIII.1.32, the sun-god Rohita, synonymous with Surya, the sun, is called the "one-footed goat." Cf. *Mysterium Coniunctionis*, par. 734.

To Abraham Aaron Roback

[ORIGINAL IN ENGLISH]

Dear Mr. Roback,   19 December 1936

I have received your big book[1] for which I thank you warmly. As a matter of fact I found it at home when I came back from my rather long trip.

Your remark has interested me very much, namely that you have made experiments about the mental differences between Jews and non-Jews and I should be much obliged to you if you could drop me a hint about your results. When I wrote about this difference I had in mind my own experiences which are not experimental but medical. There is indeed a marked difference which has much to do with the age of the race. I found something very similar in Hindus, namely an

[1] From the context of the letter this is probably Roback's *Jewish Influence in Modern Thought* (1929).

223

extension or extensibility of consciousness into the subconscious mind which is not to be found or is at least very rare with non-Jews. Also the tendency of consciousness to autonomy with the risk of severing it almost entirely from its instinctive sources. Freud is very typical in that respect. To him as to many other Jews, as I have seen with my own eyes, the re-establishment of the communication with the instincts means a true and vital find and source of satisfaction and joy. Non-Jewish people don't feel like that, they rather experience it as a restriction of moral freedom. That explains the peculiar leaning of Protestant parsons to Freudian analysis. In their hands it is a beautiful means to show a brand-new category of sins to people of which they never dreamt before.

I see that you assume that I have almost no Jewish pupils in the United States. That is not quite true. There is a number of Jewish doctors who have studied with me, but the reason why you haven't discovered them is that they are undiscoverable on account of their fear of being recognized as Jungians. The monopoly of psychoanalysis doesn't stand outsiders. So they are just afraid of deviating from the creed. As a matter of fact my first and most gifted pupils were Jews. In Europe there are however two or three who dared to show their hand and to acknowledge the origin whence they came.

I'm quite aware of the fact that Freud's statement is necessary for the Jew, yet in so far as there are non-Jews and in so far as there are even among Jews not a few who ought to see beyond, I have been forced by my patients to develop a point of view that considers the one and the other need. Unfortunately the political events in Germany have made it quite impossible to say anything reasonable about the most interesting difference between Jewish and non-Jewish psychology. The disinterested discussion of this most interesting difference is well-nigh impossible in our time of a new barbary. One risks being labelled as anti-Semite or pro-Semite without being heard at all.

I have not yet read your book carefully, but I didn't want to wait any longer to thank you for your very generous gift.

Sincerely yours, C. G. JUNG

To Alan W. Watts

[ORIGINAL IN ENGLISH]
Dear Sir,   21 December 1936

I'm sorry to be so late in thanking you for kindly sending me the "Wheel of Life."[1] I have seen it already.

As you rightly point out, it is not exactly what I meant by manda-las,[2] although figuratively it is a mandala. There are as you certainly know two kinds: the one I would call a mandala proper, namely for purposes of magic and worship, generally yoga practices. And the other, the cosmic, geographical, "scientific" mandala. The "Wheel of Life" belongs to the latter category. It is a close parallel to our Western cosmological, geographical, and physiological representations, of which you find plenty of examples in alchemistic philosophy and in the early mystical texts (f.i. Hildegard von Bingen). The Trinity is very frequently the centre. Such mandalas are usually based upon even numbers. That is as you see the reason why I said that I haven't come across Buddhist mandalas based upon 3, 5, or 6 (2 x 3).

I'm most indebted to you for mentioning the literature concerning the "Wheel."

Yours truly, C. G. JUNG

☐ Originally British, now American; author of books mainly on Eastern religion and philosophy.
[1] The Tibetan (or Indian) "wheel of life" symbolizes the world of *samsara*, the eternal cycle of birth and death, to escape from which is the aim of enlighten-ment. For an example of the wheel cf. "Concerning Mandala Symbolism," CW 9, i, Fig. 3.
[2] Cf. ibid., also *Psychology and Alchemy*, Part II, ch. 3.

To Martin Elsässer

Dear Professor Elsässer,   28 January 1937

It was a great pleasure to hear from you again.

Ende's pictures[1] are interesting but largely uninterpretable because they do not, as Goethe wants,[2] refer to something universal but to a universality that is hidden behind something unique and personal. For Ende the symbolic figure is essentially only an aesthetic problem which he flunks. The point is, as I have often found with artists, that they go chasing after the striking form but not the meaningful one.

☐ Professor of architecture at Stuttgart and chief town architect at Frankfurt am Main (1884–1957). 1933–47 in Turkey.
[1] Edgar Ende, German surrealist painter.
[2] Cf. Goethe's essay "Einfache Nachahmung der Natur, Manier, Stil" (1789), in *Kunstschriften* (Leipzig, 1923), pp. 62f.: "The more the imitation [of nature] . . . learns to arrange individual objects under universal concepts, the more worthy it will become to enter the threshold of the sanctuary."

Thus the figure of the old philosopher could just as well be a pole or a bird or a triangle or anything else. It is painfully apparent in the pictures that the painter is standing before closed doors through which, admittedly, a ray of light falls, but crookedly. This is the sickness of our modern artists, that they only paint or draw and reckon it a virtue to do anything rather than think, unlike the great artists of the Renaissance. I have always found it very difficult to discuss these problems with an artist, whereas I could have learnt a lot from Mantegna. The greatness of the Renaissance artist lies not least in the fact that he worked with the whole of his personality, while the artist of today assiduously avoids anything meaningful.

I thank you very much for your letter and wish you all the best. With greetings also to your wife,

Yours sincerely, C. G. JUNG

To Swami Devatmananda

[ORIGINAL IN ENGLISH]

Dear Sir,   9 February 1937

It is exceedingly difficult to explain the nature of the archetype[1] to somebody who does not know about the empirical material we are dealing with in psychology. The only parallel I can point to outside the psychological field is the so-called mythological motif in myths, legends, folklore, and religions. If you study such a motif you will find that it is by no means outright,[2] but a living structure representing something that could be called an image. Inasmuch as legends etc. are transmitted by tradition, the archetypes are consciously acquired, but inasmuch as archetypes are found in the mind of the insane as well as in normal dreams quite outside all tradition, archetypes appear also to be contents of the collective unconscious and their existence in the individual mind can only be explained by inheritance.

□ Portland, Oregon.

[1] In his later writings Jung developed and expanded the concept of the archetype considerably. He distinguished sharply between the irrepresentable, transcendental archetype *per se* and its visible manifestation in consciousness as the archetypal image or symbol. Moreover the archetype *per se* appears to be an *a priori* conditioning factor in the human psyche, comparable to the biological "pattern of behaviour," "a 'disposition' which starts functioning at a given moment in the development of the human mind and arranges the material of consciousness into definite patterns" ("A Psychological Approach to the Dogma of the Trinity," CW 11, par. 222 & n. 2).

[2] = straightforward?

Concerning your question about free will, the fact is that free will only exists within the limits of consciousness. Beyond those limits there is mere compulsion. Why there are people who have the will or a striving for the limitless I don't know. I'm not a philosopher, I'm an empiricist. But I admit there are such people. I know that in the East one explains the particular form of individual character by the doctrine of karma.[3] This is a doctrine which one can believe or disbelieve. Being not a philosopher but an empiricist, I'm missing the objective evidence. Science has no answer to questions which reach beyond human possibilities. We have no evidence for the objective functions of the psyche apart from the living brain. At all events there is no possibility whatever of examining such a psychological condition supposed to exist outside the human brain. We can think all sorts of things about such a hypothetical condition, but the answer is unavoidably a mere assumption which may satisfy the human desire for a faith but not the desire for knowledge.

You will find the definition of the collective unconscious in my book *Psychological Types*. The individual unconscious and the collective unconscious together form what I call the "self." You will find that definition also in *Psychological Types*.[4]

Sincerely yours, c. g. j u n g

[3] The doctrine of karma (Skt., deed, action, fate) teaches the retribution for every individual action. Combined with the doctrine of transmigration of the soul, it explains how the actions in one of the successive lives of an individual determine his fate in the next.
[4] Cf. CW 6, Defs. 16 and 46.

To Pastor H. Wegmann

Dear Pastor Wegmann,   5 March 1937

As you know, the public is beginning to get very interested in psychological discussions. We have here a Society for Practical Psychology[1] where medical psychotherapists and lay psychologists with an academic training try to come to terms with one another. These discussions would not in our opinion be complete unless we included the theologian. He, after all, is equally concerned with the problem of the soul and its manifold sufferings. So the question was

[1] Schweizer Gesellschaft für praktische Psychologie, where W. gave a lecture in June 1937 on "Seelische Heilung durch religiöse Einordnung."

recently raised in our Society whether it would not be possible to hear a theologian talk about the problem of treatment. On this occasion my thoughts turned to you, because I know it is a problem that is close to your heart.

I would therefore like to ask you whether you would be prepared to give a lecture to our Society sometime—perhaps in the coming summer semester—in which you would approach the whole problem from the theological side. I can assure you that you will have an attentive and sympathetic audience. I personally would be very grateful if you would undertake this task. In the interests of all concerned I think it is of the utmost importance that the foundations should be laid for an all-round understanding. Naturally this is possible only if all the faculties with similar interests are represented. The theological faculties are of little help to us here, for what we need are people with practical experience who alone are in a position to talk about reality.

I hope very much that you will give due consideration to our request.

Yours sincerely, c. g. jung

To H. G. Baynes

[ORIGINAL IN ENGLISH]

Dear Peter,   6 March 1937

Thank you very much for kindly sending me your two offprints.[1] I shall read them as soon as I have a few quiet moments. But you know everybody and everything keeps me busy here. I shall probably have to wait for my vacation to do some human and normal work.

Concerning the question of traumatic schizophrenia, you are free to use this term inasmuch as you have sufficient evidence to substantiate such a term. It is quite possible and indeed even probable that a specific disposition consisting in a congenitally fragile tissue can be fatally upset by an emotion. It is even a widespread experience that psychosis can be acutely produced by overwhelming emotions.

□ Helton Godwin Baynes, M.D., (1882–1943), English psychotherapist, author, and translator of several of Jung's works. Cf. his *Mythology of the Soul* (1940); *Germany Possessed* (1941); *Analytical Psychology and the English Mind* (1950). ("Peter" is a friendly nickname.) Cf. also Kuhn, 1 Jan. 26, n. 2; pls. iii, iv.
1 "The Psychological Background of the Parent-Child Relation" (read at the Medical Society of Individual Psychology, London, Oct. 1936), and "The Ghost as a Psychic Phenomenon" (read at a private meeting of the Society for Psychical Research, Nov. 1936). Both published in *Analytical Psychology and the English Mind*.

228

The insect drawings[2] you mention don't necessarily prove that there is a psychosis. They only show that there is a tendency towards a basic schizophrenic dissociation, the insects representing autonomous (Mendelian?) units that have a certain tendency to autonomy. In the same way as the cave-dweller filled the remote corners of his caves with drawings of hunting animals, so your patient tries to catch his autonomous units by drawing them. He tries to keep them in association with his conscious mind, thus decreasing the danger that they all run away in different directions and disappear altogether. The fact that he can draw them shows that his conscious mind is synthetic enough to control these little beasts which, if the control should fail, would reappear as those well-known schizophrenic personality-fragments or *insulae*. The insects that appear on the tree show that he succeeded in establishing the proper hierarchy in his unconscious. At least the picture points out that positive possibility. You know the schizophrenic disposition is rooted much deeper than the neurotic one. It really starts in the sympathetic system. I have seen the results of certain researches which are carried on by a chemist in the psychopathic hospital in Boston about schizophrenia. These results show that the physiological coordination of vegetative processes is just as much and in the same way disturbed as the mental coordination. The vegetative factors also go by themselves.

Cordially yours, C. G. JUNG

[2] Baynes was at that time engaged on the *Mythology of the Soul*, an investigation of schizophrenic dreams and drawings. Drawing 19 shows the two insects which were the subject of his question (pp. 715, 731ff.). Part of Jung's letter, modified, is published on pp. 704f.

To Pastor Fritz Pfäfflin

Dear Pastor Pfäfflin,   9 March 1937

. . .

Your idea of writing a doctoral thesis about sin is brilliant. That is something I would definitely like to know, what sin really is, seeing that theology has been talking about it for thousands of years. In my theological impartiality I would say that only the good Lord can decide, as stands clearly written in the Acts of the Apostles. Everything else is man-made law, wholly time-conditioned and relative. Men would never have talked of sin and the forgiveness of sin had

229

this not been a fundamental psychological fact that existed long before there were any laws. Deviation from the will of the gods was a preoccupation of humanity even in primeval times. In this sense "the old man" would have a very great deal to say. But this sense is far more comprehensive and in a way more inexorable than any human law. With kind regards,

Yours sincerely, c. g. jung

To Gerda Hipert

Dear Frau Hipert,   20 March 1937

You have seen quite correctly that the attitude-type remains more or less constant but that the function-type is subject to all manner of changes in the course of life. During a practical analysis you can observe an extremely interesting transition from the differentiated function to its auxiliary function and from this to its counter-function and thence to the undifferentiated or inferior function.[1]

You are right when you say that ethical values are the product of a highly differentiated feeling function. Naturally the intellect also plays a part in working out and formulating an ethic, but the decisive contents all come from feeling.

You are right, too, about the difference between men and women in relation to the idea. It is correct to say that women are more dependent on the idea and men more dependent on the primordial image. Naturally this is true only of those women in whom the idea functions at all, just as the primordial image becomes effective only when a man takes account of feeling. There is as yet no literature on the animus problem except for my wife's essay "Ein Beitrag zum Problem des Animus"[2] in *Wirklichkeit der Seele*, Rascher, Zurich, 1934.

It is true, of course, that inability to express oneself is a defect and in a deeper sense a fault in so far as it is incumbent upon people to realize their psychic contents whether in words, images, or deeds. But since different types do in fact exist, and men and women besides, one simply cannot imagine any form of words or any image

□ Leipzig.

[1] For a brief explanation of the terms used in this paragraph cf. *Psychological Types*, pars. 556, 666ff., 751, and Defs. 22, 30, 55.

[2] "On the Nature of the Animus," in Emma Jung, *Animus and Anima* (tr. Cary F. Baynes; Analytical Psychology Club of New York, 1957).

230

that could express a content with absolute validity and absolute conviction. What is the most perfect and clearest expression for one person can be a dead formula or a bewildering complication for another. This is due partly to the fact that human beings are defective in some way, but also to the fact that every conceivable expression is necessarily one-sided, for what is idea is not word and what is word is not deed, though all three should be one. Such completeness and perfection is only a religious legend but unfortunately never a reality in the usual sense of the word.

Yours sincerely, C. G. JUNG

To Rudolf Pannwitz

Dear Dr. Pannwitz,   27 March 1937

That you find Kierkegaard "frightful" has warmed the cockles of my heart.[1] I find him simply insupportable and cannot understand, or rather, I understand only too well, why the theological neurosis of our time has made such a fuss over him. You are quite right when you say that the pathological is never valuable. It does, however, cause us the greatest difficulties and for this reason we learn the most from it. Moreover hysteria presents certain peculiarities of the normal person in such exaggerated form that even in their blindness the doctors, who as a rule know the least about psychology, could not help stumbling upon them. I therefore chalk up the symptomatology of the neuroses as an involuntary achievement to man's credit, for which I am indeed grateful in my fashion. I also agree with you that the normal person is infinitely more interesting and valuable. Hence I have endeavoured to remove our "complex" psychology as quickly and completely as possible out of the realm of pathology. However, as you have rightly seen, I have landed myself in enormous difficulties by framing general formulations which are intended to explain the whole field of human experience. I had to keep to experiences that were directly accessible to me and compare them with data drawn from the whole history of the mind. This gives rise to some degree of inexactitude which makes my efforts appear provisional. It is perfectly clear to me that everything I do is pioneer work which has

□ (1881–1969), German author (then in Yugoslavia), follower of Nietzsche.
[1] Concerning Jung's negative attitude to Kierkegaard, cf. Künzli, 27 Feb. 43 and 16 Mar. 43, and Bremi, 26 Dec. 53.

still to be followed by a real laying of foundations, but there are gratifying signs that others are beginning to make forays into this territory.

I enclose a little offprint[2] which is of no further interest but only an attempt such as one might make to explain things to a doctor. It is an essay included in the *Eranos-Jahrbuch 1934* (Rhein Verlag, Zurich, 1935).

My letter is unfortunately overdue. Illness and inordinate pressure of work have prevented me from writing until now.

Yours sincerely, c. g. j u n g

[2] "Archetypes of the Collective Unconscious," CW 9, i.

To Dr. S.

Dear Colleague,   27 March 1937

As I was reading your dream[1] the thought suddenly struck me that it had almost a literary ring. Have you never thought of using this material for a two-tiered novel, one tier being played out in three dimensions, the other in four? Your dream is really the stuff artists work with. In this respect the dream is so excellent that I would conjecture that your descriptive powers are equal to the task in the world of consciousness as well. Action as we know can take place only in the third dimension, and the fourth dimension is that which actually wants to grow into our conscious three-dimensional world. This realization is man's task *par excellence*. All culture is an extension of consciousness, and just as modern physics can no longer do without four-dimensional thinking, so our psychological view of the world will have to concern itself with these problems. With best regards,

Yours sincerely, c. g. j u n g

[1] The dreamer was in prison and was trying to dispose of a manuscript on which he had been working. The prison then turned into a hospital where he was a patient. The doctor told him that he, the dreamer, had done some strange things. Then he seemed to be a doctor (which he was in real life) and tried to give an injection, either to himself or to a patient.

To J. Wilhelm Hauer

Dear Professor Hauer,   7 June 1937

Excuse my long silence, but I am so busy at present that I have practically no time to attend to my correspondence.

I have considered your suggestion and welcome the idea of a meeting. A seminar on comparative religion would be particularly valuable to us. But as I don't know how you would take to this idea, please tell me what you think about it.

The connection between race and religion, which you have in mind, is a very difficult theme. Since the anthropological concept of race as an essentially biological factor remains completely unclarified, to demonstrate a connection between religion and this scarcely definable factor seems to me almost too bold an undertaking. I myself have personally treated very many Jews and know their psychology in its deepest recesses, so I can recognize the relation of their racial psychology to their religion, but it would be quite beyond me to relate Islam or the ancient Egyptian religion to its devotees as I lack any intimate knowledge of Arab and Egyptian psychology. I would be just as incapable of establishing a real connection between the non-Semitic Berber race and the Aryan Mohammedan population of India. I have some insight into Indian psychology and have also analysed a Parsee, but would not be able to relate Parseeism, which is essentially different from the Indian religion, to what I know of the racial psychology of the Indians.

I see enormous scientific difficulties in this field which could hardly be dealt with in a seminar. Hence I would rather suggest to you a theme on comparative religion and would ask you to let me know your opinion.[1] With best regards,

Yours sincerely, C. G. JUNG

[1] No seminar on either theme was ever held.

To P. W. Martin

[ORIGINAL IN ENGLISH]

Dear Mr. Martin,   20 August 1937

I'm indeed very sorry that I have left your letter unanswered, but I was so busy that I could not find the necessary time to answer your question properly.

It is a very difficult and important question, what you call the technique of dealing with the shadow.[1] There is, as a matter of fact, no technique at all, inasmuch as technique means that there is a known and perhaps even prescribable way to deal with a certain difficulty or task. It is rather a dealing comparable to diplomacy or statesmanship. There is, for instance, no particular technique that would help us to reconcile two political parties opposing each other. It can be a question of good will, or diplomatic cunning or civil war or anything. If one can speak of a technique at all, it consists solely in an attitude. First of all one has to accept and to take seriously into account the existence of the shadow. Secondly, it is necessary to be informed about its qualities and intentions. Thirdly, long and difficult negotiations will be unavoidable.

. . .

Nobody can know what the final outcome of such negotiations will be. One only knows that through careful collaboration the problem itself becomes changed. Very often certain apparently impossible intentions of the shadow are mere threats due to an unwillingness on the part of the ego to enter upon a serious consideration of the shadow. Such threats diminish usually when one meets them seriously. Pairs of opposites have a natural tendency to meet on the middle line, but the middle line is never a compromise thought out by the intellect and forced upon the fighting parties. It is rather a result of the conflict one has to suffer. Such conflicts are never solved by a clever trick or by an intelligent invention but by enduring them. As a matter of fact, you have to heat up such conflicts until they rage in full swing so that the opposites slowly melt together. It is a sort of alchemistic procedure rather than a rational choice and decision. The suffering is an indispensable part of it. Every real solution is only reached by intense suffering. The suffering shows the degree in which we are intolerable to ourselves. "Agree with thine enemy" outside and inside! That's the problem! Such agreement should violate yourself as little as your enemy. I admit it is not easy to find the right formula, yet if you find it you have made a whole of yourself and this, I think, is the meaning of human life.

In the meantime you have received my Terry Lectures.[2] I should

□ (1893–1971), founder of the International Study Centre of Applied Psychology, Oxted, England. Cf. his *Experiment in Death* (1955).

[1] Cf. *Aion*, CW 9, ii, ch. II.

[2] *Psychology and Religion: The Terry Lectures* (1938), now in CW 11. The lectures were given at Yale University under the auspices of the Dwight Harrington Terry Foundation.

be very much obliged if you kindly looked them through, and you are only expected to correct the worst errors in orthography and style. But I have to bear it if the general style is somewhat awkward and crude. In America I'm not expected to write a flawless style. So please don't spend too much time on it. If you just read through them it will be all they need. I hope so at least! I'm very grateful to you for your willingness to give me your help.

Sincerely yours, c. g. jung

To Pastor Fritz Pfäfflin

Dear Pastor Pfäfflin,   30 August 1937

A real grounding as a psychotherapist requires systematic study, above all a training analysis. I don't think occasional consultations can replace the continuity of the analytical process. Of course you can learn all sorts of useful things from them, but that is not a professional grounding. I think you would do better to acquire as much knowledge within your own field of work as you reasonably and possibly can, and so gain sufficient understanding from daily life. In this way you will build up over the years a procedure that is peculiarly your own. After all, there must be not only psychotherapists but also theologians with psychological knowledge, otherwise it would be better to turn the whole Church into a psychological clinic. But the task of the Church is not the same as that of psychotherapy. The Church means serving the community, therapy serves the individual. There are plenty of people who can only be reached collectively.

Best thanks for your interesting review. Your honest words will be a thorn in the flesh for many. With best regards,

Yours sincerely, c. g. jung

To V. Subrahamanya Iyer

[ORIGINAL IN ENGLISH]

Dear Sir,   16 September 1937

I quite agree with you that it is a noble pursuit for any philosophy to seek a way to happiness for all mankind. It is quite obvious that

☐ Guru (teacher and spiritual guide) of the Maharajah of Mysore (cf. *Memories*, pp. 275/257). He came to Europe to represent India at the International

235

one cannot attain to this end without eradicating misery. Philosophy must find a way to accomplish the destruction of misery in order to attain to happiness. I should call it a pretty ambitious task, however, to eradicate misery and I'm not so optimistic as to believe that such a task could be accomplished. On the contrary, I believe that misery is an intrinsic part of human life, without which we would never do anything. We always try to escape misery. We do it in a million different ways and none of them entirely succeeds. Thus I come to the conclusion that a feasible thing would be to try to find at least a way how to enable people to endure the inevitable misery which is the lot of every human life. If anybody achieves at least endurance of misery, he has already accomplished an almost superhuman task. This might give him some happiness or satisfaction. If you call this happiness, I wouldn't have much to say against it.[1]

I sincerely hope that I shall see you again in India.[2] In the meantime I remain with every good wish,

Yours faithfully, C. G. JUNG

Congress of Philosophy at the Sorbonne, Paris, in 1937. Jung invited him, together with Paul Brunton, English writer on Yoga and related subjects, to Küsnacht, where they discussed problems of Indian philosophy.

[1] Walther Uhsadel (cf. Uhsadel, 4 Aug. 36), in his book *Evangelische Seelsorge* (1966), p. 121, reports a conversation he had with Jung in 1938 at his house in Küsnacht. Jung, pointing to a copy of one of the glass windows in the monastery at Königsfelden, Aargau, Switzerland, representing the Crucifixion, said: "'You see, this is the crux for us.' When I asked him why, he replied: 'I've just got back from India, and it has struck me with renewed force. Man has to cope with the problem of suffering. The Oriental wants to get rid of suffering by casting it off. Western man tries to suppress suffering with drugs. But suffering has to be overcome, and the only way to overcome it is to endure it. We learn that only from him.' And here he pointed to the Crucified."

[2] Jung had "searching talks" with Iyer on his visit to India the following year, when the British Government invited him to take part in the celebration of the 25th anniversary of the U. of Calcutta (cf. *Memories*, pp. 274ff./256ff.).

To Kendig B. Cully

[ORIGINAL IN ENGLISH]

Dear Sir, 25 September 1937

You can learn a great deal of psychology through studying books, but you will find that this psychology is not very helpful in practical

□ Westfield, Massachusetts.

life. A man entrusted with the care of souls ought to have a certain wisdom of life which does not consist of words only but chiefly of experience. Such psychology, as I understand it, is not only a piece of knowledge but a certain wisdom of life at the same time. If such a thing can be taught at all, it must be in the way of a personal experience of the human soul. Such an experience is possible only when the teaching has a personal character, namely when you are personally taught and not generally. In India since ancient times they have the custom that practically everybody of a certain education, at least, has a guru, a spiritual leader who teaches you and you alone what you ought to know. Not everybody needs to know the same thing and this kind of knowledge can never be taught in the same way. That is a thing which is utterly lacking in our universities: the relation of master and disciple. And that is at the same time the thing which you ought to have and any of your colleagues who want to have a psychological preparation.

Anybody whose calling it is to guide souls should have his own soul guided first, so that he knows what it means to deal with the human soul. Knowing your own darkness is the best method for dealing with the darknesses of other people. It would not help you very much to study books only, though it is indispensable too. But it would help you most to have a personal insight into the secrets of the human soul. Otherwise everything remains a clever intellectual trick, consisting of empty words and leading to empty talk. You may try to find out what I mean in my books and if you have a close friend, try to look behind his screen in order to discover yourself. That would be a good beginning.

Sincerely yours, C. G. JUNG

To Norbert Drewitt, O.P.

[ORIGINAL IN ENGLISH]

Dear Father,   25 September 1937

I am much obliged to you for kindly sending me your offprints and notes. It has interested me very much indeed to read them. I was particularly satisfied with the fact that you clearly understand that I am not a mystic but an empiricist. It is true however that a vivid interest in religion and religious truth has guided my research. My chief curiosity was always the question: What does the human

□ Oxford. O.P. = Order of Preachers (the Catholic Ordo Praemonstratensis).

mind, inasmuch as it is a natural involuntary functioning, produce if left to itself? Such a problem, of course, is only possible after a complete renunciation of all traditional truth, no matter how true it may be. Whatever my statements are, they are always based upon experiences, and whatever I say is never intended to contradict or to defend an existing truth. Its sole purpose is to express what I believe I have seen. Whatever I try in the way of explanation, it never intends to explain away or to recommend or to advise, its sole purpose is to make a particular kind of experience generally and humanly understandable.

I see from your writings that you make a most serious attempt to understand and clarify an exceedingly involved situation. Your standpoint is of course a positive creed, while I start from a complete lack of truth and understanding. Yet we are working at the same problem. I also am impressed by the fact of your complete sincerity and honesty. I believe therefore that whatever the book you are writing may contain, it will be an honest attempt at a reconciliation of scientific statements with revealed truth. I am inclined to believe from what I know already that such an enterprise is possible. But I wish I could talk to you once personally in order to explain to you what my standpoint is in this matter. I am afraid that I am unable to do it in a letter. It would require too much space and time. I am coming to England next spring at the beginning of April and I should much appreciate it if you would kindly allow me to call on you once during my stay in London.

Sincerely yours, C. G. JUNG

To M. H. Göring

Dear Colleague,   16 November 1937

Dr. Meier has drawn my attention to your short review of Rosenberg's book.[1] For anyone who knows Jewish history, and in particular Hasidism, Rosenberg's assertion that the Jews despise mysticism is a highly regrettable error. I would therefore suggest that we pass over this book in silence. I cannot allow my name to be associated with such lapses. With best regards,

Yours sincerely, C. G. JUNG

[1] Alfred Rosenberg, *Der Mythus des 20. Jahrhunderts* (1930). This book was the most egregious exposition and pseudo-scientific foundation of the Nazi doctrines on civilization.

To J. Heider

Dear Herr Heider,   1 December 1937

. . .

As to your question about X., I can only say the following. It frequently happens that when a person with whom one was intimate dies, either one is oneself drawn into the death, so to speak, or else this burden has the opposite effect of a task that has to be fulfilled in real life. One could say figuratively that a bit of life has passed over from the dead to the living and compels him towards its realization. In the case of X. there was probably an unfulfillment of this kind. This fact, as said, can either hold you back from life or prevail upon you to live. It is also probable that, if you are not one with yourself anyway, you get into a conflict, because the bit of life taken over from the dead is of a conflicting nature, both dead and living at once.

As a rule the undifferentiated function always lags behind real life a little and is constantly oriented to the past. In such cases the unconscious sends out compensatory hints which should be heeded if one has a positive attitude to life. If something is then undertaken, what passed over from the dead is realized in this undertaking. As you know, it need not be anything agreeable, it can also be a great difficulty because it always has to do with the still undifferentiated side of oneself and consequently calls up the inferior function. With kind regards,

Yours sincerely, C. G. JUNG

☐ Zurich.

Anonymous

Dear Dr. N.,   2 December 1937

I have the feeling that you are really going a bit too far. We should make a halt before something destructive. You know what my attitude is to the unconscious. There is no point in delivering oneself over to it to the last drop. If that were the right procedure, nature would never have invented consciousness, and then the animals would be the ideal embodiments of the unconscious. In my view it is absolutely essential always to have our consciousness well enough in hand to pay sufficient attention to our reality, to the Here and Now.

☐ Switzerland (a woman).

Otherwise we are in danger of being overrun by an unconscious which knows nothing of this human world of ours. The unconscious can realize itself only with the help of consciousness and under its constant control. At the same time consciousness must keep one eye on the unconscious and the other focussed just as clearly on the potentialities of human existence and human relationships.

I certainly don't want to interfere, but before I go to India I would beg you to reflect on this warning. With kindest regards,

Yours, CARL

To Dr. S.

Dear Colleague,   22 February 1938

The feeling of inner detachment and isolation is not in itself an abnormal phenomenon but is normal in the sense that consciousness has withdrawn from the phenomenal world and got outside time and space. You will find the clearest parallels in Indian philosophy, especially in Yoga.

In your case the feeling is reinforced by your psychological studies. The assimilated unconscious apparently disappears in consciousness without trace, but it has the effect of detaching consciousness from its ties to the object. I have described this development in my commentary on the *Golden Flower*.[1] It is a sort of integration process and emancipation of consciousness. The cross is an indication of this, since it represents an integration of the 4 (functions). It is perfectly understandable that, when consciousness detaches itself from the object, the feeling arises that one does not know where one stands. Actually one is standing nowhere, because standing has a below and an above. But there one has no below and above at all, because spatiality pertains to the world of the senses, and consciousness possesses spatiality only when it is in participation with that world. It is a not-knowing, which has the same positive character as nirvana in the Buddhist definition, or the *wu-wei*,[2] not-doing, of the Chinese, which does not mean doing nothing.

The profound doubt you seem to be suffering from is quite in order as it simply expresses the detachment of consciousness and the

[1] Cf. *Alchemical Studies*, CW 13, pars. 64ff.
[2] Cf. *The Way and Its Power* (tr. Waley), ch. XXXVII: "Tao never does; yet through it all things are done."

resultant explanation of the objective world as an illusion. The neurotic character of your scepticism is due essentially to the fact that you cannot accept positively the development that is being prepared or is already in progress but fight against it for understandable reasons: it is a figurative death against which one naturally has all kinds of objections to make.

If your shadow exhibits no inferior features you can be sure that your consciousness is living in the shade, that is, is playing a negative role. But that doesn't necessarily make you a dark horse. It only means that your consciousness is not yet able to see anything positive in this development towards not-being. As a result, the shadow naturally gets a positive value. There is indeed an important task you have left unfinished. The development now being offered to you is not accepted positively, whereas it is the meaning and purpose of all life's wisdom to go along with natural developments that spring from the functioning of the whole personality. With best greetings and wishes,

Yours sincerely, C. G. JUNG

To Boshi Sen

[ORIGINAL IN ENGLISH]

My dear Boshi Sen,   24 February 1938

Thank you very much for the two excellent pictures which I greatly enjoyed. They vividly bring back my visit at Bosepara Lane.[1]

I never mind an argument. Presumably you mean the eternal continuation of existence. India is keen on such speculations. I am as modest as an earthworm when it comes to such things. I assume nothing at all about it. As long as it is so difficult for us to understand the secrets of an atom or of the living protoplasm, we are surely not fit to touch upon a question like that of a continuation of life beyond material visibility. We don't even understand it when it is in matter, how could we hope to have any insight into it without matter? I also don't know whether continuation of life beyond earthly existence would be a good or bad thing. In such big matters I always argue that we are here and now and whatever the future here and now

□ Indian biologist, collaborated with Sir Jagadis Chunder Bose (1858–1937), the famous Indian plant physiologist and physicist. Sen was a follower of the teachings of Ramakrishna and Vivekananda (cf. Mees, 15 Sept. 47).
[1] Sen's residence in Calcutta.

241

is will be seen when it is there. If we should discover ourselves in a new garment and in a new place we shall say: Alas, once more! And we shall crawl through it as we have done hitherto.

The two greatest things of India, in my humble opinion, are the earth of the great mountain in the North and the spirit of Buddha in the South.

Please give my best regards to Mrs. Sen. I remembered her request on the way back, but I didn't feel equal to the task of writing something about India. I was still too much in it. But I will try now to formulate some of my impressions.[2] Thus later you will hear of me again.

Cordially yours, C. G. JUNG

[2] "The Dreamlike World of India" and "What India Can Teach Us," CW 10.

To Eric Benjamin Strauss

[ORIGINAL IN ENGLISH]

Dear Dr. Strauss,   26 March 1938

Thank you for your letter. I shall answer it more fully when I have Professor Göring's reply.

As you know pars. 2, 3, and 4 of our regulations allows the participation of everyone, quite apart from his political or religious convictions. The question of race is not mentioned at all. I should be much obliged if you could give me the list of those names which have aroused the discussion. I cannot and shall not exclude non-Aryan speakers. The only condition on which I insist is that everybody, Aryan or non-Aryan, refrains from making remarks apt to arouse the political psychosis of our days. If a speaker should trespass this limit, I should stop him right away. A scientific Congress is not the place to indulge in political follies.

Sincerely yours, C. G. JUNG

☐ English psychiatrist (d. 1961). He was a member of the organizing Committee of the 10th International Medical Congress for Psychotherapy at Oxford, 1938. For Jung's presidential address, cf. CW 10, pars. 1069ff.

To Erich Neumann

Dear Colleague,   4 April 1938

While sending you best thanks for your friendly letter of last July I must apologize for not having answered it until now. It arrived just before my departure for America,[1] where I had to give lectures at Yale University. On my return I had to leave almost at once for India, where I was invited to the 25th anniversary of the Indian Science Congress Association in Calcutta. I got back only a short while ago.

. . .

The dream you report, of a patient looking through a microscope at a lot of little worms that cause her illness, means a disturbance in the sympathetic system, an abnormal charge by which its smallest parts (worms) have been autonomized to an abnormal degree. As we know from experience, it is a question of contents which are unconscious on this level but, theoretically at least, are capable of synthesis because of their creative character. Whether it will come to that depends on the patient's fate and endowments and equally on an expertly guided inner development. I have always found that in such cases drawing and painting yield particularly good results. In a dream like this the problem is still in a bodily, organic state and cannot be distinguished from it. Only if the worms join together into a snake, for instance, is there any prospect of conscious realization. Parallel symbols are bacteria, small insects, etc.

When I compare the contents of your letter with what the papers say about Palestine I can easily imagine what a fantastic tension of opposites there must be in you. But such a tension is highly beneficial for the progress of your inner development as it brings out the meaning with particular clarity.

I have heard from Frau Dr. Braband,[2] whom you probably know, that attempts are being made to bring together all those who are interested in analytical psychology. In support of these efforts, I have sent some of my own books and writings to the University Library in Jerusalem.

I was very glad to hear that you have so much to do. Let's hope it goes on in this style. With best greetings and wishes,

Yours sincerely, C. G. JUNG

[1] Cf. Martin, 20 Aug. 37, n. 2.
[2] Cf. Braband-Isaac, 22 July 39.

To Edwin Schmid

Dear Colleague,   18 April 1938

I am doing excellently on your diet. The "short" walks have already stretched out to 3–6 hours. I can also go mountain-climbing again, which suits me fine. Yesterday I climbed about 800 metres without difficulty, from 900 to 1700. The heart is coping well, only the legs are a bit stiff afterwards.

Should I take *only* dextrose, for instance in tea and coffee?

I am scrubbing oil on myself with a hard brush. I hope to get some sunbathing. Up there in the snow it was too cold.

I have also dug, spread manure, and set potatoes, and besides that have written a longish paper in English.[1] As you see, I am bursting with energy. With very best thanks,

Yours sincerely, C. G. JUNG

□ Dr. Schmid was treating Jung for the amoebic dysentery he contracted during his stay in India (*Memories*, p. 280/262).
[1] Cf. Sen, 24 Feb. 38, n. 2.

To Isobel Moore

[ORIGINAL IN ENGLISH]

Dear Miss Moore,   2 May 1938

Buddha was once asked by one of his disciples why all his disciples, though redeemed, didn't possess the wonderful gifts of the fourth degree of contemplation, namely: sitting on the air, walking through walls, remembering their past lives, seeing things in the future, and touching the sun and moon. Buddha quietly turned the disciple's mind to the path of redemption and let him see how foolish it was to ask for such miracles. That is what the superior Indian thinks about the claims of the yogins.

I'm not aware of Freud having written an article on yoga. I have written such an article[1] a few years ago. It has often happened that my name has been exchanged for Freud's.

Sincerely yours, C. G. JUNG

□ Associated with Rhine's parapsychological library at Duke U.
[1] "Yoga and the West" (1936), CW 11.

To Dr. S.

Dear Colleague, 10 May 1938

In the confrontation with the unconscious there are indeed a considerable number of arid patches to be worked through. They cannot be circumvented. At such time it is a good thing to have some occupation which has the character of an *opus divinum*. Something like a careful shaping of images, such as many patients paint or carve in wood or stone. These primitive methods have the great advantage that the unconscious continues to work on these patterns, is enthralled and transformed by them. Naturally I can't go into further details as you have to take your own material for a starting-point. With kind regards,

Yours sincerely, C. G. JUNG

To Pastor Walther Uhsadel

Dear Pastor Uhsadel, 16 May 1938

Best thanks for kindly sending the writings you promised me. I read them at once with the greatest interest and particularly enjoyed your attitude to the question of psychotherapy and its relation to the cure of souls. Your reaction is exactly what I would have wished a theological reaction to be.

I am not surprised that you are accused of "catholicizing tendencies," but what does surprise me is that these people have the unity of the Church so little at heart. I simply cannot conceive that there is anything Christian about churches whose main motive is division. On the contrary, I find the catholicizing tendencies are actually a compliment, as they point to an endeavour to establish spiritual unity where human bickering creates disunity. Merely to read the order of the liturgy has something very satisfying about it, since it aptly contrasts the impersonal institution of the Church and its actions with the purely personal aspect of Protestantism and its habitual dissension.

I am taking the liberty of sending you, by the same post, some offprints of a later series of Eranos lectures.[1] There are things in them that might interest you from the theological point of view.

[1] Probably "Traumsymbole des Individuationsprozesses" (*Eranos Jahrbuch* 1935) and "Die Erlösungsvorstellungen in der Alchemie" (*Eranos Jahrbuch* 1936), now revised as Parts II and III of *Psychology and Alchemy*.

I shall always be a grateful recipient of whatever new things you care to send me. With kind regards,

Yours sincerely, C. G. JUNG

To Oscar Hug

Dear Colleague, 24 May 1938

You have misunderstood my sentence.[1] I meant that though the methods of modern physics are different from those of psychology their fundamental ideas are not.

I would not be surprised if one day we saw a far-reaching agreement between the basic formulations of psychology and physics.[2] I am convinced that if the two sciences pursue their goals with the utmost consistency and right into the ultimate depths of man they must hit upon a common formula.

So far as "your psychological way" is concerned I would cautiously add "*a* psychological way." Psychological experience has as we know plenty of other aspects. With kind regards,

Yours sincerely, C. G. JUNG

□ Zurich.
[1] No previous letter to Hug has been preserved.
[2] Cf. Jordan, 10 Nov. 34, n. 3.

Anonymous

Dear Colleague, 6 August 1938

It is remarkable how people can act so dumb when dealing with inner figures. Forgive me, but that's what you are doing. When you are treating a woman with an animus that proclaims the opinions of her father or husband, you are I hope capable of distinguishing between what the woman herself is saying and what must be ascribed to the animus. Technically you have to proceed in exactly the same way with your anima as in an actual case. Your difficulty only goes to show that the inner reality is not yet sufficiently real for you, and that is why you are in continual danger of possession which inevitably leads to an inflation. With kind regards,

Yours sincerely, C. G. JUNG

□ Germany.

To V. Subrahamanya Iyer

[ORIGINAL IN ENGLISH]

Dear Sir,   29 August 1938

Thank you for your kind letter which has brought back to me all the happy and beautiful memories of my short sojourn in Mysore, the beautiful city with the nocturnal lights on Chamundi hill.

As to your philosophical questions I generally quite agree with you. It is self-evident that there can be no happiness unless there is suffering. The German philosopher Schopenhauer said that happiness is merely the end of suffering. This is a somewhat negative definition. Inasmuch as suffering is a very positive condition happiness must be an equally positive one too. But unfortunately the fact is that the two cannot exist without each other. So much so that happiness easily turns into suffering even as the most intense suffering can produce a sort of superhuman happiness. They are a pair of opposites that are indispensable to life.

The phenomenon of life consists of a great many pairs of opposites, there is no energy without opposites. But inasmuch as you share in the opposites you are in conflict or at least in a continuous up and down of pain and pleasure. It is certainly desirable to liberate oneself from the operation of opposites but one can only do it to a certain extent, because no sooner do you get out of the conflict than you get out of life altogether. So that liberation can be only a very partial one. It can be the construction of a consciousness just beyond the opposites. Your head may be liberated, your feet remain entangled. Complete liberation means death. What I call "consciousness" would coincide with what you call "mind."

It is quite evident that the ego-complex is at the root of all complexes, since without an ego complexes couldn't be experienced at all. If you eradicate the ego completely, there is nobody left that would consciously experience. Too much ego always leads to a state of conflict, therefore it ought to be abolished. But it is the same thing as with the pairs of opposites: if you abolish the ego altogether, then you create unconsciousness. One assumes however that there is a consciousness without ego, a sort of consciousness of the atman.[1] I'm afraid this supreme consciousness is at least not one we could possess. Inasmuch as it exists, we do not exist.

---

[1] The individual soul or self, a reflection of the supra-individual Brahman, the ultimate Reality.

On this occasion I want to thank you once more for the cordial welcome you have given us in Mysore.

Hoping you are always in good health, I remain,

Yours sincerely, c. g. j u n g

To Georgette Boner

Dear Dr. Boner,   8 December 1938

My most cordial thanks for your extremely valuable reference to *Tristram Shandy*.[1] To begin with I did not have the feeling at all that I was guilty of plagiarism with my [anima/animus] theory, but in the last 5 years it has become more and more uncanny as I have discovered quite suspicious traces of it also in the old alchemists, and now the mischief seems complete since it turns out that I was discovered already in the 18th century. I can only think that Laurence Sterne drew upon the secret teachings (presumably Rosicrucian)[2] of his time. They contain the Royal Secret of the King and Queen, who were none other than the animus and anima, or Deus and Dea. With kind regards,

Yours sincerely, c. g. j u n g

☐ Swiss theatrical producer and designer, then in Paris.

[1] B. had drawn Jung's attention to a passage in Laurence Sterne's *Tristram Shandy* (first published between 1759 and 1767), in which Sterne speaks of "the two souls in every man living, — the one . . . being called the ANIMUS, the other, the ANIMA" (London, 1911, p. 133).

[2] The Rosicrucians were secret fraternities with mystic-reformatory aims. The name originates from a book by J. V. Andreae (German theologian, 1586–1654), *Fama Fraternitatis* (1614), which recounts the journeys of a legendary Christian Rosencreutz. Rosencreutz's (= Andreae's) *Chymische Hochzeit* (1616; *The Chymical Wedding*, 1690) is frequently mentioned in Jung's later writings. Cf. "Paracelsus as a Spiritual Phenomenon," CW 13, par. 228, and *Mysterium Coniunctionis*, Index s.v. Rosencreutz.

To W. Y. Evans-Wentz

[ORIGINAL IN ENGLISH]

My dear Mr. Evans-Wentz,   8 December 1938

I shall try to comply with your wishes as much as possible with reference to Book II which I shall make the chief subject of my inquiries.[1]

248

The Eastern idea which Mr. Sturdy[2] seems to share is that what I call the unconscious is consciousness, even superconsciousness. This is a metaphysical assumption of course. I remain within our ordinary Western consciousness, the only kind of consciousness I know. The nature of that psyche which reaches beyond my consciousness is essentially unknown to me. Therefore one aptly calls it the unconscious. Of course I wouldn't know of it if there were not parts of it that reach my consciousness, but the main body of this psyche is essentially unconscious to me, as its origins are equally unknown to me. We know of no consciousness that is not the relation between images and an ego. But unfortunately we have no means to ascertain that every living organism is equipped with what we call an ego. We even know of dim states of consciousness where our own ego becomes equally dimmed, yet the state is definitely psychic. From such an experience we may conclude that there is an enormous mass of psychic functioning which is not exactly conscious to an ego, or which is altogether without an ego. The latter condition would be utterly "dark," i.e., deprived of the light of consciousness. To speak of consciousness in a cell is to me a highly metaphysical assertion for which we have no evidence whatsoever. On the other hand it is easy to assume that each living organism has probably something like a psychic function. All psychic functioning without an ego has peculiar characteristics that adhere to every psychic fragment which is not the result of conscious functioning. Dreams, for instance, are not the result of conscious functioning in the main. They have therefore a peculiar character which we call unconscious. If the Indians would call sublime psychic experience "psyche" or something equivalent to it, I would agree with them, but to call it consciousness cannot be substantiated by any evidence. If the highest psychic condition is *Sunyata*,[3] then it cannot be consciousness, because consciousness is by definition the relationship between the subject and a representation. One is conscious *of* something. As long as you are conscious of *Sunyata* it is not *Sunyata*, because there is still a subject that is

---

☐ (1878–1965), American authority on Tibetan Yoga and philosophy, then in Cairo. Jung's "Psychological Commentary" to his edn. of *The Tibetan Book of the Dead* (German edn. 1935) is in CW 11.

[1] Jung had agreed to write a "Psychological Commentary" on Evans-Wentz's edition of *The Tibetan Book of the Great Liberation* (1954). Book II is entitled "The Yoga of knowing the mind, the seeing of reality, called self-liberation." The commentary, written in 1939, is reprinted in CW 11.

[2] E. T. Sturdy, Evans-Wentz's collaborator (cf. *The Great Liberation*, p. viii).

[3] The Void, the Absolute.

conscious of something. Void is even the void of consciousness, and there I completely agree with the East.

I hope to be able to do the promised bit of work in my winter vacations.

Hoping you are always in good health, I remain,

Yours sincerely, C. G. JUNG

To Heinrich Zimmer

Dear Professor Zimmer,   12 December 1938

Your little book *Weisheit Indiens*[1] arrived safely and I also found in it your gladdening dedication[2] which, however, keeps it a secret that everything I know comes from my mastery of not-knowing. This is attested by the fact that I was born in 1875, the year of the pig.[3] I shall especially enjoy the "Sinnbilder" and will read "Die Geschichte vom König mit dem Leichnam"[4] devoutly for the third time. With cordial thanks and many good wishes for the coming festivities,

Yours ever, C. G. JUNG

[1] Pub. 1938.

[2] "C. G. Jung/maestro di color che sanno/in Verehrung und Dankbarkeit" (C. G. Jung/master of those who know/in admiration and gratitude) — the Italian words refer to Aristotle in Dante, *Inferno*, IV, 131.

[3] The pig is one of the astrological signs in the Chinese zodiac. Hexagram 61 of the *I Ching*, "Inner Truth," says in The Judgment: "Inner Truth. Pigs and fishes. Good fortune," and explains that pigs and fishes are "the least intelligent of all animals," so that "the force of inner truth must grow great indeed before its influence can extend to such creatures" (tr. Wilhelm/Baynes, pp. 235f.). The *I Ching* also says (p. 273) that "the Abysmal [acts] in the pig."

[4] Two of the chapters in Zimmer's book. The second one is republished in *The King and the Corpse* (1948), pp. 202ff.

To Erich Neumann

Dear Colleague,   19 December 1938

Please don't worry about having written me such a long letter. I would have liked to know long ago what you are doing. You should not imagine me enthroned above world events on snow-covered peaks. I am right in the thick of it and every day I follow the Palestine question in the newspapers and often think of my friends there who have to live in this chaos. Unfortunately I foresaw all too clearly what was coming when I was in Palestine in 1932.[1] I also foresaw bad things for Germany, actually very bad, but now that they have come to pass they seem unbelievable. Everyone here is profoundly shaken by what is happening in Germany.[2] I have very much to do with Jewish refugees and am continually occupied in bringing all my Jewish acquaintances to safety in England and America. In this way I am in ceaseless touch with contemporary events.

I am very interested in what you have told me about your plans for work. Your experiences exactly parallel those I have had in Europe for many years. But I think you should be very cautious in judging your specifically Jewish experiences. Though it is true that there are specifically Jewish traits about this development, it is at the same time a general one which is also to be found among Christians. It is a general and identical revolution of minds. The specifically Christian or Jewish traits are only of secondary importance. Thus the patient you want to know about is a pure Jew with a Catholic upbringing, but I could never with absolute certainty characterize his symbolism—in so far as I have presented it[3]—as Jewish although certain nuances occasionally seem so. When I compare his material with mine or with that of other academically trained patients one is struck only by the astonishing similarities, while the differences are insignificant. The difference between a typically Protestant and a Jewish psychology is particularly small where the contemporary problem is concerned. The whole problem is of such overwhelming importance for humanity that individual and racial differences play a minor role. All the same, I can very well imagine that for Jews living in Palestine the direct influence of the surroundings brings out the chthonic and ancient Jewish element in a much more pregnant form. It seems to me that what is specifically Jewish or specifically Christian could be most easily discovered in the way the unconscious material is assimilated by the subject. In my experience the resistance of the Jew seems to be

---

[1] In 1932 Jung travelled to Egypt and Palestine with Prof. Markus Fierz (cf. Fierz, 30 Apr. 45, n. □). One interesting episode (reported by Fierz's son) was that when the two men alighted at Alexandria a palmist at the port read their hands. To Jung he said: "Oh, you are one of the few great men I have ever seen. I can't say more."

[2] The pogroms organized by the Nazis on the night 9/10 Nov., the so-called "crystal night," and its consequences.

[3] Cf. the dreams commented on in "Psychology and Religion" (orig. 1937), pars. 56ff. and 108ff. The case is described in much greater detail in Part II of *Psychology and Alchemy.*

more obstinate and as a result the attempt at defence is much more vehement. This is no more than a subjective impression.

The Zosimos essay[4] is the last thing of mine to be published. Still outstanding[5] are an article on India (written in English for an American magazine),[6] two lectures on the mother complex,[7] which will appear in the *Eranos-Jahrbuch 1938*, a long commentary on Zen Buddhism,[8] and finally an introduction to the individuation process for an American edition of my Eranos lectures.[9]

Dr. X. has apprised me of a detailed correspondence with you. It is clear that the devil has been up to his tricks again. As soon as one notices that, one should say no more but withdraw into oneself.

I was glad to hear that you are fully occupied, though it would be even more agreeable if you also had time to realize your great plan.[10] Hoping that you are keeping fit, and with friendly greetings,

Yours sincerely, C. G. JUNG

[4] "The Visions of Zosimos," CW 13.
[5] Jung used regularly to send Neumann copies of his books and offprints of his Eranos lectures.
[6] "The Dreamlike World of India" and "What India Can Teach Us," CW 10, first published in *Asia* (New York), XXXIX:1/2, 1939.
[7] Now combined as "Psychological Aspects of the Mother Archetype," CW 9, i.
[8] "Foreword to Suzuki's *Introduction to Zen Buddhism*," CW 11.
[9] "The Meaning of Individuation," intro. to *The Integration of the Personality* (tr. Stanley Dell, 1939), containing four Eranos lectures and one other essay by Jung. Revised as "Conscious, Unconscious, and Individuation," CW 9, i.
[10] Neumann planned to write a book on the psychological problem of the modern Jew. It remained an unpublished fragment.

To Eleanor Bertine

[ORIGINAL IN ENGLISH]

Dear Dr. Bertine,   9 January 1939

. . .

I'm sorry to hear that you are chiefly concerned with borderline cases. It is a thorny task, on the other hand a very interesting one. I remember Mrs. X. very well. She was due for a psychotic interval, not being born yet out of the mists of the Bardo life.[1] In such a case

☐ M.D., (1887–1968), American analytical psychologist. Cf. her *Human Relationships* (1958); *Jung's Contribution to Our Time* (1967). Jung's foreword to the former is in CW 18. (See pl. in vol. 2.)
[1] The state between death and reincarnation described in the Bardo Thödol, *The Tibetan Book of the Dead.*

it is of course the right thing to let people talk of their experiences during the morbid interval, because the contents of such experiences need integration into the sum-total of personality. Of course, it is most unorthodox from the psychiatric point of view to take psychotic things seriously. But for the patient it is much better to be unorthodox, since the psychiatrist doesn't know what to do with such cases. Such a treatment is always a risk as there is a delicate question of how much a patient can stand his pathological material. If the patient is unable to stand it, then there is a natural tendency at work to wall-up the experienced material. Thus if you should find a certain resistance or if you should meet with a flaring up of emotions you had better help the walling-up tendency. But if a patient can stand his material you can help him in integrating and understanding. The more a patient can understand the better, and he is protected against a complete inundation, and even if a new inundation should come along it would remain a psychotic interval which would not cause definite and irreparable destruction. I have often seen that people with a certain amount of psychological preparation were not completely destroyed by an acute psychosis. They came out of it as if out of a dream. They did not "coalesce" but retained their fluidity. If there are any congealed regions, you would find there: inaccessibility, lack of emotion, or inadequate emotions and complete immutability. In drawings you would presumably find breaking lines[2] or splinters or asymmetrical regions of destruction and dissolution.

As soon as the general condition of a patient is more or less reasonable again, one should remove him from a hospital, as the hospital atmosphere is most contagious. If Mrs. X. is quiet enough to stay at home, you surely should see her. If her emotionality increases under the treatment, then one should reconsider the hospital question. But if she is able to discuss her material without getting too much excited, the treatment ought to be continued, because there is a real chance of a far-reaching improvement. I have seen cases improving completely. It doesn't matter that the psychiatrist says afterwards that it was no schizophrenia. As you know it is indifferent to the devil what you call him.

Concerning the treatment you depend entirely upon the material the patient produces. You have to follow the ways of nature and not your own good intentions, i.e., you must leave that to the alienists. It

[2] Cf. for instance Pls. 8 and 9 in *Mysterium Coniunctionis*, and *Analytical Psychology: Its Theory and Practice*, pp. 198ff. and Figs. 14 and 15.

would certainly be a good thing for Mrs. X. if you could hold her hand as long as possible, i.e., until she can trust her own system again.

My best wishes for a happy New Year,

Cordially yours, C. G. JUNG

To V. Subrahamanya Iyer

[ORIGINAL IN ENGLISH]

Dear Sir,   9 January 1939

You are quite right, Schopenhauer was by no means in a position to have a complete insight into and an understanding of the Upanishads, since in those days the Upanishads were only known in the very imperfect Latin rendering of A. du Perron, who brought them over in the form of the so-called *Oupnekhat*[1] at the beginning of the 19th century.

I quite agree with you that deep sleep or any state of complete unconsciousness is beyond pain and pleasure, but also beyond consciousness, so that when the complete state of being beyond pleasure and pain is achieved, there is nobody there that could be conscious of it. It is true however that if somebody survives that condition, for instance by waking up from deep sleep or from unconsciousness, he might say: "I must have been unconscious, I felt nothing." Or if he has an agreeable feeling left over from his deep sleep: "I had a very good and pleasurable sleep without dreams." But while he was asleep or unconscious, he was not aware of it, at least we cannot prove that there was anybody aware of that condition.

It is of course a merely theoretical statement when I say that complete unconsciousness, i.e., a complete overcoming of pain and pleasure and ego, would be just death. By such a statement I only want to say that as long as I'm conscious of something, my mind is not contentless and not egoless, since *I* am aware of a definite state in which I find myself. I wouldn't call the ego a creation of mind or consciousness, since, as we know, little children talk of themselves first in the third person and begin to say "I" only when they have found their ego. The ego, therefore, is rather a find or an experience and not a creation. We rather might say: the empirical existence of an ego is a

---

[1] Abraham Hyacinthe Anquetil du Perron (1731–1805), French Orientalist; spent 1755–61 in the Orient, from which he returned with a large number of MSS. He translated a Persian version of the Indian Upanishads into Latin (1801–2). This translation, the *Oupnek'hat*, was the source for Schopenhauer's enthusiastic acquaintance with Indian philosophy.

condition through which continuous consciousness becomes possible. For we know that the sort of impersonal consciousness observed in little children is not continuous but of a dissociated and insular character.

I know it is a special feature of Indian thought that consciousness is assumed to have a metaphysical and prehuman existence. We are convinced that only what we call the unconscious mind, which is *per definitionem* a psyche not conscious to anybody, has prehuman and preconscious existence. What we call the unconscious is an exact replica of the Indian concept of super- or supreme consciousness. As far as my knowledge goes, however, we have no evidence at all in favour of the hypothesis that a prehuman and preconscious psyche is conscious to anybody and therefore a consciousness.

Concerning your last question I want to say that I quite agree that there is nothing in or of the material world that is not a projection of the human mind, since anything we experience and are able to express through thought is alien to our mind. Through experience and mental assimilation it has become part of our mind and thus it has become essentially psychic. Inasmuch as a material thing does not enter our consciousness it is not experienced and we cannot say for certain that it does exist. Whatever we touch or come in contact with immediately changes into a psychic content, so we are enclosed by a world of psychic images, some of which bear the label "of material origin," others the label "of spiritual origin." But how those things look as material things in themselves or as spiritual things in themselves we do not know, since we can experience them only as psychic contents and nothing else. But I cannot say that material things or spiritual things in themselves are of psychic nature, although it may be that there is no other kind of existence but a psychic one. If that is the case, then matter would be nothing but a definiteness of divine thought, as Tantrism suggests. I have no objection to such an hypothesis, but the Western mind has renounced metaphysical assertions which are *per definitionem* not verifiable, if only recently so. In the Middle Ages up to the 19th century we still believed in the possibility of metaphysical assertions. India, it seems to me, is still convinced of the possibility of metaphysical assertions. Perhaps she is right and perhaps not.

. . .

Hoping you are always in good health and active as ever, I remain, dear Sir,

Yours devotedly, c. g. j u n g

To Pastor Fritz Pfäfflin

Dear Pastor Pfäfflin,   10 January 1939

First of all I would like to express my heartfelt sympathy over the heavy loss that has befallen you.

Since you wish to know what I think about such experiences,[1] I would like to point out before anything else that there was a direct connection between the event in Africa and your consciousness. This is an undeniable fact and in my opinion there is only one explanation, namely that spatial distance is, in the psychic sense, relative. In other words, physical space is not under all circumstances a definite datum but under certain conditions is also a psychic function. One might call it psychically contractile. We must suppose that the distance between your brother's experience and your own was reduced to a minimum. From similar experiences we must conclude that this nullification of space proceeds with great speed, so that perceptions of this kind occur almost simultaneously with the accident. We can therefore speak of a psychic nullification of time as well. We could also suppose that the victim of the accident sent out a kind of radio message. But this is contradicted by the fact that occasionally details are "transmitted" which occurred only after the death—for instance, the decapitation of the body of one killed by being stabbed with a knife. In that event there can be no question of a transmission by a dying man. It is more probable that it is a perception by someone alive and seeing. Hence the psychic nullification of space and time offers a much better explanation. Accordingly the capacity to nullify space and time must somehow inhere in the psyche, or, to put it another way, the psyche does not exist wholly in time and space. It is very probable that only what we call consciousness is contained in space and time, and that the rest of the psyche, the unconscious, exists in a state of relative spacelessness and timelessness. For the psyche this means a relative eternality and a relative non-separation from other psyches, or a oneness with them. It is characteristic that your brother was amazed when you asked him whether he had sent you a message. Obviously he had not sent a message because the relative non-existence of space and time made it unnecessary. (I have expressed similar thoughts in my essay "Seele und Tod"[2] in *Wirklichkeit der Seele*.)

[1] P. had lost his brother in an accident in Africa. At the time of the accident he spontaneously experienced a conversation with this brother. The content of the conversation has not been preserved.

[2] "The Soul and Death," CW 8. Cf. also *Memories*, ch. XI: "On Life after Death."

Now with regard to the exceedingly interesting conversation you had *post mortem* with your brother, it has all the characteristic features of these experiences. For one thing, there is the peculiar preoccupation of the dead with the psychic states of other (dead) persons. For another, the existence of (psychic) shrines or places of healing. I have long thought that religious institutions, churches, monasteries, temples, etc. as well as rites and psychotherapeutic attempts at healing were modelled on (transcendental) postmortal psychic states—a real *Ecclesia Spiritualis* as the prototype of the *Una Sancta* upon earth. In the East these ideas would be by no means unheard-of; Buddhist philosophy, for instance, has coined the concept of *Sambhoga-Kaya* for this psychic existence, namely the world of subtle forms which are to *Nirmana-Kaya* as the breath-body (subtle body) is to the material body. The breath-world is thought of as an intermediate state between *Nirmana-Kaya* and *Dharma-Kaya*.[3] In *Dharma-Kaya*, which symbolizes the highest state, the separation of forms is dissolved into absolute unity and formlessness. These formulations are extremely valuable from the psychological point of view as they provide a fitting terminology for such experiences.

Naturally we can form no conception of a relatively timeless and spaceless existence, but, psychologically and empirically, it results in manifestations of the continual presence of the dead and their influence on our dream life. I therefore follow up such experiences with the greatest attention, because they show many things we dream about in a very peculiar light, where "psychological" structures appear as existential conditions. This continual presence is also only relative, since after a few weeks or months the connection becomes indirect or breaks off altogether, although spontaneous re-encounters also appear to be possible later. But after this period the feeling of the presence of the dead is in fact broken off. The connection is not without its dangers because it entangles the consciousness of the living too much in that transcendental state, resulting in unconsciousness and dissociation phenomena. This is reflected in your dream-vision of the path leading down to a lake (the unconscious). There is an antheap, i.e., the sympathetic nervous system ($=$ deepest unconsciousness and danger of dissolution of psychic elements in the form of milling ants) is becoming activated. This state takes place in you, consequently the

[3] The Universal Essence manifests itself in three Divine Bodies (*Tri-Kaya*): *Dharma-Kaya*, the body of the law; *Sambhoga-Kaya*, the body of bliss, or reflected wisdom; *Nirmana-Kaya*, the body of incarnation, or incarnate wisdom. Cf. Evans-Wentz, *The Tibetan Book of the Great Liberation*, pp. 3–4, 178, n. 1.

connection is in danger of being broken, hence your brother's admonition: "Always build on the heights!" i.e., on the heights of consciousness. "For us the depth is doom," i.e., unconsciousness is doom. Then we get into the "clouds" where one sees nothing more.

The remarkable statement that "Someone was interested in the motor cutting out" could indicate that among the crew there was someone who, through an exteriorization effect, actually caused the motor to cut out and did so because of an unrealized suicide complex. (I have seen quite a number of such effects in my time.)

With regard to contact with your brother, I would add that this is likely to be possible only as long as the feeling of the presence of the dead continues. But it should not be experimented with because of the danger of a disintegration of consciousness. To be on the safe side, one must be content with spontaneous experiences. Experimenting with this contact regularly leads either to the so-called communications becoming more and more stupid or to a dangerous dissociation of consciousness. All the signs indicate that your conversation with your brother is a genuine experience which cannot be "psychologized." The only "psychological" disturbance in it is the lake and the antheap. That was evidently the moment when, perhaps from both sides, the exceedingly difficult contact between the two forms of existence could no longer be maintained. There are experiences which show that the dead entangle themselves, so to speak, in the physiology (sympathetic nervous system) of the living. This would probably result in states of possession.

Again with especial thanks for your extremely interesting letter,

Yours sincerely, c. g. j u n g

To H. G. Baynes

[O R I G I N A L   I N   E N G L I S H]

My dear Peter,   20 January 1939

A master at Eton College, a Mr. X., has consulted me. I have sent him to you. He is at first a somewhat odd individual, but if you take into consideration what a master at a public school might be, it isn't so bad after all. He has certainly done rather funny things of which he will tell you. But I think the Harley Street specialist whom he consulted has done much funnier things.

I just want to tell you that my impression (though hastily built upon one interview) is that this man isn't really a case. He is just damn funny and has a dangerous tendency to put the wrong foot forward and to say or do everything that eventually will prove that he is crazy. But I'm absolutely positive that his feelings are still liquid. He is appreciative of a friendly and helpful attitude. He is considerate, he understands and agrees that his behaviour can seem peculiar, and he does understand that his headmaster is reasonably afraid of lunatics and that one should, therefore, not behave as if one were one. I'm pretty certain that if he has your sympathy (which he deserves, being a kindly man and jackass of an artist) you can keep him straight.

What he also needs is that you have a quiet talk with the headmaster of Eton telling him that many a don has been an odd number and that the things this man has done (at least as much as I know of them) are not very serious; that he is moreover a good teacher, apparently capable of keeping his pupils in order, and that one shouldn't fire him because it would finish him utterly, being a definite proof that he is crazy; that one should rather give him a fair chance to improve and that the headmaster might even give him occasionally some confidential and paternal advice, slapping him on the back, telling him, for instance, that one shouldn't race with the boys nor sing low songs in the solemnity of Eton.

. . .

Cordially yours, c. g. jung

To Johanna Michaelis

Dear Frau Michaelis,   20 January 1939

Your questions are not easy to answer. Your conjecture that ancient Egyptian psychology was somehow fundamentally different from ours is probably right. Those millennia had indeed quite different problems. On one side a torpid impersonal unconsciousness reigned, on the other a revealed consciousness, or a consciousness inspired from within and hence derived directly from the gods, personified in Pharaoh. He was the self and the individual of the people.[1] The spirit still came from above. The tension between above and below was undoubtedly extreme, hence the opposites could be held together only by means of equally rigid forms. The "duality" of the ruler is

□ Berlin.

[1] For the concept of Pharaoh as Osiris, first the collective and then the individual soul, cf. Neumann, *The Origins and History of Consciousness*, p. 429.

based on the primitive belief that the placenta is the brother of the new-born child,[2] which as such often accompanies him throughout life in ghostly fashion, since it dies early and is ceremonially buried. You can find detailed descriptions of this in Lévy-Bruhl's *Le Surnaturel et la nature dans la mentalité primitive*.[3] The *ka*[4] is probably a descendant of the placenta.

White and red are sacred colours in India too, for instance the temple walls are painted with white and red stripes. What they mean is not clear to me. Your interpretation as light and blood is extremely probable but one should have historical proofs.

The tension between above and below in ancient Egypt is in my opinion the real source of the Near Eastern saviour figures, whose patriarch is Osiris. He is also the source of the idea of an individual (immortal) soul. ("The Osiris of N. N.") The purpose of nearly all rebirth rites is to unite the above with the below. The baptism in the Jordan is an eloquent example: water below, Holy Ghost above. On the primitive level the totemistic rite of renewal is always a reversion to the half animal, half human condition of prehistoric times. Hence the frequent use of animal skins and other animal attributes. Evidence of this may be found in the cave paintings discovered in the south of France.

Among these customs we must also reckon the demotion of high to low. In Christianity the washing of the disciples' feet, in ancient Egypt the birth from an animal's skin.[5] Hence twice a year in India, even today, the Maharajah of Travancore, with torso bared and bare feet, must accompany the god to the bathing place with his whole court. As a further parallel there are the Shrovetide customs of the medieval Church, when the youngest lay brother took the abbot's seat and was waited upon by the older monks. Modern student initiations! Also the ritual mockery of sacred customs, the Fools' Mass in medi-

---

[2] M. referred to an example of active imagination quoted in *The Interpretation of Visions* (1940 edn., vol. 7, Lecture III, 23 Nov. 32, p. 39); "From a white placenta emerged a creature in the shape of a child." She also mentioned the dual nature of the Pharaoh (one of his appellations was "The Two Lords").

[3] Lucien Lévy-Bruhl (1857–1939), French sociologist and ethnologist, 1899–1927 professor at the Sorbonne. His book is translated as *Primitives and the Supernatural* (1936).

[4] The second self or double of the personality.

[5] According to Alexandre Moret (*Mystères égyptiens*, 1922), the Pharaoh was enveloped at the Sed festival in an animal skin representing the uterus from which he was reborn. Concerning the Sed festival, cf. Neumann, *Origins*, pp. 243ff.

eval monasteries.[6] Among the Pueblo Indians the "delight makers" (see *The Delight Makers* by Adolf F. Bandelier[7]).

It is very probable that as long as seriously observed rites exist which unite the polar opposites the balance in the life of a people will be preserved. Hence, in China, Tao rests upon the harmonious cooperation of heaven and earth. But as you can see from the *I Ching*, heaven sometimes separates from the earth, thus producing a disorderly and unfavourable state of affairs.

There are very many parallels to these questions you have touched upon, particularly to the baptismal customs, but I cannot possibly mention them all. As regards the four royal standards[8] I would only remark that, if I remember rightly, a placenta was carried along with them. There is a monograph on this, but unfortunately I cannot remember its title.

Yours sincerely, C. G. JUNG

[6] Cf. Jung, "The Psychology of the Trickster Figure," CW 9, i, pars. 458ff.
[7] New York, 1890; 2nd edn., 1918.
[8] There were in fact many more standards of the Pharaoh, but the four most closely related to him were those of the falcon, ibis, wolf, and the Royal Placenta (cf. Frankfort, *Kingship and the Gods*, 1948, p. 92).

To W. Y. Evans-Wentz

[ORIGINAL IN ENGLISH]

My dear Mr. Evans-Wentz,   9 February 1939

Thank you very much for kindly sending me Mr. Sturdy's letter. I can appreciate his standpoint and I quite agree with him that there are states of intensified consciousness which deserve the name "super-consciousness." No matter how far that "super-consciousness" reaches, I'm unable to imagine a condition where it would be completely all-embracing, i.e., where there would not be something unconscious left over. To assume something which is beyond human grasp is a prerogative of faith. It belongs to metaphysics and not to science, as it is beyond proof and experience. The question of a highly intensified consciousness however is not the important question. The point at issue is rather the question of the ego. The ego in psychology is the cognizing subject designated as "I." Thus Mr. Sturdy correctly quotes St. Paul's saying: "*I* have seen things. . . ."[1] So even in his *ekstasis* Paul himself assures us that an "*I*" has seen. Now, if his ego had been

[1] Cf. Acts 26:13: "I saw in the way a light from heaven . . ."

completely dissolved and abolished, he never could have said "I have seen," he might have said "God has seen," or rather he would not have been able to tell us even about the fact that something had been seen at all. So no matter how far an *ekstasis* goes or how far consciousness can be extended, there is still the continuity of the apperceiving ego which is essential to all forms of consciousness. It is quite true that we can be oblivious even of our body (being a doctor, I know this only too well) but that does not mean that the psychological ego does not exist any more. As a matter of fact, I am going on talking as if I were fully conscious of my ego. I form my sentences with "I" just as before and if anybody should say to me: "What you are experiencing is not your experience at all, it belongs to somebody else!" I would certainly reject such a statement. By such a rejection I would confirm the fact that it was my ego that has apperceived.

When I say that anything psychic beyond consciousness is "dark," it is quite certainly dark to me because I don't know it, but I cannot decide whether it is dark or bright in itself, simply because I don't know it. And I know no way to ascertain the existence of consciousness for instance in a caterpillar. One can only *believe* that psychic existence beyond consciousness is dark or bright.

The so-called "psychic" reactions of lower organisms are very well-known to me, but there is no proof at all that these psychic reactions are conscious to an ego, they can be merely psychic. Psyche is (as is generally known) by no means identical with consciousness, since we know that there are plenty of reactions in man of which he is completely unconscious. Such reactions can be experimentally produced, observed, and measured, and it is a fact established by thousands of experiments that the individual himself is completely unconscious of them. One could of course hold that man habitually suffers from double consciousness (double personality), but there is absolutely no evidence for such an assumption.

I cannot see why it is a mystery how the unconscious can ever become known to consciousness. It is a fact of everyday experience that formerly unconscious contents more or less suddenly emerge into consciousness. As a matter of fact our consciousness couldn't function if the unconscious psychic process didn't support it by providing it with the necessary material. For instance, if you have forgotten a name and the unconscious obstinately retains it, then you depend almost entirely upon the good will of the unconscious that it allows you to recall it. It happens very often that your memory fails you in an almost diabolical way.

I don't know what Mr. Sturdy means by "being able to control one's dreams." Can he produce dreams at will? For instance, can he say "today I'm going to dream such and such a dream"? I have never heard of such a thing. That you can learn to remember your dreams has nothing to do with "to control one's dreams." There is not one word about control of dreams in Dunne's book.[2] Inasmuch as you can remember your dreams at all, it is evident that your consciousness continues at least in a dim way through sleep, otherwise you couldn't dream and you couldn't remember the dream.

"As long as Sunyata is cognized by a subject it remains object." But when the subject enters Sunyata and becomes identical with it, the subject itself is Sunyata, namely void. And when the void is really void, there is not even a cognizing subject in it. The subject has vanished and there cannot be a consciousness of this fact, because there is nothing left any more. There can also be no memory of it, because there was nothing.

I don't know what Mr. Sturdy means when he says that telepathy and psychometry etc. ought to be considered. What is their connection with the fact that there is no consciousness without an ego that is conscious of something? Surely telepathy widens out our consciousness, but there is always an ego conscious of something. Mr. Sturdy seems to forget that I'm a psychologist who is a scientist whose duty it is to explore knowable things. The scientist sees no merit in preaching certain metaphysical convictions. Thus I accept the fact that there are people who are convinced of the existence of a personal God, or who are convinced that the psychic material which is unconscious to me is conscious to the "I" of God. I can accept that there is a belief in the Virgin Birth, the immaculate conception, in Parvati[3] being the wife of Siva, or anything under the sun, but I surely cannot suggest that this is absolute truth, because I simply have no evidence for it. I want to know what there is to be known, but I don't want to make assumptions about things of which I know that one cannot know them. Thus it is absolutely impossible to know what I would experience when that "I" which could experience didn't exist any more. One calls this a *contradictio in adjecto*. To experience *Sunyata* is therefore an impossible experience by definition, as I explained above, and it is also impossible to experience consciousness in a field of which I know nothing. You can expand your consciousness so that you even

---

[2] *An Experiment with Time.*
[3] Incarnation of the supreme goddess Kali-Durga-Sati.

cover a field that had been unconscious to you before, but then it is your ego that is conscious of this new acquisition, and there is absolutely no reason to believe then that there is not a million times more unconscious material beyond that little bit of a new acquisition. Thus agnosticism is my duty as a scientist. I don't compete with confessions of religious creeds. I never claimed to be a metaphysician and I do not sympathize with the preaching of more metaphysical convictions. We have too many of them already and too few that are really believed.

I am sure you will have a wonderful time in Heluan. I often think of the splendour of the Egyptian sun in our misty "Niflheim" (home of the mists). Though I'm thinking furiously about the fundamental psychological problems of the East, I haven't done much yet in the way of commenting on the *Great Liberation*. The time for it will be April when I shall have the necessary time. I hope that you will get my Ms. by May.

I enclose [Mr. Sturdy's] two letters.

Sincerely yours, C. G. JUNG

Anonymous

Dear Herr N.,   22 March 1939

Your first dream[1] shows that you yourself are identical with an unconscious feminine figure which as you know I call the anima. So the process you are in is a real one, but it is being falsely played out on you instead of on the anima.

The second dream[2] follows from the first. Through the identity with the anima you are driven up to a steep cliff where you find yourself in a very precarious situation. You can't hold the child because it doesn't belong to you. The icy storm goes together with the heights on which no man can live: again an expression of an unnatural and dangerous situation. In Goethe, Euphorion[3] is the child of Helen, begotten by father Faust. That is a normal situation.

Obviously the processes in Faust are real. Such things cannot possibly be "wishful fantasies." They are on the contrary the material which, when it comes up in a man, can make him go mad. This is

☐ France.
[1] The dreamer gives birth to a child.
[2] The dreamer stands on a steep cliff, beneath him a deep abyss, in an icy storm. He has a small child in his arms but cannot hold it.
[3] *Faust II*, Act 3. Cf. *Psychology and Alchemy*, CW 12, par. 243.

also true of the fourth stage of the transformation process,[4] the experience in the Beyond. It is an unconscious reality which in Faust's case was felt as being beyond his reach at the time, and for this reason it is separated from his real existence by death. It expresses the fact that he still had to "become a boy" and only then would he attain the highest wisdom. Euphorion stands for the future man who does not flee from the bond with the earth but is dashed to pieces on it, which means that he is not viable under the existing circumstances. Faust's death must therefore be taken as a fact. But like many a death it is really a mystery death which brings the imperfect to perfection.

The Paris-Helen-Euphorion episode is actually the highest stage that the transformation process has reached, but not in itself the highest, for the element Euphorion has not been integrated into the Faust-Mephisto-Paris-Helen quaternity as the *quinta essentia*.

The connections you adduce with typology are interesting but difficult. Goethe himself was an intuitive feeling type. Faust first appears as Goethe's shadow, namely as an introverted scientist and doctor (thinking and sensation). Now comes the first transformation: he discovers his countertype ("feeling is all") and at the same time realizes the projection of the anima, as is invariably the case in the analytical process. Behind Gretchen stands the Gnostic sequence: Helen-Mary-Sophia.[5] They represent a real Platonic world of ideas (thinking and sensation on the mystic level). Here Goethe divines the fact that unconscious, undifferentiated functions are contaminated with the collective unconscious, with the result that they can be realized only in part rationally but for the most part irrationally, i.e., as an inner experience.

All the rest of Part Two is closely connected with Goethe's alchemical knowledge, which no one should underestimate. I was amazed at the amount of Hermetic philosophy I found in it. For your own clarification I would urgently recommend you to take account of the thought-processes of alchemy in relation to *Faust*. By the same post I send you two offprints of my writings, "Die Erlösungsvorstellungen in der Alchemie" and "Die Visionen des Zosimos."

. . .

Now a general remark. I don't know if I am deceiving myself, but it seems to me as though you have understood the "reality character"

[4] The fourth transformation of Faust—into Doctor Marianus—after his mystery death (*Faust II*, Act 5, last scene.) Cf. ibid., par. 558.
[5] Cf. "The Psychology of the Transference," CW 16, par. 361.

of Faust's experience in a rather limited psychological or perhaps psychologizing way. Forgive me if this criticism offends you. But I had a rather uncomfortable feeling when you spoke of "wishful fantasies." The idea of a wishful fantasy is an expression taken over from Freud's personalistic psychology of neurosis, which enables the doctor to break a patient of his silly megalomania or hysterical pretensions. But this only disguises the fact that the doctor does not understand in what respect such ideas are perfectly correct. They are just as incorrect as the dream in which you give birth to a child, but in a deeper sense they are just as correct as Goethe's Paris-Helen experience. When an insane person says he is the forefather who has been fecundating his daughter for millions of years, such a statement is thoroughly morbid from the medical standpoint. But from the psychological standpoint it is an astounding truth to which the broadest possible *consensus gentium* bears witness. It is expressed in the words: *Scit et te Deum esse.*[6] Freud would say: "An incestuous wish-fantasy," because he would like to save the poor patient from a bit of obnoxious nonsense. But I would say to the patient: "What a pity you are too stupid to understand this revelation properly." In the case of Goethe's *Faust*—which I consider altogether superb—I would anathematize the expression "wishful fantasy" from beginning to end.

. . .

Yours sincerely, c. g. jung

[6] "For He [God] doth know that . . . ye shall be as gods." Gen. 3:5.

Anonymous

[ORIGINAL IN ENGLISH]

Dear Mr. N.,   22 March 1939

As you will realize it is extremely difficult to judge an individual case in which one doesn't know the *dramatis personae*.

If a young man loves a woman who could almost be his mother, then it always has to do with a mother complex. Such a union is sometimes quite useful for many years, particularly in the case of artistic persons who haven't fully matured. The woman in such a case is helped by an almost biological instinct. She is hatching the eggs. The man as the son-lover benefits by the partially sexual, partially motherly interest of the woman. Thus such a relationship can be sat-

□ U.S.A.

isfactory in every respect for an indefinite period, but the advancing years would certainly put a definite limit to it as it is not quite natural. It may be that even an artistic nature becomes so adult that the need of becoming a father and a grown-up man in general begins to prevail against the original son-attitude. When that is the case the relationship is overdue.[1]

What I say is a general rule which shouldn't be recklessly generalized. Man is a most peculiar experiment of nature and particularly in erotic respects simply anything is possible.

. . .

Sincerely yours, c. g. j u n g

[1] I.e., "has become out of date."

To A. Zarine

Dear M. Zarine, 3 May 1939

Excuse the long delay in my response; I do not always have time to answer long letters such as yours. And your questions are rather complicated.

In reading your letter I did not get the impression at all that your reasoning was morbid or unsound. The reasoning itself seems to me normal, but the way that you apply it is not very fortunate, since I question whether you have fully understood what the "transcendent function" means.

In the normal man the transcendent function operates entirely in the unconscious, which tends to continually reestablish the equilibrium. The arguments that you bring up in your letter concern the transcendent function, to be sure, but I do not think you have grasped the true nature of the process. Of course, that is quite natural, since you cannot have had the experience of a psychologist and consequently cannot picture how these things really are. Yet I do not even need to take an abnormal case for an example. There are many normal cases in which, under certain circumstances, a character opposed to the conscious personality suddenly manifests itself, causing a conflict between the two personalities.

Take the classic case of the temptation of Christ, for example. We say that the devil tempted him, but we could just as well say that an unconscious desire for power confronted him in the form of the devil.

☐ (Translated from French.) France.

267

Both sides appear here: the light side and the dark. The devil wants to tempt Jesus to proclaim himself master of the world. Jesus wants not to succumb to the temptation; then, thanks to the function that results from every conflict, a symbol appears: it is the idea of the Kingdom of Heaven, a spiritual kingdom rather than a material one. Two things are united in this symbol, the spiritual attitude of Christ and the devilish desire for power. Thus the encounter of Christ with the devil is a classic example of the transcendent function. It appears here in the form of an involuntary personal experience. But it can be used as a method too; that is, when the contrary will of the unconscious is sought for and recognized in dreams and other unconscious products. In this way the conscious personality is brought face to face with the counter-position of the unconscious. The resulting conflict—thanks precisely to the transcendent function—leads to a symbol uniting the opposed positions. The symbol cannot be consciously chosen or constructed; it is a sort of intuition or revelation. Hence the transcendent function is only usable in part as a method, the other part always remains an involuntary experience.

Naturally, these experiences appear only in people without religious convictions. For where there is a definite belief there are also definite concepts from among which a symbol can be chosen. Thus conflict is avoided, or rather the opposite does not appear, being hidden beneath a dogmatic image (Christ, for example). That is why you find no trace of the transcendent function in the psychology of a man with definite religious convictions. What the term "transcendent function" designates is really the transition from one condition to another. When a man is caught by a religious concept, he does not leave it; he stays with his religious conviction, and, furthermore, that is what he should do. If any conflict appears, it is immediately repressed or resolved by a definite religious idea. That is why the transcendent function can be observed only in people who no longer have their original religious conviction, or never had any, and who, in consequence, find themselves directly faced with their unconscious. This was the case with Christ. He was a religious innovator who opposed the traditional religion of his time and his people. Thus he was *extra ecclesiam* and in a state of *nulla salus*. That is why he experienced the transcendent function, whereas a Christian saint could never experience it, since for him no fundamental and total change of attitude would be involved.

You can find a detailed exposition of the transcendent function in Goethe's *Faust*. After his pact with the devil, Faust is transformed through a series of symbols. But Goethe could describe them only because he had no definite preconceived religious ideas. He too was *extra ecclesiam*.

The transcendent function is not something one does oneself; it comes rather from experiencing the conflict of opposites. You can find a detailed exposition of this problem in my *Psychological Types*.[1]

A semiotic representation cannot be transformed into a symbol, because a *semeion* is nothing more than a sign, and its meaning is perfectly well known, whereas a symbol is a psychic image expressing something unknown. In a certain sense the symbol has a life of its own which guides the subject and eases his task; but it cannot be invented or fabricated because the experience of it does not depend on our will.

Hoping that I have been able to give you a rather clearer idea of what I mean by the "transcendent function," I am,

Very sincerely yours, C. G. JUNG

[1] Cf. *Psychological Types*, CW 6, pars. 825–8; also "The Transcendent Function," CW 8.

To W. E. Hocking

[ORIGINAL IN ENGLISH]

My dear Professor Hocking,   5 May 1939

Thank you very much for your kind letter. It is pure pleasure to answer it.

I emphatically agree with your standpoint concerning the empirical element in religious experiences, viz. revelation. But I realize on the other hand the tremendous complication which arises from such a recognition for all forms of creeds with the sole exception of some Indian religions. The Vishnu religion, for instance, could assimilate Christ as an avatar,[1] but Buddhism would concede only a mild interest to Christ. For Christianity particularly it is true that it is altogether of the papal standpoint: *Sit ut est aut non sit*.[2] If the Christian truth is not supreme and solely valid, then it believes it has lost its *raison d'être* and, if I may express my humble opinion, it

☐ (1873–1966), professor of philosophy at Harvard. Cf. Zimmer, 14 Dec. 36.
[1] Vishnu is the supreme personification of the Absolute, the highest God. He became incarnate in Krishna, the God of the *Bhagavadgita*. Avatar: incarnation of a deity/ in this case, of Vishnu.
[2] "Let it be as it is or not at all."

would have lost it. It would instantly have to turn into a sort of philosophical syncretism. I think that this is a most serious point.

I hope that my book *Psychology and Religion* has been forwarded to you. I have discussed there the question of "individual revelation" at length. It is a point that is of daily concern to myself, since time and again I have to deal with patients whose fundamental problem is how to assimilate a religious experience that contradicts or modifies the traditional Christian truth. I take the liberty of sending you an offprint of a little paper I wrote about the Beatus Niklaus,[3] a Swiss saint who for the mere lack of money has not been canonized yet, but he is on the list. His is a typical case of a non-dogmatic religious experience. St. Francis is another more famous example.

Hoping you are always in good health, I remain,

Yours sincerely, C. G. JUNG

[3] "Brother Klaus," CW 11. Brother Klaus, or Niklaus von der Flüe, was canonized by Pius XII in 1947 and declared the patron saint of Switzerland.

Anonymous

[ORIGINAL IN ENGLISH]

Dear Mrs. N.,   22 May 1939

. . .

Regression into childhood is a very typical effect of a brain haemorrhage. I can imagine that these impressions have a strong effect upon you. The presence of a person dying (and under such conditions) has a definite effect upon one's unconscious. Such an influence makes the world unreal and strengthens the unconscious so that it often forms a vortex in which one is sucked under. Be careful that this does not happen to you! Try to touch things that remind you of your reality. I also hope that my letter will be a cool draught from another world.

I think you always have the chance to run into stormy weather at sea. With me the sea usually tries its best to imitate a mill-pond.

Mrs. X.'s great scheme of a world symbol collection[1] is certainly a great adventure. I confess my imagination cannot even grasp the scope of it, but we have heard of mountains in labour which eventually brought forth a mouse. Thus we won't disturb her. The idea itself is quite useful, but such a thing, if efficiently done, should be based on the collaboration of at least one hundred scholars.

□ U.S.A.   [1] Project of an American lady, which never materialized.

The Jewish race problem is really a crucial question, so crucial that I wouldn't know how to tackle it. It has so many aspects and every one of them leads to any amount of misunderstandings. If we were living in a calm world where a reasonable discussion would be possible and where people would be sure that they were always dealing with gentlemen, one could risk a discussion, but the general atmosphere is poisoned and overheated to such an extent that every word sounds wrong. It is an almost hopeless beginning to say something about the race problem.

I have actually reduced my work simply because I had to do it and I expect to reduce it still more in the future. I had something like a little collapse the other day on account of overworking. I feel quite all right now again, but I have to be careful. When I'm less plagued with patients my spirit grows perhaps more adventurous and then I might have some ideas again, but for the time being I have not even ideas.

Hoping you are otherwise always in good health, I remain with best wishes,

Yours cordially, c . g . j u n g

To Hugh Crichton-Miller

[O R I G I N A L   I N   E N G L I S H]

My dear Crichton-Miller, 28 June 1939

I have seen the list of the English delegates which Dr. Strauss[1] has sent to our secretary. I was surprised not to find one single name known to me. I should think that more representative men would be preferable.

I expect you are coming to the meeting. Your presence is all-important, because the English delegation does not impress me as being in any way *au courant* with the delicate situation in the International Society. I am afraid that under the circumstances certain prejudices might decide instead of common sense. Therefore I think your presence, not only as a vice-president but also as a representative of higher reason, will be indispensable. You know that I am still under the

☐ (1877–1959), English psychiatrist, founder and first medical director of the Tavistock Clinic for Functional Nerve Cases (later the Institute of Medical Psychology), London. In 1938 he became vice-president of the International Medical Society for Psychotherapy. Cf. *Hugh Crichton-Miller*, A Personal Memoir by his Friends and Family (1961), with a foreword by Jung, in CW 18.
[1] Cf. Strauss, 26 Mar. 38.

271

suspicion of being a secret Nazi agent despite all I say or do. On account of this there ought to be somebody on the board who is "above board."

Fortunately enough the Dutch have invited us to Holland for the next Congress.[2] In this way we have gained at least 2 years of indecision over against Germany.

It is also imperative that there is a person of authority present at this meeting of delegates, because I shall propose new elections. This is partially due to the fact that I want to withdraw as an international president[3] and partially to the fact that it will be necessary to take the wind out of the sails of the opposition to which I am no *persona grata* but rather a *persona suspecta*.

Cordially yours, C. G. JUNG

[2] On account of World War II this Congress did not take place until 1951, when it was held in Leiden, Holland, under the auspices of a newly constituted International Federation for Medical Psychotherapy, founded 1946.

[3] As a matter of fact Jung was re-elected as international president until such time as the application of the Italian, Hungarian, and Japanese national groups for admission had been dealt with (cf. Hoop, 26 Oct. 40, n. 1).

To Egon Freiherr von Eickstedt

Dear Colleague, 3 July 1939

While I greatly appreciate your kind request for an article on the racial problem, I regret to have to inform you that I have concerned myself far too little with racial questions to be able to say anything decent about them. Equally, the connection between bodily disposition and psychic peculiarities is still so obscure to me that I cannot venture to speculate about it. My typology is concerned only with the basic forms of psychological attitude which I could not at present identify with any physiological or anatomical dispositions.

I hope, therefore, that you will not take it amiss if I cannot fulfil your expectations. With collegial regards,

Yours sincerely, C. G. JUNG

□ German anthropologist, then editor of the *Zeitschrift für Rassenkunde* (Breslau).

To J. Meinertz

Dear Colleague, 3 July 1939

Best thanks for kindly sending me your investigation on psycho-therapy.[1]

As I see from an at present only cursory reading of your book, you give the problem of psychotherapy a central place in the discussion of modern German philosophy. This affords me the great advantage of being able to fill in the gaps in my knowledge of modern philosophy at all essential points, since I can find everything I need in your book. What Heidegger, Klages,[2] and Jaspers have to say in this respect has never affected me very deeply, for one notices the same thing in all writers who have never had to wrestle with the practical problems of psychotherapy. They all have an astonishing facility with words, which they endow with an almost magical efficacy. If Klages had had to treat a single case of neurosis he would never have brought off that thick tome on the obnoxious spirit.[3] Similarly, Heidegger would have lost all desire to juggle with words. You have done the psychotherapist a favour by cutting useful footpaths through this linguistic jungle, and at every turn he can see the most curious vistas opening out before him.

An especially delectable morsel is the way the philosophers juggle with death. I can't wait for the dissertation "How is Death Possible?" or "The Philosophical Foundations of Death." Excuse these heretical fits of mine; they spring from practical experience, where the impotence of philosophical language is revealed at its starkest.

Without a doubt your book meets an essential need, namely the necessity of a philosophical *rapprochement* with the psychotherapeutic insights that were wholly unknown to an earlier philosophy. To you, dear Colleague, belongs the honour of being a pioneer in this field. It is also greatly to your credit that you do not, like the Heidegger school, merely play verbal tricks but say something substantial. Again with best thanks,

Yours sincerely, C. G. JUNG

□ Worms.

[1] J. Meinertz, *Psychotherapie—eine Wissenschaft. Untersuchungen über die Wissenschaftsstruktur der Grundlagen seelischer Krankenbehandlung* (1939).
[2] Ludwig Klages (1872–1956), German philosopher and graphologist.
[3] One of the main works of Klages is *Der Geist als Widersacher der Seele* (The Spirit as Adversary of the Soul; 3 vols., 1937).

To Dr. S.

Dear Colleague, 15 July 1939

I am here again in October and can see you then.—Your ear troubles are very distressing. They can of course be considerably intensified or reduced by one's subjective attitude. Even an ordinary whisper can become unendurable as soon as one's inner attention is directed towards it. Conversely, it can completely disappear if one forgets it.

These phenomena can to a large extent be "overheard." As soon as one's attitude becomes autoerotic in any way, the symptoms increase. An autoerotic attitude necessarily results if, for instance, the function of relationship (Eros) is not sufficiently attended to; that is, if something that ought to be put outside oneself is left inside. That is one possibility. The other possibility is a reluctance to go along with fate, with the result that the importance of the body is abnormally enhanced. With best wishes,

Yours sincerely, C. G. JUNG

To M. R. Braband-Isaac

Dear Colleague, 22 July 1939

Your feeling of being paralyzed is a natural reaction to an over-expenditure of libido. To that extent it is a purposive phenomenon. It is, however, exploited by the animus and poisoned by interpretations. Your doubt that you are making progress is really a philosophical and not a moral or psychological issue. If, therefore, you are impressed by the fact that I knew about the deeper meaning of the Zosimos visions way back in 1912,[1] this only shows that there is something here you do not quite understand. As a matter of fact we have actually known everything all along; for all these things are always there, only we are not there for them. The possibility of the deepest insight existed at all times, but we were always too far away from it. What we call development or progress is going round and round a central point in order to get gradually closer to it. In reality we always remain on the same spot, just a little nearer to or

☐ M.D., psychotherapist; she resided in Palestine.
[1] Jung mentions these visions in *Wandlungen und Symbole der Libido* (1912); cf. *Symbols of Transformation*, CW 5, pars. 200, 484, 553 & n. 97.

further from the centre. Even as a child I had alchemical insights which would sound much more astonishing than anything I said about them in my libido book. Other people have them too. Originally we were all born out of a world of wholeness and in the first years of life are still completely contained in it. There we have all knowledge without knowing it. Later we lose it, and call it progress when we remember it again. The animus has the peculiarity of making false rationalizations about everything. When he sees that we are not covering any ground he interprets it as not progressing. A true understanding would say that there is no ground to cover and therefore no movement through space, but an inner awareness which cannot be expressed in spatial categories. Such occasions are naturally a godsend to the animus—he can then construct the most marvellous contradictions. Perhaps you will read the *Tao Teh Ching* again for a change. With best wishes,

Yours sincerely, c. g. j u n g

To Hugh Crichton-Miller

[O R I G I N A L I N E N G L I S H]

My dear Crichton-Miller, 2 September 1939

I am sorry to be so late in answering your letter. I am convinced that Prof. Göring has not properly understood your motives in proposing Dr. van der Hoop.[1] But that has little or nothing to do with his inability to understand English. It has everything to do with his general inability. Please have no feelings of inferiority on the score of your misunderstanding Prof. Göring's very simple psychology. It has surely nothing to do with your ignorance of the German language. If you suspect Göring of foolish prestige motives you are not far from the truth. The trouble we have to deal with—or we had to deal with—is rather the usual one in any international organization. What one ought to have is an official translator who faithfully renders every nonsense the speaker says. But all this—hélas!—is already an echo from the past. The devil knows how the world will look if we ever meet again. So for the time being we need not worry about

---

[1] Jung, then president of the International Society for Psychotherapy, was looking for a successor, preferably from one of the neutral countries, in order to minimize the tension between the Axis countries and the Allies. Hence C.-M. had suggested Hoop. This move was interpreted by Göring, leader of the German group, as a slight to Germany.

future congresses, delegate meetings, translators, etc. Hitler is reaching his climax[2] and with him the German psychosis.

Good luck to you. I thank you for your cooperation.

Sincerely and cordially yours, C. G. JUNG

[2] Germany invaded Poland on 1 Sept.

To M. Esther Harding

[ORIGINAL IN ENGLISH]

Dear Dr. Harding,   28 September 1939

Thank you for your kind letter. I have put you down on my list for next May and I hope I shall be able to keep the appointment, which is a difficult thing to say in the present circumstances.

There is not the ghost of a plan for my going to America during the war. Even if it were reasonable to go I wouldn't do it, because just as you realize your connection, even your identity, with your people in England, so we would feel entirely uprooted without our country. My son and three sons-in-law are with the army and one son-in-law is in Paris and his wife and children are with us in Küsnacht. I haven't been called upon yet to join one of the many useful organizations, but I'm living provisionally, expecting all sorts of possibilities. We naturally hope not to be implicated in the war, but there is only one conviction in Switzerland, that if it has to be, it will be on the side of the Allies. There is no doubt and no hesitation; the unanimous conviction in Switzerland is that Germany has lost her national honour to an unspeakable degree, and the Germans inasmuch as they still think know it too. I shouldn't wonder if the most curious things happened in Germany. The situation is completely opaque because of the inhuman terror the whole population is kept under by.

Hoping you are always in good health, I remain,

Yours cordially, C. G. JUNG

□ M.D., (1889–1971), English analytical psychologist practising in U.S.A. Cf. her *The Way of All Women* (1933; 2nd edn. 1970); *Woman's Mysteries* (1935; 2nd edn. 1971); *Journey into Self* (1956); *Psychic Energy* (1947; 2nd edn., 1963); *The 'I' and the 'Not-I'* (1965); *The Parental Image* (1965). Jung's forewords to the first, second, and fourth publications are in CW 18. (See pl. in vol. 2.)

Anonymous

[ORIGINAL IN ENGLISH]

My dear Mrs. N.,   5 October 1939

If there hadn't been such a throng of things lately I surely would have written to you long ago. It is a curious thing that the closer people are to very serious issues, the calmer they seem to be. There is of course a great deal of apprehension in Switzerland and we feel the sword of Damocles hanging over our heads. But I was recently in Basel and I found that people are carrying on as usual, despite the fact that hell can break loose at any moment. I was on a point of the frontier right between the French and German lines. You could see the French and German fortifications and all was as quiet and peaceful as possible. No noise and no shots; all the villages are evacuated and nothing stirs.

My son and my sons-in-law are, with one exception, all with the army and my daughter from Paris with her children has taken refuge with us.

Young Hans[1] has been called to the army finally! He is now in a motorized unit where he has to serve as chauffeur and mechanic, as a member of the Auxiliary Service. I suppose that he has even got a uniform which will please him very much. I occasionally get an enthusiastic postcard. Up to the beginning of September he helped me in Bollingen as long as I was there. But with the mobilization he had to join the ranks.

I myself am too old to do active service, but I have been asked to "stand for Parliament."[2] That means, a large group of people seem to want me as a member of the Conseil National (which would be the House of Commons in England). I told them that I'm no politician and they say that that was exactly why they wanted me, that they had politicians enough. I said: Well, under those conditions I can do it. I don't know exactly yet what it means; at all events it means sessions of a fortnight's duration about five or six times a year, and personally no end of boredom. By great good luck it might be that I can say something reasonable. I'm told that people want representatives who mean spiritual values. It is an interesting sign of the times. I'm only on the list and I insisted upon being put

□ U.S.A.
[1] Cf. Kuhn, 1 Jan. 26, n. □.
[2] Jung was asked to stand as candidate for the "Landesring der Unabhängigen" (National Group of Independents) but was not elected.

practically on the last line, as I still hope that I won't be elected. The elections take place somewhere at the end of October or beginning of November. So you'd better tell nobody of this very curious new development.

If I can help you in any way to get through to Switzerland I might do so through the Fremdenpolizei.

It is not exactly the time when one could be busy with a book. The atmosphere is terribly disturbed and it is quite difficult to keep out of it. The things that happen in Germany are just incredible, and the future is full of unheard-of possibilities. The feeling is entirely apocalyptic. It is just like the time when God has allowed Satan to roam on earth for one time and a half.[3] The Germans as far as I know them are partially terrified and partially drunk with blood and victory. If ever there was a mental epidemic it is the actual mental condition in Germany. Hitler himself (from what I heard) is more than half crazy. With every good wish,

Yours cordially, C. G. JUNG

[3] A contamination of Rev. 20:7–8 and 12:14.

To Dr. S.

Dear Colleague,   20 October 1939

If you do not go along with the unconscious properly, i.e., if it finds no expression through consciousness and conscious action, it piles up its libido in the body and this leads to physical innervations. Autoerotism, of course, is itself an unnatural hyper-innervation. There are, however, certain clinical differences between autoerotism and hyper-innervation caused by a blocked unconscious. In the latter case we have chiefly disturbances of the sympathetic system or psychic disturbances in the form of heightened attention to the body. The unconscious is largely identical with the sympathetic and parasympathetic systems, which are the physiological counterparts of the polarity of unconscious contents.

You won't get out of the "old house" until you have drained to the last drop what is going on there. Only then can the situation change. With kindest regards,

Yours sincerely, C. G. JUNG

To Gottlieb Duttweiler

Dear Herr Nationalrat,   4 December 1939

Although I know you have more than enough to do I would like to make the suggestion that in view of the internal difficulties in Switzerland all possible steps should be taken to prevent social unrest in the future.

As you know, mobilization has resulted in a great difference between the social position of conscripts and of persons not liable for military service. There are hundreds and thousands of soldiers whose families have been deprived of their breadwinners, while on the other hand foreigners and those not liable for military service can quietly go on earning a living and eventually take over the job the soldier has lost. This situation is bound to lead to the gravest disputes unless energetic action is taken right away to even out these inequalities.

In my opinion a political party should seize the initiative and introduce the following measure: *mobilization will be declared absolute, every Swiss citizen between the ages of 18 and 60 being counted as mobilized whether he is liable for military service or not.* Those who are not liable would be under the same regulations as the conscripts, the only difference being that the soldier would do his duty with a rifle and the non-conscript as a wage-earner. Every Swiss citizen would accordingly be put on the payroll and anything he earned above and beyond that would be used for the public good[1] for the duration of the mobilization. If this measure were introduced now, everything possible would have been done to prevent social unrest, and the soldier at the front need no longer have the uncomfortable feeling that on top of his risking his life for others he and his family are financially disadvantaged. If the war should last for a long time we shall be exposed to the greatest financial hardships anyway.

☐ (1888–1962), Swiss businessman and politician. Founder of Migros, the first Swiss co-operative retail trading society; member of the National Council, Councillor of State. Also founded the "Landesring der Unabhängigen" (cf. previous letter, n. 2).

[1] In an almost identical letter, written the same day, to his old friend Albert Oeri (cf. Oeri, 11 Dec. 20), editor of the *Basler Nachrichten* and member of the National Council, Jung specified that these funds should be made available primarily to the "distressed families of the conscripts."

Hence we need a magnanimous gesture now in order to cope with future difficulties.[2]

Yours sincerely, c. g. jung

[2] Jung's suggestion was not accepted. Instead, the Schweizerische Lohn- und Verdienstersatzordnung (Swiss Wages and Income Compensation Order) arranged compensation for financial losses caused by the mobilization.

To Erich Neumann

Dear Colleague,   16 December 1939

I was happy to hear from you again. You have obviously waited rather too long before writing to me, for your letter is so concentrated that a full-scale reaction by post is simply impossible.

Had I had your dream I would have needed either to thin it out or to round it out. When a dream assumes this legendary form, there are contents in it that should be taken up, elaborated, and rounded out through active imagination. I would have needed to dramatize the dream still more to make it yield up its secrets. The Wotan association[1] does not point to the Teutonic regression in Germany but symbolizes a spiritual movement affecting the whole civilized world (Wotan as wind-god = pneuma). This explains why Wotan also figures among Jews, though only German Jews, as I have seen many times.

The hermaphrodite[2] is certainly an archetype. It stands for a union of opposites and is probably a duality symbol equivalent to Aquarius and would thus have about the same value as the fish symbol at the

[1] N. reported a dream in which he was an old pilgrim threatened by Nazis (?). As he was about to continue his pilgrimage, there stood at his side a "son" and a "father" who turned into an old prince. The prince told the pilgrim to go in spite of the protests of the "son," in order to expiate his condemnation at a trial. The pilgrim started on his journey, taking only his slouch hat (association: Wotan's hat) and staff, without being allowed to take leave of the "son." The dream continues with the prince killing the pilgrim, but not before the pilgrim had prophesied the prince's death. Many details have been omitted in this summary.

[2] In a second dream there appeared "a gigantic hermaphrodite of cosmic proportions . . . , male in its upper and female in its lower part" (again details omitted). N. had mentioned in his letter that he was working on the problem of the meaning in Jewish religion of the polarity expressed in the hermaphrodite.

beginning of our era. As the alchemical symbolism shows, it signifies the self, whose Indian symbols are likewise hermaphroditic. (Cf. the Atman figure at the beginning of the *Brihadaranyaka Upanishad*.[3]) This problem transcends racial differences and comes from that wind of the spirit which is blowing over Europe and probably the whole world too, for in the Far East as well things are everywhere in rapid motion.

Here we are very impressed by the immediate danger of war in our own country, but for the time being everything is still in suspense.

In my lectures[4] I am discussing the Eastern attitude with the help of Yoga philosophy and the Western attitude with the help of Ignatius's *Exercitia Spiritualia*. My best wishes,

Ever sincerely, C. G. JUNG

[3] Cf. *Brihadaranyaka Upanishad*, 1.4.3 (cf. Hume, *The Thirteen Principal Upanishads*, 1934, p. 81).
[4] Lectures at the Swiss Federal Polytechnic (ETH), Zurich.

To Dr. Tochtermann

Dear Colleague,   13 January 1940

By the "creative element" you probably mean a person's creative faculty. Your question as to whether this faculty is present from the beginning is not easy to answer. There are undoubtedly cases where one can take it as certain that it was present from the start, but in other cases it seems to develop in the course of life. I personally incline to the view that this faculty, like everything else, was present from the start.

Your second question, regarding the relation between creativity and the mother complex, can be answered as follows: A creative person who has not yet developed this faculty sufficiently will generally have a mother complex, which does not mean that anyone with a mother complex is also creative. So when a mother complex is resolved by analysis, in one case a creative person will emerge, in another a timid little boy who would rather have hidden behind his mother all his life. In the first case the mother complex is unreal, in the other it is real. With collegial regards,

Yours sincerely, C. G. JUNG

☐ Bad Elster, Germany.

To Dr. Ed. Lauchenauer

Dear Dr. Lauchenauer,   16 January 1940

. . .

What the public still doesn't know and can't get into its head is that the collective man is subhuman, nothing but a beast-man, as was clearly demonstrated by the exquisite bestiality of the young German fighters during the Blitzkrieg in Poland. Any organization in which the voice of the individual is no longer heard is in danger of degenerating into a subhuman monster. With kind regards,

Yours sincerely, C. G. JUNG

☐ Aarau, Switzerland.

To Henriette Goodrich

[ORIGINAL IN ENGLISH]

My dear Mrs. Goodrich,   20 May 1940

Your very kind letter has touched me profoundly. I hope I have not to avail myself of your most generous proposition.[1] My whole family including 11 grandchildren have gone to a refuge in the mountains near Saanen.[2] All my sons[3] are with the army. Zurich is—in case of war—threatened with complete destruction, because it is just in the main line of defence. We have here the feeling as if one were sitting on a box full of dynamite that might go off in the next moment. Yet one is quiet, because it is a great fatality. For the time being I am also in Saanen, but I am planning to go back to Zurich as soon at it seems certain that the war gets stabilized in the north. Actually it looks as if Italy prefers an undisturbed Switzerland. Even the dictators mistrust each other. We are all terribly sorry for England and France. If they should lose the war, we also shall not escape the reign of the Antichrist. But we Swiss cling to our soil and we share its fate.

Thank you for your kindness!

Yours cordially, C. G. JUNG

☐ (Handwritten.) Now Mrs. Benjamin Lehmann, Saratoga, California.
[1] When the Germans started their attack on France through the Netherlands, Belgium, and Luxembourg on 10 May 1940, Switzerland also seemed in danger of invasion. G. suggested to Jung that he bring his family over to California for the duration of the war.
[2] Many Swiss left the eastern part of Switzerland, the most exposed to attack, for a redoubt in central Switzerland. Saanen is in Canton Bern.
[3] Jung refers to his son and four sons-in-law.

Jung at his desk, 1945

I

Clark University, September 1909
A. A. Brill, Ernest Jones, Sandor Ferenczi
Sigmund Freud, Stanley Hall, C. G. Jung

Eugen Bleuler

Hermann Hesse

Richard Wilhelm

H. G. Baynes

III

IV   Jung in East Africa, 1925

Count Hermann Keyserling

Olga Fröbe-Kapteyn

Heinrich Zimmer with Jung, Eranos, 1939

V

(*clockwise*) Mary Mellon; Frances G.
Wickes; Mary Churchill with Jung, 194
Victor White with Jung at Bollingen

(*clockwise*) Munich, 1930; Bailey
Island, Maine, 1936; On Lake
Zurich, 1945; C. G. Jung and Emma
Jung, Küsnacht, 1950

VII

Jung's house at Küsnacht

VIII

Anonymous

[ORIGINAL IN ENGLISH]

Dear Mrs. N.,   20 May 1940

This is just the kind of experience you needed. You trust your unconscious as if it were a loving father. But it is *nature* and cannot be made use of as if it were a reliable human being. It is *inhuman* and it needs the human mind to function usefully for man's purposes. Nature is an incomparable guide if you know *how* to follow her. She is like the needle of the compass pointing to the North, which is most useful when you have a good man-made ship and when you know how to navigate. That's about the position. If you follow the river, you surely come to the sea finally. But if you take it literally you soon get stuck in an impassable gorge and you complain of being misguided.

The unconscious is useless without the human mind. It always seeks its collective purposes and never your individual destiny. Your destiny is the result of the collaboration between the conscious and the unconscious.

I am actually in the mountains with my family and all the little grandchildren avoiding the dangers of Zurich. We all hope and pray for a British victory over the Antichrist.

Sincerely yours, C. G. JUNG

To Mary Mellon

[ORIGINAL IN ENGLISH]

My dear Mrs. Mellon,   19 June 1940

Thank you for your friendly letter, which arrived today. I send you these few words in haste, because this evening at 7 o'clock the *last*

□ (Handwritten.) Mary Conover Mellon (1904–1946) was the first wife of Paul Mellon, well known American philanthropist and art collector. 1939–40 Paul and Mary Mellon were in Zurich. Mrs. Mellon undertook psychotherapeutic treatment with Jung for asthma; the political situation of that time caused the analysis to be interrupted prematurely, but a close friendship arose between the Mellons and Jung. Mary Mellon was responsible for the establishment in 1945 of Bollingen Foundation in New York (projected as early as 1941, and named for Jung's retreat on the upper lake of Zurich). Originally, only the publication of a collected edition of Jung in English was planned, but the program of the Foundation was soon broadened; the so-called Bollingen Series includes intellectual works in various cultural spheres, which in the widest sense further the understanding of Jung's ideas. (See pl. VI.)

mail for U.S.A. will leave Switzerland. From now on all communications will be interrupted.[1] I think the night has descended upon Europe. Heaven knows if and when and under which conditions we shall meet again. There is only one certainty—nothing can put out the light within.

Every good wish to you and to your husband!

Yours affectionately, C. G. JUNG

[1] This soon proved to be an unfounded rumour.

To Karl Kerényi

Dear Professor Kerényi,   26 July 1940

Many thanks for kindly sending me your MS "Kore."[1] I have read your brilliant account of the Kore figure with the greatest interest.

When you say that an ethnologist can scarcely imagine with what feelings a classical philologist will read his material, I can say the same of the psychologist who is permitted to enjoy this lively object-lesson concerning a figure which so often crops up in his practice. Were I not so busy at present with urgent work I could hardly resist the temptation to add a psychological commentary. I don't know what you intend to do with this essay. Will you have it published soon, or will it be some time before it goes to the printer? In the latter case I would consider whether it would be possible to say something suitable, provided that such a suggestion is acceptable to you.

I am keeping your essay a while longer. But if you want it back I can send it to you at any time.

Yours sincerely, C. G. JUNG

☐ Hungarian philologist and mythologist; since 1943 in Ascona, Switzerland; lectured extensively at the C. G. Jung Institute, Zurich, and at the Eranos meetings. Author of numerous works, mainly on Greek mythology.
[1] In *Das göttliche Mädchen* (1941), with a psychological commentary by Jung; republished together with *Das göttliche Kind* as *Einführung in das Wesen der Mythologie* (Amsterdam/Zurich, 1941). *Essays on a Science of Mythology* (New York, 1949; London edn. has title *Introduction to a Science of Mythology*). Jung's commentary, "The Psychological Aspects of the Kore," is in CW 9, i.

To H. G. Baynes

[ORIGINAL IN ENGLISH]

My dear Peter,   Bollingen, 12 August 1940

This is the fateful year for which I have waited more than 25 years. I did not know that it was such a disaster. Although since 1918[1] I knew that a terrible fire would spread over Europe beginning in the North East, I have no vision beyond 1940 concerning the fate of Europe. This year reminds me of the enormous earthquake in 26 B.C. that shook down the great temple of Karnak. It was the prelude to the destruction of all temples, because a new time had begun. 1940 is the year when we approach the meridian of the first star in Aquarius. It is the premonitory earthquake of the New Age.

Up to the present moment Bollingen has escaped—together with Switzerland—the general destruction, but we are in prison. You don't see the walls, but you feel them. The newspapers are hushed and one hardly cares to read them, except for doubtful information about the war. For a while, just when I studied your book,[2] I went with all my grandchildren to the West of Switzerland because we expected an attack. Afterwards I was very busy because all doctors were with the army.

It is awkward to write, as the censor reads the stuff. But I must tell you how often I think of you and all my friends in England. I

☐ (Handwritten.)

[1] While working on the "North Africa" chapter in his *Memories* (IX, i), Jung related to Aniela Jaffé that, soon after peace was declared in 1918, he had a "visionary dream" which continued to haunt him until the outbreak of World War II: "I was returning to Switzerland from a trip in Germany. My body was covered with burns and my clothes were burnt full of holes; for I had seen fire falling like rain from heaven and consuming the cities of Germany. I had an intimation that the crucial year would be 1940." (Communication from A. J.)—In the autumn of 1913, while actually on a journey, Jung had an "overpowering vision" of a "monstrous flood covering all the northern and low-lying lands between the North Sea and the Alps. . . . Then the whole sea turned to blood." The vision was repeated two weeks later. During the spring and early summer of 1914 he had "a thrice-repeated dream that an Arctic cold wave descended and froze the land to ice" (*Memories*, pp. 175f./169). — These dreams and visions foretold the outbreak of World War I. And in 1918 he wrote: "As the Christian view of the world loses its authority, the more menacingly will the 'blond beast' be heard prowling about in its underground prison, ready at any moment to burst out with devastating consequences" ("The Role of the Unconscious," CW 10, par. 17). Cf. also "The Fight with the Shadow," ibid., par. 447.

[2] *Mythology of the Soul.*

often complain that Mr. Chamberlain did not read my interview with Knickerbocker.[3]

Your book is quite interesting and it seems as if your interpretations hit the nail on the head. Certain points would need some discussion. But one should talk, writing is too clumsy.

It is difficult to be old in these days. One is helpless. On the other hand one feels happily estranged from this world. I like nature but not the world of man or the world to be. I hope this letter will reach you and convey to you all the wishes the human heart can't suppress in spite of censors. They are human too after all.

In autumn I resume my lectures at the E.T.H. about the individuation process in the Middle Ages![4] That's the only thing with me one could call up to date. I loathe the new style, the new Art, the new Music, Literature, Politics, and above all the new Man. It's the old beast that has not changed since the troglodytes.

My dear Peter, I am with you and with old England!

Cordially yours, c. g.

[3] An interview with the American journalist H. R. Knickerbocker, "Diagnosing the Dictators," *Hearst's International Cosmopolitan*, Jan. 1939. In it Jung suggested that Western civilization might be spared the horrors of Nazi terrorism by turning Hitler's aggressive libido towards Russia, as the only way to stop Hitler making war on the West. In this way Nazism could be induced to commit suicide. The interview is included in *C. G. Jung Speaking* (in press).
[4] Alchemy I and II, Nov. 1940–Feb. 1941; May–July 1941.

To J. H. van der Hoop

Dear Colleague,   26 October 1940

As you will remember, I tendered my resignation at the meeting of delegates in Zurich, July 1939, because I was firmly resolved to give up the running of the Society. I knew for certain that conditions would arise in the future when I would no longer be in a position to do anything useful. The precipitate announcement at that time of three new national groups[1] was an unmistakable symptom of developments to come. I was induced to continue as president until such time as the said groups were accepted.

I have now endeavoured for more than a year to get the necessary documents from these groups but in no case have I succeeded. One

[1] Italy, Hungary, and Japan. The admission of these groups would have strengthened the German influence.

of them hasn't even been constituted as yet, the other hasn't sent in its statutes, and the third hasn't replied at all. Meanwhile Prof. Göring has been pressing for the acceptance of the three groups. Since I have not succeeded in carrying out the task allotted to me within a reasonable period, I have felt justified in handing this task back to the Society and making my resignation final.

This decision was welcomed by Prof. Göring, who declared that I was too old anyway to understand the new developments. Accordingly, at the last Congress of the German group in Vienna, Göring transferred the Society to Germany,[2] on the ground that Germany now had all the necessary international connections to continue the Society—connections with Holland, Denmark, Sweden, Switzerland, Hungary, Italy, and Japan. Our secretary-general, Dr. C. A. Meier, has apprised Prof. Göring of the whole legal position in a special memorandum, to which no reply has been forthcoming.

The situation now is as follows: I have handed over the business management in the interim to Dr. C. A. Meier until such time as an international meeting of delegates becomes possible again. This interim situation is perfectly understandable because no international business can be conducted under present conditions, with the result that the secretariat is, so to speak, unemployed. Dr. Meier will pay the moneys due to the German group out of the Society's funds in Switzerland. He will preserve the framework of the International Society since the Swiss group considers itself a member. The International Society consists at present of Sweden, Denmark, England, Switzerland, and Holland.

Through my resignation I have given up the management of the *Zentralblatt*. I have been accused by the Germans of making it essentially an organ of my school; hence I have given it up with pleasure. If you count the number of papers that have appeared from my pen in the *Zentralblatt*, and the few my pupils have written, you will have to admit that such an accusation is not borne out by the facts.

In Switzerland I have gone to inconceivable trouble to get the psychotherapists together, but find no support among my colleagues, which is due mainly to the sectarian resistance of the Freudians. Of late I have made no more such attempts but am now leaving it to others to do something about it. If people find I am standing in their way, it makes no difference to me to resign.

---

[2] Göring declared at this Congress—which he illegally designated as a meeting of delegates of the International Society—that the Society was *gleichgeschaltet* (conformed). The same fate befell the *Zentralblatt*.

287

Naturally in the normal course of things an international meeting of delegates should be convened, but as you well know this is not possible under the present conditions. I myself would be very pleased if a better alliance of psychotherapists in Switzerland and a closer collaboration with Holland were possible, but since my efforts in this respect have proved fruitless I must, as I have said, leave it to others. Though I am a member of the Swiss Psychotherapy Commission[3] instituted by the Psychiatric Society, and am also president of the Curatorium of a Psychotherapeutic Institute,[4] not yet functioning in Zurich because of the war, I must everywhere guard against taking any initiative, otherwise it is immediately thought that I want to monopolize everything. This idiotic prejudice is a considerable obstacle to cooperation. That this is not merely Swiss bigotry should be clear to you from the above-mentioned accusation concerning the *Zentralblatt*.

As I am no longer president, I would ask you to direct all matters relating to the Society to Dr. C. A. Meier. For the reasons stated, I want to avoid exerting any influence on the affairs of the Society so as to prevent useless upsets.

I would like to bring it to your attention that an article[5] will soon appear in the *Zentralblatt* in which I am represented as the spokesman of a bygone epoch. From this you can see how timely my resignation was. With collegial regards,

Yours sincerely, C. G. JUNG

[3] Cf. Bjerre, 8 May 36, n. 2.
[4] The Curatorium of the Teaching Institute for Psychotherapy (cf. Hoop, 14 Jan. 46, n. 1).
[5] This article, if it appeared, cannot be traced.

To H. G. Baynes

[ORIGINAL IN ENGLISH]

My dear Peter,   9 December 1940

I just got your letter of September 10th for which I was waiting a long time. Thank you very much for all the news. I can't tell you how glad I am that you and your family have escaped the danger of getting bombed that came so close to your house.

Things are all right over here up to the present moment. But we don't know what the future will bring us. I'm busy as usual and as often as I can I work in the garden to prepare a field for potatoes next spring. We are practically cut off from the world as far as supplies are concerned and have to live on our wits as well as we can. My daughter from Paris and her children are with us since the beginning of the war, happily enough. But her husband is still in Paris.

We are following the exploits of the R.A.F. with the greatest admiration and we marvel at the way the British people are carrying on. It is at least a light in the darkness which we feel very much being so close to it.

A long time ago I wrote to X., but got no answer. Have you any news from her? I wonder what she is doing.

I'm still not through with your book, because I've been interrupted by a lot of additional work and I don't get things as quickly off my hands as I used to do when I was younger.

Please give my best regards to Mrs. Baynes. I hope that your house and your family will be protected in the future as they have been in the past. Three cheers for old England!

Cordially yours, C. G.

To Mary Mellon

[ORIGINAL IN ENGLISH]

My dear Mrs. Mellon,   Bollingen, 7 January 1941

Since days I feel the necessity to write to you. Several times you appeared to me quite vividly. I know I still owe you a letter in response to yours which you wrote in October. I had a pretty miserable time then. I did not feel well, and the term brought me, besides the lectures, a mountain of practical work. My summer vacation was full of work too, and not so long as usual. Moreover that damnable war against England and the destruction of France was more than one could bear. I had to feel with England all the time as if I had to support her at least morally. The devastation of London hurt me as if it were my own country. I had to wait for my winter vacation to write letters. I have answered Mr. Mellon's letter right away though, because I felt it was immediately needed. I thank you for the beautiful camellia, which we got in time. It was really touching that you thought of us at Christmas time. Your plans for the refuge and the *hortus conclusus*[1] are really exciting. I can understand that the archi-

---

☐ (Handwritten.)

[1] *Hortus conclusus*, "enclosed garden," image often used in medieval hymns to the Virgin Mary. The passage is concerned with construction and landscaping at the Mellon house.

tect goes crazy when you tackle his unconscious so ruthlessly. But I am grateful to you that you have created something in America I really long to see. It is something that is not only in the mind but also in earth and stone. This thought gives me a feeling of peace and restfulness, something I can look forward to, beyond the abomination of war and the Nietzschean insanity of Germany. Be careful when you tread on the tiger's tail that is the American unconscious. Yours is a formidable task. The thing above all is *steadfastness* in the whirlpool of our actual world. It is now a question whether we can really hold the treasures of culture and defend them against the overwhelming onslaught of the powers of darkness. With us everything is as if frozen. People are still moving about and trains are running as usual. But automobiles have almost vanished from the streets. Food is still plentiful but everything costs more, though not yet badly. Our army concentrates in the mountains, to hold the position as long as possible.[2] But the lower country will have to be sacrificed in case of war. It would be sheer madness to attack Switzerland, but the Germans are mad. Recently we had some bombs on Zurich near the main station and several houses destroyed and a few people killed and wounded. But the bombs were British. Those Canadians are not yet up to the mark in European geography. Nobody minds, because all our sympathies are on the British side and we enjoy the Italian defeats. The news one gets from Germany is most contradictory. A German, well informed, told me that about 90% are against the régime. A Swiss from Berlin told me that the workmen openly criticized Hitler and called him a liar. Mussolini is most unpopular and the mood of the people is unsatisfactory. The young people in Germany, however, are still full of illusions, although the mood in the army has considerably dropped since England could not be overrun. People from Paris told me that the Germans are unlikely to succeed in the administration of the conquered countries since they are lacking in sufficient numbers of qualified people. Peculiarly enough, Germany seems to suffer from an increasing lack of labour, and less from food scarcity. Frau Fröbe[3] succeeded in bringing over my paper on the Trinity, one of the fruits

[2] Reference to the so-called national redoubt devised by General Guisan, consisting of numerous fortifications in the Alps in case of an invasion of Switzerland by the enemy.

[3] Olga Fröbe-Kapteyn (cf. Fröbe, 29 Jan. 34) visited the U.S.A. for several weeks in fall 1940; among other things she intended to discuss arrangements for the Eranos Conferences with the Mellons and others.

of this summer. I don't dare to send you my recent paper "Das göttliche Kind," which I produced together with Prof. Kerényi, for fear it could get lost. Parcels are still unsafe and, God knows, after a while communications cease altogether. Perhaps we will get under German domination. In that case I certainly would be silenced, which I should not mind, provided that I have still my books and a roof over my head. But I do hope to see you again. Every good wish to you!

Yours affectionately, c. g. j u n g

To Karl Kerényi

Dear Colleague,   18 January 1941

. . .

I have read *Das Aegäische Fest*[1] with great interest and it has put me in a remarkable mood. I have the feeling that a terrific lot could be said about it, chiefly from the alchemical side. I don't think Goethe was aware himself of how profoundly he was influenced by alchemy. What he read at the behest of Frl. von Klettenberg[2] hardly suffices to explain the depth of his alchemical intuition. The same astonishing empathy was at work here which you show he had with Greek mythology. You put the emphasis on the festival, and this without any doubt is in accord with the whole plan of the Classical Walpurgisnacht.[3] What chiefly fascinates me is the figure of the Homunculus, who appears in threefold form in Part II. First the Boy Charioteer, then Homunculus, and finally Euphorion. They all end in fire.[4]

Thus the feelings your book has aroused in me do not quite tally with the picture you have painted. I want to avoid at all costs wrenching out any one detail from that brilliant canvas. I must mull over

---

[1] (Amsterdam, 1941.) This book gave Jung the stimulus for writing his last great work, *Mysterium Coniunctionis* (cf. p. xiii). Concerning the Aegean Festival, see *Faust II* (tr. Wayne) Act 2, pp. 141ff.: "Rocky Inlets of the Aegean Sea."

[2] Susanne Katharine von Klettenberg (1723–74), friend of Goethe's mother, author of religious hymns and pietist essays. During the years 1760–70 she strongly influenced the young Goethe's religious views and introduced him to alchemy.

[3] *Faust II*, Act 2.

[4] The homunculus (manikin) is produced by Faust's assistant Wagner according to an alchemical prescription of Paracelsus. He and the other two *puer aeternus* figures all burst into flame.

291

your book some more. Perhaps I shall succeed in arranging my psychological material in a form that fits it better.

. . .

I hope you will continue to have patience with my incubation. I'll be writing to you again later. With kind regards,

Yours sincerely, c. g. jung

Anonymous

Dear Fräulein N.,   23 January 1941

There is much that I do not understand in your letter. If you are suffering from an inferior extraversion, then that is a fact which is nobody's fault and for which you can hold nobody responsible. It is a difficulty which is rooted in your own nature and which you can only acknowledge in an attempt to do the best you can with it.

Nor does it matter at all whether I have a high or a low opinion of you. The only thing that matters is what you do yourself. Nobody can "fence you in," as you put it. But people who have no money, for instance, are fenced in by that very fact without being able to hold anybody else responsible.

There are a whole lot of facts in your letter which you'll just have to face up to instead of tracing them back to the faulty behaviour of other people. Psychological treatment cannot rid you of the basic facts of your nature; it can only give you the necessary insight, and only to the extent that you are capable of it. There are countless people with an inferior extraversion or with too much introversion or with too little money who in God's name must plod along through life under such conditions. These conditions are not diseases but normal difficulties of life. If you blame me for your psychological difficulties it won't help you at all, for it is not my fault you have them. It's nobody's fault. I can't take these difficulties away from you, but have merely tried to make you aware of what you need in order to cope with them. If you could stop blaming other people and external circumstances for your own inner difficulties you would have gained an infinite amount. But if you go on making others responsible, no one will have any desire to stand by you with advice.

Yours sincerely, c. g. jung

☐ Switzerland.

To the Secretary of the Union Mondiale de la Femme pour la Concorde Internationale, Geneva

Dear Madame, 27 January 1941

I agree with you entirely that it would be desirable if we could make humanity more reasonable simply by instruction and by good intentions. But are good intentions enough to impress men? If they were impressionable, the last war with all its atrocities should have served as a lesson. Yet we have to assume that it produced no effect since hardly a generation later everything is forgotten. That is why it seems to me useless to try to educate men by talking to them and instructing them. Men have to be gripped, because only those who are gripped can grip others. Spirit cannot be learned, it is given to us by God's grace, which cannot be had by force or reason.

But if men of good will applied themselves to the solution of the conflicts and the causes of the conflicts in their own vicinity, and tried to free themselves from outside influences, they could at least set an example. As we know, example is more effective than admonition. In ten lectures I could not add anything at all to what I have just said. I know that this way of looking at things is neither brilliant nor inspiring, and that—precisely because of its simplicity—it would not have any popular effect. But since it is my conviction, I could not say anything else in speaking publicly. This point of view being doubtless out of key with the aim of your organization, it seems to me that you would do better not to receive me among your lecturers.

Thanking you nevertheless for your amiable intention, I am,

Yours sincerely, C. G. JUNG

☐ (Translated from French.)

To Josef Goldbrunner

Dear Dr. Goldbrunner, 8 February 1941

Very many thanks for kindly sending me your book on my psychology.[1] I read it at once and was impressed by your careful exposi-

☐ Ph.D., Roman Catholic priest. Then in Munich; now professor of theology at the U. of Regensburg, Germany.

[1] Probably *Die Tiefenpsychologie von C. G. Jung und christliche Lebensgestaltung* (privately printed, 1941).

tion and the trouble you have taken over your task, which was surely not an easy one.

A fundamental misunderstanding has crept into it, however, for which I wouldn't like to hold you entirely responsible. You evidently did not know that epistemologically I take my stand on Kant, which means that an assertion doesn't posit its object. So when I say "God" I am speaking exclusively of assertions that don't posit their object. About God himself I have asserted nothing, because according to my premise nothing whatever can be asserted about God himself. All such assertions refer to the psychology of the God-image. Their validity is therefore never metaphysical but only psychological. All my assertions, reflections, discoveries, etc. have not the remotest connection with theology but are, as I have said, only statements about psychological facts. This self-limitation which is absolutely essential in psychology is generally overlooked, whereupon this disastrous confusion arises, with the result that it looks as if I were presuming to make metaphysical judgments. Again with best thanks and kindest regards,

Yours sincerely, C. G. JUNG

To Elined Kotschnig

[ORIGINAL IN ENGLISH]

Dear Mrs. Kotschnig,   18 February 1941

Please don't believe one moment that I have less to do on account of the war. I only have less foreigners, but otherwise it's all the same as before. If you are going to ask me further questions, please have it typewritten, it's so much easier than handwriting. Also short and precise questions are much appreciated.

I'm pretty certain that psoriasis is a psychological disease, though I'm not able to establish a specific psychological cause for it. But I know that if a patient's psychology becomes cleared up so that he functions as any human being ought to function, then everything comes into the open which has been retained before. These psychological skin diseases seem to be nothing else than a sort of psychological perspiration. It is just as if the retained or dammed up contents were filtering through the skin and appearing on the surface, like saltpeter blossoming out of humid walls.

The life of X., as you describe it, is tangibly full of quantities of life not lived, but I must confess that under the circumstances you describe it's almost impossible to find a way to help her. As the old doctors assumed that such skin diseases were caused by a so-called dyscrasia—a bad mixture of humours—psychology comes to a very similar result in so far as the general attitude of the patient is more responsible for the ailment than any particular point that might be cleared up or settled by specific advice. You know how long it takes to change the whole viewpoint of the patient, yet in nearly all neuroses it is almost indispensable that the whole outlook on life undergoes a complete change. Thus X. would need a complete analysis which surely would be no easy case. . . .

Sincerely yours, c. g. jung

To Karl Kerényi

Dear Colleague,   10 March 1941
. . .

Many thanks for kindly sending me your Labyrinth book,[1] which I found extraordinarily interesting. The labyrinth is indeed a primordial image which one encounters in psychology mostly in the form of the fantasy of a descent to the underworld. In most cases, however, the topography of the unconscious is not expressed in the concentrated form of the labyrinth but in the false trails, deceptions, and perils of an underworld journey. But there are also designs which express the labyrinth idea in the skein motif (coiling serpents, meanders, etc.).

With regard to Goethe's Aegean Festival, this contains, as I think I have written you already, the intuition of a central alchemical motif, namely the *coniunctio*, which is intimately bound up with the production of the Homunculus. With an almost uncanny sureness of intuition you have touched on a central problem of the unconscious which seems to me exceedingly difficult to handle. *Das Aegäische Fest* describes one aspect of this problem, but the problem itself extends infinitely further: on the one hand via the *hierosgamos* into Gnosis and Christian mythology and thence into Indian Tantrism, on the other via the Homunculus into the psychology of alchemy. This complex of motifs is a labyrinth in itself, an indescribable tangle of problems, and I fear that my thoughts about it, although they have been going on for years, have still not got to the point where I could trust myself to say anything responsible. More-

[1] *Labyrinth-Studien* (1941).

295

over this task would cut across a plan I have been carrying around with me for some time, namely a description of the accessible processes of the unconscious, especially of the *coniunctio* motif.[2]

I am afraid that just tacking on a few remarks on the significance of the Homunculus in alchemy would be doing your beautiful book a poor service. One would have to say something to the point or else nothing at all. I would gladly have used my spring holiday for this purpose had I not been asked to deliver the address at the Paracelsus jubilee[3] this year, and I had to consent although I am no Paracelsus specialist. But as I have to mug up the philosophy of this country-man of mine because he exerted a considerable influence on later alchemy, and there are evidently few people who know anything about this particular aspect of medieval speculation, I shall have to spend my holiday pursuing the labyrinthine thought-processes of Paracelsus and in addition prepare my summer lecture. Consequently there will be no time left to devote myself to your book.

If you could wait until the summer I might, *Deo concedente*, be able to contribute something on *Das Aegäische Fest*, but it is simply impossible before. With lively regrets and best wishes,

Yours sincerely, c. g. j u n g

[2] A plan finally realized with the publication of *Mysterium Coniunctionis*, CW 14.
[3] A lecture given in 1941 on the occasion of the 400th anniversary of Paracelsus's death at Einsiedeln, his birthplace: "Paracelsus as a Spiritual Phenomenon," CW 13. — Philippus Aureolus Theophrastus Bombastus von Hohenheim, called Para-celsus, Swiss physician and philosopher (1493–1541), was the founder of a new school of medicine, at the centre of which stands the concept of man as a micro-cosm whose substances and energies are in "concordance" with those of the macrocosm.

To Carl Julius Abegg

Dear Dr. Abegg, 2 April 1941

Many thanks for kindly sending me your book.[1] It always makes me a little nervous when an author sends his work to me as a "psy-chologist" because I always suspect, perhaps unjustly, that he wants to hear something psychological from me. But that is just what I find

☐ Zurich.
[1] *Johanna, ein Schicksal* (1941).

impossible in the great majority of cases, since I am always impressed and affected not only as a professional but also as an aesthetically-minded layman, and have to imagine all sorts and conditions of men so vividly that I become completely oblivious of the author and feel obliged to appear somewhere in the story as a more or less qualified helper. I am then caught up in it and personally involved in the events, so that I react at most with exclamations but seldom or never with what the giver of the book expects from me. There is, however, one exception and that is when the author arouses my hostility, which is far from the case with your book. The quiet meditativeness that radiates from the fate you have described is rather like a verse from a hymn-book which one unexpectedly comes across again after 50 years.

Yours sincerely, C. G. JUNG

To Mary Mellon

[ORIGINAL IN ENGLISH]
Bollingen, 18 April 1941
anno miseriae

My dear Mrs. Mellon,

I should have written to you long ago, but I was kept so busy by lectures, meetings, patients, that I never found a quiet moment. On top of all I felt very tired and deeply depressed by the senselessness of this war. It is mere destruction. Why in hell is Man unable to grow up? The Lord of this world is surely the Devil. Mrs. Fröbe brought me cheerful news about yourself and the splendid work you do. She was in high spirits, as I well understand. I am missing the great world and the travelling therein and I envied her. I think such reactions are just human, all-too-human. You hardly can imagine the thickness of the black cloud suspended over Europe, and one wishes to escape from the soundless pressure of evil and dull idiocy. Excuse these lamentations! They always come first, when I have to reach out into the world to shake somebody's hand across the Atlantic. I feel then how far I am withdrawn from this world of illusion and of ever-renewed attempts at an illusory goal.

I am deeply indebted to you for all you do for the common cause. I naturally agree with the Bollingen Press idea. Little Bollingen at Yale![1] It is marvellously grotesque. In as much as I am able to

□ (Handwritten.)

[1] An original plan was to publish Bollingen Series under the auspices of Yale U. The actual publisher, beginning in 1943, was Pantheon Books Inc., a private firm under the direction of Kurt Wolff. (See Wolff, 1 Feb. 58.)

advise you I shall be only too glad to do it, but then I have to dictate letters.

Your dreams: Twin children, twin men, twin Jungs—this series suggests the projection of a dualism in yourself which, however, becomes chiefly visible in *myself*. It is probable, therefore, that it should be seen in myself rather than in yourself; in other words: it should be seen as an *objective* and not as a *subjective* problem. It is matter of a dualism in the *unconscious* (therefore projected) *personality*, which we designate as the self or the unknowable totality of man, for which I am the paradigm in your dream. You can formulate the idea in the well-known Hindu style: I am the victim and the killer, the food and the eater, I am yea and nay! My invitation means that you should come up to the level of such understanding, whose vehicle is love and not the mind. This love is not transference and it is no ordinary friendship or sympathy. It is more primitive, more primeval and more spiritual, than anything we can describe. That upper floor is no more you or I, it means many, including yourself and anybody whose heart you touch. There is no distance, but immediate presence. It is an eternal secret—how shall I ever explain it?

I wish you could come again to Ascona. But the world-wide darkness is still on the increase. I am grateful to fate that you have such dreams, otherwise the world would be rather empty in the Western Hemisphere.

I hope your husband has received my letter about mathematics.[2] Please give him my best regards! Also to Prof. Zimmer, when you see him. I had a letter from Ximena de Angulo[3] about my Zosimos. I am going to write to her. At all events you can set her mind at peace by telling her she should not worry about the German text, since the English text is carefully revised and fully reliable. My best and sincerest wishes to you!

Affectionately yours, C. G. JUNG

P.S. Excuse me sending you such an unaesthetic letter![4] We are rationed but living conditions are still normal. Of course no petrol anymore, no cars, English tobacco on the decline. Central heating very limited, general state of health therefore much better, decrease

[2] At the time, Paul Mellon had enrolled as a student in St. John's College, Annapolis, Maryland, whose curriculum is based on the "Great Books" of the Western tradition. He had written Jung about his studies in mathematics.
[3] Mary Mellon's assistant editor in the early stages of Bollingen Series, daughter of Cary F. Baynes and her first husband, Jaime de Angulo.
[4] Jung had written on both sides of the airmail paper.

of children's diseases by about 50%. No grippe to speak of! I am planting potatoes and beans. At times I feel old and rotten. But I have recovered from the worst of my fatigue. Next time I shall answer more promptly.

To Olga von Koenig-Fachsenfeld

Dear Dr. Koenig,   5 May 1941

. . .

In my opinion it is scarcely possible to correlate the various forms of neurosis with aetiological archetypes. Things are not as simple and schematic as that. So far as the aetiology of the neuroses is concerned I can only say that a neurosis ensues whenever the inner psychic situation is not in accord with the outer, and one or the other is consequently disregarded to an unwarranted extent in the effort to adapt. The classic compulsion neurosis is an exception in that it is always due to a latent psychosis, which is also the reason why it is uncurable. Its compulsions are due to inaudible voices which under certain conditions may become audible.

All attempts at specific aetiologies of neurosis and corresponding psychological formulations I consider to be artificial concepts. With kindest regards,

Yours sincerely, C. G. JUNG

☐ Ph.D., German analytical psychologist. Cf. her *Wandlungen des Traumproblems von der Romantik bis zur Gegenwart* (1935). Jung's foreword is in CW 18.

To H. G. Baynes

[ORIGINAL IN ENGLISH]

My dear Peter,   27 May 1941

Thank you very much for your long letter! Your lecturing activity is really astonishing. But I can understand that the public realizes a certain need to compensate the onesidedness of organized activities. And I can well imagine that the great cataclysm has knocked over many prejudices and false values. I have noticed similar phenomena in Switzerland, but universities of course are the last to be touched or moved, which—I suppose—is the case all over the world. The war

☐ (Handwritten.)

has brought me more work instead of less. Our young people are for long stretches of time with the army and thus I can't get rid of my patients. My public lectures at the Technical University demand a certain amount of attention. I am actually lecturing about the psychology of alchemy. For several years now I have been lecturing about the process of individuation. First I gave an account of Patanjali's Yoga Sutra,[1] then of two Buddhist treatises[2] concerning the attainment of Buddhahood. The third course was about the _Exercitia Spiritualia_ of St. Ignatius. The fourth course is about alchemy[3] as the absolute contrast to the _Exercitia_. As they are going to celebrate the 400th Anniversary of Paracelsus's death in 1541 I had to prepare a lecture about him (on invitation of course), which has taken away practically the whole of my spring vacation as I had to dive into the unfathomable chaos of Paracelsan tracts with their queer and difficult terminology. Recently I delivered two lectures at the Club about the main symbolism of the Mass (sacrifice and transubstantiation).[4] I seem to be dealing more and more with subjects not just suitable for public discussion (f.i. a lecture on the Trinity[5] at Eranos!). I have not continued my book, since I discovered that the subject I had in mind was much vaster than my limited knowledge and moreover I did not feel my approach was the right one. It seems to me that I am now on a better track. The ultimate result is perhaps no book but a series of essays or lectures.[6] The general trend is a continuation of _Psychology and Religion_. I often have interviews now with a Catholic priest,[7] an intelligent and scholarly man, who gives me a chance to get thoroughly acquainted with the Catholic mind. It is wonderful to see mediaeval mentality still at its best. At the same

[1] The four classic Yoga Sutras, compiled and commented on by Patanjali, whose historical personality is still controversial. The first three Sutras may date from the 2nd cent. B.C., the fourth is apparently later (cf. Zimmer, _Philosophies of India_, p. 282). The Yoga Sutras of Patanjali represent a philosophical systematization of ancient Yoga theories and practices.
[2] The Amitayur-Dhyana Sutra (_Sacred Books of the East_, XLIX, 1894), a Mahayana Buddhist text, and the Shri-Chakra-Sambhara Tantra, a Tantric text (in Avalon, _Tantric Texts_, VII, 1919).
[3] Cf. Baynes, 12 Aug. 40, n. 4.
[4] Later combined into the Eranos Lecture "Das Wandlungssymbol in der Messe" (_Eranos Jahrbuch_ 1940/41); now revised as "Transformation Symbolism in the Mass," CW 11.
[5] "Zur Psychologie der Trinitätsidee" (_Eranos Jahrbuch_ 1940/41), now revised as "A Psychological Approach to the Dogma of the Trinity," CW 11.
[6] The final result was _Psychology and Alchemy_, CW 12 (orig. 1944).
[7] Dr. Gallus Jud. Cf. "Symbolism in the Mass," p. 203, n. 1.

time I realize more and more the importance of the loss Protestantism has suffered. But it was tragically inevitable. Don't think, please, that I am callous in not mentioning the horrors of our time. I am confirmed in my fundamental disbelief in this world. Here we are all right so far. With every good wish I remain,

Yours cordially, C. G.

To Robert H. Loeb

[ORIGINAL IN ENGLISH]

Dear Mr. Loeb,   26 August 1941

I'm very late indeed in answering your letter[1] but I've been so busy in the last year that many letters have remained unanswered. Now I have my vacations and I can do something about it.

I'm glad to know that you have found something that alleviates your distressing symptoms.

Your idea about the image of the medicine-man being the everlasting model for the impressive doctor is quite correct. Also your comparison of Freud and myself. Freud is essentially concretistic, like Newton, and I'm chiefly impressed by the relativity of psychological phenomena.[2]

Concerning the type-problem with Freud and Adler, I admit it is an intricate one. What I meant to say was that Freud's theoretical point of view is extraverted, whereas Adler's point of view is quite introverted. Now if you read my article about the artist ("On the Relation of Analytical Psychology to Poetical Art" in *Contributions to Analytical Psychology*,[3] 1928), you will find that I discriminate between the ordinary ego-consciousness of the man and his creative personality. Very often there is a striking difference. Personally a creative man can be an introvert, but in his work he is an extravert and vice versa. Now I knew both Freud and Adler personally. I met Freud when he was already a man in his 50's. His general way of

---

□ (1883–1953), of New Rochelle, New York. — In a letter of 1921, Dr. William Alanson White (then superintendent of St. Elizabeths Hospital, Washington, D.C.) introduced L. to Jung: "Mr. L. was formerly a New York business man who became so deeply interested in analytical psychology that he gave up his business and has devoted himself almost exclusively to the study in this department of science for some months past. . . ." He was in analysis with Jung until 1923.
[1] L.'s letter is dated 18 Oct. 40.
[2] L. had compared Freud to Newton and Jung to Einstein.
[3] Now "On the Relation of Analytical Psychology to Poetry," CW 15.

living was a genuinely introverted style, whereas Adler, whom I met as a young man, being of my age, gave me the impression of a neurotic introvert, in which case there is always a doubt as to the definite type. As you know, Freud himself was neurotic his life long.[4] I myself analyzed him for a certain very disagreeable symptom which in consequence of the treatment was cured. That gave me the idea that Freud as well as Adler underwent a change in their personal type. First of all Freud, as a creative personality, had a definite extraverted point of view. In his personal psychology on the other hand, he underwent a tremendous change in his life. Originally he was a feeling type and he began later on to develop his thinking, which was never quite good in his case. He compensated his original introversion by an identification with his creative personality, but he always felt insecure in that identification, so much so that he never dared to show himself at the congresses of medical men. He was too much afraid of being insulted. Adler, I suppose, was personally never a real introvert, therefore as soon as he had a certain success he began to develop an extraverted behaviour. But in his creative work he had the outlook of an introvert. The power complex which both of them had showed in Freud's personal attitude, where it belonged. In Adler's case it became his theory, where it did not belong. This meant an injury to his creative aspect. As a matter of fact Freud was the far greater mind than Adler. Freud is a real view, Adler a sidelight, though of considerable importance.

The diagnosis of a type is extremely difficult when it is a matter of a neurosis. As a rule in such a case you see both, introversion as well as extraversion. But the one belongs to the ego-personality, and the other belongs to the shadow- or secondary personality. As is often the case, these two personalities can succeed each other in life. Either you begin your life with the shadow (putting the wrong foot forward) and later on you continue with your real personality, or vice versa. I hope I have answered your question.

Times are very hard and the atmosphere of Europe is oppressive. It is difficult to understand that there are still Americans who do not realize what the world situation really is.

Hoping you are in relatively good health, I remain,

Yours sincerely, c. g. jung

---

[4] Cf. Hanhart, 18 Feb. 57, n. 2. — Without the publication of the passage in that letter, authorized neither by Jung nor by his heirs, the editor would not have felt justified in including this (and the following) sentence.

To Heinrich Zimmer

My dear Zimmer,   26 August 1941

Heartiest thanks for your two manuscripts, "The Involuntary Creation" and "The Celtic Romance of the Soul."[1] I shall soon enjoy reading them, which I can do now as I am on holiday.

We often think of you and did so quite particularly at the last Eranos meeting, where a Hungarian Hellenist and mythologist, Kerényi, did his best to take your place for us,[2] though it didn't quite come off because there is, after all, only one Zimmer who, we concluded, is inimitable. We simply missed you! Altogether, you can hardly imagine the moribundness of this European world. Particularly here in Switzerland we have the feeling that we can only live vertically. Thank God for small mercies! But living horizontally is nice too, though completely blighted because after a few kilometers we hit the frontier and on top of that we no longer have a car. When we go on holiday my wife and I push a two-wheeled cart ahead of us with the luggage, which is not so sad but uncommonly amusing.

As you may have heard, I have been very busy of late with Catholic matters. This time I have given three lectures on the Mass.[3] I haven't published anything for a long time, otherwise I would have sent it to you.

My wife sends best greetings to you and your wife, and so do I.

Yours ever, C. G. JUNG

☐ Zimmer now lived in New Rochelle, New York.
[1] Now in Zimmer, *The King and the Corpse*, with "The Celtic Romance of the Soul" retitled "Four Romances from the Cycle of King Arthur."
[2] Kerényi lectured on "Mythologie und Gnosis" (*Eranos Jahrbuch* 1940/41).
[3] Cf. Baynes 27 May 41, n. 4 and 5.

To Mary Mellon

[ORIGINAL IN ENGLISH]

My dear Mrs. Mellon,   Bollingen, 8 September 1941

Thank you very much for your kind letter! I just got it and I answer it immediately. I wrote a long letter to you in spring. But I think you never got it. At least I heard from our post office that the letter has not been let through. I don't know why. Believe me, I often

☐ (Handwritten.)

think of you and I often wish I could see you again. But you are further away than the moon. I thought of you in Ascona, where we had a very nice meeting.

Your dream is shocking indeed. You get such dreams when you are too much identified with somebody. The unconscious then tries to throw something in between. You probably have a very living image of myself and it might keep you too much away from yourself, no matter what I am. It must be something of the sort, because all your letters emanate an immediate warmth and something like a living substance which has an almost compelling effect. I get emotional about them and I could do something foolish if you were not on the other side of the ocean. Please don't misunderstand me: I am in a healthy condition of mind, but I merely describe, with utmost honesty, that which is produced by a letter of yours. It is slightly uncanny, and it proves that there is a living connection through the non-space, i.e., an unconscious identity. Such a thing is dangerous to a certain degree, at least it can cause a certain alienation from yourself. I do consider your dream as a very necessary compensation, though a painful one. My attitude is one of honest and sincere devotion beyond all doubt. It has never changed. You don't need to do anything about it, because I think a normally functioning unconscious will compensate the trouble efficiently. It is f.i. enough to get this shock of such a poisonous dream. You know, we have to realize that no matter how much we should like to be able to talk to each other, we shall be separated for a long time, perhaps forever, if such a human concept can be applied to whatever happens after death. You know time and space are only relative realities, which under certain conditions do not exist at all. Yet our conscious life detains us within the confines of time and space. Perhaps you ought to realize the facts as they are. We don't know what is going to happen over here. Germany exhales a simply devastating atmosphere. It is well-nigh indescribable. I am not going to lecture this winter. I feel it is time to reduce my public work. A time might come when there will be nothing left but the life within.

It is splendid that Paul is with the army. It is true, he has the air of a good marksman. We know them well in Switzerland. I hope my lectures about the Mass will please you. I don't write a book about Paracelsus, only two lectures, because I have been asked to lecture about him on the occasion of the 400th return of the day of his death (1541).

Please give my best regards to Paul. Sincerely hoping that my letter will reach you, I remain yours,

Affectionately, C. G. JUNG

P.S. Can't you pull a wire and tell the Bermuda censor who I am and that I am a F.R.S. and that I got an honorary D.Sc. at Oxford? and moreover I am a thoroughly reliable individual?

To Gustav Senn

Dear friend,   13 October 1941

Best thanks for your kind letter. I was naturally very pleased that you have made a serious effort to plough through the jungle of my problematical little book.[1]

I have grappled with your book,[2] too, and am very impressed by the methodology of your Theophrastus, who could indeed be a modern scientific mind in more than one respect. I could not help marvelling at your philological exactitude. I have plumb forgotten my Greek as I have to read mainly Latin texts, Greek ones being something of a rarity in alchemy.

Kant's categorical imperative is of course a philosophical touching-up of a psychic fact which, as you have quite correctly seen, is unquestionably a manifestation of the anima.[3] A complete elucidation of this phenomenon in Kant would be possible only if we had sufficiently authentic material on his relation to his mother. This also hangs together with the fact that he never married.

I have always avoided scientific polemics because they are usually fruitless, as I have seen from many examples in my immediate vicinity. My anima constantly repeats the saying: *Magna est vis veritatis*

□ (1875–1945), professor of botany at the U. of Basel. Jung wrote the original version of "The Philosophical Tree," later revised and expanded, for a *Festschrift* on the occasion of Senn's 70th birthday. Cf. *Alchemical Studies*, p. 251n.

[1] Probably an advance copy of *Paracelsica* (1942), containing "Paracelsus the Physician," CW 15, and "Paracelsus as a Spiritual Phenomenon," CW 13.

[2] "Die Entwicklung der biologischen Forschungsmethode in der Antike und ihre grundsätzliche Förderung durch Theophrast von Eresos," *Schweizer Gesellschaft für die Geschichte der Medizin und Naturwissenschaften* (Aarau), VIII, 1933.

[3] Cf. H. Rider Haggard's *She*, where She, the anima figure, is called "She-Who-Must-Be-Obeyed."

et praevalebit.[4] With that I have come through pretty well, all things considered. Not that there weren't occasions when I would have been delighted to settle some special blockhead's hash in the time-honoured fashion.

I had hoped to meet you in Einsiedeln and was very sorry not to see you. It was an unusually fine and lively affair and the monastery did its very best.

Hoping it won't be another 40 years before we see each other again, and with best regards,

Yours, CARL

[4] "Great is the power of truth and it shall prevail."

Anonymous

Dear Dr. N.,   27 October 1941

Your dream[1] unquestionably refers to the archetypal problem of the extrusion of the soul from the body. One is forced to conclude that in your case the soul is only loosely seated in your body. It remains to be seen whether that is correct or not. However, the friendly lion in the dream seems to indicate that the looseness of the soul is not exactly desirable, since the lion compensates your condition in a very obvious way: the Zurich lion[2] represents your localized instinct, firmly rooted in your earth, just as the lion's soul—as with all animals —is securely fixed in its body. Moreover you seem prone to eczema, which not infrequently indicates that one is not properly inside one's body. It is sometimes the same with other diseases.

If you devote yourself, intentionally and intellectually, to dangerous problems such as the squaring of the circle, this is yet another indication of a tendency to get away from the body, because this problem symbolizes an irrational state of wholeness which cannot be contrived but can only be experienced. This experience cannot be brought about or discovered by even the greatest intellectual effort.

Polyps in the anal region indicate a creative impulse in that region—an impulse that is of course being misused. It is as though you were defecating yourself out of the anus, and this is a topsy-turvy procedure since you really ought to be producing yourself. But you

□ Switzerland.
[1] The dream has not been preserved.
[2] The lion is the heraldic animal of Zurich.

obviously aren't. Somewhere there is a place where you are not making yourself felt, not creating yourself. You are squeezing yourself out behind, so to speak, acting not in accordance with your instinct but in accordance with reflections or inclinations which are the very reverse of instinctively correct actions. You jump out of your skin, but backwards.

Naturally one ought to know more about your personal life, which I don't. But it is conceivable that in your dealings with those around you, you are not sufficiently self-contained and therefore need the support of the Zurich lion. The valley of darkness has to be gone through in reality and not in fantasy, otherwise one could spare oneself an infinite number of unpleasantnesses which are nevertheless important for life. I think, therefore, that if you keep as closely as possible to concrete reality and try to create yourself there and illuminate the darkness, you will be on a more normal road than when you engross yourself in squaring the circle as a substitute. This problem confronts you with the extremely tricky task of uniting the principle of the square with that of the circle. It frequently presents itself in the relationship between two people, when it is the problem of fitting a square peg into a round hole.

I hope these hints may be of some help.

Yours sincerely, c. g. j u n g

To Alice Lewisohn Crowley

[ORIGINAL IN ENGLISH]

My dear Mrs. Crowley,   20 December 1941

. . .

I begin to feel my age and whenever I get a bit too tired I also feel my heart and that is decidedly disagreeable and makes me cross with the whole world, which is damnable anyhow. I went through a period of black depression during the first 4 days.[1] Only yesterday I began to feel human again. And then your situation in Europe came back to me with a bang! I beg you to consider your life. If they are going to send you to Poland, you only can suicide yourself. Please forgive this crudeness! It is my anxiety for your life which makes me say such things. Remember, I warned you before America went to

□ (1884–1972), co-founder and director of the Neighborhood Playhouse, New York, devoted to experimental theatre. Later resided in Zurich.
[1] The Japanese attacked Pearl Harbor 7 Dec. 1941.

war. It is urgent that you do something and quick! Europe is in a desperate situation.

I am sorry and I am helpless.

Yours affectionately, C. G. JUNG

To Jolande Jacobi

Dear Dr. Jacobi,   31 December 1941

I am sorry to be answering your letter only now. Everything has got in arrears because all sorts of things have gone wrong. Also the postal service here is very slow.

There can be no doubt that Dr. X.'s statements are projections of his "Jewish" anima. This anima is *anti-Semitic*, i.e., feels the need to correct a Christianity that looks "Jewish." Dr. X. is more Protestant than he suspects, like very many educated German Catholics. Indeed at the time it needed merely the dogma of infallibility[1]—tame enough and perfectly logical in itself—to throw Germany into a veritable uproar and let loose a second schism.[2] The "Jewish" anima is therefore projected upon Jewesses, not because they are Jewish but because they are still *pagan* in their eroticism, or at least this is suspected. But this eroticism goes together with an unconsciousness which an intelligent Jewess does not have. *She upsets people by her heightened consciousness.* Naturally *you* have no hallucinations of memory, but Dr. X. has. Of course these projections are all wrong, but they are symptoms of resistances due to the above-mentioned *unconscious* assumptions. It doesn't matter what *your* convictions[3] are: you affect him as a Jewess. Anyone who has unconscious assumptions must be treated like an insane person: one must let him have them until he comes into conflict with himself. You mustn't want to do anything with him, *just let him talk.* Important conversations you should immediately note down at home so as to correct any falsifications of memory. You shouldn't worry about him too much, as you work far too intensively and penetratingly. Don't forget that

[1] The dogma of the infallibility of the pope was first defined at the Vatican Council in 1870.

[2] A group of German Catholics, under the leadership of Johann Ignaz von Döllinger, professor of theology in Munich, did not accept the dogma of infallibility and in 1871 formed a community of "Old Catholics." The movement spread to Switzerland, Austria, and some other countries without, however, gaining a large membership.

[3] Dr. Jacobi is a Catholic convert.

you are playing the all-powerful mother role. You must also be able to lose him, otherwise he will prove himself the eternal son by seeming indispensable to the mother. He detests this sweet submission and dependence and yet longs for them. You can't have any total attitude to this paradox so you must treat him like a phenomenon and want nothing for yourself. Everything you give must be given as though given up for lost, that is, sacrificed. If you have the feeling it's all been wasted, that is as it should be. He wants to get out of his mother complex, so he has to experience it again on you. And if you still haven't taken to your heels, perhaps he will discover the human being in you. Interpret and explain nothing. Watch your tongue, for it can sting. I can receive you this coming Sunday at 10 a.m. in Küsnacht. With best regards,

Yours, C. G. JUNG

To Paul Schmitt

Dear Dr. Schmitt,   Locarno, 5 January 1942

Best thanks for your New Year letter, with its welcome news that the pebbles ejected by the volcano on whose edge I am sitting have landed somewhere. It is a never-failing pleasure to hear an echo. The recognition of this bad quality in myself makes me indulgent with the vanity and sensitivity of otherwise competent authors—too long one can hear no echo, and this can easily lead to an obdurate and grim self-admiration—or the reverse. . . .

You have hit the mark absolutely: all of a sudden and with terror it became clear to me that I have taken over *Faust as my heritage*, and moreover as the advocate and avenger of Philemon and Baucis,[1] who, unlike Faust the superman, are the hosts of the gods in a

☐ (Handwritten.) Paul Schmitt, LL.D., (1900–1953), Swiss publisher and journalist, editor of the *Münchner Neueste Nachrichten* until 1933, when he had to leave Germany on account of his opposition to Naziism. Lectured at several Eranos meetings on philosophical and historical subjects.

[1] The myth of Philemon and Baucis tells how they were the only ones to offer hospitality to Zeus and Hermes when they came down to earth to test men's piety. In *Faust II* (Act 5) Faust wantonly causes the death of the couple. In his *Memories* (pp. 234f./221f.) Jung reports how the inner dichotomy between "Personality No. 1 and No. 2" (pp. 57/66) made him identify with Faust ("Two souls, alas, are housed within my breast"), and how he felt Faust's guilt as his own and that he had to expiate Faust's crime. (Cf. Keyserling, 2 Jan. 28, n. 3.) Concerning Jung's interest in the figure of Philemon cf. *Memories*, pp. 182ff./176ff.

ruthless and godforsaken age. It has become—if I may say so—a personal matter between me and *proavus* Goethe.[2] To the extent that I harbour a personal myth of this kind you are right in nosing up a "Goethean" world in me. Indeed it is there, for it seems to me unavoidable to give an *answer* to Faust: we must continue to bear the terrible German problem that is devastating Europe, and must pull down into our world some of the Faustian happenings in the Beyond, for instance the benign activity of Pater Profundus.[3] I would give the earth to know whether Goethe himself knew why he called the two old people "Philemon" and "Baucis." Faust sinned from the beginning against these first parents ($\phi i \lambda \eta \mu a$ and Baubo[4]). One must have one foot in the grave, though, before one understands this secret properly.

I wish you all the best for the New Year and hope to see you again soon after my return.

Yours sincerely, C. G. JUNG

[2] = Goethe the ancestor. There is a family tradition according to which Jung's grandfather, Carl Gustav Jung (1794–1864), was an illegitimate son of Goethe's. Although this tradition could not be proved, it amused Jung to speak of it (*Memories*, pp. 35/47 & n. 1). Cf. also Jung, 30 Dec. 59.
[3] *Faust II*, Act 5.
[4] $\phi i \lambda \eta \mu a$ = kiss. Baubo (= belly) is a Great Mother figure; in Greek mythology, a lewd old woman who succeeded in making Demeter, grieving over the abduction of her daughter Persephone to the underworld, laugh at an obscene gesture.

To Pater X.

Dear Pater,   17 January 1942

Thank you very much for your kind letter and the parcel of books. I am truly astonished at the depth and the extent of your study of yoga. As you say very rightly, some people pay no attention to yoga because they do not take it seriously, while others claim to know a great deal more about it than they actually do. Yoga, to me, is no more than a subject for research. It neither impresses nor deceives me. During my stay in India[1] I saw for myself that yoga is not at all what we think. There Hatha yoga[2] is often no more than acrobatics, or

☐ (Translated from French.) Canton Fribourg, Switzerland.
[1] Cf. Iyer, 16 Sept. 37, n. 1.
[2] Hatha Yoga aims at the achievement of perfect health and supernormal bodily

simply gymnastics; or else it is a physiological aid to concentration, an aid which these highly emotional people need very much in order to master themselves. In the course of these concentration exercises the individual gets into a dream state, or autohypnotic condition, which removes him from the world and its illusions. Since the goal of yoga is the void of deep sleep, yoga can never be a final truth for the occidental world.

Yoga seems to me, like many other similar practices, to be a wilful and technical application of a special individual experience. A descent to the greatest depth in oneself ("the ocean of divinity") is undoubtedly the ideal being followed. This encounter with the greatest in oneself must therefore be the impressive experience that is sought for again through the yoga technique. I have tried to formulate this idea in a parable on the mandala which you will find in the pamphlet on rebirth;[3] I enclose it together with a little essay on yoga[4] which I had forgotten.

With sincere regards and my best wishes for the New Year,

C. G. JUNG

---

powers. It is both a preliminary to all other Yoga disciplines and a system in itself.

[3] Offprint of "Die verschiedenen Aspekte der Wiedergeburt," *Eranos Jahrbuch* 1939; now revised as "Concerning Rebirth," CW 9, i. For the parable on the mandala see par. 233.

[4] "Yoga and the West," *Prabuddha Bharata* (1936); in CW 11.

To H. G. Baynes

[ORIGINAL IN ENGLISH]

My dear Peter,   22 January 1942

It was a great pleasure to have your letter of Nov. 23rd. It took its time in arriving, but it gave me at least an idea of what you are doing. I appreciate your letter all the more as I know how difficult it is to write letters at all. Your dealings with the clergy are interesting. What will become of the Christian Church? I will try to send you a MS of the Mass and one about the Trinity. It seems as if one or the other will be included in the English edition of an Eranosbook launched in America.[1] At the moment I am unable to give you suffi-

☐ (Handwritten.)

[1] Cf. Fröbe, 29 Jan. 34, n. ☐. "Transformation Symbolism in the Mass" appeared in *The Mysteries* (vol. 2 of Papers from the Eranos Yearbooks; 1955).

cient information: there is such a turmoil of publications, translations etc. that I have lost control. I will try whether I can procure another copy of the Red Book.[2] Please don't worry about translations. I am sure there are 2 or 3 translations already. But I don't know of what and by whom. A little book about Paracelsus is about to appear. This "religio medica" might interest you. I will send you a copy. I have given up lecturing at the E.T.H.[3] It became too much of a strain, with everything else minus the auto, which has facilitated so many things. I have done a lot of research work within the last years besides my practical obligations. A certain slowing down seems to be indicated. I cannot get reconciled to the stupidity and shortsightedness of man, nor to this world in general. We are in for a new "Katakombenmentalität,"[4] the only German invention or article "made in Germ." of lasting value. The devil has been seriously underrated within the last centuries. And the Church has played along with him in an irresponsible way. God, things are so very much worse than one likes to admit. No reason for any optimism: this world will never be better as it is already "le meilleur des mondes possibles." But it has an almost uncanny faculty of deteriorating into something infinitely worse. The Church insists too much on faith and far too little on insight and judgment. Thus the Church preserves a general credulity which the devil can make use of and *he does use it!* Childishness has been favoured, propagated and nurtured. Its result is Socialism, the *political infantilism* κατ' ἐξοχήν[5] which is always the first step toward the Leviathan. The future might easily be so bad that the Church could be forced by circumstances to give up all her childish worldliness and socialism and to turn to the spiritual problem of man, which she has so sadly neglected. I would say of the *Catholic Church* —"criminally neglected." (More sins are forgiven to the great sinner than to the petty one.)

It is all like talking about the weather in a howling storm at sea or in a snowstorm on a glacier. It does not matter and nobody hears it. The shrieking of the demons is the stillness of the spirit. It means a withdrawal unheard of, until one hears the great silence.

[2] The book in which Jung recorded his dreams and fantasies. Cf. *Memories*, pp. 188/180; also "Nachtrag zum 'Roten Buch,' " in *Erinnerungen*, p. 387.
[3] Jung had to give up his lectures, started in 1933, for reasons of health.
[4] = "catacomb mentality." Probably a reference to the need to withdraw into hiding, as the early Christians did in the catacombs.
[5] = pre-eminently, par excellence.

Hoping you are in good health and that the same is true of your family, I remain,

Yours cordially, c. g.

To Elisabeth Metzger

Dear Frau Metzger,   7 February 1942

Your conception of the archetype as a psychic gene is quite possible. It is also a plausible hypothesis that the archetype is produced by the original life urge and then gradually grows up into consciousness—with the qualification, however, that the innermost essence of the archetype can never become wholly conscious, since it is beyond the power of imagination and language to grasp and express its deepest nature. It can only be experienced as an image.[1] Hence the archetype can never enter consciousness in its entirety but remains a borderline phenomenon, in the sense that external stimuli impinge upon the inner archetypal datum in a zone of friction, which is precisely what we might describe consciousness as being. This view would do greater justice to the essentially conflicting nature of consciousness.

From the rest of your remarks I see that you have already formed trenchant views of the nature of the psyche.

Yours sincerely, c. g. jung

☐ Stuttgart.

[1] Distinction between the archetype *per se*, or psychoid archetype, and the archetypal image. Cf. Devatmananda, 9 Feb. 37, n. 1; also "On the Nature of the Psyche," CW 8, pars. 417f.

To Eugen Diesel

Dear Dr. Diesel,   10 April 1942

I am sorry that I am only now thanking you for your friendly letter and for your kindness in sending me your books.[1] I had completely forgotten that we met in Darmstadt in 1930.[2]

☐ German author.

[1] *Vom Verhängnis der Völker* (1942); the other is not identifiable.

[2] D. and Jung both lectured at Darmstadt in 1930 at a meeting of Keyserling's "Schule der Weisheit." D.'s lecture was "Die Neugestaltung der Welt," Jung's "Archaic Man," CW 10.

313

Meanwhile I have read one of them all through and part of the other and have gained some insight into the way you see our modern world. I did not know the *Verhängnis der Völker*. What strikes me is the tremendous force with which your thinking has been swept into the world turmoil and into the abysmally insoluble problem of human masses. Solutions seem to me possible only in the realm of the microcosm. The world at large still is and probably always will be the hopeless struggle of a cosmos against an eternal chaos. I am so impressed by this fact that my thoughts, as I finally had to admit, have not got beyond *hic mundus* and the *princeps huius mundi* of the New Testament. Where the road branches off towards infinite multiplicity it has come to a stop in me and I have preferred the footpath. Since then I have lost all desire to speak of multiplicity because simplicity seems to me so much more useful.

Please don't take this as a criticism of your preoccupations: I know that a mirror has to be held up to mankind. Schopenhauer has obviously had a long-lasting effect on you. I have read your book not only as a foreground phenomenon but also as a background one, and I fully understand why you must now be occupied with rendering a total account of the "human process to date." Quite rightly the question of standpoint is the most difficult of all, it was of the most concern to me, too, and therefore I had to avert my eyes from the corrupting spectacle, remembering the fate of Alypius, that friend of St. Augustine's, who wanted to keep his eyes shut at the circus—but when the crowd raised a mighty cry at the fall of a gladiator he was forced to open them again, and then, as Augustine says, he "was stricken with a deeper wound in the soul than the man he had opened his eyes to see suffered in the body."[3] It is, as you say, the most interesting theme because the most hopeful. One must never look to the things that ought to change. The main question is how we change ourselves. This standpoint is admittedly absurd, yet it is infinitely more satisfying than the absence of the Archimedean point.

I would dearly like to talk with you about this, as it seems to me, most important matter if it were possible in the circumstances, but now is not the time for horizontal movements: everyone is in the prison and can only move vertically. We have all become *katochoi tou theou*,[4] miraculously without knowing it. One can only hope that in time, by the grace of God, the shackles hung upon us will be

[3] Cf. *Symbols of Transformation*, par. 102.
[4] = "Prisoners of God."

314

sufficiently loosened for a European conversation to be conducted in quietude. Until then each must go through his incubation period.

I am taking the liberty of sending you by the same post one of my latest writings. With best regards,

Yours sincerely, C. G. J U N G

To Jürg Fierz

Dear Herr Fierz,   10 April 1942

The application of my function theory to the spirit of language seems to me difficult and problematical in so far as language is infinitely older than the differentiation of the functions. These are always present, but in such an undifferentiated state that they simply cannot be kept apart. Together they constitute the psychic functioning in general and out of this matrix is produced language, partly as objective imitation and partly as subjective imitation—that is, it expresses what the object does or what the subject does. Auditive, motor, and visual factors as well as skin sensations also play a large role. You see this particularly with primitive languages, where many words would not be understood at all without the corresponding gestures. Hence many primitives cannot have a conversation at night unless they make a fire in the light of which they can observe each other's miming.

I know little of the "objective spirit"[1] the philosophers talk about, nor in my opinion does language live of itself—it always lives from man. I think we are dealing here with the same kind of illusion as the State. People talk of the State as though it were a living entity, when in fact it is only a conventional concept that could not live for a second unless man pumped the necessary life into it.

A psychological object-lesson could probably be derived from language without too much difficulty. Take for instance the symptoms of emotion in language and the effects the emotions have upon it, emotive metaphors, etc. With kind regards,

Yours sincerely, C. G. J U N G

□ Zurich. Then student, later Ph.D., journalist, since 1950 editor of the Zurich *Tagesanzeiger*.
[1] F. mentioned the attempt of contemporary philosophy to understand language as the manifestation of an "objective spirit" independent of a psychic factor, existing and creating out of itself.

To Arnold Kübler

Dear Herr Kübler,   10 April 1942

I have been mulling over your question about the Romantics but have come to the conclusion that, fully occupied as I am with my own work at present, I could hardly muster the necessary patience to expatiate on such a contemplative theme as "Why Can't We Paint Like the Romantics Any More?" with the contemplativeness this requires. For that is what we lack at the present time—contemplativeness. If one is sitting on a volcano and can be contemplative to boot, this is a superhuman heroism which is itself a contradiction in terms. Nowadays it's no longer any use appealing to any certainties. Deep down we know that everything is tottering. When the earth quakes, there are only abrupt and disjointed fragments, but no closely woven and harmonious flower carpet. A Romantic ideal in our time would be like a figment from a feverish dream. Therefore it is much better for modern art to paint the thousand-hued débris of the shattered crockery than to try to spread a deceptive quietness over the bottomless disquiet. The grotesque, the ugly, the distorted, the revolting perfectly fit our time, and if a new certainty does not start up somewhere, art will continue to express disquiet and inhumanity.

That is all I have to say on this question. It is abrupt and disjointed, like what we are talking about.

Yours truly, C. G. JUNG

□ Swiss author and illustrator, 1941–58 editor of the Swiss monthly magazine *Du* (Zurich).

To B. Milt

Dear Colleague,   8 June 1942

Your questions[1] are not easy to answer as they touch on territory which for all the work of historical specialists still remains very much in the dark, probably because, as you quite rightly remark, the West-

□ Zurich.

[1] M. asked about the relation between symbolic and rational-conceptual thinking and to what extent the loss of the former during the Middle Ages was responsible for the alienation of scientific thought from a more general humanistic approach.

ern mind has deviated in a particular direction from its original basis. Paracelsus, it seems to me, is one of the most outstanding exponents of a spiritual movement which sought to reverse this turning away from our psychic origins as a result of Scholasticism and Aristotelianism. One can with a good conscience be in some doubt whether Paracelsus still remained in the origins or whether he got stuck in them again. The object-orientedness of the Western mind, as I am accustomed to call it, makes us forget that all knowledge is subjectively—that is, psychically—conditioned. This trend, manifesting itself first in the Church in the form of Platonism and Augustinism, succumbed to Aristotelianism. The Arabs were in a sense responsible for this development because, through their transmission of Aristotle, they threatened the Platonism of the Church. As we know, it was Thomas Aquinas who effectively parried this growing danger from the Arab side. In my view, however, it would be wrong to overestimate the philosophical importance of the Arabs. They were in the main faithful transmitters and handed down to the Middle Ages not only Aristotle but also a lot of Neoplatonic and Neopythagorean influences which became the roots of Western science. By this I mean alchemy in the first place. The quintessence of Hermetic philosophy[2] is a classical feeling for nature and is pagan *par excellence*. This *lumen naturae*[3] was bound to appear obnoxious to the Church, for which reason the philosophical tendency in alchemy did not visibly break through until about the fourteenth century.

The parallel development in China is instructive in that alchemy was there allied with Taoism and in the first centuries after Christ was pressed back by Confucianism along with Taoism and its ancient sources. But in keeping with the greater tolerance in China, alchemy resumed its philosophical flights perhaps in the eighth century, and put forth blossoms such as *The Secret of the Golden Flower*, which Richard Wilhelm brought out with my collaboration. Confucianism could in a sense be compared with the Aristotelianism of the Church.

The symbol-laden obscurantism of our medieval alchemy, which

---

[2] Hermetic philosophy is based on the *Corpus Hermeticum*, a collection of Neoplatonic, mystical, and Gnostic writings dating back to the 3rd and 4th cents. Translated and edited by Scott, *Hermetica* (4 vols., 1924–36).

[3] The *lumen naturae*, light of nature, plays an important role in the work of Paracelsus, where it is a source of enlightenment based on experience side by side with enlightenment through revelation. Cf. "Paracelsus as a Spiritual Phenomenon," CW 13, pars. 148ff.

317

strikes us as almost pathological, was due not least to the necessity of disguising the paganism of the alchemists' views because of the mortal danger of falling foul of the Holy Inquisition. Since the essential source of knowledge in Hermetic philosophy was the *lumen naturae*, or individual revelation, it is altogether understandable that the revelation administered by the Church could not tolerate a second one. Consequently, those deep springs bubbling up from nature, i.e., from the depths of the psyche, were largely blocked and the psychic component of our cognitive processes was excluded from the purview of consciousness.

As I have had the good fortune to go more closely into the psychology of Orientals, it has become clear to me that anything like a question of the unconscious—a quite notorious question for us—simply doesn't exist for these people. In the case of the Indians and Chinese, for instance, it is overwhelmingly clear that their whole spiritual attitude is based on what with us is profoundly unconscious. It was therefore left to psychopathology rather than, say, theology to discover that a quite substantial portion of our psyche has disappeared—to wit, the so-called unconscious. So it is not in the least surprising, but actually certain on *a priori* grounds, that we should find the nearest analogy to our "unconscious" in alchemy and Hermetic philosophy, and all we have really done today is unwittingly to take up again that spiritual quest whose exponent among many others was Paracelsus. Our Western intellectualistic and rationalistic attitude has gradually become a sickness causing disturbances of the psychic equilibrium to an extent that can hardly be estimated at present.

If you like to call the attitude of Paracelsus experimental, then the result of the experiment was that he got the practical outcome of the Church's Aristotelianism, namely the objectification of nature, really going. As to the other side of him, one can safely say it was not a success. The adversities of his time saw to it that he remained stuck in occultism, thanks to the fact that that age had as little a conception of psychology as Catholic philosophy has today. The psyche as an object of scientific study had still to be discovered.

I don't know whether I have answered your questions adequately, but you know as well as I do how complicated and far-reaching are the factors that have to be considered. With collegial regards,

Yours sincerely, c. g. j u n g

To Alice Lewisohn Crowley

[ORIGINAL IN ENGLISH]

My dear Mrs. Crowley,   20 July 1942

Your dream[1] of June 26th—the Arab—has anticipated several of my dreams this month, in which I was in Africa, I myself wearing a long shoka (something like a long white shirt). This figure refers to Mercurius,[2] for I first dreamt of Mercury[3] as a young Arab prince whom I had to push under water. This is what happens to Mercury!

Your dream of July 6th is also to the point. I dreamt of an Eastern prophet, followed by a woman who was almost hypnotized by his prophetic stammerings. Clearly my anima being completely fascinated by my shadow, who in his place is seized by the spirit of life (Mercury!).

"Being naked" often means "accessible to all influences." Having no persona[4] is a state of self-being regardless of the world of conditioned relations.

I am awfully busy on my Mercury material and I had to live it, i.e., it caught hold of me, played the transformation of Mercury on my own human system and gave me incidentally a remarkably miserable fortnight.[5] Your dreams have caught some of it. I am all right again, but not yet through with my material.

Yours cordially, C. G. JUNG

[1] The dream has not been preserved.

[2] Jung was at the time preparing his lecture "Der Geist Mercurius" (*Eranos Jahrbuch* 1942), now revised as "The Spirit Mercurius," CW 13. Mercurius is the most elusive and paradoxical figure in alchemy with innumerable significations, for which reason he was called *Mercurius duplex* and was sometimes regarded as an hermaphrodite. He symbolizes both the lowest *prima materia* and the highest *lapis philosophorum*, as well as the chthonic god of revelation and transformation (Hermes). Psychologically, he represents the collective unconscious (ibid., par. 284).

[3] *Memories*, pp. 242f./229f.

[4] The "mask" which the individual presents to the world, his function of adaptation to it. Cf. *Two Essays*, pars. 243ff., and *Psychological Types*, pars. 800f.

[5] In an English letter of 28 July Jung wrote: "For the time being I am still immersed in Mercury, who, as he will always try to, has dissolved me almost and just failed to separate me limb from limb." Cf. *Mysterium Coniunctionis*, par. 357, where the King, after drinking quantities of a "special" water (Mercurius as *aqua permanens*), exclaims: "I am heavy and my head hurts me, and it seems to me as though all my limbs were falling apart."

To Margaret Erwin Schevill

[ORIGINAL IN ENGLISH]

Dear Mrs. Schevill,   1 September 1942

Your letter has reached me with considerable delay but it has arrived. I think you could risk sending me a copy of the manuscript[1] without which I wouldn't be able to say much in the way of an introduction. At all events it would be a poor sort of thing, since my mind is not actually preoccupied with Indian lore. I'm deeply immersed in mediaeval thought rather, though I have recently read Wheelwright's book about the Navajo Creation Myth,[2] which is very interesting in a way. Such a detailed recording of the primitive mind shows the extraordinary interwovenness of a definite natural milieu with the archetypal collective pattern, a picture which is surely most bewildering inasmuch as the numberless plants and animals and the peculiar atmospheric conditions are strange to you. Intimate knowledge of them, however, is indispensable for the understanding of the specific value of just such a plant or such an animal.

On the whole I think the mail is safe. Recently I got quite a number of letters and even books from the U.S.

Hoping you are always in good health, I remain,

Yours sincerely, C. G. JUNG

☐ Margaret Schevill Link (1887–1962), American ethnologist, of Arizona. As a student of literature and art she had worked for some time with Jung and became interested in the myths of the Navaho Indians. Cf. her *Beautiful on the Earth* (1945), *The Pollen Path* (1956). (Cf. also Mirabal, 21 Oct. 32.)
[1] Presumably *Beautiful on the Earth*, though Jung did not write an introduction for it.
[2] Mary C. Wheelwright, *Navajo Creation Myth* (1942).

To Margareta Fellerer

Dear Frau Fellerer,   3 October 1942

Thank you very much for the excellent photographs. I am glad to hear you are on the mend again. I can vouch for it that nothing is so invigorating and healing as the mountain air. This year I was again in the mountains, first in the Valais and then really high up.

As one grows older one must try not to work oneself to death un-

☐ Professional photographer living in Ascona (d. 1971), who had made many beautiful photographs of Jung and other speakers at the Eranos meetings.

necessarily. At least that's how it is with me. You are probably quite right about mobilizing the creative forces, only with me it is rather different. I can scarcely keep pace and must watch out that the creative forces do not chase me round the universe at a gallop. No mobilization for me! I have to coax myself soothingly, with great assiduity and attentiveness, not to do too much. This summer it took me about two months in order to be able to do nothing again. But as everything is the other way round with women, I presume that your formula is absolutely right for the female sex. And judging by other experiences of mine that's just what they do. To put it briefly, one might say: with women the inner pressure must be raised with some pumped-in carbonic acid, but it is advisable for a man to fix a spigot on the barrel so that he does not leak away completely. Maybe the latter formula is too subjective.

It seems to me that the secret of growing old properly is to consume oneself wisely and avoid being consumed. With best greetings and wishes,

Ever sincerely yours, C. G. JUNG

To J. B. Rhine

[ORIGINAL IN ENGLISH]

Dear Dr. Rhine, 5 November 1942

Thank you for your kind letter. I'm very much interested in your new parapsychological enterprise[1] which you promise. If I have any comments to make I shall not hesitate to send them to you for any kind of use you choose for them. If ever I am able to say something about extra-sensory perception I would certainly give the paper to you, because your journal would be the only suitable place for such an article.

I have sent the photograph[2] and hope it will have reached you in the meantime.

I often mention your work to people over here and I think it is of the greatest importance for the understanding of certain peculiar phenomena of the unconscious. In our practical work we come across

---

[1] R. wrote that he was "going into some problems of the parapsychological field" and asked for Jung's comments later on. The new problems concerned psychokinesis, the direct action of the mind on matter (cf. Rhine, 1 Apr. 48, n. 2). He also asked Jung to let him have his "general views on extra-sensory perception and allied phenomena" for the *Journal of Parapsychology* (pub. at Duke University).
[2] A photograph of himself sent at R.'s request.

peculiar telepathic influences which throw a most significant light on the relativity of space and time in our unconscious psyche.

I quite agree with you that once we are in possession of all facts science will look very peculiar indeed.[3] It will mean nothing less than an entirely new understanding of man and world.

Hoping you are always in good health, I remain,

Yours sincerely, c. g. j u n g

[3] R. mentioned a phenomenon similar to Jung's "exploded knife" (cf. Rhine, 27 Nov. 34) and added: "These inexplicable cases are very tantalizing, but of course we must remember that all sciences begin with comparatively inexplicable phenomena. What a science must come eventually from the full explanation of such occurrences, taking them at their face value!"

To Wellmann W. Schmied

Dear Sir,   5 November 1942

With regard to your question about the black sun, Baudelaire's "soleil noir"[1] is by no means an exception. The idea of a counter earth occurs, for instance, in the Pythagorean system,[2] and we find the *sol niger*[3] in alchemy, also the *ignis niger*.[4]

The corresponding idea of a black moon does not exist, because this would coincide with the new moon and so is already anticipated. The moon plays a considerable role with women,[5] while the sun-vision occurs both with women and men.

The question of women's initiation pictures is obscure in so far as the archetypal material in this respect is not nearly so extensive as men's. This for the simple reason that the initiations were evolved

☐ Davos, Switzerland.

[1] Cf. Baudelaire, *Le Spleen de Paris* (1869), XXXVI, Le Désir de Peindre: "Je brûle de peindre celle qui m'est apparue. . . . Je la comparerais à un soleil noir." Also Gérard de Nerval's famous "El Desdichado" (*Les Filles du Feu*, 1954): "Ma seule Étoile est morte,—et mon luth constellé / Porte le Soleil noir de la Mélancholie." Cf. Pierre, 3 Dec. 52, n. ☐.

[2] According to Philolaos, a follower of Pythagoras, the centre of the universe is formed by the central fire; nearest to it is the counter-earth, next comes the earth, then the moon, the sun, the planets, and the fixed stars.

[3] Cf. *Psychology and Alchemy*, par. 140 and Fig. 34.

[4] *Ignis gehennalis*, the fire of hell, which is associated with the *sol niger*. Cf. *Mysterium Coniunctionis*, par. 113.

[5] Ibid., pars. 222ff.

and handed down chiefly by men. Nevertheless there are all sorts of clues in Greek mythology (also in primitive psychology). I would particularly draw your attention to the figures of Hecate, Demeter, and Kore, and the Magna Mater. It is this last figure that plays the most important and most repellent role in female initiations. The "terrible"[6] refers to her. You will find something about it in Kerényi and Jung: *Einführung in das Wesen der Mythologie* (Pantheon Akademische Verlagsanstalt, Amsterdam and Leipzig, 1941). Much of interest also in H. Thurnwald: *Menschen der Südsee* (Enke Verlag, Stuttgart, 1937).

Yours sincerely, C. G. JUNG

[6] S. mentioned the case of a woman who could not tell her dreams because they were "too terrible." She died shortly afterwards.

To Franzizka Baumgarten-Tramer

Dear Dr. Baumgarten-Tramer,   21 November 1942

Many thanks for kindly sending me your paper "Zur Geschichte des Rorschachtests,"[1] which I have read with pleasure.

Inspired by Justinus Kerner's *Kleksographien*,[2] I made a whole collection of inkblots back in my high school days, because these irrational configurations stimulated my fantasy activity so delightfully that they often afforded me day-long enjoyment. I was therefore particularly amused when I heard that Rorschach was using the same technique to determine psychic peculiarities, which was doubtless a fruitful undertaking.

I look forward to further papers from you.

Yours sincerely, C. G. JUNG

☐ (1889–1970), Swiss psychologist, professor at the U. of Bern.
[1] *Schweizer Archiv für Neurologie und Psychiatrie* (Zurich), 50 (1942), 1–3. The inkblot tests were developed by the Swiss psychiatrist Hermann Rorschach (1884–1922). Cf. Rorschach, *Psychodiagnostics* (1942).
[2] Justinus Kerner (1786–1862), German physician and poet. He was particularly interested in paranormal phenomena, and Jung cites his book *The Seeress of Prevorst* (orig. 1829; tr. 1859) frequently in "On the Psychology and Pathology of So-called Occult Phenomena," CW 1. In *Kleksographien* (1857) Kerner describes his method of producing pictures by making symmetrical blots of various materials.

To Karl Srnetz

Dear Colleague, 19 December 1942

It would be very nice indeed if it should turn out that the Chwolson[1] is obtainable. Meanwhile I would like an older edition of the Vulgate and Septuagint and should be grateful if you could get these texts for me.

Your views concerning the effect of psychotherapy are absolutely correct. In practice we have to take into account all the contributions and statements that have ever been made about the psyche. That is why I have said that every psychological theory is a subjective confession. Naturally everyone will speak of his own contribution. If he didn't, he'd be making no contribution at all. But by speaking of it he gives the impression that it is the only thing he can see, or the reader gets the erroneous idea that with each renewal of standpoint everything else has been superseded. Naturally this is a fallacy. Depending on the peculiar nature of the case the most primitive therapeutic methods can achieve even better results than the most refined. When we speak of drawing, for instance, this is only a minimal auxiliary method. In certain cases this tactic has a very good effect and in other cases it means nothing. Here again it is not a matter of a world-shaking innovation. Also, scientifically and theoretically important statements have no psychotherapeutic value in themselves, as they are only verbal formulas without any life of their own. Usually when a writer or any other artist makes fraudulent use of psychology he falls into his own trap, because art can no more be fashioned from concepts than from the Pythagorean theorem. Theoretical formulations give one absolutely no idea of the practice, which is infinitely more multifaceted and alive than any theory could convey. Nor is it the task of theory to paint a picture of life, but rather to create a workmanlike language which is satisfied with conventional signs. With collegial regards,

Yours sincerely, C. G. JUNG

☐ Zwittau, Czechoslovakia.

[1] D. Chwolson, *Die Ssabier* (1856). There were two Sabaean sects, the one a semi-Christian sect of Babylonia, the other the Harranite (or pseudo-Sabaean) sect of Mesopotamia. The latter considered Ion, a son of Mercury, to be their ancestor ("The Visions of Zosimos," CW 13, p. 60, n. 4). Magic, astrology, and human sacrifice played a part in their religion. The Harranite treatise "Liber Platonis quartorum" (in *Theatrum chemicum*, V, 1622) is quoted and commented on in *Psychology and Alchemy*, CW 12, pars. 366ff.

To Alice Lewisohn Crowley

[ORIGINAL IN ENGLISH]

My dear Mrs. Crowley,   Bollingen, 19 December 1942

Thank you ever so much for all the good and—oh so useful things! Is it not a nice time when food reigns supreme? Hans[1] was very helpful and owing to his help I could manage an important part of my winter program, viz. woodchopping. We have felled 3 trees and have chopped them up handsomely. It was a pious wish to invite you to one of our gorgeous dinners and it remained one without attaining full maturity. The reason was that we barely could finish our work this evening. We had to do the last bit by the light of a lantern. Spring or summer is a more suitable time anyhow.

My very best thanks and cordial wishes for the New Year—yes, one still goes on wishing as if there were a time ahead, when wishes can fulfil themselves. Let us hope that there is.

Yours affectionately, C. G. JUNG

☐ (Handwritten.)
[1] Cf. Kuhn, 1 Jan. 26, n. ☐.

To Aniela Jaffé

Dear Frau Jaffé,   Bollingen, 22 December 1942

Heartiest thanks for the very welcome and edible Christmas present you have destined for me. I hope you haven't stinted yourself of these things! To me they come most opportunely, especially here in Bollingen where one is a bit pinched.

Your dream[1] is very remarkable in that it coincides almost literally

☐ (Handwritten.) Aniela Jaffé, originally of Berlin; 1955–61 Jung's secretary and collaborator; editor of the Swiss edition of these Letters. Recorded and edited *Memories, Dreams, Reflections*. Cf. also her "Bilder und Symbole aus E.T.A. Hoffmanns Märchen 'Der Goldne Topf,' " in Jung's *Gestaltungen des Unbewussten* (1950); "Hermann Broch: Der Tod des Vergil," *Studien zur Analytischen Psychologie C. G. Jungs* (1955); *Apparitions and Precognitions* (tr., 1963; Jung's foreword is in CW 18); *The Myth of Meaning* (tr., 1970); *From the Life and Work of C. G. Jung* (tr. 1971).
[1] "I am in a deep cellar, together with a boy and an old man. The boy has been given an electric installation for Christmas: a large copper pot is suspended from the ceiling and electric wires from all directions make it vibrate. After some time there are no more wires; the pot now vibrates from atmospheric electric oscillations."

with my first systematic fantasy,[2] which I had between the ages of 15 and 16. It engrossed me for weeks, always on the way to school, which took three-quarters of an hour. I was the king of an island in a great lake like a sea, stretching from Basel to Strassburg. The island consisted of a mountain with a small medieval town nestling below. At the top was my castle, and on its highest tower were things like copper antennae which collected electricity from the air and conducted it into a deep vault underneath the tower. In this vault there was a mysterious apparatus that turned the electricity into *gold*. I was so obsessed with this fantasy that reality was completely forgotten.

It seems to me that your dream is an important contribution to the psychology of the self. Through the self we are plunged into the torrent of cosmic events. Everything essential happens in the self and the ego functions as a receiver, spectator, and transmitter. What is so peculiar is the symbolization of the self as an apparatus. A "machine" is always something *thought up*, deliberately put together for a definite purpose. Who has invented this machine? (Cf. the symbol of the "world clock"![3]) The Tantrists say that things represent the *distinctness of God's thoughts*. The machine is a microcosm, what Paracelsus called the "star in man."[4] I always have the feeling that these symbols touch on the great secrets, the *magnalia Dei*.[5] With best greetings and cordial thanks,

Ever sincerely yours, C. G. J.

[2] *Memories*, pp. 8off./86ff.
[3] *Psychology and Alchemy*, pars. 307ff.
[4] Cf. "Paracelsus as a Spiritual Phenomenon," CW 13, pars. 163, 188; "On the Nature of the Psyche," CW 8, par. 390.
[5] Possibly a Paracelsan term, meaning "The great things of God."

Anonymous

Dear Dr. N.,   6 January 1943

Permit me a few remarks on the content of your letter of 25 December 42. It seems to be that you have very many opinions. But if one wants to understand something, it is advisable to have no opinions and to learn to weigh the facts carefully. In the case of dreams, for instance, you completely overlook the fact that it is not a question of mere phenomenology but of actual determinants which can only be discovered by carefully taking up the whole dream context. You also assume that what you know about a dream is everything that can be known about it. But that isn't so at all. There are still very many things behind and besides, which one needs to know in order to understand a dream properly. Incidentally, you can give up from the start trying to understand your own dreams, because everywhere you will strike your own blind spot. Maybe you are of the opinion that you don't have one, but I would advise you to drop this opinion if you want to get anywhere. Maybe, too, you want to get nowhere and therefore your opinions are quite particularly dear to you. One can thoroughly deceive oneself about oneself in this respect. At all events your mental situation is thoroughly conducive to dreams about burglars. One always has such dreams when there is something outside that wants to get inside, but is kept outside with the greatest cunning.

Dreams do not "jumble up the personalities." On the contrary, everything is in its proper place, only you don't understand it.

As to the dream of the mountaineer,[1] I knew my colleague. He, too, was a man who lived by his opinions and continually made his reckoning without the host. In his case I didn't need to prophesy anything at all, for I knew only too well that he was walking on air and could fall through at any moment, which was what actually happened because he took my warning for a mere opinion that could be offset by umpteen other opinions. Unfortunately my opinion was on the side of fact while his wasn't.

Certainly telepathy is a phenomenon conditioned by space and time. But it demonstrates the relativity of space and time, and this is something I didn't invent. You might consult your countryman, Prof. Jordan[2] in Rostock, on this question.

You seem to have very strange ideas about religion. Rightness is not a category that can be applied to religion anyway. Religion consists of psychic realities which one cannot say are right or wrong. Are lice or elephants right or wrong? It is enough that they exist. Here you show your very defective sense for facts which you compensate by masses of opinions. I have a scientific training and hence an entirely different standpoint which is obviously alien to you in every respect. Thus for me religious statements are not opinions but facts that one

□ Germany.
[1] In the dream the dreamer, a passionate mountaineer, "stepped out into space from the top of a mountain." For details of the case, see "Child Development and Education," CW 17, pars. 117ff.
[2] Cf. Jordan, 10 Nov. 34.

can look at as a botanist at his plants. The criterion is the old dictum: *Quod semper quod ubique quod ab omnibus creditur.*[3] The science of religion including the psychology of religion has to come to terms with this fact. No opinions prevail against it.

The question of dream psychology is a very difficult topic which can be discussed with some prospect of success only if one has the necessary rudiments of knowledge together with thorough practical experience. The fact of having dreams is not nearly enough. You also have a digestive system but this is not nearly enough to make you a physiological chemist.

Yours very truly, c. g. jung

[3] "What is believed always, everywhere, and by everybody." From Vincent of Lerins, *Commonitorium*, 2: "Likewise in the Catholic Church itself it should be our particular concern to hold fast to what is believed everywhere at all times by all men."

To Arnold Künzli

Dear Herr Künzli,   4 February 1943

Many thanks for kindly sending me your well-meaning review of my little book.[1] Believing as I do that you are endeavouring to do justice to my conceptions, I venture to draw your attention to one questionable item which has often enough been the object of my curiosity and occasional investigation. I cannot, to be sure, maintain that the latter has ever been crowned with success. Permit me, therefore, to molest you also with my questions. They have to do with that general fault-finding with my scientific attitude which is customary in Switzerland.[2] Supposing that my attitude really does exhibit such easily recognizable faults, how do you square this with the fact that I unite at least seven honorary doctorates upon my unscientific and/or benighted head? I am, by your leave, an honorary member of the

☐ (Handwritten.) Arnold Künzli, then a student, now Privatdozent for political philosophy at the U. of Basel.
[1] A review of "On the Psychology of the Unconscious," CW 7, in *Der Zürcher Student*, Jan., 1943.
[2] K. wrote in his review that "much in Jung is still the romantic vision of a creative spirit, occasionally at the expense of scientific empiricism." In another review, published in the same issue of *Der Zürcher Student*, of a book by D. Brinkmann, *Probleme des Unbewussten* (1943), K. spoke of the "romantic character of the unconscious in C. G. Jung."

Academy of German Scientists and Physicians, a Fellow of the Royal Society, Doctor Scientiae of Oxford and Harvard University, and was one of the four guests of honour and representatives of Swiss science at the Tercentenary of the latter University. Do these august bodies really consist of nothing but simpletons incapable of judgment, and is the Philosophical Faculty of Zurich University the brain of the world?

I would be sincerely grateful to you if you could enlighten me how it comes that the conception of science prevalent in Germany, England, America, and India,[3] by virtue of which I was awarded degrees as a *scientist*, does *not* satisfy the scientific and theoretical requirements of the Philosophical Faculty of Zurich. I would be all the more obliged for your kind information since I have never yet succeeded in discovering in what way my theories or methods run counter to the nature of empirical science and must therefore be condemned by the undisputed authority of the last-named worshipful corporation.

I reject the term "romantic" for my conception of the unconscious because this is an *empirical* and anything but a philosophical concept. This is not altered by the fact that I share the initials "C.G." with Carus[4] and like him use the word "unconscious." He was a philosopher, I am not. I do not "posit" the unconscious. My concept is a *nomen* which covers empirical facts that can be verified at any time. If I posited the archetypes, for instance, I would not be a scientist but a Platonist. *Philosophically* I am old-fashioned enough not to have got beyond Kant, so I have no use for romantic hypostases and am strictly "not at home" for philosophical opinions. People can only prove to me that certain facts do not exist. But I am still waiting for this proof.

Since your goodwill is apparent from your review I would expressly like to emphasize that I am not saddling you personally with the attitude of the Philosophical Faculty. Your review was only the indirect cause of a renewed stirring of curiosity, combined with the hope of hearing something that would help to counteract my evidently only local scientific inferiority. With best thanks,

Yours sincerely, C. G. JUNG

---

[3] Jung also received honorary degrees from the universities of Benares, Allahabad, and Calcutta.

[4] Carl Gustav Carus (1789–1869), German physician and philosopher. In his *Psyche* (1846) he uses the term "unconscious," basing himself on Schelling's romantic *Naturphilosophie*.

To Arnold Künzli

Dear Herr Künzli,   13 February 1943

Many thanks for your friendly answer.[1] One must certainly grant it the predicate "common sense." I now see more clearly the terminological possibilities of a Babylonian confusion of tongues when one seriously sets about studying science as an object instead of practising it.

It goes without saying that every age has its presuppositions, which are the more difficult to lay by the heels the more one tries to jump over one's own head. I don't believe in such a futile philosophical undertaking. Even Kant, for all his critiques, constantly employs the concepts that were current in his century. Poring over such work, a future age may find entertainment in a past one. Therefore I prefer to cling on to the deed, to what we can achieve with the means at hand. If it should later turn out that these means were not as good as those we shall have in a hundred years' time, this is no reason for mortification today, since we know quite well that the better which is to come would never have hatched out had we not begotten the best that is possible now, however imperfect it may be. I regard all speculations that exceed our capacities as sterile griping and at the same time a pretext for covering up one's own infertility. This kind of criticism leads only to the mastery of complicated banalities, the Platonic exemplar of which is embodied for me in the philosopher Heidegger. With best regards,

Yours sincerely, C. G. JUNG

[1] K. referred to the impossibility of "scientific" dream interpretation, since science had here reached a point where "irrational forces, creative intuition, and inspired association" had to come to its assistance.

To Arnold Künzli

Dear Herr Künzli,   Einsiedeln, 28 February 1943

Your kind letter has reached me in the dark forest where I am snatching the air for a few days. I have nothing against your views if critical analysis, as you want it to do, not only judges by the presuppositions of the past but also takes account of the facts which the

☐ (Handwritten.)

330

present has brought to light. Philosophical criticism must, to my way of thinking, start with a maximum of factual knowledge if it is not to remain hanging in mid air and thus be condemned to sterility. I can put up with any amount of criticism so long as it is based on facts or real knowledge. But what I have experienced in the way of philosophical criticism of my concept of the collective unconscious, for instance, was characterized by lamentable ignorance on the one hand and intellectual prejudice on the other. Brinkmann's book on the unconscious[1] is an exception. A work like this—and here I entirely agree with you—is a most welcome clarification of concepts and hence a valuable stepping-stone to the future. I have no objection whatever to objective studies of this kind, since they meet all the requirements of the scientific attitude. They discard unconscious subjective prejudices, whereas Heidegger bristles with them, trying in vain to hide behind a blown-up language. Here he shows his true colours. Only listen to one seminar on psychiatry and then you will know where this language can also be heard. At Brinkmann's lecture in the SGPP[2] the contrast between his normal language and the twaddle he read out from Heidegger was positively comic. This struck not only me but my psychiatric colleagues as well. The substance of what he read out was unutterably trashy and banal, and Brinkmann could just as well have done it to make Heidegger ridiculous. At any rate that is the effect it had. Heidegger's *modus philosophandi* is neurotic through and through and is ultimately rooted in his psychic crankiness. His kindred spirits, close or distant, are sitting in lunatic asylums, some as patients and some as psychiatrists on a philosophical rampage. For all its mistakes the nineteenth century deserves better than to have Heidegger counted as its ultimate representative. Moreover this whole intellectual perversion is a German national institution. England can oblige only with James Joyce and France with surrealism. Italy remains tame with her Benedetto Croce, who should actually be dated 1850. For all its critical analysis philosophy has not yet managed to root out its psychopaths. What do we have psychiatric diagnosis for? That grizzler Kierkegaard also belongs in this *galère*. Philosophy has still to learn that it is *made by human beings* and depends to an alarming degree on their psychic constitution. In the critical philosophy of the future there will be a chapter on "The Psychopathology of

[1] Cf. Künzli, 4 Feb. 43, n. 2.
[2] Schweizerische Gesellschaft für Praktische Psychologie, Zurich, where Brinkmann read a paper on Feb. 9 entitled "Das Gerücht als massenpsychologisches Phänomen."

Philosophy." Hegel is fit to bust with presumption and vanity, Nietzsche drips with outraged sexuality, and so on. There is no thinking *qua* thinking, at times it is a pisspot of unconscious devils, just like any other function that lays claim to hegemony. Often *what* is thought is less important than *who* thinks it. But this is assiduously overlooked. Neurosis addles the brains of every philosopher because he is at odds with himself. His philosophy is then nothing but a systemized struggle with his own uncertainty.

Excuse these blasphemies! They flow from my hygienic propensities, because I hate to see so many young minds infected by Heidegger. Best regards,

Yours sincerely, c. g. jung

To Arnold Künzli

Dear Herr Künzli,   16 March 1943

That Kierkegaard[1] was a stimulating and pioneering force precisely because of his neurosis is not surprising, since he started out with a conception of God that had a peculiar Protestant bias which he shares with a great many Protestants. To such people his problems and his grizzling are entirely acceptable, because to them it serves the same purpose as it served him: you can then settle everything in the study and need not do it in life. Out there things are apt to get unpleasant.

I am, to be sure, a doctor, but even more than that I am concerned with the saving good of man, for I am also a psychiatrist. I would have said to Kierkegaard straight off: "It doesn't matter what *you* say, but what *it* says in you. To *it* you must address your answers. God is straightway with you and is the voice within you. You have to have it out with that voice." Whatever stuffing Kierkegaard had in him would then have been plain to see. A changed man, certainly, but a *whole* one, not a jangling hither and thither of displeasing fragmentary souls. True creative genius does not let itself be spoilt by analysis, but is freed from the impediments and distortions of a

---

[1] In a letter of 27 Feb. 69 K. wrote to the editor: "I must have asked Jung in a letter of which I have no copy his opinion on divers problems of a psychological nature which had occurred to me during my study of Kierkegaard." He was working at the time on his Ph.D. thesis on the problem of anxiety (*Angst*) in Kierkegaard. In 1948 he published *Die Angst als abendländische Krankheit. Dargestellt am Leben und Denken Sören Kierkegaards.*

neurosis. Neurosis does not produce art. It is uncreative and inimical to life. It is failure and bungling. But the moderns mistake morbidity for creative birth—part of the general lunacy of our time.

It is, of course, an unanswerable question what an artist would have created if he had not been neurotic. Nietzsche's syphilitic infection undoubtedly exerted a strongly neuroticizing influence on his life. But one could imagine a *sound* Nietzsche possessed of creative power without hypertension—something like Goethe. He would have written much the same as he did, but less strident, less shrill—i.e., less German—more restrained, more responsible, more reasonable and reverent. Jacob Burckhardt might have been a friend to him.

Neurosis is a justified doubt in oneself and continually poses the ultimate question of trust in man and in God. Doubt is creative if it is answered by deeds, and so is neurosis if it exonerates itself as having been a phase—a crisis which is pathological only when chronic. Neurosis is a protracted crisis degenerated into a habit, the daily catastrophe ready for use.

To the question whether anxiety is the subject or object of the philosophers, I can only answer: anxiety can never be the object unless it is, or was, first the subject. In other words, anxiety, as affect, always *has us*, wherefore we say—*lucus a non lucendo*[2] and euphemistically!—"*I have anxiety.*"[3] The philosopher starts from the anxiety that possesses him and then, through reflection, turns his subjective state of being possessed into a perception of anxiety. Question: is it an object worthy of anxiety, or a poltroonery of the ego, shitting its pants? (Compare Freud, "The ego is the seat of anxiety,"[4] with Job 28:28, "The fear of the Lord, that is wisdom.") What is the "anxiety of the ego," this "modestly modest" overweeningness and presumption of a little tin god, compared with the almighty shadow of the Lord, which is the fear that fills heaven and earth? The first leads to apotropaic defensive philosophy, the second to γνῶσις θεοῦ.[5]

Would you have the time and inclination to review Walter Ehrlich's *Der Mensch und die numinosen Regionen* (Chur, 1943)?

---

[2] Lit. "the [word] forest [derives] from not shining"—a famous example of spurious etymology (in Quintillian, *De institutione oratoria*, I, 6, 34), by which the meaning of a word is derived from its opposite.

[3] This German construction is unavoidable here in order to preserve the play on words, which seems untranslatable otherwise. "Ich habe Angst" would ordinarily be translated "I am afraid." [Tr.]

[4] "The Ego and the Id," Standard Edn. 19, p. 57.

[5] = "knowledge of God."

A philosopher who leaves the "sham science" of psychology far below him and with godlike nimbleness bestrides the rainbow bridge of hypostases without being seized with vertigo. We empirical worms stare up at the heights, gawping.

I can send you the book if you would care to do it. The review would be for the new *Zeitschrift für Psychologie* (not more than 3-4 typewritten pages, preferably less).[6] With best regards,

Yours sincerely, C. G. JUNG

[6] K.'s review was published in *Schweizer Zeitschrift für Psychologie*, II (1944).

To Karl Kerényi

Dear Professor Kerényi,   2 May 1943

On my return from a holiday in the country, where I devoted myself to working on the land, I find your Labyrinth book,[1] which I have begun reading with the greatest interest. Your kind dedication[2] has given me much pleasure. Please accept my best thanks.

It was no small surprise to me to learn that you are on a so to speak official mission in Switzerland and will be here for some time.[3] I must congratulate you on this, for great as is the honour for Switzerland in sheltering you as a representative of the Hungarian intelligentsia, it must be equally pleasant for you personally to live for a change in a country not at war.

Please convey my compliments to your wife. With best greetings and thanks,

Yours sincerely, C. G. JUNG

☐ (Handwritten.)
[1] *Labyrinthos. Der Linienreflex einer mythologischen Idee* (1941).
[2] "Munus auctoris Kerényi" (gift of the author, Kerényi).
[3] K. had been sent to Switzerland by the Hungarian Prime Minister, Miklos Kallay, who tried secretly to maintain contact with the Allies in spite of Nazi domination. (Communication by K. to editor.)

To Jolande Jacobi

Dear Dr. Jacobi,   Bollingen, 26 August 1943

. . .

The mistake you are making consists in your being drawn too much into X.'s neurotic problem. This is evident from the fact, for instance,

334

that your animus is trying like mad to interpret when there is nothing to be interpreted. *Why* does he say he has other relationships? Why indeed! As though anyone knew. He just says it. That is very nice of him, inconsiderate, truthful, tactless, unpremeditated, confiding, etc., etc. If you knew the *real* reason you would also know who X. was at his birth and at his death. But we shall only find that out in the Hereafter. He has absolutely no reason he can state, it has simply happened and can be interpreted quite superfluously in a hundred different ways, and no single interpretation holds water, being merely an insistence which, once made, only has the effect of driving him into further whimsical and uninterpretable reactions. In reality his irrational behaviour represents the conscious and unconscious sides of the anima, and is absolutely necessary in order to gain insight into her, just as in general he needs a bevy of women in order to grasp the essence of this glamorous figure. Of course he is still too naïve to notice this. But you, just as naïvely, have intruded yourself as an anima figure into this witches' sabbath and are therefore caught up in the dance as though you were nothing but an anima. Wherever you stick a finger in out of "love" or involuntary participation you will burn it, for it is not involvement that is expected of you, but objective, disincarnate observation, and if you want to snatch something out of it for the heart—and no reasonable objection can be made to this—you must pay for it in blood, as was always so and always will be. At least one must keep one's head out of it so as not to be eaten up entirely by emotional ape-men. Where there are emotional ties one is always the disappointed disappointer. This one has to know if one wants, or is forced, to participate correctly.

. . .

With cordial greetings,

Yours sincerely, C. G. JUNG

To Aniela Jaffé

Dear Frau Jaffé,   3 September 1943

Your letter was very interesting. The situation with the *Golden Pot*[1] seems to be that the masculine and feminine principles, spirit

☐ (Handwritten.)
[1] E.T.A. Hoffmann's story "Der Goldne Topf." Cf. Jaffé, 22 Dec. 42, n. ☐.

and life, are in a state of unconscious conflict which is excluded by consciousness.

The macrocosmic relationship presents a great difficulty. It shows itself symptomatically first in the form of an urge to make the microcosmic relationship objective, external, tangible. The *coniunctio* of the masculine and feminine halves of the self is apt to overpower the individual and force him into physical, i.e., cosmic, manifestation. You want to illuminate the world as Luna (I as Sol). But every archetype, before it is integrated *consciously*, wants to manifest itself physically, since it forces the subject into its own form. The self in its divinity (i.e., the archetype) is unconscious of itself. It can *become conscious only within our consciousness*. And it can do that only if the ego stands firm. The self must become as small as, and yet smaller than, the ego although it is the ocean of divinity: "God is as small as me," says Angelus Silesius.[2] It must become the thumbling in the heart.[3] The *hierosgamos* takes place in the vessel. In principle you are not the goddess, I am not the god, otherwise man would cease to be and God would not have been born. We can only stretch out our hands to each other and know of the inner man. Superhuman possibilities are not for us.

I am wrestling just with this problem of the *coniunctio*, which I must now work up as the introduction to *Aurora Consurgens*.[4] It is incredibly difficult. Cordial greetings,

Ever sincerely yours, c. g. j u n g

P.S. The one standing behind my face (the masculine part of the self) calls to your "Elisabeth,"[5] who is the feminine half. In this world both are thumblings (homunculi). God, the greatest, becomes

[2] Angelus Silesius (Johannes Scheffler; 1624–77), German mystic. Quotation from his *Cherubinischer Wandersmann* (1657–74), Book I (*The Cherubinic Wanderer*, tr. W. R. Trask, 1953). Cf. *Psychological Types*, par. 432.

[3] *Katha Upanishad*, 4.13: "That Person in the heart, no bigger than a thumb, burning like flame without smoke, maker of past and future, the same today and tomorrow, that is Self." Quoted in *Symbols of Transformation*, par. 179; cf. also par. 178 for similar quotation from *Shvetashvatara Upan.*, 3.13.

[4] This "introduction" turned into the vastly expanded *Mysterium Coniunctionis*, CW 14. *Aurora Consurgens*, ed., with a commentary, by Marie-Louise von Franz, was published in 1957 as vol. III of this work; tr. (separate work), 1966.

[5] J. reported a dream in which a male figure standing behind Jung's face addresses a female figure standing behind the dreamer's face by the name of Elisabeth.

in man the smallest and most invisible, otherwise man cannot endure him. Only in that form of the self does God dwell in the macrocosm (which he himself is, though in the most unconscious form). In man God sees himself from "outside" and thus becomes conscious of himself.

All this in support of your difficult work on the *Golden Pot*!

Anonymous

[ORIGINAL IN ENGLISH]

My dear Mrs. N., 6 September 1943

Your relation to Mrs. X. seems to be disturbed by the "wolfsoul." As you pointed out, envy, competition, feelings of inferiority etc. arose between you. With reference to myself there is also the factor of jealousy, the latter of a very elementary sort. One is—hélas—never at the end of that seemingly endless *animal tail,* which one cannot cut off but only tolerate or suffer. Mrs. X. is less aware of it and takes what she knows more lightly, whereas you take it almost too seriously, at least with the whole weight of a hard fact. It is however a "relative" fact. With an introvert—on account of his inferior Eros —it weighs more and seems to be more important. But the extravert should teach him to look a bit more away from it. As Lord Beaconsfield said: "Important things are not so very important," etc. She constellates your shadow naturally and it gives you a nice feeling of inferiority, thus far quite healthy. Only don't take it too seriously and don't believe that Mrs. X. has not her private hell too. Everybody has, but it is the extravert's particular game to show the least of trouble and to cause the most of it. Don't rely too much on your inferior Eros, and keep even smarting relations. You learn a lot from them. If your animus misbehaves, then you have not used your feelings. Social feelings are never 100% pure gold but consist of about 40% make-up. This is no deception but an altruistic endeavour and produces a good conscience, a thing not to be despised.

Don't worry yourself too much (wolfishness against oneself). Worry Mrs. X. This is better.

Yours cordially, C. G. JUNG

Anonymous

Dear N. N.,   10 September 1943

Here I send you merely a greeting to tell you that I have understood your letter. I have thought much about prayer. It—prayer—is very necessary because it makes the Beyond we conjecture and think about an immediate reality, and transposes us into the duality of the ego and the dark Other. One hears oneself speaking and can no longer deny that one has addressed "That." The question then arises: What will become of Thee and of Me? of the transcendental Thou and the immanent I? The way of the unexpected, not-to-be-expected, opens, fearful and unavoidable, with hope of a propitious turn or a defiant "I will not perish under the will of God unless I myself will it too." Then only, so I feel, is God's will made perfect. Without me it is only his almighty will, a frightful fatality even in its grace, void of sight and hearing, void of knowledge for precisely that reason. I go together with it, an immensely weighty milligram without which God had made his world in vain. Best wishes,

Yours ever, JUNG

□ (Handwritten.)

To Emil Egli

Dear Dr. Egli,   15 September 1943

Many thanks for kindly sending me your book, *Der Schweizer in der Landschaft*.[1] I entirely agree with the pages you have marked. The more so as my thoughts have often moved along similar lines. At one time I related the idiosyncrasies of Paracelsus[2] to his early environment and also dropped similar hints in my answer to Keyserling's exposé of Switzerland.[3] I am deeply convinced of the—unfortunately—still very mysterious relation between man and landscape, but hesitate to say anything about it because I could not substantiate it rationally. But I am fully persuaded that if you settled a Siberian tribe for a few hundred years in Switzerland, regular Appenzellers would come out in the end. It is probably a matter of something like psychic mimicry.

[1] Bern, 1943.
[2] Cf. "Paracelsus," CW 15, pars. 2–4.
[3] "The Swiss Line in the European Spectrum," CW 10.

Altogether your book makes very interesting and delectable reading. Again with best thanks,

Yours sincerely, C. G. JUNG

To Carl Hamburger

Dear Colleague,   9 October 1943

Colours are only a partial instance of the question of clarity in general. Just as consciousness is largely reduced in dreams, so is the completeness of the image. Hence there are many dreams which are entirely abstract. Eidetic clarity is a function of the intensity of the residual consciousness in the dream. Exactly as in the waking state, when with restricted consciousness the clarity of the image is reduced too. Thus colours are by no means wholly absent in dreams, but only when the perceiving consciousness is on a relatively low level. With collegial regards,

Yours sincerely, C. G. JUNG

□ Canton Vaud, Switzerland.

To Pastor H. Wegmann

Dear Pastor Wegmann,   19 December 1943

Your review of Dr. Aeppli's book in the NZZ[1] delighted as much as it interested me, particularly because Köhler's review of Aeppli's last book[2] was so deplorably compromising. I admire your review for its courage, manliness, and honesty, qualities we so often painfully miss but which are vitally important for "Protestantism" (in the best sense of this unfortunate term). It is indeed quite wrong for the "reformed Church" to want to act in every respect like the Catholic. The latter possesses the whole wealth of tradition, the former is poor and should be poor, since it must relinquish all our yesterdays again and again in order to live wholly in the ever-procreative spirit which

□ (Handwritten.)
[1] "Begegnung mit dem Traum," Neue Zürcher Zeitung, 17 Dec. 1943, review of the Swiss psychotherapist Ernst Aeppli's Der Traum und seine Deutung (1943).
[2] Ludwig Köhler, professor of theology in Zurich, had, under the pseudonym Hugo Ratmich, reviewed Aeppli's Lebenskonflikte (1932) in the Neue Zürcher Zeitung, 12 Dec. 42.

339

is its truest foundation. What it leaves behind is always the *katho-licon*,[3] and what it finds before it is the presence of God in the living individual human being, the only place where God can be met with beyond a peradventure. And if it is not an *ecclesia spiritualis*, then it is nothing but a Catholic memory, for which there is certainly much to be said, or there could not be so many people who are satisfied with the anamnesis alone. Its supreme and unique meaning, it seems to me, is that it lives in and with the creative spirit and shares its adventures, tragedies, perils, and triumphs. The Catholic Church arranges the codification of memories and the lessons of history so much better. The conservation of so much classical paganism is of inestimable value. Therefore the Catholic is the *Christian* Church par excellence. But a confession of faith in the Holy Spirit is beyond Christ (for which I politely beg your pardon) and hence, it seems to me, more helpful for the attainment of salvation (which still hasn't materialized) than that backward-looking memory of the prefiguring God-man who prepared the way for the Paraclete. And it is the Paraclete that represents the revelation of God in the individual-as-he-is, the nothing-but-man.

This is but a token of my gratitude to you for having made me feel in your review something one so often longs to hear and so seldom does hear—an avowal of the living presence of the spirit.

Yours sincerely, C. G. JUNG

[3] Universal remedy or formula.

To Arnold Künzli

Dear Herr Künzli,   12 January 1944

Having been away from home for some time I am only now getting down to answering your kind letter with your review.[1] Above all I want to thank you heartily for the excellent review, which I'm sorry to hear must be printed in abbreviated form. This is yet another reminder of the fact that I have to be presented to my contemporaries only as a third-class passenger. It all hangs together with Switzerland being a hundred years behind the times. Compared

☐ (Handwritten.)
[1] MS. of a review of *Psychology and Alchemy*, *Schweizer Monatshefte* (Zurich), XIII:12 (Mar. 1944).

with Pulver's review,[2] yours has the great merit of singling out the essential, which remains invisible with Pulver, and not only with him but with all the others as well, so that it then looks as if one had actually said nothing. I don't hold it against the Swiss for being *officially* one of the most unspiritual nations in Europe, on the contrary I sympathize, since their spirituality consists in their fear of the spirit. They still have, thank God, sufficient instinct to avoid its dangers and to enjoy poets who have been dead for a hundred years or, if more recent, are insignificant. In our age of worldwide deracination it is a veritable blessing that there are still people who are immune to the spirit, or at least take serious pains to skirt round everything the spirit might mean with all conceivable circumspection. This shows true respect for the spirit, even though it is sometimes a hard job to play the role of the tabooed with good grace. Therefore I wouldn't care to belong to any other nation, for even a positive evaluation of the spirit, however enjoyable it may momentarily be for an author, always degenerates into capriciousness: you then *have* the spirit, or think you have, and are thus relieved of the obligation to fear it. Then the spirit comes in the form of the devil, as the cruel fate of Germany shows. Perhaps you could place the *whole* review with a Swiss daily? *Bund? Basler Nachrichten?* With best regards,

Yours sincerely, c. g. j u n g

[2] Max Pulver, "Vermächtnis unter Lebenden. Zu C. G. Jungs *Psychologie und Alchemie,*" *Neue Zürcher Zeitung,* 6 Nov. 43.

To Emma von Pelet

Dear Frau von Pelet,   Bollingen until 15 January 1944

. . .

John Pordage,[1] English mystic and alchemist of the 17th century, says that "our inner earth" and "our inner heaven" are "spotted"

☐ Resident of Ascona (d. 1968). Worked chiefly as translator from English into German. Among her translations are works of Vivekananda, M. E. Harding's *Psychic Energy,* and Suzuki's *The Doctrine of No-Mind.*
[1] John Pordage (1607–1681), English physician and alchemist, rector of Bradfield, Berkshire. Leading member of the Philadelphians, a religious mystical sect founded by Jane Lead (or Leade; 1623–1704), which based its teachings on the writings of the German mystic Jakob Boehme (1575–1624). Cf. "The Psychology of the Transference," CW 16, pars. 506ff.

with the *peccatum originale* of Luciferian pride. Psychologically this means collective guilt,[2] for we all have within us that fiery devil who has seized power in Germany thanks to the boundless unconsciousness and arrogance of the individual. It is a madman's fate that will irresistibly run its course and would do so also in us if we were to break the authority of the law within us and our contract with ourselves. But this does not prevent us from being continually licked round by the flames of hell. All of us have to atone, inwardly and outwardly, for this guilt of unconsciousness. With best regards,

Yours sincerely, C. G. JUNG

[2] Cf. Ullmann, 25 May 45, n. 1.

To Karl Kerényi

Dear Colleague,   6 July 1944

Your recent communications on Asklepios interested me enormously. Immediately after your visit I discovered a treatise[1] which till now I had never deemed worthy of closer study. In it I found that Sulphur is not only *medicina* but also *medicus*. It reports a dream-vision in which two figures, Sal and Sulphur, quarrel and suddenly Sal deals Sulphur an incurable wound.[2] From this wound—evidently a borrowing from the gospel passage *"flumina de ventre Christi"*[3]— flows a stream of milk. Diana comes from a grove to bathe in it. A prince, passing by, burns with love for her, she reciprocates, but at this juncture she sinks below the surface and the prince, hastening to her rescue, is drowned likewise. Whereupon their souls rise up out of the stream, etc.

The two are naturally Sol and Luna—the brother-sister pair— who originally gave birth to Sulphur.

This vision reminds me of what you told me about Koronis. May I ask you to name the passages in your texts? With your permission I would like to refer to your findings.[4] It would help to fortify the

[1] By the Moravian alchemist Michael Sendivogius (1566–1646), entitled "Tractatus de sulphure" (*Musaeum Hermeticum*, 1678; tr. *The Hermetic Museum*, 1953). The treatise is summarized in *Mysterium Coniunctionis*, CW 14, par. 144.
[2] Cf. ibid.
[3] = "rivers from the belly of Christ." Cf. John 7:38; also Rahner, "Flumina de Ventre Christi," *Biblica* (Rome), XXII (1941).
[4] Koronis was the mother of Asklepios, his father being Apollo. Asklepios was saved from the dead body of Koronis, who had been killed by Apollo's sister

minds of my readers if, in danger of getting lost in this abstruse chaos, they felt the solid ground of Greek mythology under their feet. So it was with me, as I have already told you. I had almost lost the courage to publish this farrago. With best thanks in advance,

Yours sincerely, C. G. JUNG

Artemis as punishment for her unfaithfulness with Ischys. Cf. Kerényi, *Asklepios: Archetypal Image of the Physician's Existence* (1959), pp. 93ff. Jung refers to K.'s research on Asklepios in *Mysterium Coniunctionis*, par. 144, n. 157.

Anonymous

Dear Frau N.,   11 July 1944

What happens after death[1] is so unspeakably glorious that our imagination and our feelings do not suffice to form even an approximate conception of it. A few days before my sister died[2] her face wore an expression of such inhuman sublimity that I was profoundly frightened.

A child, too, enters into this sublimity, and there detaches himself from this world and his manifold individuations more quickly than the aged. So easily does he become what *you* also are that he apparently vanishes. Sooner or later all the dead become what we also are. But in this reality we know little or nothing about that mode of being, and what shall we still know of this earth after death? The dissolution of our time-bound form in eternity brings no loss of meaning. Rather does the little finger know itself a member of the hand. With best regards,

Your devoted C. G. JUNG

[1] This letter is especially significant since Jung himself had been close to death after a severe cardiac infarct at the beginning of 1944. He gives a vivid description of the visions he had during his illness in *Memories*, ch. X. The illness accounts for the long gap in the letters between Jan. and July.
[2] She died in 1935.

To Karl Kerényi

Dear Professor Kerényi,   1 August 1944

Many thanks for kindly allowing me to make use of your MS.[1] I have not only read it with the greatest interest but also enjoyed the quite special atmosphere of this work. You have succeeded admirably in conveying a sense of the mysterious background and depth of the healing process. It seems as if the inclusion of the landscape only gave the interpretation of the myth its perfect form. That, too, you have brought off superbly. I only hope the medical readership of the *Ciba-Zeitschrift*[2] will gain as much from your work as I did!

Yours sincerely, C. G. JUNG

[1] Of *Asklepios: Archetypal Image of the Physician's Existence*.
[2] Where the original version of the above book was published by Ciba A. G., (Basel, 1948) as *Der göttliche Arzt*.

To Jürg Fierz

Dear Dr. Fierz,   7 August 1944

The question of the daemonic[1] is on the one hand simple and on the other exceedingly complicated. It could best be discussed in terms of case material; that is, you would have to tell me of the case you are chiefly concerned about. Generally speaking the daemonic is that moment when an unconscious content of seemingly overwhelming power appears on the threshold of consciousness. It can cross this threshold and seize hold of the personality. Then it is possession, which can naturally be personified in many forms.

If you would like to talk with me personally sometime I am gladly at your disposal. Perhaps you would arrange with my secretary an hour that suits both of us.

Yours sincerely, C. G. JUNG

[1] F. inquired about Jung's interpretation of the daemonic, particularly in connection with Goethe's use of the term in *Dichtung und Wahrheit*, Book 20, and asked what manifestation of the unconscious it represented.

To Alwine von Keller

Dear Frau von Keller,   21 August 1944

Best thanks for your long letter. I have heard nothing from Frau X. for a long time. I only hope things are going better with her. She is indeed a problem, like all Germans today.

I am very grateful to you for news about Zimmer,[1] for I have had but little. Like the physician who attended me, Dr. Haemmerli,[2] he died on the eve of his fame. This seems to be a particularly critical moment. There is indeed a great danger in being praised before the eve. That is why one's fate always strives for posthumous recognition. It would almost have done away with me too, for the sole reason that I was appointed professor in Basel.[3]

I am extremely glad that this year's Eranos meeting went off very well without me.

By the beginning of winter I hope to have got my wits together again so that I can also think of other people. Meanwhile with best thanks and friendly greetings,

Yours sincerely, c. g. jung

☐ Pupil of Jung's, analytical psychologist (d. 1966).
[1] Zimmer died in U.S.A. in Mar. 1943.
[2] Dr. Theodor Haemmerli died in Apr. 1944. Cf. Memories, pp. 293/273, where he is referred to as "Dr. H."; also Jung's letter of 25 Oct. 55 to H.'s brother.
[3] In 1942 Jung gave up his lectures at the Swiss Federal Polytechnic, Zurich, because of ill health. In 1943 he accepted a chair for medical psychology at the U. of Basel, but again had to resign on account of his heart attack.

To H. Irminger

Dear Herr Irminger,   22 September 1944

After having been prevented from doing so by a long illness, I have now read your MS. First of all, I would like to thank you for having taken so much trouble to show me how the Catholic doctrine completes and perfects my psychological writings. You also wonder—rightly, from your point of view—why I don't declare my belief in God and return to the bosom of the Church.

It may interest you to know that I once received a letter from an "alchemist," that is, from a man who still believes in the medieval art of gold-making, who informed me that I understood nothing whatever of the true alchemy, but that if I did I would avow my faith in it. When I was in India, the philosophers there assured me that their enlightened philosophy was infinitely further advanced than mine, whereas I still languished in the darkness of Ahamkara,[1]

[1] Ahamkara ("I-maker"), is the world of ego-consciousness.

Maya, etc. No doubt a Persian sufi[2] would find my remarks about Chadir[3] very jejune and, by thoroughly instructing me in his mysticism, would show me the way to salvation.

All critics of this kind have one thing in common: with a couple of more or less polite remarks they all without exception pass over the *facts* I have presented and verified, which do not interest them in the least, and want to convert me to their special credo.

My dear Sir! *My pursuit is science,* not apologetics and not philosophy, and I have neither the capacity nor the desire to found a religion. *My interest is scientific, yours evangelical,* therefore you write an apologia for Catholic doctrine, which I have never attacked and don't want to attack. These two standpoints are mutually exclusive so that any discussion is impossible. We talk at cross purposes and charge through open doors.

As a scientist I have to guard against believing that I am in possession of a final truth. I am therefore put in the wrong from the start, since I am not in possession of the truth, which is solely on the side of my opponent. Consequently, the only thing that matters for you is that I should emerge from my benighted error and acknowledge the truth of the Catholic doctrine. As a Christian, of course, I take my stand on the Christian truth, so it is superfluous to want to convert me to that.

In my writings I naturally remain below the heights of every religious system, for I always go only as far as the psychological facts I have experienced permit me. I have no ambition to profess or support any one faith. I am interested solely in the facts.

On this empirical foundation every religion has erected its temple, and the two intolerant ones among them, Christianity and Islam, vie with each other in raising the totalitarian claim that their temple is the only right one.

Though I know little of Catholic doctrine, that little is enough to make it an inalienable possession for me. And I know so much about Protestantism that I could never give it up. This lamentable indecision is what you, with so much psychological acumen, censure as a "complex." Now with regard to this indecision I must tell you that I have consciously and deliberately decided for it. Since no man can serve two masters, I can submit neither to one creed nor to the

[2] Lit. "clad in wool." Adherents of Sufism, a mystical development of Islam.
[3] Chadir (or Khidr) is the enigmatic, immortal knower of divine secrets; he figures in the 18th Sura of the Koran and plays an important role in Sufism. Cf. "Concerning Rebirth," CW 9, i, pars. 240ff.

other, but only to the *one* which stands above the conflict. Just as Christ is eternally being sacrificed, so also he hangs eternally between the two thieves. There are good Catholic and Protestant Christians. If the Church has suffered a schism, then I must be satisfied with being a Christian who finds himself in the same conflict Christendom is in. I cannot disavow my brother who, in good faith and for reasons I cannot invalidate with a good conscience, is of a different opinion. You yourself express the view that dire abuses within the Church played no small part in causing the schism. I can only agree with this and would draw your attention to the fact that a far more terrible schism has occurred in our own day, namely the Antichristian movement which *rules* Russia and Germany. The Church in both its denominations is causally implicated in this schism too. The cause, to be sure, is no longer the profligacy of the declining 15th century, but rather a loss of spiritual authority which, it seems to me, is due to the inability of the Churches to come to terms adequately with the scientific spirit. Science seeks the truth because it feels it does not possess it. The church *possesses* the truth and therefore does not seek it.

The fact of Antichristianity posits a far deeper schism which is infinitely harder to hold together than Catholicism and Protestantism. This time it is a Yes and No to Christianity as such.

When a crack runs through a house, the entire building is affected and not merely one half of it. The house is no longer as trustworthy as before. A conscientious builder does not try to convince the owner that the rooms on either side of the crack are still in an excellent condition, but will set to work on the crack and seek ways and means to mend it. The splendid and costly furnishings of the rooms will interest him only in so far as he is intent on saving the rooms. He has no time to wander around admiringly, exclaiming that they are the most beautiful in the world, when there is already a creaking in the beams.

As a doctor I am interested only in one thing: how can the wound be healed? It is quite certain that the schism can never be repaired by each side extolling its advantages to the other instead of lamenting their woeful inability to establish peace. While mother and daughter bicker, there comes the enemy of both, the Antichrist, and shows these Christians who are squabbling about *their* truth what *he* can do—for in egotism he outbids everybody.

Anyone who wants to, or has to, heal this conflict is faced with the hell of a mess: he sees that the European is only half a Christian.

He will become a whole one only when he can also stand on his left leg. The doctor has to treat both sides, for the whole man suffers when he is sick and not merely the half.

This is the reason why I try to establish facts *on which the two sides can unite.* (It is also the reason why I get kicks from both sides.) Every hardening of the denominational standpoint enlarges the crack and diminishes the moral and spiritual authority of Christianity, as everyone outside the Church can plainly see. But certain people are as though smitten with blindness.

It is naturally much *easier* to cling obstinately to a credo and assert its absolute validity. In this way you avoid any personal conflict but fuel the general one instead. Usually this is called egotism, but I call it blindness and bigotry when one party still believes it can finally settle the other's hash. Even the Antichrist, who is a past-master of this method, deceives himself mightily in this respect (thank God!).

As much as the Christian is bound to be convinced of the moral value of his own submission, he should not require or even expect it of others, for this totalitarian claim destroys his humility, even when it is cunningly hidden behind an impersonal mask.

As a doctor I am continually concerned with the victims of the great schism of our time. For this reason I cannot, through onesided denominationalism, throw the seekers of healing out on their necks, for they have come straight from the battlefield of the schism. The *tertius gaudens*[4] of the domestic squabble is the Antichrist, who has not by a long shot sprung only from German Protestantism or the venality of the Church of the Czars, but also from the eminently Catholic soil of Italy and Spain. Every Church must beat its breast, as must every European: *mea culpa, mea maxima culpa! None is right,* and therefore the scientifically minded man of today says: Let us go and seek the facts upon which all could unite, for opinions that have sprouted into totalitarian truths are the source of never-ending strife which no one wants to end.

I was amazed to see that you too have not understood the concept of the "self." How on earth did you come by the idea that I can replace God, and by means of a concept? As a scientist I cannot after all assert that "God" does something, for how can I prove that the specific cause is "God"? For this I would need a proof of God, which we have long known can be nothing but a begging of

[4] = "the third who laughs."

the question. I can, if need be, still demonstrate the existence of a wholeness supraordinate to consciousness, but of its own nature it defies description. This "self" never in all one's life takes the place of God, though it may perhaps be a vessel for divine grace. Such regrettable misunderstandings are based on the assumption that I am an irreligious man who doesn't believe in God, and to whom, therefore, one only needs to show the way to belief. These critics remind me of a certain Benedictine Father who, in the 18th century, wrote a book in which he demonstrated that Greek mythology was nothing but alchemy. The poor chap didn't know that alchemy grew out of mythology.

Thus, with commendable patience and undoubted goodwill ("He who loves his child chastises it"), and despite my stupendous and obdurate folly, you want to bring me to the goal and consummation of my life's work, and whither do you lead me? To the very spot from which I started, namely to that still medieval Christianity, which failed not only four hundred years ago but is now more of a failure than ever and in the most terrible way. The German Army is supposed to consist of Christians, and the larger half of it of Catholics at that.

Why don't people read my books conscientiously? Why do they gloss over the facts?

Germany dreams of world domination and is getting it in the neck with a vengeance. Likewise, Christianity dreams a noble dream of catholicity and is not only split up in itself but largely disowned even in its Western homeland. And people do not see that I am gathering *for tomorrow* the factual material which will be desperately needed if the European of the future is to be convinced of anything at all. The denominationalist is interested only in apologias and propaganda. Scientific responsibility means nothing to him. Nowadays he is invariably a *laudator temporis acti*. The kerygma[5] of the early centuries poured forth *new spirit* and it worked like fire. But the salt has lost its savour and salts no more. Hence that *granum salis* is also missing which my critics would need in order to correct their projections and to open their drowsy eyes wide enough to see reality: nowhere and never have I denied God. I start from a positive Christianity which is as much Catholic as Protestant, and I endeavour in a scientifically responsible manner to point out those empirically graspable facts which make the justification of Christian

---

[5] Preaching, declaration of religious truth.

and, in particular, Catholic dogma at least plausible, and besides that are best suited to give the scientific mind an access to understanding. I expect no gratitude from spiritual and clerical pride, merely a little less blindness. I know, however, of a few high-ranking clerics who appreciate my labours. It is by no means in the interests of the Church if insufficient understanding ventures too far. People should read authors who take as positive a stance towards Christianity as I do rather more carefully and reflect before trying to convert them to what is already an object of their greatest concern.

Have you never noticed that I do not write for ecclesiastical circles but for those who are *extra ecclesiam*? I join their company, deliberately and of my own free will outside the Church, and should I on that account be branded a heretic, I answer: "The savourlessness of the salt serves the work of Antichrist."

In my view it is utterly wrong to criticize my scientific work, which does not claim to be anything except scientific, from any other standpoint than that which alone is appropriate to the scientific method. Confessions of faith are, as we know, not the business of science. I would be sinning against the modesty proper to science if I said anything more, or other than, what can be gleaned from the facts. I once described the archetype as an *imprint* which presupposes an *imprinter*.[6] Science can never assert that the imprinter is "God," since that can never be proved. Just as I restrict myself to the facts, any proper criticism that deserves a hearing must likewise concern itself with these facts, and either prove that they do not exist or that their interpretation runs counter to scientific principles. Should the facts be inconvenient for any kind of creed, then they are not to be got rid of by an authoritarian fiat or by faith. Anyone who tries to do so immobilizes himself and remains irretrievably behind world history. Instead of such purposeless criticism I would far rather have a scholarly Catholic collaborator who with understanding and goodwill would correct my theologically defective mode of expression, so that I could avoid everything that looks even remotely like a criticism, let alone a devaluation, of Church doctrine. I am so profoundly convinced of the immeasurable significance of the Church that I would wish to spare her all unnecessary difficulties.

You may discern from the length of my letter the interest I evince in your work, in spite of the fact that you have charged with excessive vehemence through a door I have long kept open.

Yours sincerely, C. G. JUNG

6 *Psychology and Alchemy*, pars. 15f.

To Rudolf Bernoulli

Dear Colleague,   5 October 1944

Your very friendly letter gave me great pleasure. I am indeed slowly getting better, but it is real slow! Fortunately I can go on with my scientific work and am at present engrossed in the secret of the Chymical Wedding.[1]

Nowadays, certainly, the number of hermetics[2] has grown increasingly small. But it was never particularly large, because the *aurea catena*[3] they write about does not run through schools and conscious tradition but through the unconscious. Hermeticism is not something you choose, it is a destiny, just as the *ecclesia spiritualis* is not an organization but an *electio*.

I hope that your health, too, which had been shaky for so long, has now righted itself again. With best regards,

Ever sincerely yours, C. G. JUNG

☐ (1880–1948), professor of the history of art at the Swiss Federal Polytechnic, Zurich.
[1] Probably a reference to his work on *Mysterium Coniunctionis* (cf. par. 104). In a more specific sense it could also refer to Christian Rosencreutz's *The Chymical Wedding* (cf. Boner, 8 Dec. 38, n. 2), which is discussed in "The Psychology of the Transference," CW 16, pars. 407 & n. 18, 416, 500, itself an "offshoot" of *Mysterium Coniunctionis* (cf. p. xv) and first published in 1946.
[2] B. had written: "Even if the number of conscious hermetics has become very small you prove that quite a few hermetic elements are alive and kicking in our unconscious."
[3] The "golden chain" of alchemy, the series of wise men of whom the first was said to be Hermes Trismegistos, Thrice Greatest Hermes, identified with Thoth, the Egyptian god of learning, and as such considered the father of alchemy.

To Adolf L. Vischer

Dear Colleague,   10 October 1944

I hear from Dr. X. and incidentally also from Basel that there is a possibility of my friend Kerényi getting a lectureship. I have heard this news with joy and interest. Since the time of Bachofen[1] there

☐ Swiss physician, lecturer (emeritus) in gerontology at Basel, member of the Curatorium of the University. (Cf. White, 27 Dec. 47.)
[1] Johann Jakob Bachofen (1815–1887), Swiss sociologist and cultural historian. He was professor of Roman Law at the U. of Basel and resigned in 1844. His

351

has been an unredeemed debt on the part of philology and Kerényi is a good opportunity for redeeming this debt. In his own field he is a pioneer. His work was highly esteemed even by Reitzenstein[2] and I can confirm from my own experience that he has a positive genius for feeling his way into the structure and meaning of Greek fable. As a matter of fact that was the deeper reason for our work together. His interpretation and exposition of mythology not only afford extremely valuable parallels with the psychology of the unconscious but are also a veritable fountainhead of psychological insights which are of the greatest help especially in interpreting unconscious processes. Kerényi would be a good acquisition for any university as he brings with him a new and living spirit which is often lacking to an alarming degree precisely in the Philological Faculty.

I would gladly have written to you earlier about this matter had I not assumed that it was already lined up.

So far I have made a satisfactory recovery but can do only a small part of my work. Nevertheless I can cope with my scientific obligations. But this only with care, patience, and slowness. If you come to Zurich sometime, it would be a pleasure to see you again. With best regards,

Yours sincerely, C. G. JUNG

pioneer research on "mother right" and on the primacy of matrilineal descent was largely disregarded in academic circles. Cf. *Myth, Religion, and Mother Right* (A selection from his writings; Bollingen Series, 1967).
[2] Richard Reitzenstein (1861–1931), German philologist and historian of religion.

To Max Pulver

Dear Dr. Pulver,   2 November 1944

Many thanks for kindly sending me your interesting and timely book.[1] The third chapter seems to me particularly valuable. Regarding the problem of evil and power, it has always struck me as significant that "Macht" [power] is derived from "machen" [to make]; and since "making" is a specific activity of man, one might come to the conclusion that the characteristic expression of human life bears

□ (1889–1952), Swiss author and graphologist.
[1] *Person, Charakter, Schicksal* (1944).

the stamp of evil and that in consequence the Anthropos[2] is really Lucifer. Again with thanks and kind regards,

Yours sincerely, C. G. J U N G

[2] The Original Man, man in his ideal, archetypal totality and one of the symbols of the self.

To H. Irminger

Dear Herr Irminger,   20 November 1944

. . .

Allow me to express my astonishment that you lay so much stress on my being "reft asunder," as though this were something extraordinary that ought not to be. Have you still not noticed that the Church, indeed Christianity itself, is reft asunder? Do you deny the existence of the schism or of Antichristianity? As Christians and human beings we are therefore reft—moreover does not Przywara S.J. write somewhere about a "rift"?[1] On this rift we are all crucified. I am conscious of this fact in myself as well as in my fellow men, among whom there are some very *positive* Christians. It is scarcely possible that you are unconscious of the conflict within yourself (which is just what being "reft asunder" means). Even the Christian Paul had that man of violence, Saul as the angel of Satan,[2] to buffet him in the face. One shouldn't evade this conflict by escaping into a premature and anticipated state of redemption, otherwise one provokes it in the outside world. And that is of the devil.

Yours sincerely, C. G. J U N G

[1] Erich Przywara, S.J.; the "rift" is mentioned in his *Deus semper maior*, I, pp. 71ff.
[2] Cf. II Cor. 12:7.

To Hugo Rahner, S.J.

Dear Colleague,   20 November 1944

Very best thanks for kindly sending me your beautiful book.[1] Leafing through it, I was immediately struck by the poem of Paulinus

☐ S.J., professor of Church history and patrology at the U. of Innsbruck, Austria.
[1] *Mater Ecclesiae* (1944).

of Nola, especially the verse: "Out of this mother is born the Ancient as well as the Infant. . . ."[2]

Just now I am busy with the motif of the king's birth in alchemy.[3] There is in alchemy an author who was an English clergyman in the 15th century.[4] He calls the king the *antiquus dierum.*[5] All this Senex-Puer symbolism has to do with the renewal of the ageing god in Ancient Egypt.

The passage in Paulinus forces on me a question I really didn't want to ask you because it seems absurd: are there, in a way I don't suspect, any ideas in the patristic literature that might refer to the senescence of the Deity? Although this thoroughly pagan thought seems completely impossible to me, the insistence on the old man who is reborn as a child nevertheless has a suggestive affinity with the Egyptian motif.

You were kind enough to put a copy of your "Gottesgeburt"[6] at my disposal. As it is a bound copy I assume that I should return it to you. It has been lying around so long because of my illness and till now I have unfortunately had no opportunity to make excerpts from it. May I keep it for a while longer?

Allow me to take this opportunity not only to thank you for your beautiful new book, but also to express the gratitude we all feel for your work on patristic symbolism, which for us is extraordinarily valuable. Your researches help to bridge that difficult gap which separates the modern consciousness from the living myths of antiquity. With best regards,

Yours sincerely, C. G. JUNG

[2] St. Paulinus (353–431), bishop of Nola. The verses occur in Poema 25 (cf. *Mysterium Coniunctionis*, par. 375).
[3] Ibid., pars. 368ff.
[4] Sir George Ripley (1415–1490), Canon of Bridlington, author of *Cantilena Riplaei* (ibid., par. 370, n. 67).
[5] "Ancient of Days." Cf. ibid., par. 374.
[6] "Die Gottesgeburt," *Zeitschrift für katholische Theologie* (Innsbruck), LXIII (1939), LXIV (1940).

To Karl Kerényi

Dear Colleague,   23 November 1944

Very many thanks for kindly sending me your *Töchter der Sonne.*[1] I marvel at the range and speediness of your publishing activity, not to mention the profundity of your mythological interpretations. For me your writings are each time an unalloyed joy, affording a stimulating glimpse into backgrounds I cannot always, or cannot yet, take in. Your new book, too, is a veritable treasure-house of hints and pointers to fleeting impressions and memories of my wanderings in the realm of alchemy and the unconscious.

Yours sincerely, c. g. j u n g

[1] Zurich, 1944.

To Pastor Ernst Fischer

Dear Pastor Fischer,   21 December 1944

The article you sent me in the Volksblatt[1] may refer to a dream but the development is literary so that one can never be quite certain how much invention is mixed up with it.

The dream is not uninteresting and was obviously dreamt by a very religious person. We know, of course, that what happens in the dream is a drama taking place on one's own interior stage, where the dreamer is the actors, the libretto, the theatre, and the public rolled into one. Here the dreamer witnesses how his wife and daughter suddenly vanish as though rapt up to heaven. This is undoubtedly a process of dissociation which the dream by projection extends to any number of other families. If we take this bit as genuine, we would have to conclude that the dreamer is suffering from a dissociation affecting not only himself but his whole circle.

His dissociation consists in a splitting-off of the feminine element in the unconscious, which in Western languages is designated by anima, psyche, and their cognates, all of the feminine gender. These dissociations usually occur when consciousness has in one respect or another strayed too far from its natural basis and consequently gets into conflict with its natural preconditions. This is such a common phenomenon in the history of culture that for the purpose of healing such dissociations reconciliation rites were instituted which frequently took the form of the *hierosgamos*. Even in Christianity we have this symbolism in the *nuptiae agni*[2] and in the union of the *sponsus*

☐ Basel.
[1] As there are numerous Swiss papers called *Volksblatt*, the article could not be identified.
[2] Rev. 19:7ff. Cf. *Mysterium Coniunctionis*, index *s.v.* Marriage of the Lamb.

Christ with the *sponsa ecclesia*.[3] This reconciliation symbolism as a cure for psychic dissociation is found in most religions. Even in the strongly masculine Jewish religion we have the love symbolism of the *pardes rimmonim*[4] and the ultimate union of the Shekhinah with the sponsus Tifereth.[5]

The dissociated state is itself a morbid one and people who run around in such a state are liable to infect others. The excitement emanating from this article tends to rouse the naïve reader to expect some kind of miracle, which is not altogether as it should be. I therefore always advise my patients, when they have significant dreams of this nature, to regard them as messages directed to their own private address (*somnia a Deo missa!*), and I would have given the same advice to the writer of this article. On top of that, he lays himself bare before the eyes of the knowledgeable. It would be another matter if together with the dream he had made an insightful confession of his own state. But from lack of knowledge this was obviously impossible.

Hoping I have given a satisfactory answer to the complicated questions raised by the article, I remain,

Yours sincerely, C. G. JUNG

[3] Ibid., *s.v.* Christ and the Church.
[4] "Orchard of Pomegranates." Cf. Song of Songs 4:13.
[5] The Shekhinah is the Glory of God, thought of as feminine, who is united with Tifereth, Beauty, the name of the sixth Sefira (more frequently called "Rahamim," Compassion) in the Kabbalistic system of the ten Sefiroth representing the "stages in the revelation of God's creative power" (Scholem, *Major Trends in Jewish Mysticism*, 1941, p. 13).

To Allen W. Dulles

[ORIGINAL IN ENGLISH]

My dear Dulles,   1 February 1945

Since after my illness I get interested once more in the affairs of the world, the various ways of propaganda began to interest me. German propaganda tries inevitably to hollow out a moral hole with

☐ (1893–1969), American diplomat. During World War II he was a leading official of the Office of Strategic Services (OSS), the American intelligence agency, with an office in Bern which was in communication with the anti-Nazi circles within Germany. During his stay in Switzerland he paid Jung several visits. In 1950 he became deputy chief of the Central Intelligence Agency (CIA), and in 1953 its chief.

the hope of an eventual collapse. A better propaganda appeals to the moral strength and not to the feebleness of the enemy.

As far as the psychological effectiveness of Allied propaganda is concerned, it strikes me that the best things that have appeared so far are General Eisenhower's proclamations to the German people.

These proclamations, couched in simple, human language which anyone can understand, offer the German people something they can cling to and tend to strengthen any belief which may exist in the justice and humanity of the Americans. Thus they appeal *to the best* in the German people, to their belief in idealism, truth, and decency. They fill up the hole of moral inferiority, which is infinitely better propaganda than destructive insinuations.

General Eisenhower certainly should be congratulated.

Sincerely yours, C. G. JUNG

To Kristine Mann

[ORIGINAL IN ENGLISH]

My dear Dr. Mann,   1 February 1945

Eleanor Bertine has already given me the news of your illness[1] in a letter I received a few days ago. I wish I could talk to you personally, but one is so far from each other and it is such a long time we are separated from the rest of the world that one feels quite hopeless about a communication. We don't trust even our letters to be capable of jumping over the abyss which yawns between us and the wide world. Still I hope that a good star conveys my letter to you.

As you know, the angel of death has struck me down too and almost succeeded in wiping me off the slate.[2] I have been practically an invalid ever since, recovering very very slowly from all the arrows that have pierced me on all sides. Fortunately enough my head has not suffered and I could forget myself in my scientific work. On the whole my illness proved to be a most valuable experience, which gave me the inestimable opportunity of a glimpse behind the veil. The only difficulty is to get rid of the body, to get quite naked and void of the world and the ego-will. When you can give up the crazy will to live and when you seemingly fall into a bottomless mist, then

☐ M.D., (1873–1945), American analytical psychologist, a founder of the Analytical Psychology Club of New York and of its library, now named in memory of her. (See pl. in vol. 2.)
[1] She was dying of cancer.
[2] Cf. Anon., 11 July 44, n. 1.

the truly *real* life begins with everything which you were meant to be and never reached. It is something ineffably grand. I was free, completely free and whole, as I never felt before.[3] I found myself 15,000 km. from the earth and I saw it as an immense globe resplendent in an inexpressibly beautiful blue light. I was on a point exactly above the southern end of India, which shone in a bluish silvery light with Ceylon like a shimmering opal in the deep blue sea. I was in the universe, where there was a big solitary rock containing a temple. I saw its entrance illuminated by a thousand small flames of coconut oil. I knew I was to enter the temple and I would reach full knowledge. But at this moment a messenger from the world (which by then was a very insignificant corner of the universe) arrived and said that I was not allowed to depart and at this moment the whole vision collapsed completely. But from then on for three weeks I slept, and was wakeful each night in the universe and experienced the complete vision. Not I was united with somebody or something—*it* was united, *it* was the *hierosgamos*, the mystic Agnus. It was a silent invisible festival[4] permeated by an incomparable, indescribable feeling of eternal bliss, such as I never could have imagined as being within reach of human experience. Death is the hardest thing from the outside and as long as we are outside of it. But once inside you taste of such completeness and peace and fulfillment that you don't want to return. As a matter of fact, during the first month after my first vision I suffered from black depressions because I felt that I was recovering. It was like dying. I did not want to live and to return into this fragmentary, restricted, narrow, almost mechanical life, where you were subject to the laws of gravity and cohesion, imprisoned in a system of 3 dimensions and whirled along with other bodies in the turbulent stream of time. There was fulness, meaning fulfillment, *eternal* movement (not movement in time).

Although your letter is dated Nov. 27th/44, I hope that my answer will reach you. Your letter arrived today and I am writing at once.

Throughout my illness something has carried me. My feet were not standing on air and I had the proof that I have reached a safe ground. Whatever you do, if you do it sincerely, will eventually become the bridge to your wholeness, a good ship that carries you

[3] The following description is a condensation of *Memories*, pp. 289ff./270ff.
[4] Ibid., pp. 294/274.

358

through the darkness of your second birth, which seems to be death to the outside. I will not last too long any more. I am marked. But life has fortunately become provisional. It has become a transitory prejudice, a working hypothesis for the time being, but not existence itself.

Be patient and regard it as another difficult task, this time the last one.

I greet you, CARL G. JUNG

To Pastor Max Frischknecht

Dear Pastor Frischknecht,   7 April 1945

Thank you for kindly sending me your book.[1] Permit me a few objective remarks: you stumble over the term "self." This nomenclature is no invention of mine. It existed with the same meaning for the same thing thousands of years before I did. Following Bacon's scientific rule, *principia explicandi praeter necessitatem non sunt multiplicanda*,[2] I was obliged to choose this concept or else prove that it meant something different. I could not furnish this proof. Certainly the concept was—and in Indian scholastic philosophy today still is—metaphysical, because philosophy at this level always includes psychology. The metaphysical nature of a concept did not prevent physics, for instance, from operating with the (thoroughly metaphysical) concept of aether right down to the time of the theory of relativity. One must only apply the necessary reservations befitting a working hypothesis, as Kant did when he called the *Ding an sich* a "merely negative borderline concept." You yourself have quoted what I say about the self in this respect.

You also seem to overlook the fact that every assertion about something that is unknowable must of necessity be *antinomian* if it is to be true, also that natural data (e.g., the maximum density of water at 4° C.) are always *irrational*. Since scientific statements are

---

☐ Basel.

[1] *Die Religion in der Psychologie C. G. Jungs* (1945).

[2] "Explanatory principles should not be multiplied beyond the necessary." The proposition, in the form "Entia non sunt multiplicanda praeter necessitatem," is associated with the English scholastic William of Occam (*ca.* 1300–1349) and is known as "Occam's Razor." It had already been taught by Duns Scotus (*ca.* 1265–1308), one of the greatest mediaeval philosophers.

inductive, starting as they do from irrational data, they are bound to be irrational in so far as they are descriptive. Only deductions are logical. My scientific methodology is nothing out of the ordinary, it proceeds exactly like comparative anatomy, only it describes and compares psychic figures.

Comparative anatomy swarms with primary forms, archetypes—a term which I mentioned only in passing as deriving from Augustine.[3] Actually it occurs earlier, in Cicero (Epist. XII to Pomponius Atticus, 5) and in the *Poimandres*[4] (ed. Scott, I, 8a). Does anyone expect a zoologist to represent the primary form of the vertebrates or of the individual organs as stamped by God's own hand? After all, we are no longer living in the 18th century, when zoology began with Genesis ch. 1. Or would you accuse a physiologist of making a God of the living body when he describes it as a self-regulating system? Is the God-image, which has functioned as a psychic factor in man everywhere since the remotest times, as the *consensus omnium* attests, absolutely identical with God? I expressly emphasize that it isn't and that there is no justification for such an assumption. Does one found a new religion every time one busies oneself with the psychology of comparative religion? As the case of Overbeck[5] shows, one can even make a distinction between the history of the Church and theology.

Although my honesty may be doubted (unfortunately I have never discovered why) I would consider it extremely dishonest—and what is still worse, bigoted and stupid—if a psychologist were to assert that the God-image does not have a tremendous effect on the psyche. For the scientist this has nothing to do with the theological question of God's existence, as he is concerned simply and solely with the phenomenology of psychic dominants,[6] whether they be called God,

---

[3] St. Augustine (354–430) does not use the term "archetypus" but formulates the idea of it in *De diversis quaestionibus*, LXXXIII, where he speaks of "ideae principales." Cf. "Archetypes of the Collective Unconscious," CW 9, i, par. 5.

[4] The "Poimandres" (of Hermes Trismegistus) is the first book of the *Corpus Hermeticum*. The passage referred to is Εἶδες ἐν τῷ νῷ τὸ ἀρχέτυπον εἶδος ("you have seen in your mind the archetypal image"); cf. Scott, *Hermetica*, I, p. 116, where ἀρχέτυπον εἶδος is translated as "archetypal form." In the second book, "A Discourse of Hermes Trismegistus to Asclepius," there occurs at par. 126 the phrase τὸ ἀρχέτυπον φῶς, "the archetypal light" (Scott, I, p. 140).

[5] Franz Overbeck (1837–1905), Swiss theologian, friend of Nietzsche's. Although professor of theology at Basel he became estranged from Christianity. Cf. Overbeck, *Selbstzeugnisse* (ed. Tauber), 1966.

[6] A term occasionally used for the archetypes, e.g., CW 7, pars. 377, 388.

Allah, Buddha, Purusha, Zeus, planets, zodia, or sex (as Philippians 3:19, "whose God is their belly," rightly says).

Science cannot assert that God stamped his own archetype, neither can it say that the archetype engenders God, nor does it say anything of the sort. But it has the right to make statements about the observable psychic effects of an archetype. It does not have to take instruction from anyone in this matter, least of all from a nonprofessional.

Your opinion that I am an atheist is pretty bold, to say the least. Have I ever said "God could not live for a second without me"? That was Angelus Silesius,[7] whose atheism has still to be proved; the whole Indian East says it too, and the charge of atheism would be equally out of place. What do you know, may I be permitted to ask, about my religious convictions? Do you conclude from my preoccupation with alchemy that I also believe in Mercurius or am an ἑρμητικός?[8] The teacher is not always a tyro, the psychiatrist not invariably mad, and the prison chaplain not an obvious criminal.

If you have formed the peculiar notion that I am proclaiming a religion, this is due to your ignorance of psychotherapeutic methods. When for instance the heart no longer functions as it has always functioned, it is sick, and the same goes for the psyche, whose functioning depends on archetypes (instincts, patterns of behaviour, etc.). The doctor sees to it that the heart gets into its old rhythm again, and the psychotherapist must restore the "original pattern," the original ways in which the psyche reacts. This is done, today as several thousand years ago, through the "anamnesis" of the archetype. I can't help it that religions *also* work with archetypes (in the Christian, i.e., the Catholic, Church there is even a *cura animarum*!). But as the Medical Faculty is at least as old as the Theological Faculty it is idle to start quarrelling about priorities. I could just as well accuse the parson of dabbling in medicine because he works with archetypes, and even more so the doctor of godlessness and messing about with religion because he does the same. He was doing this when parsons still wore leopard skins and danced to the drum.

Don't you think one should judge a thing only if one has *some* knowledge of it, and a man only if one knows him *well*? Don't you think that hearsay and personal resentment are not exactly the most

---

[7] The quotation occurs in his *Cherubinic Wanderer* (orig. 1657–74), Book I; cf. also *Psychological Types*, par. 432.

[8] = a hermetic.

reliable foundations for judgment? You say, quite rightly, that you (or "we," as you so modestly put it) "ought not to be guided simply by personal feeling." My dear Pastor, I beg you with all due deference to read through your book again, critically and with this proviso in mind.

I am grateful to you for your efforts to present my concept of the self as accurately as possible. This idea seems to have become a stumbling-block ever since Origen and Meister Eckhart were accused of heresy, whereas in the East it is *mani padme*, "the jewel in the lotus," or *hiranyagarbha*,[9] the golden seed, the "conglomerate soul." Cf. the verses:[10]

> The first man and the last is Christ alone,
> All men do spring from him, in him are one.

Well, well: "Unto the Christians a stumbling-block, unto the Jews foolishness."[11]

Yours very truly, c. g. j u n g

[9] In *Rig Veda* X, 121 the attribute of the creator-god Prajapati, who creates himself as the golden seed arising from the primordial waters.
[10] Angelus Silesius, Book 5.
[11] Ironical version of I. Cor. 1:23: "But we preach Christ crucified, unto the Jews a stumbling-block, and unto the Greeks foolishness."

Anonymous

Dear Fräulein N.,   Bollingen, 23 April 1945

I am sorry to hear you are ill. Your news reached me when I was all of a dither and had to settle everything in a hurry—and I can't hurry any more. Even so I will send you a sign of life, for since yesterday I have been in Bollingen. Writing was simply impossible before, as I had to have time for myself and my tasks. Just now some hard chunks of reality have hit you, and hit all the harder because I have spoilt you, but you needed spoiling in order to approach closer to the earth, where you could get at the stone. Hardness increases in proportion to the speed of approach.

Wishing you a good recovery,

Yours ever, c. g. j u n g

To Markus Fierz

Dear Professor Fierz,   30 April 1945

I am taking the liberty of enclosing a page of the MS for the new edition of one of my books.[1] There is a thought here that touches on the realm of physics. I should be most grateful for your views on this point. Naturally I feel very unsure when I set foot on alien territory, particularly one that is so studded with intricate problems. But Jordan's ideas[2] have given me courage, so that I have ventured to establish a connection which came to me quite unexpectedly.

With best regards, ·

Yours sincerely, C. G. JUNG

☐ Swiss physicist, then professor of theoretical physics at Basel, since 1945 professor at the Swiss Federal Polytechnic, Zurich.
[1] *Psychologie und Erziehung* (1946), revised version of *Analytische Psychologie und Erziehung* (1926), now "Analytical Psychology and Education," CW 17.
[2] Cf. Jordan, 10 Nov. 34, n. 2.

To Fritz Blanke

Dear Colleague,   2 May 1945

The "Bear-skinned"[1] comes into the category of unorthodox beings, more specifically that of werewolves, "doctor animals,"[2] leopard men,

☐ (1893–1967), professor of divinity at the U. of Zurich.
[1] B. inquired about Nicholas von der Flüe's vision of the "man with the bearskin." In this vision the Blessed Brother Klaus saw a divine pilgrim whom he seemed to have identified with Christ, and whose clothes changed into a bearskin, glistening with gold (cf. von Franz, *Die Visionen des Niklaus von der Flüe*, 1959, p. 81). In "Brother Klaus" Jung discusses the Trinity vision (cf. n. 12 infra) but mentions the Bear-skin vision only in passing (par. 487). In a letter to Mary Mellon of 24 Sept. 45 (not published in this selection) Jung reports an incident which throws light on the role of Nicholas von der Flüe in Swiss psychology. He writes: "We lived [during the war] in ghostlike suspension and in an unbelievable sort of unreality, never too sure of our existence. Several times it hung on a hair that we were invaded. We hardly dared to believe in a miracle. But it came off. My son is an officer in a Catholic infantry regiment. He told me that his soldiers had the collective vision of the blessed brother Niklaus von der Flüe, extending his hands towards the Rhine to ward off the German troops approaching our frontiers. The blessed Brother is actually going to be canonized in Rome. It is nice to have such protective saints. . . ."
[2] Magicians or daemonic beings appearing in the form of animals. Cf. *Symbols of Transformation*, par. 503: *Two Essays*, par. 154, n. 5.

and "Beriserkr."[3] The man charged with *mana*,[4] or numinous man, has theriomorphic attributes, since he surpasses the ordinary man not only upwards but downwards. Heroes have snake's eyes (Nordic: *ormr i auga*), are half man half serpent (Kekrops, Erechtheus), have snake-souls and snake's skin; the medicine-man can change into all sorts of animals. Among the American Indians, certain animals appear to the primitive medical candidate; there is an echo of this in the dove of the Holy Ghost at the unearthly baptismal birth (when the Christ came to Jesus). Another echo is the "Brother Wolf" of St. Francis.[5] Characteristic of the Germanic mentality of Brother Klaus is the figure of the pilgrim reminiscent of Wotan, for whom "die Wütenden" [the raging ones], the Bear-skinned, are an excellent match. Evidently the figure of Christ appears here in two forms: 1. as a pilgrim who, like the mystic, has gone on the *peregrinatio animae*;[6] 2. as a bear whose pelt contains the golden lustre. In alchemy the bear is one of the theriomorphic symbols of transformation, like the dragon, lion, and eagle. (See *Psychology and Alchemy*, fig. 90.) These are all stages of spiritual transformation, like the κόραξ, λέων,[7] etc. of Mithraism. In alchemical mysticism there finally arises out of the lion (or bear) the *aurum philosophicum* in the form of a *novus sol*, i.e., the golden lustre. (Folklore and alchemy interpenetrated at a very early date!)

The meaning of the vision may be as follows: on his spiritual pilgrimage and in his instinctual (bear-like, i.e., hermit-like) subhumanness Brother Klaus recognizes himself as Christ. This runs parallel with his manifest adoption by God the Father and God the Mother.[8] The brutal coldness of feeling[9] that the saint needed in

[3] Berserker, "the bear-skinned," were in Nordic mythology people who could assume the form of bears; Nordic warriors who fought with frenzied fury were called Berserkers. Cf. "Wotan," CW 10, pars. 386, 389.

[4] Mana, the primitive (Melanesian) concept of supernatural power, of something extraordinarily potent. Cf. "On Psychic Energy," CW 8, par. 52, 44, pars. 123ff.; *Two Essays*, II, Part Two, ch. IV: "The Mana Personality."

[5] In ch. XXI of *Fioretti di San Francesco*, a 14th cent. collection of legends about St. Francis of Assisi (1181–1226), the story is told of how St. Francis tamed the wild wolf of Gubbio and addressed him as "Brother Wolf."

[6] = peregrination of the soul.

[7] = raven, lion.

[8] Brother Klaus saw in a vision how "God the Father and God the Mother laid both arms on his shoulders and thanked him for having helped their son" ("Brother Klaus," pars. 485f.); then in another vision he saw the son dressed in clothes identical with his own.

[9] Brother Klaus left his wife and ten children after fifteen years of marriage.

order to abandon his wife and children and friends is encountered in the subhuman animal realm. Hence the saint throws an animal shadow. (Analogies: Antichrist, the Temptation. *Quid mihi et tibi es, mulier?*)[10] Whoever can suffer within himself the highest united with the lowest is healed, holy, whole.

The vision is trying to show him that the spiritual pilgrim and the Beriserkr are both Christ, and this opens the way to forgiveness of the great sin which holiness is. (*Sine peccato nulla gratia!*[11]) He is frightened to death by God's wrath (Trinity vision[12]) because this wrath is aimed at him, who has betrayed his nearest and dearest and the ordinary man for God's sake.

Yours sincerely, C. G. JUNG

[10] John 2:4: "Woman, what have I to do with thee?"
[11] "Without sin no grace."
[12] In this vision Brother Klaus "saw the head of a human figure with a terrifying face, full of wrath and threats," whereupon "overcome with terror he instantly turned his face away and fell to the ground." ("Archetypes of the Collective Unconscious," CW 9, i, pars. 12ff.; "Brother Klaus," par. 478.) On account of its terrifying and therefore heretical character this vision was later adjusted to dogmatic concepts and brought into connection with the Trinity picture in the parish church at Sachseln (where Brother Klaus had been baptized) and called the "Trinity vision."

To Markus Fierz

Dear Professor Fierz,   7 May 1945

Best thanks for your prompt and detailed answer, which I found very satisfactory. I am particularly pleased with your suggested change[1] on p. 25, which is much more promising than my version.

I quite agree with your view that the situation indicated in this sentence is similar to the situation in psychology where discrimination is the precondition of knowledge, only it seems to me a sidetrack which, though entirely right in itself, does not, as you yourself remark, quite fit into the context of my argument. The ego-complex consists of all conscious contents, since consciousness is the exponent of the whole personality. Hence its contents are also of a personal

[1] The changed passage occurs in "Analytical Psychology and Education," par. 163: "As physics has to relate its measurements to objects, it is obliged to distinguish the observing medium from the thing observed, with the result that the categories of space, time, and causality become relative."

nature and must be distinguished from those of the objective psyche. My argument is concerned with a more general reflection, namely the reconstruction of the physical process as a psychic process. The parallel to this is the idea that the psychic process would, conversely, also be "reconstructed" as a physical process. The physical reconstruction would differ from the psychic in that it is not really a construction but would have to be conceived as an end-state or as an influence on the physical process, much as Schrödinger conceives it in his new English publication *What Is Life?*[2]—an influencing of the physical processes by the psychic. The materialistic premise is that the physical process causally determines the psychic process. The spiritualistic premise is the reverse of this. I think of this relationship in the physical sense as a reciprocal one, in which now one side and now the other acts as a cause. One could also say that under certain conditions the physical process reflects itself in the psychic, just as the psychic does in the physical. Of the utmost importance, it seems to me, is your information that the result of a measurement is essentially conditioned by the very nature of the measurement. From this it is evident that an objective and absolute measurement is actually impossible. Nevertheless a certain amount of measurement and a certain amount of knowledge of the physical are rendered possible by the psychic. We would have to conclude that a certain moulding and influencing of the physical process by the psychic are objectively present. Whether this can be proved is naturally another matter. If, faced with a reciprocal relationship, we can speak of an Archimedean point at all, then in my view such a point would be at least theoretically possible, since for the physical world there is an "outside" in the psychic, and consequently the physical would be an "outside" for the psychic at least in theory.

Your idea that the behaviour of physical processes is essentially conditioned by the physicist's method and mode of observation is very interesting. If we apply this idea to psychic processes, then psychological observation would also be prejudicial to the behaviour of the psyche. In both cases the physical as well as the psychic would be needed for the purpose of complementation, from which it follows that an approximately adequate knowledge of the physical could be completed by psychic complementation and, conversely, that any psychological knowledge could be completed only by knowledge of

[2] Erwin Schrödinger, *What Is Life?* (1944). Schrödinger (1887–1961), Austrian physicist, received the Nobel prize in 1933 for his work on wave mechanics.

the physical. In accordance with your view, psychology would be faced with the difficult task of explaining what the explanation of the physical as a psychic process actually means, and physics would be faced with the equally impossible task of explaining what are the physics of psychological theory. Actually this seems to me possible only if, by a combination of physical and psychic knowledge, one could reach a plane above and beyond the present dichotomous mode of observation by virtue of being in possession of both standpoints. I have a vague recollection that Pauli once said something similar.

I still have a lot of thinking to do as regards your opinion that the moral commitment of psychological knowledge[3] involves a crucial difference between this and the physicist's knowledge. At the moment I could not say anything adequate. The moral "ought" is certainly, in itself, a genuine phenomenon, but whether it signifies a radical difference still seems to me somehow questionable. Again with best thanks,

Yours sincerely, c. g. j u n g

[3] F. wrote: "Therefore I do not know whether it is not just the mathematical unequivocality but the moral non-commitment of physics which can be understood as a justification for the peculiar equivocality of psychology, which on the other hand is morally committed."

To Albert Oeri

Dear friend, 7 May 1945

Best thanks for your interesting article on "The Vanished One."[1] I had seen it already as I often read the *Basler Nachrichten*. I particularly liked the historical parallels and your remark that Hitler represents the heights and the depths of the German nature with painful exactitude. He really is the incarnation of the German's psychopathic inferiority, which also accounts for the German's feeling of national inferiority. The inferiority complex is always found just at the place where it does not belong.

Your article reminds me that a little while ago I wrote something

[1] Oeri, "Der Verschwundene," *Basler Nachrichten*, 5/6 May 1945. Article on Hitler, whose death was then still shrouded in darkness. Thus, as at the death of Friedrich Barbarossa (cf. *Symbols of Transformation*, par. 287, n. 36), the legend arose that he had only disappeared and would one day return.

which I am still not sure whether I can use or not.[2] I would like to submit it to your excellent judgment, so that you can tell me what you think of it and whether one can say such things out loud at all without being suspected of utter crankiness. At bottom I am convinced of the soundness of my reflections, but making them plausible is another matter. So I would first like to hear your opinion before anything further is done with this cuckoo's egg. In any case please regard it simply as grateful response to your pungent remarks about Germany.

With best thanks and kind regards, JUNG

[2] Probably "After the Catastrophe." Cf. Ullmann, 25 May 45, n. 2.

To Pastor Paul Métraux

Dear Pastor Métraux,   23 May 1945

. . .

Protestantism is above all a religion for adults—if it is understood. The Catholic Church is a mother, but the role played by Protestantism is more that of the father. Protestantism makes the child into a man, and every man has a different point of view. Therefore the fact that Protestantism is divided seems to me to be precisely the guarantee of its vitality. I consider this dissociation a sign of life with nothing basically alarming about it. I am convinced that Protestantism answers a fundamental human need, because Catholicism puts too much church between God and man, whereas—for the weak—Protestantism does not put enough between God and man. As far back as the Old Testament we can see that most courageous men were only just able to bear the presence of God.

. . .

Yours sincerely, C. G. JUNG

□ (Original in French.) Métraux (d. 1965) was editor-in-chief of *Semeur Vaudois*, Journal de l'Église Nationale (Lausanne).

To Hermann Ullmann

Dear Dr. Ullmann,   25 May 1945

As you correctly surmise, the text of the interview[1] was not submitted to me before publication. As is regularly the case nowadays, apparently, the interviewer prints only what he understands, putting everything in black and white and suppressing a number of vitally important conditional or parenthetical remarks.

Unfortunately the crucial concept of collective guilt[2] was left hanging in mid air—this seems to have created the greatest furore. Germany's collective guilt consists in the fact that it was undoubtedly the Germans who started the war and committed the unspeakable atrocity of the concentration camps. In so far as they were Germans and such things happened inside the German frontier, all Germans are befouled. Furthermore, all Europeans are besmirched by these happenings since they took place on European soil. This collective guilt is not a moral or a judicial construction but a psychological fact which in itself is irrational; in other words, if these things had happened in Switzerland and I crossed the French frontier with a Swiss passport and the French official remarked affably "Oh un cochon de Suisse," I would regard it as natural and logical. One only wishes the Germans could take this to heart and not commit the tactical blunder of insisting in and out of season that nobody knew of the concentration camps and nobody could have done anything about them, etc. It is and remains a fact that these things happened in Germany and that it was Germans who did them. Obviously we all know that there were also people in Germany who suffered under these things and fought against them. But it is important that the Germans in general should admit their guilt and not foist it off on others. They have even ventured to assert that the English are to blame for the concentration camps because they did not stop Hitler's coming to power.

As to the psychopathic inferiority[3] of the Germans, such happenings betray an alarmingly high degree of instability. 10% is putting it very low. I reckon with the same percentage among the Swiss. I wish you, as an outsider, could have attended German, French, English, and American congresses, to mention only one of the possible forms of social contact. There you could have made a collection of weird and wonderful experiences. What one then experienced in

□ German author.

[1] "Werden die Seelen Frieden finden?" *Weltwoche* (Zurich), 13:600, 11 May 1945. Now "The Postwar Psychic Problems of the Germans" in C. G. *Jung Speaking* (in press).

[2] Jung dealt explicitly with the problem of German collective guilt in "After the Catastrophe," first published in June 1945 in *Neue Schweizer Rundschau* (Zurich), XIII:2; now in CW 10.

[3] Cf. ibid., pars. 419, 423; also "Epilogue to Essays on Contemporary Events," ibid., pars. 465, 479.

the way of tactlessness, crudity, rudeness, etc. from the German side counterbalanced the no doubt amiable qualities of many Germans. For 30 years we have experienced nothing but Germany's threat to her neighbours or shameful violation of them, or else her wails for understanding. They were supposed either to knuckle under to Germany or understand and love her. But what is Germany's duty to Europe? "Collective guilt" raises just this question: What is Germany's debt to Europe after everything she has done in these 30 years? That is what Europe wants to hear from Germany. It is therefore impossible for the individual German simply to shake off this obligation by laying the blame on others, for instance the wicked Nazis. Nor can we Europeans shake off the German atrocities in the eyes of Indians or Americans. So if a Pueblo Indian should one day say to me "You Europeans are worse than ravaging beasts," I would have to agree politely, for in no circumstances should I win his just estimation by shaking off from the start every trace of complicity.

. . .

Yours sincerely, C. G. JUNG

To Albert Oeri

Dear friend,   26 May 1945

Very many thanks for your kind assessment of my half-baked concoction[1] which I myself found unsatisfactory. You are quite right, of course: it is too pessimistic, or rather, it has a pessimistic effect on people who are brought up to expect their piece of cake still in this world. Why aren't they told betimes that the "prince of this world" and "lord of the air" takes good care that the tastier morsels are snapped up by the wicked ones they envy so much, and that marriage is not the end but the beginning of the romance? The misery is that you can't tell "people" anything whatever; you can tell it only to individuals. Nevertheless, I shall have to write something about the concept of collective guilt that will stir people up.[2]

Thanks for the detailed news of your daughters, especially Regula,[3]

[1] Probably the interview cited in the preceding letter, n. 1.

[2] "After the Catastrophe."

[3] Regula Rohland-Oeri, by marriage a German. In the last days of the war she was able to escape from Berlin to Switzerland with her two small children. Cf. Rohland-Oeri, 23 Dec. 50.

who was much in our minds during those catastrophic times. Please give her my greetings. I would be interested to see her again one day.

All the best, JUNG

To Jolande Jacobi

Dear Dr. Jacobi,   12 June 1945

I would answer your question as follows: It is a fact that intelligence and psychological preparation in cases of schizophrenia result in a better prognosis. I therefore make it a rule to give anyone threatened with schizophrenia, or the mild or latent schizophrenic, as much psychological knowledge as possible, because I know from experience that there is then a better chance of his getting out of the psychotic interval. Equally, psychological enlightenment after a psychotic attack can be extraordinarily helpful in some circumstances. I am not convinced that schizophrenia is absolutely fatal any more than tuberculosis is. I would always recommend psychological education to patients at risk as a measure of prophylactic hygiene. Like neurosis, psychosis in its inner course is a process of individuation, but one that is usually not joined up with consciousness and therefore runs its course in the unconscious as an ouroboros.[1] Psychological preparation joins the process to consciousness, or rather, there is a chance of its being joined, and hence of the individuation process having a healing effect.

Hoping I have answered your question satisfactorily, and with best regards,

Yours sincerely, C. G. JUNG

[1] The snake that bites its own tail (cf. *Psychology and Alchemy*, Figs. 7, 13, 20, 46, 47, 108, 147, 253). The term is used here as an image of an unconscious circular process without effect on consciousness. But the (o)uroboros as a mandala and image of the alchemical *opus circulare* can symbolize the conscious process of individuation. Cf. *Aion*, pars. 297, 407.

To Hedwig Boye

Dear Dr. Boye,   6 July 1945

So your dreams have come true! Allow me to express my heartfelt sympathy over the great loss you have suffered. The fact that your mother really did die shows that dreams have an objective significance and by all human standards must be regarded as messages. This is wonderful and makes for reconciliation.

Ever sincerely yours, C. G. JUNG

☐ (Handwritten.) The letter is addressed to a refugee from Poland whose mother had stayed behind in Warsaw. In 1944 she had several dreams about the death of her mother. The mother had in fact died shortly after the Warsaw rising of Aug./Sept. 1944. — Cf. her *Menschen mit grossem Schatten* (1945).

To Pastor Max Frischknecht

Dear Pastor Frischknecht,   17 July 1945

Thank you for your letter and essay. I, too, think that your youth is still an encumbrance to you. But it seems to me that certain obligations are laid even upon youth. I have read your essay with interest. As you yourself regard it with a critical eye, I will raise no further objections. I am only interested to know how you come to grips with the fact that in the Old Testament Satan is one of God's angels and a member of the heavenly choir and thus part of the divine substance. (A relative separation first occurs in the Book of Job.) I hope it has become clear to you in the meantime that the archetype, as a psychological datum, does not delineate any historical God and therefore cannot be identified with any existing ideas of God. I can only repeat: I am not a theologian but an empiricist who can establish only the possibility, given by the archetype, of no matter what ideas of God.

I hope you will have an opportunity to make the necessary corrections, since it should be in the interests of the theologian today not to block still further the approaches to an understanding of religion by misconceptions that can so easily be removed. I call it tragic blindness when theologians, of all people, accuse me of psychologism, or—how stupid can they get?—of worshipping the self. The chief difficulty, it seems to me, is that the theologian preaches away just as though he had an old heathen congregation before him that had still heard nothing of the great news from Palestine. By so doing he completely misses the mark with modern man. He would do better to think a bit more so as to make his preaching *understandable*. Why does he go on pouring new wine into old bottles?

Why is he not glad when science tenders him some help? After all, nobody believes any more that His Reverence is filled with the Holy Ghost every Sunday morning. And how does Luther know that the Holy Ghost is not a *sceptic*? This is theological presumptuousness. The spirit bloweth where *it* listeth and not where Calvin with his *providentia specialis*[1] wants it to blow. Does theology still not know the harm it does to the religious life?

Perhaps, my dear Pastor, you will allow an old man, who has had some experience of life and the world, to offer you the above points for reflection. You still have a long stretch of the road before you, and the future will call the theologian to account as never before. Nowadays people want to *understand* and not just be harangued in an edifying manner. I hear over and over again: "Well, I knew ages ago what the parson says about it, but that's no help to me." Why do the young complain that not a flicker of light comes from the Church? This question cannot leave anybody cold who still has some truck with Christian civilization. The theologian today must *know* a bit more about the human soul if he wants to address it. I once told Archbishop Temple:[2] "Send me an intelligent young theologian. I will lead him into the night of the soul so that one of them at last may know what he is actually dealing with." But nobody came. Naturally they knew it all already, and much better. That is why the light has gone out.

Yours sincerely, C. G. JUNG

[1] Calvin's "special providence" is the special operation of the Holy Spirit in the faithful, who are thus raised to a life of holiness.
[2] William Temple (1881–1944), Archbishop of Canterbury.

Anonymous

Dear N.,   19 July 1945

That's the way it is. Life is indeed profit and loss. Whenever the apples perfume the air, paradise is soon coming to an end. You can face eternity properly only when you have "forgotten the world." And if everything turns out all right, it wasn't all that bad. Better to feel the weight of the earth too much than to hang out over the edge of it.

□ (Handwritten.) To a woman.

Everything went very logically and is on the positive side, that is, you have really lived it even though it is not what you actually wanted. It is a hot summer.

I wish you all the best,

Ever sincerely yours, C. G. JUNG

To Hugo Rahner

Dear Professor Rahner, 4 August 1945

I feel the need to thank you at once for your kind birthday letter even before reading your contribution to the Festschrift.[1] I must let you know with all speed how much I enjoyed everything.

I have read your essay on the archetype[2] with great interest. It seems to me that the main difficulty is that you have a different conception of it from the modern scientific one which is the indispensable tool today. I could not possibly reach my contemporaries with a different concept. Of course I fully appreciate your objections if I accept the Scholastic premise, but it seems to me that the Scholastic standpoint is neither adequate nor suitable for the needs of an empirical science. You will realize that it is impossible for me to argue with you personally about this. What would need discussing is the difference of the centuries and of a radically altered view of the world. I won't voice any opinion on the justification for one or the other standpoint since, as a non-philosopher, I do not consider myself competent. I only know the one thing I have already pointed out, that Scholastic language and its presuppositions are no longer appropriate for contemporary man if one wants to give him any understanding of the human psyche. I know this not *a priori* but from repeated experience.

From your essay on magical herbs I have already seen quite enough to whet my curiosity to the highest pitch. I must, however, read the volume in the proper sequence and so far have not got to the core of it, which your study represents. Even so I am convinced that I shall find quite marvellous things in it, and one could not wish for

---

[1] A special *Eranos Jahrbuch* (XII, 1945) published in honour of Jung's 70th birthday, under the title *Studien zum Problem des Archetypischen*. R.'s contribution was "Die seelenheilende Blume, Moly und Mandragora in antiker und christlicher Mystik" (tr. as "Moly and Mandragora in Pagan and Christian Symbolism," in Rahner, *Greek Myths and Christian Mystery*, 1963).

[2] "Archetypus," in *Christliche Kultur*, supplement to the *Neue Zürcher Nachrichten*, 20 July 1945.

a more beautiful birthday present. The fact of your having participated in these festivities in such a friendly and personal way has made a deep impression on me and I am quite particularly grateful to you.

I hope to see you again in Ascona this year and once more shake you by the hand. As soon as I have read your contribution I will write again and give you my impressions. Meanwhile with best greetings and heartiest thanks,

Ever sincerely yours, C. G. JUNG

To Olga Fröbe-Kapteyn

Dear Frau Fröbe,   Bollingen, 20 August 1945

The opus consists of three parts: insight, endurance, and action. Psychology is needed only in the first part, but in the second and third parts moral strength plays the predominant role. Your present situation is the result of pressure of circumstances which are unavoidable. It is *conflicts of duty* that make endurance and action so difficult. Your life's work for Eranos was unavoidable and right. Nevertheless it conflicts with maternal duties which are equally unavoidable and right. The one must exist, and so must the other. There can be no resolution, only patient endurance of the opposites which ultimately spring from your own nature. You yourself are a conflict that rages in itself and against itself, in order to melt its incompatible substances, the male and the female, in the fire of suffering, and thus create that fixed and unalterable form which is the goal of life. Everyone goes through this mill, consciously or unconsciously, voluntarily or forcibly. We are crucified between the opposites and delivered up to the torture until the "reconciling third"[1] takes shape. Do not doubt the rightness of the two sides within you, and let whatever may happen, happen. Admit that your daughter is right in saying you are a bad mother, and defend your duty as a mother towards Eranos. But never forget that Eranos is also the right thing and was latent within you from the beginning. The apparently unendurable conflict is proof of the rightness of your life. A life without inner contradiction is either only half a life or else a life in the Beyond, which is destined only for angels. But God loves human beings more than the angels. With kindest regards,

Yours sincerely, C. G. JUNG

□ (Handwritten.)
[1] The "uniting symbol" as the symbol of creative union.

AUGUST 1945

To Karl Kerényi

Dear Professor Kerényi,   20 August 1945

Your study on the Heros Iatros,[1] filled to the brim and overflowing with meaning, has given me particular joy, for which—albeit with unforgiveable tardiness—I thank you most heartily. I won't mention the numerous reasons for procrastination, but above all I had to read the whole book first. I am always profoundly impressed by the riches of Greek mythology, which have hitherto been presented so paltrily. You touch the fragments with the magic wand of your intuition, and behold! they fly together into recognizable figures. The motif you are dealing with is excitingly rich in associations and full of pregnant allusions. Concerning Machaon[2] there is in alchemy an ancient author (most alchemists were physicians) by the name of Elbo Interfector.[3] The stag[4] also appears as a cognomen of Mercurius or as Actaeon[5] and the wounding plays a great and mysterious role, as indicated in the saying: *bellida pax, vulnus dulce, suave malum.*[6]

I am looking forward to seeing you in Ascona again. With cordial thanks,

Ever sincerely yours, C. G. JUNG

☐ (Handwritten.)
[1] K.'s contribution to the *Festschrift* was "Heros Iatros. Ueber Wandlungen und Symbole des ärztlichen Genius in Griechenland."
[2] Machaon, son of Asklepios, appears in the *Iliad* (2, 721f.) as physician, and is wounded by Paris (11, 505ff.). He had his own cult place at Gerenia.
[3] Cf. *Mysterium Coniunctionis*, par. 316.
[4] *Psychology and Alchemy*, par. 518 and fig. 240.
[5] Actaeon, a keen hunter, was turned into a stag by Artemis as punishment for surprising her while bathing; he was chased and killed by his own hounds.
[6] "A warring peace, a sweet wound, a mild evil" (John Gower, d. 1408, *Confessio Amantis*, ed. G. C. Macaulay, II, 1899–1902, p. 35). These words are used as a motto to the Introduction of "The Psychology of the Transference," CW 16.

To P. W. Martin

[ORIGINAL IN ENGLISH]

Dear Mr. Martin,   20 August 1945

I was very pleased with your kind letter of June 4th. It is long ago since I heard of you last.[1] Happily enough we have been spared in Switzerland. So easily it could have happened that the Germans

[1] Cf. Martin, 20 Aug. 37.

376

would have invaded our country too. It would not have been so easy as France or Austria though. We were decided to fight.

I'm glad to know that you are still interested in the psychology of the unconscious. I know it is exceedingly difficult to write anything definite or descriptive about the progression of psychological states. It always seemed to me as if the real milestones were certain symbolic events characterized by a strong emotional tone. You are quite right, the main interest of my work is not concerned with the treatment of neuroses but rather with the approach to the numinous. But the fact is that the approach to the numinous is the real therapy and inasmuch as you attain to the numinous experiences you are released from the curse of pathology. Even the very disease takes on a numinous character.

I hope it won't take so long any more until travelling becomes possible again. We have been secluded from the rest of the world for about 5 years. In the days before the radio it would have been very bad indeed, but the radio was very helpful in this war. One always could keep in touch with the decent world beyond that infernal hovel of lies and crimes.

Please remember me to Mrs. Martin!

Yours cordially, C. G. JUNG

Anonymous

[ORIGINAL IN ENGLISH]

Dear Mrs. N.,   31 August 1945

Above all I must ask your pardon for the considerable delay of my answer to your letter of March '45. The moment peace came a real avalanche of letters descended upon me. Before that I was safely secluded from contact with the world and I was spared many hundreds of letters. Now I am in the frying pan, particularly so since my 70th birthday, when the flood of letters became even worse. Ever since my illness I can never get through with my correspondence and I suffer from a chronic bad conscience. Now you know under what conditions I'm writing to you.

I must thank you for kindly sending me Read's book about Education and Art.[1] Unfortunately I'm unable to share your enthusiasm. I am not particularly fond of the famous potpourri: Psychology-Art-Education. Each thing in itself is quite nice, but together it becomes

[1] Herbert Read, *Education through Art* (1943).

377

an awful sauce. I'm sorry, I'm too critical, but I cannot overcome this idiosyncrasy.

. . .

I'm glad to know that you managed to get through this terrible war without serious mishap. I was glad of the news about people in England. The insular feeling we developed in Switzerland during the war is decidedly persistent. We had the feeling as if we were on an island of reason and mental balance and outside there was nonsense. It simplified the world considerably. Of course we cannot maintain such an attitude for ever, but for the time being it is not yet far from being right. We got the necessary shock from the atomic bomb, yet cannot do anything about it. I heard several people saying: Well it would be quite right if they would blow the earth and everything upon it down to hell for ever!

Hoping you are always in good health, I remain,

Yours sincerely, C. G. JUNG

To J. B. Rhine

[ORIGINAL IN ENGLISH]

Dear Dr. Rhine,   18 September 1945

Your letter[1] was a great joy to me. I have often thought of you in these last years and I also often mentioned your name and your experiments to many people.

I wish I could fulfil your wish[2] but having a scientific conscience I feel very hesitant about it since, being a doctor, my observations are all of a clinical kind, which means that they are unavoidably subjective to a certain extent, and never systematic as they are all isolated cases and facts which form a rather incoherent mass that would look like a collection of anecdotes. I despise such a way of dealing with this matter and I would much prefer to be in a position to deal with coherent material collected along certain scientific lines. Of course, I have had quite a number of noteworthy experiences, and you know how it is: the circumstances and persons involved, though

[1] R. recalled "the delightful occasion of the luncheon party in New York." It took place in the summer of 1937 when Jung was in the U.S.A. for his Terry Lectures at Yale, and was the only time he and Rhine met personally.

[2] That Jung write down his observations and reflections on parapsychological problems. He did so to some extent in "Synchronicity: An Acausally Connecting Principle" (orig. 1952), and also in Memories, esp. ch. XI: "On Life after Death."

indispensably important for the explanation of the facts, cannot be described in a way that would convince the outsider. It would all look hopelessly haphazard and pretty flimsy. As you assume, I have thought a great deal about parapsychological facts and I tried to establish certain connections, but I always refrain from talking publicly about such matters for the above-mentioned reasons. But, seeing your point of view, I'm quite willing to tell you whatever I have thought if that is of any value to you. In this case I should propose that you put certain questions to me[3] about things that interest you and I will try to formulate my answers so far as I'm able to do so. It might give me a certain lead to talk about matters which otherwise wouldn't occur to me.

Parapsychology plays a subtle part in psychology because it lurks everywhere behind the surface of things. But, as the facts are difficult to catch, their theoretical aspect is still more elusive on account of its transcendent character. When certain people hold that it is something like a fourth dimension, they don't seem to be very far off the truth.

During the war my health wasn't too good. As a matter of fact I was seriously ill and having reached the biblical age of 70, I'm none too efficient any more, though I have done a decent amount of scientific work lately. I can't omit to warn you that I perhaps don't know so much about parapsychology as you suspect me to do. It is not exactly my field, and therefore I don't feel very competent to talk much about it. There is only a faint possibility that you will find something of value in the maze of my thoughts.

Hoping you are always in good health, I remain,

Yours sincerely, C. G. JUNG

[3] R. took up this suggestion in a letter of 30 Oct.; Jung's answers appear in his letter to Rhine of Nov. 45.

To Susan R. Bach

[ORIGINAL IN ENGLISH]

Dear Mrs. Bach,   26 September 1945

Thank you for your kind birthday wishes. I was very interested in your "report" of what you have been doing during these years of war.

☐ Analytical psychologist, originally in Berlin, practising since 1939 in London. Cf. her *Spontaneous Paintings of Severely Ill Patients* (Documenta Geigy, Acta Psychosomatica, Basel, 1969).

As you rightly suspect I'm rather flooded with letters and can only gradually work my way through an avalanche of paper.

I'm really grateful to you that you tell me how much my work has been of help in your very specific work with people uprooted through the accidents of war. I always had a sort of hunch that whatever I had learnt about the unconscious was due to a somewhat similar but internal catastrophe in my psychic neighborhood and that the war outside was a repetition on the collective scale. Although I was fully aware of the most incredible powers of evil lurking in the depths, I never expected such a gigantic outburst of abysmal horrors.

I congratulate you on your splendid work which must be a great satisfaction to yourself.

Yours sincerely, c. g. j u n g

To William G. Mather

[O R I G I N A L   I N   E N G L I S H]

Dear Professor Mather,   26 September 1945

Your letter interested me very much. Your idea that primitive methods or religious exercises have something to do with the experience of the unconscious is perfectly correct. I suppose you mean to say that these people are white people and not Hopi Indians or something of the sort that celebrate snake dances. If I'm right in assuming that you mean white sectarians,[1] then it is obviously a matter of the phenomenon peculiar to colonial settlers.

Inasmuch as civilized white people settle down on virgin soil their unconscious assimilates the peculiar nature of the country. So much so that even their children begin to resemble to a certain extent the autochthonous population of that country. In Africa and in India you observe a violent resistance in the white man against the primitive or exotic country in which he lives. In Africa, for instance, I observed that the settlers there either hate that country or they just love it. In either case (if they are real settlers, and not only transient officials that serve their 20 years of exile) they *nolens volens* begin to get assimilated by the soil and they develop a very curious mentality. It is just as if the unconscious part of their psyche was sinking down into the peculiar phenomenon "going black."[2] You can observe

☐ Professor of agricultural economics, Pennsylvania State College.
[1] M. asked Jung's opinion about white religious sects in America.
[2] The observed fact that white people living in a coloured or primitive environ-

380

how these people get lured away unconsciously from their civilized sphere.

Even in America you can observe similar things: for instance the students' most remarkable initiation ceremonies that above all resemble Indian rituals. No wonder if sects show similar symptoms: in the case you mention the relation to snakes which always represents the integration of the chthonic (earth-) element. To the same chapter belongs the positive or negative emphasis on sex. It is practically the same whether you emphasize sex through affirmation or negation. It simply means sex is all-important. If it is denied it simply means the chthonic element is all-important, yet in a hostile way. In the other case it is understood as something positive. The torture of the body, for instance, which is so frequent with primitives, shows merely the importance of the body. And very often you cannot tell which is the greater pleasure: granting chthonic lusts or denying them.

All this has nothing to do with theology or other spiritual factors. It is chiefly the question of the overwhelming tendency of the unconscious to get rooted in the soil. You can observe similar phenomena in Europe, where nature can have an overwhelming influence, as for instance the sea or barren islands or lonely parts of the country or mountainous regions as in Switzerland. In Switzerland we have many sects which have something in common with those of Wales and other mountainous parts of Britain. Invariably they have mostly a very peculiar relation to sex either in a positive or a negative way.

Hoping I have answered your question to your satisfaction, I remain,

Yours sincerely, C. G. JUNG

---

ment unconsciously take on the characteristics of the natives. Cf. "Mind and Earth," CW 10, and "Complications of American Psychology," ibid., par. 962.

To Father Victor White, O.P.

[ORIGINAL IN ENGLISH]

Dear Father White,   26 September 1945

It was a great pleasure and surprise to me to receive your interesting articles[1] about my psychology. Owing to the fact that I celebrated

□ (1902–60); Dominican priest; in 1945 he was professor of dogmatic theology at Blackfriars, Oxford. Cf. his God and the Unconscious (1952, with a foreword by Jung, now in CW 11), and Soul and Psyche (1960). (See pl. VI.)

my 70th birthday this summer I have not yet emerged from the floods of correspondence that have invaded me. Thus I can only thank you today for your kindness and beg your pardon that I am so late in answering your letter.

I'm highly interested in the point of view the Church takes with reference to my work. I had many discussions with Catholic priests in this country too and it is on my instigation that Catholic scholars have been invited to the Eranos lectures[2] of which you presumably have heard. We enjoy now the collaboration of an extremely competent scholar of patristic literature, Professor Hugo Rahner, S.J., of Innsbruck University. Quite a number of Catholic publications[3] have been occupied with my psychology in this country too and there are some among them which are really very understanding. I must say that I never would have expected so much appreciation and real understanding from the theological quarter. Owing to rather obvious reasons Protestant theologians are rather reticent and they don't know yet whether I should be condemned as a heretic or depreciated as a mystic. As you know, mysticism and hereticism enjoy about the same bad reputation in Protestantism. So there is not much hope for me left from that side.

I shall certainly read your articles with greatest interest and then I will avail myself of the pleasure of writing to you again in order to tell you what my reactions were. For the time being I can only thank you for your kindness.

Yours sincerely, c. g. J U N G

[1] *The Frontiers of Theology and Psychology* (The Guild of Pastoral Psychology, Lecture No. 19, 1942); "St. Thomas Aquinas and Jung's Psychology," *Blackfriars*, XXV:291 (June 1944); "Psychotherapy and Ethics," ibid., XXVI:305 (Aug. 1945); and "A Postscript" to the last-named article, being a reply to criticisms of Jung's attitude to religion contained in J. C. Flugel, *Man, Morals, and Society* (1945). The first and last of these papers are included in revised form in *God and the Unconscious* (ch. IV, V, VIII; cf. Preface, pp. ixf.).

[2] Ernesto Buonaiuti (1881–1946), professor of the history of early Christianity at the U. of Rome; Henri-Charles Puech, professor of the history of religion at the Collège de France; Hugo Rahner, professor of church history and patrology at the U. of Innsbruck.

[3] Cf. Gebhard Frei, "Die Bedeutung der Forschung über das Unterbewusstsein," *Neue Schweizer Rundschau*, July 1943. Jung may also have had in mind the meeting of the Philosophische Gesellschaft Innerschweiz in Jan. 1945, with lectures by A. W. Willwoll, "Vom Unbewussten im Aufbau des religiösen Erlebens," and Frei, "Die Religionskunde und das Unbewusste," both in Emil Spiess (ed.), *Rätsel der Seele* (1946).

To Father Victor White

[ORIGINAL IN ENGLISH]

My dear Father White,   5 October 1945

In the meantime I have finished reading the pamphlets you kindly have sent to me. My first reaction was: what a pity that you live in England and that I don't have you at my elbow when I am blundering in the wide field of theological knowledge. You must grant me attenuating circumstances though: besides all the other things I had to learn, I arrived only very late at the treasure-house of patristic wisdom, so late in fact that my limited powers didn't suffice any more to acquire all that would be needed to elucidate and explain the perplexities of modern psychological experience. Excuse the irreverential pun: you are to me a white raven inasmuch as you are the only theologian I know of who has really understood something of what the problem of psychology in our present world means. You have seen its enormous implications. I cannot tell you how glad I am that I know a man, a theologian, who is conscientious enough to weigh my opinions on the basis of a careful study of my writings!

My temperamental empiricism has its reasons. I began my career with repudiating everything that smelt of belief. That explains my critical attitude in my *Psychology of the Unconscious*. You should know that this book was written by a psychiatrist for the purpose of submitting the necessary material to his psychiatric colleagues, material which would demonstrate to them the importance of religious symbolism. My audience then was a thoroughly materialistic crowd,[1] and I would have defeated my own ends if I had set out with a definite creed or with definite metaphysical assertions. I was not and I did not want to be anything else but one of them. My principle was always not to seek the place where I might do something useful, but to do it where I actually was. I was impressed with their utter lack of knowledge in matters of symbolism and I wanted to do my best to provide it for them. Only too late I have discovered that it wasn't my colleagues at all but very different people who became interested in my work. I have tried to accommodate myself to the psychiatric and medical mind, hardened and often made cynical through the relentless onslaught of brutal and cruel facts and the depravity of mankind.

---

[1] Jung's early association with the psychoanalytical school came to an end with the publication of *Wandlungen und Symbole der Libido*, 1912; see Freud, 13 Dec. 10, n. 5.

Thus, when I said that God is a complex,[2] I meant to say: Whatever He is, He is *at least* a very tangible complex. You can say, He is an illusion, but He is at least a psychological fact. I surely never intended to say: He is *nothing else* but a complex. Naturally when my book got into the hands of readers outside my psychiatric sphere they read it with very different eyes. Hence many mistakes! My book was originally nothing but a reprint from a psychiatric periodical,[3] which was supposed to be read by doctors chiefly. Concerning my gnoseological standpoint at that time please see note 42, p. 307, Engl. edit. of *Psychology of the Unconscious.*[4]

You have rendered justice to my empirical and practical standpoint throughout. I consider this as a very meritorious act, since most of my philosophically or theologically minded readers overlook my empiricism completely. I never allow myself to make statements about the divine entity, since that would be a transgression beyond the limit of science. It would therefore be unfair to criticize my opinions as if they were a philosophical system. My personal view in this matter is that man's vital energy or libido is the divine pneuma all right and it was this conviction which it was my secret purpose to bring into the vicinity of my colleagues' understanding. When you want to talk to scientists you cannot start with a religious creed. You have to show the facts and let them draw their own conclusions. You also cannot say that man's goal is actually realized in God, you must again show facts demonstrating in what the goal is realized. What you can show in this respect is the symbol of the self, a well-defined psychological phenomenon, which anybody may call God, but the scientists cannot prove it to be God. As a scientist I must give a wide berth to anything dogmatic or metaphysical, since it is not the scientist's task to preach the Gospel. But it is precisely what the theologian has to say, namely

---

[2] Cf. *Symbols of Transformation*, par. 128: "Psychologically . . . God is the name for a complex of ideas grouped round a powerful feeling." Also ibid., par. 89 and n. 29. (The passages were also in the original 1912 edn.; see *Psychology of the Unconscious*, New York, 1916, pp. 95, 71; London, 1921, pp. 52, 38.)

[3] *Wandlungen und Symbole* first appeared in the *Jahrbuch für psychoanalytische und psychopathologische Forschungen*, III (1911) and IV (1912).

[4] "Here it is not to be forgotten we are moving entirely in the territory of psychology, which in no way is allied to transcendentalism, either in positive or negative relation. It is a question here of a relentless fulfilment of the standpoint of the theory of cognition, established by Kant, not merely for the theory, but, what is more important, for the practice . . ." (*Psychology of the Unconscious*, 1916, p. 529, n. 42; 1921, p. 307, n. 42); Jung deleted this note in *Symbols of Transformation*.

that the dogma is the hitherto most perfect answer to and formulation of the most relevant items in the objective psyche and that God has worked all these things in man's soul. The scientist however cannot prove such an assertion, he can only try his best in his limited sphere.

I sympathize fully with you when you say: "The task before us is gigantic indeed."[5] It is enormous and I marvel at the intellectual pachydermia of those who ought to know better and who didn't take notice apparently, or worse—who try to get rid of the octopus by the most futile arguments. I have frequent discussions with Catholic as well as Protestant theologians. As a rule they are astonishingly innocent of actual psychological experience and often they seem to have forgotten the wisdom of the Fathers. It is all very well to have it summarized most beautifully by St. Thomas Aquinas,[6] but when it comes to the interpretation of man's living soul you need actual knowledge. It is far from me to depreciate concepts and formulas. On the contrary I envy you and all those enjoying full possession of Scholastic philosophy and I would surely be among the first to welcome an explicit attempt to integrate the findings of psychology into the ecclesiastical doctrine. I am sure I should draw the greatest benefit from it. I am grateful for every hint you dropped in your papers. I was for instance most interested in what you said about the problem of the Third Person.[7] I wish you would enlighten me about this subject a bit more. Could you tell me about the sources where I can find more enlightenment? You can perhaps imagine my feelings of inadequacy when I have to tackle such a problem at short notice. It is usually so, that I keep quiet for years about such intricate matters as for instance the Trinity. But all of a sudden the subject comes up in a discussion or in a lecture and somebody deals with it in a really inadequate way, then I feel somebody ought to say something more to the point and I am launched utterly unprepared, only supported by my experience with practically nothing on the other, the theological side. There I would need some solid theological help. I realize that it can come only from the Catholic side, as the *sola fide* standpoint[8] of the Protestant has lost the tradition of the doctrine

[5] "Psychotherapy and Ethics," p. 298.

[6] In White's "St. Thomas Aquinas and Jung's Psychology," pp. 209–19. Thomas Aquinas was a member of the Dominican Order, founded by St. Dominic in 1216.

[7] *The Frontiers of Theology and Psychology*, p. 18.

[8] "By faith alone": Luther's teaching of justification by faith alone, based on the

too much to be useful in disentangling the knots in the empirical material. This collaboration has been realized to a certain extent as I enjoy the most valuable help of Prof. Hugo Rahner, S.J., at Innsbruck University. He is an authority on the ἑρμηνευτική [9] of the Fathers. But I see him only rarely and it is most difficult to find out how far his psychological understanding reaches. I think he is too careful. Do you know the *Eranos-Jahrbücher*? Do you read German? There is stuff for you. If you read German I should like to send you my book *Psychology and Alchemy*, much better than the badly translated *Integration of the Personality*,[10] which was forced out of my hands by the thrift and "pep" of an American publisher. There will be an English edition of *Psychology and Alchemy* within the next year.[11]

I owe you special thanks for kindly remembering my seventieth birthday. The Eranos circle has dedicated to me a Festschrift in which you will find a brilliant paper by Rahner about Moly and Mandragora[12] and an equally remarkable essay by Layard on the subject of primitive marriage-classes and the virgin archetype.[13]

You accuse me of repudiating the divine transcendence altogether. This is not quite correct. I merely omit it, since I am unable to prove it. I don't preach, I try to establish psychological facts. I can confirm and prove the interrelation of the God-image with other parts of the psyche, but I cannot go further without committing the error of a metaphysical assertion, which is far beyond my scope. I am not a theologian and I have nothing to say about the nature of God. There is no place for subjective confessions in science. Whatever I say about "God" is said about the image *expressis verbis*. And the image *is* relative, as you yourself have stated.

It is again a matter of to-whom-you talk. My public does not consist of theologians but of utterly worldly, educated people of our day. When you talk of God, they do not know of *what* you talk, since such ideas have been dismissed long ago as nebulous fantasies. I show

---

theology of St. Paul, as against the then current Roman doctrine of justification by works.

[9] Hermeneutics, science of interpretation, more especially of the Bible.

[10] *The Integration of the Personality* (New York, 1939; London, 1940). Chs. 1–3 now in CW 9, i; 4–5 in CW 12; ch. 6 in CW 17.

[11] Actually it appeared in 1953. Cf. Rhine, 18 Feb. 53, n. 4.

[12] Cf. Rahner, 4 Aug. 45, n. 1.

[13] John Layard, "The Incest Taboo and the Virgin Archetype," *Eranos Jahrbuch* XII (1945).

facts to them and not metaphysical assertions which they cannot grasp. If I were talking to peasants I certainly would talk about God, since I know that they know of what I am talking. *It is of the highest importance* that the educated and "enlightened" public should know religious truth as a thing living in the human soul and not as an abstruse and unreasonable relic of the past. People must be taught to see where they come in, otherwise you never bridge the gulf between the educated mind and the world of dogmatic ideas, which they comprehend nowhere and which moreover offend their reason. If the Reformers for instance had ever understood what the Holy Mass is or what the *ritus* in general stands for, they would certainly not have abandoned it. The appalling lack of understanding threatens the Christian religion with complete oblivion. You cannot preach to a man who does not understand the language. To shout and to repeat makes no sense. But you feel as I do, that the theologian ought to learn a new language. What if St. Paul had talked on the ἀγορά [14] as if he were in a synagogue? Understanding begins with the individual mind and this means psychology. It is a gigantic task indeed to create a new approach to an old truth. More than once I have put the question to my theological friends: what about new wine in old skins? The old way of interpreting has itself to be interpreted, this time with the help of science. This method can reach the modern mind as I have seen in many cases. I do not combat the Christian truth, I am only arguing with the modern mind. We have known for long and sufficiently well how things ought to be, but we do not know how to bring them about. This is my main concern. People are not to be lured any more by the promises of Heaven and Hell, they want to understand. I cannot "tell" my patient, I have to seek him and I must learn his language and think his thoughts, until he knows that I understand him correctly. Then only is he ready to understand me and at the same time the strange language of the unconscious, that tells him of eternal truths, and incidentally he will discover that he has heard similar things before. That's the practical way. But to get there you have to avoid "suggestions."

Well—a long letter! Not my style at all. "It" has made an exception in your case, my dear Father, because "it" has appreciated your conscientious and far-sighted work.

Yours sincerely, C. G. JUNG

[14] = market-place.

To Arthur Gloor

Dear Herr Gloor,   29 October 1945

I have glanced through your manuscript[1] and concentrated chiefly on the part where you speak of psychology. It is not quite clear what you want me to do. I can only confirm that the use you make of psychological viewpoints is essentially correct in so far as you concern yourself with the personality of the artist. You judge him, it seems to me, very fairly, also the Romantics in general. It is another matter when you come to the psychology of art, but your hero seems to have done nothing of boast in this field. The work of art has its own specific psychology[2] which is sometimes notably different from the psychology of the artist. Were it not so, the work of art would not be autonomous.

Your opinion that the unconscious is "kept under" by the pursuit of art might be improved on as follows: So long as Christian dogma expressed the essence of the unconscious in well-nigh perfect fashion, the unconscious had no chance to manifest itself except in a purely personalistic and therefore insignificant way. In Romanticism it appeared as a collective phenomenon, but Romanticism is not the first symptom of this slipping of the unconscious out of the well-structured dogmatic forms of the Middle Ages. Very early on we had Christian mysticism and alchemy with its heterodoxy as manifestations of the unconscious in the grand manner.

. . .

It always amuses me when people say they dismiss psychology. It would never occur to me to dismiss literary studies or aesthetics because they too are concerned with certain aspects of the human psyche, and I can never understand with what justification my colleagues in other professional fields can dismiss psychology out of hand. I would never dream of putting psychology in the place of aesthetics or the like. On the other hand it is obvious to every child that the artist has a human psyche whose qualities are at least similar to those of ordinary mortals. I understand the resistance better in the case of philosophers, since psychology saws off the branch they are

☐ Zurich.
[1] Of E.T.A. Hoffmann. *Der Dichter der entwurzelten Geistigkeit* (1947).
[2] Cf. "On the Relation of Analytical Psychology to Poetry," "Psychology and Literature," "Ulysses," "Picasso," all in CW 15.

sitting on by wickedly robbing them of the illusion that they represent the absolute spirit.

Yours truly, C. G. JUNG

To Laurence J. Bendit

[ORIGINAL IN ENGLISH]

Dear Dr. Bendit, 12 November 1945

I have read your essay on Paranormal Cognition[1] (P.C.) with greatest interest and I fully agree with you in all your general statements. There are only some minor points which I want to comment on. The fact, for instance, that you couldn't find a word about the famous ψ^2 in my writings is merely due to the misfortune that a considerable part of my work is not translated. You would have found not only an acknowledgement of "telepathy" but also an example of P.C. in Kerényi and Jung: *Einführung in das Wesen der Mythologie* (Amsterdam 1941, p. 230 f.).[3]

I'm acquainted with P.C. and I have seen many a case of it. The reason why I haven't said more about it publicly is that I don't like to talk about things which are difficult to prove.

I include P.C. in the concept of intuition,[4] "perception by the way of the unconscious." Sensation[5] is perception in absolute time and space, intuition is perception in relative time and space, or "elastic" time[6] and ditto space. Dunne[7] is by no means the first to have recognized the prophetic quality of dreams. Any old medicine man 10,000 years ago has done so.

What's wrong with intuition? Is there any difference between "perception by the way of the unconscious" (i.e., you don't know how you get it) and P.C. which is also "perception in an unknown way"?

☐ M.D., British writer on psychological and religious subjects.

[1] *Paranormal Cognition, Its Place in Human Psychology* (1944).

[2] The Greek letter *psi*, abbreviation for *psi* phenomena = psychic or parapsychological processes such as extra-sensory perception (ESP), psychokinesis (PK), and telekinesis (TK), alleged movements without physical contact or at a distance.

[3] "The Psychological Aspects of the Kore," CW 9, i, pars. 334–8.

[4] *Psychological Types*, Def. 35.

[5] Ibid., Def. 47.

[6] "Synchronicity," CW 8, par. 840.

[7] *An Experiment with Time.*

Or does P.C. claim to know what P.C. is? I confess I don't know how to make a difference between intuition and P.C.

I like your little book, and I appreciate your unorthodox attitude in that case where it was chiefly a matter of an insufficient adaptation to P.C. I suppose you have also seen cases where P.C. developed under the influence of analytical treatment? I am fully aware of the extraordinary importance of such phenomena, which transcend our actual means of understanding. They give you a certain feeling of hopelessness. This has been one of the main reasons why I tried to explore the unconscious from another side, which seemed to be more accessible than the "parapsychological" phenomena, which are, at least for the time being, far beyond the reach of our actual mental capacity, although I always kept them in mind and left a place for them in my definition of intuition. Physiology has not done so yet, but it ought to leave room for paraphysiology, which comes in where it is a question of materialization. I have seen enough of this phenomenon to convince me entirely of its existence. Being an honorary member of the British and American SPR[8] I have read almost all the important publications in this field. All this on top of my own experiences has led me to the conclusion that space as well as time and matter are relative to the psyche, i.e., they are to a certain extent psychic functions. I discussed this problem with Rhine whose experiments with the space and time factor prove my hypothesis with sufficient evidence. I don't know whether Rhine has already published his experiments concerning the psychic influences on mechanical dice-throwing.[9] They prove, as far as I know, the extension of psychic relativity to matter. If this is true, my hypothesis would be at least a point of view from which a theoretical handling of P.C. and paraphysiology could start.

I should like to send you something in exchange for your book but unfortunately I have no copies left of my English translations. Not knowing whether you are sufficiently acquainted with the German language I don't dare to send you one of my German publications, but let me know in case you do read German.

Sincerely yours, C. G. JUNG

[8] Society for Psychical Research.
[9] Described in Rhine, *The Reach of the Mind* (1948).

To Pastor H. Wegmann

Dear Pastor Wegmann,   20 November 1945

Best thanks for your letter. The position you have taken interests me greatly; it gives me a chance to look more closely at my own attitude. You are right, of course: Meyer catholicizes.[1] As you say, he takes the Scriptures *tale quale*—ostensibly: but, if I am not deceived, he has a streak of mysticism which gives his picture a special character. The result is that the *tale quale* standpoint appears almost *irrelevant* compared with his supramundane vision of an interpretation that comes as close as possible to the ancient Church. I find him unpalatable only when he modernizes in style and language and thus steps out of his "ekstasis." When I visualize the content of the book as understood in its best sense, I discover something in it that is somehow similar to my own way of looking at things. Not that I believe in verbal inspiration or that I find no contradictions and human peccadillos in the text; but the revelatory character imputed to it and the sometimes farcical thoughts are an integral part of his vision. And it is this that interests me in its totality. When Meyer amplifies and interprets he speaks to me out of its fullness; indeed, it is as though he were caught up uncritically in this visionary world and were ambling along its highways and byways, laden with everything that the centuries have piled on top of this primordial phenomenon. A strange and rare spectacle in modern Protestantism, methinks, so far as my limited knowledge goes!

At the Paracelsus Jubilee in 1941 I heard a Benedictine sermon, during which the jackanapes took it into his head to present the Catholic view as "agréable." How much better it would have been if he had been inspired by a supramundane vision of the nature and attributes of the Trinity and so conveyed some idea of that primordial phenomenon from which all Christian doctrine originally sprang. "*Et mortuus est Dei filius, prorsus credibile est, quia ineptum est. Et sepultus resurrexit; certum est, quia impossibile est.*"[2]

For the primordial is indeed the supramundane, which the world

---

☐ Zurich.

[1] Cf. W. Meyer, I *Korinther* 11–16, *Leib Christi* (1945). He was a follower of Karl Barth (cf. Oeri, 4 Jan. 29, n. 7).

[2] "And the son of God died, which is immediately credible because it is absurd. And buried He rose again, which is certain because it is impossible." Tertullian, *De carne Christi*, II, 5.

knoweth not and is incapable of judging, which cannot be got at with any logic or criticism, and which can only be amplified and interpreted but never made "agréable." I only wish the theologians would accept the Kabbala[3] and India and China as well, so as to proclaim still more clearly how God reveals himself. If in the process Christianity should be relativized up to a point, this would only be *ad majorem Dei gloriam* and would do no harm to the meaning of the Christian doctrine. For all this is true and much else besides. Minor inconsistencies and obscurities can be left to the purists; but the great incompatibles, such as the being and non-being of God, his person and his non-person, and the *coincidentia oppositorum*[4] in general, belong to the picture of the divine paradox.

It seems to me strangely beside the point if Protestants think they can adopt a critical, deliberative attitude towards God's revelation in its totality. I think one can only speak out of the torrent of divine images, and in such a way that the continuity of tradition is not broken, otherwise one gets unawares into the *cul de sac* of subjective opinion. *Quod semper, quod ubique, quod ab omnibus creditur*[5] should be the guideline for the theologian, since he is speaking out of and to the depths of an *anima naturaliter christiana*[6] which recognizes no subjective deals with God, even though the individual psyche enforces them because all life dwells only in individual carriers. But it is just this fragmentation that has to be compensated by a continual recollection of the *veritates catholicae.*

It seems to me that Meyer has lived up to this need as fully as possible, if not in all particulars then at least in the general sense that he is speaking on a plane beyond the empirical Church and its ecclesiasticism. I sense that he is dreaming of a catholicity which wants to embrace the tree of the Church as a whole. To what extent his attempt is a success or a failure I, an incompetent layman, cannot judge.

[3] Cf. Nanavutty, 11 Nov. 48, n. 5.

[4] Nicholas of Cusa (Cusanus) (1401–64), defined God as a *coincidentia oppositorum* (cf. "The Psychology of the Transference," CW 16, par. 537). This concept, transferred to the psychological plane, plays an important role in Jung's psychology as the "union of opposites." As a symbol of wholeness or psychic totality, the self is the supreme *coincidentia oppositorum* (cf. *Symbols of Transformation,* par. 576).

[5] Cf. Anon., 6 Jan. 43, n. 3.

[6] "The soul is by nature Christian." Tertullian used this definition in *Apologeticus adversus gentes pro Christianis.*

I should be glad to hear from you sometime what you think of my "thoughts out of season."[7] With best regards,

Yours sincerely, c. g. j u n g

7 Allusion to Nietzsche's *Unzeitgemässe Betrachtungen* (tr., *Thoughts Out of Season*).

Anonymous

Dear Herr N.,   23 November 1945

When moral weakness[1] is coupled with a relatively good intelligence, as seems to be the case with you, one must use this intelligence when the ethical sense fails. This trite bit of wisdom cannot teach you any psychotherapy, but you must understand it and simply apply it yourself. If you can make this minimal use of your intelligence, you are saved. If not, not.

Yours truly, c. g. j u n g

☐ Switzerland.
1 N., who was awaiting trial for a petty offence, asked for advice as to how not to succumb to similar temptations in the future (he was at the time on probation for a similar offence committed two years before).

Answers to Rhine's Questions   [ORIGINAL IN ENGLISH]
November 1945

1) I consider parapsychology as a branch or discipline of general psychology, more especially of the psychology of the unconscious.

☐ As suggested by Jung (Rhine, 18 Sept. 45) R. submitted the following questions:
1. What do you think is the proper relation of parapsychology to the general science of psychology?
2. What is your view of the mind-body relation, and to what extent is parapsychology of help on this question?
3. What, in your judgment, has parapsychology taught us regarding the character of the human psyche?
4. To what extent do you see a useful relation between parapsychology and psychiatry?
5. Can you interpret the experimental findings of parapsychology in extrasensory perception and its apparent reach beyond the limits of space and time as we think of them, in terms of your views of the human personality? I would par-

2) The psychology of the unconscious has much to say about the mind-body relation (psychogenic disturbances of the physiological functions). Parapsychology is apt to demonstrate the existence of phenomena of a psychic nature, which influence material objects or create physical bodies in a place where no such or similar matter was before. Thus parapsychology may elucidate the problem of how the living is shaped and continuously reshaped through the unconscious psyche.

3) Parapsychology has shown above all that the psyche has an aspect of a relative-temporal and relative-spatial character. It has shown, moreover, that the unconscious psyche has a faculty to influence matter detached from bodily contact and to assemble matter beyond the reach of the body to such a degree that it appears as a physical body perceptible to our senses as well as to the photographic plate.

4) I see, for the time being at least, no "useful" connection between parapsychology and psychiatry. It is as yet a merely scientific problem, but as such of the highest importance. Parapsychological phenomena appear not infrequently in the beginning of psychoses, perhaps less frequently during the course of such diseases.

5) I can explain extra-sensory perception only through the working hypothesis of the relativity of time and space. They seem to be *psychically* relative, i.e., what one calls absolute space, for instance, only exists in the world of macrophysical aspects. In the microphysical world the relativity of space and time is an established fact. The psyche, inasmuch as it produces phenomena of a non-spatial or a non-temporal character, seems to belong to the microphysical world. This would also explain the obvious non-spatial nature of psychic existences such as thought etc. and the fact of precognition. In so far as the psyche is an energic phenomenon, it has mass, but mass of microphysical extension or weight. From this fact we can derive material effects of the psyche.

As the relativity of time and space includes the relativity of causality, and as the psyche partakes of relative time-space, it also relativizes causality and therefore enjoys, in so far as it is microphysical, an at least relative independence of absolute causality. (Chinese philosophy says that as long as things are in the North-East, i.e., before

---

ticularly appreciate having your account of how precognition can be explained in your terms. Does this allow for volitional freedom?
Jung's answers give his preliminary formulations which were clarified seven years later in his work on synchronicity.

they have risen, they can be altered. When they have entered the East, they take their unalterable course.) The fact that the future can be occasionally foreseen does not exclude freedom in general, but only in this particular case. Freedom could become doubtful only if everything could be foreseen.

Viewed from the psychological standpoint, extra-sensory perception appears as a manifestation of the *collective unconscious*. This particular psyche behaves as if it were *one* and not as if it were split up into many individuals. It is *non-personal*. (I call it the "objective psyche.") It is the same everywhere and at all times. (If it were not so, comparative psychology would be impossible.) As it is not limited to the person, it is also not limited to the body. It manifests itself therefore not only in human beings but also at the same time in animals and even in physical circumstances. (Cf. the oracle technique of the *I Ching* and character horoscopes.) I call these latter phenomena the synchronicity of archetypal events. For instance, I walk with a woman patient in a wood. She tells me about the first dream in her life that had made an everlasting impression upon her. She had seen a spectral fox coming down the stairs in her parental home. At this moment a real fox comes out of the trees not 40 yards away and walks quietly on the path ahead of us for several minutes. The animal behaves as if it were a partner in the human situation. (One fact is no fact, but when you have seen many, you begin to sit up.)

. . .

The bread-knife is still in my possession.[1] The table is gone.

[1] Cf. Rhine, 27 Nov. 34.

To Pastor H. Wegmann

Dear Pastor Wegmann,   6 December 1945

Your standpoint, I think, is sufficiently clear. I have nothing against it in principle, since Protestantism stands or falls by it. There must be individual freedom in Biblical exegesis. The only question seems to be whether this freedom should be exclusive or not. Being gripped by Christ, as you yourself say, is no unambiguous matter. Even those who persecute him are gripped by him. For one person he is a human being, for another God.

Now, the sermon is not a dialogue between two individuals but an address to a collectivity consisting of widely divergent minds. Hence, quite rightly, *the* gospel should be preached, i.e., something that has the support of a consensus. One can, it seems to me, go to extremes in two opposite directions: one man preaching his subjective standpoint, the other moving exclusively along traditional lines. The one stirs up polemics, the other peters out in conventionality. One need not, however, go to extremes, but only remember that the community has different needs. Thus the fact that there is a genuine religiosity in the Catholic Church proves the existence of a need for fixed and immovable ideas and forms. But you also come across this need with Protestants, particularly as the Bible guarantees no solid foundation.

You mention for instance the Book of Job. For every thinking person the question arises: What about God's omniscience? What, above all, about his morality? He dickers with the devil, lets himself be bamboozled by him and torments the wretched Job simply because he is unsure of himself. It is as if a potter made a bet with his apprentice as to whether the pot he had fashioned would go kaput if he hurled it to the ground. What does the pot, which in this case is a human being, say to that? What does it mean when he calls upon God to help him against God? And how does this conception of God square with the New Testament one? How, come to that, does the layman square it with the ambiguous figure of Christ, not only with the discrepancy between the Synoptic and the Johannine Christ but also with the biographically elusive, so-called "personal" figure? It took many centuries of the most strenuous mental effort to produce anything like a unified conception which a "keen" Protestantism deems itself entitled to cold-shoulder.

This discontinuity gives me much food for thought. I always have the feeling of being torn up by the roots. Protestantism *pur sang* strikes me as something dynamic but unbalanced which, lacking a counterweight, plunges ahead and dissolves into countless subjectivisms. If I had any say in the matter I would suggest calling this manifestation of the *individuation process*, now emerging more and more clearly, no longer a *denomination* and not squeezing it into an ostensible Church, since Protestantism is by its very nature anti-ecclesiastical. A Church must have a common foundation, and that foundation is certainly not the Bible nor is it the figure of Christ, which has provoked the most divergent views among the theologians themselves. Why the devil didn't the Protestant theologians of the day travel to the Tridentinum[1] when safe conduct was nevertheless

[1] The Ecumenical Council of Trent (1545–63) was convened by Paul III to

assured them? The Protestants are equally to blame for it that the evolutionary process within the Church has not proceeded more rapidly. The individuation process is a development on the native soil of Christianity. But Protestantism is not a Church and will not be a Church, and particularly not a Counterchurch, although it is rooted in the Church, namely the primitive Church and its tradition.

Whatever the specialist may think about Meyer's exegesis, I regard it as a signpost that should not be overlooked. He brings the foundations of Protestantism closer again to the primitive Church and allows the lone wanderer, the fate-marked heretic (significantly derived from αἱρεῖν, to take, choose, decide for something!) to divine something of that maternal foundation where he is connected with the whole of Christendom. And since the outpoured Holy Ghost is himself a great heretic, he also inflicts αἵρεσις, choice and agonizing decision, on all those solitaries who disturb and loosen up the *Ecclesia* by enriching her—provided of course that they can and want to link back to a maternal Church. Whether the earthly Church recognizes this linking-back or not is perhaps a painful, personal, subsidiary question. The main thing is that the linking-back should occur in the spirit, and in a spirit of childlikeness and humility. Should the earthly Church not be present at this act, then the case is no different from that of the priest who, in the absence of a congregation, celebrates the Mass by himself. The space the congregation otherwise fills will not be empty, and if the mother does not succour her children, then the grandmother will, who always intervenes when the mother fails. The grandmother is less exclusive than the mother. The Magna Mater has already had pagan children and as *Ecclesia spiritualis* she embraces a Christendom as huge as it is fragmented.

You write that the Protestant dynamism is endangered by the spirit of tradition. In my opinion this danger appears only where the dynamism of the Holy Ghost is at work, that is, where a solitary heretic must strike a new path through the primeval jungle. But where the "Holy Ghost" can be damped down by tradition, it is no longer a question of a "holy" Ghost—who cannot be damped down —but of a man-made secession which had probably better be stopped. In Protestantism diversionary tactics have virtually been elevated into a principle, which on the one hand hinders the linking-back to the

solve the serious problems of the time, and in particular to deal with the schismatic tendencies rampant since Luther.

immemorial collective origin and on the other hand renders any agreement on what has been achieved impossible. Because of his narrow spiritual foundation the Protestant is constantly driven into spiritual arrogance, of which, as you know, we have some terrifying examples before our eyes. The Catholic, however, has to squander his best energies in papering over the crumbling Church walls, while the religious problems slip out of his hands into those of the Protestants, who create the greatest confusion by carrying them to extremes.

Meyer's book has opened my eyes again to the truly neurotic situation of the Christian today. The highest cultural principles of the West glower at each other across the schism—the Christian is split within himself. Therefore it is quite possible that the devil will overrun the world. A universal Church would have more authority than a split one. It is clear that the Catholic Church cannot give up her claim to catholicity without collapsing into nothing. If on the other hand Protestantism were to give up its ambitious claim to be itself a Church, it would have lost nothing but only gained itself, whole and complete. You cannot have both, Church *and* freedom, and if both want both undiminished, no Solomon will be found to pronounce judgment. Anyone who wants both must sacrifice something on both sides. The tragedy is that the two creeds cannot bring this to pass. *Ecclesia semper catholica aut nihil*,[2] but Protestantism culminates in the individual. The claim of the Church is legitimate in principle, and so is the individual's. To share in the tradition the Protestant would definitely have to sacrifice some of his subjectivism and spiritual arrogance, and for the sake of catholicity the Church would have to make some radical exceptions to the rule.

Forgive me, my dear Pastor, that this letter has turned out so long. Your decisive standpoint has enabled me to formulate my thoughts about the schism in the Church. And for that I am sincerely grateful to you. With best regards,

Yours sincerely, C. G. JUNG

[2] "The Church is forever Catholic or nothing."

To Pastor Fritz Buri

Dear Pastor Buri,   10 December 1945

Very many thanks for kindly sending me your book, *Die religiöse Ueberwindung der Angst*.[1] I have been waiting for a rejoinder to

Pfister's book[2] from theological quarters. I myself cannot agree with Pfister. First and foremost because fear is a fundamental reaction of nature. Kierkegaard's view that animals have no fear is totally disproved by the facts. There are whole species which consist of nothing but fear. A creature that loses its fear is condemned to death. When "cured" by missionaries of their natural and justified fear of demons, primitives degenerate. I have seen enough of this in Africa whatever the missionaries may say. Anyone who is afraid has reason to be. There are not a few patients who have to have fear driven into them because their instincts have atrophied. A man who has no more fear is on the brink of the abyss. Only if he suffers from a pathological excess of fear can he be cured with impunity.

Second, where the religions are concerned, they deliver from fear and at the same time create fear, even Christianity, and that is right because one person has too much, another too little. Absolute deliverance from fear is a complete absurdity. What about the fear of God? Doesn't God ordain fearful things? Has Pfister no fear if both legs are broken for him and in the end he must dangle from a meat-hook through his chin? Does no fear warn him of danger to body and soul? Has he no fear for the life of his sick child? A man without fear is a superman. I don't like supermen. They are not even likeable. If Christ in Gethsemane had no fear, then his passion is null and void and the believer can subscribe to docetism![3]

Third, religions are not by any means mere fear-constructs. Far be it from me to deny the existence of apotropaisms, but like all religious phenomena, they go back to something that the biologist can only describe as a basic instinct of human nature. His science does not entitle him to assert that religions are revelations of the divine spirit, which they very easily might be although we are unable to prove it. In this sense I must describe every religious idea as a "fiction" since, formally at any rate, it is a conflation of imaginative possibilities. On the other hand, we can be sure that it is not motivated by any conscious intention, rather it "happens" to man on an unconscious level (unconscious = unknown). That is the utmost sci-

---

□ Bern.

[1] Bern, 1945.

[2] Pfister, *Das Christentum und die Angst* (1944). (Concerning Pfister cf. Ferenczi, 25 Dec. 09, n. 5.)

[3] Docetism, a heresy of the early Christian Church, taught that Christ was born without any participation in physical matter and that accordingly his body and his suffering were not real but only apparent.

ence can establish. The wonder does not lie in the content of the "fiction" but in the existence of the fiction, even if it should be a conscious device used for illegitimate purposes (e.g., banishing fear). But it is putting the cart before the horse to explain all dogmas and rites as apotropaic fear-constructs. It is not only a scandal if theologians entertain such notions, but psychologically false as everyone knows who has had a religious experience, and as is also proved by the investigation of primitive rites. It verges directly on atheism to try to reduce the religious function to anything other than itself. . . .

Fourth, as a psychotherapist I do not by any means try to deliver my patients from fear. Rather, I lead them to the reason for their fear, and then it becomes clear that it is justified. (I could tell you a few instructive stories in this respect!) If my patient understands religious language, I say to him: Well, don't try to escape this fear which God has given you, but try to endure it to the end—*sine poena nulla gratia!*[4] I can say this because I believe I am a religious man and because I know with scientific certainty that my patient hasn't invented his fear but that it is preordained. By whom or what? *By the unknown.* The religious man calls this *absconditum*[5] "God," the scientific intellect calls it the unconscious. Deriving fear from repression is a neurotic speculation, an apotropaism invented for cowards; a pseudo-scientific myth in so far as it declares a basic biological instinct unreal and twists it into an *Ersatz*-formation. One could just as well explain life as a flight from death or love as an evasion of the hate which one hasn't the courage to muster. They are neurotic artifices with which one diddles hysterics out of the only meaning they have (which lies precisely in their neurosis), naturally with the best but unendurably shallow intentions.

I hope you will not take it amiss if I hazard the conjecture that you may have read rather too little of me. I infer this from the difficulties which my manner of expression seems to cause you. *Fictio* and *imaginatio* have for me their original, full meaning as important activities that concern not only man but God. (*Deus imaginatur mundum. Trinitas imaginata in creatura.*)[6] Formal dogma is *fictio s. imaginatio*; but its origin, its very existence, is a *revelation* of hidden

---

[4] "Without punishment no grace."
[5] The hidden (God).
[6] "God imagined the world. The Trinity is imaged in the creature." In spite of exhaustive inquiries the source remains unidentified. But cf. von Franz, *Aurora Consurgens: A Document Attributed to Thomas Aquinas*, p. 186, n. 141: "God created all visible things through imagination (φαντασία) and manifests himself in everything. . . . Thus the creative fantasy of God is contained in the visible

contents which are not in accord with the *mundus sensibilis*. (Hence Tertullian's unsurpassable paradox.[7])

In the hope that it will make my standpoint somewhat clearer to you I am taking the liberty of sending you my little book *Psychology and Religion*, as a token of gratitude for the rich stimulation your book has afforded me.

Yours sincerely, C. G. JUNG

---

world" (paraphrase of Scott, *Corpus Hermeticum*, I, p. 158). Cf. also *Psychology and Alchemy*, pars. 396, 399.

[7] Cf. Wegmann, 20 Nov. 45, n. 2.

To Count Hermann Keyserling

Dear Count,   10 December 1945

I was glad to hear through Mr. X. how you are. It is wonderful how you have come through this catastrophe. Let us hope conditions will gradually improve. Here in Switzerland we are still rationed, but can't complain about anything since we were miraculously spared the Nazi madness. I see from numerous examples that the Germans still have no conception of the mood of the world against Germany. The catastrophe overshadows the whole world. The seed of evil is sprouting everywhere. With best greetings and wishes,

Yours sincerely, C. G. JUNG

☐ (Handwritten.)

To Pastor H. Wegmann

Dear Pastor Wegmann,   12 December 1945

Your friendly letter of 8.XII was just what I wanted to hear from you—namely your clear and unmistakable attitude to the question of the Church. In truth I didn't know that you think so critically in this matter. But I must admit your arguments are right, for I think from the religious standpoint likewise, if not even more radically. Your previous letter did not bore me in the least; on the contrary, I fear I have been a nuisance to you with my preoccupations and would therefore beg your forgiveness for writing to you again so soon. I must, however, overcome my scruples because the problem of religion— apart from its subjective importance—is gradually swelling to cosmic

401

proportions parallel with contemporary events. That is, I do not believe that reason can be the supreme law of human behaviour, if only because experience shows that in decisive moments behaviour is precisely *not* guided by reason but rather by overpowering unconscious impulses. There is nothing to cope with the latter but their own equivalent, something that adequately expresses their nature, gives them name and shape. There thus arises in consciousness a receptacle, so to speak, into which the unconscious onslaught can pour and wherein it can assume cultural form. If this does not happen, there is unquestionably a danger that the onslaught will express itself as cataclysmically as an avalanche. This form has always been given by religion, never by reason.

The problem is particularly urgent today because civilized humanity will soon have arrived at the crossroads where it can use the atom bomb. The effect of the uranium bomb has proved disappointing. The new plutonium bombs being produced on the assembly line are said to be 150 times more effective! Thus the suicide of human civilization has moved appreciably closer, and chain reactions will be discovered in the future which will endanger the planet. Nearly 2000 years ago the world entered the last month of the Platonic year, the aeon of Pisces, and developed chiliastic expectations. A thousand years ago these came to light still more clearly,[1] and now, nearly 2000 years after Christ mankind has the instrument in its hands with which it can prepare the end and assuredly will if a third World War does not come soon and smash the power of those nations which might *also* develop the atom bomb unless—*and this is the only hope*—the great reversal comes, a universal retreat from Marignano.[2] I can imagine this as nothing other than a religious, world-embracing movement which alone can intercept the diabolical impulse for destruction. That is the reason why the question of the Church grips me so urgently, for the Church is the one worldly authority where spirit in the religious sense moves the brute masses. The Church would have her *raison d'être* if she could save mankind or at least civilization. I well know that it is useless for the single individual to rack his brains

[1] At the end of the first millennium numerous heretical sects arose such as the Bogomils, Cathars, Albigenses, Brethren of the Free Spirit, Beghards, the Holy Ghost movement of Joachim of Flora, and others. Cf. *Aion*, pars. 139, 225ff.

[2] In 1515 the French king Francis I defeated the Swiss fighting for Milan at Marignano, northern Italy. This defeat was a major turning-point in Swiss history, as it shattered the hope of maintaining for Switzerland the status of a European power and inaugurated the attitude of neutrality which she has adopted ever since.

over it, but one must nevertheless talk about it. Therefore I *embêtier* you with another long letter for which I must ask you to forgive me. I know it is childish or superstitious but I feel a little comforted in the knowledge that I have got it off my chest.

Naturally I don't expect an answer unless your pen sets itself in motion of its own accord. With best regards,

Yours sincerely, C. G. JUNG

To Paul Schmitt

Dear Dr. Schmitt,   20 December 1945

I see from your letter, for which best thanks, that you are laid up in a clinic again. I had thought your malaria had come to a standstill, but this is obviously not so. I find it very regrettable that you must plague yourself with so many bodily disturbances. It almost seems as if the *ignis vitae* of which you write were coming out at the wrong place as fire. In alchemy there is an ἀναζωπύρωσις,[1] by which is presumably meant a transformation of the destructive fiery spirit into a *spiritus vitae*. You are in the midst of an inner confrontation with yourself which is of the highest general importance. We all have to contribute our mite to this problem. Occasionally we must also inquire whether something that wants to go upwards has not taken a false route downwards into the body.

.   .   .

With kindest regards,

Yours sincerely, C. G. JUNG

[1] *Anazopyrosis*, quickening by fire, an expression to be found in the "Book of Komarios," which according to Jung dates from the 1st cent. A.D. Cf. von Franz, *Aurora Consurgens*, p. 368.

To the owner of this book: Dr. Jürg Fierz

Writing a prefatory note to these *diversa* gives me a peculiar feeling. A collection of my essays from various times and situations of life is rather like a grasshopper with type on its feet jumping through

□ A dedication which Jung wrote for a bound volume of his own offprints prepared by F., literary editor of the *Weltwoche* (cf. Fierz, 10 Apr. 42, n. □). Although, strictly speaking, not a letter it is included here for the sake of its personal expression and human interest.

the world of ideas, leaving occasional traces behind it; and it requires a considerable effort of imagination to reconstruct from the zigzag track of these footprints the nature of the animal that produced them. I envy no one this task, as I myself have a distaste for auto-biography. The immense expanse of vaguely recognizable objects in the world has lured me forth to those twilit border zones where the figure I have meanwhile become steps towards me. The long path I have traversed is littered with husks sloughed off, witnesses of countless moultings, those *relicta* one calls books. They conceal as much as they reveal. Every step is a symbol of those to follow. He who mounts a flight of steps does not linger on them, nor look back at them, even though age invites him to linger or slow his pace. The great wind of the peaks roars ever more loudly in his ears. His gaze sweeps distances that flee away into the infinite. The last steps are the loveliest and most precious, for they lead to that fullness to reach which the innermost essence of man is born.

Küsnacht, 21 December 1945   C. G. JUNG

To J. H. van der Hoop

Dear Colleague,   14 January 1946

It made me very happy to hear from you again after these terrible years. I have often thought of you and felt tempted to write to you. But I didn't because I was afraid of compromising you. On account of my critical utterances I was "marked down" by the Gestapo, my books were banned in Germany, and in France they were for the most part destroyed.

During the last five years I have succeeded in establishing pleasant working relations with my one-time opponents, some of the leading minds among the Freudians here. We have founded a "Teaching Institute for Psychotherapy"[1] at the University, directed by a Cura-torium of nine doctors. The "Institute" consists in regular lectures being held. The Curatorium, to which some ten guests are invited, meets regularly every fortnight for common scientific work. At present we are concerned with the psychology of the transference.

[1] Founded in Zurich, May 1938. Its president was Jung, its secretary Gustav Bally. Among the lecturers were Jung, Hans Bänziger, Bally, M. Boss, Th. Bovet, K. Binswanger, R. Brun, Kielholz, Alphonse Maeder, H. W. Maier. According to

404

Even the president of the Psychoanalytical Society[2] takes part. The transactions are pervaded by a thoroughly positive spirit, and the discussions are fruitful and in every way enjoyable.

I can only hope and wish that no one becomes "Jungian." I stand for no doctrine, but describe facts and put forward certain views which I hold worthy of discussion. I criticize Freudian psychology for a certain narrowness and bias, and the Freudians for a certain rigid, sectarian spirit of intolerance and fanaticism. I proclaim no cut-and-dried doctrine and I abhor "blind adherents." I leave everyone free to deal with the facts in his own way, since I also claim this freedom for myself. I can thoroughly approve the facts Freud describes and the way he treats these facts provided they stand the test of critical reason and common sense. I diverge only when it comes to interpreting the facts, which Freud conceived in a demonstrably unsatisfactory way. Since the psyche is not personal only and not only of today, we have to draw upon the psychology of primitives as well as the history of the mind in explaining them, avoiding at the same time certain medical and biological prejudices. An example of faulty method would be Freud's *Totem and Taboo*[3] or *The Future of an Illusion*.[4] Here doctrinaire assumptions led to erroneous conclusions. His conception of the incest problem is also unsatisfactory.

The fact that it was just the Allied representatives who would not allow me to resign from the Presidium of the International Medical Society for Psychotherapy is now taking its revenge on me, as I am suspected of collaboration with the Nazis. For instance, I have been blamed for the death of 600 Jews.[5] These insinuations originate demonstrably with the Freudians. This is called scientific discussion!!

---

a communication from Dr. K. Binswanger, Jung was particularly interested in creating an Institute in which the various analytical schools could cooperate, and he drew up statutes for this purpose. He was greatly disappointed when his plans —which also included the psychological training of physicians, the training of school psychologists, the establishment of psychotherapeutic clinics at universities —were frustrated by the opposition of existing institutions. For this reason the Teaching Institute was dissolved in 1948.

[2] This seems to be an error. The two members of the Swiss Psychoanalytical Society taking part in the meetings were Bally and Bänziger, but not the president, Phillip Sarasin, who lived in Basel.

[3] Standard Edn. 13.   [4] Standard Edn. 21.

[5] Jung refers to the unfounded rumour that he was a visitor to Berchtesgaden. In fact one of Hitler's doctors had asked him, by telephone from Munich, to examine the Führer psychiatrically as the latter's pathological symptoms had increased. Jung refused. — Cf. Anon., 5 Oct. 39.

I should be glad to welcome you again in Zurich. For me long journeys are unfortunately out of the question; my cardiac infarct has left me with a lasting scar and a correspondingly low cardiac performance. I hope you are now recovering from the terrible time of suffering. For us the uncertainty and the constant alerts were not easy to bear, but nothing in comparison with what Holland suffered and what we could follow only from a distance with impotent rage. Heyer had the impertinence to write to me recently that he was only an "ideologist," of course no Nazi.

If there is anything I can do for you please let me know. With best regards and wishes,

Yours sincerely, c. g. JUNG

To Alexander Willwoll, S.J.

Dear Professor Willwoll,   14 January 1946

Many thanks for kindly sending me your interesting essay.[1] I admire the thoroughness of your documentation and the objectivity of your argument in a field that assuredly contains much that is irritating to philosophers and theologians. Personally it makes me sad to see how the spokesmen for the humanities often toil and moil over my writings only to reduce all my conceptual variants to a common denominator. The philosopher should always bear in mind that our *point de départ* is different, since I approach the problems from the scientific, empirical side: what he calls "ideas" I observe and describe as *entia*, just like a botanist his plants, a zoologist his animals, and a chemist his substances. I am not out to build a conceptual system, but use concepts to describe psychic facts and their peculiar modes of behaviour. For a zoologist a bear, regardless of its Himalayan, Siberian, European, or American genus, is always a bear, and the empirical psychologist proceeds in the same way with psychic *entia*. What he would call the *accidentia* of ideas is for the philosopher and even more for the theologian just the essential thing. This can hardly be anything but irritating. It is therefore very much to your credit that you have succeeded in treating my concepts with so much goodwill and objectivity.

Yours sincerely, c. g. JUNG

☐ S.J., (1887–1961), Swiss Catholic psychologist.
[1] "Vom Unbewussten im Aufbau des religiösen Erlebens," in Emil Spiess (ed.), *Rätsel der Seele* (1946).

406

To Hans Meyer

Dear Colleague,   30 January 1946

I was very interested in your paper and will see if it can be placed with the *Neue Schweizer Rundschau*. At all events I will recommend it to the editor as the first German attempt to get at the problem psychologically. I can only agree with your reflections. You have set yourself a frame of reference that restricts the problem to the actions and sufferings of Germany. To go beyond that would probably not be appropriate at the moment, even though the argument as such would have to be carried further, to the point where it embraced all Europe. Germany is an isolated instance at present, but she represents merely the tip of an iceberg. European man, indeed man in general, has for the first time in his history dropped out of the original scheme of things and is growing up in a world which he has robbed of every influence on his psychic life and now loads him with a crushing responsibility. At the same time fate has pressed the atom bomb into his hands and with it the means of destroying himself for good and all.

In the face of this situation there is naturally a compensating reaction in the unconscious, whose outcome, considering the ineffectuality of our consciousness, could have no other consequences than a catastrophe. In reality, however, a tremendous revolution in Christianity has long been due, since our erstwhile religious views have been overtaken by events and need a reformation. 400 years ago it was Germany who performed this service for the world. The unconscious is pure nature, with the result that what stands behind the bad foreground is a natural fact beyond good and evil. It always depends on human comprehension whether the archetypal content of the unconscious will take a favourable or a nefarious turn. The unconscious is the future in the form or disguise of the past. It is not a "wish" but a "must."

What happens when man introjects God? A superman psychosis, because every blockhead thinks that when he withdraws a projection its contents cease to exist. Insight, insight! I have tried all my life to din a bit of understanding into people. May others have better luck. With collegial regards,

Yours sincerely, C. G. JUNG

☐ Hamburg.

To Pastor Max Frischknecht

Dear Pastor Frischknecht,   8 February 1946

Since it is apparent from your friendly letter and your essay[1] that you are struggling to understand my views correctly, I am taking the liberty of writing you a very long letter.

Your careful study on the terrifying vision of the Blessed Brother Klaus,[2] for which I thank you very much, made interesting and enjoyable reading. I agree entirely with what you say up to the point (p. 36) where you raise the question of the transcendent reason for the vision. Your alternative is either "metaphysical God" or Brother Klaus's "own unconscious." This is the *caput draconis!*[3] Unwittingly and unawares you impute to me a theory which I have been fighting against for decades, namely Freud's theory. As you know, Freud derives the religious "illusion" from the individual's "own" unconscious, that is, from the *personal* unconscious. There are empirical reasons that contradict this assumption. I have summed them up in the hypothesis of the *collective unconscious*. The personal unconscious is characterized by the fact that its contents are formed personally and are at the same time individual acquisitions which vary from man to man, so that everyone has his "own" unconscious. The collective unconscious, on the contrary, is made up of contents which are formed personally only to a minor degree and in essentials not at all, are not individual acquisitions, are essentially the same everywhere, and do not vary from man to man. This unconscious is like the air, which is the same everywhere, is breathed by everybody, and yet belongs to no one. Its contents (called archetypes) are the prior conditions or patterns of psychic formation in general. They have an *esse in potentia et in actu* but not *in re*,[4] for as *res* they are no longer what they were but have become psychic contents. They are in themselves non-perceptible, irrepresentable (since they precede all representation), everywhere and "eternally" the same. Hence there is only one collective unconscious, which is everywhere identical with itself, from which everything psychic takes shape before it is personalized, modified, assimilated, etc. by external influences.

---

[1] "Das schreckliche Gesicht des Klaus von Flüe," *Theologische Zeitschrift* (Basel), II:1 (1946).

[2] Cf. Blanke, 2 May 45, n. 12.

[3] = "head of the dragon," an alchemical concept symbolizing the union of highest and lowest. Cf. *Mysterium Coniunctionis*, pars. 140f.

[4] Potential and active existence, but not in reality (as a thing).

In order to clarify this somewhat difficult concept I would like to take a parallel from mineralogy, the so-called crystal lattice.[5] This lattice represents the axial system of the crystal. In the mother liquor it is invisible, as though not present, and yet it is present since first the ions aggregate round the (ideal) axial points of intersection, and then the molecules. There is only the *one* crystal lattice for millions of crystals of the same chemical composition. No individual crystal can speak of *its* lattice, since the lattice is the identical precondition for all of them (none of which concretizes it perfectly!). It is everywhere the same and "eternal."

The theological parallel is the idea of *likeness to God*. There is only *one imago Dei*, which belongs to the existential ground of all men. I cannot speak of "my" *imago Dei* but only of "the" *imago Dei*. It is the principle by which man is shaped, one and the same, immutable, eternal.

Al-Ghazzali[6] sees in the "virtue" by reason of which the stone falls the will of Allah, Schopenhauer the blind Will,[7] the physicist gravitation. Would the modern theologian contest the right of the physicist to propound a theory of gravitation? Maybe with the observation that this theory maintains that the stone falls *merely* for physical reasons, whereas obviously the process can only be explained in a correct and satisfactory manner if the stone falls by God's will?

When, more than 30 years ago, I spoke of God as a "complex of ideas,"[8] an *image* therefore, I only meant that a God-image is present in man, not, be it understood, in his conscious mind but in his unconscious, where it is inaccessible to criticism and arbitrary modification. People instantly accused me of atheism.

I have never asserted that Brother Klaus's vision of God sprang from his personal unconscious, but rather from that—we may well say—mysterious sphere of suprapersonal factors which somehow

---

[5] This example of the crystal lattice is used, rather loosely, for the first time in 1929, in "The Significance of Constitution and Heredity in Psychology," CW 8, par. 221. It occurs again in "Psychological Aspects of the Mother Archetype" (orig. 1939), CW 9, i, par. 155, and in the revised text (1948) of "The Psychological Foundations of Belief in Spirits," CW 8, par. 589, n. 6.

[6] Abu Hamid Mohammed al-Ghazzali (Algazel) (1058–1111), Moslem theologian and mystic, leading representative of Sufism.

[7] Schopenhauer, in *The World as Will and Idea* (orig. 1819), defined the Will as the ultimate reality and principle of all existence. In itself the Will is blind and unaffected by conscious motives; it receives knowledge of itself only through the world of ideas by which it recognizes itself as the will to live.

[8] Cf. White, 5 Oct. 45, n. 2.

underlie man. Because this sphere is antecedent to man and is a *sine qua non* of his psychic life, I allow myself to call this "psyche" (or whatever it may be) "divine" in contradistinction to "human," since even the theologians do not hesitate to conceive likeness to God as an *imago DEI* and hence *divine*. To the "simple" human psyche there is now attached this *imago Dei*, which complicates its simplicity somewhat. Incidentally, my use of "divine" is not to be understood *sensu strictiori*: in the ancient pharmacopoeia there is a *lapis divinus*,[9] and in alchemy a ▽ *divina s. ὕδωρ θεῖον*,[10] (which also means sulphuric acid).

Your difficulty in understanding my way of looking at things is due to the incommensurability of standpoint. As a theologian you adopt the standpoint of the *scientia divina* and see the world through God's eye. As a scientist I see with merely human eyes, judge by means of human understanding, and presume to no other knowledge than is afforded me by scientific insight. I can therefore only establish that Brother Klaus did not see his image as a concrete, material figure in space, that it was not the product of delirium or intoxication, but was on the contrary "psychogenic," i.e., a psychic fact to be evaluated as a spontaneous product of certain processes in the "unconscious." This "unconscious" consists, as I have said, of empirically demonstrable, subliminal contents (or contents that have become subliminal), and to that extent it is designated the "personal unconscious" and may therefore be considered altogether "psychic" (in contradistinction to "somatic"). But over and above this there seem to be contents which cannot be explained as individual acquisitions (they correspond to the complicated instinctual dispositions in the animal kingdom). They correspond to the inherited modes of behaviour which are present *a priori* at any time. (Crystal lattice!) They influence psychic behaviour and express themselves in psychic forms; hence we speak of them as psychic contents, a *façon de parler* which does not accord badly with their phenomenology. At bottom we naturally don't know what their nature is since we know only their numinous effects. We know as little about their origin as about the origin of cosmic rays. *Beyond that I know nothing.* So-called "spiritual" existences are verifiable for me only as psychic (likewise, of course, all "metaphysical" existences). This is the standpoint of the scientist and phenomenologist, to whom the thousand years of

[9] = divine stone. Cf. *Psychology and Alchemy*, par. 159.
[10] = divine water (▽ was the alchemical sign for water). Cf. *Mysterium Coniunctionis*, par. 119, n. 45.

the Middle Ages have demonstrated *ad oculos* that there is the phenomenon of a consensus which claims the right and the capacity to explain the world from God's standpoint. The scientist will only affirm that at all times and in all places there have been and still are very many people who think "theologically" and not "scientifically." He does not by any means contest the possibility and possible validity of this thinking, only he doesn't think like that.

The concept of the unconscious *posits nothing*, it designates only my *unknowing*. I affirm only the evident fact that the vision rose up from the ground of the psyche. Beyond this ground there are only precarious conjectures. But this is just where the *scientia divina* steps in, declaring it possesses a sure knowledge of all the things science doesn't know. This assertion, I willingly admit, is uncommonly interesting but not verifiable, so is not an object of scientific study in so far as it claims to be more than a phenomenon. Science is human knowledge, theology divine knowledge. Therefore the two are incommensurable.

It is clear that theology has to "secularize" the psyche, for measured against the Creator all creatures are "bad earthen pots."[11] Souls, human beings, things, planets, the worlds of fixed stars shrink before God's eye into miserable ephemerids. The ridiculously small eye of the scientist beholds vastnesses in the deeps of nature and their equivalents in the psyche. The merest trifles appear wonderful to him, as for instance this paltry psychic organism to which such wonderful things happen. The scientist must be content with the poverty of his merely human knowledge. The theologian sits on top of a gigantic mountain, while the scientist toilsomely climbs up it way down below. I do not dispute the possibility that the vision was sent to the blessed brother by God himself. But how should I *know* that this was so? If I don't *know* something, neither do I know what I should *believe* about it, unless, for reasons unknown to me, I am *compelled* to believe. But in the latter event my scientific conscience would say: "That too is a phenomenon the reasons for which you know nothing about."

It seems to me, therefore, that it is I who have to make my standpoint clear to the theologian rather than he his to me, which I am so intimately familiar with for historical and personal reasons. It seems to me I would have no difficulty in thinking theologically. But I find that theologians do not understand the scientific viewpoint.

---

[11] *Faust II*, Act 2. Cf. *Psychology and Alchemy*, par. 204.

411

How comes it, for instance, that you tax me with "theology"? Is the physicist with his gravitation or any other theory also going in for "theology"? (Certainly he competes with the theologian al-Ghazzali!)

Marginal notes:

1. There is no difference in principle between interpretation and projection. Even the wave theory of light is a projection or it wouldn't need a parallel particle theory.

2. I too slipped up over the source of "Deus est sphaera." The dictum does not come from Alanus de Insulis[12] either, but from a Hermetic treatise entitled *Liber Hermetis* or *Liber Trismegisti*, which exists only in manuscript form. (Codd. Paris. et Vatic.) Cf. M. Baumgartner, in *Beiträge zur Geschichte der Philosophie des Mittelalters*, 2nd ed., IV, 118: *Deus est sphaera infinita, cuius centrum est ubique, circumferentia nusquam.*[13]

Yours sincerely, C. G. JUNG

P.S. I hope you will excuse this critical discussion. I always regret it when theologians take up a defensive position on the erroneous assumption that I want to put something else in the place of theology. On the contrary, I thought that theologians, in view of their apologetics, would be glad of psychological proofs which corroborate the rightness of their statements also on empirical grounds, even though this is possible only to a modest degree. I have found that the little I have to put forward has helped a great many people to *understand* the facts of religion. The $\chi\acute{\alpha}\rho\iota\sigma\mu\alpha$[14] of faith is not granted to all.

[12] Alain de Lille (*ca.* 1128–1202), French theologian and Latinist.
[13] "God is an infinite sphere whose centre is everywhere and the circumference nowhere." Concerning the origin of the saying cf. "A Psychological Approach to the Dogma of the Trinity," CW 11, par. 229, n. 6, and *Mysterium Coniunctionis*, par. 41, n. 42. Further documentation in J. L. Borges, "Pascal's Sphere," *Other Inquisitions* (1964).
[14] Charisma, a gift or favour bestowed by God.

To Father Victor White

[ORIGINAL IN ENGLISH]

My dear Father White,   13 February 1946

My answer to your kind letter comes very late indeed: I have a bad conscience. There are certain reasons, however, that may excuse my long silence. For a number of weeks I felt very low on account of a grippe in the head and in the intestines and besides this ailment I was caught in the grips of a book that eats me alive if I don't write it.[1] As I must still see certain patients, give consultations, write letters etc., my time for work is very short.

This evening I shall give a report about the way you conceive of my psychology before a group of doctors,[2] who regularly come to my house every fortnight. Once I mentioned a parallel you draw between St. Thomas' philosophy and my psychology, which remark met with great interest. They asked me to give them fuller details. On this occasion I went through your pamphlets again and found a point which I forgot to mention in my previous letter. It is in your article "St. Thomas Aquinas and Jung's Psychology" (*Blackfriars* XXV, 216): "Jung's substitution of indetermined 'libido' for Freud's determined 'sexuality' was a challenge," etc. (9th line from the bottom). Your statement as to the transformability of instinct is correct in the main, yet it could give cause for criticism from biological quarters. Instinct as seen from a biological standpoint is something *extremely conservative,* so much so that it seems to be almost inalterable. This is a fact one should not overlook in talking to a scientist. It is a regular fact in the animal kingdom. It is only man that shows a certain unreliability concerning the functioning of his instincts, and it is only civilized man who is capable of losing sight of his instincts to a certain extent and under certain conditions. If he is nothing but instinctive he collides with his civilization, and if he gets a bit too far away from his instinctive basis he gets neurotic. There is a certain optimum between the two extremes. Transformation of instinct, therefore, can only concern a small part of it and it takes untold thousands of years until a noticeable change is effected. This is the transformation envisaged by the biologist. But the kind of transformation which the psychologist has in mind is something else and cannot be compared to the biological effect, as it is not a "real" change such as is understood by a natural scientist. It is rather a "psychological" change, a change brought about by a psychological superstructure: a relatively small amount of instinctive energy (i.e., energy of the instinct) is led over into another form, i.e., a thought- or feeling-form (idea and value) upon the basis and with the help of a pre-existing archetype. This is done for instance by a ritual anamnesis of an archetypal figure. You can observe this procedure

[1] Possibly *Aion* (1951) or *Mysterium Coniunctionis.*
[2] Cf. Hoop, 14 Jan. 46, n. 1.

413

in nearly all renewal or rebirth mysteries: there is an invocation and dramatic representation of the (spiritual) ancestor and his deeds. The δεικνύμενον[3] and δρώμενον[4] "constellate" (or stimulate) the latent analogous archetype in the μύσται,[5] and its inherent fascination causes the instinctive energy (libido) to deviate from its original, biological course and to adhere to its spiritual counterpart. See for instance the hermeneutic conception of the Cantic. Cant., where Christ corresponds to the "spiritual ancestor" or archetype of man (as *Adam secundus*),[6] while the fundamental instinctive basis is represented by an indubitable erotic situation.

I am most grateful to you for the information about St. Thomas and for the interesting news. I had no idea that my work would find so much attention.

. . .

Hoping you are always in good health, I remain,

Yours sincerely, C. G. JUNG

[3] = what is shown.
[4] = what is acted.
[5] = initiates.
[6] The Second Adam = Christ. Cf. *Mysterium Coniunctionis*, par. 144, and "Answer to Job," CW 11, par. 625. Cantic. Cant. = Song of Songs (AV: Solomon).

To Pastor Olivier Vuille

Dear Pastor Vuille,   22 February 1946

Your question raises a problem which is not easy to solve. If Hosea were a modern man his language would lead us to suppose that he had a special rapport with his mother, since the way he expresses himself denotes a great preponderance of feeling. But it would be dangerous to conclude this about the ancient prophet, since the biographical details, which alone would permit us to draw such a conclusion, are absolutely lacking. We have only one *text* whose singular content and peculiar language could be understood as coming from other sources than the author's particular personality. And it must not be forgotten that this personality was speaking as a prophet. This fact prevents us from making use of a personalistic psychology, since what a prophet imagines is derived far less from his personal unconscious than from the collective unconscious and can be explained only by the latter. It is preferable, therefore, to ex-

□ (Translated from French.) Canton Vaud.

414

plain Hosea's imagery by the archetype of the "divine marriage"—
an image that he must have encountered frequently in his pagan
environment—than to derive it from a personal idiosyncrasy. In the
same way that we cannot deduce the principal ideas of *Faust* from
Gothe's attitude toward his parents, we are unable to make such
deductions about Hosea, a man who lived in psychological conditions
so different from our own that we can hardly imagine them. Thus
I cannot allow myself to make personalistic interpretations, especially
as the language of prophecy does not seem to me to arise from the
personal imagination but rather from collective imagery. Here again
—as in great poetry, religious experiences, prophetic dreams and
visions—archetypal images are the causal factors, and they have little
to do with the prophet's individual disposition. Hosea's way of representing the relationship between the Divinity and his people as a
marriage[1] is completely explicable in the spiritual atmosphere of
Palestine and Syria in his time, where the idea of the *hierosgamos*
played a great part.

I am taking the liberty of enclosing a study by one of my students,[2] which I hope you will return at your convenience. In it you
will see the method we use for studying the psychology of cases like
this.

With best regards, C. G. JUNG

[1] Cf. Hosea 1:2. Hosea married a harlot at Yahweh's command. In those days a
harlot was considered holy (the Hebrew word for holy is *kadosh*, for harlot
kedesha, the holy one).
[2] Riwkah Schärf, "Die Gestalt des Satans im Alten Testament," later published
in Jung's *Symbolik des Geistes* (1948). Tr. *Satan in the Old Testament* (1967).

To Pastor A.F.L. van Dijk

Dear Pastor van Dijk,   25 February 1946

The question of meditation is really a problem of the first order.
I have read your brochure and gather that you want to put spiritual
exercises on a Protestant basis. Two different ways have developed in
the West. One is historical and probably originates in Benedictine
contemplation[1]—Benedictine mysticism, the Victorines,[2] and in par-

□ Kampen, Netherlands.
[1] St. Benedict of Nursia (*ca.* 480–543) laid down as one of his rules for monastic
life silence as an aid to contemplation.
[2] A congregation of canons at St. Victor's church in Paris, founded by William

415

ticular the *Itinerarium* of St. Bonaventura.[3] Then we have the exercises of Loyola, stemming from Islam. All these various Christian methods of contemplation and meditation have one thing in common: the image to be meditated upon as well as the kind of meditation are presented to the candidate from outside. This meditation can do no more than merely fill out the image given. If you want to compare the technique of modern psychotherapy with these old methods, you could understand it as something similar, since here too certain contents are reflected upon and observed though the system is different. In psychotherapy, dreams are subjected to meditative observation[4] for the purpose of restoring the broken connection between consciousness and the unconscious or integrating the latter's contents. In this case, of course, no external object is prescribed for conscious meditation, it is always provided by the unconscious. This kind of psychic experience goes back historically to philosophical alchemy, and in ecclesiastical tradition has superficial connections with the sects of the Free Spirit (13th cent.).[5] The two Christian trends have a considerably deeper connection with the psychology of Origen.[6] But the real source is to be found outside and prior to Christianity in those peculiar psychic processes reported by Apuleius in his *Metamorphoses*,[7] and in the Mithras Liturgy,[8] the Acts of Thomas and of John.[9]

.   .   .

With best thanks for your brochure,

Yours sincerely, C. G. JUNG

---

of Champeaux (1070–1121). The mystical element played a predominant role in their teachings.

[3] Known as "Doctor Seraphicus" (1221–74), Franciscan theologian. For him mystical contemplation of God was the highest activity of man. The full title of the work is *Itinerarium mentis ad Deum*, which contains a variant of the saying "God is an infinite sphere . . ." (cf. Frischknecht, 8 Feb. 46, n. 13).

[4] Or "active imagination." Cf. Keyserling, 23 Apr. 31, n. 2.

[5] Brethren of the Free Spirit, a heretical sect originating in Southern Germany. Cf. *Aion*, par. 139.

[6] The most scholarly theologian of Christian antiquity (ca. 185–253). For his psychology cf. *Psychological Types*, pars. 21ff., and *Aion*, par. 336. His teachings were condemned at the fifth Ecumenical Council at Constantinople (399); among other things he taught that the devil would be saved in the end (ibid., par. 171, n. 29). Cf. also Rahner, "Das Menschenbild des Origenes," *Eranos Jahrbuch* 1947.

[7] Latin author, born *ca.* 123 A.D. at Madauros in Africa. The *Metamorphoses,* or *The Golden Ass,* is an apparently autobiographical novel describing the hero's life and initiation into the mysteries of Isis and Osiris.

[8] A Greek papyrus stemming from the Alexandrian school of mysticism (cf. Dieterich, *Eine Mithrasliturgie,* 1903). Jung made use of its symbolism in *Symbols of Transformation,* CW 5, pars. 143f., 149ff., and in "The Concept of the Collective Unconscious," CW 9, i, par. 105.

[9] Cf. James, *The Apocryphal New Testament* (1921), pp. 364ff. and 228ff. The former dates from the 3rd cent. and is the most famous of the Gnostic Acts; the latter from 2nd cent.

Anonymous

Dear Spouses!   10 April 1946

Since your letter of 10.I.46 is signed X. and Y. the above salutation seems to me a fitting one, especially as it is obviously the intention of Y. to present themselves not as a unity but as a masculo-feminine duality. I must offer my apologies to the highly esteemed Spouses for the long delay in composing this letter, which tenders them my thanks. The writer is an old man, no longer very efficient, who turns out to be a bad swimmer in the flood of paper that threatens to drown him, more particularly since the so-called peace and with it the international post have invaded our previously so apprehensive and yet so pleasantly isolated country. Later, when the roving Anglo-Saxon can cross our borders again, I shan't be able to read any letters at all let alone write them. I can only hastily wave a handkerchief and then only as if by accident. But since the masculine half of the *coniunctio* that has introduced itself is a poet, he can assuredly concoct as many answers as he likes from me, and thus bring a soft glow into the—so I hear—Chinese eyes of the feminine half. For of this royal pair, which is forever one and yet two, an old Master says: *Omnia in se habet, quod indiget.*[1]

Herewith the limping messenger from the Sesame Mountain[2] bids farewell and extends friendly greetings to the honoured pair from

C. G. JUNG

☐ (Handwritten.)

[1] "It [the *lapis*] has in itself everything it needs." Cf. *Aion,* par. 220.

[2] The name of a Swiss "Volkskalender" (popular calendar).

To Bernhard Milt

Dear Colleague,   13 April 1946

Very tardily I am at last getting down to answering your kind letter of 28 November 45. By way of excuse I can only plead that I have not yet regained my former working capacity. I beg you, therefore, to pardon my negligence.

You raise in your letter the question of the archetype of the self. As you rightly suppose, this archetype is not so much a working hypothesis as something that is found. There are, as I have shown for instance in *Psychology and Alchemy* with the help of empirical material, typical symbols in dreams which, *faute de mieux*, I have called symbols of wholeness or of the self. I have also gone into the reasons for this nomenclature. I have often asked myself whether the term "archetype" (primordial image) is a happy one. In general I find it most disadvantageous to let neologisms run riot in any science. The science then becomes too specialized in an unjustifiable way and loses contact with the world. I therefore prefer to use terms that are also current in other fields, at the risk of provoking occasional misunderstandings. For instance, Jakob Burckhardt applied the term "primordial image" to *Faust*,[1] and with every conceivable psychological justification. Equally, I believe, the word "archetype" is thoroughly characteristic of the structural forms that underlie consciousness as the crystal lattice underlies the crystallization process. I must leave it to the philosopher to hypostatize the archetype as the Platonic *eidos*. He wouldn't be so far from the truth anyway. The expression is much older than Augustine. It is found with a philosophical stamp as far back as the *Corpus Hermeticum*, where God is called the "archetypal light." In Augustine, who was still a Platonist, the archetype has absolutely the connotation of a primordial image, and so far as it is meant Platonically it does not agree at all badly with the psychological version. The old Platonic term differs from the psychological one only in that it was hypostatized, whereas our "hypostatization" is simply an empirical statement of fact without any metaphysical colouring.

Frischknecht is wrangling with me badly. I get a letter from him from time to time. Recently I had to spell it out to him that the theologian looks at the world through the good Lord's eyes, but the

☐ Zurich.
[1] Cf. *Symbols of Transformation*, par. 45, n. 45.

418

scientist only through human eyes. In his essay on Brother Klaus he has not even noticed that he has tacitly imputed to me Freud's personalistic standpoint, without remarking that this is just what I have been criticizing Freud for these last 30 years. Basically I have every sympathy with the difficulties of the theologian. It is no small matter to have to admit that in the end all dogmatic assertions are human statements—with, as I always emphasize, quite definite psychic experiences underlying them. Considering the extraordinary difficulty of epistemological self-limitation it is really not surprising that any number of misunderstandings come about. I am quite sure that if I had chosen any other term for the archetype, misunderstandings of another colour would have cropped up, but they would have cropped up anyhow. With collegial regards,

Yours sincerely, C. G. JUNG

To Father Victor White

[ORIGINAL IN ENGLISH]

Dear Father White, 13 April 1946

I was very pleased with your letter and I hasten to answer it at once. It is a nice idea of yours that you want to come out to Switzerland between July and September. The time that would suit me best would be between the 12th and 27th of August. I should like you to consider yourself as my guest during your stay here. I shall be in the country, on the upper part of the lake of Zurich, where I have a little country place. If you are a friend of the simple life you will have all the comfort you need. If your tastes should be too fastidious you would find it a bit rough. To give you an idea: I do my own cooking and chop my own wood and raise my own potatoes. But you have a decent bed and a roof over your head and we shall have plenty of time to discuss anything under the sun. As to clerical garments, you need no disguise whatever, since we shall be in a Catholic country, not very far from the famous monastery of Einsiedeln.[1] But I warn you to bring something old and disreputable with you so that you spare your good clothes, and a pair of light shoes for occasional sailing on the lake.

In alchemy you find many references to the *homo quadratus*,[2]

[1] In Einsiedeln, a town in Canton Schwyz, there is a beautiful Benedictine monastery founded in the 10th cent. It is also a place of pilgrimage.
[2] W. cited an article on the subject in the 1945 issue of the *Harvard Theological*

which is always an allusion to *mercurius quadratus*, i.e., the *hermai*.[3] The *quadratura* is a symbol for totality.

Yours sincerely, C. G. JUNG

Review. The *homo quadratus* or *Mercurius quadratus* refers to the totality of the four elements. Cf. *Psychology and Alchemy*, CW 12, par. 172.
[3] Marble or bronze pillars. Cf. ibid., Fig. 63.

To Laurence J. Bendit

[ORIGINAL IN ENGLISH]

Dear Dr. Bendit,   20 April 1946

I do remember X. and I'm sorry to hear that he died. He was my patient once. I'm glad to know that his end was correct.

Concerning Ascona I must say that the meetings continued throughout the whole war. You should apply as soon as possible to Mrs. Fröbe (Casa Gabriella, Ascona-Moscia, Tessin) for tickets. The meeting will take place at the end of August. It would be a great pleasure to meet you there and to discuss matters with you.

Your views about extra-sensory perception are not fundamentally different from mine. It's only the definition which I was criticizing. People are apt to consider intuition as something quite particular, something much "higher" than sensory perception. As you know I call intuition *any kind* of perception which takes place in a way that cannot be explained by the function of the senses. Intuition of divine thoughts or of a small tumour in the bone is in no way different as the nature of an object has nothing to do with the function of intuition. It has to do with it just as little as the faculty of seeing with the nature of the object which you see. It is always the function of seeing or hearing, the nature of which does not depend upon the object. I do not make the difference between intuition as a merely unconscious perception and a hypothetical intuition which would produce say a pneumatic truth. Whether intuition takes place in a normal state of mind or in an ecstasy or in a delirium, it is always the same function which in certain cases however reaches an acuteness or an autonomy which it does not in other cases. But there are people with an unusual faculty of thinking or reasoning or with an extraordinary sense-perception; for instance there are chamoix-hunters in our country who see the stars in bright sky during daytime, etc.

This is the reason why I classify any kind of extra-sensory perception under the term of intuition,[1] no matter what the object is.

Inasmuch as any function of consciousness can be directed, controlled, differentiated, intuition also can be practised and differentiated. That you can perceive things which your senses would not allow you to catch hold of or your thinking would not allow you to infer forms an additional problem. It forces us to speculate about the nature of time and space. The fact that extra-sensory perception is real proves that time and space are psychically relative. That means that they can be more or less annihilated. If that is the case, an extreme also is possible where time and space don't exist at all. If a thing is capable of non-existence then we must assume that it is also capable of absolute existence. We know that time and space are indispensable and inalterable conditions of our three-dimensional world, what you call the world of the soma. The non-existent space and time cannot be an object of our observation. Therefore there is no possibility of proving that they do not exist. The most we can know is that under certain psychic conditions time and space reveal a certain elastic quality, i.e., a psychic relativity, where they begin to behave as if they were dependent upon the psyche. From this fact I conclude that the human psyche (and presumably the animal psyche too) has a non-spatial and a non-temporal quality, i.e., a relative power to make time and space non-existent. This would speak in favour of a relative immortality, as only in time can something come to an absolute end, but in relative time it can only come to a relative end. Concerning space we would come to the conclusion that the psyche is only to be located relatively. In other words, the whereabouts or the extension of the psyche in space is relatively uncertain.

Concerning spirit (pneuma) I want to say that spirit and matter are a pair of opposite concepts which designate only the bipolar aspect of observation in time and space. Of their substance we know nothing. Spirit is just as ideal as matter. They are mere postulates of reason. Therefore I speak of psychic contents that are labelled "pneumatic" and others "material."

I'm much obliged to you that you mention a possible translator of my writings. The great difficulty of translating my works consists

---

[1] Later, Jung expanded his conception of ESP phenomena, considering them as "meaningful coincidences" or "synchronistic" events. Cf. "Synchronicity," CW 8, esp. par. 840.

in the fact that one rarely finds a translator who is educated enough to understand my technical language or my thought. I have a thoroughly humanistic training and my language is imbued with all sorts of allusions which are completely dark to somebody lacking an academic training. (. . .)

Yours sincerely, C. G. JUNG

To J. Allen Gilbert

[ORIGINAL IN ENGLISH]

Dear Dr. Gilbert,   20 April 1946

Your letters[1] have reached me after all. It was a great pleasure to see that you haven't changed yet, you have continued the "rhinoceros walks."[2] I remember vividly those tracks of the pachyderm in the African jungle, and still more the smooth footpaths of the hippopotamus whose customs are of clock-like regularity. I was very glad to see, too, that you have discovered how great the analyst's modesty is in speaking of "analysis" instead of "programmatic synthesis." There is a reasonable amount of certainty that we can show a patient what there is, but we cannot hand out the thing which he ought to do. Because it is so difficult to do something about one's own life, we are also careful not to reveal too much to an individual what he might be expected to do or what the tasks of his life would be leading him to, because we know how difficult it is to do anything at all. So when a patient complains that he knows exactly what he might do, I say: Well, you are in the position of everybody who knows what he might do; he has now to set to work to do at least something of it and to find out how to do it. There would be no difficulty in life if one always knew beforehand how to do a thing. Life is some sort of art and not a [straight] rail or a ready-made product to be had at every corner.

Your plan to submit to an experiment[3] like a rabbit would be quite a good idea if you would have the courage to do it by your

[1] The letters are dated 10 Oct. 44 and 17 Sept. 45.
[2] G., himself an analyst and physician, had been in analysis with Jung for several months in 1926/27. At that time Jung had a dream about him in which G. appeared as a wounded rhinoceros that "created great havoc; the feeling was one of concern and pity." In his letter of 1945 G. mentioned "the fear that possessed you in the presence of my rhinoceros tracks."
[3] An experiment in introversion.

422

own means. I could only show you how to introvert, but such an experience wouldn't be your own if anybody else put you through it. The point is just that *you* can put yourself through it, as anybody would who tried to live his own life. Nobody can live it for you or instead of you. Your life is what you try to live. If I should try to put you through something it would be my life and not yours. At your age[4] I shouldn't worry any more what one could do with your life. You should rather think of what *you* still can do with it. And in your place I wouldn't seek such an experiment as it is already near at hand, because the end of life will put you exactly into what you always tried to get into. But unfortunately you tried it in an indirect way and under the guidance of somebody else. But when you die, nobody else will die for you or instead of you. It will be entirely and exclusively your own affair. That has been expected of you through your whole life, that you live it as if you were dying. So it will happen to you as it happens to most people. They die in exactly the same ways as they should have lived. Good Lord, how many impersonations do you reckon you need to understand this simple truth?

As I see from your letter, you are still going strong and I hope that you will continue still for a while in the same way. That is a fair chance for you to meditate a bit deeper about how one ought to live.

Yours sincerely, C. G. JUNG

[4] At the time of his last letter G. was 78. He died at 81.

To Eugene H. Henley

[ORIGINAL IN ENGLISH]

My dear Henley,   20 April 1946

I should have written to you long ago to thank you for your kindness and generosity. The tobacco has safely arrived and I must say that Granger[1] has remained my true love. I hope that you have received the two books I sent you. I'm having another one sent to you.

Ever since my recovery I have been very busy and I only have to be careful not to overwork. There is so much to do and particularly such a flood of letters that I hardly can keep up with it. For some time the current affairs ate up whatever time was left to me and so

☐ Ph.D., (1884–1968), American analytical psychologist.
[1] Name of an American pipe tobacco.

all my personal correspondence had to go by the board for a while. I now have my spring vacations and can atone for some of my sins at last. I'm up at Bollingen and enjoy a most beautiful spring. I can sail my boat again which gives me no end of pleasure.

I have read with great interest all the news about conditions in America. We only get some scarce information through the papers and it isn't always very clear. Having been shut off from the world for such a long time, one is no longer *au courant* with the status of the world in general. Our so-called peace is a troubled affair and the greatest part of Europe is still in hysterics. No wonder really! The mental and moral, social and financial catastrophe is simply gigantic. The mental and moral devastation is the one I'm chiefly concerned with, since we begin now to get more immediate and personal acquaintance with the facts of the atrocities of the war. We see now the people who have been in the bombed cities and have undergone the nightmare of hell. The mentality created by the Nazis in Germany is really a study in itself. People were horrified by my assertion that the Germans were psychopaths,[2] but this is really a very mild judgment considering the spiritual catastrophe of the German mind.

I have seen a great deal of X. In a way he has pleased me very much. He is running his job very efficiently and he could really do something pretty great. But he gets into drink from time to time and then he is just damn foolish, so that one is never too sure that he doesn't get mixed up in a fatal scandal. In that respect he is— excuse me—typically American, as he is unexpectedly efficient in one way and in another way as astonishingly childish. A European of his calibre would be far less efficient because he would be just too childish, and he would be far less childish because he would be cleverer. There is a great distance between the ego and the shadow in an American and that is the reason why so many of your boys get on with the Germans so well—because there is something similar in the Germans, namely the great tension between the positive and the negative pole. The only difference is that in the American the tension exists between the civilized and the primitive man, in the German between the cultural man and the devil. This is one of the reasons why the Americans are easily led astray or influenced by the Germans. I think there is no small danger for your boys in Germany. I see it also in X., who is always in danger of getting too much under their influence. They are so damn plausible, like old Hitler, who may

[2] Cf. Ullmann, 25 May 45, n. 3.

roast in hell for ever. But I must say this for him: he was an eye-opener! He has even opened my eyes several inches. You quote in your letter my saying that I had no illusions. Against this statement I must say that before the Hitler era I still had some illusions which have been radically destroyed by the prodigious efforts of the Germans. I really had not thought that man could be so absolutely bad. I thought he could be evil, but evil has at least a certain character, while evil in Germany was rotten. It was a carrion of evil, unimaginably worse than the normal devil. Since Germany is not on the moon, I have drawn my conclusions for the rest of mankind.

Conditions in Switzerland are somewhat better than during the war, though our bread-ration has been reduced again to 250 gr. a day, which isn't bad since we have more possibilities of other foodstuffs than in other countries. During the war I cultivated my own fields. I have raised corn, potatoes, beans and lately even wheat, also poppy for oil. We have eaten polenta like Italians. It isn't so bad, but not very interesting.

My best regards to Mrs. Henley,

Gratefully yours, C. G. JUNG

To Wilfrid Lay

[ORIGINAL IN ENGLISH]

Dear Mr. Lay, 20 April 1946

It was a great pleasure to have a letter from your hand. Its contents have pleased me very much as they convey essential things. You have understood my purpose indeed, even down to my "erudite" style. As a matter of fact it was my intention to write in such a way that fools get scared and only true scholars and seekers can enjoy its reading.

I admire you very much for having learned and apparently mastered the difficult Chinese language. I never got so far and that is the reason why I feel hopelessly handicapped in the further pursuit of the intricacies of *I Ching*. I once had the immodest and rather foolish fantasy of writing a commentary on the *I Ching*, but I soon recognized the enormity of such a task and the absolute inadequacy of my equipment.

☐ (1872–1955), American teacher and writer on psychology. Cf. in translator's note (by C. F. Baynes) to the *I Ching*: "[Dr. Lay] learned Chinese for the sole purpose of reading the *I Ching*."

I'm not as old as you are yet, but I must say that not very long ago I recognized the immense truth of being the *hsiao jên*.[1] Such an understanding is indispensable to anyone who wants to understand what you very rightly formulate as equipollence.[2] Only the *hsiao jên* contains the *chên-jên*,[3] who is the universal basis for your equipollence.

Your method of unravelling the mysteries of a quotation, namely by looking up its context, is very subtle and I must say elucidating. Curiously enough it coincides absolutely with my method of dream-interpretation.

What you say about "this so-called peace," which apparently doesn't make you particularly happy, doesn't refer any more to the Pax Romana of olden times. It is now, as you have noticed, a Pax Americana. It should fill you with pride if you are still accessible to political illusions. To me this peace is no peace at all. I think there is no such thing as peace, since even a peaceful democracy like Switzerland is nothing but a mitigated civil war which we are wise enough or small enough to entertain chronically in order to escape worse issues. Man, on the whole, is a fool and remains a fool. Yet it is apparently indispensable to believe in a better future. It never has been better, however, it has only been new and apparently incomparable, so that people have always been puzzled whether it could not be perchance the long hoped-for better future.

. . .

Hoping you are always in good health, I remain,

Yours sincerely, C. G. JUNG

[1] Lit. "little man." The "little man" is frequently referred to in the *I Ching*; his fate is to suffer and accept (cf. Hellmut Wilhelm, "Das Zusammenwirken von Himmel, Erde und Mensch," *Eranos Jahrbuch* 1962, pp. 342f.). Richard Wilhelm, in his German translation of the *I Ching*, used the term "gemeiner Mensch" (common man), which in Mrs. Baynes's English version is rendered "inferior man." According to a communication from Hellmut Wilhelm, the term *hsiao jên* in the *I Ching* does not carry a derogatory meaning although it acquired this in later writings, particularly those of the Confucian school; so perhaps "common man" would express the double meaning more accurately.
[2] L.'s concept of "spiritual equipollence," according to which "everyone has a soul, and has as much chance as anyone else of becoming conscious of its extent."
[3] The "true man," the perfect man of Taoist philosophy. Cf. *Mysterium Coniunctionis*, par. 490, and "The Philosophical Tree," CW 13, pars. 432f.

Anonymous

[ORIGINAL IN ENGLISH]

My dear N., 28 April 1946

. . .

Yes, your trouble has very much to do with the dissolution of the ego. It is the ego that doubts, hesitates, lingers, has emotions of all sorts, etc. In your *patientia* you have your Self. You have missed nothing and you have failed nowhere, you simply suffer from things that happen to you. No matter how you interpret them. The ego wants explanations always in order to assert its existence. Try to live without the ego. Whatever must come to you, will come. Don't worry! Your mood on dawn (April 7th) tells you everything. Don't allow yourself to be led astray by the ravings of the animus. He will try every stunt to get you out of the realization of stillness, which is truly the Self.

. . .

Yours cordially, c . g .

□ The addressee is a woman.

To Robert Eisler

Dear Dr. Eisler, 25 June 1946

What I said in *Two Essays* about archetypes in the animal psyche[1] was only an aside. I hazard the conjecture, which is based on certain experiences, that the lowest layers of our psyche still have an animal character. Hence it is highly probable that animals have similar or even the same archetypes. That they do have archetypes is certain in so far as the animal-plant symbioses clearly demonstrate that there must be an inherited image in the animal which drives it to specific instinctive actions. I have dealt with this point only in one essay: "Instinct and the Unconscious"[2] (in *Contributions to Analytical Psychology*, Kegan Paul, London, 1928).

An offprint of my lecture "Archetypes of the Collective Unconscious" follows by the same post. I have also asked my publisher to

□ Ph.D., (1882–1949), Austrian writer on comparative religion, philosophy, and archaeology, then residing in England.
[1] Cf. CW 7, par. 109: "There is nothing to prevent us from assuming that certain archetypes exist even in animals."
[2] Cf. CW 8, pars. 268, 277.

send you a copy of my *Psychology and Alchemy*, which of all my writings is probably the most concerned with archetypes.

Yours sincerely, C . G . J U N G

Anonymous

[O R I G I N A L   I N   E N G L I S H]

My dear N.,   6 July 1946

I have been waiting for a sign of your existence since you vanished from the scene of my ordinary surroundings, and I often wondered what you are doing and how you are faring. The leap from Zurich and its remoteness into the seething pool of New York must have been a real *tour de force.* . . . I don't wonder that introversion has actually no chance with you. Moreover it would be too fantastic even to think of introversion under your present circumstances. A tough and cold-blooded extraversion is the only thing that carries you across the stormy sea of your manifold activities.

I have, as you rightly surmise, just begun my vacations in Bollingen. I enjoy sailing, the lapping of the water against the bow and the gentle breeze of the mornings. No mental activity—except the elaboration of attractive menus. Yesterday I had the visit of a French Carmelite monk, a learned man, interested in the psychology of religion. Our main theme was the Devil and the demons.

I hope you are reckless enough to take care of yourself. My very best wishes.

Yours affectionately, C . G .

☐ The addressee is a woman.

To Joachim Knopp

Dear Herr Knopp,   10 July 1946

1. An author by the name of Jakob Lorber[1] is unfortunately not known to me.

2. With regard to homoeopathy you are quite right in considering

---

☐ Düsseldorf.

[1] K. asked for information about a certain Jakob Lorber (1800–1864) who, according to him, had kept a record of an "inner voice," starting in 1840.

it a continuation of alchemical practice. This is indeed so. I recommend you to take a look at the writings of Hahnemann.[2] You will find them listed in any encyclopedia.

3. Regarding organic illness (accidents, injuries, etc.) it can be stated with certainty that these things do at least have psychological syndromes, i.e., there is a concomitant psychic process which can sometimes also have an aetiological significance, so that it looks as though the illness were a psychic arrangement. At any rate there are numerous cases where the symptoms exhibit, in a positively remarkable way, a symbolic meaning even if no psychological pathogenesis is present.

4. One cannot say that every symptom is a challenge and that every cure takes place in the intermediate realm between psyche and physis. One can only say that it is advisable to approach every illness from the psychological side as well, because this may be extraordinarily important for the healing process. When these two aspects work together, it may easily happen that the cure takes place in the intermediate realm, in other words that it consists of a *complexio oppositorum*, like the *lapis*. In this case the illness is in the fullest sense a stage of the individuation process.

5. I don't know under what conditions you could study in Switzerland. But I would advise you to write tentatively to the Dean of the Medical Faculty [in Zurich]. Someone there might be able to help you. I myself have long since given up lecturing at the University, nor do I lecture any more at the Federal Polytechnic. So in this respect I can give you no information.

Unfortunately I don't know any psychotherapist for you now in Germany who has my confidence. Some of these people are dead, some have disappeared. As you know, my teachings were suppressed as much as possible in Germany both before and during the "era." Consequently, though I am very well known in Anglo-Saxon countries only a very few people know me in Germany—a land of the dead as you rightly say.

Yours truly, C. G. JUNG

[2] Samuel Hahnemann (1775–1843), German physician, founder of homoeopathy. His main work is *Organon of the Rational Art of Healing* (orig. 1810).

429

To Fritz Künkel

Dear Dr. Künkel, 10 July 1946

This is to acknowledge with thanks the receipt of the books of Stewart Edward White.[1] I have read them conscientiously, and I would know from these books what sort of problem you are confronted with even if I hadn't seen it from your letter.

The really important book is *The Unobstructed Universe*. The other two do not rise much above the level of the general run of spiritualistic literature, of which I made a thorough study for a long time in my earlier days in order to find out the meaning of this movement. Already then it became absolutely clear to me that the whole spiritualistic movement is pervaded by an unconscious urge to allow the unconscious to reach consciousness. This phenomenon shows that even today our consciousness is still much too split off from the unconscious, which leads to a psychic uprooting of man. This also explains why practically everybody falls victim to some kind of -ism, with the result that any cause, however reasonable in itself, gets a pathological streak. The wildest breaking away of consciousness from the natural order of things has, of course, been witnessed in Germany, but we see the same phenomenon in other nuances and gradations throughout the whole world of the white man. Even the yellow Japanese have gone to blazes. They have obviously learnt so much from the uprooting and corresponding madness of the white man that they no longer consulted the *I Ching* before and during the war. In the first World War Japanese statesmen always consulted it in important affairs of state, as I know from Richard Wilhelm.

Although *The Unobstructed Universe* is written in a ghastly style, it contains ideas of fundamental importance which, despite the barbarous setting, seem to me significant enough to be taken seriously.

☐ M.D., (1889–1956), German psychotherapist, emigrated to U.S.A. and settled in Los Angeles, California. Originally a follower of Alfred Adler, he became sympathetic to Jung's ideas.

[1] American author (1873–1946). He wrote over 40 books but became known mainly through his "Betty Books," in which he recorded the statements made by his wife during trances (cf. *The Betty Book*, 1937; *Across the Unknown*, 1939). After the death of his wife he received communications from her through a medium. He collected these messages in *The Unobstructed Universe* (1940). Jung's foreword to the German translation of this book (*Uneingeschränktes Weltall*, 1948) is in CW 18. Cf. also "The Psychological Foundations of Belief in Spirits," CW 8, par. 599.

Their concurrence with the findings of the psychology of the unconscious is positively amazing. The compensatory drive of the unconscious towards conscious realization stands out particularly clearly; that is to say our consciousness is largely dissociated from the unconscious so that a reconnection is of the utmost importance. This is also a basic principle of analytical psychology. Equally worth noting is the introverted attitude necessary for this, without which the unconscious contents could not be assimilated. The fact that they appear in the form of personifications (spirits) is not at all surprising. Firstly it has been from time immemorial the traditional form of unconscious compensation, and secondly there is no possibility of proving with certainty that it is really not a question of spirits. But the proof that it *is* a question of spirits is equally difficult if not impossible. As we know, the proof of identity is extraordinarily difficult to furnish, though all sorts of people have tried. One may be entirely convinced subjectively, but that is a long way from being an objective proof. I can't imagine any method whereby an objective proof could be furnished. The proofs that White gives are not in themselves convincing since every single one of them could be explained by the actually existing knowledge in the unconscious (cryptomnesia,[2] clairvoyance, etc.). I once discussed the proof of identity for a long time with a friend of William James,[3] Professor Hyslop[4] in New York. He admitted that, all things considered, all these metapsychic phenomena could be explained better by the hypothesis of spirits than by the qualities and peculiarities of the unconscious. And here, on the basis of my own experience, I am bound to concede he is right. In each individual case I must of necessity be sceptical, but in the long run I have to admit that the spirit hypothesis yields better results in practice than any other.

The success of this book is not surprising either. We are living again in a postwar period in which, as after the first World War, a veritable wave of spiritualism is sweeping mankind. A further point

[2] "Hidden memory," recollection of forgotten or repressed experiences as though they were new and original ideas. Cf. "Cryptomnesia," CW 1.
[3] American psychologist and philosopher (1842–1910), professor at Harvard. He became interested in psychical research; his best known investigations in this field were with the American medium Mrs. Piper, which convinced him of the genuineness of her mediumship.
[4] James Hervey Hyslop (1854–1920), American psychologist, professor at Columbia University; he did extensive work on psychical research in which he, like William James, first became interested through his sessions with Mrs. Piper.

of agreement with the psychology of the unconscious is the idea of the elasticity of space and time. I coined this same term many years ago and have used it in my lectures without knowing anything about this book. The extraordinary emphasis White lays on consciousness also agrees with our view that the dawning of consciousness, indeed consciousness itself, is the all-important goal of human evolution.

Since *The Unobstructed Universe* is not handicapped by any knowledge of psychology, the author is completely unaware of the fact that his Betty, who manifests herself as his *femme inspiratrice*, is also present in him even if his Betty had never died or had not existed at all. For this reason I do not call this feminine figure Betty but anima. The figure of Anne[5] behaves towards Betty as the mother archetype (the Great Mother) behaves towards the ego in the psychology of women. She represents the feminine aspect of the self. This point is of particular interest as it does not fit in with the psychology of a man. If Betty were nothing but an anima, in the case of a man there would have to be a masculine figure corresponding to Anne, namely the Wise Old Man. In this respect, then, Betty behaves like a real woman and not like an anima. This seems to indicate that she is herself rather than an anima figure. Perhaps, with the help of such criteria, we shall one day succeed in establishing, at least indirectly, whether it is a question of an anima (which is an archetype never lacking in masculine psychology) or of a spirit. I must own that with regard to Betty I am hesitant to deny her reality as a spirit; that is to say I am inclined to assume that she is more probably a spirit than an archetype, although she presumably represents both at the same time. Altogether, it seems to me that spirits tend increasingly to coalesce with archetypes. For archetypes can behave exactly like real spirits, so that communications like Betty's could just as well come from an indubitably genuine archetype. On the other hand, it must be emphasized that by far the greatest majority of communications are of purely psychological origin and appear in personified form only because people have no inkling of the psychology of the unconscious.

You are quite right when you say that in these circumstances it would be the task of a practical psychology to offer the public handier concepts than the subtleties of analytical psychology. In actual practice one finds oneself again and again in the position of having to

[5] Anne (or "Lady Anne") is one of the figures appearing in *The Unobstructed Universe*; according to Betty's communications, a Scottish lady of superior intelligence and wide knowledge who had lived in the 16th cent. and "collaborated" with Betty.

make do with the terminological crudities of science. I would like to draw a radical distinction between psychology as a science and psychology as a technique. In practice I have no compunction, if the case seems to me sufficiently certain, in speaking simply of spirits— albeit with the proviso that these spirits may be partly or entirely mere personifications of unconscious tendencies and sooner or later are integrated into consciousness and then vanish. I have observed plenty of such cases, where the unconscious first appeared in spirit form— spirits which later, after discharging their contents into consciousness, disappeared again.

Your view that the collective unconscious surrounds us on all sides is in complete agreement with the way I explain it to my pupils. It is more like an atmosphere in which we live than something that is found *in* us. It is simply the unknown quantity in the world. Also, it does not by any means behave merely psychologically; in the cases of so-called synchronicity it proves to be a universal substrate present in the environment rather than a psychological premise. Wherever we come into contact with an archetype we enter into relationship with transconscious, metapsychic factors which underlie the spiritualistic hypothesis as well as that of magical actions.

The best idea in *The Unobstructed Universe* is perhaps that of frequency.[6] It is an idea that dawned on me too during my attempts to explain the relative reality of metapsychic phenomena. The parallel White draws with the nature of thought seems to me to hit the mark very aptly. Thought has no quality in common with the physical world except its intensity, which in mathematical terms may be considered as frequency. You observe a distinct heightening of this intensity or frequency in all cases where either an archetype manifests itself or, owing to an absolute *abaissement du niveau mental*,[7] the unconscious comes actively into the foreground, as in visions of the future, ecstasies, apparitions of the dying, etc.

I would like to see the book translated if only it were written more sensibly, but there is so much insufferable gabble in it that it would

---

[6] White devotes a chapter to "Frequency." According to Betty's and Anne's communications, frequency is the essence of movement, and thought is psychological movement. Each stage in the development of consciousness has its individual frequency.

[7] "Lowering of the mental level," a term coined by Pierre Janet in *Les Obsessions et la psychasthénie* (1903) to explain dissociations, automatisms, and other psychic disturbances. Jung makes frequent use of the term in explaining neurotic, psychotic, and also synchronistic phenomena.

only scare off an educated European public, for no one likes picking out the pearls from such a journalistic morass. But the book has stimulated me no end, and for this I am most grateful to you. With best regards,

Yours sincerely, C. G. JUNG

Anonymous

Dear Sir, 10 July 1946

By parental power is usually understood the influence exerted by any person in authority. If this influence occurs in childhood and in an unjustified way, as happened in your case, it is apt to take root in the unconscious. Even if the influence is discontinued outwardly, it still goes on working in the unconscious and then one treats oneself as badly as one was treated earlier. If your work now gives you some joy and satisfaction you must cultivate it, just as you should cultivate everything that gives you some joy in being alive. The idea of suicide, understandable as it is, does not seem commendable to me. We live in order to attain the greatest possible amount of spiritual development and self-awareness. As long as life is possible, even if only in a minimal degree, you should hang on to it, in order to scoop it up for the purpose of conscious development. To interrupt life before its time is to bring to a standstill an experiment which we have not set up. We have found ourselves in the midst of it and must carry it through to the end. That it is extraordinarily difficult for you, with your blood pressure at 80, is quite understandable, but I believe you will not regret it if you cling on even to such a life to the very last. If, aside from your work, you read a good book, as one reads the Bible, it can become a bridge for you leading inwards, along which good things may flow to you such as you perhaps cannot now imagine.

You have no need to worry about the question of a fee. With best wishes,

Yours sincerely, C. G. JUNG

☐ Resident of Germany.

To J. B. Priestley

[ORIGINAL IN ENGLISH]

Dear Mr. Priestley,   17 July 1946

· · ·

Since I saw you I have read several of your novels and plays and I enjoyed them very much. I was particularly impressed by the two aspects of your personality. Your one face is so much turned to the world that one is surprised again and again to meet another face which is turned to the great abyss of all things. I just wanted to tell you my impression as I want to let you know how much I appreciate the superhuman faculty of looking at things with a straight and with an inverted eye.

Yours gratefully, C. G. JUNG

☐ English novelist, playwright, and critic. This letter was sent in by P. in the form printed here.

Anonymous

Dear N.,   20 July 1946

I think you are expecting rather too much of people without giving sufficiently of yourself. One has to stand *below* others if one wants something to drop down from them into one's lap. Since you are up to your ears in the inkpot again, I politely invite you to call in on me most ceremoniously next Wednesday afternoon at 4 o'clock. Here there are no higher personages but chiefly snails who are enchanted with the rain. With best greetings,

Your sighing grandfather, C. G. JUNG

☐ (Handwritten.) The addressee is a man.

To Eleanor Bertine

[ORIGINAL IN ENGLISH]

Dear Dr. Bertine,   25 July 1946

· · ·

I'm just spending a most agreeable time of rest in my tower and enjoy sailing as the only sport which is still available to me. I have just finished two lectures for the Eranos meeting of this summer.[1]

[1] Combined as "Der Geist der Psychologie," *Eranos Jahrbuch* 1946; published

It is about the general problem of the psychology of the unconscious and its philosophical implications.

And now I have finally rest and peace enough to be able to read your former letters and to answer them. I should have thanked you for your careful reports about Kristine Mann's illness and death long ago,[2] but I never found time enough to do so. There have been so many urgent things to be done that all my time was eaten up and I cannot work so quickly any longer as I used to do.

It is really a question whether a person affected by such a terrible illness should or may end her life. It is my attitude in such cases not to interfere. I would let things happen if they were so, because I'm convinced that if anybody has it in himself to commit suicide, then practically the whole of his being is going that way. I have seen cases where it would have been something short of criminal to hinder the people because according to all rules it was in accordance with the tendency of their unconscious and thus the basic thing. So I think nothing is really gained by interfering with such an issue. It is presumably to be left to the free choice of the individual. Anything that seems to be wrong to us can be right under certain circumstances over which we have no control and the end of which we do not understand. If Kristine Mann had committed suicide under the stress of unbearable pain, I should have thought that this was the right thing. As it was not the case, I think it was in her stars to undergo such a cruel agony for reasons that escape our understanding. Our life is not made entirely by ourselves. The main bulk of it is brought into existence out of sources that are hidden to us. Even complexes can start a century or more before a man is born. There is something like karma.

Kristine's experience[3] you mention is truly of a transcendent nature. If it were the effect of morphine it would occur regularly, but it doesn't. On the other hand it bears all the characteristics of an *ekstasis*. Such

---

in revised form as "Theoretische Ueberlegungen zum Wesen des Psychischen," *Von den Wurzeln des Bewusstseins* (1954); now "On the Nature of the Psyche," CW 8.

[2] Cf. Kristine Mann, 1 Feb. 45. M. had died on 12 Nov. 45.

[3] About 3 or 4 months before her death, while in hospital with a good deal of pain, depressed and unhappy, Dr. Mann saw one morning an ineffable light glowing in her room. It lasted for about an hour and a half and left her with a deep sense of peace and joy. The recollection of it remained indelible, although after that experience her state of health worsened steadily and her mind deteriorated. Jung felt that at the time of the experience her spirit had left her body.

a thing is possible only when there is a detachment of the soul from the body. When that takes place and the patient lives on, one can almost with certainty expect a certain deterioration of the character inasmuch as the superior and most essential part of the soul has already left. Such an experience denotes a partial death. It is of course a most aggravating experience for the environment, as a person whose personality is so well known seems to lose it completely and shows nothing more than demoralization or the disagreeable symptoms of a drug-addict. But it is the lower man that keeps on living with the body and who is nothing else but the life of the body. With old people or persons seriously ill, it often happens that they have peculiar states of withdrawal or absent-mindedness, which they themselves cannot explain, but which are presumably conditions in which the detachment takes place. It is sometimes a process that lasts very long. What is happening in such conditions one rarely has a chance to explore, but it seems to me that it is as if such conditions had an inner consciousness which is so remote from our matter-of-fact consciousness that it is almost impossible to retranslate its contents into the terms of our actual consciousness. I must say that I have had some experiences along that line. They have given me a very different idea about what death means.

I hope you will forgive me that I'm so late in answering your previous letters. As I said, there has been so much in between that I needed a peaceful time when I could risk entering into the contents of your letter.

My best wishes!

Yours sincerely, C. G. JUNG

To Margaret Erwin Schevill

[ORIGINAL IN ENGLISH]

Dear Mrs. Schevill,   25 July 1946

Thank you very much for your kind birthday-letter which has reached me a day before the eventful date.

The idea of a seminar for old people is not bad at all, although it would be exceedingly difficult to find suitable material along which one could develop the ideas that deserve to be talked about. It could be done however in an absolutely unpremeditated way in the form of questions and answers. Of course all of the people ought to be seriously concerned with the question of death or should have felt the touch of it at least.

437

I'm sorry to hear that Mr. Schevill died. I did not know it. I hope he had an easy death and not such a terrible agony as for instance Kristine Mann. I'm terribly sorry X. has to suffer from cancer, in her case cancer really comes too early and it is a mean way of killing people anyhow. But nature is horrible in many respects. It is a fact that the body very often apparently survives the soul, often even without a disease. It is just as if the soul detached itself from the body sometimes years before death actually occurs, or sometimes with perfectly healthy people who are going to die within a short delay by acute illness or accident. As far as we know at all there seems to be no immediate decomposition of the soul. One could almost say, on the contrary.

It is curious that you mention the problem of transference and its importance for the problem of death. I'm just about to publish a book about the psychology of transference,[1] where I try to elucidate its problems with reference to its metapsychical aspects.

I'm glad to hear that your books thrive. Mine do too! Actually I'm enjoying my summer vacations and I'm full of the best intentions to restrict my work with patients to the utmost, and you know that the way to hell is always paved with good intentions. You know, for old people, the concept of "next year" or something of the sort is always problematic since one has learned that time is a most relative thing and can come to a complete end whenever it chooses.

It would be nice to see you again if you come across the dividing ocean.

Cordially yours, C. G. JUNG

[1] "The Psychology of the Transference" (orig. 1946), now in CW 16.

To Erich Neumann

Dear Dr. Neumann,   5 August 1946

I mustn't keep you waiting any longer although I am far from having finished reading everything you sent me.[1] I am particularly impressed by the lucidity and precision of your formulations. My further impressions must wait and I plead for patience. You can

□ (Handwritten.)
[1] The MS of his *The Origins and History of Consciousness* (1954; orig. 1949). Jung's foreword is in CW 18.

scarcely imagine how overloaded I am with work, above all with letters. Recently I had to cope with about 100 letters in 14 days. Hardly were the postal connections with abroad re-established than tempests of letters blew in. Also it rained MSS which are particularly bothersome. Besides that I had to see patients and give an eye to my own work. Since my illness I am no longer as efficient as before and have to spare myself a bit. The result is I get nowhere. I always wanted to write to you but each time something intervened that had to be settled immediately, so that I never found the leisure to write you anything substantial. I have also been thinking how we could get you over to Europe again, but I see no way at present. Conditions here are difficult, as you can imagine, and everything is uncertain. We live on our cultural island as before, but all round us is sheer destruction, physical and moral. One has to shut one's eyes to do anything sensible oneself. Germany is rotted beyond description. Letters I get from there are with few exceptions either infantile or pig-headed or hysterical, which more than anything else confirms that my diagnosis of Germany's spiritual condition was right.

In France, England, and Switzerland it is now Catholic scholars who are taking an interest in my psychology. For the rest, a book by a Reformed theologian Dr. H. Schär, *Religion und Seele in der Psychologie C. G. Jungs*,[2] has just been published (Rascher, Zurich). It might interest you. It is very good and positive. The author is lecturer on the psychology of religion at the University of Bern. I have just finished 2 lectures on "The Spirit of Psychology" for Eranos. They are discussions of principle. I'll send you an offprint. Also my little book on transference is to appear soon. It's a risky business, but when you are old you can say more than when life is still ahead.

The situation in Palestine seems to be very difficult indeed. The new age is being born with endless pains.

Recently I ran into X. while visiting one of my Kabbalistic pupils. He is an interesting phenomenon. He gets into the unconscious through the roof and as the corns[3] on his feet are blind he can't see what he's climbing down into.

Meanwhile with best greetings and wishes,

Ever sincerely yours, C. G. JUNG

[2] *Religion and the Cure of Souls in Jung's Psychology* (1950; orig. 1946). Cf. also his *Erlösungsvorstellungen und ihre psychologischen Aspekte* (1950).
[3] In German, "Hühneraugen," hen's eyes.

To J. B. Priestley

[ORIGINAL IN ENGLISH]

Dear Mr. Priestley,   9 August 1946

Thank you very much for the copy of your talk and for the book.[1] I have read both in the meantime. I cannot say how much I enjoyed your most luminous and comprehensive talk. It is really remarkable how you succeeded in getting your vast subject together and making a whole of it. I must say I have never seen a better summary of my main ideas in such a concise form. It is a masterpiece.

I have also read your novel with greatest interest. I was particularly impressed by the way in which you make your figures real. They are complete characters. The next impression was the atmosphere you give to places and situations. As a psychologist I could not help noticing your extraverted hero, who lives the better part of a human life forgetting nothing but himself and his fatal relatedness to certain human beings. An introvert would have forgotten the greater part of the world in order to work out the secret of his relationship to the little girl and her mystery. And she would have married him as soon as possible in order to show him that she is no mystery at all. But Gregory needed 30 years and a bad slump into a prolonged brown study in order to remember himself. The most impressive dissolution of the magic family represents one of the most characteristic experiences of an extravert. An introvert—if the gods are favourable to him —might discover how positively, even magically attractive people can be. He would also need 30 years or more. Your novel has given me the chance of meeting some more individuals and of sharing some more human lives. We live in so many lives and so many lives live in us, that's where you take it. My best thanks!

Yours truly, C. G. JUNG

[1] P. gave a BBC talk "Description of a Visit to Carl Gustav Jung" on 18 June 1946 and sent Jung a copy together with his *Bright Day* (1946).

To Jolande Jacobi

Dear Dr. Jacobi,   19 August 1946

. . .

You are much too sensitive to gossip. As soon as one has anything to do with analysis one becomes the butt of rumours. If I had listened to them I would have been dead long ago. Better to listen to your dreams than to the mouthings of human lemurs.

. . .

My best wishes!

Yours ever, c. g. jung

To Roger Lyons

[ORIGINAL IN ENGLISH]

Dear Mr. Lyons,   12 September 1946

I'm fully aware of the fact that it must be a most bewildering business to a rational American to collide with such strange a psychology as mine. It seems to be full of the most unwarrantable contradictions. On the one hand you ought to know more about my work and on the other hand you have no chance to talk to me. I understand that such a situation is more or less incomprehensible but I should advise you to read something about Zen Buddhism. I have written a little introduction to one of Suzuki's books[1] and you might get hold of one of his volumes. That would give you a certain idea of what you are up against.

One can indeed use analysis as an escape and one has to be quite particularly careful in your case that such a thing does not happen, because you must learn to use your own powers and the more one helps you to do so, the more one hinders you. There must be a certain optimum and this consists in seeing me and not seeing me, both in the right proportions. The right proportion, however, cannot be established by man alone. It will be established by peculiar circumstances over which we have little or no control. Presumably you come across myself in the right moment and then you gain something, but if you try to force circumstances it is quite likely that you don't hit it off. Our last meeting in Ascona was absolutely on the right line. Such a thing can happen again. In the meantime you must hunt alone and seek it where you find it.

Yours sincerely, c. g. jung

□ An American, then studying in Zurich; now a foreign service officer, United States Information Agency.
[1] "Foreword to Suzuki's *An Introduction to Zen Buddhism*," CW 11. The foreword was originally published in Suzuki, *Die grosse Befreiung: Einführung in den Zen Buddhismus* (1939).

To Ernst Anderes

Vir Magnifice! 22 September 1946

Permit me to thank you and the University once again for the invitation to Winston Churchill's reception[1] and quite particularly for the honour of seating me next to the illustrious guest. Conversation with him, however, made no small demands on one's tact and ingenuity, as I was constantly in doubt as to how much question and answer I might expect from that very tired man. Nevertheless I thank you for one of the most interesting experiences of my life. With collegial regards,

Yours very sincerely, C. G. JUNG

☐ (1883–1952.) Then professor of gynaecology, later Rector of Zurich U.
[1] 23 Aug.–16 Sept., Churchill spent a holiday in Switzerland, and afterwards visited Bern and Zurich. In Bern the Swiss Government arranged a reception, and in Zurich the University—where Churchill gave a famous address—arranged a dinner. On both occasions Jung was present, and in Zurich was seated next to Churchill, apparently at the behest of Churchill whose daughter Mary was interested in Jung's work. (See pl. VI.)

To Erlo van Waveren

[ORIGINAL IN ENGLISH]

Dear Mr. van Waveren, 25 September 1946

It has taken a very long time until I was able to get so far in my correspondence that I could answer your letter. One could say that the whole world with its turmoil and misery is in an individuation process. But people don't know it, that's the only difference. If they knew it, they would not be at war with each other, because whosoever has the war inside himself has no time and pleasure to fight others. Individuation is by no means a rare thing or a luxury of the few, but those who know that they are in such a process are considered to be lucky. They get something out of it, provided they are conscious enough. Of course it is a question whether you can stand such a procedure. But this is the question with life too. Millions of people couldn't stand it, as you know from recent events. Individuation is just ordinary life and what you are made conscious of. If anybody should marvel at it, he must have been unprepared for what life holds in store for everybody. My best wishes!

Yours sincerely, C. G. JUNG

☐ Analytical psychologist, in New York City.

442

To Jolande Jacobi

Dear Dr. Jacobi,   27 September 1946

I congratulate you on your productivity! It is indeed in all brevity a whole compendium of erotic problems.[1] I have suggested only a few, mostly stylistic, alterations in the text, with pencil. The "man who carries his Eve within him"[2] comes from alchemy and not from the "mouth of the people," at least so far as I know this collective organ. I hope very much that you have recovered to some extent. Your news that Churchill was not bored at our table was a great relief. Conversation with him was no easy matter since he directed his answers mostly to the House of Commons.*

With best greetings,

Yours sincerely, C. G. J U N G

* I nearly fell over with astonishment when I discovered that I had been seated next to Churchill—and at a University dinner too! "There will be signs and wonders. . ."!

[1] "Der Schattengeliebte und das Rautendelein," *Du* (Zurich), no. 11, Nov. 1946.
[2] Cf. *Hermetis Trismegisti Tractatus vere Aureus*, 1610: "Our Adamic hermaphrodite, though he appears in masculine form, nevertheless carries about with him Eve, or his feminine part, hidden in his body." Quoted in Jung, "Psychology and Religion," CW 11, par. 47 & n. 22; cf. also *Mysterium Coniunctionis*, par. 545.

Anonymous

Dear N.,   7 October 1946

It is not a simple matter to write to you. I am trying to put myself in *your* shoes so as to give you an intelligible answer. You are obviously not yet in a position yourself to form any conception of the mood of the world towards everything and everybody that comes from Germany. Every personal relationship is overshadowed by what has happened, since everybody was affected by it in the most personal way. Had, for instance, the Germans visited Switzerland, you would not now be able even to write to me any more. I really do not know what your attitude is to these facts and real possibilities that hung over us like doom year after year, or rather, how you judge their

□ Germany. To an analytical psychologist (male), a friend and pupil of Jung's.

443

effect on non-Germans. From the answer of your Swedish acquaintance you surely must have seen that there are any number of difficulties which, as I have discovered from the many letters I have received from Germany, are hardly appreciated in Germany itself. For us non-Germans they are on the contrary only too plain.

The letters from my German acquaintances invariably begin where they left off in 1939 or earlier. These people obviously approach one as though nothing had happened in between, except for a few untoward accidents like disease, getting bombed out, losing a relative, etc. They take it entirely for granted that individual relationships are something extramundane, or that the individual exists in himself, apart from his family and nation, and therefore has no solidarity with them let alone any responsibility for them. This curious emancipation is like anticipating the highest goal of psychic differentiation and has a chilling effect on the ordinary mortal, rather like that of a Zen Master on the Christian Westerner. Anyone who has attained this emancipation has reached nirvana and thus made himself unreal. There is nothing wrong with that, only one would not expect such a person to turn to people again. That would be too spooky and moreover lacking in style. Had the average German really attained this liberation from the social coil by a special act of grace, then the mass phenomenon of a "people's community" would be inexplicable. But since a mass movement did in fact exist, the emancipation of the individual must be spurious since it needed compensating. Accordingly the truth would be that the German, like every civilized person (not to mention the primitive!), is answerable for his family and his nation. He must take into account his relation to the surrounding world if he wants to spare himself some very unpleasant experiences. He would do well to realize the views and sensitivities of other people who feel a solidarity with their country if he is not to miss the mark completely. A non-German would presuppose sufficient family responsibility, both in himself and others, not to take it as a matter of course that if he were in the German's shoes he would be received with open arms. If, for instance, my family had done a mortal injury to another family, or ruined them, I would certainly not take the restoration of friendly relations with a member of that family for granted; on no account could I ignore the attitude of my family as completely as my German correspondents do. This impressive peculiarity of German psychology has led me to conclude that there must be a remarkable unconsciousness of the collective responsibility of the individual. This fact might also explain the peculiar susceptibility to mass psychosis, which compensates the deficiency of consciousness in the most effective way, *but downwards* (hence the leftward-turning swastika!).[1]

I realize that you may feel my answer thoroughly absurd, but I would remind you that it was not *we* who had the mass psychosis. I would have maintained a tactful silence had you not expressed the earnest wish to have an answer from me. I think you should no longer take German psychology as self-evidently valid, but must consider the reactions of foreigners if you want to establish any relations with representatives of the so-called "second-class" nations. I know that in the sphere of your individual consciousness you do not think like that. But I miss in your letter the consciousness of collective responsibility, which for us is an indispensable requirement not only of politeness but of human feeling in general. I know that this condition is very difficult for you because to you it seems so ridiculous. But I do not doubt that if you take the trouble to think it through thoroughly you will see the logic of it.

Recently a letter burst into the house from Bruno Goetz,[2] the writer, in which he expressed the wish to visit me immediately. I replied that it was too painful for me to talk with Germans as I had not yet got over the murder of Europe. Whereupon he drenched me with a flood of literary vituperation. To which I rejoined: Q.E.D. Herr Goetz with his thoughtful answer has once again, but unconsciously, ridden roughshod over the feelings of the non-German in true Teutonic fashion, in order to intoxicate himself with the elation of his noble anger. This is no longer seasonable. The Herrenvolk has become obsolete; the stupendously harmless Herr Goetz still doesn't know that. As a matter of fact he knows nothing at all, and appears mightily justified in his own eyes. I am sorry for these people who have failed to hear the cock crowing for the third time.

If I had belonged to a secret society which had tried to murder you in a disgraceful way and you had miraculously escaped, it is not altogether improbable that you would feel some hesitation towards me. With kind regards,

Yours sincerely, C. G. JUNG

[1] The leftward-turning swastika denotes movement towards the unconscious; cf. "A Study in the Process of Individuation," CW 9, i, par. 564.
[2] German writer; cf. his *Das Reich ohne Raum* (1925), cited in "Wotan," CW 10, par. 384.

Anonymous

[ORIGINAL IN ENGLISH]

Dear N.,   7 October 1946

Thank you for your letter. Within the last weeks I had a sort of bad conscience, always thinking that I should write to you, but I had such a hectic time this summer that correspondence was pushed into the background. I lost about half of my vacations because of Eranos, a Congress,[1] and Mr. Churchill's visit to Switzerland. The latter event was interesting in so far as I had a chance to meet Mr. Churchill at close quarters and also his most charming daughter Mary. The reception Churchill had in Zurich was something you really have missed. Churchill told me afterwards that it was the best and most impressive reception he ever had in his life.

· · ·

Yours cordially, C. G. JUNG

☐ U.S.A. (a woman).

[1] A joint meeting in Zurich of the Zürcher Naturforschende Gesellschaft and the Schweizerische Naturforschende Gesellschaft in Sept. 1946, when a "Section for Practical Psychology" was founded as part of the latter Society.

To Fritz Verzar

Dear Colleague,   31 October 1946

Please forgive me for having kept you waiting so long for my answer. Lately I have had so much to do that it simply wasn't possible to give your letter the attention it deserved. But now I will delay no longer and tell you my reaction.

I am quite convinced that something ought to be done to make mankind aware of the tremendous dangers of the path they are travelling. In some respects people are already aware that the situation is extremely dangerous, as the universal fear of war proves. It is self-evident that it would be highly desirable to humanize humanity, but when one sees the struggle the great powers have in order to reach any kind of agreement on apparently the most reasonable meas-

☐ 1930–56 professor of physiology at the U. of Basel; from 1957 Director of the Institute for Experimental Gerontology. — He asked Jung for help in his endeavour to abolish the death penalty since "there is no problem that can be redeemed or improved by death."

446

ures for the well-being of the world at large, and how they fail because one or the other refuses to be talked to or cannot give way, this becomes even more impossible when certain moral questions are touched upon. To be sure, a general agreement could be reached that human beings should not murder each other, but this would instantly be circumvented by sticking them in labour camps in Siberia, for instance, where people are not exactly murdered but are housed and fed so that they can work, and where they then perish of various diseases, while all the time the State refuses to admit that it has murdered them. The Americans are certainly a very humane nation, or at least imagine they are, but this does not prevent so-and-so many Negroes from being lynched every year. Moreover I have some doubts whether it would not have been more humane, for instance, to shoot Grand Admiral Raeder,[1] as he wished, instead of putting him behind bars for 30 years. I at any rate would prefer to be shot than to spend even 10 years in prison. When one knows how the prisoners degenerate morally and spiritually, and under what torments, one is no longer 100 per cent convinced that the death penalty would not be far more humane. Only for outsiders, who have never been inside, is penal servitude not a hellish cruelty. I know many cases from my psychiatric experience where death would have been a mercy in comparison with life in a prison.

Unfortunately you can't preach to people, for if it really worked the world would long since have been converted to Christianity and then there would be no crime any more. But that is just the difficulty, that you get nowhere with teaching and telling people. What was the end-result of hundreds of years of Christian education in Germany? The barbarism was not touched by it in the slightest, and God knows enough was said every Sunday from all the pulpits in Europe. I know from my practice what it takes to drive even the simplest, most obvious truth into people. In certain cases it is simply impossible, and these are not even madmen but people who in their private life are considered absolutely *compos mentis*. Of course governments could do something, but nowadays when you want anything from any government you are referred to the world situation, which causes the governments enough headaches as it is and leaves them no time to think about how the death penalty could be abolished or human

---

[1] Grand Admiral Erich Raeder (1876–1960), Commander-in-Chief of the German Navy, 1935–43. At the Nuremberg trials he was sentenced to imprisonment for life, but was freed in 1955.

life made sacred. Fundamentally, no one is convinced enough of the absolute value and sanctity of man to guarantee him his life under all circumstances. You can see that with damages for fatal accidents: a man's life is worth ca. 5000 frs. And it is unfortunately true that the more he values his own life the less he values that of his fellow man. After what has happened in Germany I have lost the last vestiges of any illusions I may have had about man's capacity for improvement. If it is not possible to bring about any change in human consciousness we shall not succeed, either, in realizing an ideal which is acknowledged by all reasonable people anyway but founders again and again on the savage unreason and unconsciousness of humanity in general. Sure I would be hopeful and would do everything in my power to support your endeavours if only I saw the slightest possibility of their meeting with success. But unfortunately I know that no outcry and no discussion can alter things in the least. With best regards,

Yours sincerely, C. G. JUNG

To Father Victor White

[ORIGINAL IN ENGLISH]

Dear Father White,   6 November 1946

Your dream[1] is very much to the point! I had all sorts of feelings or "hunches" about you and about the risks you are running. We are indeed on an adventurous and dangerous journey! But the guiding principle is the "wind" i.e., the πνεῦμα. Norway is the northern country, i.e., the intuitive sector of the mandala.

. . .

If you could get me just one or two specimens of the ordinations against alchemy,[2] I should be most obliged.

[1] In his first letter after visiting Jung in August W. mentioned a dream in which he was sailing, with Jung at the helm, from Norway to England. They were passing through perilous rocks at great speed, but there was no feeling of fear "because the wind was taking care of us."

[2] No answer can be found in W.'s letters. These ordinations could refer to the Papal Decretal *Extravagantis* of John XXII in 1317 (tr. J. R. Partington, "Albertus Magnus on Alchemy," *Ambix*, London, I:1, 1937). Partington states that "the study and practice of alchemy were forbidden several times to the Franciscans in the period 1272–1323 . . . and to the Dominicans between 1273 and 1313 . . . with penalties increasing from imprisonment to excommunication, the scandal going on, it is said, in spite of severe prohibitions."

I am most interested in what you are going to write and I shall certainly write a preface[3] if you wish me to do so.

After the congresses[4] I had to spend about 5 days participating in the reception of Mr. Churchill in Bern as well as in Zurich. At the last dinner I even had the seat beside him. He was very tired, more than I was. Afterwards I had to settle down to a careful overhauling of my Eranos lectures.[5] I have just given them the last touch. They have grown in size, as I have inserted some rather extensive material illustrating the multiple "luminosities" of the unconscious,[6] representing the "conscious-like" nuclei of volitional acts (presumably identical with archetypes). I hope this is not too Chinese. I have included St. Ignatius of Loyola's vision of the serpent with the many eyes[7] as a most unorthodox piece of evidence.

Thank you for the photos! They are good and a pleasant souvenir of your visit to Switzerland. I hope your next one will not be postponed too far! I wish I could travel more easily. But I am kept down through too many things. Presently I must make up my mind to tackle my dangerous paper about the psychology of the H. Trinity.[8]

The Latin text of *Aurora Consurgens* is in the British Museum. A rare print of 1625. The title of the volume is: *Harmoniae Inperscrutabilis*,[9] etc.

Hoping you are always in good health and in good spirits,

Yours, C. G. JUNG

[3] Possibly the foreword to W.'s *God and the Unconscious* (1952), now in CW 11.

[4] Cf. Anon., 7 Oct. 46, n. 1.

[5] Cf. Bertine, 25 July 46, n. 1.

[6] "On the Nature of the Psyche," CW 8, pars. 388ff.

[7] Ibid., par. 395.

[8] "A Psychological Approach to the Dogma of the Trinity," CW 11.

[9] Full title: *Harmoniae inperscrutabilis chymico-philosophicae sive Philosophorum antiquorum consentientium decades duae*, ed. Johannes Rhenanus (Frankfort, 1625). *Aurora Consurgens* appears therein as "Aurora sive Aurea hora," Decas II, pp. 175–242.

To Father Victor White

[ORIGINAL IN ENGLISH]

Dear Father White,   18 December 1946

Thank you for your dear letter. It is a great consolation to know that one's included in the prayers of fellow beings. The *aspectus*

mortis[1] is a mighty lonely thing, when you are so stripped of everything in the presence of God. One's wholeness is tested mercilessly.
An accumulation of drugs however necessary has made a complete
rag of myself. I had to climb out of that mess and I am now whole
again. Yesterday I had a marvellous dream: One bluish diamond,
like a star high in heaven, reflected in a round quiet pool—heaven
above, heaven below.[2] The *imago Dei* in the darkness of the earth,
this is myself. The dream meant a great consolation. I am no more
a black and endless sea of misery and suffering but a certain amount
thereof contained in a divine vessel. I am very weak. The situation
dubious. Death does not seem imminent, although an embolism can
occur anytime again. I confess I am afraid of a long drawn-out
suffering. It seems to me as if I am ready to die, although as it looks
to me some powerful thoughts are still flickering like lightnings in a
summer night. Yet they are not mine, they belong to God, as everything else which bears mentioning.

Please write again to me. You have a purity of purpose which is
beneficial. Thank you for the records, quite interesting!

I don't know whether I can answer your next letter again. But let
us hope. Gratefully,

Yours, C. G. JUNG

☐ (Handwritten in pencil.)

[1] Over a month earlier Jung had had a very serious heart embolism. His letter
is written by hand, apparently lying down. It is the first of a long series of handwritten letters, often of many pages, showing his great personal interest in the
correspondence with W., who seemed able to give Jung what he felt he needed
most: a man with whom he could discuss on equal terms matters of vital importance to him. It is significant that with the growing estrangement over the
problem of the *privatio boni* (cf. White, 31 Dec. 49, n. 11) the handwritten
letters are replaced by dictated, typed ones, except for the very last two (25 Mar.
60, 30 Apr. 60), written during W.'s fatal illness. About three-quarters of Jung's
letters to him, comprising all the important discussions of psychological and
religious problems, are published in this selection, but some of a too private
nature are omitted.

[2] From the alchemical saying:

Heaven above	All that is above
Heaven below	Also is below
Stars above	Grasp this
Stars below	And rejoice.

Cf. "The Psychology of the Transference," CW 16, par. 384.

To Georgette Boner

Dear Dr. Boner, 17 March 1947

Belated thanks for your magnificent present![1] I am slowly recovering from my illness and have to push my correspondence very much into the background so as not to overload myself.

I shall read the book on my spring holiday in Locarno and I have already admired the splendid illustrations. What especially amazes me is the empathy with which you have drawn in the Chinese style. The legend is something I set an extraordinarily high value on, for it is saturated not only with worldly wisdom but with an unwitting profound psychology which grows quite naturally out of the earth. It is downright marvellous to see how the Chinese have tended their psyches as they do their gardens and yet cripple the feet of their women and indulge in all manner of cruelties. But it is also said that the Aztecs, precisely because of their terrible gory religion, were the gentlest and most childlike of men. Just the reverse with us and our sweet Christianity!

I have also heard that your father died at an advanced age. Please accept my heartfelt sympathy.

Yours sincerely, C. G. JUNG

□ Zurich.
[1] Wu Ch'êng-ên, *Monkeys Pilgerfahrt; Eine chinesische Legende*, tr. Georgette Boner and Maria Nils from Arthur Waley's English version, *Monkey* (1942), with 76 drawings by B. (1947).

To Jakob Stahel

Dear Colleague, 17 March 1947

Cordial thanks for your friendly picture postcard and kind remembrances. I have—touch wood!—only good to report. I keep to my daily regime: two hours of scientific work in the morning, and in the afternoon a rest plus a visitor. I now go for a walk twice a day for about ¾ of an hour. Things are already going a bit better, though not yet brilliantly. On Thursday I go to Locarno, Hotel du Parc.

I am sorry you're having such beastly weather, I walk in all weathers and am glad I can do it, thanks to your efforts. I hope you are making

□ M.D., (1872–1950), Jung's doctor. After his death his son, R. Stahel, became Jung's doctor until Jung's death in 1961.

451

a good recovery. The rest will do you good too. With best wishes, also to your wife,

Yours gratefully, C. G. JUNG

To Father Victor White

[ORIGINAL IN ENGLISH]
Locarno, until 10th of April
27 March 1947

My dear Victor,

As you see I avail myself of your kind permission to call you by your first name. I hope you will reciprocate by calling me C.G. which is the current designation of my unworthy "paucity." Well—I have to apologize for not having answered your interesting letters. The reason is: I have been completely swamped by an article which I had to elaborate for a new edition. It is that risky thing about the Holy Trinity. My efficiency is still very restricted and thus I have to drop everything else when I have to do something that really demands attention. I have finished the paper now. It is going to appear in a book called *Symbolik des Geistes*. The book will include Dr. Schärf's essay on Satan[1] and two other papers of mine, "Psychologie des Geistes"[2] and "Der Geist Mercurius."[3] In the meantime I have read your paper about Revelation[4] with the greatest interest. I must say it gave me a new light on St. Thomas. His views are really astonishing. It looks now very much more possible that he is the author of the *Aurora Consurgens*.[5] I thank you very much that you let me have your paper. With your kind permission, I should like to quote something of it in my paper on the Trinity. I think his angels and demons are simply wonderful.

. . .

□ (Handwritten.)

[1] Cf. Vuille, 22 Feb. 46, n. 1.

[2] First published in *Eranos Jahrbuch* 1945; retitled "Zur Phänomenologie des Geistes im Märchen," now "The Phenomenology of the Spirit in Fairytales," CW 9, i.

[3] First published in *Eranos Jahrbuch* 1942; now "The Spirit Mercurius," CW 13.

[4] "St. Thomas' Conception of Revelation," *Dominican Studies*, I:1 (1947); also in abbreviated form as "Anthropologia rationalis (The Aristotelian-Thomist Conception of Man)," *Eranos Jahrbuch* 1947. The lecture, slightly revised, is now ch. VII: "Revelation and the Unconscious," in W.'s *God and the Unconscious*.

[5] Cf. von Franz, *Aurora Consurgens: A Document Attributed to Thomas Aquinas* (1966), p. xi, n. 9.

X. is indeed on the right track in suspecting subatomic physics to be in secret league with psychology. I am hovering over that point too and keep my mind busy with digesting physical facts and theories. As soon as I get back to Zurich, I will read your paper once more, looking up the thing I want to quote. It is of course that excellent point that revelation has more to do with good imagination than with good morals.[6] I should even say that there is only a good prophet when the devil has caught hold of one of his legs. I beg your pardon! I suppose you had to be mighty tactful in your paper; there are some pretty vertiginous corners. That is of course because St. Thomas is really a great man quite apart from his saintliness.

I am looking forward to the summer. The weather here is execrable. For 10 days it is just pouring and no sunshine whatever. It even has snowed down to the 900 m. level. In Zurich the weather is much better. It has helped my concentration on my work. I shall not lecture in Ascona. Working out my last lecture[7] has given me no end of trouble. It has gone into print. But no proof sheets yet. I have not seen O. yet, since I avoid patients.

Hoping to see you in Ascona!

Yours cordially, C. G. JUNG

[6] In a letter of Jan. 1947 W. mentioned "St. Thomas' repeated assertion that to be a good recipient of revelation what is needed is 'not good morals but a good imagination.'" Cf. "Dogma of the Trinity," par. 289, n. 1.
[7] "On the Nature of the Psyche" (cf. Bertine, 25 July 46, n. 1).

To Professor Loewenthal

Dear Professor Loewenthal,   11 April 1947

I have read your letter with interest. I think you are quite right when you correlate the concept of intro- and extraversion with all conceivable intro- and extrapetal tendencies. My typology is based exclusively on biological data. I have myself brought it into relationship with the biological fact that when many eggs are produced the protective instinct is little developed or not at all, whereas with few eggs it is very strongly developed.[1] If you go into the ontogenetic and phylogenetic prehistory of intro- and extraversion, you necessarily

☐ Ramoth-Hashavim, Palestine.
[1] *Psychological Types*, par. 559.

453

come across all the polarities you mention. At the same time the concept itself becomes increasingly generalized until it finally loses its psychological applicability. But that is the fate of all psychological concepts. If they are traced back to their biological foundations they become so imprecise that they lose their psychological meaning. This is not to say that tracing types of consciousness back to instinctive data is superfluous. To understand their structure a knowledge of the biological foundations is essential. But since it is the nature of psychological concepts to point forwards, in the sense of an entelechy,[2] their specific meaning consists in the apprehension of complicated psychic facts. They lose this meaning, as said, when they are looked at retrospectively, in terms of their origin. They then dissolve into extremely general biological conditions.

I don't know whether you have read Jeans's[3] critique of Kant's conception of space. At any rate one would now have to formulate the apriorism of the so-called space category rather differently than was possible in Kant's day. The three-dimensionality of space is an unconscious precondition which is not to be confused with an apriori judgment.[4] This is where Jeans's critique comes in, demonstrating that space cannot be an apriori *judgment*. Its psychological reality is that of an *archetype*, i.e., it is just as unconscious as this and just as effective as this, which is why I have called the archetypes "dominants." It was just this point in your letter that interested me most, since at present I am very much concerned with apriori categories.

Yours sincerely, C. G. JUNG

[2] "That which carries its goal in itself," a term used by Aristotle to describe the active force inherent in the organism which turns potentiality into actuality and so leads to the attainment of the pre-existent goal.

[3] Sir James Hopwood Jeans (1877–1946), English mathematician, physicist, astronomer, professor of applied mathematics at Cambridge and Princeton. Cf. his *The Mysterious Universe* (1930) for criticism of Kant.—To Kant space and time were only *a priori* categories of cognition, having no reality outside these conditions.

[4] A judgment independent of a necessary premise based on experience.

To Eleanor Bertine

[ORIGINAL IN ENGLISH]

Dear Dr. Bertine,   17 April 1947

I have recovered so far from my illness that I can do my scientific work again and also enjoy life once more. I feel almost as well as I did before my illness, but I have to be even more careful not to overwork. I must live leisurely. My illness was due chiefly to the terrific conflict between practical work with patients and my creative scientific work. In my illness I found that there was a mountain of thoughts which I should get into shape and of which I hadn't known that they existed. I'm now trying to catch up with my unconscious fertility. I have a feeling as if I were the ancestral mother of the rabbits.

You could have come over this summer just as well as next year. You wouldn't shorten our rations. If *you* don't eat what the hotels in Switzerland offer you, then somebody else will devour it. We don't get it in either case. But I must say our rationing system is most efficient and we have enough food and of a very decent quality. I should have liked to see you again after such a long time. Of course, if you come over, you must realize that I am no longer capable of delving into the mysteries of your private psychology, as the remnant of my creative power has to be reserved for my own use. This is decidedly no joke. It is a very serious thing when you sin against this law. I can answer questions and I can discuss anything under the sun provided that it doesn't draw on my creative resources. And when you do analysis you have to do it by application of your creativeness. That is why I avoid personal analytical activity now. Hoping you are always in good health,

Yours cordially, C. G. JUNG

To Richard Otto Preiswerk

Dear Cousin,   21 April 1947

Many thanks for your interesting letter, in which you confirm all my forebodings about the Near East.[1]

I have recovered pretty well from my recent illness but must still take care not to overwork. I was very pleased to hear that you are taking an interest in my ideas. I am sending you through my publisher a small book,[2] which is a short introduction to the psychology

☐ M.D., (1884–   ), practising in Alexandria, Egypt; Jung's cousin on his mother's side (her maiden name was Emilie Preiswerk).

[1] In a letter of 1 Apr., P. mentioned the dangers arising from the nationalistic tendencies in Egypt.

[2] Probably *Ueber die Psychologie des Unbewussten* (1943); now "On the Psychology of the Unconscious," CW 7.

of the unconscious. It is a remarkable thing about psychotherapy: you cannot learn any recipes by heart and then apply them more or less suitably, but can cure only from one central point; and that consists in understanding the patient as a psychological whole and approaching him as a human being, leaving aside all theory and listening attentively to whatever he has to say. Even a thorough discussion can work wonders. It is of course essential for the psychotherapist to have a fair knowledge of himself, for anyone who does not understand himself cannot understand others and can never be psychotherapeutically effective unless he has first treated himself with the same medicine. Otherwise he never knows what he is doing. You don't get anywhere with such facile, general doctrines as that neurosis consists of repressed sexuality and the like. The psychotherapist must be a philosopher in the old sense of the word. Classical philosophy was a certain view of the world as well as of conduct. For the oldest authorities of the Church even Christianity was a sort of philosophical system with a code of conduct to match. There were philosophical systems for a satisfying or happy way of living. Psychotherapy means something of the sort too. It must always deal with the whole man and not merely with organs. So it must also proceed from the whole of the doctor.

I think that if you immerse yourself in my thought-processes without regarding them as a new gospel, a light will gradually go up for you about the nature of psychotherapy. There is, by the way, a Frenchman in your vicinity who seems to be *au courant*: Godel in Ismailia, Suez Canal Hospital. Recently he invited me to spend the spring holiday there. Unfortunately the invitation came too late, and the travel difficulties lamented by you plus my still far too shaky health decided me to choose the quieter part. One is no longer so young that one can afford to go a-venturing. Previously anything like that would have had definite attractions.

It is sad that you can't come over this year. But I can understand that under the present difficult conditions a journey would be as disagreeable for you as it would for me. It is a shame everything has to go to the devil, but human beings are such fools that they obviously deserve no better fate. With best greetings and wishes,

Yours, [CARL]

To Father Victor White

[ORIGINAL IN ENGLISH]

My dear Victor,   23 April 1947

You are a more conscientious letter writer than I am. I have been eaten up by work. But now there is a lull—most welcome indeed. I have just finished the MS of *Symbolik des Geistes*. From now on it will take quite a while until it is printed. I had to revise my paper "Geist der Psychologie"[1] ("Geist" meaning the same as f.i. in *Esprit des Lois*)[2] completely. It has increased in size considerably. I quite understand that it is very difficult to catch my meaning from the very sketchy first form of the paper. I think we agree that the unconscious is psychic, i.e., a sort of mind. Yet it is unc. since it is not associated with ego-consciousness, which is precisely the reason why it is "unconscious." Though it might be conscious to another subject, an alter ego, it is at all events severed from the ego. Yet it has according to its effects a psychic nature, or at least we assume it has. I have covered these points in the new edition. The paper is now going into print and I will send you an offprint as soon as copies are available.

I have made a great effort to explain what I mean by "psychic": I call those biological phenomena "psychic" which show at least traces of a *will that interferes with the regular and automatic functioning of instincts.*[3] This formulation raises a mountain of problems, f.i., Who is the subject of this will? What is the "knowing" coupled with every volitional act? etc. I have dealt with these questions to the best of my ability in the enlarged paper, so you'd better wait for it. I have gone once more through your splendid essay "De Revelatione."[4] I think, if you would give a short survey of *The Psychology of St. Thomas* at the Eranos meeting,[5] you would fulfil our expectations. You must realize that your public appreciates the demonstration of a mediaeval psychology which is strange to our ears. We are not used to it as your colleagues are. Moreover a genius like St. Thomas, who takes into consideration the action of angels and demons, will be accepted with the greatest attention, because it gives us a chance to understand how a mediaeval mind tackled the mod-

---

☐ (Handwritten.)

[1] "On the Nature of the Psyche."

[2] *De l'Esprit des Lois* (1748), the monumental work of the French political philosopher and historian Charles de Montesquieu (1689–1755).

[3] Cf. "On the Nature of the Psyche," CW 8, pars. 371ff.

[4] Cf. White, 27 Mar. 47, n. 4.

[5] This suggestion led to W.'s Eranos lecture; cf. ibid.

ern problem of the collective unconscious. Thus a part of your essay on St. Thomas, if you arrange it a bit for the occasion, would do. The psychological conceptions of Aristotle[6] have already been dealt with. Since St. Thomas was influenced by Avicenna,[7] the latter's views might deserve some attention.

. . .

O. is still torn asunder by the opposites inside a dense cloud of inflation. But his is a big problem. I am no more strong enough to tackle it myself. I have seen him. I can only hope that by the grace of God some light will dawn upon him. I know what's wrong, but how can I bring it home to him? He won't lap it up. No cause for optimism in his case!

X.—yes, I think she would be giving headaches right and left. I got them too as long as she was on the premises. "God protect me from my friends" said Bismarck. So do I. But I have heard nothing of what she is up to recently.

When you come to Zurich before Eranos, I hope you will give us the pleasure of putting you up in the style of last year.

Yours cordially, C. G. JUNG

[6] Probably Walter Wili, "Probleme der Aristotelischen Seelenlehre," *Eranos Jahrbuch* 1945.
[7] Latinized form of Ibn Sina (980–1037), the greatest Arab philosopher and physician.

To Mr. O.

[ORIGINAL IN ENGLISH]

Dear Mr. O.,   30 April 1947

Having studied your dream-material and having had a personal impression of your actual state of mind I have come to the conclusion that there is something wrong in the whole handling of your case, in spite of the fact that everything seems to be correct. The fact is that you have an uncannily extensive material one can hardly hope to cope with, at least I couldn't muster the amount of energy that would be required to deal with your dreams properly. In order to keep up with them one would need at least 3 hours a week. As you know, the principle of my technique does not consist only in analysis and interpretation of such materials as are produced by the unconscious, but also in their synthesis by active imagination. Of the latter I have seen nothing yet. But this is precisely the "technique" which seems to be indicated in your situation. You are not only informed enough but also intelligent enough to go on for a long stretch on the assumption that I'm buried and that there is no analyst for you under the changing moon except the one that is in your own heart. As you will understand, this does not mean at all that you analyse and interpret your dreams according to the rules of the thumb, but that you do what we call in the German language the "Auseinandersetzung mit dem Unbewussten,"[1] which is a dialectical procedure you carry through with yourself with the aid of active imagination. This is the best means I know to reduce an inordinate production of the unconscious. It doesn't seem right that a man like yourself is still dependent upon analysts. It is also not good for you, because it produces again and again a most unwholesome dissociation of your opposites, namely pride and humility. It will be good for your humility if you can accept the gifts of the unconscious guide that dwells in yourself, and it is good for your pride to humiliate itself to such an extent that you can accept what you receive. I don't intend to behave as if I were a corpse already. I'm therefore quite willing to help in your attempt in this direction, but I refuse in your own interest to plague myself with your material which is only helpful when you acquire its understanding by your own effort. Pride is a wonderful thing when you know how to fulfil its expectations. Did you never ask yourself who my analyst is? Yet, when it comes to the last issue, we must be able to stand alone *vis à vis* the unconscious for better or worse.

. . .

Yours sincerely, C. G. JUNG

[1] This term is usually translated in CW as "coming to terms with the unconscious."

To Mr. O.

[ORIGINAL IN ENGLISH]

My dear Mr. O.   2 May 1947

I'm somewhat astonished that you haven't learned yet to apply what I call "active imagination," as this is the indispensable second part of any analysis that is really meant to go to the roots. I wish you would carefully study what I have written about it in *Die Beziehungen zwischen dem Ich und dem Unbewussten.*[1] It is true, not much has been published about this subject. Most is contained

[1] "The Relations between the Ego and the Unconscious," CW 7.

in my Seminars. It is too difficult a subject to deal with before a merely intellectual public.

The dream[2] you write about is suggestive in that respect: it is a *massa informis*[3] which is meant to be shaped. It shouldn't go down the sink as it is always expected to do, it must remain on the surface, because it is the *prima materia*[4] of whatever you are going to do about it. The point is that you start with any image, for instance just with that yellow mass in your dream. Contemplate it and carefully observe how the picture begins to unfold or to change. Don't try to make it into something, just do nothing but observe what its spontaneous changes are. Any mental picture you contemplate in this way will sooner or later change through a spontaneous association that causes a slight alteration of the picture. You must carefully avoid impatient jumping from one subject to another. Hold fast to the one image you have chosen and wait until it changes by itself. Note all these changes and eventually step into the picture yourself, and if it is a speaking figure at all then say what you have to say to that figure and listen to what he or she has to say.

Thus you can not only analyse your unconscious but you also give your unconscious a chance to analyse yourself, and therewith you gradually create the unity of conscious and unconscious without which there is no individuation at all. If you apply this method, then I can come in as an occasional adviser, but if you don't apply it, then my existence is of no use for you.

Yours sincerely, c. g. jung

[2] A mass of yellow substance grew under the hand of the dreamer. He tried to wash it down the kitchen sink but the drain was blocked and the mass didn't go down.

[3] Alchemical term for the original chaos containing the divine seeds of life.

[4] The term *prima materia* is often used synonymously with that of the *massa informis* (or *massa confusa*). Cf. *Psychology and Alchemy*, Index.

To Erna Asbeck

Dear Frau Asbeck,   7 May 1947

Precognitive dreams can be recognized and verified as such only when the precognized event has actually happened. Otherwise the greatest uncertainty prevails. Also, such dreams are relatively rare.

☐ Wuppertal, Germany.

460

It is therefore not worth looking at the dreams for their future significance. One usually gets it wrong.

Yours truly, c. g. jung

To Mr. O.

[ORIGINAL IN ENGLISH]

My dear O.,   7 May 1947

Your material is, as I feared, much too rich! It needs a tremendous amount of mental work to reduce it.

Your first vision where your Beatrice appears contains a point where I can show you how you can come in. Beatrice, as an anima figure, is most certainly a personification; that means, a personal being created in this shape by the unconscious. You can safely assume that this is the shape your anima has chosen in order to demonstrate to you how she looks. Such a huge Beatrice is surely an unexpected sight. Instead of reacting to this rather amazing sight, you are satisfied with continuing your vision. But the natural thing would be that you make use of the opportunity and start some dialogue with your anima. Anybody who feels natural about such things would follow his surprise and put a question or two to her: why she appears as Beatrice? why she is so big? why you are so small? why she nurses your wife and not yourself? Etc. You also might ask her—since she is the "messenger of the grail"—what that funny thing is with that orange? what the magic ring means? what is the matter with all those animals? Treat her as a person, if you like as a patient or a goddess, but above all treat her as something that does exist. Moreover, in this vision you get right under the influence of your anima, and that's the reason why she begins to feed your wife, because your wife becomes underfed when you fall for your anima. Therefore you must talk to this person in order to see what she is about and to learn what her thoughts and character are. If you yourself step into your fantasy, then that overabundance of material will soon come to more reasonable proportions. But since you are giving free rein to your intuitions you are just swamped by it. Keep your head and your own personality over against the overwhelming multitude of images and aspects. You can do that, as I tell you, by stepping into the picture with your ordinary human reactions and emotions. It is a very good method to treat the anima as if she were a patient whose secret you ought to get at.

Yours sincerely, c. g. jung

461

To Albert Jung

Dear Colleague,   20 May 1947

The interpretation of the figure of Sophia, in the context in which I mentioned it, can only be done with the material handed down from antiquity, and there the interpretation is very simple. She is the Sapientia Dei, as she appears in the Wisdom of Solomon. To this Sophia is dedicated the Hagia Sophia of Byzantium. From the proper name Sophia are derived the names of saints, among them the so-called "Wicked Sophie."[1] The Hagia Sophia or Sancta Sapientia has of course nothing to do with witches, but Wicked Sophie can probably be connected with the witch-hunts, for the inclemency of the weather was frequently attributed to witches. Sophia cannot be brought together with Eve, since Eve has nothing to do with magic, but she probably can with Adam's first wife, Lilith.[2] The "Eternal Feminine"[3] in *Faust* is the Sapientia Dei, who is this same Sophia. It cannot be doubted that since such figures always have a shadow, Sophia has one too. This shadow would be a perversion of the divine into the dark and magical. Naturally this is the witch, or the arch-sorceress Hecate, who, three-headed and three-bodied, represents the lower equivalent of the Trinity (psychologically, the lower function triad). You will find a description of these curious trinitarian overlappings in my Eranos lecture, "Die Psychologie des Geistes"[4] (*Eranos-Jahrbuch* 1945).

Permit me a perhaps indiscreet question concerning your name: are you related to Dr. A. Jung, the gynaecologist in St. Gallen? He was a student friend of mine. With collegial regards,

Yours sincerely, C. G. JUNG

☐ Physician and analytical psychologist, now professor at Fribourg U., Switzerland. (No relation of C. G. Jung.)

[1] J. asked for an explanation of the term "Böse Sophie" (Wicked Sophie) used for the last of the proverbial cold days, May 12–15. The three others are named Pankratius, Servatius, and Boniface. The German word for them is the "Eisheiligen" = Ice Saints.

[2] Lilith, a night demon mentioned in Isaiah 34:14, was according to Jewish legend Adam's first wife. AV translates the Hebrew "Lilith" as "screech owl"; DV has "lamia." Cf. *Mysterium Coniunctionis*, par. 489, and *Symbols of Transformation*, CW 5, pars. 369f.

[3] "The Eternal Feminine leads upwards and on": the concluding words of *Faust II*.

[4] Cf. "The Spirit in Fairytales," CW 9, i, pars. 430ff.

To Mr. O.

[ORIGINAL IN ENGLISH]

Dear O.,   20 May 1947

The two animals that maul each other under water represent a fight of opposites in your unconscious. The fight takes place there because it doesn't take place in your consciousness. It forms a tail-devouring *Ouroboros* to the exclusion of yourself and that's the reason why you are still a baby and have such a huge anima on account of it. But even a baby can grow up and assert itself. Small babies *do* assert themselves, as a matter of fact. If you creep inside your anima-mother you simply go to sleep and then the animals can go on mauling each other into eternity. — If there are many diamonds or many oranges that is a disintegration and multiplication of the One. Of course it's wrong, but it derives from the fact that you allow yourself to be torn asunder. That's the baby-state all right and the mauling. It's all very well to feel dependent upon the whole world, but this is not the point. The point is that you are *not* dependent and that you begin to feel yourself as *not* dependent. It is all escapism to feel dependent. By such an attitude you just lame yourself and that's the reason why you cannot put yourself upon your own feet. The right way is your own way, and you should make yourself go on that way. That will lead you somewhere. — I'm not intending to discuss dreams with you. I want to see you at your own work first. Please consider every word I say in this letter. Perhaps it puts some light into you.

Yours sincerely, C. G. JUNG

To Julia Schmid-Lohner

Dear Frau Schmid-Lohner,   20 May 1947

I think I can set your mind at rest in regard to your question whether the days of the gospel are numbered. People will read the gospel again and again and I myself read it again and again. But they will read it with much more profit if they have some insight into their own psyches. Blind are the eyes of anyone who does not know his own heart, and I always recommend the application of a little psychology so that he can understand things like the gospel still better.

Yours sincerely, C. G. JUNG

☐ Biel, Switzerland.

To Oluf Berntsen

[ORIGINAL IN ENGLISH]

Dear Sir, 18 June 1947

Thank you very much for kindly sending me the interesting book by Paul Petit[1] which I didn't know. I have read it with the greatest interest. I'm absolutely of the same conviction as he is, that there is a *telos*[2] in each community. But I should add that this *telos* is a summation of the individual *tela*. Each man has his *telos* and inasmuch as he tries to fulfil it he is a real citizen. The community is nothing without the individual and if a community consists of individuals that do not fulfil their individual *telos*, then the community has no *telos* or a very wrong one. That is the reason why the "confirmisme social se transforme en idolâtrie, quant il devient fin en soi."[3]

Please give my best regards to Dr. Vischer[4] if you see him.

Yours gratefully, C. G. JUNG

□ Basel.

[1] *Résistance spirituelle* 1940–42 (Paris, 1947), edited and introduced by Jacques Madaule, and with a poem by Paul Claudel; extracts from Petit's open letters and articles in *La France Continue*, a clandestine paper appearing in Paris during the German occupation. Petit was denounced and beheaded in Cologne, August 1944.

[2] Goal, end.

[3] Quotation from Petit's article "20 mars 1941" in the above-mentioned book. The article criticized Pétain's appeal to the French people to make a "redressement intellectuel et moral."

[4] Cf. Vischer, 10 Oct. 44, n. □.

To Erminie Huntress Lantero

[ORIGINAL IN ENGLISH]

Dear Mrs. Lantero, 18 June 1947

Please forgive the long delay of my answer to your letter. It is not neglect that has hindered me from answering it sooner.

Your dilemma Agape-Eros[1] is a most interesting problem. There is indeed a big gap between the concept of Agape and the one of Eros. The former has a definitely intellectual and ethical character, while the latter, as I apply it, has very much more the quality of an

□ L.'s letterhead reads: "Religion in Life. A Christian Quarterly. Editorial Offices, New York."

[1] "Agape," charity, love, meaning love for God, spiritual love. In the NT it also signifies "love feast," the common meal taken by the early followers of Christ and sometimes connected with the Eucharist. Cf. Jude 12, "feasts of charity."

empirical concept formulating certain observable psychological facts. Of course, I did not invent the term Eros. I learnt it from Plato. But I never would have applied this term if I hadn't observed facts that gave me a hint of how to use this Platonic notion. With Plato Eros is still a daimonion or daemonium in that characteristic twilight in which the gods began to change into philosophical concepts during the course of centuries. As I am thoroughly empirical I never took a philosophical concept for its own sake. It was a word to me, which designated something tangible and observable, or it meant nothing. Thus when I tried to formulate the keynote of the general masculine attitude I fell upon the term Logos which looked to me to be the right word for the observed facts. The same when I tried to formulate a woman's general attitude I came upon the word Eros. Logos, being an intellectual something, naturally has the character of discrimination which is the essential basis of any intellectual judgment. Eros, on the other hand, is a principle of relatedness,[2] and since I wanted to apply a characteristic term for relatedness it was naturally the word Eros which presented itself. I didn't take this word[3] from anybody. I took it from my vocabulary and I said in so many words what I meant by it, namely a principle of relatedness. I took this term and not the term Agape, because relatedness is a natural feature of human psychology, but Agape is not. It is a very specified ethical concept. Eros is nothing of the kind. That is the reason why you find, as you say, Eros not only in the ancient Chinese religion but in many primitive religions as well.

As my whole psychology derives from immediate experience with living people, it is a matter of course that my concept of Eros also originated in immediate experiences. My experience is a medical one in the first place, and only in the course of many years I began to study comparative religion and I also studied primitive psychology, partially in the field. But all that came afterwards and it merely substantiated what I had found with modern individuals. There is not one single thing in my psychology which is not substantiated essentially by actual experiences.

To my knowledge this idea of Eros has not been anticipated in modern literature, simply because nobody else has based it upon immediate observation.

Sincerely yours, c. g. j u n g

---

[2] L. asked about the origin of Jung's definition of Eros as "the basic feminine principle of relatedness." Cf. "Woman in Europe," CW 10, pars. 255ff.

[3] I.e., as a psychological term.

To Pastor Werner Niederer

Dear Pastor Niederer,   23 June 1947

It was very kind of you to write to me at such length. I like to get reactions from my public, otherwise I am easily overcome by a feeling of isolation in the contemporary spiritual world.

I can only agree with your thoughts. Last year I saw an English Dominican[1] who spontaneously admitted that *everything* depended on whether the Church would go along with modern psychological developments or not. I was very surprised to hear that from a *Catholic* theologian. I wouldn't have gone so far. But it does seem to me that it would be appropriate if theology at least knew about the existence of the unconscious. This would be facilitated by St. Augustine's "Noli foras ire, redi ad te ipsum, in interiore homine habitat veritas."[2] Above all it must be understood that there is *objective psychic existence,* and that psychological explanation is not necessarily psychologizing, i.e., subjectivizing. The conception of dogma must be reviewed. I once reproached the late Dr. Temple, Archbishop of Canterbury, with the fact that in the "Doctrine of the Church of England" the dogma of the Virgin Birth is hedged about with qualifications and thus thrown in doubt. A concretistic understanding of it is thus made more difficult, and so it should be, I now think, for "spirit" is not *materia cruda* but air, fire, and aether, *volatile volatilior,*[3] a *quinta essentia.* Dogma is *credibile quia ineptum.*[4] To be understood at all it must be understood *typice—* in modern terms, *archetypally.* In our example Virgin = ANIMA *quae non novit virum.*[5] She does not conceive by man, but conceives God himself by God himself. That seems to me much better and more understandable, for such things can be observed and experienced.

So regarded, the dogmas gain new life, even the homoousia controversy[6] comes alive again. My new book *Symbolik des Geistes* is soon going to press. In it questions of dogma are discussed.[7]

☐ (Handwritten.) Zurich.
[1] Father Victor White.
[2] "Go not outside, return into thyself: truth dwells in the inner man." Augustine, *Liber de vera religione.* Motto to "A Psychological Approach to the Dogma of the Trinity."
[3] = more volatile than volatile.
[4] = credible because absurd. Cf. Wegmann, 20 Nov. 45, n. 2.
[5] = the soul which did not know man.
[6] Homoousia is the concept of the three Persons of the Trinity being of the

In your office as pastor you must not think aloud—for the sake of the weaker brethren. But one should know that symbols, even though not understood discursively, still have an effect on simple souls. We doctors have to speak the vernacular with many of our patients too.

Yours sincerely, c. g. j u n g

---

same substance (consubstantial) as against the homoiousia concept asserting the *likeness* of their substance. Cf. *Psychological Types*, par. 31.
[7] Published in 1948; contains the essay cited in n. 2 supra.

To Erich Neumann

Dear Colleague,   1 July 1947

The only disturbing term that struck me as I read your first volume[1] was the so-called "castration complex." I regard this term not only as an aesthetic mistake but also as an erroneous overvaluation of sexual symbolisms. This complex actually has to do with the archetype of sacrifice, a far more comprehensive term and one which takes account of the fact that for primitives sex does not have anything like the significance it has for us. In primitive psychology one must always bear in mind that the search for food, or hunger, often plays a decisive role. Thus the symbols of sacrifice are not just castrations or derivates of the same, as is especially obvious when you consider the taboos, all of which have a sacrificial meaning. The tabooing of words or syllables, for instance, can only be derived from castration by sheer force. Rather we must look at actual or alleged castration in the light of the archetype of sacrifice, which would make all these manifold forms far easier to understand in an unobjectionable way. The term "castration complex" is much too concretistic for my taste and too one-sided, although there are plenty of phenomena to which it proves perfectly applicable. But I would have avoided everything that gives the appearance of deriving psychic events from a specific instinct. We must put the essence of the psyche at the beginning as a phenomenon *sui generis* and understand the instincts as being in a special relationship to it. If we don't do this, all psychic differentiation is at bottom "nothing but." And then what does one do with a castrated Origen?[2]

[1] First part of the MS of *The Origins and History of Consciousness*.
[2] Origen castrated himself in literal interpretation of Matthew 19:12: ". . . there

467

This is the only point I must take exception to. For the rest I must say that I deeply admire your lucid exposition, crammed full of ideas. I have spoken with Rascher and he says he is ready to take on the book, but not until next year because of business reasons. An unavoidable lowering of prices is expected, and this makes all publishers hesitant. If I should come across anything else I will let you know. I shall now scrutinize your smaller writings[3] more closely, as there is a chance that Rascher will eventually bring out a collection of them. But this question has not been clarified yet. So you see that since things are going better with me I am busying myself with your affairs and doing my best to facilitate publication. But it's not all that simple in view of the scope of your work. Meanwhile with best regards,

Ever sincerely yours, C. G. JUNG

---

be eunuchs, which have made themselves eunuchs for the kingdom of heaven's sake." Cf. *Psychological Types*, pars. 21ff.

[3] Not identifiable in detail. Among them was the first draft of *Depth Psychology and a New Ethic* (1969; orig. 1949).

To M. Esther Harding

[ORIGINAL IN ENGLISH]

Dear Dr. Harding, 8 July 1947

At last I am through with your huge MS.[1] I allowed myself to make some pencil marks on it. . . . You write "noumenous." This word derives from Lat. *numinosum* (powerful) and not from the Greek νοούμενον = *noumenon*, which means: thought (part. pass.). The correct English rendering of *numinosum* would be "numinous."

You have heaped together practically the whole of analytic experience. Thus your treatise will be a most helpful instrument in the hands of practical analysts. I was quite surprised by the masterful way in which you dealt with the undoubtedly difficult problems of the individuation process and with the intricacies of alchemical symbolism. Your book is a remarkably clear survey of analytical psychology. You have a decidedly pedagogic vein, which makes your book readable even to a person of average intelligence. (In spite of

[1] *Psychic Energy: Its Source and Goal* (1948), with a foreword by Jung, now in CW 18; 2nd edn., 1963: *Psychic Energy: Its Source and Transformation*.

468

the "average" it seems to be pretty rare!) My heartiest congratulations.

Yours cordially, C. G. JUNG

P.S. I don't know T. S. Eliot. If you think that his book[2] is worthwhile, then I don't mind even poetry. I am only prejudiced against all forms of modern art. It is mostly morbid and evil on top [of that].

I am sorry that you couldn't come across the ocean this year. In spite of the fact that I feel more or less all right again, I more and more consider existence as something provisional and I realize now very often that I am doing a certain thing for the last time. It has a somewhat peculiar ring. For untold years it has happened for the first time that I could not plant my potatoes and my corn any more and weed has overgrown my piece of black earth, as if its owner were no more. Things and exterior life slip past me and leave me in a world of unworldly thought and in a time measured by centuries.

I am glad that you and others carry on the work I once began. The world needs it badly. It seems to come to a general showdown, when the question will be settled whether the actually existing man is conscious enough to cope with his own demons or not. For the time being it seems to be a losing fight. It would not be the first time that darkness has fallen upon a whole civilization and Master Eckhart been buried for 600 years. Ships of 1500 tons have been built again only after 1700 years and the mail began to function in Europe only in the second half of the XIX century as it functioned in Roman times. Switzerland has become an island of dreams amidst ruins and putrefaction. Europe is a rotting carcass. Towards the end of the Roman Empire they made attempts and had insights similar to mine.

[2] According to a communication from H., this was either *Murder in the Cathedral* or *The Waste Land*, or possibly she sent both.

To Jolande Jacobi

Dear Dr. Jacobi,   8 July 1947

. . .

I must confess I was against the C. G. Jung Institute[1] only from aversion to the prominence given to my name. However, that can

□ (Handwritten.)

be changed. It is not easy to get accustomed to the thought that "C.G. Jung" designates not merely my private person but something objective as well. Your article[2] is excellent. Where do you get all this interesting information from? Your various avocations are really remarkable. I can soon say with Schopenhauer: *legor et legar* (I am read and shall be read). I am making efforts to be lazy. I wish I could grant you respite too.

Cordially yours, C. G. JUNG

[1] The C. G. Jung Institute in Zurich was founded 24 Apr. 1948; J. had taken an active part in the preparatory work. Jung's address on that occasion is in CW 18.
[2] "Die Tiere bei der Christgeburt," *Du* (Zurich), no. 8 (1947).

To Hermann Berger

Dear Herr Berger,   12 July 1947

I am sorry to be so late in answering your letter. Illness has prevented me from attending to my correspondence.

I can answer your most essential question, namely my attitude to Buddhism, by saying that Buddhism means just about as much to me as Christianity. Only it is rather more old-fashioned and less suitable for Western people.

Yours sincerely, C. G. JUNG

☐ Stuttgart.

To Günther Däss

Dear Herr Däss,   12 July 1947

. . .

As regards the "centre"[1] you are quite right: the pairs of opposites in German psychology have flown to extremes because the centre has got lost. This centre was indirectly produced by an infernal deception through the figure of the Führer. This happens in all societies where the spiritual centre has dropped out. Only in this spiritual centre is there any possibility of salvation. The concept of the centre was called by the Chinese Tao, which the Jesuits in their day translated as Deus. This centre is everywhere, i.e., in everybody,

☐ Stuttgart.
[1] D. wrote about the guilt of the German people in "relinquishing the centre."

470

and when the individual does not possess this centre he infects all the others with this sickness. Then they lose the centre too. *Deus est circulus cuius centrum est ubique circumferentia vero nusquam!*[2]

Yours sincerely, c. g. jung

[2] Cf. Frischknecht, 8 Feb. 46, n. 13.

To Pastor Walther Uhsadel

Dear Pastor Uhsadel,   12 July 1947

I was very pleased to hear from you again after such a long time. I am looking forward to your book,[1] which you said you'd send me. I haven't yet seen Thurneysen's *Lehre von der Seelsorge.*[2] Now that you have drawn my attention to it, I must take a look at it. It would indeed be a great surprise to me if anything at all should come out of dialectical theology[3] that might be of practical interest to human beings. I have never succeeded in making any contact whatever with this theology, and it has always remained dark to me exactly what the dialogue is supposed to consist of. To me it seems completely absent. I have more contact with the opponents of dialectical theology and also with Catholic theologians, whom I find especially interesting. I have dabbled a bit with the Church Fathers, more particularly the heresiologists. My medical experience has increasingly compelled me to come to terms with Christian symbolism and here the Church Fathers were a great help. A little while ago I sent a new book, *Symbolik des Geistes*, to press; there are all sorts of things in it that might, indeed should, interest a theologian. However, as is usual with us, it will be some time before the book is out.

If ever you get a chance to come to Switzerland I should of course be very glad to see you. If you should see Frau Dr. Froboese,[4] please give her my greetings.

Yours sincerely, c. g. jung

☐ Cuxhaven, Germany.
[1] *Umweg zur Kirche*; the book was never published.
[2] Eduard Thurneysen, closely connected with the development of dialectical theology.
[3] A new movement in Protestantism, strongly influenced by Kierkegaard and fully developed by Karl Barth. Cf. Oeri, 1 Jan. 29, n. 7.
[4] Felicia Froboese-Thiele (1890–1971), M.D., German analytical psychologist. Jung's introduction to her *Träume—eine Quelle religiöser Erfahrung?* (1957) is in CW 18.

To Heinz Westmann

Dear Mr. Westmann,   12 July 1947

Best thanks for your letter and your news about the Present Question Conference.[1] The theme is indeed very interesting: "What is the critical problem in human relationships today?" Human relationships today are threatened by collective systems, quite apart from the fact that they are still, or always were, in a dubious and unsatisfactory condition. The collective systems, styled "party" or "State," have a destructive effect on human relationships. And they can easily be destroyed, too, because individuals are still in a condition of unconsciousness which cannot cope with the tremendous growth and fusion of the masses. As you know, the main endeavour of all totalitarian States is to undermine personal relationships through fear and mistrust, the result being an atomized mass in which the human psyche is completely stifled. Even the relation betwen parents and children, the closest and most natural of all, is torn asunder by the State. All big organizations that pursue exclusively materialistic aims are the pacemakers of mass-mindedness. The sole possibility of stopping this is the development of consciousness in the single individual, who thereby is rendered immune to the lure of collective organizations. This alone keeps his soul alive, for its life depends on the human relationship. The accent must fall on conscious personalization and not on State organization. The latter inevitably leads to the blight of totalitarianism.

In this sense I wish your undertaking every success. I am writing you this instead of a special greeting and leave it to you to make what use you will of this letter. With best regards,

Yours sincerely, C. G. JUNG

☐ Analytical psychologist, originally of Berlin; 1937–55 practising in England, since then in U.S.A.
[1] The second Present Question Conference, organized by W. and the psychiatrist Eric Graham Howe, took place in Birmingham, Aug. 1947.

To Erich Neumann

Dear Colleague,   Bollingen, 19 July 1947

What I can do for your extremely valuable works I will do with pleasure. Unfortunately everything has been greatly delayed by my illness, which cost me a tidy ½ year. In old age time presses and the years become ever fewer, i.e., it is plain to behold: *Utendum est aetate, cito pede labitur aetas / Nec bona tam sequitur quam bona prima fuit!*[1]

I cannot deny the justification for the term "castration complex" and still less its symbolism, but I must dispute that "sacrifice" is not a symbol. In the Christian sense it is actually one of the most important symbols. The etymology[2] is obscure: there is as much to be said for *offerre* [to offer] as for *operari* [to effect, to be active]. "Sacrifice" is both active and passive: one *offers* a sacrifice and one *is* a sacrifice. (Both together in the sacrifice symbolism in the Mass!) It is the same with *incest,* for which reason I had to supplement it with the concept of the *hierosgamos.* Just as the pair of concepts "incest/hierosgamos" describes the whole situation, so does "castration/sacrifice." Couldn't one, to proceed cautiously, say instead of castration complex castration *symbol,* or castration *motif* (like incest motif)?

You have still to go through the experience of being misunderstood. The possibilities are beyond conception. Perhaps you had better insert in your text a short explanation of the negative and positive aspects of the symbol, right at the beginning where you speak of the castration complex.

I very much hope it will be possible for you to come to Switzerland. At the moment I am enjoying my urgently needed holiday in my tower on the Upper Lake. Our Club wants to found a "C.G. Jung Institute for Complex Psychology." Preparations are already in progress. Frau Jaffé will be secretary. She has written a magnificent essay on E.T.A. Hoffmann which I shall publish in my *Psychologische Abhandlungen.*[3]

I am doing pretty well, but feel the burden of my 73 years. With best regards,

Your devoted C. G. JUNG

☐ (Handwritten.)

[1] "Hurry with the time, for time rushes with fleet foot, and that which follows is not as good as the one that was." Ovid, *Ars amatoria,* 3, 65.

[2] The German word for "sacrifice" is *Opfer,* offering. Cf. *Psychology and Alchemy,* par. 417.

[3] The essay was published in *Gestaltungen des Unbewussten = Psychologische Abhandlungen,* VII.

To Pastor Werner Niederer

Dear Pastor Niederer,   Bollingen, 5 August 1947

Best thanks for your kind birthday wishes! Please would you also express my thanks to your wife. Your sermon on God is indeed timely. It implicitly demands the tremendous task of *following* Christ (which is precisely not an *imitatio!*); this demand *is* God addressing himself to man. But "he that is near me is near to the fire," and where God is nearest the danger is greatest.[1] The man of today is still boundlessly infantile, and therein lies the great danger and the continual incentive for the theological outlook to be equally infantile. Caution is indicated. The way up Mont Blanc consists of many little steps. But a beginning must be made. With best regards,

Yours sincerely, C. G. JUNG

☐ (Handwritten.)
[1] Cf. Corti, 30 Apr. 29, n. 4 and 5.

To Aniela Jaffé

Dear Aniela,   Bollingen, 10 August 1947

I thank you with all my heart for your response to my "Trinity": I couldn't imagine a more beautiful one. It is a "total" reaction, and it had a "total" effect on me too. You have perfectly imaged what I imagined into my work. It again became clear to me from your letter how much one misses when one receives no response or a mere fragment, and what a joy it is to experience the opposite—a creative resonance which is at the same time like a revelation of the feminine being. It is as though a wine, which by dint of toil and sweat, worry and care has finally become mature and good, were being poured into a precious beaker. Without this receptacle and acceptance a man's work remains a delicate child, followed with doubting eyes and released into the world with inner anxiety. But when a soul opens to the work, it is as though a seed were lodged in good earth, or the gates of a city were closed in the evening, so that it can enjoy surer repose.

I thank you.

Cordially, C.G.J.

☐ (Handwritten.)

To Olga Fröbe-Kapteyn

Dear Frau Fröbe, 16 August 1947

The dissolution of the transference often consists in ceasing to describe the nature of one's relationship as "transference." This designation degrades the relationship to a mere projection, which it is not. "Transference" consists in the illusion of its uniqueness, when seen from the collective and conventional standpoint. "Uniqueness" lies simply and solely in the relationship between individuated persons, who have no other relationships at all except individual, i.e., unique ones.

Of course it is all right with me if the lectures begin at 9.30.

Kindest regards,

Ever sincerely, C. G. JUNG

To B. V. Raman

[ORIGINAL IN ENGLISH]

Dear Prof. Raman, 6 September 1947

I haven't yet received *The Astrological Magazine*, but I will answer your letter nevertheless.

Since you want to know my opinion about astrology I can tell you that I've been interested in this particular activity of the human mind for more than 30 years.[1] As I am a psychologist I'm chiefly interested in the particular light the horoscope sheds on certain complications in the character. In cases of difficult psychological diagnosis I usually get a horoscope in order to have a further point of view from an entirely different angle. I must say that I very often found that the astrological data elucidated certain points which I otherwise would have been unable to understand. From such experiences I formed the opinion that astrology is of particular interest to the psychologist, since it contains a sort of psychological experience which we call "projected"—this means that we find the psychological facts as it were in the constellations. This originally gave rise to the idea that these factors derive from the stars, whereas they are merely in a relation of synchronicity with them. I admit that this is a very

☐ R.'s letterhead reads: "Raman Publications, Proprietor B. V. Raman; The Astrological Magazine (India's Leading Cultural Monthly)."
[1] Cf. Freud, 12 June 11.

curious fact which throws a peculiar light on the structure of the human mind.

What I miss in astrological literature is chiefly the statistical method by which certain fundamental facts could be scientifically established.

Hoping that this answer meets your request, I remain,

Yours sincerely, C. G. JUNG

To Udo Rukser

Dear Herr Rukser,   6 September 1947

Your conjecture that the prolongation of the cross downwards signifies a predominance of the unconscious is not improbable. I have always regarded this prolongation as a moving upwards of the triad which goes together with the Christian Trinity symbol, i.e., with the predominance of the so-called "upper triad"[1] representing the spirit. The more strongly the spiritual element comes to the forefront, the greater the danger of its becoming identical with consciousness. There then supervenes, as you correctly surmise, a compensatory emphasis on the unconscious.

You are also right when you conjecture that a one-sided orientation of consciousness always leads to a counter-reaction. The greater the danger of mass-mindedness, the stronger the emphasis on the individual. The fact, for instance, that our age has truly discovered the unconscious comes under this head, as well as the widespread interest in psychology, which to begin with looked like an exclusively subjective affair. But with psychology the real man becomes a problem, that is to say the individual, for there are no other men except individuals. In this movement, widely supported by the public, there is already an attempt to combat mass-mindedness and the resultant totalitarianism. The interest in psychology has the inevitable consequence that individual self-awareness is heightened, which we know from experience is the best weapon against the devastating influence of the mass psyche. If this movement forges ahead and increases in

□ R.'s letterhead reads: "Deutsche Blätter. Für ein europäisches Deutschland, gegen ein deutsches Europa. Quillote, Chile."

[1] The "upper triad" needs the "lower triad" symbolizing the chthonic, feminine element for its completion. Cf. "The Phenomenology of the Spirit in Fairytales," CW 9, i, pars. 425ff. Concerning the prolongation of the cross downwards, cf. "The Philosophical Tree," CW 13, par. 334, and its inversion in Fig. 26.

476

scope, the greatest threat to our civilization would be checked. But if the reaction fails, we must inevitably look forward to further frightful catastrophes, for mass man breeds mass catastrophe. The greatest dangers today are the huge mass States like Russia and America. However, history teaches that such monsters are usually short-lived. That at least is a hope! With kind regards,

Yours sincerely, C. G. JUNG

To Gualthernus H. Mees

[ORIGINAL IN ENGLISH]

Dear Dr. Mees, 15 September 1947

I'm very sorry indeed that I had no chance to answer your three letters[1] which I have received in the last years. First I couldn't because we were surrounded on all sides by the Nazis and later on I had two serious illnesses which have prevented me from coping with my enormous mail. Thus I'm also late in answering your last letter which somehow got snowed under.

I often thought of you and I'm very sorry to hear that you had a bad time. I hope that by now you have recovered completely from your ailments.

I was very much interested in your news about the Maharshi.[2] I'm well aware of the fact that my very Western criticism of such a phenomenon as the Maharshi was rather upsetting to you. I consider a man's life lived for 65 years in perfect balance as most unfortunate. I'm glad that I haven't chosen to live such a miracle. It is so utterly inhuman that I can't see for the life of me any fun in it. It is surely very wonderful but think of being wonderful year in year out! Moreover I think it is generally much more advisable not to identify with the self. I quite appreciate the fact that such a model is of high paedagogical value to India. Right now such a wonderful example of balance would be most needed in the Punjab or in Calcutta or in the respective governments of Hindustan and Pakistan.[3]

☐ Dutch sociologist whom Jung had met in India, and pupil of Shri Ramana Maharshi. He founded his own ashram in Travancore.

[1] One letter is from 1944, another from 1945, and the last from Feb. 1947.

[2] Jung edited Zimmer's book on the Maharshi, *Der Weg zum Selbst: Lehre und Leben des indischen Heiligen Shri Ramana Maharshi aus Tiruvannamalai* (1944) (Zimmer died in 1943) and wrote an introduction to it: "The Holy Men of India," CW 11.

[3] The partition of British India into the two Dominions of India and Pakistan in July 1947 was followed by the mutual massacre of Indians and Moslems.

477

Concerning Zimmer's book I must say that I had no hand in its publication except that I took it in hand to be published by my Swiss publisher. Thus I was fully unaware of how the text came into existence or what its defects are. I had to leave the entire responsibility to my friend Zimmer who was a great admirer of the Maharshi.

I'm sorry that I was under the impression when we met in Trivandrum[4] that you introduced your friend Raman Pillai[5] as a remote pupil of Shri Ramana. This however doesn't matter very much, since the basic coincidence of most of the Indian teaching is so overwhelmingly great that it means little whether the author is called Ramakrishna[6] or Vivekananda[7] or Shri Aurobindo,[8] etc.

I only hope that you didn't endanger your health too much! It must be awful to live in a continuous sweat-bath for 6 months of the year. I should much appreciate it if you could once enlighten me about the Maharshi's daily activities. I wonder wherein his self-realization consists and what he actually did do. We know this running away business from parents etc. with our saints too![9] But some of them have done something tangible—if it was only a crusade or something like a book or the *Canto di Sole*.[10] I had a chance, when I was in Madras, to see the Maharshi, but by that time I was so imbued with the overwhelming Indian atmosphere of irrelevant wisdom and with the obvious Maya of this world that I didn't care any more if there had been twelve Maharshis on top of each other. I was profoundly overawed and the black pagoda of Bhuvaneshvara[11] took all the air out of me. India is marvellous, unique, and I wish I could stand once more on Cape Comorin[12] and know once more that this

---

[4] During his stay in India, in 1938, Jung was invited to give two lectures at the U. of Trivandrum, capital of Travancore.

[5] Jung refers to Raman Pillai, without mentioning his name, in "The Holy Men of India," par. 578: "In Trivandrum . . . I ran across a disciple of the Maharshi. He was an unassuming little man . . . modest, kindly, devout, and childlike . . . a man who had absorbed the wisdom of the Maharshi with utter devotion . . . I acknowledge with deep gratitude this meeting with him."

[6] Indian holy man and ascetic (1834–1886). Cf. ibid., pars. 958, 962.

[7] Indian religious reformer, pupil of Ramakrishna (1862–1902).

[8] Shri Aurobindo Ghose (1870–1950), religious reformer.

[9] For instance, Niklaus von der Flüe. Cf. Blanke, 2 May 45, n. 9.

[10] The *Canto di Sole* of St. Francis of Assisi.

[11] Presumably the ruined sun temple at Konarak, to which a road leads from Bhuvaneshvara. The "Black Pagoda," Surya Deul, is famous for its erotic sculptures. Cf *Memories*, pp. 277f./259f., and "What India Can Teach Us," CW 10, par. 1013. Cf. also *Aion*, par. 339, n. 1.

[12] Cape Comorin is the southernmost point of India.

world is an incurable illusion. This is a very helpful and salutary insight, when you must not live daily in this damn machinery and these undeniable realities which behave exactly as if they were real.

I'm sending this to the address you gave me in Holland, hoping that it will be forwarded to you if you have left.

Yours sincerely, C. G. JUNG

To Dr. S.

Dear Colleague, 8 October 1947

I gather from your description[1] that you are indeed climbing too high. Sanskrit and India really are a bit much. You must turn back to the simple things, just as your dream[2] says, to the forest. There is the star. You must go in quest of yourself, and you will find yourself again only in the simple and forgotten things. Why not go into the forest for a time, literally? Sometimes a tree tells you more than can be read in books. With best wishes,

Yours sincerely, C. G. JUNG

[1] S. was undergoing a psychological crisis accompanied by severe anxiety states. He mentioned that for the last five years he had been studying Sanskrit and Indian philosophy.
[2] The dreamer finds himself at a terminal moraine (= pile of débris at the foot of a glacier). On the other side there is a dark forest in which a single star shines with a very bright light.

To Father Victor White

[ORIGINAL IN ENGLISH]

Dear Victor, Bollingen, 19 December 1947

Our letters seem to feel that they have to cover a great distance![1] I have expected your letter with considerable curiosity and it confirms what I thought would be your immediate reaction. It's all very bewildering. Wylie's book,[2] I find, is a most remarkable picture of the things a European has great difficulty to understand. Certainly

☐ (Handwritten.)
[1] W. had gone to the U.S.A. on a lecture tour.
[2] Philip Wylie, *Generation of Vipers* (1942), a virulent criticism of the American scene. In his chapter on "Common Women" he discussed the phenomenon of the American "Mom," the "destroying Mother." Jung had met him in the U.S.A. in 1936. (Cf. Wylie, 22 Dec. 57.)

such a book would be utterly impossible in Europe because it kills itself. Yet to my mind nobody can foretell the effect it may have upon the average American. Don't forget that "Mom" has not turned into a mother from a lovely girl on account of nothing but maturation. The animus of women is an answer to the spirit which rules the man. It has its origin in father's mind and shows what the girl has received from the lovely, kind, and incompetent father. His family weakness on the other hand he owes to the animus of his mother and thus the evil is handed on from generation to generation. I don't think that Wylie's book defeats its own ends in America. The general hide is enormously thick. W. is ethical, but he does not—not yet—understand religion. That is the reason why his outlook on a further moral development is so peculiarly hazy and so incredibly shallow. But that is decidedly no reason why it should not appeal to the American appetite, which ever so often prefers sawdust instead of real food.

You remember my unsympathetic dream figure of the dry Jesuit logician?[3] Not very long after I wrote to you, I simply had to write a new essay I did not know about what. It occurred to me I should discuss some of the finer points about anima, animus, shadow, and last but not least the self.[4] I was against it, because I wanted to rest my head. Lately I had suffered from severe sleeplessness and I wanted to keep away from all mental exertions. In spite of everything, I felt forced to write on blindly, not seeing at all what I was driving at. Only after I had written about 25 pages in folio, it began to dawn on me that Christ—not the man but the divine being—was my secret goal. It came to me as a shock, as I felt utterly unequal to such a task. A dream told me that my small fishing boat had been sunk and that a giant (whom I knew from a dream about 30 years ago)[5] had provided me with a new, beautiful seagoing craft about twice the size of my former boat. Then I knew—nothing doing! I had to go on. My further writing led me to the archetype of the God-man and to the phenomenon of synchronicity which adheres to the archetype. Thus I came to discuss the Ἰχθῦς[6] and the then new aeon of ♓ 0°

[3] The dream has not been preserved.
[4] Cf. Aion, chs. III, II, and IV.
[5] Possibly a dream Jung had when working on Psychological Types: a small horse was trying to pull a large ocean liner to the pier. Suddenly a giant appeared, slew the little horse, and pulled the liner into dock.
[6] Aion, chs. VI and VIII–XI are a comprehensive investigation of the symbolism of the zodiacal sign Pisces, particularly in connection with the Christ figure and the "Christian aeon" (= first millennium).

(following ♈ 30°), the prophecy of the Antichrist and the development of the latter from 1000 A.D. in mysticism and alchemy until the recent developments, which threaten to overthrow the Christian aeon altogether. I have found some beautiful material.

Last night I dreamt of at least 3 Catholic priests who were quite friendly and one of them had a remarkable library. I was the whole time under a sort of military order and I had to sleep in the barracks. There was a scarcity of beds, so that two men had to share one bed. My partner[7] had already gone to bed. The bed was very clean, white, and fresh and he was a most venerable looking, very old man with white locks and a long flowing white beard. He offered me graciously one half of the bed and I woke up when I was just slipping into it. I must say that up to now I have handled the problem of Christ strictly on the level with the dogma, which is the leading thread through the maze of "my" unthought thoughts.

Ad "neurosis": I mean, of course, that it is as a rule better to leave neurotics to themselves as long as they do not suffer and seek health. There is enough of a task for the psychotherapist.

I am glad to hear that "they"[8] gave you a hearty welcome in New York. Please give them my best regards.

The conditions in England[9] are indeed lamentable. Perhaps it is just as well that you have more dreams to deal with than to write. The latter can wait, but what you are meant to be cannot wait. My best wishes for Xmas and New Year,

Yours cordially, C. G.

[7] Cf. White, 30 Jan. 48, par. 4 ("Something similar happened in my dream. . .").
[8] On the strength of a letter of introduction from Jung, W. had been very warmly received by the Analytical Psychology Club of New York.
[9] Many of the wartime restrictions regarding rationing, etc., were still in force.

To Father Victor White

[ORIGINAL IN ENGLISH]

My dear Victor,   27 December 1947

I am so "distrait" by my writing that I forgot a most important point about which I should have asked you: There exists a plan to create an "Institute of Analytical Psychology" ("Institut für complexe Psychologie") in Zurich.[1] A "comité" has been elected, consisting of

□ (Handwritten.)
[1] The C. G. Jung Institute.

5 persons[2] (C. A. Meier, Dr. K. Binswanger, Dr. Jolan Jacobi and Dr. L. Frey-Rohn and myself), who are preparing the list of the actual founders. I have been asked to write to you whether you would be inclined to allow us to put your name on that list. You risk no further obligations. We only hope you would add the moral authority of your name to the new enterprise. We have already the names of Gebhard Frei,[3] Prof. of modern philosophy at the collegium Sacerdotale in Schöneck, Prof. Pauli, physicist and Nobel prize man, Prof. Gonseth,[4] mathematician, E.T.H., Rob. de Traz,[5] French-Swiss novelist of fame, Ad. Vischer[6] of the Curatorium Universitatis Basiliensis, etc. Your name would be in good society. Personally I should be much obliged to you if you could do us this pleasure.[7] In return you will receive further particulars about the Institute. I have written a longish letter to you, which probably goes by slow mail. So this forgotten item may reach you before the letter which should have contained it. What I am "distrait" about is depicted in that letter.

As I am getting on in age and as I am going to be gathered to my ancestors and avatars within a measurable time, the Institute is meant to carry on the work. My former English Seminars[8] are already substituted by a number of lectures and courses about dream psychology, ps. of fairy tales, selected topics from the Old Testament, ps. of the Gilgamesh Epos, ps. of the Renaissance (XV cent.) [These lectures] are to be consolidated in the form of an Institute. The Psych. Club [contributes] the rooms, the use of the library and a sum of money.

I am very busy just now, but tomorrow I am going to Bollingen for a fortnight.

Cordially yours, C. G.

---

[2] All the other four members were analysts and personal pupils of Jung. Together with him they later formed the first Curatorium of the Institute.

[3] Cf. Frei, 13 Jan. 48.

[4] Ferdinand Gonseth (b. 1890), mathematician and philosopher; 1920-29 Professor at Bern and Zurich; since then professor of higher mathematics at the Swiss Federal Polytechnic (E.T.H.), Zurich.

[5] Robert de Traz (b. 1884), Swiss novelist and critic; for some time editor of the *Revue de Genève*.

[6] Cf. Vischer, 10 Jan. 44.

[7] W. accepted this suggestion and became a founder member of the C. G. Jung Institute.

[8] Cf. Körner, 22 Mar. 35, n. 1.

Anonymous

From a letter of condolence, 1947

. . . I was grieved for him. Now he has vanished and stepped outside time, as all of us will do after him. Life, so-called, is a short episode between two great mysteries, which yet are one. I cannot mourn the dead. They endure, but we pass over. . .

To Pastor Jakob Amstutz

Dear Pastor Amstutz, 8 January 1948

Many thanks for kindly sending me your book on Rilke.[1] I am reading it with pleasure, especially as I was always aware, since getting to know Rilke, of how much psychology there was hidden in him. In fact he came up against the same field of experience that has engrossed me for decades, though I approach it from a very different angle.

Yours sincerely, C. G. JUNG

☐ Then of Bern, now professor of philosophy and religion, Juniata College, Huntingdon, Pennsylvania.
[1] *Die Seelsorge Rilkes* (1948).

To Canon H. G. England

[ORIGINAL IN ENGLISH]

Dear Sir, 8 January 1948

I'm sorry to be so late in answering your kind letter. I'm somewhat overwhelmed by my correspondence and find it very difficult to cope with it.

It is by no means easy to answer your questions as it is a matter of the exceedingly problematic relations between theology and psychology. First of all, therefore, I must ask you to remember that I don't claim to be a theologian; I'm moving entirely within the limits of a natural empirical science. This is important to know, as it dictates a certain terminology which doesn't coincide with theological explanations. Thus, above all, the concept of the unconscious. We call that psychological sphere unconscious because we cannot observe it

☐ Exeter, England.

483

directly. We only observe certain effects of it and from them we draw
certain conclusions as to the nature and condition of possible contents of the unconscious. You could also say: the sphere of the unconscious is a sphere of the unknown psyche about which we say
nothing by calling it the unconscious. We do not say that *it* is conscious or unconscious, it is only unconscious to us. What it is in itself
we do not know and do not pretend to know. If you call it the
universal consciousness we cannot contradict you, we can only confess our ignorance as to its real state. But if you call it universal consciousness, then it is the universal consciousness of God. If you make
such an assumption, then the difficult question arises as to where the
definitely evil influences that derive from the unconscious come
from—these influences which you rightly identify with the symbol
of the dragon.[1]

The dragon is the devil of old. I'm quite ready to accept that term,
because it describes definite psychological experiences, as "God" does.
But psychology can only confirm that the highest and the lowest,
the best and worst impulses derive from the sphere of the unconscious psyche. That is the utmost we can say within the limits of
science.

Instead of St. George[2] you could use the more general symbolism
of Christ and the devil. St. George is a more personalistic formulation of the same. The saint is surely the conscious ego, but not the
persona, because we don't assume that St. George is merely a mask
hiding the real self. Persona is what you want to impress people with
and what they force you to assume as a role. Therefore it is called a
mask. The sword, which you identify with the Logos, is properly interpreted on the assumption that St. George symbolizes Christ, as no
one else would be capable of wielding the Logos. But if you take St.
George as a human being, then it would be his discriminating faculty
and this is the main characteristic of consciousness, that it is discriminating, chiefly by means of the intellect. Thus the sword very
often represents the intellect or discriminating values. The dragon in
this case would be the whole length of the shadow, namely the human plus the animal (ape) -shadow in man.

The anima, being psychologically the female counterpart of the
masculine consciousness, based upon the minority of female genes in
a masculine body, has a decidedly dual aspect. She functions like a

[1] E. defined the dragon as "the shadow which abides in the unconscious."
[2] He identified St. George with the "ego of the Christian personality" and
equated this, wrongly, with the "self-conscious persona."

persona, being a link between the collective unconscious and the conscious, just as the persona is a link between the real personality and the external world.[3] Her dual aspect is due to the fact that the effects of the collective unconscious are dual in their aspect too. Thus the anima can transmit not only good influences but also evil ones. As a matter of fact, she is not rarely the worst daemon in a man's life. We like to imagine that God is all light, but S. Johannes à Cruce[4] has the truly psychological notion of the darkness and the seeming remoteness of God as an effect of the divine presence. This state of darkness is by far the most trying and most dangerous part of the mystical experiences. It feels like a void and this is precisely what Buddhism cultivates as the most desirable state of Nirvana. The Buddhists reach it in exactly the same way as Christian mystics do, namely by excessive self-abnegation. At least this is true of classical Buddhism. It is not so true of its later developments, as for instance in Zen.

It is generally true that consciousness must win a victory over the powers of darkness. But as darkness is not wholly subject to our moral valuation, since it seems to be one of the divine characteristics, it remains a question whether the dragon is to be considered as wholly evil. This question, however, is a most intricate one. The serpent as well as the dragon and other reptiles usually symbolize those parts of the human psyche which are still connected with the animal side of man. The animal still lives in him: it is the old saurian that is really the dragon, and therefore the dragon is a very proper symbol. These parts of the psyche are most intimately connected with the life of the body and cannot be missed if body and consciousness are to work together soundly. Therefore a certain amount—or better an uncertain amount—of darkness has to be allowed, because it is vitally necessary if the body or the mind is to live at all. Many neuroses come from the fact that too good a victory has been won over the body and its dark powers. Old Drummond,[5] for instance, used to lament over the awful moods of pious people. Those were the cases where the old serpent has been too cruelly mauled by too spiritual a consciousness. One would have found in analysing these people that there was no small amount of greed and vanity in their spiritual aspirations. The

[3] Cf. *Two Essays* (1966 edn.), par. 507, sec. 6.
[4] St. John of the Cross, Spanish monk, "Doctor of the Church" (1542–91). His main work is "The Dark Night of the Soul" (continuation of his "Ascent of Mount Carmel"), tr., J. A. Peers, *Works* (1943).
[5] James Drummond (1835–1918), English Unitarian scholar.

medical psychologist knows that he is treading on dangerous ground here and therefore he goes warily when it comes to the question of victories over darkness.

This is admittedly no theology, but it is a question of mental and physical health. We think that, when God made animals, He equipped them with just those needs and impulses that enable them to live according to their laws. We assume that He has done the same with man. In a way the animal is more pious than man, because it fulfills the divine will more completely than man ever can dream of. He can deviate, he can be disobedient, because he has consciousness. Consciousness is on the one hand a triumph and a blessing, on the other hand it is our worst devil, which helps us to invent every thinkable reason and way to disobey the divine will. O yes, things are far more difficult than they ought to be! Thus we welcome everybody who says that things are simple.

I have made an honest attempt to answer your questions as fully as possible. It is too bad that most of my recent work has not been translated into English. Otherwise I could refer you to some works which deal with these questions more amply.

Sincerely yours, c. g. j u n g

To Gebhard Frei

Dear Dr. Frei,   13 January 1948

In your essay,[1] which I have read with great interest, you have given a fair and in all essentials correct presentation of my views. Your remarks about the "self" and "God," on which you lay particular stress, I find very apt. As you will see, I have taken the liberty of making a few comments in your MS, which though not very considerate of me may perhaps be of service to you.

The great difficulty is the clash between scientific and epistemological thinking on the one hand and theological and metaphysical thinking on the other.

With regard to the self, I could say that it is an equivalent of God.

☐ (1905–68), professor of philosophy and comparative religion at the Theological Seminary of Schöneck, Switzerland.
[1] MS of "Zur Psychologie des Unterbewussten," *Annalen der philosophischen Gesellschaft Innerschweiz und Ostschweiz,* 1948. The essay, titled "On Analytical Psychology," appeared as an Appendix to Victor White's *God and the Unconscious.*

That sort of thing puts the wind up the theologians because it looks as if a "God-substitute" had been created. To the psychologist this is so absurd that he would hesitate to credit anybody with such stupidity. He would put it like this:

When I say "God" this is a *psychic image*. Equally, the self is a psychic image of the transcendent, because indescribable and inapprehensible, wholeness of man. Both are expressed empirically by the same symbols, or symbols so similar that they cannot be distinguished from one another. Psychology is concerned simply and solely with experienceable images whose nature and biological behaviour it investigates with the help of the comparative method. This has nothing whatever to do with God *per se*. How can any man in his right senses imagine he could subtract anything from or add anything to God? If I have 20,000 frs. and I say it is 50,000 I shall soon find out that my real 20,000 have not increased by a cent. After all, I am not such a lunatic that people could credit me with the idea of intending to create a God-substitute. How could any man replace God? I can't even create a lost button with my imagination but have to buy myself a new real one!

The mistake, it seems to me, is that these critics actually *believe only in words*, without knowing it, and then think they have *posited* God. Because they don't know this, it appears projected on to me in the accusation that *I* am manufacturing a God. This accusation is so unbelievably absurd because at the very most I speak of an *imago Dei*, as I have repeatedly emphasized in countless places, and I am not like the idiot who believes that the image he sees in the mirror is his real and living I.

My thinking is *substantive*, but theological-metaphysical thinking is in constant danger, as the above instance shows, of operating with substanceless words and imagining that the reality corresponding to them is then seated in heaven.

What *else* could the theologian show? Well, Christ is in us and we in him! Why shouldn't the workings of God and the presence of the υἱὸς τοῦ ἀνθρώπου[2] in us be real and experienceable? I thank God every day that I have been permitted to experience the reality of the *imago Dei* in me. Had that not been so, I would be a bitter enemy of Christianity and of the Church in particular. Thanks to this *actus gratiae* my life has meaning, and my inner eye was opened to the beauty and grandeur of dogma. I can see that the Church is my mother, and that

[2] = Son of Man.

the spirit of my father leads me away from her to the battlefield of the world, where every day the light is in danger of being extinguished for me by the *princeps huius mundi,* the stifling darkness of unconsciousness. Avidya[3] is a cardinal evil for the Buddhists too. It is probably *the* sin and *malum kat' exochen.*[4]

The tension you feel between the Church and psychology does not, in my opinion, lie in morality but in psychic facts, namely conflicts of duty, which in the last resort come from our having no sure judgment about good and evil, and the more psychological insight we acquire the more we see how fearfully the two of them interpenetrate. The evil of the good and the good of the evil are—unfortunately, unfortunately!—ineffaceable facts. Psychology is as little to blame for this as zoology for lice. It merely knows about them, and whoever wants to remain unconscious (thereby serving the devil) therefore hates and suspects psychology. The reigning prince of this world shuns the light of knowledge like the plague. If good did not have its evil side and vice versa, the notion that God could lead his miserable little creature into temptation would be an absurd blasphemy. It would then be a simple matter always to decide for the good. But in reality it needs the highest consciousness and the greatest perspicacity to reach even a halfway intelligent decision. Many people pride themselves on this spirit of perspicacity, but Christ says: μακάριοί εἰσιν οἱ πτωχοὶ τῷ πνεύματι ὅτι ὄψονται τὸν θεόν.[5] Nothing makes us so deeply conscious of our poverty as the problem of good and evil. Did it please the Pharisees that Christ consorted with publicans and whores? What did he say to Peter about eating unclean beasts?[6] Why did the Lord commend his deceitful and unjust steward because he had done φρονίμως?[7]

It would perhaps be advisable if you got it into your public's head that my psychology does not deal in banalities and platitudes but with the most difficult problems it is possible to imagine, which can only be compared with those of microphysics. They are not my invention, but I sweat at them.

Please excuse this long letter! You may gather from it how very

---

[3] Ignorance, nescience, or—psychologically—unconsciousness; one of the five "klesas" or impairments which prevent man from realizing his essential nature.

[4] See Baynes, 22 Jan. 42, n. 5.

[5] "Blessed are the poor in spirit, for they shall see God" (cf. Matthew 5:3 & 8).

[6] Cf. Acts 10:10ff. and 11:4ff. The Lord said: "What God hath cleansed, that call thou not common."

[7] = wisely, prudently. Cf. Luke 16:8.

concerned I am to get into a right relationship with Catholic thinking in particular, for this is the precondition, which cannot be thought
out of existence, for solving the difficult problems with which the
psychology of the unconscious confronts us. With best regards,

Yours very sincerely, C. G. JUNG

To Antonios P. Savides

[ORIGINAL IN ENGLISH]

Dear Professor Savides, 13 January 1948

Thank you for your kind wishes for the New Year. I must say I
have some dark recollection[1] of you, but it's rather blurred.

An autobiography is the one thing I'm not going to write.[2] Such
things are never quite true and they cannot be made true. I've seen
enough autobiographies in my lifetime and the essential things were
lacking in every one of them. The true things can be guessed from
my scientific work, provided that the reader is bright enough to draw
intelligent conclusions. My best wishes!

Yours sincerely, C. G. JUNG

[1] They had met at the Harvard Tercentenary Conference of Arts and Sciences
in 1936, where Jung lectured on "Psychological Factors Determining Human
Behaviour," CW 8.
[2] Jung's remarks are particularly interesting in view of his later *Memories*.

To Pastor Jakob Amstutz

Dear Pastor Amstutz, 23 January 1948

Thank you very much for the extremely interesting picture.[1] It is
a kind of St. George, whose lower half is a dragon. A most unusual
picture! It is as though consciousness were aware that the dragon is
the lower half of man, which indeed and in truth is the case. One
can therefore take this picture as a representation of the inner conflict or of its opposite—an expression of the fact that dragon and hero
actually belong together and are one. This insight can be documented
from mythology and would have far-reaching consequences if it were
examined from the point of view of comparative religion. With best
thanks,

Yours sincerely, C. G. JUNG

[1] Tracing of the keyplate of an old Bernese barn.

To Father Victor White

[ORIGINAL IN ENGLISH]

Dear Victor,   30 January 1948

Many thanks for your personal willingness to contribute to our endeavours![1] I have not yet heard from Rome.

Many thanks also for the other contents of your letters! It took me a while to digest everything properly. I am particularly glad that you have sent me your dream you had at a time (1945) when you did not yet know me personally. It is very helpful to me. Your interpretation is quite correct as far as it goes. Of course the dream leads up to our personal discussion; it paves the way to it. Thus I am still left somewhat as the representative of the argument pro S. Spiritu.[2] But the argument started in yourself. It is quite clear that the unconscious insists rather vehemently upon the problem of the S. Spir., which I can confirm from many of my own dreams, including the one I have sent to you, i.e., the one about the *senex venerabilis*.[3] In your dream you are separated from me and connected with me by an anima-figure,[4] as by the *platform*,[5] by which you are either separated from the sea or enabled to reach it. Further on in Zurich you must celebrate Mass *among the women*.[6] The female factor, i.e., the anima, is the bridge and the *conditio sine qua non*. The unknowable *Veritas Prima*[7] solved the problem for the time being.

The emphasis on the anima means of course the totality of man: male plus female = conscious plus unconscious. Whatever the unconscious and whatever the S. Spir. is, the unconscious realm of the psyche is the place where the living Spirit that is more than man manifests itself. I should not hesitate to call your dream a manifestation of the S. Spir. that leads you on to deeper understanding, away from the narrowness of formulas and concepts to the living truth.

☐ (Handwritten.)

[1] Cf. White, 27 Dec. 47, n. 7. W.'s letter has not been preserved, but from Jung's next sentence it appears that W. had tried to interest the higher Catholic authorities in Rome in the C. G. Jung Institute.

[2] In W.'s dream Jung was talking about the Holy Ghost as manifested in the unconscious.

[3] The dream mentioned in White, 19 Dec. 47, par. 3.

[4] Jung's wife was sitting between them.

[5] He was outside a house by the seashore, but separated from the sea by a raised platform.

[6] He had to celebrate Mass in a nuns' chapel.

[7] The dream ends with W. explaining to Jung "St. Thomas Aquinas' teaching about Faith in the Unknown and Unseen Veritas Prima."

Something similar happened in my dream,[8] of which, unfortunately, I have given you the mere outlines. While I stood before the bed of the Old Man, I thought and felt: *Indignus sum Domine.*[9] I know Him very well: He was my "guru" more than 30 years ago,[10] a real ghostly guru—but that is a long and—I am afraid—exceedingly strange story. It has been since confirmed to me by an old Hindu.[11] You see, something has taken me out of Europe and the Occident and has opened for me the gates of the East as well, so that I should understand something of the *human* mind.

Soon after this particular dream, I had another one continuing a subject alluded to in the former dream, viz. the figure of the priest, the head of the library. His carriage and the fact that he unexpectedly had a short grey beard reminded me strongly of my own father. The second dream[12] is very long and has many scenes, of which I can only relate the last one. In all parts of the dream I was concerned with my father. In the last scene I was in *his house* on the ground floor, very much preoccupied by a peculiar question which had been raised at the beginning of the dream: "How is it possible that my mother celebrates her 70th birthday in this year 1948 while I am reaching my 74th year?" My father is going to answer it and he takes me up with him to the first floor by way of a narrow winding staircase in the wall. Coming out on the 1st floor, we find ourselves in a (circular) gallery, from which a small bridge leads to an isolated cuplike platform in the centre of the room. (The room has otherwise no floor, it is open down to the ground floor.) From the platform a narrow staircase, almost a ladder, leads up to a small door high up in the wall. I know this is *his* room. The moment we enter the bridge, I fall on my knees, completely overcome by the sudden understanding that my father is going to lead me into the "supreme presence." By sympathy he kneels at my side and I try to touch the ground with my forehead. I almost reach it and there I woke up.

The peculiar 1st floor is exactly like the famous *diwan-i-khas* (hall of audience) of Akbar the Great[13] in Fatehpur-Sikri, where he used

---

[8] See n. 3 above.

[9] "I am not worthy, Lord."

[10] The fantasy of Philemon who represented "superior insight." Cf. *Memories*, p. 183/176.

[11] Ibid., p. 184/177.

[12] Ibid., pp. 218f./207f.

[13] Ibid. Akbar the Great, Jalal ud-Din Mohammed (1542–1605), the greatest of the Mogul emperors of India. Fatehpur-Sikri was one of his capitals.

to discuss philosophy and religion with the representatives of all philosophies and all creeds.

Oh yes, it is my way all right. I don't despise the fish.[14] I am glad you share it with me. I can eat fish on Fridays. I have brethren and sisters in the spirit and where once I felt godforsaken and really lonely, there was my guru. Surely there is something the matter with the solitary man;[15] if he is not a beast, he is conscious of St. Paul's words: τοῦ γὰρ καὶ γένος ἐσμέν.[16] The Divine Presence is more than anything else. There is more than one way to the rediscovery of the *genus divinum* in us. This is the only thing that really matters. Was there ever a more solitary man than St. Paul? Even his "evangelium" came to him immediately and he was up against the men in Jerusalem as well as the whole Roman Empire. I wanted the proof of a living Spirit and I got it. Don't ask me at what a price.

When I said that the Protestant has to digest his sins alone, I really meant: he must carry them, because how can God take him with his sins if he does not carry them? if he has been relieved from the weight of his burden?

Concerning "barracks"[17] you are quite right; they mean submission and discipline, of which I could tell you a very long story indeed. Whoever has clearly understood what it means: *Qui fidelis est in minimo,*[18] is overwhelmed with the dire necessity of submission and discipline of a subtler kind than the *regula S. Benedicti*. I don't want to prescribe a way to other people, because I know that my way has been prescribed to me by a hand far above my reach.

I know it all sounds so damned grand. I am sorry that it does, but I don't mean it. *It* is grand, and I am only trying to be a decent tool and don't feel grand at all.

Happily the cloud of sleeplessness has lifted recently. My brain had been too active. My paper about the Ἰχθύς[19] has disturbed the tranquillity of my mind in its deepest layers, as you can imagine.

---

[14] In a letter of 3 Jan. 48 W. reported a dream in which he and Jung were having a meal together on a Friday. W. was surprised when Jung asked him to pass the fish to him, since he, as a non-Catholic, was under no obligation to abstain from meat.

[15] In the same letter W. quoted Aristotle's words: "The solitary man is either a beast or a god."

[16] Acts 17:28: "For we also are his offspring." Quotation from the Stoic Aratus of Soli, *Phaenomena*.

[17] Cf. White, 19 Dec. 47, par. 3.

[18] Luke 16:10: "He that is faithful in that which is least."

[19] Cf. White, 19 Dec. 47, n. 6.

In a Catholic Journal (published by Routledge and Sons)[20] a somebody "condemns" my Essays on Cont. Hist.[21] because my attitude to religion and to rational philosophy is, as he says, "ambiguous." *O sancta simplicitas*!

I hope that your writing is progressing and that you enjoy your interesting holiday in U.S. I have just read Kravchenko's book on Russia.[22] Worth reading! You get an idea of the *princeps hujus mundi* and his remarkable works.

Cordially yours, c. g.

P.S. My mother = anima is younger than myself.[23] When I was 3 years old I had my first anima-experience,[24] the woman that was *not* my mother. It means a lot that escapes me for the time being.

[20] According to a communication from Routledge & Kegan Paul, London, they never published a Catholic journal.
[21] *Essays on Contemporary Events* (1947). The essays are republished in CW 10 and 16.
[22] Victor Kravchenko, *I Chose Freedom* (1947). He was a former Soviet spy whose revelations about conditions in Russia and Russian espionage created a sensation.
[23] Cf. the statement in Jung's second dream that his mother was 70 when he was reaching 74.
[24] *Memories*, p. 8/22f.

To P. Bächler

Dear Herr Bächler,   8 March 1948

Please forgive me for the delay in thanking you for your letter and for kindly sending me the little book about the apparition at Fatima.[1] I had already read the book with the greatest interest and am now very happy to possess it.

When you say that modern psychology is doing preparatory work for the Church *nolens volens*, you are deceiving yourself a little.

□ Bern.
[1] Possibly Gonzaga da Fonseca, *Maria spricht zur Welt; Geheimnis und weltgeschichtliche Sendung Fatimas* (tr. from the Italian), 1943. In 1917 three Portuguese children claimed to have had several visions of the Virgin and to have received a heavenly message in a field near the village of Fatima. These visions aroused great interest and in Oct. 1917 a crowd of 70,000 people claimed to have seen the sun spin and descend towards the earth on the spot where the "Lady in White" appeared. Cf. Jung, "Flying Saucers: A Modern Myth of Things Seen in the Sky," CW 10, par. 597.

There is very much conscious purpose in what I say, for I am persuaded that the Christian Church is one of the most powerful instruments for keeping the great masses more or less right in the head.

The book has faced me with problems which I cannot brush under the table, but unfortunately I cannot give you more information without involving you in the thought processes of a scientific person which would probably appear very strange. At all events I cannot omit to thank you cordially for your thoughtful gift.

Yours sincerely, C. G. JUNG

To Pascual Jordan

Dear Professor Jordan, 1 April 1948

I received your interesting book *Verdrängung und Komplementarität*[1] a little while ago. Unfortunately a thorough study of it has not yet been possible, but I hope to get down to it soon.

Although parapsychological problems lie on the extreme edge of my field of research, I still follow with great attention the new developments which one frequently encounters in psychology in regard to these phenomena. Some time ago I took the liberty of sending you what I have written recently on this subject.[2] I hope my essay has reached you in the meantime.

Here we are discussing with Pauli the unexpected relations between psychology and physics.[3] Psychology as might be expected appears in the realm of physics in the field of theory-building. The outstanding question is a psychological critique of the space-time concept. On this point I have just made a strange discovery[4] which I would first like to check out with Pauli from the physical side. If I should publish anything about it in the near future I will not fail to let you know. Again best thanks for your book,

Yours sincerely, C. G. JUNG

---

[1] Hamburg, 1947. The book is cited in "Synchronicity," CW 8, par. 862, n. 55, as "concerning the relations between microphysics and the psychology of the unconscious."

[2] "Der Geist der Psychologie," *Eranos Jahrbuch* 1946; now "On the Nature of the Psyche," CW 8, which contains important reflections on the relations between psychology and modern physics. Cf. pars. 414ff., 434ff.

[3] Ibid., pars. 439–40 & n. 130.

[4] This may refer to the quaternios mentioned in White, 21 May 48, par. 2/3.

To J. B. Rhine

[ORIGINAL IN ENGLISH]

Dear Dr. Rhine,   1 April 1948

I've read your book[1] with the greatest interest and I thank you very much for sending me more than one copy. People read it a lot over here and I have recommended it to several physicists interested in psychological and parapsychological matters. I think it is one of the greatest contributions to the knowledge of unconscious processes. Your experiments[2] have established the fact of the relativity of time, space, and matter with reference to the psyche beyond any doubt. The experimental proof is particularly valuable to me, because I am constantly observing facts that are along the same line. My chief concern is the theoretical problem of the connection between the psyche and the time-space-continuum[3] of microphysics. We have some discussions over here with physicists concerning this matter. I think I'm going to write something about it when I have worked through the maze of symbolism which leads up to this very modern problem.

Unfortunately my most recent books are not yet translated into English, otherwise I would have sent you one of my recent writings. A general English edition of all my works is under way, so I hope it will not be too long before I can send you something which might interest you.[4]

Sincerely yours, C. G. JUNG

[1] *The Reach of the Mind* (1948).
[2] Experiments with long-distance card-guessing, dice-throwing, psychokinesis. Cf. "Synchronicity," pars. 833ff.
[3] Whereas physics before the relativity theory distinguished between a three-dimensional space and an independent time, the development of the theory led to a view in which space and time are joined together in a four-dimensional space-time continuum.
[4] The first vol. of the CW to appear was 12, *Psychology and Alchemy*, in 1953.

To Dr. S.

Dear Colleague,   1 April 1948

The phenomenon you describe[1] really does point to the fact that unconscious contents, which normally are projected on top of each

[1] S. described the spontaneous feeling of events about to take place which had taken place the same way before, and how images of these events appeared to him

other just like Galton's photographs, have come closer to consciousness but are not sufficiently charged with energy to cross the threshold. There are various reasons for this. Consciousness may not be ready for them, there being no corresponding conceptions in it by means of which the unconscious could be apperceived. Or there is a fear of these contents, or they are too weak for somatic reasons, since a certain amount of energy is required to bring unconscious contents to apperception. I therefore counsel patience, don't exert yourself too much, but regard this matter as a kind of growth process which must run its natural course. Give yourself a rest as much as you can, and transform your fear into the expectation and hope that these contents will one day become conscious for you. There is no question at all of schizophrenia. That would arise only if these contents were charged with so much energy that they inundated your consciousness. It is essential that you don't upset yourself unnecessarily. As a rule such contents need time to attract sufficient libido to reach a state where they are capable of becoming conscious. The more they enrich themselves with energy, the more differentiated and clearer they become, and it is very possible that, once they have got that far, your attention will be drawn to them in dreams.

Preoccupation with Indian philosophy is not altogether harmless.[2] Psychologically considered, it is on a par with Scholasticism, i.e., an exclusive realism[3] which is thoroughly prejudicial to the tasks of the present. It is probably this preoccupation which has released in you a defensive compensation coming from the unconscious. Nevertheless we can learn something from India, namely an inner-directed attention and contemplation which must, however, refrain from all intellectual anticipation and should form no views about what the unconscious is or might be. With best regards,

Yours sincerely, C. G. JUNG

---

without becoming understandable, "as if different films were projected simultaneously and on top of each other."

[2] Cf. Jung's warning to Dr. S., 8 Oct. 47.

[3] The school of mediaeval philosophy which, in contradistinction to nominalism, "affirms . . . that general concepts exist in themselves after the manner of Platonic ideas." *Psychological Types,* par. 41.

To Jolande Jacobi

Dear Dr. Jacobi,   15 April 1948

I understand what Fordham[1] means but it doesn't agree at all with my view of the objective psyche.[2]

We also speak of the "objective world," by which we do not mean that this objective world is the one we are conscious of. There is no object of which we are totally conscious. So, too, the collective unconscious becomes conscious in part and to that extent it is then a conscious object. But over and above that it is still present unconsciously, though it can be discovered. It behaves exactly like the world of things, which is partly known, partly unknown, the unknown being just as objectively real as that which is known to me. I chose the term "objective psyche" in contradistinction to "subjective psyche" because the subjective psyche coincides with consciousness, whereas the objective psyche does not always do so by any means.

I wanted to let you know my exact position so that you can make use of this definition if necessary.

. . .

With friendly greetings,

Yours sincerely, c. g. j u n g

[1] Dr. Michael Fordham (cf. Fordham, 8 June 54, n. ☐) had suggested reserving the term "objective psyche" for those aspects of the collective unconscious which appear in consciousness. Cf. *The Life of Childhood* (1944), p. 2, and *The Objective Psyche* (1948).
[2] The origin of the term may be found in "Basic Postulates of Analytical Psychology," CW 8, par. 666. Cf. *Psychology and Alchemy*, par. 48, where the objective psyche is synonymous with the unconscious. It is the "objective knowledge of the self" manifested in the collective unconscious as distinct from the "subjective consciousness of the ego." Cf. *Aion*, pars. 251–2.

To J. A. Howard Ogdon

[ORIGINAL IN ENGLISH]

Dear Mr. Ogdon,   15 April 1948

Although I haven't yet finished reading your interesting book,[1] I don't want to postpone the expression of my gratitude. I can say

☐ Manchester, England.
[1] *The Kingdom of the Lost* (1947).

that I have already learned quite a number of things from it. I'm slowly ploughing along, taking it in gradually. Although it is by no means the only autobiography of a cured psychosis, yours is unique owing to your psychological and general education. This enables you to formulate and express in suitable terms what other former patients failed to formulate.

Concerning your view about Hatha-Yoga I can confirm your ideas entirely. Yoga as well as other "mystical" practices imitate nature and that explains their efficacy. Yoga postures are imitations of catatonic gestures, postures and mannerisms. One could say that the classical catatonic condition is a fixed or congealed Yoga mechanism, i.e., a natural tendency released under pathological circumstances. This is to be interpreted as a teleological attempt at self-cure, as it is a compensatory process produced under the stress of the schizophrenic dissociation of the mind. The dissociation leads to a sort of chaotic disrupture of the mental order and the catatonic tendency tries to bring about an order, however pathological, creating fixed positions over against the relentless flow of associations. The *prana*-discipline[2] has practically the same effect. It concentrates the psychic energy upon the inner ways in which the *prana* flows. The localization in the brain is doubtful, but in general it is correct to assume that the unconscious processes are chiefly located in the lower centres of the brain from the thalamus downwards.

Thank you again for the kind gift of your book,

Yours sincerely, C. G. JUNG

[2] *Prana* = vital wind, life breath, equivalent of the Greek pneuma; the discipline consists of exercises in breath control.

To Walter Lewino

[ORIGINAL IN ENGLISH]

Dear Sir,   21 April 1948

I'm sorry to be so late in answering your letter. I've been overburdened with work lately and I very often cannot attend to my correspondence personally for a long time.

No doubt the anima has a very important aspect as a giver of wisdom. She is the *femme inspiratrice par excellence*. She derives her wisdom from her "father"—in dogma [they are] represented by

□ Paris.

Mary [= anima] and God [the] Father,[1] viz., Holy Ghost. "In the womb of the mother dwells the wisdom of the father." Thus the anima is always associated with the source of wisdom and enlightenment, whose symbol is the Old Wise Man.[2] As long as you are under the influence of the anima you are unconscious of that archetype, i.e., you are identical with it and that explains your preoccupation with Indian philosophy. You are then forced to play the role of the Old Wise Man. The archetype fulfils itself through you. Only when you discriminate between yourself and this wisdom do you become aware of the male archetype of the spirit. The anima is the road that leads to it and appears to be also the source of it, but it is an appearance only. She herself is the archetype of mere life that leads into experiences and awareness. Indian thought (f.i., Ramakrishna and many others) is based upon a mentality still "contained in the mother,"[3] because the general mood of India is matriarchal. Our Western consciousness has undergone a differentiation of the parental images: we have father and mother. We even dispossessed the mother, making her less divine than the father. Lately, however, the archetype of the mother is decidedly developing inside the Catholic Church, aided by remarkable miracles (Assisi and Fatima), also the attempts at bringing about the official recognition of the *conclusio* that Mary has been taken up to heaven together with her body.[4] It is most difficult to compare the Indian mentality with ours. It could be compared, however, with the mood of Scholastic philosophy, but that is for us about 600 years ago.

Thank you for the pictures you've sent me.

Sincerely yours, C. G. J U N G

[1] Jung's meaning here is not clear; the added words are an attempt at clarification.
[2] The Wise Old Man is the archetype of spirit and meaning. Cf. "Archetypes of the Collective Unconscious," CW 9, i, pars. 74, 79.
[3] Cf. the Great Mother goddess Kali.
[4] The "attempts" later led to the promulgation of the dogma of the Assumptio Mariae in 1950. Cf. White, 25 Nov. 50, n. 2.

To C. R. Birnie

Dear Dr. Birnie,

[ORIGINAL IN ENGLISH]

14 May 1948

. . .

I have never come across a case where a woman actually had a child by her own father, but I've seen a number of cases where such consequences might easily have happened, i.e., incest with father and mother. The actual event of incest means nearly always a terrific blow to the psychic structure, except in cases of very primitive minds. The incest has the importance of a real trauma. Its effect is a fixation to the time and the circumstances of the incest as well as to the person of the perpetrator. This is the meaning of the dream that repeats itself in your case.[1] She is still her father's prisoner. A dream that repeats itself always refers to one and the same psychological situation that lasts as long as the dream repeats itself. The unconscious brings up the fact as a sort of compensatory act with the intention that it should be remembered and introduced into consciousness. As it [incest] is a trauma it is always held at bay and is partially repressed. It cannot be assimilated and so the dream brings it back in the more or less vain hope that consciousness will be able to assimilate it. It can be assimilated provided that consciousness understands the symbolic meaning of the event. Consciousness, of course, is exclusively fascinated by the external moral and factual aspect of the act. But that is not enough: the main point is that incest arouses an archaic level of mind (which I call the collective unconscious) in which one finds a highly archaic meaning of paternal incest.

When one has to treat such a condition, one ought to get the patient to reproduce the (unconscious) fantasies round the incest, applying the method of active imagination if the dreams don't produce the necessary stuff.

. . .

There is an interesting difference between maternal and paternal incest as the former is more archaic and affects the feeling life of the son. Paternal incest on the other hand is of a more recent nature and affects the mind of the daughter, because the father has to do with everything that is mental and spiritual. In such a case a thorough explanation of the mental and spiritual implications of the incestuous act is unavoidable, since its nature is highly symbolical and as a rule refers to the sacred mysteries of the faith, namely to the myth of Mary who gives rebirth to her father in producing his

□ London.
[1] B. reported the recurrent dream of a woman of 35 who "at the age of 23 had a child by her supposed father." In the dream "she was locked in a dark room with a window" and "a door outside which her father stood." It was the actual room in which her father had locked her "from early childhood in order to coerce her into sexual acts."

son ("qui de sa fille fit sa mère").[2] In the mediaeval representations of the Antichrist you always find a careful description of how the father (the devil) has sexual intercourse with his daughter and thereby produces the Antichrist. This is one of the classic representations of the archetype of paternal incest. I'm afraid it is a pretty complicated business.

. . .

Sincerely yours, C. G. JUNG

[2] "[God] who made his daughter into his mother." Quotation from Chrétien de Troyes, 12th cent. poet, author of *Le Conte du Graal*. For the reverse of this process cf. Dante, *Paradiso*, XXXIII, 1: "O Virgin Mother, daughter of thy son."

To Father Victor White

[ORIGINAL IN ENGLISH]

Dear Victor! 21 May 1948

Finally I am able to write to you. I thank you very much for your excellent lecture on Gnosticism.[1] I much admire your balanced judgment and your just evaluation of a subject that has been so often represented in a wrong light and misunderstood by all sorts of comprehensible and incomprehensible prejudices. Your presentation of the Pistis Sophia[2] is excellent. Among the patristic writers about Gnosticism I missed Hippolytos,[3] the most thorough and the most intelligent of all. Epiphanius,[4] who shares the former's lot, does not deserve much praise. Your paper has made me think: *Have I faith or a faith or not?* I have always been unable to produce faith and I

□ (Handwritten.)

[1] The lecture was read to the Analytical Psychology Club of New York, 20 Feb. 48, and to the Guild of Pastoral Psychology, London, 10 Dec. 48; published Apr. 49 as Lecture No. 59.

[2] = Trustful Wisdom, title of a Gnostic work in Coptic; tr. Mead, *Pistis Sophia* (1921).

[3] Bishop of Portus Romanus (d. *ca.* 230), Greek writer of the Early Church. His writings, rediscovered only in the 19th cent. and at first attributed to Origen, are an indispensable source for the teachings of Gnosticism. His *Philosophumena; or, The Refutation of All Heresies* (tr. 1921) is copiously quoted in Jung's later works, under the title *Elenchos*.

[4] Epiphanius, bishop of Constantia (*ca.* 315–402), Church Father who in his youth was greatly influenced by Gnostic teachings. His main work is *Panarion*, a treatise on heresies.

have tried so hard that I finally did not know any more what faith is or means. I owe it to your paper that I have now apparently an answer: faith or the equivalent of faith with me is what I would call *respect*. I have respect for the Christian Truth. Thus it seems to come down to an involuntary assumption in me that there is something to the dogmatic truth, something *indefinable* to begin with. Yet I feel respect for it, although I don't really understand it. But I can say my life-work is essentially an attempt to understand what others apparently can believe. There must be—so I conclude—a rather strong motive-power connected with the Christian Truth, otherwise it would not be explicable why it influences me to such an extent. My respect is—mind you—involuntary; it is a "datum" of irrational nature. This *is* the nearest I can get to what appears to me as "faith." There is however nothing specific in it, since I feel the same kind of respect for the basic teachings of Buddhism and the fundamental Taoist ideas. In the case of the Christian Truth one would be inclined to explain this *a priori* respect through my Christian education. Yet the same cannot be said in the case of Buddhism, Taoism and certain aspects of Islam. Hindu theology curiously enough never had the same appeal, although it has gripped my intellect at times quite powerfully.

Gnosticism has renewed its vitality with me recently, as I was deeply concerned with the question of how the figure of Christ was received into Hellenistic nature-philosophy and hence into alchemy. A little book[5] has grown out of such studies within the last months. It will be, I am afraid, a shocking and difficult book. It has reduced me to a most curious attempt to formulate the progress of symbolism within the last two thousand years through the figure of 4 quaternities[6] based upon 2 quaterniones of the Naasenes[7] as mentioned by Hippolytos. The first one is the so-called Moses-quaternio.[8]

. . .

Well, it is a mad thing, which I cannot explain here but it seems *hellishly important* in so far as it winds up with the physical time-space quaternio.[9] The whole seems to be logically watertight.

I feel reasonably well and hope you do the same. You must have

---

[5] *Aion.*

[6] Ibid., ch. XIV. The quaternios are on pp. 227, 231, 236, 238.

[7] A Gnostic sect in which the serpent (*naas* from Hebrew *nachasch*) occupied a central place of worship. Cf. *Psychology and Alchemy*, par. 527.

[8] Here follows a sketch, with short commentary, of the quaternio in *Aion*, p. 227.

[9] Ibid., p. 252.

had an interesting time. A Jesuit professor of theology at Louvain[10] is coming to see me next week. They begin to sit up. Looking forward to the summer, when I hope to see you again at Bollingen,

Yours cordially, c. g.

[10] Probably Father Raymond Hostie. At that time, however, he was not a professor of theology but still a seminarist at Louvain. Later he became professor of the Faculty of the Society of Jesus in Louvain and wrote a book, *Du mythe à la réligion*, 1955 (tr., *Religion and the Psychology of Jung*, 1957), of which Jung disapproved strongly (cf. Hostie, 25 Apr. 55).

To Henry A. Murray

[ORIGINAL IN ENGLISH]

My dear Murray,   2 July 1948

A few days ago I received your very kind letter and the book on "Sentiments"[1] you have published together with Christiana. I am glad to have this document of American psychology. You see it is so interesting to study the way in which one tackles this subject.

I am glad to know after such a long lapse of time—and what a time—that you are both well and active. I wish I could still as actively partake in the affairs of the world. But reaching soon the station No. 74 of my trek through the lands, deserts, and seas of this three-dimensional world, I feel the burden of my years and the work not yet done. Everything goes slowly and rest is indicated between times of work, although I cannot complain about my general state of health.

I was greatly surprised to hear of 52 weeks of discussion in which my name occurred. Hélas—there is so much one does not know! I am grateful to know that I was not altogether forgotten. I don't know who that peculiar friend is who told you of my alleged saying that you were a barren tree. Surely such a thing has never been said by myself, since after I read your former book[2] I confidently expected some more along the same lines. I sincerely hope you don't believe what people say about me. If *I* did, I should have buried myself long ago. I have gone through your new book cursorily, but I shall read it as soon as I have some leisure to do it with the necessary con-

[1] H. A. Murray and C. D. Morgan, *A Clinical Study of Sentiments* (Genetical Psychological Monographs, No. 32, 1945); an investigation in depth of the strength of certain dominant values in eleven college students.
[2] *Explorations in Personality* (1938).

centration. You must have seen much during the war, strange countries as well as strange people. We have lived in a prison for 6 years, of which 5 years were spent in more or less continuous apprehension of inevitable extinction. I had to settle down to a 50:50 certainty of a quick or protracted end through a bullet or a concentration camp—and no possibility of action, please, except in a world not to be reached by any Gestapo of the world.

I am looking forward with great pleasure to your promised study about Melville.[3] I have begun to understand why a university professor has to postpone dealing with animae and the like as he also better keeps away from incubi, sylvani, nymphae, and salamandrae. It is such a long, long way from behaviouristic psychology without man to a psychology of man. I am greatly interested in the question of how you will set about to produce an "embracement or the integration of the opposite." The opposite is a concrete object, and what if the subject should happen to be disinclined to integrate the subjective opposite corresponding to the object? In other words: how will America proceed to embrace Russia without realizing that the Kremlin is right below the threshold of her own consciousness? Attempts in this respect have not been exactly hopeful yet. It is of course a banal truth, which I emphasize time and again, that without the unconditional reality of the object no projection can ever be discovered or withdrawn.

18th of July. Here I have been interrupted for many days by an intestinal grippe affecting the liver. That is how it is in these years when one is old and without resistance.

I cannot quite agree with your opinion about "individuation." It is not "individualization" but a conscious realization of everything the existence of an individual implies: his needs, his tasks, his duties, his responsibilities, etc. Individuation does not isolate, it connects. I never saw relationships thriving on unconsciousness. You—on the other side—have had the unique experience of men doing splendid team work during the war. We over here had the experience of helpless formidable masses shoved into hell. I have seen the German "Arbeitsbataillone," Mussolini's reception in Berlin, etc. Wonderful team work—one idea for all—two million people on Tempelhoferfeld cheering "unisono," all meant to be roasted in burning oil and slowly starved to death. Le Bon[4] does not mean theories, he means

---

[3] M. was then working on two chapters: "Introduction to *Pierre*, by Herman Melville," and "In Nomine Diaboli, an analysis of *Moby Dick*," both unpublished.
[4] Le Bon, *The Crowd, A Study of the Popular Mind* (orig. 1895).

the facts. It is difficult to get around them. What about the masses headed by your ape man Lewis?[5] What about the Russian avalanche of 200 million slaves? You say you feel that something should be done along the line of an agreement. Exactly, quite my idea. But what are you going to do with that mass mentality of the leaders, mostly downright criminals or lunatics (of the reasonable variety, particularly dangerous!)? Indeed something should be done, but unfortunately the men in the Kremlin understand only their own argument, i.e., violence and ruthlessness. That is what you are up against. How could you deal with Hitler? Well it is the same with Russia. Nothing short of the atom bomb will register there.

In the week following Aug. 22nd I ought to be at the Eranos meeting in Ascona near Locarno. It would be a great disappointment not to see you while you are in Europe. In the beginning of September I shall be back in Küsnacht or in the tower in Bollingen about 40 km. from Zurich.

Well this is a long letter, I am afraid—too long! I should be very glad indeed to see you here if you can manage at all.

My best regards to Christiana!

Cordially yours, C. G. JUNG

[5] John L. Lewis (1880–1969), American labour leader; from 1920 president of the powerful United Mine Workers of America; 1935–40 president of the Congress of Industrial Organizations. In *ca.* 1948 Lewis was involved in disputes with the U.S. Govt. over labour policies.

To Erich Neumann

Dear Colleague,   17 August 1948

Yesterday I finished reading your lecture.[1] I can only express my admiration for the way you have mastered your difficult task. It has turned into a really excellent account of the problem of mysticism in general, as lucid as it is thorough. Mysticism has probably never been subjected to such comprehensive treatment as in this work of yours. I felt a quite special sympathy with the saint who buys firewood instead of a fur coat.[2] It is well that you haven't said less, and

[1] "Der mystische Mensch," *Eranos Jahrbuch 1948*; tr. "Mystical Man," *The Mystic Vision* (1968).
[2] Cf. Buber, *Tales of the Hassidim*, II (1949), p. 274. In this story a famous rabbi is called a Zaddik (the Hebrew term for a righteous man) in a fur coat.

505

more would have been unwise. τῷ καιρῷ πρόσεστι πάντα τὰ καλὰ (all good depends on right measure).

I thank you for your work. With best regards and wishes,

Yours sincerely, C. G. JUNG

Explanation: "One man buys a fur coat, another buys firewood. . . . The first wants to warm only himself, the second wants to warm others as well."

To Father Victor White

[ORIGINAL IN ENGLISH]

My dear Victor,   Bollingen, 24 September 1948

Your letter reminds me that no sooner had you left[1] I discovered, nicely stowed away in my mail bag, your article in *Commonweal*.[2] Sorry! I never opened that bag, because I felt rather rotten in the beginning of my vacations. I am very grateful to you that you took up the revenging sword in my favour. Reinhold's article is immeasurably stupid and prejudiced. There is such a thing as intellectual responsibility of which R. seems to be unaware. Such people poison the spiritual atmosphere.

In my rather distracted mental state I quite forgot to ask you a question which has been on my mind for a long time: it is the *Anima Christi*. I refer to the meditation on the *anima Christi* in the *Exercitia Spiritualia S. Ignatii*. What is the a. Christi? Has Christ an "anima"? By which I mean "soul." Christ is God. Has God a soul? It cannot very well be the human *anima rationalis*, which would have no place beside God. It seems as if God were His own soul. But what does the "Anima Christi" mean then?[3]

I should be much obliged if you would kindly enlighten me about the teaching of the Church in this respect. No hurry! You are probably busy enough after your long absence.

[1] On his return from the U.S.A., W. stayed with Jung 6–14 Sept.

[2] "The Analyst and the Confessor," *Commonweal*, 1948; now ch. 9 of *God and the Unconscious*.

[3] W.'s answer in a "most helpful and comprehensive letter" (cf. White, 8 Jan. 49) has not been preserved. — The Council of Chalcedon, 451, formulated the doctrine of the two natures of Christ as "at once truly God and truly man of reasonable soul and body." As God he is pure spirit and thus has no soul; as man he has man's *anima rationalis*. — The psychological aspects of the *anima Christi* are dealt with extensively in Jung's E.T.H. Lectures, 1939/40, on the *Exercitia Spiritualia of St. Ignatius of Loyola*.

For a fortnight we have here a real summer. I was so full of pep that I have overdone my wood-chopping a bit. I have to keep quiet now, writing letters and doing some scientific work on the Antichrist.[4] You remember the two fishes Satan discovered swimming on the dark waters?[5] They have perhaps some connection with the two martyrs (*testes*) in the Apocalypse.[6] A mediaeval text says about them: *Sibylla nuncupat eos duo stellas.*[7] This might refer back to the *coniunctio* of Jupiter and Saturn at Christ's nativity. Just as *duo stellas* announced the first coming of Christ, so they appear to be the *praesagium* of His second coming. Jupiter and Saturn are a contrast: ♃ is *beneficus*, ♄ is a typical *maleficus*, the *sol niger*[8] of the alchemists. It is remarkable that the *praesagium* consists in either case in a *complexio oppositorum*. It would point to a secret intention to make a *mediator oppositorum* of Christ, i.e., an incarnation of the archetype of the Self.

By the way: the earliest use of the word ἀρχέτυπος I have just found occurs in Philo: *De Opificio mundi*, I, §69,[9] referring to the εἰκόν θεοῦ . . . κατὰ τὸν τῆς ψυκῆς ἡγεμόνα νοῦν.[10] Hitherto I had believed that it first occurs in the *Corpus Hermeticum*: θεὸς τὸ ἀρχέτυπον φῶς.[11] S. Augustinus does not use "archetypus" as I once erroneously surmised,[12] only the idea, but it occurs in *Dionysius Areopagita*.[13] Hoping your weather is as fine as ours.

Yours cordially, C. G.

[4] The Antichrist is discussed at considerable length in *Aion*; see Index.

[5] Mentioned in a heretical text of the Cathars, a 12th–13th cent. sect who rejected the authority of the Pope and the Catholic Church, and were wiped out in the Fourth Crusade. The text is quoted in *Aion*, pars. 225ff.

[6] Rev. 11:3–12.

[7] "The Sibyl names them two stars."

[8] Black sun or "counter-sun" (cf. Schmied, 5 Nov. 42, n. 1), the shadow of the sun or the sun itself in its negative aspect. It also symbolizes the alchemical states of *nigredo*, blackness (cf. Neumann, 5 Jan. 52, n. 11) and *putrefactio*, both necessary for the achievement of the opus.

[9] Cf. "Archetypes of the Collective Unconscious," CW 9, i, par. 5, and *Mysterium Coniunctionis*, par. 761.

[10] "The images of God, in respect of the mind, the sovereign element of the soul."

[11] "God the archetypal light." Cf. "Archetypes of the Collective Unconscious," par. 5.

[12] Cf. Frischknecht, 7 Apr. 45, n. 3.

[13] Unidentifiable Christian Neoplatonic writer of the 5th cent. whose writings exerted a great influence on mediaeval thought. The word ἀρχέτυπος occurs in his *De divinis nominibus*, 2.5; 4.1; and in *De coelesti hierarchia*, 3.3.1; 3.3.7; 4.3.1. (Cf. CW 9, i, par. 5.)

To Sally M. Pinckney

[ORIGINAL IN ENGLISH]

Dear Miss Pinckney,   30 September 1948

Although the dangers of the individual identifying with the collectivity are very great indeed, the relationship between these two factors is not necessarily negative. It has its very positive aspects too. As a matter of fact a positive relationship between the individual and society or a group is essential, since no individual stands by himself but depends upon symbiosis with a group. The self, the very centre of an individual, is of a conglomerate nature. It is, as it were, a group. It is a collectivity in itself and therefore always, when it works most positively, creates a group. This is the reason, for instance, why such a thing as the New York Club exists at all. Such a oneness demands a positive expression which can be found only in an interest common to all members of a group. Starting from such a consideration the Psychological Club of Zurich has founded the new Institute,[1] the Curatorium and lectors of which are all members of the group.

It would certainly be of greatest interest to the welfare of the New York Club if a way could be found to direct its energies into some such channel. Of course you wouldn't be in the position to found an institute for teaching analytical psychology, but there are many other useful activities of which I got a certain idea through reading your Bulletin. It is quite a clever piece of work and quite valuable as to its information. It would, for instance, be highly interesting to know of books or articles in which analytical psychology is mentioned, criticized, reviled or praised. It would also be of greatest value to hear critical and prejudiced voices. As you know, one learns most through resistances and difficulties. In this kind of work, where intelligent reading is chiefly needed, many members of your Club could be assigned to special tasks.

I'm very sorry to be so late with my answer. I have been ill in the meantime and I couldn't pick up the lost threads until just now.

Yours sincerely, C. G. JUNG

☐ Editor of the *Bulletin of the Analytical Psychology Club of New York*. On behalf of the Bulletin Committee she asked Jung to contribute a statement "on the positive values to the individual of group participation." His contribution— this letter—was published in the *Bulletin*, X (Sept. 1948).
[1] The C. G. Jung Institute, Zurich, founded Apr. 1948.

To Dr. S.

Dear Colleague, 30 September 1948

Fear is aggressivity in reverse. Consequently, the thing we are afraid of involves a task. If you are afraid of your own thoughts, then your thoughts are the task. Hence you are absolutely right in your argumentative letter about the spirit. It was just my intention to reduce such complications to their primary form. In this respect my essay[1] is certainly exoteric, but in this very exotericism lies a quite special esotericism, since spirit is aboriginal and probably always an *agens per se*, and can therefore never be caught in intellectual form. It is a primordial phenomenon. But from the empirical, psychological standpoint one can also call it a quality which attaches to certain psychic contents in contradistinction to the material, concrete label. With kind regards,

Yours sincerely, C. G. JUNG

[1] "The Phenomenology of the Spirit in Fairytales," CW 9, i.

To Herbert Read

[ORIGINAL IN ENGLISH]

Dear Mr. Read, Pro tempore on Rigi, 17 October 1948

As I have read your *Green Child*[1] I feel under a certain moral obligation to thank you for kindly calling my attention to its existence. I feel not naturally drawn to what one calls "literature," but I am strangely attracted by genuine fiction, i.e., fantastical invention. Inasmuch as fantasy is not forced and violated by and subjugated to an intellectually preconceived bastard of an idea, it is a legitimate and authentic offspring of the unconscious mind and thus far it provided me with unadulterated information about the things that transcend the writer's conscious mind. Most writers hate this point of view. But I assume that you do not, otherwise you would not have shoved your book anywhere near my vicinity. I have read it right through in one day and it gave me a rumbling in the depths that kept me awake for the better part of the night. It is, above all, wonderfully English:

☐ (Handwritten.) Sir Herbert Read (1893–1968), English poet, novelist, art critic, co-editor of CW. (See pl. in vol. 2.)

[1] *The Green Child* (1935). The green folk are the inhabitants of an underworld country to which Siloen, the green girl child, takes Olivero, the hero of the story.

you go to bed without any particular forebodings and with no plans or intuitions whatever and you wake up in the morning being the unaccountable proprietor of 30,000 square miles of virgin country, where you can't help being immensely useful and efficient. Happily enough you don't know that you never were really there, since you discover after 20–30 years that the thing you really meant has been left behind in your native village. What you rediscover is a compensation for all the things you have professed and lived for a lifetime. This green folk—*hélas*—was real enough, but had a hell of an existence during your absence. What lovely unconventional things you have missed! From most enjoyable promiscuous baths up to the highest regions of wisdom! Here my Acheron began to shake. You touched upon the alchemical arcanum *par excellence*, the philosophers' stone, a really enormous problem that is actually very much on my mind indeed. The shocking thing is that the Stone symbolizes a most highly spiritual idea, namely that age-old and universal image of the Anthropos (f.i. Christus = ὁ υἱὸς τοῦ ἀνθρώπου). What does it mean that Spirit itself, even the divine πνεῦμα is stone, or that stone's spirit?[2] Such ideas are by no means intellectual inventions, on the contrary they are authenic products, natural growths of the unconscious. There is nothing arbitrary about them.

In your story the two worlds don't touch each other, i.e., their point of contact is rather painful. It is a case of either/or. This is quite true, even immensely so. The right hand does not know what the left is groping for. This is our worldwide "psychologie à compartiment." An old alchemist reading your novel would have wept for sheer joy. It did not make me weep, but it tricked my mind into action and I had to solve all the riddles you have dished out. So f.i. your number 5,[3] where there ought to be a 4, and why is this underworld so green[4] and mouldy and so circular and so purgatorylike? I don't want to submerge you with the outbursts of my funny mind. I just wished to give you at least a taste of the reactions your book has released. They are meant to be a small token of my gratitude for a day of intense enjoyment and interest.

Yours sincerely, c. g. JUNG

[2] Cf. *Psychology and Alchemy*, par. 405.
[3] There are always groups of five in the country of the green folk: 5 judges, 5 benches with 5 bearded men, etc. In alchemy the number 5 plays an important role as the quincunx and quintessentia.
[4] Cf. "The Spirit in Fairytales," par. 406.

To Fritz Blanke

Dear Colleague,   10 November 1948

Very many thanks for kindly sending me your book on Brother Klaus.[1]

The fact that Brother Klaus, on his own admission and according to the reports of reliable witnesses, lived without material sustenance for twenty years is something that cannot be brushed aside however uncomfortable it may be. In the case of Therese of Konnersreuth[2] there are also reports, whose reliability of course I can neither confirm nor contest, that for a long period of time she lived simply and solely on holy wafers. Such things naturally cannot be understood with our present knowledge of physiology. One would be well advised, however, not to dismiss them as utterly impossible on that account. There are very many things that earlier were held to be impossible which we know and can prove to be possible today.

Naturally I have no explanation to offer concerning such phenomena, but I am inclined to think it should be sought in the realm of parapsychology. I myself have observed materialization processes and verified that at the area of the body surface from which ectoplasmic materializations emanated, the degree of ionization of the atmosphere touching the skin was sixty times the normal. That is to say, ionized molecules were passing in or out at that point, which evidently lead to the production of that whitish (luminous?) mist from which materialized portions of the body take shape. If such things can occur, then it is also conceivable that persons in the vicinity of the medium might act as a source of ions—in other words, nourishment might be effected by the passage of living molecules of albumen from one body to another. This seems to me to offer a possible approach to an explanation. Unfortunately these things have been far too little investigated at present. This is a task for the future.

Your little book is very interesting, and I was glad that you didn't dismiss out of hand the statements of the saint, which are probably reliable, but have taken them seriously. Again with best thanks,

Yours sincerely, C. G. JUNG

☐ This letter was published, with revisions, in *Neue Wissenschaft* (Olten and Fribourg), 1950/51, as "The Miraculous Fast of Bruder Klaus." In its revised form it is included in CW 18.

[1] *Bruder Klaus von Flüe* (1948).

[2] Therese Neumann (1889–1962), generally known as Therese of Konnersreuth, stigmatized since 1926, when she claimed to have re-experienced Christ's Passion.

To Albert Jung

Dear Colleague,   10 November 1948

Best thanks for kindly sending me your writings.[1] I am sincerely grateful to you for your sympathetic and intelligent exposition. I find it particularly meritorious that you have taken all this trouble to inculcate a little psychology into the doctors. Doctors in general not only have a repugnance to reading voluminous books, they also have a regular horror of thinking, for which they have ceased to be trained ever since their high-school days. It therefore remains uncommonly difficult for them; so difficult, indeed, that they can read the simplest of my books only with beads of sweat on their brows, if at all. In the end, of course, psychology is only an outlying frontier of medicine, but in its practical aspects it is so important that at least the psychiatric side of medicine will not be able to avoid acquiring some knowledge of the nature of the psyche, which after all is the essence of bodily life.

The Innerschweizer Philosophengesellschaft[2] seems to be taking a lively interest in my psychology. I get word of it occasionally from Professor Gebhard Frei, who has lectured on this subject.[3] I wish you all luck with your lecture. At least you have the advantage of an audience which has a more pertinent conception of the psyche and its symbolism than the medical public. Again with best thanks,

Yours sincerely, C. G. JUNG

[1] Various reviews of Jung's books, including a review of *Symbolik des Geistes* and other essays in *Aerztliche Monatshefte* (Schwarzenburg), Heft 4 (1948).
[2] This Society, whose members are predominantly Catholic priests, is part of the Swiss Society for Philosophy.
[3] Cf. Frei, 13 Jan. 48, n. 1.

To Piloo Nanavutty

[ORIGINAL IN ENGLISH]
Dear Miss Nanavutty,   11 November 1948

I'm sorry to be so late in answering your kind letter of October 19th. As you know I'm old and no more able to take care of my correspondence as I should.

☐ At that time a research student at Girton College, Cambridge, England; originally from India.

Title-page of Blake's "Genesis" MS.: see Nanavutty, 11 Nov. 48

There is no objection against your reading my volumes on Zarathustra.[1] They have nothing to do with Zarathustra the prophet, of course. And they should be read with criticism, since they are merely notes taken by members of my audience which I never corrected. They certainly contain quite a number of mistakes. I should also prefer it if you would refrain from quoting the notes in your writings.

Thank you very much for your interesting offprint.[2] Blake's picture[3] is very interesting. The caricature of the four zoa of Ezechiel[4] in this form, which you suppose to be due to the *peccatum originale*, represents exactly what the Kabbala[5] calls the four *achurayim*[6] which form the outermost shells of the world together with the *septem reges lapsi*[7]—the fallen seven kings that mean aeons preceding the actual one. They have the general meaning of impure spirits. The Kabbala was accessible to non-Hebrew students through Knorr von Rosenroth's *Kabbala Denudata*[8] of 1684, where you find the necessary data in the index latinus under "cortices."

I find Blake a tantalizing study, since he has compiled a lot of half- or undigested knowledge in his fantasies. According to my idea,

---

[1] Cf. Körner, 22 Mar. 35, n. 1.

[2] Piloo Nanavutty, "A Title-page in Blake's illustrated Genesis Manuscript," *Journal of the Warburg and Courtauld Institutes* (London) (1947), 114ff.

[3] The picture is a black and white reproduction (ill. 33) of one of Blake's two coloured title-pages for the Genesis MS (*ca.* 1826). The conventional symbols of the four evangelists are used to represent Blake's Four Zoas (Urthona, Urizen, Luvah, Tharmas) in his Prophetic Books, but all of them are in caricatured form, expressing the degeneracy of spirit, intellect, passion, and body. In their entirety they show, according to N., "Blake's conception of the fall of man." See illustration (by permission Henry E. Huntington Library and Art Gallery).

[4] The "four living creatures" in Ezekiel 1:5ff. and 10:8ff.; also the "four beasts" in Rev. 4:6ff. and 5:6ff.

[5] The Kabbalah, the Jewish mystical tradition, extends from the 1st cent. to the present. The printed literature comprises about 3,000 texts, and many more have never been printed. The two most important texts are the *Sefer Yetsirah* (Book of Creation), written between the 3rd and 6th cent., and the *Sefer Ha-Zohar* (Book of Splendour), 13th cent. Cf. Scholem, *Major Trends in Jewish Mysticism*.

[6] Cf. "A Study in the Process of Individuation," CW 9, i, par. 575, n. 115: ". . . the four Achurayim are the so-called 'back of God.'"

[7] Ibid.: "The seven kings refer to previous aeons, 'perished' worlds."

[8] Christian Knorr von Rosenroth (1636–89), Christian Kabbalist. *Kabbala denudata* is a Latin translation of several Kabbalistic writings and passages from the *Zohar*, together with essays on the meaning of the Kabbalah. Rosenroth is frequently cited in *Mysterium Coniunctionis*; see its Index *s.v.* Knorr von Rosenroth, and a saying of his forms the motto to "The Psychology of the Transference," CW 16.

they are an artistic production rather than an authentic representation of unconscious processes. He lived at a time when such incredible concoctions were fashionable. I felt that I should know a great deal of that contemporary most unsavoury literature if I made a serious attempt to get at the proper interpretation of his pictures.

I have had a letter from your sister and am just going to write to her.

Yours sincerely, C. G. JUNG

To Father Victor White

[ORIGINAL IN ENGLISH]

Dear Victor,   16 December 1948

The spirit prompts me to write to you.

It is quite a while ago since I have heard of you and very much longer since I have heard you really. I may be all wrong, but I confess to have a feeling as if when you were in America a door had been shut, softly but tightly. I don't want to disturb you, but I feel as if I ought to tell you about my fantasy, so that you know my side of the picture at least. I know there are things somewhere too damned difficult to be even mentioned, but they should not cut you off entirely. It is not bad for you to get a breath from the great wind of the world occasionally and from all the dark things "that go bump in the night." That is why I take the liberty of knocking at your door. I suppose you are very busy. Don't feel pressed for an answer, please! I am looking for my own peace and that is the reason why I tell you about my qualms. Having done so I recline in my grandfather's chair going on dreaming about Virgil's *"Tityre, tu patulae recubans sub tegmine fagi. . ."*[1]

Light that wants to shine needs darkness.

Cordially yours, C. G.

□ (Handwritten.)
[1] Cf. Virgil, *Eclogue*, I, 1: "Tityrus, thou liest canopied beneath thy spreading beech."

To Erich Neumann

Dear Colleague,   December 1948

Please forgive me for writing to you by hand, but I can concentrate my thoughts better that way. The MS of *Myst. Coniunct.* is still not

514

in travelworthy form, also the last chapter has not yet been written. But there are various MSS which are more or less ready for press and of which copies can be sent to you.

Your book on ethics[1] has come out here and is already kicking up so much dust that the time may come when I have to state my position. The question has been raised at the Institute whether it is advisable under the circumstances to make use of your kind permission and bring out the book in the series. It is feared that this would be prejudicial to future discussion, also that the Institute would be committed to certain formulations even if only morally or to outward appearances. A small Institute still weak in the legs cannot risk too many opponents (sidelong glances at the University and Church!).

I have read your book a second time and again had a very strong impression and with it the certainty that it will come like a bombshell. Your formulations are brilliant and often razor-sharp; they are provocative and aggressive—shock troops in the open where nothing, unfortunately, was to be seen before. Naturally the enemy will concentrate his fire on such an exposed detachment. It is just the transparently clear, unambiguous formula that is most endangered because it has an exposed side. No war is waged without losses, and with a stalemate one gets nowhere. Even the title "New Ethic" is a clarion call: Aux armes, citoyens! Here we shall get a whiff of poison gas and some clobbering about the head. In Tel-Aviv you run the risk of Egyptian bombs.

I am not quarrelsome but combative by nature and I cannot conceal from you my secret pleasure. But I shall have to act worried and if necessary discharge my duty as commandant of the fire brigade. Your writings will become a *petra scandali* but also the most potent impetus for future developments. For this I am profoundly grateful to you. With best regards,

Very sincerely yours, C. G. JUNG

☐ (Handwritten.)
[1] *Depth Psychology and a New Ethic* (tr., 1969).

To Alwine von Keller

Dear Frau von Keller,   Bollingen, 2 January 1949

As I am in Bollingen and your letter came at a favourable hour, I can at last get down to answering you.

That at the end of the year one is disposed—and particularly in our well-advanced youth—to backward glances is not to be wondered at. I too am in a retrospective phase and am occupying myself, for the first time in 25 years, thoroughly with myself, collecting my old dreams and putting them together. There are all sorts of strange things among them. How little one still knows of the "unconscious"! (Blessed be this non-prejudice-evoking term!)

I would like to take this opportunity of drawing your attention to a book: *The Various Light* by Monica Redlich, London 1948. The author is unknown to me but writes about things that are not unknown to me. It will interest you.

If you don't get this year's *Eranos-Jahrbuch* I would like to send you my essay "On the Self"[1] when the offprints come out.

My health has its ups and downs mostly because I still don't really know what one can or cannot do when one will soon be 74. My last illness was overwork. I have to tell myself twice a day: not too much! Snail's pace and rests in between and a change of snail-horses. Nevertheless I have succeeded in finishing a new paper on mandalas[2] which is to appear this year.

I have regretted very much that I shan't be able to come to this year's [Eranos] meeting. I must still look out for my liver. I am like an old car with 250,000 km. on its back that still can't shake off the memory of its 20 horsepower. Nevertheless, I console myself with the thought that only a fool expects wisdom. With every good wish for the New Year,

Yours ever, C. G. JUNG

☐ (Handwritten.)
[1] "Ueber das Selbst," *Eranos Jahrbuch 1948*, now *Aion*, ch. IV: The Self.
[2] "Ueber Mandalasymbolik," *Gestaltungen des Unbewussten* (1950), now "Concerning Mandala Symbolism," CW 9, i.

To Father Victor White

[ORIGINAL IN ENGLISH]

Dear Victor,   Bollingen, 8 January 1949

Thank you cordially for your nice human letter![1] I know now at least where you are. I was afraid America had spirited you away altogether. It is of course just like me to forget your most helpful and

☐ (Handwritten.)
[1] This letter appears to have been lost.

comprehensive letter about the *anima Christi*,[2] i.e., to forget to thank you. As a matter of fact I felt particularly grateful to you for having answered my request so thoroughly. Such things happen to me time and again and always have happened, namely that my feelings or a certain kind of them are suddenly no more in sight, especially in that moment when I should acknowledge them. That's how the inferior function behaves.

. . .

Your cryptic remarks about "synchronistic effects" on Dec. 16th arouse my curiosity, since I feel peculiarly innocent as to ulterior motives of my letter. This feeling of innocence may prove the contrary. I am sorry you can't tell me more about it. On my side it was an inner urge that prompted me to write. I felt a need to hear from you. The effect America had upon you looks exactly like something that went right through to the unconscious, whence it will appear again after a more or less prolonged incubation, in a new form.

The combination of priest and medicine man is not so impossible as you seem to think. They are based upon a common archetype, which will assert its right provided your inner development will continue as hitherto. It is true, the "fringe" of new things is always made up of funny figures. I imagine we could have observed very similar lunatics among the early Christian followers, f.i. those people who were cured of possession. After all, England and our old world is your *Rhodus, hic salta!*[3] One's anxiety always points out our task. If you escape it you have lost a piece of yourself, and a most problematic piece at that, with which the Creator of things was going to experiment in His unforeseeable ways. They are indeed apt to arouse anxiety. Particularly so, as long as one can't see below the surface. The independent mind in you is subject and object of the divine experiment. . . . If you feel isolated in England, why don't you make one of your *fratres* into a real brother in the spirit? When I came to Zurich, the most materialistic city of Switzerland, there was nobody ready-made for my needs. I then shaped some for me. They were meant for this experience. One could see it from their dreams.

Sorry this is a long letter again. Don't trouble to answer it.

Yours cordially, c. g.

---

[2] Cf. White, 24 Sept. 08.

[3] "Hic Rhodus, hic salta" (Here is Rhodes, here jump!), from Aesop's *Fables* ("The Braggart"), in which a man boasts of an enormous jump in Rhodes and is challenged to prove his prowess.

To Markus Fierz

Dear Colleague,   12 January 1949

May I ask you a mathematical question? During my illness in 1944 I had, after my heart embolism, an interval of syncope (?) or amnesia (?) and can remember no outer perceptions. Instead I had an unusually impressive vision[1] in which, among other things, I saw the earth from a great distance. What interests me is how great this distance was. Clues are: my whole field of vision was filled with a segment of the earth's sphere. At the top left I saw the northwestern edge of the earth. At the bottom right, on the edge of my field of vision, was Ceylon, and on the left the whole of India. I could vaguely make out Persia, Arabia, the Red Sea and, high up to the left, the Mediterranean, also the northeastern coast of Africa. The question is: How far distant from the earth was my standpoint[2] in order to take in this area?

I hope very much that answering this question will not give you too much trouble. With best thanks in advance,

Yours sincerely, c. g. j u n g

[1] *Memories*, pp. 289ff./270f.
[2] Approximately 1000 miles. Ibid., p. 290/270.

To Jürg Fierz

Dear Dr. Fierz,   13 January 1949

Above all you must realize that I am not in the habit of interfering with my pupils. I have neither the right nor the might to do that. They can draw such conclusions as seem right to them and must accept full responsibility for it. There have been so many pupils of mine who have fabricated every sort of rubbish from what they took over from me. I have never said that I stand "uncompromisingly" behind Neumann.[1] There is naturally no question of that. It should be obvious that I have my reservations.

If you want to understand Neumann properly you must realize that he is writing in the spiritual vacuum of Tel-Aviv. Nothing can come out of that place for the moment except a monologue. He writes as he fancies. No doubt this is provocative, but I have found that pro-

[1] Neumann's *Depth Psychology and a New Ethic* had aroused considerable controversy (cf. Neumann, Dec. 1948).

vocative books are by no means the worst. They get people's goat only because such people cannot be reached in any other way.

If people want to know what I think about these things they have my books, and everyone is free to listen to my views. They could just as well read my books instead of getting worked up about Neumann. If I recommend his book it is chiefly because it shows the sort of conclusions you come to when you ruthlessly think out ethical problems to the end. One must also remember that Neumann is a Jew and consequently knows Christianity only from the outside; and further, that it has been drastically demonstrated to the Jews that evil is continually projected. For the rest—where confession is concerned—it is indeed the case that if a person does not regard something as a sin he has no need to confess it. If Neumann recommends the "inner voice" as the criterion of ethical behaviour instead of the Christian conscience, this is in complete agreement with the Eastern view that in everybody's heart there dwells a judge who knows all his evil thoughts. In this respect Neumann also stands on the best footing with very many Christian mystics. If the mentally insane assert the same thing, that has always been so, only one should know that the voices of the insane are somewhat different from what Neumann calls the inner voice. Many insane people play themselves up as ethicists *par excellence* with no encouragement from Neumann. There is of course no external justification for the inner voice, for the simple reason that nobody knows what is good and what evil. It would all be terribly simple if we could go by the decalogue or the penal code or any other moral codex, since all the sins catalogued there are obviously so pointless or morbid that no reasonable person could fail to see how fatuous they are. Ethical decision is concerned with very much more complicated things, namely conflicts of duty, the most diabolical things ever invented and at the same time the loneliest ever dreamt of by the loneliest of all, the Creator of the world. In conflicts of duty one codex says Whoa there! and the other says Gee up! and you are none the wiser for it. It is an actual fact that what is good to one appears evil to the other. You have only to think of the careworn mother who meddles in all her son's doings—from the most selfless solicitude of course—but in reality with murderous effect. For the mother it is naturally a good thing if the son does not do this and does not do that, and for the son it is simply moral and physical ruin—so scarcely a good thing.

You are quite right when you say that Neumann's individual ethic makes far heavier demands on us than the Christian ethic does. The only mistake Neumann commits here is a tactical one: he says out loud, imprudently, what was always true. As soon as an ethic is set up as an absolute it is a catastrophe. It can only be taken relatively, just as Neumann can only be understood relatively, that is, as a religious Jew of German extraction living in Tel-Aviv. If one imagines one can simply make a clean sweep of all views of the world, one is deceiving oneself: views of the world are grounded in archetypes, which cannot be tackled so easily. What Neumann offers us is the outcome of an intellectual operation which he had to accomplish for himself in order to gain a new basis for his ethic. As a doctor he is profoundly impressed by the moral chaos and feels himself in the highest degree responsible. Because of this responsibility he is trying to set the ethical problem to rights, not in order to give out a legal ukase but to clarify his ethical reflections, naturally in the expectation of doing this also for the world around him.

In reading such a book you must also consider what sort of a world we are living in. You know, perhaps, that today Christianity is relativized by the splitting of the Church into so-and-so many million Catholics and so-and-so many million Protestants and that Bolshevism reigns supreme from Thüringen to Vladivostok—and on top of this there is an East with several billion non-Christians who have their views of the world too. Since this world is one world we are faced with the question: How do we come to grips with it? We cannot simply restrict ourselves to *our* view of the world, but must perforce find a standpoint from which a view will be possible that goes a little step beyond the Christian as well as the Buddhist, etc. As a Christian you must exert yourself and make it your daily preoccupation to bridge the woeful conflict in the Church by finding a mediating position. One cannot be simply Protestant or Catholic. That is much too facile, for in the end the one is the other's brother and this cannot be got rid of simply by declaring one of them invalid. Neumann postulates a position which in the deepest sense is valid for everyone. If there is an inner deciding factor it must be valid for all men. The question is only: Is there an inner voice, i.e., a vocation? Undoubtedly there isn't for 99% of humanity, just as a whole lot of things don't exist for this vast majority for the simple reason that they don't know about them. There isn't even a quite ordinary hygiene which would be valid for more than about 90% of humanity, let alone a corresponding moral code. If ethical decision is not in the last resort somehow inherent in human nature, then the case is completely hopeless, for no book of laws has lasted in the long run.

Subjectively I am absolutely convinced of the inner deciding factor and my practical work with patients aims exclusively at bringing it to consciousness. What you can learn from moral codes and manuals of morality and penal codes are practicalities which no intelligent person will overlook. But no book of laws has ever been written for conflicts of duty and there alone does the real ethical problem begin. There alone will you learn ethical responsibility. Everything else is settled by adaptation and plain horse sense. I do not regard it for a moment as particularly meritorious morally for a person to avoid everything that is customarily considered a sin. Ethical value attaches only to those decisions which are reached in situations of supreme doubt. That is the question that burns Neumann's soul and in this he has my support, no matter whether my position is relativized or not. I am no opportunist, but I observe in this respect certain fundamental ethical principles and not utilitarian ones.

If I were to write about ethics[2] I would naturally not express myself like Neumann. But neither am I the Neumann who has been pushed by an atrocious fate into a militant counterposition. If he has confronted the world with a difficulty which so-and-so many people have to torment themselves with, it does not surprise me in the least and I shall not fault him for that. Nor can I regret it if these so-called Christians are tormented a bit. They have richly deserved it. They are always gabbling about Christian morality and I would just like to see someone for once who really follows it. They can't muster even the slightest understanding for Neumann, let alone brotherly love. I only wish the Christians of today could see for once that what they stand for is not Christianity at all but a god-awful legalistic religion from which the founder himself tried to free them by following his voice and his vocation to the bitter end. Had he not done so there would never have been a Christianity. It is quite certain that the "community" will be outraged by this problem of an individual ethic, but that must be so for the question nowadays is: Community of whom or with whom? Not community as such, for we have always had that and what was the result? The "people's community" in Germany and suchlike. It is high time people reflected how they are constituted or what is the constitution of the thing they want to introduce into a community. A bad cause is not made better by multiplying it by 10,000 and 100 rapscallions do not add up to a single decent man.

As a first rule for book-reading I would recommend you always to

[2] Cf. "A Psychological View of Conscience," CW 10.

consider *who* the author is. We should have learnt by now that thoughts expressed by words never represent anything absolute, and that only the clueless make themselves new garments out of the rags of thought. With best regards,

Yours sincerely, c . g . j u n g

To Gebhard Frei

Dear Professor Frei,   17 January 1949

Many thanks for kindly sending me your recent paper on magic.[1] The question of the "subtle body"[2] interests me too. I try, as my custom is, to approach the problem from the scientific angle. I start with the formula: $E = M$, energy equals mass. Energy is not mere quantity, it is always a quantity of something. If we consider the psychic process as an energic one, we give it mass. This mass must be very small, otherwise it could be demonstrated physically. It becomes demonstrable in parapsychological phenomena, but shows at the same time that though it obeys psychic laws it does not obey physical laws, being in part independent of time and space, which means that psychic energy behaves as though time and space had only relative validity. Thus psychic energy can be grasped only by means of a 4- or multidimensional schema. This can be represented mathematically, but not envisaged. Atomic physics does the same for quantitatively measurable facts. The psychologist, however, sees no possibility as yet of quantitatively measuring his facts. He can only establish them, not explain them. There are, undoubtedly, synchronistic effects with a "vitalizing" force, i.e., phenomena which are not only synchronistic but also allow the conjecture that psychic energy influences living or inert objects in such a way that, as though "animated" by a psychic content alien to them, they are compelled to represent it somehow or other. These effects do not come from consciousness but from an unconscious form of existence which appears to be permanently in a merely relative spatio-temporal, i.e., 4- or multidimensional state. Psychic contents in this state act as much *outside* me as *in* me, just as much *outside* time as *in* time.

[1] "Magie und Psychologie," *Neue Schweizer Rundschau* (Zurich), No. 48, 1948/49, pp. 680-88.
[2] In parapsychology, the theory that psychic phenomena in the form of the "subtle body" can manifest themselves as physical phenomena. Cf. C. A. Meier, "Psychosomatic Medicine from the Jungian Point of View," *Journal of Analytical Psychology* (London), VIII:2 (July 1963), 111ff.

I think this much can be concluded with sufficient certainty. Of course it isn't an explanation but merely an attempt to formulate conclusions which seem to follow from the empirical premises. The psychic seems to me to be in actual fact partly extraspatial and extratemporal. "Subtle body" may be a fitting expression for this part of the psyche. With best regards and cordial thanks,

Yours very sincerely, C. G. JUNG

To Eugene M. E. Rolfe

[ORIGINAL IN ENGLISH]

Dear Mr. Rolfe,   3 March 1949

I'm sorry to have kept your manuscript[1] so long, but I wanted to have it thoroughly researched, in which purpose I have been helped by a friend.

The first part of your book is a quite interesting attempt to apply the idea of wholeness to the individual in the light of your own experience, but in the second part you fall more and more a victim to the idea of a collective solution.

You say in your letter that you had a dream while writing the first stages of your book, namely that you were going to have a child, and that in the later stages you dreamt that you had a baby small but like yourself, and that at the end you were afraid that it was a miscarriage. I'm afraid that these dreams apply to your book inasmuch as the second part and the end are premature attempts to translate your individual experiences into a collective application, which is impossible. You cannot teach a certain kind of morality or belief; you must be it. If you are it, then you can say what you want and it works. But you are not out of the woods yet. For instance, you entirely neglect the fact that man has an anima that plays the dickens with him—you married her and the shadow rolled into one. Under those conditions it is almost impossible to realize one's own anima, because her reality is all the time right under your nose and it is always pointed out to you that she is your wife.

It is a great temptation in our days, when one talks to Germans, to look for a sort of collective teaching or a collective ideal, but you

☐ London.

[1] "The Idea of Humanity" (unpublished). Jung liked the first chapters on the subjective reality of the Godhead and the stages of life, but was doubtful about the later ones on the Christian doctrine of the family. (For R.'s later writings cf. Rolfe, 1 May 54, 19 Nov. 60.)

find only words that don't carry. But if you are a really integrated personality, in other words, if you know all about your shadow and all about your anima (which is worse), then you have a hope to be the truth, namely truly yourself and that is a thing that works. I could repeat the words of an early Christian Papyrus which says: "Therefore strive first to know yourselves, because ye are the city and the city is the kingdom."[2]

. . .

I hope you will not mind the almost rude directness of my letter. It is well-meant, as I know that if you should succeed in publishing the book as it is now, it would be no success whatever, or it would have a wrong effect. I should therefore advise you to keep the manuscript unpublished until the most important question of the shadow and the anima has been duly settled.

Sincerely yours, c. g. JUNG

[2] Oxyrhynchus Papyrus 654, ii, in Grenfell and Hunt, *New Sayings of Jesus and Fragments of a Lost Gospel* (1904), p. 15. The exact words are: "(strive therefore?) to know yourselves . . . (and?) ye shall know that ye are in (the city of God?) and ye are (the city?)." Cf. also James, *The Apocryphal New Testament* (1924), pp. 26f.

To Henri Flournoy

Dear Colleague,   29 March 1949

I have just read your sympathetic report of my work with particular pleasure. Thank you for the interest you have been good enough to take in the objective exposition of my ideas.

It interested me very much, however, to find in your epilogue a few references to the archetypes which seem to me to contain some misunderstandings. I do not deny the existence of facts whose existence Freud has proved. I do not believe in theories and have no

☐ (Translated from French.) Henri Flournoy, son of the Swiss psychiatrist Théodore Flournoy (1854–1920). T. Flournoy's translation of the "Miller Fantasies," i.e., "Quelques Faits d'imagination créatrice subconsciente" in *Archives de psychologie* (Geneva), V (1906), formed the starting point for Jung's *Symbols of Transformation*. Jung describes the role he played in his development in *Erinnerungen, Träume, Gedanken*, pp. 378f. (this section is omitted in the English and American ed.). In *Memories*, p. 162/158 he refers to him as his "revered and fatherly friend."

intention at all of replacing his theory with another. What I intend is to demonstrate new facts—the existence of archetypes, for example —whose existence, moreover, has already been accepted by other sciences: in ethnology as *représentations collectives* (Lévy-Bruhl); in biology (Alverdes[1]); in history (Toynbee); in comparative mythology (Kerényi, Tucci,[2] Wilhelm, and Zimmer, representing ancient Greece, Tibet, China, and India); and in folklore as "motifs." The well known idea of the "behaviour pattern" in biology is synonymous with that of the archetype in psychology. As the term "archetypus" clearly shows, the idea is not even original; this notion is found with the same significance as early as in Philo Judaeus, in the *Corpus Hermeticum*, and in Dionysius the Areopagite. My inventiveness consists in nothing but the fact that I believe I have proved that archetypes do not appear only in the "migration of symbols"[3] but in the individual unconscious fantasies of everyone without exception. I have furnished proof of this in several large volumes which unfortunately have not yet been published in French. As I see it, the idea of a psychic "pattern of behaviour" is not at all astonishing, since the similarity of autochthonous psychic products was admitted to be a fact even by Freud. His is the honour of having discovered the first archetype, the Oedipus complex. That is a mythological and a psychological motif simultaneously. But obviously it is no more than a single archetype, the one representing the son's relationship to his parents. So there must be others, since there is still the daughter's relationship to the parents, the parents' relationship to the children, the relationships between man and woman, brother and sister, etc. Very probably there are also "patterns" representing the different ages of man, birth, death, etc. There are any number of typical situations, each represented by a certain innate form that forces the individual to function in a specifically human way. These are the same as the forms that force the birds to build their nests in a certain way.

[1] Friedrich Alverdes, German zoologist. Cf. Jung, "Instinct and the Unconscious," CW 8, par. 282, n. 12, citing Alverdes, "Die Wirksamkeit von Archetypen in den Instinkthandlungen der Tiere," *Zoologischer Anzeiger* (Leipzig), CXIX, 9/10 (1937).

[2] Giuseppe Tucci, Italian Orientalist, professor of the religion and philosophy of India and the Far East at the U. of Rome. Lectured at Eranos 1953 on "Earth as Conceived of in Indian and Tibetan Religion, with Special Regard to the Tantras."

[3] One of the theories for explaining the concordance of myths and symbols among different civilizations is that they were transmitted by migration and tradition. Cf. "Constitution and Heredity in Psychology," CW 8, par. 228.

Instinct takes a specific form, even in man. That form is the archetype, so named because unconscious thought expresses itself mythologically (*vide* Oedipus). I am only continuing what Freud began, and I often regret that the Freudian school have not known how to develop their master's fortunate discovery.

In reading your epilogue, I asked myself whether you mistrust my qualifications or my scientific competence as the Freudians generally do. There is undoubtedly a basis for your criticism, but unfortunately I do not know the reasons for it, and it would be most useful to me to know them. No one has yet been able to prove my hypothesis false. Freud himself certainly did not think it necessary to know Greek mythology in order to have an Oedipus complex (and neither do I, for that matter). Obviously the existence of an archetype—that is to say, the possibility of developing an Oedipus complex—does not depend on historical mythologems. What is the logical error in this reasoning?

I have never been able to discover the slightest difference between incestuous Greek fantasy and modern fantasy. Undoubtedly incestuous fantasy is pretty universal and obviously it is not unique in being able to express itself through a mythologem. What more natural conclusion can we draw than that we are dealing here with a generally human disposition, which is instinctive and innate, as instinct is with all animals? How else can we explain identical or analogous products among tribes and individuals who could not have known of the existence of parallel creations? Do you really believe that every chick invents its own way of breaking out of the egg? Or that every eel makes an individual decision to start for the Bermudas, as though the idea were entirely novel? Why don't people take into account the thoroughly documented facts that I present in my alchemical studies? But they don't read those books, and they are satisfied with quite puerile prejudices, like the one that I mean inherited ideas, and other nonsensical things!

So—while I admire the conscientious way you presented my essays —I admit that I cannot help being somewhat sorry that you could not avoid making such a derogatory reference without the slightest proof or explanation. After your fine attempt to be strictly objective, a confession of your Freudian faith would perhaps have been enough to ease your conscience. But it seems to me you could have done that without disqualifying the heretic.

I do not habitually write letters of this sort. But I thought I should make this exception in view of the personal esteem which has always characterized my relations with both your father and yourself. I am, dear colleague,

Yours with best regards, c. g. jung

To Emma von Pelet

Dear Frau von Pelet,   Bollingen, 4 April 1949

Your gift was a great joy! Joh. Peter Hebel[1] is our Basel poet *par excellence*, and I spent my whole youth at the mouth of the Wiese,[2] of which Hebel sang. I fear you have deprived yourself in leaving this heirloom to me. My heartiest thanks!

What comes to you from the world, and what you answer, constitute your relation to the world. Just this is "going out into the world." For the time being you are doing so in the disguise of translations.[3] This is as good a work as any other. Fruitful introversion is possible only when there is also a relation to the outside.

If Shanti[4] is too much for you, you must draw in your horns until you have found a tolerable mean. You shouldn't let yourself be put upon—that would be a serious weakness. Finding the right measure is also a way of relating to the world. With cordial thanks and kind regards,

Yours sincerely, c. g. jung

☐ (Handwritten.)
[1] Johann Peter Hebel (1760–1826), Swiss poet.
[2] The river Wiese flows through Klein-Hüningen, where Jung's father took up residence in 1879. Cf. *Memories*, p. 15/29.
[3] Cf. Pelet, 15 Jan. 44, n. ☐.
[4] The house where P. lived, near Ascona.

To Aniela Jaffé

Dear Aniela,   Bollingen, 12 April 1949

Your letter dropped in on me at a time of difficult reflection. I'm sorry I can't tell you anything more. It would be too much. Also, I haven't yet reached the end of my thorny path. Hard and burdensome insights[1] have come to me. After long wanderings in the darkness,

☐ (Handwritten.)
[1] Jung was at that time working on *Aion*, which contains the seeds of many ideas eventually formulated in "Answer to Job" and "Synchronicity."

glaring lights have gone up which mean I don't know what. At any rate I know why I need the seclusion of Bollingen. It is more necessary than ever. . . .

I congratulate you on the completion of "Séraphita."[2] Though it didn't help Balzac to turn aside from the self, one would like to be able to. But I know one would have to pay for it even more dearly. I wish I had a Jahwe Sabaoth as a κύριος τῶν δαιμόνων.[3] I understand more and more why I nearly died and I can't help wishing I had. The draught is bitter. With cordial greetings,

Yours ever, c. g.

[2] J. gave two (unpublished) lectures at the Psychological Club, Zurich, on the life of Balzac and his novel *Séraphita*.
[3] = Lord of the Daemons.

Anonymous

Dear Colleague,   25 April 1949

I have glanced through your symbological essay.[1] You have all sorts of good ideas, but you lack the intellectual discipline and scientific method which are of the utmost importance in this field. Without them one goes adrift and achieves no reliable results. There is also a psychological danger because symbolic material constellates your unconscious, and if you then do not handle the material according to strict scientific rules, but only sniff out intuitive analogies, your unconscious is broken up instead of synthetized. I must *warn* you of this danger! I would advise you to single out *one* specific question, for instance the shape of the numerals 0-9 in Roman or Arabic, and investigate this problem with scientific exactitude, avoiding all digressions.

I would also advise you to get in touch with Fräulein Dr. Schärf[2] at the Institute, so that she can give you the necessary methodological guidance. Doctors seldom have a differentiated thinking, since their studies give them no training in this respect. But in psychology it is indispensable.

It is *very important* for your mental health that you should on the one hand concern yourself with psychic material but on the other hand should do so as systematically and accurately as possible, other-

☐ (Handwritten.) Switzerland.
[1] An attempt to interpret certain modern Arabic numerals as symbolic images.
[2] Cf. Vuille, 22 Feb. 46, n. 1.

wise you are running a dangerous risk. Do not forget that the original meaning of all letters and numbers was a *magical* one! Hence the "perils of the soul."[3] There are good beginnings in your work, but it is still too wild, too disordered, too *disjunctive*. With best wishes,

Yours sincerely, C. G. JUNG

[3] The fear of primitives of the dangers threatening their souls, resulting in a "loss of soul" or, in psychological terms, dissociation of consciousness. Cf. Frazer, *The Golden Bough*, Part II: *Taboo and the Perils of the Soul*.

To Armin Kesser

Dear Herr Kesser,   18 June 1949

I would like to thank you very much for your amiable review of my book *Symbolik des Geistes*.[1] You have succeeded in handling this difficult material in a way that gives the reader a real impression of my ideas.

I would only like to draw your attention to one small discrepancy: seen in psychological perspective, the concept of the self cannot be described as a *summum bonum*. I have never done so anywhere. This would be a contradiction in terms, since the self by definition represents the virtual union of all opposites. It cannot be described as a *summum bonum* even in the metaphorical sense, because it is not a *summum desideratum* but rather a *dira necessitas* which is characterized by all the corresponding unpleasant qualities. Individuation is as much a fatality as a fulfillment. The psychology of the self is not philosophy but an empirical process which, being a natural process, could run its course smoothly if it did not take a tragic turn in man by colliding with his consciousness.

Yours sincerely, C. G. JUNG

□ (1906–1966), Swiss art and literary critic.
[1] In *Neue Zürcher Zeitung*, No. 1194, 11 June 1949 and No. 1223, 15 June 1949.

To Markus Fierz

Dear Professor Fierz,   22 June 1949

I have read your great paper in the *Eranos-Jahrbuch* with avid interest.[1] I find it extraordinarily stimulating.

However, I am turning to you in another matter, namely the enclosed manuscript which Pauli has prompted me to write.[2] It is a putting together of my thoughts on the concept of synchronicity. Since physicists are the only people nowadays who would be able to deal with such a concept successfully, it is from a physicist that I hope to meet with critical understanding although, as you will see, the empirical basis seems to lie wholly in the realm of psychic phenomena.

I should be extraordinarily grateful if you would be kind enough to go over my thinking critically, and grateful too for any criticism you may offer. Unfortunately I am moving in very difficult and obscure territory where reason can easily go astray. But as the problem seems to me of first-class importance, I would not like to neglect anything that might help the discussion.

I hope I am not making too heavy demands on your valuable time. With best thanks in advance,

Yours sincerely, C. G. JUNG

[1] "Zur physikalischen Erkenntnis," *Eranos Jahrbuch 1948*.
[2] Probably a draft of the later Eranos lecture "Ueber Synchronizität," *Eranos Jahrbuch 1951*, now "On Synchronicity," CW 8, Appendix, pars. 969ff.

To Virginia Payne

[ORIGINAL IN ENGLISH]

Dear Miss Payne,   23 July 1949

I do remember the Clark Conference of 1909.[1] It was my first visit to the United States and for this reason my recollections are particularly vivid, although I must say that the details of the Conference itself have largely disappeared. But I do remember some incidents.

I travelled on the same boat with Professor Freud who was also invited and I remember vividly our discussion of his theories. We chiefly analysed our dreams during the trip and also during our stay in America and on the way back. Professor William Stern[2] from Breslau was on the same boat, but Freud didn't feel particularly enthusiastic about the presence of an academic psychologist. No wonder, because his position of pioneer in Europe was not particularly enviable. I still sympathize entirely with his negative feelings, since I enjoyed the same fate for over 30 years.

[1] P. asked Jung for his recollections of this Conference (cf. Forel, 12 Oct. 09, n. 1), on which she was writing her doctoral thesis at the U. of Wisconsin.
[2] (1871–1938), German psychologist, professor of psychology at the Universities of Breslau and Hamburg; from 1933 in U.S.A.

Two personalities I met at the Clark Conference made a profound and lasting impression on me. One was Stanley Hall,[3] the President, and the other was William James whom I met for the first time then. I remember particularly an evening at President Hall's house. After dinner William James appeared and I was particularly interested in the personal relation between Stanley Hall and William James, since I gathered from some remarks of President Hall that William James was not taken quite seriously on account of his interest in Mrs. Piper[4] and her extra-sensory perceptions. Stanley Hall had prepared us that he had asked James to discuss some of his results with Mrs. Piper and to bring some of his material. So when James came (there was Stanley Hall, Professor Freud, one or two other men and myself) he said to Hall: "I've brought you some papers in which you might be interested." And he put his hand to his breastpocket and drew out a parcel which to our delight proved to be a wad of dollar bills. Considering Stanley Hall's great services for the increase and the welfare of Clark University and his rather critical remarks as to James' pursuits, it looked to us a particularly happy rejoinder. James excused himself profusely. Then he produced the real papers from the other pocket.

I spent two delightful evenings with William James alone and I was tremendously impressed by the clearness of his mind and the complete absence of intellectual prejudices. Stanley Hall was an equally clear-headed man, but decidedly of an academic brand.

The Conference was noteworthy on account of the fact that it was the first time that Professor Freud had an immediate contact with America. It was the first official recognition of the existence of psychoanalysis and it meant a great deal to him, because recognition in Europe for him was regrettably scarce. I was a young man then. I lectured about association tests and a case of child psychology.[5] I was also interested in parapsychology and my discussions with William James were chiefly about this subject and about the psychology of religious experience.

As far as I remember we didn't make many contacts with psychologists or psychiatrists with the exception of old Dr. Putnam,[6]

[3] American psychologist (1844–1924), professor of psychology and President of Clark University. Cf. *Memories*, p. 366/337. (See pl. II.)
[4] Cf. Künkel, 10 July 46, n. 3.
[5] "The Association Method" and "The Family Constellation" (CW 2), and "Psychic Conflicts in a Child" (CW 17).
[6] James Jackson Putnam (1846–1915), American physician, professor of neurology at Harvard; a founder of the American Psychoanalytical Association.

who curiously enough was an adept of Hegel's philosophy. Apart from that he was an unprejudiced, very human personality whom I liked and admired.

Since it was our first stay in America we thought it all very strange and we felt we didn't speak the same mental language as our American surroundings. I had many discussions with Professor Freud about the peculiar American psychology which, to myself at least, was more or less enigmatical. I only got the gist of it when I came back in 1912.[7] Then only did I begin to understand the main and distinctive features of American compared with European psychology.[8]

We spent a very interesting week in Dr. Putnam's camp in the Adirondacks and continued to be bewildered by the peculiar ways and ideas of the many native guests at that camp. It was a large party of about 40 people.

I cannot remember much of the papers presented at the Conference, nor of other discussions that took place, but we felt very much that our point of view was very different and that there hardly existed a bridge between the then prevailing American views and our peculiar European standpoint.

It is not for me to judge the effect on psychiatry in general, since this is a specifically American development which I haven't followed up. The influence of psychology on psychiatry is still very small for obvious reasons. In any great institution there is no time at all for individual investigation—at least it is so in Europe, and the number of alienists I have taught is quite small.

Hoping I have been able to give you at least an idea of my recollections of the Clark Conference, I remain,

Yours sincerely, C. G. JUNG

[7] In Sept. 1912 Jung gave a series of lectures on "The Theory of Psychoanalysis" (CW 4), at Fordham U., New York.
[8] Cf. "The Complications of American Psychology," CW 10.

To Hélène Kiener

Dear Fräulein Kiener,   13 August 1949

In my paper "Der Geist der Psychologie" (*Eranos Jahrbuch 1946*) I have shown, with the help of historical material, that the collective unconscious was compared symbolically with the starry sky—in par-

□ Analytical psychologist, Strasbourg.

ticular by Paracelsus.[1] I have devoted a whole chapter to the unconscious as a "multiple consciousness."[2] I cannot possibly repeat this whole chapter for you. I would advise you to ask the Strasbourg University Library if the paper could be sent to you from the Basel University Library. Unfortunately I have no more copies of it.

To substantiate a factual analogy between the unconscious and the cosmos is an almost insoluble task. Nor can one cite the supposed planetary arrangement of electrons round the atomic nucleus, as this is only a controversial model by means of which certain physicists have envisioned the mathematical relation between electrons and the atomic nucleus. I use a similar image to represent the relation of the archetypes to the central archetype of the self. This is no proof of actual identity or similarity, its only basis being that the explanation employs the same image in order to make certain irrepresentable relationships more or less conceivable. This is true also of the historical symbols for the nature of the unconscious which I have discussed in the above paper. It is not only possible, but for certain reasons quite probable, that the collective unconscious coincides in a strange and utterly inconceivable way with objective events. I have tried to formulate this coincidence as synchronicity and just now am engaged on a work of this kind. But one cannot say that the coincidence is reflected in the analogy of planetary laws of motion or the starry sky. We have here, as you see, a very difficult problem which you would do well to leave alone. For your purposes it is enough that an analogy between the starry sky and the unconscious has existed from very early times, at least as a symbol.

Otherwise I have nothing to remark. With best regards,

Yours sincerely, C. G. JUNG

[1] Cf. "On the Nature of the Psyche," CW 8, pars. 390ff.
[2] Ibid., ch. 6.

To Erich Neumann

Dear Colleague,   Bollingen, 28 August 1949

As a result of numerous disturbances I have so far managed to read through only rather more than half of your MS.[1] Even for an educated

☐ (Handwritten.)
[1] Possibly the MS of "Die mythische Welt und der Einzelne," *Eranos Jahrbuch 1949.*

lay public it is very difficult because it takes too much for granted. Very interesting for me, because admirably thought out. Only, you do tend to apostrophize the unconscious too pessimistically. It would be advisable to counter every negative remark with a positive one, otherwise one gets the impression of a catastrophic tragedy with no grace from above. But that doesn't accord with experience: "God helps the valiant." For the rest, I have no essential corrections to report. I am particularly impressed by your thoroughness in thinking the problems through. But don't forget that behind this cloud of thought there sits a public which will scarcely be in a position to penetrate it. Meanwhile with best regards,

Yours sincerely, C. G. JUNG

To Dorothy Thompson

[ORIGINAL IN ENGLISH]

Dear Mrs. Thompson, 23 September 1949

It is a pleasure to receive the letter of a normally intelligent person in contrast to the evil flood of idiotic and malevolent insinuations I seemed to have released in the U.S.A.[1]

Well, you know I am just as deeply concerned with the extraordinary as well as uncanny situation of the world as you are yourself. (By the way, I have read quite a number of your political comments and admired their practical intelligence and common sense!)

□ (1894–1961), American journalist; worked as a reporter in Germany but was expelled in 1934 because of her anti-Nazi sentiments.

[1] An acrimonious controversy had arisen in the U.S.A. over the award, by the Fellows in American Letters of the Library of Congress, of the Bollingen Prize in Poetry to the poet Ezra Pound in 1949. Articles published in *The Saturday Review of Literature* (11 and 18 June) arbitrarily dragged Jung into the conflict, presenting him as a Nazi and anti-Semite by the method of misquotation, quotation out of context, and insinuation. The only connection with Jung lay in the name of the award, in which the name "Bollingen" appears simply because it was the Bollingen Foundation (named after the village where Jung had his country retreat) that had put the money ($1000) at the disposal of the Library. The articles were followed by a long correspondence in which, again quite arbitrarily and without relevance to the original issues, opponents of Jung came up with unfounded accusations based on the same methods of falsification. Concerning the award to Pound cf. "The Case against the Saturday Review of Literature," *Poetry* (Chicago), 1949. — Dorothy Thompson mentioned the controversy in her letter (10 Sept.) to Jung, referring to the "mendacity and malice" of his opponents.

I could say quite a lot about the actual dilemma of the world from my psychological point of view. But I am afraid it would lead too far afield into realms of psychological intricacies which would demand a great amount of explanation.

I will try to be simple. A political situation is the manifestation of a parallel psychological problem in millions of individuals. This problem is largely *unconscious* (which makes it a particularly dangerous one!). It consists of a conflict between a conscious (ethical, religious, philosophical, social, political, and psychological) standpoint and an unconscious one which is characterized by the same aspects but represented in a "lower," i.e., more archaic form. Instead of "high" Christian ethics, the laws of the herd, suppression of individual responsibility and submission to the tribal chief (totalitarian ethics). Instead of religion, superstitious belief in an *ad hoc* doctrine or truth; instead of philosophy, a low-grade doctrinary system which "rationalizes" the appetites of the herd; instead of a differentiated social organization, a meaningless chaotic agglomeration of uprooted individuals kept under by sheer force and terror and blindfolded by appropriate lies; instead of a constructive use of political power with the aim of attaining an equilibrium of freely developing forces, a destructive tendency to extend suppression over the whole world through attaining mere superiority of power; instead of psychology, use of psychological means to extinguish the individual spark and to inhibit the development of consciousness and intelligence.

You find this conflict in nearly every citizen of any Western nation. But one is mostly unconscious of it. In Russia, which has always been a barbarous country, the unconscious half of the conflict has reached the surface and has replaced civilized consciousness. That is what we fear might happen to ourselves too. We are afraid of this schizophrenia all the more since Germany has clearly demonstrated that even a civilized community can be seized by such a mental catastrophe as it were overnight (which proves my point).

Thus we have got to realize:

1. We are not immune.
2. The destructive powers are right there in ourselves.
3. The more unconscious they are, the more dangerous.
4. We are threatened from within as well as from without.
5. We cannot destroy the enemy by force; we should not even try to overcome Russia, because we would destroy ourselves, since Russia is—as it were—identical with our unconscious, which contains our instincts and all the germs of our future development.

535

6. The unconscious must be slowly integrated without violence and with due respect for our ethical values. This needs many alterations in our religious and philosophical views.

The West is forced to rearmament. We have to be ready for the worst. Europe must be organized by the U.S.A. *à tort et à travers* if needs be. And it will be of vital importance to the U.S.A. *But no attack! Under no condition!* Russia can only defeat herself. We cannot defeat our instincts, but they can inhibit each other and they do if you allow them to run freely within certain limits, i.e., only so far that they don't just kill you. You shoot when you are threatened in your very existence, not when you are merely hurt in your feelings or in your traditional convictions.

The accumulation of weapons, though indispensable, is a great temptation to use them. Therefore watch the military advisers! They will itch to pull the trigger. Russia is certainly on the warpath and it is only fear of those who are in the know that holds her back. Your country is already at war with Russia, like the *drôle de guerre* 1939/40. *There is no reason and no diplomacy that will effectively deal with Russia*, because there is an *elementary drive* in her (as was the case with Hitler!).

I see the main trouble not in Russia but in Europe, which has become a vital extension of the U.S.A. The great question is whether the historically differentiated nations of Europe can be sufficiently welded together to form a unified bloc. Apart from military defensive measures the organization of Europe forms the foremost and most difficult task of American policy.

I should like to call your attention to my little book: *Essays on Contemporary Events* (Kegan Paul, London, 1947), where you will find some further contributions to the great problem of our time. It seems to me that at the bottom of all these problems lies the development of science and technology, which has destroyed man's metaphysical foundation. *Social welfare has replaced the kingdom of God.*

Earthly happiness can only be attained through somebody else's misfortune, as wealth grows at the expense of poverty. "Social welfare" has become the lure, the bait and the slogan for the uprooted masses, which can only think in terms of personal needs and resentments; but they don't see that there is no escape from the law of compensation. Their Marxist philosophy is based upon the conviction that the river once in the future can be persuaded to flow upwards. They don't see that they themselves have to pay for this stunt by unending suffering. Much better to know, therefore, that life on this earth is balanced between an equal amount of pleasure and misery, even when it is at its best, and that *real progress* is only the psychological adaptation to the various forms of individual misery. Misery is relative. When many people possess two cars, the man with only one car is a proletarian deprived of the goods of this world and therefore entitled to overthrow the social order. Germany was not in possession of world-supremacy, therefore she was a "have-not."

We all think in terms of social welfare. That is the big mistake, because the more you economize on the vulgar forms of misery, the more you are ensnared by new, unexpected, complicated, intricate, incomprehensible variants of unhappiness such as you have never dreamt of before. Think of the almost uncanny increase of divorces and neuroses! I must say I prefer a modest poverty or any tangible discomfort (f.i. no bathroom, no electricity, no car, etc.) to those pests. The bit of social progress attained by Nazi Germany and Russia is compensated for by police terror, a new and very considerable item on the list of miseries, but an inevitable consequence of "social welfare." Why not "spiritual welfare"? There is no government on earth bothering much about it. Yet spiritual adjustment is *the* problem.

If we understand what Russia is in ourselves, we know how to deal with her politically.

Ancient Rome, not knowing how to deal with its own social problem, viz. slavery, succumbed to the onslaught of barbarous tribes. The Christian Middle Ages withstood the first Asiatic wave and the second (the Turks). Now the world is confronted with the third. The great danger is that we are not up to our own spiritual problem like old Rome. Technology and "social welfare" provide nothing to overcome our spiritual stagnation, and they give us no answer to our spiritual dissatisfaction and restlessness, on account of which we are threatened from within as from without. We have not understood yet that the discovery of the unconscious means an enormous spiritual task, which *must* be accomplished if we wish to preserve our civilization.

I hope you will forgive the unsystematic way in which I represent my ideas you wanted to hear of. My attempt is, I know, very incomplete, but I cannot write a whole book. Nevertheless I hope that you can perceive at least something.

Yours sincerely, C. G. JUNG

To Georg Krauskopf

Dear Herr Krauskopf,   31 December 1949

Your book *Die Heilslehre des Buddha*[1] has arrived safely. I can perfectly understand your preference for Buddhism. It is something magnificent. I have visited the holy places of Buddhism in India[2] and was profoundly impressed by them, quite apart from my reading of Buddhist literature. If I were an Indian I would definitely be a Buddhist. But in the West we have different presuppositions. No Hindu pantheon lies behind us, instead we have a Judaeo-Christian background and a Mediterranean culture, consequently different questions await an answer. Buddha would settle our account too early, and then it would go with us as it did when we European barbarians had that sudden and shattering collision with the ripest fruit of antiquity—Christianity—not to the advantage of our inner development.[3] Something in us has remained barbarian; in India things are different. But we aren't Indians.

Soon I shall get down to reading your book with the greatest interest. Buddha "gets" me again and again. By way of criticism I would only remark that I regret very much not having the footnotes in the text. This makes the reading of the book uncommonly tiresome, and I hope that in a later edition you will put the footnotes in the text where they belong. For me books that have the annotations at the back are almost unreadable. With best thanks,

Yours sincerely, C. G. JUNG

□ Stuttgart.
[1] Waiblingen, 1949.
[2] *Memories*, pp. 274ff.
[3] Cf. Schmitz, 26 May 23.

To Ernesto A. C. Volkening

Dear Dr. Volkening,   31 December 1949

As you rightly remark, the concept of the archetype is a very complex affair. The archetype is a psychologically experienceable factor, i.e., archetypally constructed images are produced by the unconscious. Obviously these images, so far as their specific content is concerned, are always dependent on local and temporal conditions. But the ground-plan of these images is universal and must be assumed to be

□ Bogotá, Colombia.

538

pre-existent, since it can be demonstrated in the dreams of small children or uneducated persons who could not possibly have been influenced by tradition. The pre-existent pattern is irrepresentable because it is totally unconscious. It functions as an arranger of representable material. Thus the archetype as a phenomenon is conditioned by place and time, but on the other hand it is an invisible structural pattern independent of place and time, and like the instincts proves to be an essential component of the psyche.

. . .

With best wishes for the New Year,

Yours very sincerely, c. g. j u n g

To Father Victor White

[O R I G I N A L   I N   E N G L I S H]

My dear Victor,   31 December 1949

Before the old year goes to end, I should like to write to you—a thing I tried a while ago, but never found time enough. First we had (at the end of Oct.) a regrettable accident: my wife fell in the corridor (slipping on a carpet) and broke her right arm in the shoulder— a nasty fracture indeed. I had her in the hospital for 2 months. Then I myself was laid up with a gastric grippe and a troublesome liver; then Marie-Jeanne Schmid[1] came down with a similar ailment, knocking her out completely. My correspondence and other obligations could go and did go up the chimney, i.e., they just dropped into Nirvana. Now I am reasonably well again and can write to you. You have kept me busy for a while with your *correctio fatuorum*[2] in *Dominican Studies*. I found it very interesting and illuminating and

☐ (Handwritten.)

[1] Marie-Jeanne Schmid (now Frau Boller-Schmid), Jung's secretary from Apr. 1932–Sept. 1952, the date of her marriage.

[2] = "correction of fools," referring to W.'s review of *Eranos Jahrbücher* 1947 and 1948 in *Dominican Studies* (Oxford), II:4 (Oct. 1949). He wrote an appreciation of "Ueber das Selbst" (*EJ* 1948), the later ch. IV of *Aion*, but criticized Jung for his "misunderstandings" of the doctrine of the *privatio boni* and for his "quasi-Manichaean dualism," calling his "somewhat confused and confusing pages . . . another infelicitous excursion of a great scientist outside his orbit . . . and a brief and unhappy encounter with scholastic thought." (The *privatio boni* is not discussed in ch. IV of *Aion* but in ch. V: "Christ, A Symbol of the Self," which W. must have read in MS form. Cf. par. 112, n. 74: "My learned friend Victor White, O.P., in his *Dominican Studies* (II, p. 399) thinks he can detect a Manichaean streak in me. . . .")

it has forced me to go as far back as *Basilius Magnus*,[3] who is the perpetrator of *omne malum a homine*[4] (Hom. II. in *Hex.*—Migne, [P.G.] XXIX, col. 37 sqq.): τῆς ἐν ἑαυτῷ κακίας ἕκαστος ἑαυτὸν ἀρχηγὸν γνωριζέτω.[5] Evil originates out of a διάθεσις ἐν ψυγή.[6] and thus it is οὐχὶ οὐσία ζῶσα.[7] It merely derives from ῥαθυμία,[8] from carelessness and negligence which are obviously μὴ ὄν[9] as they are merely psychological. And so it is today: reduce something to a whim or an imagination, then it vanishes into μὴ ὄν, i.e., nothingness. I firmly believe however that psyche is an οὐσία.[10] I also took a dive into St. Thomas, but I did not feel refreshed afterwards. All and sundry disregard the fact that good and evil are the equivalent moieties of a logical judgment. They also omit to discuss at the same time the eternity of the devil, hell and damnation, that are certainly not μὴ ὄν and equally not good (i.e., good only to the heavenly spectators). This *privatio boni*[11] business is odious to me on account of its dangerous consequences: it causes a negative inflation of man, who can't help imagining himself, if not as a source of the [Evil],[12] at least as a great destroyer, capable of devastating God's beautiful creation. This doctrine produces Luciferian vanity and it is also greatly responsible for the fatal underrating of the human soul being the original abode of Evil. It gives a monstrous importance to the soul and not a word about on whose account the presence of the Serpent in Paradise belongs!

The question of Good and Evil, so far as I am concerned with it,

[3] Basil the Great (*ca.* 330–79), bishop of Caesarea.

[4] "All evil comes from man." From Basil's *Hexaemeron*, a series of sermons on the opening verses of Genesis and an exposition of the Psalms. For this and the following quotations cf. *Aion*, pars. 81ff.

[5] "Each of us should acknowledge that he is the first author of the wickedness in him" (par. 83).

[6] "condition of the soul" (ibid.).

[7] "not a living entity" (ibid.).

[8] "carelessness, indifference, frivolity" (par. 85).

[9] = that which does not exist, non-being.

[10] = substance, essence.

[11] The Catholic doctrine of the *privatio boni* maintains that evil is the privation or absence of good and has no substance or reality of its own. Jung strongly objected to this view: for him good and evil were equally real as polar opposites. These two contradictory views—the theological-metaphysical and the psychological-empirical—played an ever-increasing role in the discussions between Jung and White, and led to a growing estrangement. For Jung's view cf. *Aion*, esp. pars. 74f., 89f., 98; for the Catholic, White's *God and the Unconscious*, p. 75, n. 1 and *Soul and Psyche*, esp. ch. 9: "The Integration of Evil."

[12] Here Jung made an obvious slip by writing "Good," which would not give the sense he intended.

has nothing to do with metaphysics; it is only a concern of psychology. I make no metaphysical assertions and even in my heart I am no Neo-Manichean;[13] on the contrary I am deeply convinced of the unity of the self, as demonstrated by the mandala symbolism. But dualism is lurking in the shadows of the Christian doctrine: the devil will not be redeemed, nor shall eternal damnation come to an end. Origen's optimistically hoping or at least asking whether the devil might not be redeemed in the end was not exactly welcomed.[14]

As long as Evil is a μὴ ὄν, *nobody will take his own shadow seriously.* Hitler and Stalin go on representing a mere "accidental lack of perfection."[15] *The future of mankind very much depends upon the recognition of the shadow.* Evil is—psychologically speaking—*terribly real.* It is a fatal mistake to diminish its power and reality even merely metaphysically. I am sorry, this goes to the very roots of Christianity. Evil verily does not decrease by being hushed up as a non-reality or as mere negligence of man. It was there before him, when he could not possibly have a hand in it. God is the mystery of all mysteries, a real Tremendum.[16] Good and Evil are psychological relativities and as such quite real, yet one does not know what they are. For this reason they should not be projected upon a transcendent being. Thus you avoid Manichean dualism without *petitiones principii* and other subterfuges. I guess I am a heretic.

You must have had an interesting time in Spain. I had indeed not the faintest idea of what an English College in Valladolid would do.

I know you must criticize me. I am decidedly not on the winning side, but most unpopular right and left. I don't know whether I deserve to be included in your prayer. Yet there is a consolation that has reached me across the gulf of an aeon: καὶ ὅ που εἷς ἐστιν μόνος, λέγω, ἐγώ εἰμι μετ'αὐτοῦ.[17]

With all good wishes for a successful and happy New Year.

Yours cordially, c . g .

[13] Manichaeism was a syncretistic, Gnostic religion inaugurated by Mani of Babylonia, *ca.* 215–77. It is strictly dualistic, based on the eternal conflict between light and darkness, good and evil.

[14] *Aion,* par. 171 & n. 29.

[15] *Ibid.,* pars. 74, 96.

[16] The German theologian Rudolf Otto (1869–1937), in his book *The Idea of the Holy* (tr. 1926; orig. 1917), defined the *Tremendum* as an aspect of the *numinosum,* "numinosity," which for him was the central characteristic of the Divinity.

[17] ". . . and where there is one alone I say I am with him" (James, *The Apocryphal New Testament,* Oxyrhynchus Papyrus 1, logion x, p. 27).

To Serge Moreux

Dear M. Moreux,   20 January 1950

While I thank you for your kind letter, I must tell you that unfortunately I am obliged to limit my activity for reasons of age and health, and so it will not be possible for me to write an article for the projected number of *Polyphonie*.

Music certainly has to do with the collective unconscious—as the drama does too; this is evident in Wagner, for example. Music expresses, in some way, the movement of the feelings (or emotional values) that cling to the unconscious processes. The nature of what happens in the collective unconscious is archetypal, and archetypes always have a numinous quality that expresses itself in emotional stress. Music expresses in sounds what fantasies and visions express in visual images. I am not a musician and would not be able to develop these ideas for you in detail. I can only draw your attention to the fact that music represents the movement, development, and transformation of motifs of the collective unconscious. In Wagner this is very clear and also in Beethoven, but one finds it equally in Bach's "Kunst der Fuge."[1] The circular character of the unconscious processes is expressed in the musical form; as for example in the sonata's four movements, or the perfect circular arrangement of the "Kunst der Fuge," etc. I am with best regards,

Yours sincerely, C. G. JUNG

☐ (Translated from French.) Serge Moreux, director of *Polyphonie, Revue Musicale* (Paris), asked for a contribution on "the role of music in the collective unconscious" to be published in an issue entitled "La musique et les problèmes de l'homme."
[1] "The Art of Fugue" (1749/50), Bach's last and one of his grandest works, consisting of 19 fugues on an identical theme and its variants, all in D minor.

To Edmund Kaufmann

Dear Minister,   January 1950

Permit me, as a foreigner, the liberty of claiming your valuable time in a matter affecting your state. I am writing to you at the instiga-

☐ Then minister of finance for the state (German *Land*) of Württemberg-Baden, at its capital, Stuttgart.

tion of Dr. W. Bitter,[1] director of the Psychotherapeutic Teaching Institute in Stuttgart. The existence of this Institute is threatened, partly as a result of financial difficulties, but for the other and most important part through the union of neurologists under the leadership of Prof. Kretschmer. The Institute trains not only physicians but also laymen for psychotherapeutic work. For professional and prestige reasons, this work is a thorn in the flesh of psychiatrists and professional neurologists. We have had the same trouble in Switzerland and are still suffering from it. However, with a great effort I have succeeded in pushing it through that lectures on the psychology and therapy of the neuroses shall be held at the Medical Faculty here. And two years ago an Institute similar in principle to the Stuttgart one was founded in Zurich.

Today, with the exception of London, Berlin, and Zurich, there is no University or Medical Faculty or any other Institute where the necessary specialists and their assistants receive an adequate amount of psychological training. The Stuttgart Institute is a praiseworthy exception.

The tremendous spread of neuroses in our time makes it imperatively necessary that physicians and their assistants should be trained in psychology. As there are far too few specialists (precisely because they have not been psychologically trained at the Universities), the medical psychotherapist as well as a Psychotherapeutic Institute are dependent on the collaboration of trained laymen. In my very extensive international practice I have for decades had lay assistants and could not have managed without their help. There were and there are simply not enough doctors who have any reliable training in psychotherapy. This requires a thorough knowledge of psychology which is not taught at psychiatric clinics.

Psychotherapeutic Teaching Institutes are of great social importance and fill a painful gap in the University medical curriculum. Though I am a doctor myself—*medicus medicum non decimat*[2]—I must nevertheless state with regret that it is just the doctors who are the greatest hindrance to our endeavours. The professional spirit is always inimical even to the most useful innovation. One has only to think of the lamentable attitude of the medical profession to antisepsis and the combatting of puerperal fever! Again and again I am confronted with the positively abysmal ignorance of my near col-

---

[1] Cf. Bitter, 12 July 58, n. □.
[2] "Physician does not decimate physician."

leagues, the psychiatrists, as regards the psychology and treatment of the neuroses. Compared with our European backwardness, at least psychosomatic medicine is making considerable headway in America.

It would therefore be a cultural act of far-reaching significance if the flourishing Stuttgart Institute could be kept alive.[3]

In the hope, dear Minister, that you will not take offense at the free expression of my views, I remain, with respectful regards,

Yours very truly, C. G. JUNG

[3] The Institute still exists and plays an important part in the training of psychotherapists.

To Aloys von Orelli

Dear Colleague, 7 February 1950

I have read through your MS with interest and found it correct. I only feel somewhat doubtful when you equate "affectivity" with feeling. Affectivity is emotionality and I would like to distinguish it strictly from feeling, which, if differentiated, is a rational (value) function, whereas affects always remain spontaneous products of nature. Only in its undeveloped, primitive state is feeling contaminated with emotions, this being the distinguishing-mark of undifferentiated feeling.

"Morbus Schlemihl"[1] is an admirable invention!

Page 9. The formulation that individuation takes place even without marriage, by way of introspection and meditation, is a bit too positive. To avoid misunderstandings, one would immediately have to add that a responsible relationship of whatever kind is essential, otherwise that particular side of the individual remains undeveloped.

Page 10. It is questionable whether the union of animus and anima can be described as a *unio mystica*. The only certain thing is that the *hierosgamos* is a mythological parallel. The *unio mystica* is more a dissolution of the ego in the divine Ground—a very different experience.

☐ Swiss psychiatrist and psychotherapist; director of the psychiatric clinic "Hohenegg," Meilen, near Zurich; later practising in Basel.
[1] In Adelbert von Chamisso's story "Peter Schlemihls wundersame Geschichte" (1814) the hero sells his shadow, and the name "Schlemihl" has become proverbial in Germany for a person who is the constant victim of unforeseeable incidents resulting in all kinds of misadventures.

544

As for your question about the primacy of the intellect or of feeling, I would point out that I have answered it in my essay "Woman in Europe" by saying that feminine psychology is generally characterized by the principle of Eros and masculine psychology by the principle of Logos. This point is discussed at some length.

I should be very glad to receive you for a talk, only I can't do it at once because I am going on holiday next week. Afterwards I could see you on Tuesday, 21 February, at 8 p.m. if this time suits you. Meanwhile with collegial regards,

Yours sincerely, C. G. JUNG

To Hans E. Tütsch

Dear Dr. Tütsch, 23 February 1950

With regard to your question I must advise you that the only information I have at my disposal is what has appeared in the newspapers. From this one can draw only speculative conclusions but nothing certain can be made out.

It is altogether possible that, through physio-moral torture, deprivation of sleep, systematic poisoning with an opium derivative or a similar toxin, a man can be demoralized and made so suggestible that he will do another's will simply to avoid further torment. Threatened with exquisite physical tortures, most of us would give in long beforehand and confess whatever was wanted. Since we have not used torture for the last 150 years in our administration of justice, we are totally ignorant of the psychic effects of torture. Only in the concentration camps have we been able to see what devastating effects torture has on the morale of the individual. I don't think one need envisage any specific chemical means as an explanation of the astonishing statements of the accused.

I would rather not write an article about it since, as you see, the question is undecided for me for lack of sufficient information.

Yours very truly, C. G. JUNG

□ Foreign editor of the *Neue Zürcher Zeitung*, asked for a contribution on the psychological aspect of the Russian trials, in particular those in Budapest of the Englishman Edgar Sanders and the American Robert A. Vogeler.

To Edward Whitmont

Dear Colleague, 4 March 1950

I have read your paper with great interest. Your approach to the problem of psychophysical parallelism seems to me correct in all essentials, so far as I can judge this from the psychological side.

The difficulty this problem comes up against is that what we can grasp psychologically never goes deep enough for us to recognize its connection with the physical. And conversely, what we know physiologically is not sufficiently advanced for us to recognize what would form the bridge to the psychological. If we approach from the psychological side we come up against the phenomena I have termed archetypes. If I am not mistaken, these irrepresentable formations, in their whole mode of action, correspond to the "patterns of behaviour" in biology, since they seem to represent the basic forms of psychic behaviour in general. To know what these forms are in themselves, we would have to be able to penetrate into the whole mystery of the psyche. But this is totally unconscious to us, because the psyche cannot lay itself by the heels. We can do no more than carefully tap out the phenomenology that gives us indirect news of the essence of the psyche. Similarly—from the other side—physics is tapping its way into irrepresentable territory which it can visualize only indirectly by means of models. Both sciences, the psychology of the unconscious and atomic physics, are arriving at concepts which show remarkable points of agreement. Here I will mention only the concept of complementarity.[1]

□ M.D., analytical psychologist, originally Austrian, now practising in New York. Cf. his *The Symbolic Quest* (1969).

[1] According to Niels Bohr (cf. Haberlandt, 23 Apr. 52, n. 3), complementarity is based on the experience that microphysical structures show different aspects when observed under different experimental conditions. Pauli defined it as representing "the free choice of the experimenter (or observer) to decide . . . which insights he will gain and which he will lose; or, to put it in popular language, whether he will measure A and ruin B or ruin A and measure B" (Jung, "On the Nature of the Psyche," CW 8, par. 440; cf. also par. 439, n. 130, and C. A. Meier's definition in par. 440. Meier was the first to draw attention to the parallel between complementarity in psychology and physics). Thus different experiments and observations complement each other, a well-known example being the wave model of the electron which is complementary to the particle model. With regard to psychological complementarity there is a terminological difficulty: "complementarity" or "complementation" has to be distinguished from "compensation." Whereas the latter is of a dynamic character, balancing the one-sidedness of the conscious attitude, the former does not so much balance and regulate the

If we consider the psyche as a whole, we come to the conclusion that the unconscious psyche likewise exists in a space-time continuum, where time is no longer time and space no longer space. Accordingly, causality ceases too. Physics has reached the same frontier. Since the one line of research proceeds from within outwards and the other from without inwards, and there is no hope of our reaching the point where the two meet, there is nothing for it but to try to find points of comparison between the deepest insights on both sides. But this is where the above-mentioned difficulty comes in: our knowledge of the instincts, i.e., of the underlying biological drives, is very inadequate, so that it is only with the greatest difficulty and great uncertainty that we can equate the archetypes with them. And when it comes to the chemistry of albumen, in my view all possibilities of comparison cease altogether.

There is, however, another possibility that should not be lost sight of, and that is synchronicity, which is basically nothing other than *correspondentia*[2] more specifically and more precisely understood, and was as we know one of the elements in the medieval explanation of the world. It is conceivable—and there are facts pointing in this direction—that an archetypal situation will reflect itself also in physical processes. Thus, as early as the dream-book of Artemidorus, we come across the case of a man dreaming that his father perished in a fire, and after a few days the dreamer himself died of a high fever.[3] I have observed such things. These correspondences can go still further and give rise to the most curious meaningful coincidences. This question could be answered more or less satisfactorily only if the dreams of physically ill persons were systematically investigated. One might then be able to see what dream motifs correspond to what physical states. But no investigations of the sort have yet been made.

---

conscious attitudes as supplement and widen the scope of consciousness. It is thus of a more mechanical nature. The concept of compensation is closely connected with one of Jung's most important discoveries: that the psyche is a self-regulating system. Cf. "The Transcendent Function," pars. 159f., "General Aspects of Dream Psychology," pars. 488ff., "On the Nature of Dreams," pars. 545ff., all in CW 8.

[2] Concerning *correspondentia* cf. "Synchronicity," CW 8, pars. 924ff.

[3] Artemidorus Daldianus, 2nd cent. A.D., Greek soothsayer and interpreter of dreams. He is best known for his *Oneirokritika*, mainly a compilation from earlier authors. For details of the case in question cf. Jung, ed., *Man and His Symbols* (1964), p. 78 (Jung's chapter, also in CW 18).

Your approach is somewhat along these lines. As you know, these ideas were brought to a high pitch of development by Paracelsus. Today it is a question of finding conclusive proofs. If one wants to work this field, one encounters the further difficulty that the statistical method of science, which alone furnishes adequate proofs, stands in a relationship of complementarity to synchronicity. This means that when we observe statistically we eliminate the synchronicity phenomenon, and conversely, when we establish synchronicity we must abandon the statistical method. Nevertheless, the possibility remains of collecting a series of individual instances of correspondence, each instance throwing its own light on the phenomenon of synchronicity. It would be conceivable, for instance, that salt has a general biological significance and efficacy which correspond in some way to the symbolic significance of salt. But this constatation could be substantiated only by a large number of individual observations. I think this would be a very difficult undertaking as long as we know so little about the nature of synchronicity, which, incidentally, has nothing to do with synchronism but connotes a meaningful coincidence which is not necessarily synchronism in the strict sense.

. . .

With collegial regards,

Yours sincerely, c . g . j u n g

To Marie Ramondt

Dear Frau Ramondt,   10 March 1950

While thanking you for kindly sending me your offprint[1] I must apologize for the delay in answering your letter. I had to get the paper read by somebody else first since my knowledge of Dutch is not sufficiently fluent.

If I understand you correctly, you hold the view that primitive material cannot be interpreted because it is not just a statement of the psyche but also a statement—and an important one—of the surrounding world. This is very true up to a point. For the primitive the unconscious coalesces with the external world, as can plainly be seen from the numerous projections of the primitive consciousness. Here one can hardly speak of an ego-world relationship, since the

☐ Utrecht, Holland.
[1] Published in *Volkskunde*, a publication of the Royal Dutch Academy of Sciences, Amsterdam, but unidentifiable.

ego as we understand it barely exists. The primitive consciousness is an immersion in a stream of events in which the outer and inner world are not differentiated, or very indistinctly so. Perhaps I have not understood you correctly, but it seems to me that such material can be interpreted with due regard to its conditions. Not, of course, in such a way that the significance of the Christian cross could be applied to a medicine-man's vision of a cross. That would be putting the cart before the horse. The primitive simply brings us nearer to the archetypal foundations of the later significance of the cross, and in our interpretations we must naturally take account of the primitive's mentality—that with him the outer world has as much to say as the inner world, since with the primitive the unconscious is just as much outside as inside.

The unconscious, as we know it today, came into existence in its present form only through the differentiation of consciousness. With the primitive the inside is infinitely more an outside, and vice versa, than with us. It must be admitted, however, that for our differentiated mentality the reconstruction of that primitive semi-consciousness is no simple matter. When you interpret primitive fairytales, for instance, whose contents are nevertheless clearly formed, this difficulty becomes very apparent because you sense that objects have aspects for the primitive which we would never dream of. To interpret primitive visions one must be intensely aware of this interweaving of the external object with the psychic state. Indeed, among relatively primitive Europeans, too, there are dreams which on account of this contamination are extraordinarily difficult to interpret. But this is not to say that those motifs which at later stages of cultural development lead to well-formed ideas cannot also be found in their most primitive form, but lacking a certain accent of value and hence a corresponding clarity.

Yours sincerely, C. G. JUNG

To Raymond F. Piper

[ORIGINAL IN ENGLISH]

Dear Dr. Piper,   21 March 1950

I am sending you the two photographs[1] you wanted and also the picture of a third mandala[2] which has not been published yet. I have nothing against your using them.

---

[1] P., professor of philosophy at Syracuse U., New York, asked permission to use two illustrations from *The Secret of the Golden Flower* (1 and 6) for a book

The conditions under which such a mandala picture is produced in the course of treatment are very complex. I have given a description of such a process[3] in a book which is just about to be published in German: *Gestaltungen des Unbewussten* (Rascher & Cie., Zurich). The book also contains a number of hitherto unpublished reproductions of mandalas.[4] It would lead much too far if I should attempt to give you a full description of the psychological background of the two pictures in the *Golden Flower*.

All I can tell you is that the painter of No. 1 is a young woman, born in the East Indies,[5] where she spent her first 6 years. Her difficulty was a complete disorganization caused by her coming to Europe into an entirely different milieu where she couldn't adapt on account of the fact that she had been imbued by the Eastern atmosphere. She got into a highly neurotic state in which she couldn't cope with herself any longer. The unconscious produced chaotic dreams and she was filled with confusion. In this state I advised her to try to express herself by making pictures. She made quite a number of them which she developed out of a few lines without knowing where they would lead to. These mandalas helped her to restore order in her inner life.

The other picture[6] is by an educated man about 40 years old. He produced this picture also as an at first unconscious attempt to restore order in the emotional state he was in which had been caused by an invasion of unconscious contents.

The third mandala was designed by an artistically gifted patient of mine, a woman of about 50 years. It represents a labyrinth, i.e., it is based upon a labyrinthine design with 4 entrances, one in the middle of each side, and one exit in the centre near the central quaternity. It represents all the shapes and forms of life, a veritable ocean of organic life through which man must seek his way to the central goal. This is what the woman herself says. It is a fair representation of the individuation process. Amidst the wealth of figures

---

of his on "Cosmic Art." These mandalas are also reproduced in "Commentary on *The Secret of the Golden Flower*," CW 13, and in "Concerning Mandala Symbolism," CW 9, i, Figs. 9 and 28.

[2] See illustration.

[3] In "A Study in the Process of Individuation," CW 9, i.

[4] "Concerning Mandala Symbolism."

[5] Although born in Java, the painter was of European origin. Cf. "Mandala Symbolism," pars. 656–9, and "The Realities of Practical Psychotherapy" (1966 edn.), Appendix, par. 557, referring to the same case.

[6] "Mandala Symbolism," Fig. 28 and par. 682. Jung painted this mandala.

Mandala by a patient: see Piper, 21 Mar. 50

there are two outstanding points, the one a moon and the other a wheel. The moon represents the essence of woman's nature and the wheel the course of life, or the cycle of birth and death (according to the Epistle of James III, 6).[7] The 4 entrances are allegorized by representatives of the 4 elements. It is one of the most remarkable examples of such drawings I ever came across. The drawing was produced in an absolutely spontaneous way.

As to Eastern mandalas I should say that there should be quite a number of them to be found in your oriental collections in America. San Francisco seems to be a place where you can get them occasionally from oriental dealers. Also the Musée Guimet in Paris has a number of extraordinarily fine specimens.

Yours sincerely, C. G. JUNG

[7] The New English Bible has "the wheel of our existence"; AV "the course of nature."

To Jolande Jacobi

Dear Dr. Jacobi,   24 March 1950

I have heard that tomorrow you celebrate your 60th birthday. I wouldn't want to miss this opportunity of expressing my hearty felicitations. Above all, this is the day when I must remember with gratitude all the persevering and self-sacrificing work you have done throughout the years to spread and develop my ideas. I can only hope and wish that your health will continue to sustain your characteristic energy and working capacity so that the latter remain undiminished without detriment to the former. To this end I also wish you that wise limitation which is the art to be learnt in the 7th decade.

In multos annos!

In enduring friendship, C. G. JUNG

☐ (Handwritten.)

To Emanuel Maier

[ORIGINAL IN ENGLISH]

Dear Professor Maier,   24 March 1950

I must apologize for the long delay in answering your letter of January 16th. I'm a very busy man and suffer from an overwhelming correspondence which I'm hardly able to cope with.

I know Hesse's work and I know him personally. I knew the psychiatrist who treated him. He died several years ago. Through him Hesse received some influences originating in my work (which show for instance in *Demian, Siddhartha,* and *Steppenwolf*).[1] It was about that time (1916) that I made Hesse's personal acquaintance. The psychiatrist was Dr. J. B. Lang.[2] He was a very curious, though extremely learned man, who had studied oriental languages (Hebrew, Arabic, and Syrian) and was particularly interested in Gnostic speculation. He got from me a considerable amount of knowledge concerning Gnosticism which he also transmitted to Hesse. From this material he wrote his *Demian.* The origin of *Siddhartha* and *Steppenwolf* is of a more hidden nature. They are—to a certain extent— the direct or indirect results of certain talks I had with Hesse. I'm unfortunately unable to say how much he was conscious of the hints and implications which I let him have. I'm not in a position to give you full information, since my knowledge is strictly professional.

I have never done any systematic work on any of Hesse's novels. It would be, I admit, an interesting psychological study, particularly from the standpoint of my theoretical conceptions. It is possible for anyone sufficiently aware of my work to make the necessary applications. Unfortunately my time doesn't allow me to go into detail, because this would amount to a new dissertation which would demand an extra amount of work which I'm not able to produce.

I should be very much interested to know about the results of your researches.

Yours sincerely, C. G. JUNG

☐ M., Professor of German at the U. of Miami (Florida), was working on a dissertation (N.Y.U., 1953) "The Psychology of C. G. Jung in the Works of Hermann Hesse." It was never published and the MS is now in the Hesse Archiv, Marbach, Württemberg. — Jung's letter was published in an essay by Benjamin Nelson, "Hesse and Jung. Two Newly Recovered Letters," *The Psychoanalytic Review* (New York), vol. 50 (1963), 11–16. See also below, Addenda (2).
[1] *Demian* (orig. 1919), *Siddhartha* (orig. 1922), *Steppenwolf* (orig. 1927).
[2] Josef B. Lang, M.D., (1881–1945), psychotherapist in Lugano, an early pupil of Jung's who later separated from him. Cf. his "Zur Bestimmung des psychoanalytischen Widerstandes" and "Eine Hypothese zur psychologischen Bedeutung der Verfolgungsidee," both in Jung (ed.), *Psychologische Abhandlungen,* I (1914). — In his *Demian,* Hesse modelled the figure of Pistorius on Dr. Lang, then about 35. See Hesse, 3 Dec. 19, n. 2, in Addenda (1).

To Gilles Quispel

Dear Dr. Quispel,   21 April 1950

Please forgive me for the long delay in answering your question.[1] I have so much to do and such an enormous correspondence that I often cannot catch up with it with my limited resources. It can easily happen that a letter I would have most liked to answer is submerged for a long time in the flood of other, less important ones.

It is of course extremely difficult, in judging Gnostic images, to tell how much is genuine inner experience and how much is philosophical superstructure. All the same the enumeration of the many Naassene symbols for the One in Hippolytos shows with reasonable certainty that in many instances they are genuine primordial images. How far back the immediate experience behind these images lies, in other words, to what extent they are traditional, is another question. That they may be spontaneous experiences we know from our experience with patients, where any knowledge of tradition must be definitely excluded. Thus the pictures they occasionally draw are very often spontaneous recreations of images which have a religious and historical significance.

When Valentinus[2] employs the word *apokoktein*[3] for the separation of the shadow, he may well have been thinking of the mythological usage of this word, for the separation of the shadow signifies the cutting off of the chthonic side. It does not seem exactly probable to me that when Christ cuts off his shadow this is an immediate visionary experience, but chiefly a philosophical idea very drastically expressed.

It is different with the image of the winged man.[4] This is very much older than *Phaedrus* (it occurs for instance in Babylonia).

☐ Professor of ancient Church history at the U. of Utrecht; authority on Gnosticism.

[1] Concerning the relationship of spontaneous experience and philosophical interpretation in Gnostic myths.

[2] The most prominent exponent of Gnosticism, born in Egypt, *fl.* 2nd cent. A.D.

[3] Q. mentioned that Valentinus applied this term, "used for the dismemberment of e.g. Attis," to the "cutting off of the shadow" in the sense of "the stripping off of passions." Cf. *Aion*, par. 75, n. 23.

[4] Referring to the threefold sonship of the Gnostic Basilides (2nd cent.). Cf. ibid., par. 118: "The second son . . . received 'some such wing as that with which Plato . . . equips the soul in this *Phaedrus*.' " Concerning the Babylonian reference cf. *Symbols of Transformation*, Pl. XIX, the Winged Gilgamesh.

Coming now to the egg, this egg or uterus is not restricted to the Greek sphere but occurs also in India as *hiranyagarbha* (golden seed). Finally, the breaking of the vessels[5] is a figure of speech which occurs practically everywhere. It need not be a primordial experience at all. I think very many symbols simply derive from language and linguistic metaphors. On the other hand, I think it most unlikely that philosophy produces mythology. Philosophy can produce allegory but not genuine mythology, since this is far older. It does, however, have affinities with philosophy through its budding philosophical ideas. These ideas are then worked out in philosophy. Their mythological aspect would amount to their involution. But this never leads to mythology, only to allegory. Philosophical interpretation and primordial image are always found side by side, as you quite rightly remark, for nothing promotes philosophical reflection as much as the experience of primordial images. This is also the case with dreams: when an unconscious content emerges into consciousness, it can effect this transition only by clothing itself with the ideas existing in consciousness, thereby becoming perceptible. As to how things look in the unconscious, that is beyond our ken. Hence I define the archetypes as irrepresentable forms which clothe themselves with different material varying with each experience.

The archetypal character of certain traditional images can probably never be established as due to an immediate primordial experience. One can conclude that the experience expresses an archetype only by demonstrating, through comparative research, that the same or very similar images occur in quite other cultures and also as verifiable primordial experiences in modern individuals. The historical explanation of a symbol has therefore always to be sought first in its own cultural sphere, and then one must demonstrate the occurrence of the same or similar symbols in other cultural spheres in order to support the assertion that it is an archetype. But this assertion becomes absolutely certain only when the image can be found in a modern dream, and moreover in an individual who has never had any contact with the corresponding traditions. That, at any rate, is the procedure I follow.

Hoping I have answered your question, I remain,

Yours very sincerely, C. G. JUNG

[5] Cf. Kirsch, 18 Nov. 52, n. 4.

To Father Victor White

[ORIGINAL IN ENGLISH]

Dear Victor! 12 May 1950

. . .

Your metaphysical thinking "posits," mine doubts, i.e., it weighs mere names for insufficiently known οὐσίαι. That is presumably the reason why you are able to integrate a shadow μὴ ὄν, while I can only assimilate a substance, because for "positing" thinking "non-being" is just as much an *ens* or ὄν as "being," i.e., a conceptual existence. You are moving in the universe of the known, I am in the world of the unknown. That is, I suppose, the reason why the unconscious turns for you into a system of abstract conceptions.

. . .

I hope you can manage to come up to Switzerland whenever you are in the vicinity.

Yours cordially, c. g.

☐ (Handwritten. This letter (of which the first part, the interpretation of a dream of W.'s, has been omitted) is in answer to a letter of 4 May in which W. said: "For the moment I do indeed feel that *that* discussion [of the *privatio boni*] has reached deadlock. What is so perplexing to me is the fact that it is precisely your psychology which has enabled me to *experience* evil as the *privatio boni*. For my part I can give no meaning at all to psychological terms like 'positive-negative,' 'integration-disintegration' if evil is NOT *privatio boni*. Nor can I see any motive for 'integrating the shadow'—or any meaning in it either—if the shadow is not a good deprived of good!" Jung returns to this subject in his letter of 9–14 Apr. 52.

To Joseph Goldbrunner

Dear Herr Goldbrunner, 14 May 1950

Permit me, as one who is, in a manner of speaking, both known and unknown to you, to express my best thanks for your objective and sympathetic exposition of my psychology.[1] There are indeed few authors, as you yourself have probably observed, who could wring from themselves an objective evaluation of my work. So much the more reason for me to be sincerely grateful to you for your achievement. I would gladly content myself with an unqualified apprecia-

[1] *Individuation; A Study of the Depth Psychology of Carl Gustav Jung* (1955; orig. 1949).

tion of your book but for a few points which seem to me to require clarification.

You rightly emphasize that man in my view is enclosed in *the* psyche (not in *his* psyche). Could you name me any idea that is *not* psychic? Can man adopt any standpoint outside the psyche? He may assert that he can, but the assertion does not create a point outside, and were he there he would have no psyche. Everything that touches us and that we touch is a reflection, therefore psychic.

That my psychology is wholly imprisoned in the psyche is a fact that cannot be otherwise. You would not, presumably, object that geology treats of nothing but the earth, or that astronomy only circles round the starry sky?

Psychology is, strictly speaking, the science of conscious contents. Its object therefore is not metaphysical, otherwise it would be metaphysics. Does one hold it against physics that it is not metaphysics? It is self-evident that all objects of physics are physical phenomena. Why should psychology be the only exception to this rule?

Everything that man conceives as God is a psychic image, and it is no less an image even if he asseverates a thousand times that it is not an image. If it were not, he would be unable to conceive anything at all. That is why Meister Eckhart says, quite rightly, "God is pure nothing."

As an empirical science, psychology can only establish that the unconscious spontaneously produces images which have always been spoken of as "God-images." But as the nature of the psyche is wholly unknown to us, science cannot establish *what* the image is a reflection of. We come here to the "frontier of the human," of which G. von Le Fort[2] says that it is the "portcullis of God." In my private capacity as a man I can only concur with this view, but with the best will in the world I cannot maintain that this is a verifiable assertion, which is what science is all about in the end. It is a subjective confession which has no place in science.

It is equally out of place to say that individuation is *self-redemption.* This is precisely what it is not. As you yourself have described so beautifully, man exposes himself to all the powers of the non-ego, of heaven and hell, of grace and destruction, in order to reach that point where he has become simple enough to accept those influences, or whatever it is we call "God's will," which come from the Unfathomable and whose source lies behind those same psychic images

[2] Gertrud von le Fort (1876–1971), German Catholic writer.

which both reveal and conceal. How one could see through this "hoarding" is, frankly, beyond my comprehension. How can one see, think, or conceive that which is non-psychic? Even if I aver that it is not psychic, it is still my conception standing before the unknowable fact; and if it is non-psychic then it cannot be conceived at all.

We take it for granted that images are reflections of *something*. In so far as this something is supposed not to be psychic, it is necessarily inconceivable—even the spectacular blue of the sky does not exist in physics but is expressed by the mathematical concept of wave-lengths. Am I, then, to declare that because I see blue, blue exists in itself and is not psychic? That would be against my better knowledge and therefore immoral.

I am deeply impressed by man's proneness to error and self-deception. I therefore deem it a moral command not to make assertions about things we can neither see nor prove, and I deem it an epistemological transgression if one nevertheless does so. These rules hold good for empirical science; metaphysics holds to others. I recognize the rules of empirical science as binding upon myself. Hence no metaphysical assertions will be found in my writings, and, n.b., *no denials of metaphysical assertions*.

Hoping that these explanations may perhaps be of service to you, I remain,

Yours very sincerely, C. G. JUNG

To Roscoe Heavener

[ORIGINAL IN ENGLISH]

Dear Mr. Heavener,   16 May 1950

I cannot tell you exactly why and under what circumstances Adler separated from Freud. The general reason—as I heard then—was that Freud couldn't see Adler's point of view. This I can confirm: Freud indeed couldn't see that Adler's views were justified by facts.

I have written very often about my disagreement with Freud. First of all he couldn't accept my idea that psychic energy (libido) is more than sex instinct, and that the unconscious does not only wish but also overcomes its own wishes. I couldn't agree with Freud's claim that the technique of psychoanalysis is identical with his sex-theory. I also couldn't agree with his theory of dreams as wish-fulfillments. Freud, I'm afraid, misunderstood theoretical doubt or

☐ Colmar, Pennsylvania.

557

criticism as a personal resistance and I couldn't agree with him that his view was right. Those were the main points that made a cooperation impossible and that is also the reason why I had to separate from him.

Yours sincerely, C. G. JUNG

To Philip Magor

[ORIGINAL IN ENGLISH]

Dear Mr. Magor, 23 May 1950

I have thought a long time over your request, because I don't know exactly what I could tell you. You are sure to know the home-truth that prayer is not only of great importance but has also a great effect upon human psychology. If you take the concept of prayer in its widest sense and if you include also Buddhist contemplation and Hindu meditation (as being equivalent to prayer), one can say that it is the most universal form of religious or philosophical concentration of the mind and thus not only one of the most original but also the most frequent means to change the condition of mind. If this psychological method had been inefficient, it would have been extinguished long ago, but nobody with a certain amount of human experience could deny its efficacy.

This is about all I can tell you in a few words. Otherwise I should have to write a whole treatise.

Sincerely yours, C. G. JUNG

☐ London.

To Oskar Splett

Dear Dr. Splett, 23 May 1950

I must confess that your question is very difficult to answer, and I would ask you to take my remarks as more or less hypothetical.

I, too, doubt whether the term "early maturation" is the right one. Like you, I would rather speak of a kind of "watchfulness" or "increased awareness." This phenomenon can in fact be observed in all those countries which were directly affected by the war, most of all those where war or revolution were worst. Above all, probably, with the "Besprisornji," Russia's hordes of orphaned children. It is

☐ Munich.

558

less a matter of real maturation than of premature watchfulness and a one-sided intensification of instinctive tendencies. If by maturation is meant an expansion of consciousness or a rounding-out of the personality, then "early maturation" is quite wrong. In the vast majority of cases consciousness is not expanded but contracted; instead there are sharp ears, wide-open eyes and increased cupidity—the very things we can also observe with primitives under similar conditions. Only in exceptional cases is there an accelerated, real maturation; the majority show a regressive development back to the primitive. I regard this development as a direct consequence of political and social upheavals, and it seems to me that such phenomena are less observable in a more peaceful atmosphere than elsewhere. I am thinking, for instance, of Switzerland and America, where the people escaped the effects of the war.

Since I have not undertaken any thorough researches in this field my opinion is based only on general impressions.

Yours sincerely, c. g. j u n g

Anonymous

Dear Dr. N.,   10 June 1950

You get nowhere with theories. Try to be simple and always take the next step. You needn't see it in advance, but you can look back at it afterwards. There is no "how" of life, one just does it as you wrote your letter, for instance. It seems, however, to be terribly difficult for you *not* to be complicated and to do what is simple and closest to hand. You barricade yourself from the world with exaggerated saviour fantasies. So climb down from the mountain of your humility and follow your nose. That is *your* way and the straightest. With kind regards,

Yours sincerely, c. g. j u n g

☐ (Handwritten.) To a woman.

To Chang Chung-yuan

[ORIGINAL IN ENGLISH]

Dear Sir,   26 June 1950

I have read your pamphlet[1] with great interest and I can tell you that I fundamentally agree with your views. I see Taoism in the same

559

light as you do. I'm a great admirer of Ch'uang-tze's philosophy. I was again immersed in the study of his writings when your letter arrived in the midst of it.

You are aware, of course, that Taoism formulates psychological principles which are of a very universal nature. As a matter of fact, they are so all-embracing that they are, as far as they go, applicable to any part of humanity. But on the other hand just because Taoist views are so universal, they need a re-translation and specification when it comes to the practical application of their principles. Of course it is undeniable that general principles are of the highest importance, but it is equally important to know in every detail the way that leads to real understanding. The danger for the Western mind consists in the mere application of words instead of facts. What the Western mind needs is the actual experience of the facts that cannot be substituted by words. Thus I'm chiefly concerned with the ways and methods by which one can make the Western mind aware of the psychological facts underlying the concept of Tao, if the latter can be called a concept at all. The way you put it is in danger of remaining a mere idealism or an ideology to the Western mind. If one could arrive at the truth by learning the words of wisdom, then the world would have been saved already in the remote times of Lao-tze. The trouble is, as Ch'uang-tze rightly says, that the old masters failed to enlighten the world, since there weren't minds enough that could be enlightened. There is little use in teaching wisdom. At all events wisdom cannot be taught by words. It is only possible by personal contact and by immediate experience.

The great and almost insurmountable difficulty consists in the question of the ways and means to induce people to make the indispensable psychological experiences that open their eyes to the underlying truth. The truth is one and the same everywhere and I must say that Taoism is one of the most perfect formulations of it I ever became acquainted with.

Sincerely yours, C. G. JUNG

□ Ph.D., 1947–53 professor of Chinese classics at the Asia Institute, New York; lectured at the Eranos meetings 1955, 1956, 1958. Now professor of philosophy, U. of Hawaii.

1 "An Interpretation of Taoism in the Light of Modern Philosophy," unpublished; expanded as *Creativity and Taoism* (1963).

To Sibylle Birkhäuser-Oeri

Dear Frau Birkhäuser,   13 July 1950

As unfortunately so often happens (when one is as old as I am), *l'esprit d'escalier*[1] is beginning to play its unwelcome role. Your case went on tormenting me until I finally discovered what it was that I did *not* tell you: letting the unconscious come up is only the first half of the work. The second half, which I failed to mention, consists in *coming to terms with the unconscious*. The fantasy you gave me to read shows no sign of this. I do not know whether I am justified in concluding that you have no knowledge of this important task. You will find an example of it in "The Relations between the Ego and the Unconscious," describing the case of a young man who in fantasy sees his fiancée fall into a crack in the ice and lets her drown.[2] You must step into the fantasy yourself and compel the figures to give you an answer. Only in this way is the unconscious integrated with consciousness by means of a dialectical procedure, a dialogue between yourself and the unconscious figures. Whatever happens in the fantasy must happen to *you*. You should not let yourself be represented by a fantasy figure. You must safeguard the ego and only let it be modified by the unconscious, just as the latter must be acknowledged with full justification and only prevented from suppressing and assimilating the ego. Here you need the support of a *woman*. A man always stirs up the unconscious too much. I recommend either my wife or Frl. T. Wolff.[3]

Well, I have now salved my bad conscience.

Yours sincerely, c. g. j u n g

☐ Analytical psychologist (1914–1971), fourth daughter of Albert Oeri. Cf. letter to her husband, Birkhäuser, 2 Nov. 60.
[1] A thought that comes to mind too late.
[2] CW 7, par. 343. Actually this is an example of passive fantasy, as the text makes clear. Jung obviously meant to give an example of active imagination. Cf. Keyserling, 23 Apr. 31, n. 2.
[3] Jung's close collaborator and friend. Cf. Kirsch, 28 May 53, n. 1.

To Gustav Graber

Dear Colleague,   14 July 1950

Your special issue for my birthday,[1] together with your kind foreword, was a great surprise and joy to me. I am particularly impressed

561

by the large number of contributors and their excellent contributions, and I appreciate the pains the editor has taken to bring together so many good things. Anticipating my 75th birthday, which has yet to be celebrated, the Festschrift as a whole is a notable résumé of such ideas of mine as have taken root in the minds of my contemporaries. One's 75th birthday is a moment when one looks back with one laughing and one lachrymose eye on the long path one has left behind, hoping also that it will be of some benefit to one's fellows. It is therefore a comfort to see that not a few seeds have fallen on fruitful soil.

I thank you with all my heart for having procured me this joy, as well as all the others whose exertions have contributed to the success of the work. In gratitude,

Yours sincerely, C. G. JUNG

□ (Handwritten.)
1 G., editor of the Swiss monthly *Der Psychologe* (Schwarzenburg), had brought out a special issue in honour of Jung's 75th birthday: *Komplexe Psychologie*, II:7/8 (July/Aug. 1950).

To Manfred Bleuler

Dear Colleague,   19 August 1950

Your kind letter with wishes for my birthday came as a surprise and joy. I was very touched to receive such a cordial message from my old place of work, where everything that happened afterwards had its beginning. All the more so as I have never had the pleasure of meeting you in your later years. I remember you only as a small boy at a time which for me lies in the far-off past.

All the more vivid in my memory are the impressions and the encouragement I received from your father, to whom I shall always be grateful. Not only am I deeply indebted to psychiatry, but I have always remained close to it inwardly, since from the very beginning one general problem engrossed me: From what psychic stratum do the immensely impressive ideas found in schizophrenia originate? The questions that resulted have seemingly removed me far from clinical psychiatry and have led me to wander all through the world. On these adventurous journeys I discovered many things I never yet

□ Professor of psychiatry at the U. of Zurich; 1942–70 director of the Burghölzli Clinic; son of Eugen Bleuler.

dreamt of in Burghölzli, but the rigorous mode of observation I learnt there has accompanied me everywhere and helped me to grasp the alien psyche objectively.

While thanking you for your cordial message I would also like to ask you to convey my gratitude to all those who were kind enough to sign your letter. With collegial regards,

Yours sincerely, c. g. jung

To Hermann Hesse

Dear Herr Hesse,   19 August 1950

Among the many messages and signs my 75th birthday brought me, it was your greeting that surprised and delighted me most. I am especially grateful for your *Morgenlandfahrt*,[1] which I have set aside to read at a quiet moment. Since my birthday, however, this quiet moment still hasn't arrived, for I am swamped with a flood of letters and visitors beyond my control. At my age it means going "slow and with care," nor is my working capacity what it was, especially when you have all sorts of things on your programme which you want to bring to the light of day. I have made a late start with them, which may well be due to the difficulty of the themes that have dropped into my head.

Allow me to reciprocate your gift with a specimen of my latest publications[2] bordering on the domain of literature. Meanwhile you too have moved up into the higher age bracket and so will be in a position to empathize with my preoccupations. With best thanks,

Yours sincerely, c. g. jung

[1] *The Journey to the East* (orig. 1932).
[2] Probably *Gestaltungen des Unbewussten* (1950), which contains "Psychology and Literature," CW 15.

To Ernesto A. C. Volkening

Dear Colleague,   19 August 1950

Many thanks for your kind wishes and also for your offprint. Unfortunately I am not on an intimate footing with Spanish, so I am having a report made of your essay.

Your argument with the Freudian school leaves ample room for discussion, for the simplification which makes the psyche coincide with such an important instinct as sexuality has something beguiling and seductive about it. Especially at the present time, which is distinguished by its iconoclastic tendencies, this simplification is dangerous, because it disposes of an extremely complicated and difficult subject, the psyche, in a form acceptable to common prejudice. It is generally overlooked that the psyche cannot of necessity be based only on the instinct of sexuality, but rests on the totality of the instincts, and that this basis is only a biological foundation and not the whole edifice. Reducing the total psyche to its darkest beginnings not only devalues it but shifts the problem on to an inadmissibly simple plane, rather as if one were to reduce man to a cell, which, highly complicated though it is, even in the form of an amoeba is constructed very much more simply than a man. Thus, in his passion for simplification, Freud could explain the neuroses—up to a point—on the principle of repression, but completely overlooked the psychology of the repressive principle itself, which proves to be even stronger than instinct and also belongs to the nature of the psyche, as has already been said very aptly by the old alchemist Demokritos: *Natura naturam superat.*[1]

I understand very well that anyone approaching it from the standpoint of medicine or the physical sciences will find my psychology difficult or incomprehensible, because it does not reduce the psyche to simple processes but leaves it in all its complexity—not describing the edifice only as a foundation and deriving the whole from the part, but making it, in its immensity and boundless multiplicity, an object for scientific description and elucidation.

Hence I value it all the more that you have found your way through these difficulties to a real understanding of my psychological endeavours.

I am taking the liberty of sending you a recent publication in which you will find perhaps the most thorough analysis of a product of Romanticism.[2] With collegial regards,

Yours sincerely, c. g. j u n g

[1] Demokritos (pseudo-Demokritos), ancient alchemist, *ca.* 1st–2nd cent.: "Nature conquers nature."
[2] Jaffé, "Bilder und Symbole aus E.T.A. Hoffmanns Märchen 'Der Goldne Topf,' " *Gestaltungen des Unbewussten.*

To Charles Lichtenthaeler

Dear Colleague,   7 November 1950

Although the curious personality of Paracelsus is certainly not without interest for the psychologist, it is his ideas that interest psychology especially. Indeed, I have devoted a book, *Paracelsica* (Rascher, Zurich, 1942) to the most important of his ideas. Among them, the idea of the *theorica*[1] is particularly interesting to psychology. Through his *theorica* Paracelsus gave the patient some idea of his malady, and so enabled him to assimilate it psychologically.

In addition, a good acquaintance with the fundamental facts of the unconscious is to be found in Paracelsus' esoteric doctrine, and it is very important, particularly for the treatment of neuroses, to be acquainted with the symbolic forms that are expressive of pathogenic contents. These ideas were developed symbolically by Paracelsus in his *Vita Longa*.[2] (See my *Paracelsica*.) Paracelsus passed on his knowledge of the fundamental facts of the unconscious to his pupils (and especially to Gerard Dorn)[3] but they were lost later, thanks to the rise of rationalism and scientific materialism. Not until just recently have unconscious pathogenic causes been rediscovered. It is in this connection that the work of Paracelsus is of great interest to psychologists. But obviously his ideas are extremely difficult to elucidate, and I realize that for a doctor, whose experience has not familiarized him with the large part that is played by the unconscious background of neuroses and psychoses, Paracelsus' ideas are almost incomprehensible.

Hoping that you will find this a sufficient answer to your question, I am,

Very sincerely yours, C. G. JUNG

☐ (Translated from French.) Charles Lichtenthaeler, at that time co-founder with A. Rollier of the Swiss University Sanatorium for Tuberculosis; since 1963 professor of the history of medicine at Hamburg.

[1] Cf. "Paracelsus the Physician," CW 15, par. 41.

[2] "Paracelsus as a Spiritual Phenomenon," CW 13, pars. 169ff., 213ff.

[3] Gerardus Dorneus (Gerard Dorn), physician and alchemist of the late 16th cent., of whose writings Jung made copious use in *Psychology and Alchemy, Aion,* and *Mysterium Coniunctionis.* Dorn's treatises are contained in *Theatrum chemicum,* I, 1602.

To Father Victor White

[ORIGINAL IN ENGLISH]

Dear Victor,   25 November 1950

I thank you very much indeed for kindly sending me *The Life of the Spirit*.[1] I have read your article with the greatest attention and interest. Well, you have succeeded in putting the *petra scandali*[2] very much in evidence. Concerning the *universale*,[3] you know, I have not much to say if I refrain from drawing conclusions and from speculating about the possible psychological consequences of the new dogma. It is a fascinating subject, which is intensely discussed in Zurich. It has released a series of dreams in me concerned with further developments, i.e., consequences of the new situation. Quite against my expectation the declaration has stirred up something in the unconscious,[4] viz. in the archetypal world. It seems to be the hierosgamos motif: the cut-down tree has been brought into the cave of the mother, in this case: the hold of a ship. It takes up so much space that the people living in the cave are forced to leave it and to live outside exposed to wind and weather. This motif refers to the night-sea-journey of the hero in the belly of the great fish-mother.[5]

The *universale*, as you so neatly put it, is the *interesting* aspect of the dogma. The *particulare*,[6] on the other hand, is the thing—as

---

[1] W.'s essay on "The Scandal of the Assumption" in *Life of the Spirit* (a *Blackfriars Review*), V:53/54, Nov./Dec. 1950. This particular issue of the *Life of the Spirit* was devoted entirely to "The Assumption in the Life of the Christian."

[2] = "the stone of stumbling," Isaiah 8:14. The title of the essay was a crack at the "many earnest and honest minds" that had been "scandalized" by the definition of the Assumptio Mariae, 15 Aug. 1950. The Papal Bull *Munificentissimus Deus* declaring the Assumption an article of faith was published 1 Nov. 1950, after W.'s essay was printed.

[3] See n. 6 infra.

[4] Jung's dream reported in the following lines.

[5] Jung took the dream as referring to the dogma of the Assumption, a connection which is made clear in a later letter (cf. White, 10 Apr. 54), where he talks of the Attis cult: the Attis tree carried into the cave of the Great Mother Kybele (*Symbols of Transformation*, par. 639) is an analogy of the hierosgamos of Christ and Mary. In the dream the tree is brought into the hold of a ship which Jung interprets as the mother's cave.

[6] The two chapters of W.'s essay are entitled "The Scandal of Particularity" and "The Scandal of Universality." The former dealt with the problem of the Assumption of one particular person, the Virgin Mary; the latter with the criticism of those who could not accept its universal, cosmic significance, i.e., its archetypal aspect.

you obviously realize—that takes my breath away. If the miracle of the Assumptio is not a living and present spiritual event, but consists of a physical phenomenon that is reported or only believed to have happened some 2000 years ago, then it has nothing to do with the spirit, or just as little as any parapsychological stunt of today. A physical fact never proves the existence and reality of the spirit. It only tries to concretize the spirit in material visibility. Certainly the life and reality of the spirit are in no way demonstrated by the fact that 2000 years ago a body disappeared or other miracles happened. Why should one insist upon the historical reality of this particular case of a virgin birth and deny it to all the other mythological traditions? This insistence is particularly curious because it adds nothing to the significance of the idea; on the contrary it diverts the interest from the all-important spiritual aspect to a very questionable and completely irrelevant physical phenomenon. I can only explain this peculiar *tour de force* as an attempt to prove the existence of the spirit to a coarse and primitive mind unable to grasp the psychic reality of an idea, a mind needing miracles as evidence of a spiritual presence. It is more than probable that the idea of the Assumptio did not begin its real life in apostolic times but considerably later. The miracle of the Assumptio obviously began to operate noticeably from the VI century onwards only. If the A. means anything, it means a spiritual fact which can be formulated as the integration of the female principle into the Christian conception of the Godhead. This is certainly the most important religious development for 400 years.

I am enclosing an article that has appeared in *Neue Zürcher Zeitung*.[7] It does not insist upon the concretistic historicity of the miracle but rather upon the Christian nature of the idea. I have not seen the text of the "definition" yet. Could you lend me a copy? Please return the article as I want to keep it. To judge from this article, the "definition" does not insist upon the reality, but rather upon the *belief in the reality* of the Assumptio and thus upon the *reality of the idea*. As you put it, it sounds rather like blatant materialism, which arouses the strongest objections. If the A. is an essentially concrete historical fact, then it is no more a living spiritual experience. It degenerates into a merely synchronistic effect in the past, just as interesting and curious as the departure of Elijah[8] or

---

[7] "Das neue Dogma und die Bibel," N.Z.Z., 26 Nov. 1950, by Otto Karrer, a Catholic professor of theology.
[8] II Kings 2:1–12.

the sensational disappearance of Enoch.[9] It is a mere side-stepping of the real problem, viz. the symbol of the A., whereas the really and only important factor is the living archetype forcing its way into consciousness. When insisting on historicity you risk not only the most awkward and unanswerable questions, but you also help everybody to turn his eyes away from the essential idea to the realistic crudity of a merely physical phenomenon, as it is only physical phenomena that happen in a distinct place at a distinct time, whereas the spirit is eternal and everywhere. Even the *corpus subtile* is only relatively within time and space. If we designate the A. as a fact in time and space we ought to add that it happens really in eternity and everywhere, and what we perceive of it through our senses is corruptible matter, i.e., we don't see it, but we infer or believe in the idea. The conclusion took not less than 1900 years to reach its finale. Under those conditions it seems to me preposterous to insist upon concrete historicity. But if you say: I believe that Mary endowed with her *corpus glorificationis* (i.e., characterized by almost "corporeal" distinctiveness) has attained her place in the vicinity of the Deity, I can agree with you. This seems to be also Mr. Karrer's opinion,[10] and, as he points out, Mary wouldn't be the only one. There seems to be a certain traditional consensus that a life of religious wholeness (i.e., a conscious integration of the essential archetype) justifies the hope for a distinct existence in eternity. The extension of such a consideration to Mary seems to be well within the scope of Christian philosophy.

Yours cordially, c . g .

[9] Gen. 5:18–24.
[10] See n. 7 supra.

To Hanna Oeri

Dear Dr. Oeri,   23 December 1950

The great tiredness I saw and felt in my friend on my visit to Basel has now run speedily to its end. The dead are surely not to be pitied—they have so infinitely much more before them than we do—but rather the living who are left behind, who must contemplate the fleetingness of existence and suffer parting, sorrow, and loneliness in time.

☐ The wife of Albert Oeri.

I know what Albert's death must mean to you, for with him my last living friend has also departed. We are but a remnant of the past, more and more so with each coming year. Our eyes turn away from the future of the human world in which our children, but not ourselves, will live. Enviable the lot of those who have crossed the threshold, yet my compassion goes out to those who, in the darkness of the world, hemmed in by a narrow horizon and the blindness of ignorance, must follow the river of their days, fulfilling life's task, only to see their whole existence, which once was the present brimming with power and vitality, crumbling bit by bit and crashing into the abyss. This spectacle of old age would be unendurable did we not know that our psyche reaches into a region held captive neither by change in time nor by limitation of place. In that form of being our birth is a death and our death a birth. The scales of the whole hang balanced. With heartfelt sympathy,

Yours sincerely, C. G. JUNG

To Regula Rohland-Oeri

Dear Regula, 23 December 1950

I would like to express my heartfelt sympathy on the death of your father, with whom I was bound for so long in true friendship. When the vital forces fail, when participating in life is an effort, and the great tiredness settles over everything, death brings the boon of sleep. Once the world has sunk down, there is no desire to see it rise up again. It is only we, the living, who have lost something, and lament this loss. All things pass away, graves are the milestones of existence. For the young, the death of the parents opens a new chapter of life. They are now the carriers of life and the present, and nothing hangs over them any more except an as yet unfulfilled destiny. May you go towards it with all the courage it needs.

Most cordially, C. G. JUNG

□ Oeri's third daughter. Cf. Oeri, 26 May 45, n. 3.

ADDENDA

ADDENDA

(1)

To Hermann Hesse

Dear Herr Hesse,   3 December 1919

I must send you my most cordial thanks for your masterly as well as veracious book: *Demian*.[1] I know it is very immodest and officious of me to break through your pseudonym; but, while reading the book, I had the feeling that it must somehow have reached me via Lucerne.[2] Although I failed to recognize you in the Sinclair sketches in the *Neue Zürcher Zeitung*,[3] I always wondered what sort of person Sinclair must be, because his psychology seemed to me so remarkable. Your book came at a time when, once again, I was oppressed by the darkened consciousness of modern man, and by his hopeless bigotry, as Sinclair was by little Knauer.[4] Hence your book hit me like the beam of a lighthouse on a stormy night. A good book, like every proper human life, must have an ending. Yours has the best possible

□ (Handwritten.) See Hesse, 28 Jan. 22, n. □.

[1] Berlin, 1919 (tr. 1965). The novel appeared originally under the pseudonym of its hero-narrator "Emil Sinclair." H. borrowed the name from Isaak von Sinclair (1775–1815), diplomat and author, and a friend of the poet Hölderlin, whom H. greatly admired. — The true author was generally unknown until June 1920, when Hesse officially acknowledged authorship. (The editor is indebted to Professor Ralph Freedman, Princeton U., for this information.)

[2] In 1916 H. had a serious breakdown, for which reason he went to the Sanatorium Sonnmatt, near Lucerne. There he was advised to consult Dr. J. B. Lang, a medical psychotherapist and pupil of Jung's. The therapeutic relationship soon developed into a close friendship. The analytical interviews went on from May 1916 to Nov. 1917, altogether about seventy sessions, each lasting up to three hours. The fruit of these interviews was *Demian*, written explosively in 1917 (and to a lesser degree H.'s *Märchen*, 1919 [tr. *Strange News from Another Star*, 1972]).—This information is taken from Hugo Ball, *Hermann Hesse, sein Leben und sein Werk* (Berlin, 1927). Also cf. Maier, 24 Mar. 50.

[3] E. Sinclair, "Der Europäer; Eine Fabel," *Neue Zürcher Zeitung*, 4 and 6 Aug. 1918 (nos. 10026, 10032); tr. "The European," in *If the War Goes On . . .* (1971).

[4] A fellow-student of Sinclair's, a lost creature, looking for the saviour in Sinclair.

ending, where everything that has gone before runs truly to its end, and everything with which the book began begins over again—with the birth and awakening of the new man. The Great Mother is impregnated by the loneliness of him that seeks her. In the shell burst[5] she bears the "old" man into death, and implants in the new the everlasting monad, the mystery of individuality. And when the renewed man reappears the mother reappears too—in a woman on this earth.

I could tell you a little secret[6] about Demian of which you became the witness, but whose meaning you have concealed from the reader and perhaps also from yourself. I could give you some very satisfying information about this, since I have long been a good friend of Demian's and he has recently initiated me into his private affairs—under the seal of deepest secrecy. But time will bear out these hints for you in a singular way.

I hope you will not think I am trying to make myself interesting by mystery-mongering; my *amor fati* is too sacred to me for that. I only wanted, out of gratitude, to send you a small token of my great respect for your fidelity and veracity, without which no man can have such apt intuitions. You may even be able to guess what passage in your book I mean.

I immediately ordered a copy of your book for our Club library.[7] It is sound in wind and limb and points the way.

I beg you not to think ill of me for my invasion. No one knows of it.

Very sincerely and with heartfelt thanks, c. g. jung

---

[5] Sinclair, as a soldier in the first World War, has a vision of "a mighty, godlike figure with shining stars in her hair . . . and the features of Frau Eva [Demian's mother]" giving birth to thousands of stars. One of the stars seems to seek him out: "The world was shattered above me with a thunderous roar": he is hit by a shell splinter. In a field hospital he finds himself lying beside the mortally wounded Demian.

[6] As this letter came to light only after the present volume was in page proof, nothing definite has as yet been ascertained about the allusions in this and the following paragraph. More research is needed. But it is probable that the "small token of my great respect" was a copy of Jung's *Septem Sermones*, where the Gnostic figure of Abraxas plays a key role. The "passage in your book" may refer to the beginning of ch. 5 of *Demian*: "The bird is breaking its way out of the egg. The egg is the world. He who wishes to be born must first destroy a world. The bird flies to God. The name of the god is Abraxas." The winged egg and Abraxas appear in a Gnostic mandala painted by Jung in 1916: *The Archetypes and the Collective Unconscious*, CW 9, i, frontispiece and p. xi. Cf. also Theodore Ziolkowski, *The Novels of Hermann Hesse* (Princeton, 1965), pp. 111 ff.

[7] The Psychological Club of Zurich.

574

(2)

In amplification of Maier, 24 Mar. 50:

From Hermann Hesse to Emanuel Maier

Dear Mr. Maier,   [? April 1950]

Being a friend of discretion, I have not opened Jung's letter.

In 1916 I underwent an analysis with a doctor friend of mine who was in part a pupil of Jung's. At that time I became acquainted with Jung's early work, the *Wandlungen der Libido*,[1] which made an impression on me. I also read later books by Jung, but only until around 1922 because thereafter analysis did not greatly interest me. I have always had respect for Jung, but his works did not make such strong impressions on me as did those of Freud. Jung will already have written you that, in connection with an evening of readings I gave as the guest of Jung's Zurich Club, I also had several analytic sessions with him around 1921.[2] Then too I got a nice impression of him, though at that time I began to realize that, for analysts, a genuine relationship to art is unattainable: they lack the organ for it.

With kind regards, H. HESSE

☐ As published in an essay by Benjamin Nelson, *The Psychoanalytic Review*, 50:3 (Fall 1963); see Maier, 24 Mar. 50, n. ☐. The translation (slightly revised) is published here with permission of Mr. Heiner Hesse and of *The Psychoanalytic Review*. — According to Nelson (p. 12), the copy "bears neither a date nor point of origin on its face." The above date is adduced in relation to Jung's letter to Maier.

[1] *Wandlungen und Symbole der Libido* (1912).

[2] Cf. the following letter. Mr. Heiner Hesse has recalled, in a private communication to Professor Ralph Freedman, that his father had several analytical sessions with Jung in Feb. and Apr. 1921. This was at a time when he was unable to complete his novel *Siddhartha* (1922; tr. 1951). Cf. Ziolkowski, *The Novels of Hermann Hesse*, pp. 150-51.

From Hermann Hesse to Hugo and Emmy Ball

. . .   Zurich, [? April 1921]

I'm up and down. City and work are very tiring, but I live in a very beautiful spot high up near the forest on the Zürichberg, and occasionally

☐ From a copy of the original in the Hesse Archiv, Marbach, kindly made available by Professor Ralph Freedman, with permission of Mr. Heiner Hesse. The translation is Professor Freedman's. — Hugo Ball was one of Hesse's closest friends from the time of their meeting, 1919, until Ball's death, 1927. At Hesse's

I see dear people. But my psychoanalysis is giving me a great deal of trouble, and often Klingsor[1] feels old and incorrigible, the summer is no longer his.

I shall stay here still longer, the fruit I have bitten into has to be eaten to the full. Dr. Jung impresses me very much.

I am so glad to know that waiting for me down in the Ticino are not just chestnut forests and typewriter, but also dear friends.

I send greetings to both of you in Agnuzzo and to forest and lake from the bottom of my heart.

Yours, H. HESSE

suggestion, the publisher S. Fischer commissioned Ball to write the first authorized Hesse biography (see above, Hesse, 3 Dec. 19, n. 2).

[1] The allusion is to Hesse himself, as he liked to use the names of his heroes and in 1919 had completed the story "Klingsors letzter Sommer" (pub. 1920; tr. *Klingsor's Last Summer*, 1971).

The Collected Works of C. G. JUNG

The Collected Works of C. G. JUNG

Editors: Sir Herbert Read (d. 1968), Michael Fordham, and Gerhard Adler; executive editor, William McGuire. Translated by R.F.C. Hull (except vol. 2).

(*continued*)

* Published 1957; 2nd edn., 1970.   † Published 1973.

2 (*continued*)

Psychophysical Investigations with the Galvanometer and Pneumograph in Normal and Insane Individuals (by F. Peterson and Jung)

Further Investigations on the Galvanic Phenomenon and Respiration in Normal and Insane Individuals (by C. Ricksher and Jung)

Appendix: Statistical Details of Enlistment (1906); New Aspects of Criminal Psychology (1908); The Psychological Methods of Investigation Used in the Psychiatric Clinic of the University of Zurich (1910); On the Doctrine of Complexes ([1911] 1913); On the Psychological Diagnosis of Evidence (1937)

*3. THE PSYCHOGENESIS OF MENTAL DISEASE

The Psychology of Dementia Praecox (1907)
The Content of the Psychoses (1908/1914)
On Psychological Understanding (1914)
A Criticism of Bleuler's Theory of Schizophrenic Negativism (1911)
On the Importance of the Unconscious in Psychopathology (1914)
On the Problem of Psychogenesis in Mental Disease (1919)
Mental Disease and the Psyche (1928)
On the Psychogenesis of Schizophrenia (1939)
Recent Thoughts on Schizophrenia (1957)
Schizophrenia (1958)

†4. FREUD AND PSYCHOANALYSIS

Freud's Theory of Hysteria: A Reply to Aschaffenburg (1906)
The Freudian Theory of Hysteria (1908)
The Analysis of Dreams (1909)
A Contribution to the Psychology of Rumour (1910–11)
On the Significance of Number Dreams (1910–11)
Morton Prince, "The Mechanism and Interpretation of Dreams": A Critical Review (1911)
On the Criticism of Psychoanalysis (1910)
Concerning Psychoanalysis (1912)
The Theory of Psychoanalysis (1913)
General Aspects of Psychoanalysis (1913)
Psychoanalysis and Neurosis (1916)
Some Crucial Points in Psychoanalysis: A Correspondence between Dr. Jung and Dr. Loÿ (1914)
Prefaces to "Collected Papers on Analytical Psychology" (1916, 1917)
The Significance of the Father in the Destiny of the Individual (1909/1949)
Introduction to Kranefeldt's "Secret Ways of the Mind" (1930)
Freud and Jung: Contrasts (1929)

‡5. SYMBOLS OF TRANSFORMATION (1911–12/1952)

With Appendix: The Miller Fantasies

* Published 1960.   † Published 1961.
‡ Published 1956; 2nd edn., 1967.

*6. PSYCHOLOGICAL TYPES (1921)
With Four Papers on Psychological Typology (1913, 1925, 1931, 1936)

†7. TWO ESSAYS ON ANALYTICAL PSYCHOLOGY
On the Psychology of the Unconscious (1917/1926/1943)
The Relations between the Ego and the Unconscious (1928)
Appendix: New Paths in Psychology (1912); The Structure of the Un-
conscious (1916) (new versions, with variants, 1966)

‡8. THE STRUCTURE AND DYNAMICS OF THE PSYCHE
On Psychic Energy (1928)
The Transcendent Function ([1916]/1957)
A Review of the Complex Theory (1934)
The Significance of Constitution and Heredity in Psychology (1929)
Psychological Factors Determining Human Behaviour (1937)
Instinct and the Unconscious (1919)
The Structure of the Psyche (1927/1931)
On the Nature of the Psyche (1947/1954)
General Aspects of Dream Psychology (1916/1948)
On the Nature of Dreams (1945/1948)
The Psychological Foundations of Belief in Spirits (1920/1948)
Spirit and Life (1926)
Basic Postulates of Analytical Psychology (1931)
Analytical Psychology and *Weltanschauung* (1928/1931)
The Real and the Surreal (1933)
The Stages of Life (1930–1931)
The Soul and Death (1934)
Synchronicity: An Acausal Connecting Principle (1952)
Appendix: On Synchronicity (1951)

**9. PART I. THE ARCHETYPES AND THE
COLLECTIVE UNCONSCIOUS
Archetypes of the Collective Unconscious (1934/1954)
The Concept of the Collective Unconscious (1936)
Concerning the Archetypes, with Special Reference to the Anima Concept
(1936/1954)
Psychological Aspects of the Mother Archetype (1938/1954)
Concerning Rebirth (1940/1950)
The Psychology of the Child Archetype (1940)
The Psychological Aspects of the Kore (1941)
The Phenomenology of the Spirit in Fairytales (1945/1948)
On the Psychology of the Trickster-Figure (1954)
Conscious, Unconscious, and Individuation (1939)
A Study in the Process of Individuation (1934/1950)
Concerning Mandala Symbolism (1950)
Appendix: Mandalas (1955)

(*continued*)

* Published 1971.
‡ Published 1960; 2nd edn., 1969.
† Published 1953; 2nd edn., 1966.
** Published 1959; 2nd edn., 1968.

* Published 1959; 2nd edn., 1968.   † Published 1964; 2nd edn., 1970.
‡ Published 1958; 2nd edn., 1969.

The Psychology of Eastern Meditation (1943)
The Holy Men of India: Introduction to Zimmer's "Der Weg zum Selbst" (1944)
Foreword to the "I Ching" (1950)

*12. PSYCHOLOGY AND ALCHEMY (1944)
Prefatory note to the English Edition ([1951?] added 1967)
Introduction to the Religious and Psychological Problems of Alchemy
Individual Dream Symbolism in Relation to Alchemy (1936)
Religious Ideas in Alchemy (1937)
Epilogue

†13. ALCHEMICAL STUDIES
Commentary on "The Secret of the Golden Flower" (1929)
The Visions of Zosimos (1938/1954)
Paracelsus as a Spiritual Phenomenon (1942)
The Spirit Mercurius (1943/1948)
The Philosophical Tree (1945/1954)

‡14. MYSTERIUM CONIUNCTIONIS (1955–56)
AN INQUIRY INTO THE SEPARATION AND
SYNTHESIS OF PSYCHIC OPPOSITES IN ALCHEMY
The Components of the Coniunctio
The Paradoxa
The Personification of the Opposites
Rex and Regina
Adam and Eve
The Conjunction

**15. THE SPIRIT IN MAN, ART, AND LITERATURE
Paracelsus (1929)
Paracelsus the Physician (1941)
Sigmund Freud in His Historical Setting (1932)
In Memory of Sigmund Freud (1939)
Richard Wilhelm: In Memoriam (1930)
On the Relation of Analytical Psychology to Poetry (1922)
Psychology and Literature (1930/1950)
"Ulysses": A Monologue (1932)
Picasso (1932)

§16. THE PRACTICE OF PSYCHOTHERAPY
GENERAL PROBLEMS OF PSYCHOTHERAPY
Principles of Practical Psychotherapy (1935)
What Is Psychotherapy? (1935)

(continued)

* Published 1953; 2nd edn., completely revised, 1968.
† Published 1968.   ‡ Published 1963; 2nd edn., 1970.
** Published 1966.
§ Published 1954; 2nd edn., revised and augmented, 1966.

* Published 1954.

INDEX OF PERSONS

INDEX OF PERSONS

The INDEX contains the names of addressees (printed in capital letters), persons mentioned directly and indirectly in the letters, and those mentioned in the introduction. After an addressee's name appear first the page numbers of the letters by year, and thereafter references, if any, in other letters, etc. At the first reference to an addressee, as well as many of the other persons indexed, there is usually an explanatory note. (Volume 2 will contain a general index to both volumes.)